The Complete Work of

MICHELANGELO

The Complete Work of

MICHELANGELO

REYNAL AND COMPANY
in association with William Morrow and Company
NEW YORK

FOREWORD

by Mario Salmi

The centenary of a great figure in thought or science, poetry or art, always serves to call the attention of the public and the interest of scholars to him, or rather to accentuate the attention and interest, and to promote commemorative publications, usually in large numbers.

When the great man is an artist, then in these days of people who read little and of technical processes of illustration which have made such advances, magnificent books of plates appear with incredible speed, with sparse texts that cannot strike deep, even when they are carefully prepared, making their appeal merely to the curiosity of a superficial culture.

As could have been foreseen, the Fourth Centenary of the death of Buonarroti, that lofty and many-faceted genius, has called forth publications of this kind in far greater numbers than the centenary of any other great master would have evoked. And this despite the fact that from the Cinquecento down to the present Michelangelo has the richest bibliography that any artist has ever had, for the most part to be sure, dating from the last half of the nineteenth century and from the twentieth. This is quite understandable. On the one hand, we know more about the complex personality of the master because of the publication of the poems in their true form, and of the letters; on the other, the methods of art history have become keener, enabling it to rediscover Michelangelo, by studying the documents, or by iconology or a study of form, or by deeper penetration in the realm of the spirit, something which is indispensable in the case of a figure like him.

The work of Michelangelo has been variously evaluated: as the beginning of the modern age, as a revival of the irrationality of the Middle Ages, as an expression of the late Renaissance, or as an anticipation of the Baroque. In point of fact, it is anchored in the times of the artist, that is, the high Renaissance, with aspects that go beyond the classicizing serenity of the early Renaissance in a heroic vision, nourished by sorrow, sublimely absolute.

From the old sources, and from Michelangelo's poems and letters, we get to know his character, his intellectual formation, his religious convictions, his political ideals. We see today how all these things influenced his art, and how his art in turn was linked with the political contingencies of the time and to the religious crisis and its resolution by Europe, with events, that is, that shed a dark dubious light on the first half of the sixteenth century. When, at the National Academy of the Lincei, we spoke of Michelangelo the man as indissolubly linked to Michelangelo the artist, we felt justified in saying that in his work he not only expressed himself in admirable fashion but also, without being aware of it, succeeded in interpreting in representational terms the great historical change of his times, in reflecting the implicit political ideals and religious torments of many spirits contemporary and near to him. And we concluded by saying: " The name of Michelangelo is linked with a universality that is even broader than the esthetic, one that is identified with the very life of the Cinquecento. When we consider that at all times men have professed, and profess, their political ideals, and have had, and have, their religious crises, that is, sentiments bound up with our very nature, by the mysterious power of genius, Buonarroti's art, so committed and so deeply felt, rises to a universality that expands to the entire world and remains perennial."

I think that what we have said enables us to explain the tremendous fascination that Michelangelo has had and still keeps.

But, to return to our starting point, important volumes and serious contributions have appeared in 1964, and in particular the contributions at two Congresses: one on Michelangelo, held in Florence and Rome, June 15 to 21, and one on Art History, at Bonn, September 14 to 19, at which a special section was devoted to Buonarroti.

The present work is not to be confused with books written for a particular occasion. Various contributors to it deal with the various aspects of this complex personality: the artist, the thinker, the writer.

Their names, belonging to different generations, may rank as a synthesis of various aspects of modern criticism of the remarkable figure we are dealing with. It is significant, therefore, that the work will be published after the end of the Michelangelo year, in order not to overlook the results of the most recent research published in connection with the event, and to present the most up-to-date bibliography on the artist, the writer and the thinker. We have sought in this way to honor Michelangelo by a work that to a great extent sums up our knowledge and critical trends at this moment in art history, with the aid of rich illustrative material, prepared by the Editor with love and generosity.

I

THE HISTORIC AND ARTISTIC PERSONALITY OF MICHELANGELO

by Charles de Tolnay

Michelangelo in his period

MICHELANGELO AND FLORENCE

Some facts on the life of Michelangelo will help us understand certain aspects of his artistic individuality, despite the fact that he did not mold his life according to his artistic ideal nor seek to reflect his own existence directly in his art. Although it is true that he saw in his art the image of a higher, heroic world, it is also true that his life remained the modest one of the old-time Florentine craftsman. However, the facts that he passed his youth and maturity in Florence and descended from an ancient family of Florentine citizens are useful for understanding some essential aspects of the art and spirit of Buonarroti.

The family of the Simoni-Buonarroti had been established in Florence for more than three hundred years when Michelangelo was born; his ancestors, of the Guelf party with one exception, had often held public office, especially in the second half of the fourteenth century and the first half of the fifteenth, in their district of Santa Croce. The financial decline of the family began with the artist's grandfather and imposed a modest way of life on his family and that of his son Lodovico, Michelangelo's father, without ceasing to respect ancient traditions and the conventions of their social class.[1]

It is significant, however, that young Michelangelo did not feel bound to class prejudices, as is shown by the fact that he chose art as his vocation against the wishes of his father and uncle, who regarded it as unworthy of the prestige of their house. Michelangelo on the other hand seems to have been proud of it, so that for a long time he signed his letters " Michelagniolo scultore." He did not care for social conventions, since he liked to be with artisans, stone-cutters, and lowly artists; that is, " lower-class people." This leaning of his towards the lowly was also shown in his sympathy for the popular radicalism of Savonarola's republic, even though he never was a member of the " piagnoni." It would appear that this sympathy was not reciprocated, for he never received a commission from that republic.

He did, however, become the most appreciated artist in the State under the republic of Pier Soderini, supported by the lordly families of Florence.[2]

His solidarity with the common people is further proved during the siege of Florence (1529-30), under Gonfaloniere Carducci, when he too fought for the desperate defence of the city, in contrast with the great families, who wanted to arrive at a compromise with the Medici pope.[3] Down to the last years of his stay in Rome, when he was at the height of his glory and wealth and the intimate of Cavalieri and Vittoria Colonna, he still loved the company of Florentines.[4]

However, he remained a son of his class in his relationships with his family; clear proof of this is his filial devotion to Lodovico and his constant interest in his brother's affairs. After Leonardo, the oldest of his brothers, had entered the Dominican order, Michelangelo, as the senior brother, took over the responsibility for the family, which he felt so deeply that he took more care of the fortune of the Buonarroti than he did of his own, and treated his brothers with the same authoritativeness that his father had practiced toward him. Whenever he could, he bought houses and land in his district; and later he succeeded in arranging marriages for his niece Francesca and his nephew Leonardo with two prominent houses of Florence, the Guicciardini and the Ridolfi.

The loss of his mother when Michelangelo was only six must have had its effect in forming his personality, and might explain the type of Madonnas, lacking in maternal tenderness, that he did in his youth. Later he sought to make up for the absence of motherly affection by his devotion to Vittoria Colonna, who became an " ideal mother " to him. And a role almost like that of " ideal parents " in the development of his art was played by his patrons: benevolent, like Lorenzo de' Medici in his early youth, or Paul III and Julius III in Rome, later; or severe, like Julius II. The popes set Michelangelo gigantic artistic tasks, thereby spurring on his enthusiasm for the work. They did not, however, interfere directly, except in the initial phases; and not even then very effectively since the artist tended to break free of the prescriptions, vague by the way, laid down by his patrons and follow the voice of his internal inspiration.

Of his friends, only two had any considerable influence on his inspiration; both came from a much higher social class than his own. One was Tommaso de' Cavalieri, a Roman patrician of great beauty and vast culture, who became his " spiritual brother " and inspired in him an exalted mystical conception of earthly beauty as an image of the Divine idea. The other was Vittoria Colonna, Marchioness of Pescara, a member of one of the noblest families in Italy, who was Michelangelo's spiritual guide when, as his old age came on, he was seized with a deep religious fervor.

Michelangelo's art and poetry were strongly affected by two spiritual trends. Platonism and Neoplatonism inspired many of his works. He was initiated into them by his familiarity during his youth with Politian, with Landino, and probably with Ficino, Pico and Benivieni, at the court of the Medici; but there was also the influence derived from the study of Dante, Petrarch and the *Canzoniere* of Lorenzo de' Medici. In Platonism he was to find a metaphysical justification for his amorous passions for the Beautiful Cruel Lady, for Cavalieri and Vittoria Colonna. The second spiritual trend was represented by the " Catholic Reformation," which attracted him in his youth with the sermons of Savonarola and Bible reading. Later, during his Roman period, it influenced him by means of the doctrine of justification by faith alone, into which he was initiated by Vittoria Colonna.

What the Florentine landscape must have given Michelangelo is not immediately visible in his art because, according to his esthetic ideas, nature in its accidental appearances could have no place in his creations. It should be remembered, however, that not even the most abstract and ideal art is entirely independent of its environment; art, as the oldest esthetics, Aristotle teaches, is " mimesis," that is, imitation of the essence or idea of nature. The incomparable topographical position of Florence is marked by the fact that the city seems to be at the center of various rings of hills and mountains that surround, almost embrace, it.[5] This position must undoubtedly have contributed to developing in the artist a sense of the symmetry and order hidden in the complex structures of nature. The cubic geometry inherent in the forms of this landscape, which has the aspect of a natural garden, with its hills in steps and terraces and its lines of vines, olive trees, cypresses and pines, certainly favored the development of the feeling for pure and regular forms in Buonarroti. The limpid atmosphere, the clarity of the outlines of things, the sharp, almost geometrical, contrast of light and shade on them, must have been a determinant element in the development of the Master's plastic sense. The sinuous contours of the peaks of the Apennines could have contributed towards developing his sensibility for the rhythmic values of line and movement, which were to take on such basic importance in Michelangelo's nudes. The hardness and tenacity of his character seem to have had affinities with the dry compact nature of the landscape around Florence. It is true that many of these qualities of the Florentine landscape had long been assimilated and incorporated into Tuscan works of art; Michelangelo must certainly have made this experience his own.

It is no wonder then that the accent of his art is Tuscan. His mode of being was Florentine: passionate, bold, proud and at the same time reserved and severe. In the internal tension of his seemingly calm figures with their precise and yet musical outlines, in the penetrating and almost scientific definition of the structure of the plastic form, always subordinated to a vigorous synthesis, his art is typically Florentine. The character would remain of the essence even after Buonarroti had made a universal language of the Florentine idiom and, in his last works, renounced the determinateness of particular forms.

Virtually everything that is known about the artistic formation of Michelangelo as a boy is hypothetical, except the fact that he felt his vocation early and entirely spontaneously: " the boy preferred (instead of going to grammar school) to go to churches to draw and watch the painters working there," we are told by the first biographers, Vasari, Condivi and Varchi. Thus, he began as self-taught. Very likely the frescoes in the chapels of the churches of Florence were his first models. There he could learn the secrets of expressing monumentality and simplicity in the human figure. It is significant that the twelve- or thirteen-year-old boy felt himself attracted, evidently by virtue of an internal affinity, not to the recent frescoes done by artists in vogue at that time, but to those a century or two earlier—the works of the founders of the new art, Giotto and Masaccio, on whom the contemporary art was based. There he recovered the deepest roots of the Tuscan monumental tradition.

By means of these copies the boy enriched the concepts of his models with direct observation of reality; and soon he was using the same method in studying the classical statuary of antiquity. But the realistic references in these copies, rather than making him rely on empirical nature, were used to emphasize ideal reality; namely, the majesty and dignity of his figures.

It was probably on the advice of Francesco Granacci (Condivi) that in April 1488 Michelangelo was placed in the *bottega* of Domenico and David Ghirlandaio, masters from whom he may have learned the techniques of ink drawing and fresco. But the year after, Michelangelo left the *bottega* for the " free school " of sculpture founded by Lorenzo the Magnificent at the time in the Medici Garden near San Marco. We know that the Garden was full of ancient sculptures that could have inspired the young artist; it was probably there that he learned the technique of sculpture from the head of the " school," Bertoldo di Giovanni. We have nothing left of what Michelangelo did during the year he spent in the school of the Garden; but what he did in the two following years, as a guest of the Magnificent in the Palazzo in Via Larga, enables us to gauge his development. The works are the *Madonna della Scala*, a small but monumental " flattened relief," is a Donatello redone according to ancient stelae or gems. Here we already see that for Buonarroti antiquity was not a period of the past that he saw at an historical distance. His interest in it was not of an archeological nature; rather, he identified antique statuary with the world of archetypes.

Among the things that inspired the precocious youth, we further mention the fifteenth-century prints that he, it would seem, consulted from time to time. Like those, for example, of Antonio

1 " Madonna della Scala." Florence, Casa Buonarroti.

2 " Madonna della Scala " (left side view).

3 Battle of the Centaurs (right side view). Florence, Casa Buonarroti.

4 Battle of the Centaurs. Florence, Casa Buonarroti.

Pollaiolo, a master in the representation of the anatomical nude. His print, entitled the *Battle of the Nudes*, seems to have been Michelangelo's inspiration on more than one occasion.

The theme was a favorite one of the Florentine Quattrocento. Verrocchio too had treated it in a painting that is now lost, but is mentioned by Vasari. It is a sort of compendium of the nude human body, seen in various movements and from different points of view. In the bas-relief, the *Battle of the Centaurs*, also done by Michelangelo when he was a guest of Lorenzo the Magnificent, the artist treated this Florentine subject in accordance with the artistic principles of the battles represented on ancient sarcophagi and a technique influenced by Giovanni Pisano. *The Battle of Cascina*, which he wanted later to execute in the Hall of the Great Council in the Palazzo Vecchio, can only be understood as a new version of the theme of the " compendium of the nude." Once again, all the figures here are nudes, arranged symmetrically in three planes, one behind the other, as in Pollaiolo's cut. But Michelangelo's composition is denser and the figures assume attitudes from famous classical statues. The outcome is a world of living statues, half marble and half flesh, which the artist once again seems to identify with the archetypes; that is, they represent not the old saying that " art is an ape of nature." Here the assumption is that empirical nature is an imitation of the sublime world of statues. It was Florentine Platonism that provided a basis for this " transcendent realism." Even the 11

Last Judgment, which is all nudes, can be considered from a certain point of view as a final embodiment of this type of representation of the " compendium of the nude."

It is understandable that Michelangelo, having thus early realized his affinity with the Tuscan masters of the Trecento and first half of the Quattrocento, could not have any great enthusiasm for the works of his first teachers, the brothers Ghirlandaio; works that were only derivations from the works of others. Nor could the influence of his friend Granacci have been of fundamental importance for him, since Granacci's style was only a derivation from that of the young disciples of Verrocchio.

Such then must have been the most essential artistic nutriments of Michelangelo's Florentine education. To finish off this listing, we should like to mention the influence that Leonardo had on him, which may perhaps be seen for the first time in the *Pietà* in St. Peter's and later, especially, in the works of the years 1501-1505, when Michelangelo had returned to Florence. Buonarroti, although he felt himself to be an antagonist of Leonardo, twenty-three years older than he was, could not escape being influenced by him. Leonardo had introduced a new " gentle style " into Florentine art, based on deeper knowledge of empirical existence, while revealing the musical harmony that rules the life of the universe. Michelangelo was struck by the fascination of this new style, which had great success in Florence at the beginning of the new century. The Virgins done during his Florentine period (1501-1505) are like dialogues with Leonardo's lost cartoon for St. Anne with the Virgin, exhibited and greatly

admired by the Florentines in 1501. However, while Leonardo revealed the physico-spiritual harmony of domestic life, the Virgins of Michelangelo are solitary sibyls, who foresee the catastrophe, that is the Passion of Christ. Affinity with the spirit of Savonarola, whose sermons the young Buonarroti heard with deep interest, is evident in these works. At first, perhaps, there was nothing more than an analogy in their spiritual attitudes; it cannot be shown that Savonarola inspired the *Madonna della Scala*, since that relief was earlier than the Dominican's sermons on the prophetic spirit of the Virgin (1493-1494). It would seem, rather, that Michelangelo's attitude is derived from the Virgins by Giovanni Pisano and Donatello, enriched by a personal Stoic content.

Along with conventional or hereditary religious practices, which meant a great deal to him, there was in Michelangelo a profoundly personal interior religious feeling, which must necessarily have been stimulated by Savonarola's words. The criticisms of the external practices of the Church, the conviction that it needed reform from inside it, the conception of faith as independent of external ceremonies, the belief in justification more through faith than through works: all these ideas of Savonarola's were to yield their fruits later, when in Rome, Michelangelo, thanks to Vittoria Colonna, came in contact with the " Catholic Reformation " movement.

Although he was born at Caprese, and had passed virtually half of his life far from Florence, Michelangelo felt himself totally a son of the city. Like Dante, he addressed it with tender epithets: it was his " nurse," "the nest where I was born, " or " the precious joy," or " the lady of angelic form." He loved the city so much that he had personal relationships with some of its buildings; Santa Trinità was " his lady," Santa Maria Novella " his spouse." We know that, especially in his maturity and late years, he was proud of the ancient Florentine

9 Battle of the Centaurs (lower view).

10-11 Battle of the Centaurs (left and right oblique views with skimming light).

nobility of his family, which as he said had paid the Commune " taxes for three hundred years." He tried to instill this pride in his nephew. When he was away from Florence, even for a short time (in Bologna, in Venice, or in Rome), he suffered from nostalgia. And towards the end of his life he felt that his thirty years in Rome had been a voluntary exile from Florence. He always cherished the hope of returning to Florence, where he wanted to be buried; his desire was carried out by the efforts of his nephew Leonardo. During his stay in Rome he sought the company of Florentines, many of whom were political exiles; he brought his assistants from Florence, not having any confidence in the ability of Romans; he even had the wine for his table brought from Florence. When he was away, he had masses said in Florence for the success of his works (for example, for the bronze statue of Julius II in Bologna, or for the Sistine vault). His interest in political events in his city was intense, even after many years in Rome.

He was not always gentle towards his compatriots. On occasions, either for personal reasons of the moment, or from memories of the way that Dante had been treated, he called the Florentines an " ungrateful people."

The Florentines, for their part, very soon began to admire in Michelangelo, first the great artist and later the great citizen; then the great man, whom they called " *il divino;*" and towards the end of his life they spoke of him as the " most holy old man." On February 12, 1560, Benedetto Varchi wrote him from Florence, in the name of all the Florentines: " ...all of this city desires humbly to be able to see you and thus honor you from close at hand as it now does from afar... Your Excellency would do a great kindness to rejoice and honor your country by your presence ".[6]

Michelangelo's political ideas, an inheritance from the Guelf convictions of his family, were likewise altogether Florentine and are inseparable from his love for his city.

More than once, in important works he embodied his Florentine republican ideals. The first large statue he carved was a *Hercules*, the true symbol of Florence, done when he was only seventeen, after the death of Lorenzo de' Medici (April 1492). He completed it on his own initiative, without having any commission, probably to attract the attention of rich art lovers with a spectacular work. A bozzetto preserved in Casa Buonarroti, hitherto believed to be a study for the marble *David*, is actually a model done in preparation for this *Hercules*, which was lost in 1713. Rubens made a drawing of it (Paris, Louvre). The Michelangelesque quality of Rubens' copy is obvious, in both the attitude and the modelling. Hercules is shown as a young hero, standing, his head turned to one side, the club resting on the ground, diagonally behind the leg; the left arm hangs loosely by the side; the figure seems in repose, but at the same time is full of tension; in transitory balance between repose and action, the hero seems to be gauging his strength and that of an invisible enemy. The overall effect is that of a statue of antiquity; in point of fact, the initial idea is derived from a type of ancient statue that is still known today in various copies. But the aggressiveness of the attitude, the drapery that comes down along the left leg and in part behind the back, the left hand, muscular and richly articulated but almost negligent, suggesting potential power, are inspired by statues of Donatello's, such as the *St. George*, the *St. Mark* or the *Jeremiah*. Michelangelo is thus endeavoring to rejuvenate the basic source of inspiration, derived from Florentine tradition, that is Donatello, giving it a decisively classical aspect.

We know that from the thirteenth century on Hercules was represented as one of the patrons of the city of Florence, and was shown as such on old seals. One of them bears the inscription: " Herculea clava domat Fiorentia prava." (With Hercules' club Florence curbs infamy.) This explains the posture of Michelangelo's *Hercules*.

12-13 Bacchus. Florence, Bargello National Museum.

14 Legs of Bacchus and the satyr (right side view).

In the marble *David* that Michelangelo began to carve about nine years later, the artist once more applied his conception of the heroic nude, already embodied in the *Hercules*. *David* is but a new version of the *Hercules*, inverted like a mirror image. The tension is present in the *David* as well, despite the apparent calm of the pose. The commission for executing this work was given to Buonarroti on August 16, 1501, twelve days after the adoption of the new republican constitution. It may be that this even suggested to the artist the idea of representing David, not as the adolescent of Biblical tradition but as a young hero.

Michelangelo seems to have tried thereby to set up a moral and physical prototype that should inspire the citizens to defend the republic and its " just government." It was a novelty to represent David in this way, as a nude youth, lacking the traditional attributes: the sword and Goliath's head, and armed only with the sling—and even that hidden behind him. The statue does not represent the moment of triumph, as previous Florentine statues on the same subject had, but the permanent virtues of David: the " vigilance," " fortitude " and " anger " that the Florentine humanists regarded as the greatest of civic virtues. According to Coluccio Salutati, anger is a vice only when it disturbs clarity of judgment; it is a virtue when it urges the citizens on to the defense of freedom. Michelangelo fused the type of the *David* with the type of the *Hercules*, thereby giving greater emphasis to the expression of vigilance, fortitude and anger as virtues, erecting a monument to the " warrior citizen," conformably to the definition formulated by Leonardo Bruni and picked up by Machiavelli. About seventy years earlier, similar historical conditions had inspired Donatello to create in his *St. George* (now in the National Museum) the image of the " warrior citizen," defender of the republic. It might be said that Michelangelo's *David* is a transposition of Donatello's *St. George* into a heroic classicizing key.

Vasari already made the assertion that the statue has republican political significance: " As he [that is, David] had defended his people and governed it with justice, so he who governed that city [Florence] should boldly defend it and justly govern it."

After 1508 the government of the republic planned to set up, balancing the *David*, at the other side of the entrance to the Palazzo della Signoria, a gigantic group of Hercules and Antaeus, since Hercules is, like David, in Vasari's words, " an emblem of the Palace." This block, like the block for the *David*, was entrusted to the artist by Pier Soderini, Gonfaloniere for life of the republic and a friend of Michelangelo's. But in 1525 Clement VII (Medici) took the block away from Buonarroti and gave it to Baccio Bandinelli, an enemy of the republic and of Michelangelo. After the fall of the Medici in 1528, the republic took the block away from Bandinelli and gave it back to Buonarroti, who then decided to make it into Samson with two Philistines. Finally, after the fall of the last Florentine republic, the Medici Pope had the block given back to Bandinelli, who in 1534 did the group of *Hercules and Cacus* that is still in front of the entrance to the palace. As we see, the changing fortunes of the block are parallel to those of the political power in Florence, and reflect the clash of wills of the republicans and of the Medici and their party.

Late evidence of the concern with Florentine politics that was felt by Michelangelo, then already living in Rome, is the bust of *Brutus* in the National Museum, probably done between 1539 and 1540. In form it goes back to the type of the Roman busts of Caracalla, with their powerful style, but in spirit it symbolizes the Florentines' aspiration to liberty. The theme was suggested to Michelangelo by Donato Giannotti, a friend of his, an ardent republican, formerly secretary of the last republic and by now an exile in Rome. Michelangelo certainly must have had discussions with Giannotti on the tragic fate of the Florentine republic and the problem of tyrannicide. In the dialogue by Giannotti, Buonarroti says: " It is clear therefore that he who kills a tyrant is not committing homicide, by killing not a man but a beast. Therefore Brutus and Cassius did not sin when they killed Caesar... since they did not kill a man, but a beast clothed in the image of man." [7] The sentence seems to reflect the ideas of Michelangelo as expressed in the bust, full of anger and indignation, though restrained by an iron will. (Contradictory statements are attributed to Michelangelo by Giannotti, in which the artist seems at the same time to wish to justify the punishment of Brutus and Cassius in Dante's *Inferno*.) The opinion cited was also expressed by Michelangelo as a poet, in a madrigal in which Florence, personified as a beautiful woman, consoles the citizens in their lamentations over the fact that " a single man seizes what is given to so many " with the words: " with great fear [the tyrant] gets no delight from the great sin." The epigram on the *Night* (abt. 1545) reveals that at that time Buonarroti regarded the fall of the republic as the death of liberty. However, he gave this political significance on the statue only a quarter of a century after it had been conceived. Originally, the *Night* had a philosophical content and, as Condivi said, represented " all-consuming time."

15 Head of Bacchus.

16

Of the large architectural units decorated with cycles of figures, Michelangelo executed only one in Florence, the Medici Chapel, to which he put his hand in the years of his maturity, from 1520 to 1534, but which remained unfinished. In it, too, the basic inspiration came from Florentine tradition: the organization of the architecture in dark grey pietra serena stone points to the model of Brunelleschi's *Old Sacristy*. Into the order of the dark grey pietra serena stone he inserted the architecture of niched tombs of white marble, which, too, in the last analysis, derive from the niched Florentine tombs of the Quattrocento. Michelangelo, however,

17 The satyr's head.

16 Legs of Bacchus and the satyr (right side-front view).

brought this tradition to perfection, in that he conceived all the elements, panels, tombs, doors and shrines, according to a single plan following the principle of rigorous correspondence and symmetry. This was the first funerary chapel designed on a unitary plan. The white marble portions emerging from the framework of dark grey pietra serena stone seem at first sight to be façades of houses for the dead; that is, the funerary chapel becomes the meeting place of two interpenetrating ontological spheres: the contingent world opens upon the world of transcendence. The latter is the habitation of the deceased, an idea well known from the Etruscan tombs; but the apotheosis of the dukes is likewise an idea inspired by antiquity. The figures of the dukes are not recumbent, but seated at the vertex of a stepped pyramid of allegorical forms, whose development is almost independent of the architecture. This position of the dukes is intended to express their spiritual triumph, their apotheosis. It is a strange, in fact a unique instance of syncretism, this realm beyond the grave, a synthesis of the pagan Hades and the Christian Paradise, as if the artist wished to suggest to us that the two concepts of the life beyond the grave rise from a common human source. The idea of the allegories of Time, like the idea of the River Gods (which were to occupy places below the Allegories, but were never executed), in all probability representing the four rivers of Hades, seem to have been inspired by the Phaethon of Plato (Oeri). For Michelangelo, it would seem, Platonism was a philosophical doctrine of existential importance, which enabled him to grasp the mechanism that connects death and the resurrection of the soul. We note that the slender figures of the Medici Chapel

17

3

are a return to the proportions of Florentine work, after he had modified that canon in Rome when doing the Sistine, in keeping with the spacious tastes of the Eternal City.

These would be the most essential data for realizing the contribution of Florence to the development of the Master's spiritual and artistic personality.

We now ask what Michelangelo gave Florence. Here we must limit ourselves to a brief enumeration.

He cannot be said to have transformed the face of Florence, as he later did in Rome. In Florence, a city essentially of the Middle Ages and Early Renaissance, there were so many works of architecture that no commissions of great importance could be entrusted to Michelangelo. Nevertheless, he left the seal of his personality on the principal ecclesiastical and civil monuments already in existence.

He wished his *David*, the symbol of republican liberty, to be set up in front of the façade, on an axis with the tower, alongside the great gate of the Palazzo della Signoria, in order to

18 Pietà (right side view from below). Rome, St. Peter's.

20 Christ's head in the Pietà of St. Peter's.

19 Pietà (left side view from below).

bring out the significance of the Palazzo itself, the seat of the republican government. And in the great fresco that he was to have done for the Hall of the Council, commemorating the victory of the Florentines over the Pisans at Cascina, he desired once again to celebrate the civic virtues of the "warrior citizen."

As for religious edifices, Michelangelo worked on the Cathedral, on San Lorenzo, and on Sant'Apollonia; omitting mention of minor works.

The Consuls of the Arte della Lana commissioned him to make statues of the twelve Apostles in marble larger than life; they were probably to have been placed in front of the piers of the *chori* to decorate the interior of Santa Maria del Fiore. As we know, Michelangelo began only one of these statues, the powerful *St. Matthew* (Accademia), a roughed-out marble block that has always been considered a typical example of his way of working marble.

He then took up the problem of finishing the drum of the dome of Santa Maria del Fiore, its cornice and the frieze, all of which had been left incomplete. In 1507-1508 the workers of the Cathedral had discussed completing these portions. Michelangelo, indignant at the work started on the design by Baccio d'Agnolo, Simone del Pollaiolo and Giuliano da San Gallo, which was obviously out of harmony with Brunelleschi's monumental dome, derided them, comparing their little gallery to a "cage for crickets" (Vasari). Because of his intervention work was stopped on this loge above the frieze. He then made drawings for organizing the drum, and a model that has been lost; the drawings, preserved at Casa Buonarroti, show that his intention was to preserve the effect of the entire outline of Brunelleschi's dome and to have his work in keeping with its monumental style.

Finally, there may be another trace of the Master's work in the interior of the cathedral, one that has been all but forgotten since the eighteenth century, although Bocchi (1571 and 1591),

18

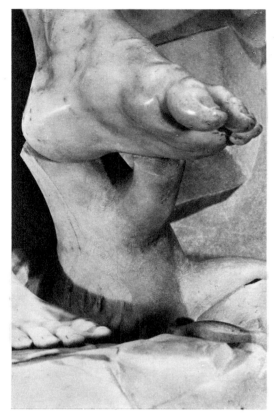

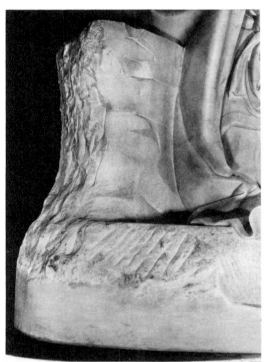

21-22 Christ's foot; support and drapings of Maria (left side view), in the Pietà.

Richa (1754-1772) and Lalande (1768) have already attributed it to Michelangelo. This is the design of the pavement around the choir of the cathedral, done in white, red and black marble, from 1520 to 1524, according to Landucci and Lapini. The original pavement of the choir, of which there is an old engraving, shows the design of an octagon in diminishing trapeziums; it is an imitation of an octagonal dome made classical by soffited coffers. (The chapel to the east of the choir still has a pavement like the one described.) The idea of having the decoration of the pavement reproduce a theme of the ceiling was ancient, but had been forgotten during the Middle Ages. The resumption of this tradition at the beginning of the sixteenth century could be attributed to Michelangelo or his successors, since he applied this principle in the Reading Room of the Laurentian Library as well.

In San Lorenzo, the ancestral church of the Medici, Michelangelo, by Leo X's wishes, was to have done a monumental façade, which was never carried out but for which we have a number of designs and a wooden model (Casa Buonarroti). It will be seen from the drawings and the model that the statues were of great importance in the architectural structure, which served as a framework for a sort of Santa Conversazione of the most important saints of Italy. Between 1531 and 1533, he did in this church, at the order of Clement VII, the delicately shaped reliquary tribune that is still in existence.

The designs for the Laurentian Library were likewise conceived by the artist as a unitary plan, like those for the Medici Chapel. So far as we know, this is the first library in which the architecture was invented by the artist *ad hoc* for its purpose, and not, as had previously been done, as a repetition of three-aisled church architecture. In the final version the artist intended to create a rhythmic relationship among the projected spatial units. His intention was to remove the visitor to the Ricetto i. e. Vestibule from the everyday world and predispose him to the spiritual labor facing him in the reading room. Michelangelo achieved this primarily by his new and dynamic architectural decoration, by his unusual staircase and by the filtered light, but the effect would have been even more impressive if he had been able to make the cycle of statues that he had designed for the shrines of the Ricetto i. e. Vestibule. We know nothing of the program for this cycle, but we believe it probable that the statues were to have represented the "illustrious men" of ancient and Italian poetry and philosophy, a suitable theme for the decoration of a library.

Among the lesser architectural works he did around Florence, we note the windows with curved supports of the Medici Palace (the original drawing for which is still preserved at Casa Buonarroti), the north portal of San Lorenzo and the portal of S. Apollonia. These two portals can now be attributed to Michelangelo with certainty on the basis of two drawings of the time (abt. 1556) as yet unpublished, which we identified a few years ago: they are inscribed, "by Michelangelo's hand." It may be that the side door of the Church of Gesù Pellegrino (Via San Gallo) was done after a design by the Master, as Richa tells us.[8]

Almost all of Michelangelo's architectural works in Florence are either projects for details or work done inside buildings, and hence could not affect the outward face of the city. Nevertheless, the master's genius left its imprint on a structure that is of importance for the physiognomy of Florence, the bridge of Santa Trinita. The conception cannot, in fact, be due to Ammannati alone, whose style was rather dry and static, even though he was in charge of building the bridge. We, therefore, feel that the late lamented Kriegbaum was correct when in 1941, on the basis of a letter from Vasari to Grand Duke Cosimo I, dated 25-IV-1560, he attributed the idea of the bridge to Michelangelo; that is the idea of having only three

23 The dead Christ, in the Pietà.

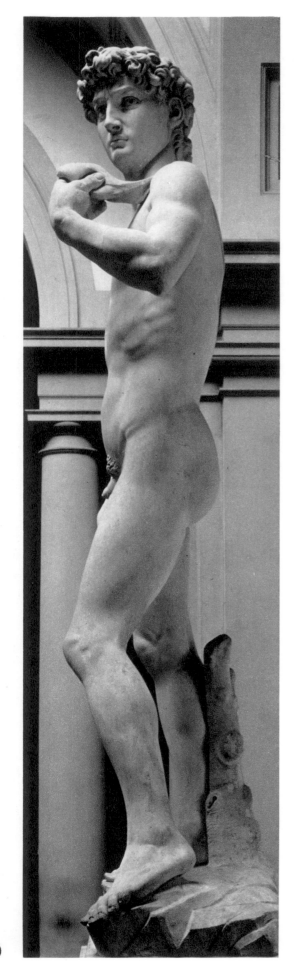

arches, separate from each other, resting on only two short piers, which made it possible to develop the continuous curving line of the embankments. And the elongated arches, too, elegantly expressing the tension and elasticity of the structure, have a dynamic quality that belongs rather to the style of Michelangelo (*cf.* his low vault for the Ricetto of the Farnese Palace) than to that of Ammannati, who yet worked out the idea of his master in the moldings and scrolls.

As we shall repeat below, Michelangelo remained a Florentine even when living away from his city. At the end of his life, although he had been living in Rome for a long time, he returned to the Florentine idiom, lean, long, sharp in proportions, in his last two *Pietà*. It is significant that in his drawings for the dome of St. Peter's (Haarlem, Lille, Oxford) he drew his inspiration from Brunelleschi's Florentine dome in the structure of the two sheels, in the proportions of lantern and dome, and in the form which, intead of being hemispherical, tends to rise, thanks to its high profile.[9]

MICHELANGELO IN BOLOGNA

We now proceed to analyze the changes in Michelangelo's style during his two stays in Bologna: in 1494 and from the end of 1506 to early in 1508.

Bologna lies in the moist and fertile plain of the Po, at the foot of rolling hills. Unlike Florence, with its austere cubical forms sharply cut out in stone, the aspect of the city is characterized by softer forms in brick and friable stone. Whereas the Florentine spirit in architecture tends towards problems hard to solve, Bologna almost always tends towards solutions that are easier to obtain. The arches are broader here and on more massive pilasters or columns, while in Florence the arches are more resilient in appearance and supported by the lithest of columns. This divergence in character can be seen even in the towers of the palaces. In the Palazzo Vecchio in Florence the tower rises above projecting battlements and rests on consoles; it has so fierce an appearance as to seem miraculously balanced above the building. The tower of the Palazzo Comunale in Bologna, more robust in its proportions, is solidly supported by the walls of the building behind the battlements and does not have the aggressive aspect of the Florentine tower.

Michelangelo did not feel at ease in the environment of Bologna, as his letters show, full of nostalgia for his city; and this despite the presence in Bolognese artistic culture of an aspect with which he must have felt a deep affinity, the works of the Sienese sculptor of the late Middle Ages, Jacopo della Quercia. It must have seemed to Michelangelo that in della Quercia he had discovered one of his spiritual ancestors. In his broad soft drapery, in the spiritual passion that animates his figures, Jacopo is a master of the late Gothic who had succeeded in integrating into his style the new monumental masculine idiom of the Florentine founders of the Renaissance, Donatello and Masaccio. He also knew the statuary of antiquity. In his figures he sought to fuse the movement of the Late Gothic with the heroic attitudes of the early Florentine Renaissance; but while his Florentine contemporaries were producing realistically concrete works, those of Jacopo, with their fluid forms, directly expressing the movements of the spirit, are lyrical and pathetic. Their almost volcanic aspect must have impressed Michelangelo, especially since that trait was already manifest in his first works, as can be seen in the *Battle of the Centaurs*. He must have found in Jacopo's works a justification for his own passionate quality. The encounter with the Sienese was the most important event of this stay in Bologna, and an echo of it runs through his works, from the *Bacchus* to the *Creation of Adam* or the *Creation of Eve*, or in the *Original Sin* of the Sistine vault. Jacopo's monumental conceptions, embodied in reliefs of small dimensions (S. Petronio), were translated by Michelangelo into monumental compositions on a much larger scale.

Michelangelo could get other inspirations at Bologna from a renewed contact with the spirit of Savonarola, who had lived for a time in the monastery of San Domenico in that city some years earlier. The spirit of the Dominican must have been present when the young Michelangelo was commissioned by the monks to execute three statuettes to complete the tomb of St. Dominic, which had remained uncompleted. The awareness of the lofty mission of mounting guard over the tomb of the Founder, which is so effectively expressed in the three statuettes, could be derived from the still vivid memory of Savonarola.

During this first period in Bologna Michelangelo made his debut as a poet as well. He had to read aloud to his patron, Giovanni Francesco Aldrovandi, the Italian poets, Dante, Petrarch and Boccaccio (Vasari). It may be at this time that he wrote his first love sonnets, in a style that was still Petrarchian.

During his second stay in Bologna, where he had been summoned by Julius II (who was seeking a reconciliation with Michelangelo after the artist's flight from Rome when the commission for the pope's tomb had been withdrawn), Buonarroti was commissioned to make the model for a bronze statue, larger than life, showing the pope enthroned and intended for a place above the main portal in the façade of San Petronio. He made the model, showing the pontiff seated, with the keys in his left hand and the right hand raised in a violent gesture, which made contemporaries wonder whether it was a blessing or a threat. This statue seems to have been a compensation for Michelangelo for the failure to do the great seated figures in the second zone of the tomb of Julius II in 1505. It anticipated the dramatic seated figures of prophets in the Sistine vault and the second version of the *Moses*. In any event, this statue (destroyed in 1511 by the indignant people of Bologna) seems to have been Florentine in type, following the type of Pollaiolo's bronze statue of *Innocent VIII* in St. Peter's. But we do not know whether there were any stylistic elements derived from della Quercia, either in the drapery or in the facial expressions.

MICHELANGELO IN ROME

Michelangelo never felt himself to be a Roman; even after long years in Rome he continued to feel himself a Florentine and to seek out the company of his compatriots. Nonetheless, contemplation of the great lines of the landscape of Latium, the classical sculptures, more numerous here than in Florence, and the majestic ruins of the Terme and ancient Basilicas, revealed to him an ideal of beauty that combines breadth and proportion, and that led him to revise his " keen " Florentine idiom.

The vast dimensions of Roman landscape and art met one of the needs of his spirit: titanism. It is obvious that in his repeated contacts with Rome he gave ever newer and larger dimensions to his works. In 1496, when he came there for the first time, for a stay of over four years, the city was still provincial and in full decadence under Alexander VI Borgia. No wonder that it did not as yet leave any decisive imprint on the artist; the *Pietà* of St. Peter's shows a language that is essentially Florentine in the reduction of the third dimension to a relief-like treatment of the group, and for the exquisite sharp chiseling of the drapery and the faces.

26 Legs of David (left rear-side view).

Rome was a much different place when Michelangelo returned in the spring of 1505. Thanks to Julius II, it had become once more aware of its glorious past. It is unlikely that Michelangelo could have conceived an ensemble of such majesty as the first project for the tomb of Julius II without the inspiration of the Roman mausoleums and triumphal arches. It should be noted, however, that the overall conception of this project was, to be sure, inspired by Roman grandeur, but the individual statues that go to make it up still have the elongated forms of the Florentine style.

During the third Roman period, from 1508 to 1514, largely still under Julius II, we see a change in the single figures as well, which become broad and powerful with rhythmic curving lines. The monumentality of the composition of the Sistine vault is not limited merely to the grand architectural framework, which was inspired by the Roman arches of triumph, but is also expressed in each of the figures. In the pale changing colors of the vault, in contrast with the clear cool tones of the Doni Madonna, we may perhaps see a reflection of the gentle air and light of the Eternal City. The three statues that he did at that time for the tomb of Julius II (the two slaves of the Louvre and the *Moses*) are likewise conceived in that monumental Roman idiom.

We have already noted that as soon as the master returned to Florence, where he remained until 1534, he adapted his style to the *genius loci*, in the Medici Chapel, giving up in part the Roman fullness of form and resuming the slender Florentine proportions. The movements of the figures in this Chapel are full of contrasts and tensions, and the " serpentine figure " has taken the place of classic contraposition. All this conformed to the taste of Florentine art even in the time of Clement VII, when the first works appeared of such Mannerists as Pontormo and Rosso, who belonged to a later generation than Michelangelo.

When Buonarroti returned to Rome in 1534, there to remain until he died, he took up the majestic Roman idiom once more in the figures of the *Last Judgment* and the frescoes of the Cappella Paolina; the drawings of this period likewise attest a return to the sweep and grandeur of the forms of Rome. Frontal contraposition replaces the serpentine figure of the Florentine period. However, the style has a simplified appearance as compared with that of the Sistine vault and bears the imprint of a new gravity. While still maintaining the enclosed and heavy outlines, he seems, from about 1550 on, to spiritualize the material. In this last Roman period he puts in the place of the concept of space as a system of closed hierarchical spheres, a space that is continuous and infinite, filled with dynamic forms and magnetic stresses, which for the first time succeeds in expressing the real space of the universe peopled by innumerable "planets."

These developments in his style were matched by changes in his life. Michelangelo, now at the summit of fame, was connected with the highest ranks of society. The old Florentine craftsman, proud of his sculptor's craft, now refused to be considered as such, " like those that have a *bottega*," and wanted to be called simply " Michelagnolo." It is only from this time, 1540 on, that we find evidences of his pride in the nobility of his house.

Towards the end of his long life he returned, as we have noted, to the Florentine idiom of slender proportions and sharp forms, in the Florence *Pietà* and the so-called *Rondanini Pietà*, even though they were works done in Rome.

Like an exile dying in a foreign land, whose lips go back to the accents of his mother tongue, Michelangelo, near death in Rome, went back to the Florentine accent.

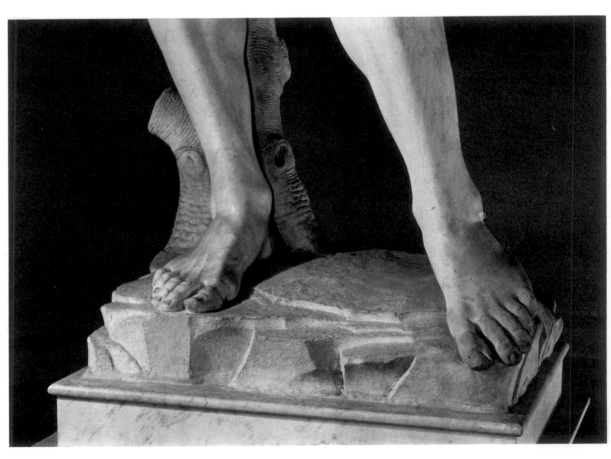

27-28 Head and torso (right side view) and feet (front view) of David.

29 Doni Holy Family. Florence, Uffizi.

For his part, Michelangelo gave back to Rome as much or more as it had given him. He gave the Eternal City a new face, restoring to it, for the first time since antiquity, a feeling for imperial dimensions and grandeur, corresponding to and expressing the spirit of the historical past and the eternal mission of Rome, ideal capital of humanity.

When Michelangelo came back to Rome in 1534 for his long last stay, the most important city planning problems, unlike the situation in Florence, were still unsolved, after centuries of neglect. The greatest temple of Christianity awaited reconstruction in conformity with the monumental conceptions of the time; the civic center, the Campidoglio, was in a state of rack and ruin, awaiting organization and the erection of grand buildings around it; the most monumental residence of the city, the Farnese Palace, was still unfinished; the gates of the city, like Porta Pia, had to be decorated. All these tasks fell to Michelangelo, who succeeded, by his latest architectural works, in expressing the prestige of the Eternal City.

This monumental grandiose quality that Buonarroti reconquered was never lost again. It became the dominant characteristic of Rome throughout the Baroque, neoclassicism, and even in the eclecticism of the nineteenth century. And it is not yet extinct.[10]

[1] On Michelangelo's family, see the researches of K. Frey in *Jahrbuch der Preussischen Kunstsammlungen*, 1885, pp. 189 ff., and Tolnay, *Michelangelo*, Vol. I, pp. 3 ff. and p. 42.

[2] Cf. Giorgio Spini, " The Political Quality of Michelangelo " in *Rivista Storica Italiana*, 1964, pp. 557 ff.

[3] Cf. Giorgio Spini, *art. cit.*

[4] Cf. K. Frey, *Sammlung ausgewählter Briefe an Michelangelo Buonarroti*, Berlin 1899, p. 238.

[5] Leonardo Bruni in *Laudatio Florentiae Urbis* (about 1404) had already stressed the importance of the beauty of the site of Florence.

[6] Cf. K. Frey, *Dichtungen des Michelangiolo Buonarroti*, Berlin 1897, p. 537.

[7] Cf. *Dialoghi* by Donato Giannotti, ed. De Campos, p. 93.

[8] Richa, *Chiese di Firenze*, Vol. V, p. 300.

[9] There are reflections in Florence, after 1550, of Michelangelo's Roman architectural style, as in Ammannati's courtyard of Palazzo Pitti and Buontalenti's palaces. The heavier forms, the more highly accentuated and projecting profiles and the fanciful combination of the elements of Renaissance architecture in the late Michelangelo are evident here. Hence, it may be said that Michelangelo dominates the architecture of his city even when he is no longer there.

[10] Although influences of the late Middle Ages and the fifteenth century are evident in Michelangelo's works, and on the other hand his forms prefigure those of Mannerism and the Baroque, we hold that Michelangelo is essentially a son of his times, since he primarily " expressed the spiritual anxieties, his own and those of his time," as we have said elsewhere (cf. *Enciclopedia dell'Arte*, Vol. IX, p. 266). He expressed religious anxieties at the time of the schism, longing for political liberty at the moment of absolutism, and the transcendental Platonic philosophy in an age of empiricist philosophy. The spiritual stresses of the historical moment became the warp of his creation, especially during the Roman period. Michelangelo, expressing them in his works of art, consciously or unconsciously made an essential contribution towards bringing them into the open.

30 Virgin and Child with St. Giovannino dei
Pitti (left oblique view). Florence, Bargello
National Museum.

The artistic character of Michelangelo

METHODS OF WORK

The works of Michelangelo enable us to take an active part in his creative procedures, more so than is possible with other artists of the time. Unlike them, Michelangelo does not give us closed forms as static objective entities but presents them in their " becoming," often leaving them only roughed out. Some of his sculptures are seen emerging gradually from the shapeless block, like images of the creative process as such. Often we can trace in the marks of the chisel the successive stages of the progress of the work, and thereby share in the effort of the artist, recreating and completing the "unfinished" block in our imagination. This may be one of the reasons why today the works of Michelangelo still seem an inexhaustible source of energy, and beholding them still strengthens our creative powers.

The Master himself evoked the phases of the creative process in the most efficacious manner, and for the first time in the history of art, in the frescoes of the Sistine Chapel vault, in the cycle of the creation of the world, in which God appears as the archetype of the creative artist. There can be no better guide than these pictures in our present study; they are better than and supplant certain Freudian hypotheses and theories as to the automatism of the subconscious during the creative act. Jacques Maritain has shown that the preconscious factor in the poetic intuition is not identical with the Freudian subconscious.[11]

Michelangelo depicted the initial phase of creation in the *Separation of Light and Darkness*, the fresco in which he revealed the preconscious state of the spirit whose arms try laboriously to make headway against the nebulous chaos surrounding it. It is a subconscious striving towards light and clarity, an instinctive movement without a rationally defined aim. Michelangelo must have lived through this picture of the initial phase of creation as clear experience, so much so that he succeeded in transferring it altogether and objectively into his representation of God the Creator. Dante described this initial preconscious state in his *Purgatory* (IX, 13-18):

> At the hour...
> ...when our mind is freer
> From the flesh and it is less assailed with cares,
> It is almost a diviner in its visions.

The second phase of the creative process consists in the projection of the internal image that Michelangelo called " the image of the heart." This moment is exemplified in the fresco on the *Creation of the Sun and the Moon*, in which the Divine creative energy, as a consequence of its superabundance, flows directly into the heavenly bodies. This emergence of internal images is captured by Michelangelo in rapid sketches and little models in plastic substances. The first sketches that Michelangelo set down (which the Italians of the Cinquecento called, significantly, " thoughts ") took form all at once; as Vasari says, they were produced " by the fury of art," the fury that we see in the expression on the face of *God the Father* in this fresco.

Michelangelo's " thoughts " consist of only a few essential lines and are left in an unfinished state, but they manifest the quality of " boldness " that Vasari and Lodovico Dolce mistakenly connected with the quality of " facility," whereas actually in Michelangelo it was an effect of his volcanic temperament. These " thoughts " are the notes of a man seeking to capture, rapidly but with precision, an internal vision that is incredibly concrete. The need of putting the internal image down on paper at high speed led Michelangelo to use typical abbreviations, a kind of stenography. To indicate an arm or a leg it was enough for him to draw convex curves, getting smaller and smaller and ending in a hand or a foot, likewise barely indicated. These abbreviations almost always are a sure proof of the Master's hand.

We are not always in opposition to determine the priority between the sketch and the sculptured model. Some of the sketches were executed directly on a wax model, and in them we see the arms of the model broken. On the other hand, we have some models that were preceded by a sketch. Actually, the question of the priority of the sketch or the sculptural model is of secondary importance. What matters is the fact that Michelangelo first expressed his monumental ideas in a small format, whether in a drawing or sculpture.

This is not to say that he did not sometimes make large models, but it would seem that this happened relatively late, from the time of the Medici Chapel on (e.g., the model for a river god in the Accademia in Florence). We do not know, however, whether he made these large-scale models for preparing his work in marble, as was the practice of his contemporaries, or whether they were intended to give a provisional idea of the entire composition to his patron.

As a rule the main idea grew or multiplied in Michelangelo's imagination. He often duplicated the same conception in order to achieve a symmetrical balanced composition, as happened, for example, in the vault of the Sistine Chapel and in the Medici Chapel, where he repeated an identical or similar motif in reverse. Apropos of this, it also happens sometimes that a figure that Michelangelo had conceived in his youth reappears reversed in a later work, but always in a more developed form. For instance, the *Hercules* of his youth (which, as has been said, we know from the model in Casa Buonarroti and an ink drawing by Rubens) was developed in reverse nine years later in the marble *David*.

More surprising, perhaps, is the use of the same motif for entirely different subjects. Thus, for example, a Tityus, a Zeus, a Ganymede is transformed directly, virtually without change, into a " Christ risen;" or, on the contrary, a religious subject, such as the *Christ* of Santa Maria sopra Minerva in Rome, is used again as a pagan subject, in this case becoming a *Victory* (Florence, Palazzo Vecchio). The initial motif is always developed, however, becoming larger in its proportions and freer in movement. This kind of development can also be observed in the great cyclic works, in which the first ideas appear rather modest in comparison with the monumental amplitude of the final version (e.g., the Sistine Vault, Medici Chapel, *Last Judgment*).

The next phase of the creative process consisted in working the first idea out in detailed studies, accurately done from life; for them, Michelangelo used his apprentices as models, for both the male and the female figures. In them he developed the poses and movements, studying the plastic stresses and the changes in the muscles. Going beyond the immediate purpose for which the drawings were done, he succeeded in giving them such sculptural perfection that they are true works of art in and of themselves. They present " absolute plastic form," independent, that is, of any environmental influence; so much so that Michelangelo could not transfer these studies as they were into the final version, in which he had to give up the richness of the modeling, replacing it, however, with other qualities of equal value. For example, a unified rhythmic contour. The relative calm that went with this third creative phase is the same that shows in the face and action of the serene *God the Father* separating the waters from the land.

Detail studies also accompanied performance of the fourth phase, in which the Master came into contact with the material of which the work was to be made. This phase is analogically shown in the fourth fresco of the series, the *Creation of Adam*, in which we see the Creative Spirit approach matter and animate it, communicating the divine spark.

At this point the initial idea must be adapted to the requirements of the material. The conception of the organic body with its life and its free and independent movements, as it appears in the first sketches, must be redimensioned in sculpture according to the requirements of the stereometric block, or, in fresco, according to the form of the wall surface.

When working on a sculpture, Michelangelo tried in the first place to use the rough chisel to transform the geometrical and crystalline planes of the block, giving it the aspect of an animated substance, a sort of primordial *hyle*. That is, he did not accept the marble as nothing but hard inert stone; he sought at once to imbue it with life, dissolving its rigidity. Even the part of the block that was to form the base of the statue was treated as animated material and not as an architectural form, as was done in Gothic sculpture, nor as a naturalistic *trompe-l'œil*, in the manner of the Quattrocento and later of the Baroque.

After the block had thus been animated, Michelangelo drew the contour of the figure on the frontal surface and, in figures in the round, on the side surfaces as well. Working with the punch, he then picked out the drawn contour and then, leaving the outstanding points intact, went down to the deeper levels with the gradin, which left a diagonal hatching on the marble whose function was to define the plastic modeling.

Thus, Michelangelo worked on the entire figure at once, with the resultant advantage of having it all before him at all times and at all the stages of the work. The side views were not developed separately but came out as the work progressed. The back of the figure was done last. After having sketched the forms and liberated them from the material, the Master came back to them at various times, working one layer at a time, and thus gradually bringing the figure closer and closer to perfection (Wenzel and Vermehren).

At each of these stages Michelangelo produced a true work of art. That is why he could sometimes stop at one of these stages, leaving the work intentionally " uncompleted." Another result of this technique is that the form seems to be enclosed within its own space, that is, within the block (A. von Hildebrandt).

This working procedure has points of contact with those used by the oldest sculptors: the Egyptians, the Greeks of the archaic period, the Romanesque and the Proto-Gothic sculptors (for instance, the statue-columns of the cathedrals). The difference between archaic sculpture and that of Michelangelo does not lie in the technique but in the spirit, the " concept " as he himself put it. In Buonarroti's work the figure, although contained within the boundaries of the block, tries ceaselessly to liberate itself, while in archaic works the figure conforms passively to the outline of the block.

Thus, Michelangelo's figures seem to emerge gradually from the material and come to life in successive stages: from the roughing out to the gradin work to the polished surfaces. There are no sudden contrasts of texture, no effects derived from the contrast of rough and delicately polished areas, as was to be the case later with Rodin. It is clear, from an analysis of Michelangelo's technique, that in him the " uncompletedness " is not the result of applying an a priori principle, but a calculated esthetic judgment that was formed spontaneously during the work, and at the same time. In Rodin, even though he was influenced by Buonarroti's

31 Virgin and Child with St. Giovannino dei
    Pitti (lower oblique view).

32-33 Virgin and Child with St. Giovannino dei
       Pitti (left and right side views).

technique, the unfinished portions were the precise results of an a priori calculation; the rough regions were intended to bring out the surface beauty of the polished regions, which often took on an erotic connotation.

In no case has all the preparatory work done by Michelangelo been preserved. Sometimes we have the first idea, in the form of a sketch, and then the final result. It would be instructive to compare the two aspects, even though the intermediate stages are lost. One instance is the relief for Bartolomeo Pitti in the Museo Nazionale; the Chantilly sketch identified by us (1928) is probably the first " thought " for this relief. In it the position of the body, seen three-quarters, turned toward the right, with the head turned in the opposite direction, the right arm resting in the lap: all correspond to the Madonna of the relief. And yet we can not speak definitely of a drawing *ad hoc*, since the sketch does not necessarily represent a " Virgin " (as it would in a sketch by Leonardo or Raphael, where the subject is identifiable from the outset), but simply a young woman. Even without knowing the purpose for which the sketch was done, there is no doubt that Michelangelo inserted it into the final version of the tondo, broadening the composition to fill the entire circular space of the block. He placed the two children symmetrically to the right and left of the Madonna and repeated the form of the tondo in the drapery, the borders and the folds of the mantle. He gave the Virgin's body and head an erect posture, accenting it with two vertical lines on either side of the axis: the arm and the fold falling straight from the knee. Michelangelo went deep into the block to obtain three planes: after the plane in high relief (with the head and right leg of the Virgin and the log on which she is seated), there is a second plane (with the right arm of the Virgin and the Child Jesus) and finally a third plane, in bas-relief

34-35 St. Matthew (side-front views). Florence, Academy of Fine Arts.

36 St. Matthew's head and torso.

(with the head of the infant St. John). Further carving out of the concave background gave further prominence to the relief. On all three figures, the cross-hatching produced by the gradin is plainly visible; and to the left can be seen a region worked with the rough chisel. There is no polished portion. By the standards of Quattrocento sculpture this would be considered an unfinished relief; but actually, all the artistic idea is entirely expressed in it.

It seems to me that the final version of this work is a synthesis between the conception of Michelangelo, namely the sibylline Madonna to which the young woman of the drawing was elevated, and the structure set up in three planes inspired by the very nature of the marble. By following the requirements of the material, therefore, the spiritual message comprised in the form of the sibylline Madonna is brought out more strongly.

The *Rebellious Slave* of the Louvre, done for the tomb of Julius II, is another instance of the way in which the outline of the block determined, up to a certain point, the artistic form and hence the spiritual message of the artist. If we compare the rapid initial sketch (now in Oxford) with the statue in the Louvre, we find that the right leg, which in the " thought " was half-hidden behind the left leg, in the statue leans vigorously on a base that still keeps the form of the block; the breastplate, which in the sketch was behind the right leg, as in some classical examples (the *Dioscuri* of Montecavallo), does not appear in the statue; in the drawing the arms are tied behind the back, while in the statue the right arm, following the outline of the block, goes vertically down the hip, while the left arm is bent at a right angle on the back, to adapt to the front and side planes of the block; the head, which in the sketch projected forward and was turned towards the spectator, stays within the limits of the block 29

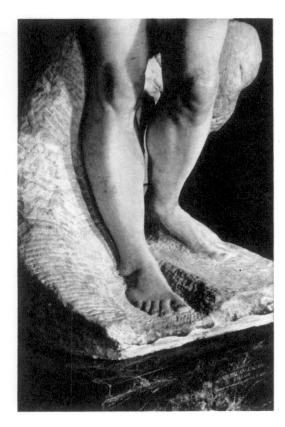

37 Legs of the Dying Slave (left side-front view). Paris, Louvre.

38-39 Torso and legs of the Rebel Slave (right rear-side and side-front views). Paris, Louvre.

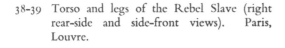

in the statue, and is twisted upwards. This is the only point at which Michelangelo introduces the dolorous expression of the *Laocoon*, here, at least in part, a result of the nature of the block. And this is one more instance of the way in which the necessity of adapting to the material intensifies the spiritual message of the work.

A different case is a " concetto " that never arrived at its final version, but of which we have a small model and the drawings for it, showing the preliminary phases of the work. We refer to a little wooden model for a Crucifix, still unpublished, an instance that has escaped the notice of scholars, despite the fact that it has been on exhibition at Casa Buonarroti for a long time.

The sturdy proportions of the body, the modeling (on the torso, for example, where the chest appears projecting and the abdomen hollowed, as if at the last breath), the form and modeling of the knees, the vertical position of the legs close together, the mass of hair treated so as to form a sort of helmet: all this is matched in the group representing Christ Crucified between the Virgin and St. John, now generally assigned to the Master's late period (1550-55).

On the basis of the triangular outline of a block drawn on the back of the *Crucified of Windsor* (Cat. 437 *verso*), we had supposed at first that this group of drawings had been done by the Master in preparation for a marble sculpture. But two letters recently exhibited in the Laurentian Library [12] contain evident references to a project of Michelangelo's for carving a wooden crucifix. The first of them was written August 1, 1562 by a certain Lorenzo Mariottini in Rome to Leonardo Buonarroti, nephew of Michelangelo, in Florence. It says: [Michelangelo] "...would like to make a crucifix in wood, and...would like you to send him all the

◁ 40 Legs of the Dying Slave (right rear-side view).

41 Torso of the Dying Slave (right rear-side view).

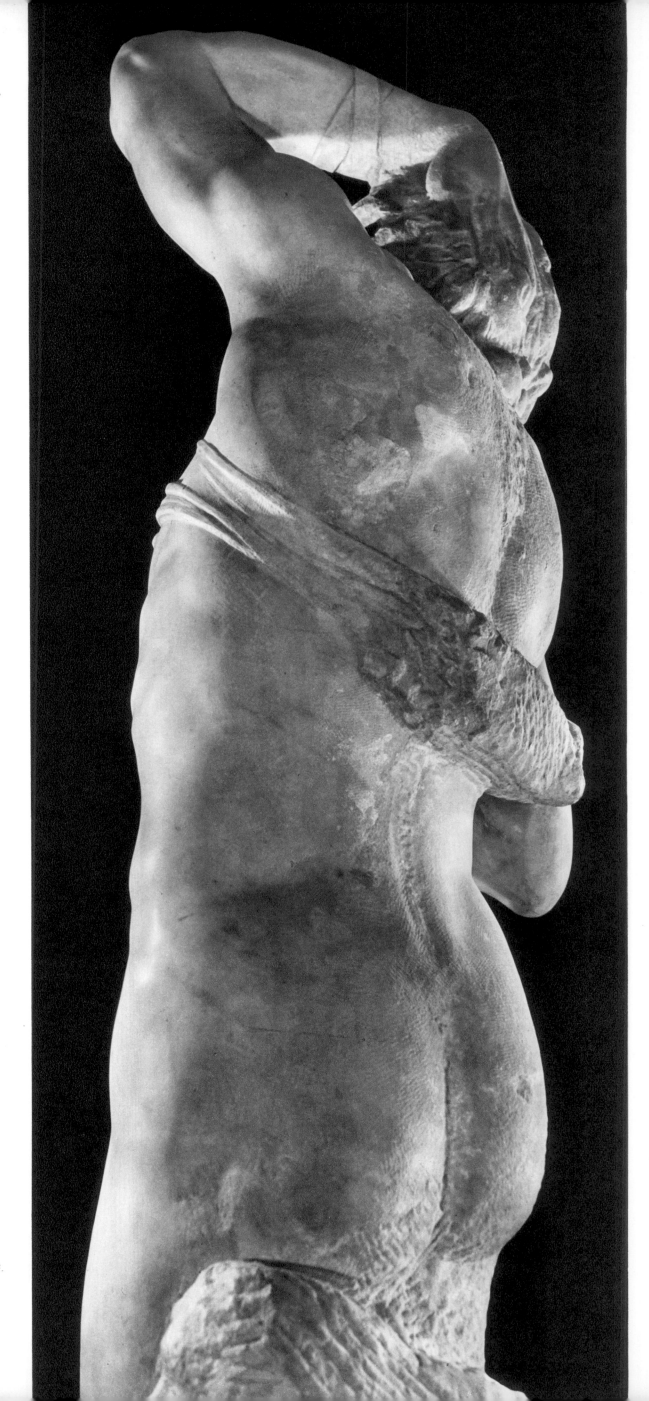

42 Torso of the Rebel Slave (rear view).

tools necessary for that kind of work." The second letter is dated the next day; it was written by Cesare Bittino from Rome to the same addressee; it contains the same request, with the added detail that the wood should be linden.

Beyond enabling us to date the wooden model in Casa Buonarroti (Fig. 106-108), these two letters make it possible to propose a more precise date for the group of drawings mentioned, which are so close stylistically to the model. That is, they must have been done about the summer of 1562.

Here we should stress the perfection that Michelangelo's mastery had attained, for he did the model directly in wood, giving it the " body and softness of marble." In this instance he did not obey the precept, codified a little later by Vasari (I, 166 ff.) that " if one wishes figures in wood to come out perfectly, he must first make a model in wax or clay."

For the model Michelangelo used a piece of wood wider than thick, triangular in shape, not unlike the block drawn on the back of the Windsor sheet mentioned above; he used the broader part for the top in order to get the arms in, although in any event, later they were broken off. He began to work it from the front, as he was in the habit of doing for a marble block, keeping the original form of the piece of wood at the top and the bottom, in the parts not carved. The surface was modeled by hollowing out the wood with a concave tool like a kind of spoon. A rough surface was produced.

Since Michelangelo left the piece " unfinished," the light seems to vibrate uniformly on it. The forms do not appear closed and isolated, but combined with the surrounding atmosphere, so that the unity of effect is more evident. The figure breathes with life, despite the immobility of the outward pose and the material of the wood; thanks to its fusion with the surrounding atmosphere, it seems almost to be spiritualized. The effect corresponds entirely to that of the drawings of the group mentioned above, in which the modeling is scarcely suggested and the repeated contours form a halo around the figures. In the drawings, however (with the exception of the *Crucified* of Codice Vaticano 3211), the head of Christ drops on the chest, while in the model it rests on the right shoulder, a position made necessary by the dimensions of the piece of wood.

Today, too, we can follow out the process of development by which Michelangelo succeeded in eliminating all movement in the pose of Christ. In the drawing of the *Crucified* of the Louvre (Inv. 842 r.), which can be dated as 1557 by the architectural drawing on the verso (and is thus five years earlier than the model and the group of drawings that we are discussing), the body is still animated with life and movement, and the head is raised as in the *Crucified* done more than ten years earlier for Vittoria Colonna. In Windsor Drawing No. 437, however, which was done later (one of those in the group we are concerned with), the body is still in motion but the head has dropped. Finally in the drawing in the British Museum (Cat. No. 82) and the one in the collection of Count Seilern (London), as in the wooden model, Michelangelo gives up all outward movement in the figure, which becomes axial, in order to achieve an image that is even more expressive of the interior drama.

The *Rondanini Pietà* is a special case, since here an original version in marble, in an advanced state, seems to have been intentionally destroyed in part and radically altered by the Master, to fit a new conception (Fig. 93-96).

In the small black chalk sketches (Oxford), the *Descent from the Cross* is depicted in two compositional types. Both show the body of Christ in vertical position carried toward the tomb either by a single figure (that of the Virgin) or by two (probably Joseph of Arimathea and Simon of Cyrene). In all of the sketches Michelangelo accentuated the contrast between the weight of the body and the effort made by the standing figures to hold it up. (Here it should be noted that in his late period Michelangelo took the closed form of the block into account even in his " thoughts.") The sketch at the extreme right of the sheet gives us the clue to a mental reconstruction of the original version in marble, which still contains some of the elements of that original: for example, the polished legs of the Christ; his right arm now detached from the upper portion of the block; and the head of the Virgin, at first turned upwards to the left (an attitude that can still be traced in the marble by an eye, part of the nasal septum and the veiled forehead). The proportions of this first version in marble were sturdier, as can be seen from the arm just mentioned. The polished legs, which are sharper, were probably done about 1555.

About nine years later Michelangelo, now near death, destroyed all the parts that projected beyond the central axis of the block, that is, the original head and part of the torso of Christ, thus wiping out the antithesis between the passive weight and the effort to support it. He cut down the dimensions of the figures and carved the new body of the Christ directly out of the portion of the block assigned to the Mother; he got the new head of the Son from the right shoulder of the Madonna: from her loins came the new arms of the Christ; he changed the position of the Virgin's head to correspond with the new head of the Son, all in all, perhaps following a subconscious impulse, coming close to the medieval presentations, in which the Madonna is alongside her suffering Son, in the act of supporting Him and showing Him to the faithful (as still can be seen, for example, in the fresco of San Miniato al Monte).

In Michelangelo's group, however, we do not find any gesture aimed at the spectator. The Mother and Son are alone. At first, perhaps, the Master wanted to depict the Virgin in the act of supporting the corpse of Christ; but now she bends over Him from above and the

46 Right side-front view of Moses.

45 Left side-front view of Moses.

36

two bodies fuse to form a single being from which all strength has departed, which is bowed and persists only by an action of Grace. This is an attitude that reflects the spiritual and physical state of the old sculptor at the time he was engaged in that work, only six days before his death, as Daniele da Volterra reports in a letter. The sunken shapes of the face of Christ seem concave, seen in profile, as if mummified, suggesting an image of Michelangelo himself after his death.

Only rarely have documents come down to us illustrating the most important creative phases up to and including the final version. This is the case for the three great cyclical works: the vault of the Sistine, the Medici Chapel and the *Last Judgment*. Analysis of this case will enable us to get a fuller vision of the dialectics of Buonarroti's creative process.

In the vault of the Sistine Chapel he took as his starting point " a certain compartmentation filled with ornament," a combination of rectangular and circular compartments with which he intended to fill the flattened barrel vault, at the same time planning to decorate the pendentives with twelve Apostles. The inspiration came to him from decorations of old ceilings that Pinturicchio had copied in the vault of the choir of Santa Maria del Popolo, but Michelangelo included the pendentives in the decoration of the vault (see the drawing in the British Museum). Subsequently, he simplified and unified this system of decoration, alternating broader and narrower frames to make the decoration of the vault harmonize with the structure of the walls of the Chapel. For each pilaster there was now a band running the width of the vault and joining it to the pilaster opposite.

After these attempts, however, which conformed to the Renaissance taste of Rome, Michelangelo was not satisfied, and said to the pope that the projects were a " poor thing," asking permission to make changes. Julius II gave him a free hand ("... that I should do as I wished in the vault.")

He, therefore, decided to decorate the lunettes as well, abandoning the flat decoration that he had planned hitherto, and inserting an architectural system with incidents and figures. His intention was to unify the entire structure of the vault, as if it were a system totally independ-

47 Arm and leg of Moses (right side-front view).

49 Head and torso of Moses (view from above).

48 Hand and beard of Moses (left side-front view).

ent of the organization already present on the chapel walls. At the same time, though, he wanted to maintain the integrity of the curved surface of the real vault and express its form, mass and inherent stresses in an ideal order. This he succeeded in doing, considering the vault as a monolith on which he was to carve a high relief in three planes, and which consisted of a framework that supported and enclosed the figures of varying dimensions, positions and movements, and all the incidents. It seems, therefore, that the creative imagination took fire suddenly when Michelangelo let himself be inspired by the real form and mass of the curved vault and decided to adorn it with figures. Whereas other contemporary artists would have seen here only the alternative between a flat decoration of the vault or an illusionist one that would contradict the form and mass of the real vault, Michelangelo succeeded in producing an autonomous drawing that retained the true form, mass and stresses of the vault, converting those qualities into artistic values, representational or architectural.

Similar to that of the Sistine vault is the development of the artistic idea of the *Last Judgment*. The first request, made by Clement VII in 1534, contemplated decorating the central portion of the altar wall of the Sistine Chapel with a Resurrection of Christ, to be done above the altarpiece of Perugino and also above two historical pictures that the same artist had already painted there. In the preparatory drawings for the *Resurrection* we already find the nude, beardless and Apollonian Christ that was to appear in the center of the *Judgment*.

Subsequently, probably under Paul III, the entire project was changed to a *Last Judgment*; whether at the pope's request or Michelangelo's, we do not know. The first sketch we have of the *Judgment* (in Bayonne) is traditional in inspiration. In it, Christ appears surrounded

50-52 The Risen Christ. Rome, Santa Maria sopra Minerva.

by the Heavenly Tribunal, which is made up of the Virgin and the Apostles, seated six to the right and six to the left. During the Middle Ages this Tribunal was usually shown on the same plane and at the same level as the Christ. Giotto had introduced an innovation; he arranged the Tribunal almost in a semicircle and his example was followed by the great painters of the early fifteenth century. There are Byzantine instances, however, in which the Apostles are shown surrounding Christ, to form a complete circle. Although in all probability Michelangelo did not know of these Byzantine examples, he conceived a similar structure. For the first time, a real human situation was evoked in a *Last Judgment:* the Apostles are not seated motionless on their thrones, but on clouds and reacting differently to the Divine announcement; some of them are terrified, others lean forward to intercede, still others look down in pity at the fate of the sinners. Here, too, Michelangelo identifies with his figures, projecting his own feelings into them as no artist had done before him. He is present in each of his creations, as a great writer is always present in every character in his works.

In a drawing in Casa Buonarroti, later than the one we have been speaking of, Michelangelo omits the theme of the seated Tribunal. The Virgin is depicted as the guide of Humanity, tending towards Heaven as if to invade it. The theme of the Virgin guiding Humanity was an invention of Giotto's; but where he had expressed the theme in the hieratic solemnity and slow motions of the elect, Michelangelo once again identifies with the efforts and struggles of

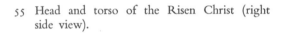

53 Head and torso of the Risen Christ (right rear-side view).

55 Head and torso of the Risen Christ (right side view).

54 The Risen Christ (left side-front view).

40

yearning Humanity, to the point of replacing the traditional structure of superposed horizontal zones by a new structure with vertical currents in opposite directions.

The later phases that led up to the final version have not come down to us. In the fresco Michelangelo rejected the theme of the interceding Virgin; here (as the late Mrs. Coor noted) she is shown as withdrawn into herself in the pose of the classical motif of the Crouching Venus. All the figures around Christ are standing, magically attracted and at the same time held at a distance from Him. At this point the Master sought to adapt the composition to the requirements of the huge wall and its structure. It was cut up by the cornices of the two side walls, making it necessary to break the unified movement of the Casa Buonarroti drawing in accordance with these cesuras into horizontal divisions (Wilde). But the movement is present within these divisions, and is transferred from one group to another, creating a kind of rotation about the Divine Judge who, as its immobile center, seems to express cosmic fatality.

Up to the present we have tried to reconstruct, more or less, the method that Michelangelo was in the habit of following in executing his works. We have seen that in the initial phase he had no intention (unlike many of our best modern artists) of creating a new and surprising personal language. Instead he either started from tradition, especially the classical and the Early Renaissance (but strangely enough, as we have said, not from the tradition of his immediate predecessors); or he took his themes directly from nature, reorganizing them in accordance with the canons of his own taste; or he developed conceptions taken from previous works of his own. He sought to develop an artistic heritage to its utmost consequences, bringing it to perfection on the principles of monumentality, symmetry and contrast. But all this did not satisfy him; and then, as if illuminated by a new revelation, he rejected what he had done up to that point and, in the final version, recreated his initial idea, but after expanding it by the spiritual experience, as if he had transferred himself at last into his figures, and had finally understood the requirements of the material, namely, the integrity of the block or the surface of the wall. The result was a new and bolder style that cannot be classified as either Renaissance or Mannerist or Baroque. It is rather a transformation of the Tuscan heritage of monumentality, sublimated by the principles of classic art. Michelangelo may,

56 Head and torso of the Risen Christ (left side-front view).

6

therefore, be said to have become, despite himself, the creator of a new period in the history of art, whose effects are still living and vital in our generations.

The new photographs in this chapter are intended to illustrate some of our observations on the characteristic way in which Michelangelo treated marble and the sacred respect he had for the material.

It will be noticed that in his reliefs, unlike artists prior to him, he left a border of marble around the composition (Fig. 1, 4, 30). This respect for the material is already felt in the *Madonna della Scala*, done in the crushed relief technique he had learned from Donatello's works. In the lower portion of the *Centauromachia*, which is a middle relief, Michelangelo left the vein of the marble which shows the original thickness of the block. He had removed it, however, in the upper portion which he left unfinished, and had begun to take it off along the sides as well; but would seem to have had second thoughts about it at a certain point. It should also be noted that although the shape of the block was rectangular and flat, he cut out the figures in relief, giving the composition a convex form with the parts projecting most arranged in the center. The figures are distributed in three planes, one behind the other, with the lower ones in greater relief, and, strangely, with the figures of the protagonists carved on the second level rather than the first.

In the *Pitti Madonna*, in the National Museum, the parts in the highest relief are those that are spiritually the most important; namely, the heads of the Madonna and the Christ Child. Here once again Michelangelo transformed a flat surface into a convex one, but one that is now in the service of the most important point of the composition: it serves, that is, to accentuate the figure of the Madonna, who is sitting on a log, on which the vein of the marble can be seen. In order to give the convexity still more relief, Michelangelo cut out the background of the composition, making it concave (Fig. 30-33).

He carved his statues by hammering at the block while it was horizontal on the floor, as can be seen from a 1527 woodcut [13] showing Michelangelo at work.

Michelangelo cut out his statues similarly to the way used for the reliefs, that is, going from one plane to another and working in depth. Since the back of the figure was cut on the part of the block that was touching the ground, many of his statues have been left unfinished, or only sketched, precisely in this portion.

His respect for the material is also seen in the way in which he treated the bases of the statues. Michelangelo treated the bases realistically, that is, imitating rocks or tree trunks, only in works of his youth, such as the *Bacchus* (Fig. 12, 16), the *Pietà* in St. Peter's (Fig. 21), the *David* (Fig. 26, 28). It happens for the last time in the *Christ* of Santa Maria sopra Minerva, in which, however, the hand of a journeyman can also be seen. Curiously enough, there are two bases here, both imitating rocks: the first one, from the block of the figure, rests on a second base that seems to have been added later. However, there were no naturalistic intentions involved in the realistic treatment of the base; in differentiating the details, Michelangelo stopped short of losing sight of the unity and homogeneity of the substance. This explains the large planes of the rocks and the strange softness of the tree trunks.

In most of his statues the base is treated as a geometrical form consisting of one or two steps, without any geometrical rigidity of form but rich in almost imperceptible irregularities

57 Torso and legs of the Risen Christ (right side view).

58-59 Legs of the Risen Christ (front and right side views).

that give animation (see the bases of the *St. Matthew*, the *Dying Slave*, the *Rebellious Slave* and the *David-Apollo*). In the bases of the *Moses*, the *Victory*, the *Leah* and the *Rachel*, although they are finished, the discreet irregularity of form is likewise present. The base of the *Rondanini Pietà* is an exception, but it was evidently redone later. This treatment was a technical discovery by Michelangelo, and the bases of these statues have an artistic value of their own, since they are evidence that for Buonarroti even the subordinate portions of the statue should bear the stamp of Michelangelo's art. As we have indicated above, the unfinished figures of the master are visibly homogeneous with the rude material from which they seem to be liberating themselves. Still more surprising is the fact that even in the finished statues the same homogeneity is revealed. For example, in the draping of the *Moses* or the *Medici Madonna* we feel the vividness of the original material; here too the Master stopped short of destroying the effect of unity with a naturalistic treatment.

As has been said, the creative principles of Michelangelo's great compositions are inspired or determined by the material and by certain formal facts that occupy a primary position in the creative process and are illuminated by a spiritual vision that transforms them.

In his cyclical works, in which he was free to invent the design of the entire architectural structure and of the figures, Michelangelo conceived three superposed horizontal zones, which corresponded to the hierarchical sequence leading from earthly life to heavenly and then to the empyrean. The zones are separated by frames and marked by architectural forms that are heavier toward the bottom and lighter above, differentiated by various orders of figures. The architectural system is not conceived by Michelangelo as a skeleton to which the figures are subordinated and into which they are inserted, as in the Gothic, but as a background out of which the figures are cut out to become virtually autonomous. This division of the composition into superposed zones must have corresponded to the hierarchical spheres well known to antiquity and to the Middle Ages, which inspired, for example, the façades of cathedrals and, in Italy especially, the structure of pulpits and fountains: images, that is, abbreviations of the order of the cosmos. These structures of universal significance are permanent in the cyclical works of Michelangelo; the façade of San Lorenzo and the first version of the tomb of Julius II were designed according to this principle, with three superposed zones inhabited by three orders of figures illustrating this hierarchical sequence.

The composition of the vault of the Sistine Chapel was inspired first of all by the preexistent form of the ceiling. The first drawings for it show how he took as his starting point the pendentives, which he wished to bind to the smooth surface of the vault proper. The already existing organization of the pavement and the decoration of the walls of the chapel suggested to him the idea of carrying their line up to the ceiling. In the final version, however, all the elements of the painted architecture were unified, taking on the form of a framework in which the artist succeeded in expressing the tensions inherent in the vault itself. At the same time, this architectural structure served to house the great figures of the Prophets and Sibyls. The openings in the framework gave on a higher sphere. Figures of differing dimensions and categories served to interpret the forces that were present in the vault itself. The principle of sequence from the bottom to the top, that is, from the lunettes, through the zone of the " seers " up to the ideal heaven, was kept and completed by a sequence in the longitudinal axis going from the entrance to the altar. Every figure had its set place within this architectural system, as had already been the case in the tomb of Julius II.

In the design of the Medici Chapel, the dimensions of the plan were already fixed and corresponded to those of the Old Sacristy. In the architectural organization of the walls and the structure of the tombs we once more see an expression of the hierarchical sequence through the three horizontally superposed zones, decorated with images of earthly life, the spirits of the dead on the second level, and finally the empty thrones of the souls become divine. Here, too, is expressed a spiritual progression in the successive planes, one behind the other, on which the lowest figures are also those nearest to the spectator and the highest ones are most remote. The innovation that Michelangelo introduced was that the figures no longer respect the architectural lines but are now combined in triangular form in front of the architecture proper of the tomb. The two superposed systems are, however, seen together in their unity as a polyphonic contrapuntal composition (A. E. Popp).

In the *Last Judgment*, on the other hand, the three zones are present only vaguely, although down to the time of Michelangelo they had traditionally formed the structure of the subject. With the exception of the *Christ* and the *Virgin*, all other hierarchical distinctions among the figures have disappeared; there are not even any figurative marks to distinguish the elect from the damned, the angels from the saints or the humans. All the orders are linked by a circular movement turning around Christ, so as to give the impression that the same figures that are rising on one side will be seen descending on the other. Thus, the hierarchical structure, a closed image of the universe, is here replaced by a vision of a homogeneous infinite space, full of the planetary motion of moving bodies, which is also the first representation of the modern macrocosm.

A final step in the direction of doing away with the tripartite composition can be seen in the two frescoes of the Cappella Paolina, in which it was replaced by gyratory motions, as in the *Last Judgment*. In this way Michelangelo came to free himself from the hierarchical structure of the universe that had come down in tradition, and for the first time expressed a conception that was to have its first exponent in philosophy in Giordano Bruno, and that was to be the world view of modern science. This unification of the universe in a rotatory motion to which all the figures are subject has no immediate precedent, and could only be compared with the images of what Vasari calls " the machine of the universe " and " the wheel of fortune," from which, however, any true and proper planetary motion in space is absent.

MICHELANGELO'S THEORY OF ART — PRINCIPAL PERIODS
IN THE DEVELOPMENT OF MICHELANGELO'S ARTISTIC PERSONALITY

Condivi reports that Michelangelo wished to write a theory of art: " An ingenious theory he had discovered by long practice."

Even before Condivi, in Giannotti's *Dialogues* (p. 42), Michelangelo states this intention. However, the treatise was never written by him. To reconstruct it more or less approximately, we have only a bit here and there in his letters and some of his poems. Indirect sources are some passages in Francisco de Hollanda, Varchi and Vincenzo Danti in his *Il primo libro delle perfette proporzioni*, 1567.

We have attempted elsewhere to reconstruct this theory of art of Michelangelo's (*The Art and Thought of Michelangelo*, 1964, p. 83 ff.). Here we confine ourselves to indicating the essential points of his new doctrine. It seems to us that this theory of Michelangelo is based on the conviction that the artist should seek in his work to imitate " the perfect intentional form of nature " (Danti); that is, its idea. Thus, Michelangelo added a new dimension to the artistic theories of the Renaissance. Prior to him, artists still followed Ghiberti's definition, " but proportionality only creates pulchritude," while Michelangelo sees beauty in the correspondence of the form to the idea, since " beauty depends on the final aim "; that is, on the adaptation of the form to the aim. For Michelangelo, proportion is no longer quantitative but qualitative; " it is an intellectual measure."

He discards proportions fixed a priori, such as Alberti, Leonardo and Dürer looked for.

Since Michelangelo abandoned naturalistic portrayal of the empirical world, it is not surprising that he did not approve the style of the works of the Flemish, Spanish and German painters, as well as those of various Italian realistic painters of the 1400's (Francisco de Hollanda).

The extensive universalism in portraying the manifold aspects of nature that Leonardo called for in the painter was not accepted by Michelangelo. Instead, he sought to arrive at a universalism in depth. For him, all the aspects and forces of the macrocosm should be comprised in the human body.

The periods of Michelangelo's artistic development arose out of the interaction of biological phases and spiritual organization.

The youthful period was marked by absorption and assimilation, in arduous study of everything that he felt was akin to his personality, in the art of the past and in that of the Tuscany of his own time (especially ancient statues and those of the Early Renaissance). We do not see in him a gradual emancipation from his masters, as is usually the case; from the very outset it is impossible not to see and identify his powerful mode of feeling, seeing and expressing existence. His youthful works already manifest the entire vision that characterized him, still vague in expression only because he did not yet possess technical mastery and deepened knowledge of anatomy and perspective.

He began to surmount these deficiencies in his first Roman period (1496-1501) and in the Florentine period immediately thereafter (1501-1505). We see in the works of these periods (as in the *Pietà* of St. Peter's or the Bruges *Madonna*) his success in organizing his overall vision and making it concrete in forms that have become precise; sharply chiseled in the marble. The same can be seen in his conception of the nude. The forms of the *Battle of the Centaurs*, pulsating with life but still generic, later become anatomically correct, and we feel the structure and play of the muscles (in the *Bacchus*) under the softness of the flesh and finally arrive (in the *David*) at vigorous monumental forms that precisely express the entire internal structure of the human body tense for action.

Michelangelo's maturity has a rhythm marked by the scansion of his great cyclical works, in which he seeks to arrive at a balance between his original overall vision and the technical wisdom he had acquired. We may therefore speak of the " heroic " period of the tomb of Julius II (first version) and the vault of the Sistine Chapel, in which his genius creates with thunderous power. Then we may speak of the " elegiac " period of the Medici Chapel, in which the artist's creativity takes on a contemplative attitude, disclosing the flow of life through the forms. Finally, we can speak of the " tragic " period of the *Last Judgment*, in which the human being, despite its titanic nature, is overpowered by cosmic forces.

The stylistic imprint of these great works is also found in other lesser works done more or less at the same time.

60 Legs of the David-Apollo (right side view). Florence, Bargello National Museum.

61-62 David-Apollo (left side view and right side view of the head and torso).

These three phases of Michelangelo's maturity had as their epilogue the old age of the final fourteen years in Rome, in which Buonarroti did not execute any cyclical works, as he had not in his youth. While his youthful period was rich in all sorts of stylistic experiments, his old age was characterized by a single manner (not in one art only, but in all three) in which the antinomies inherent in the great epochs of his maturity are reconciled on a single level. The forms are spiritualized and merge into a new unity; they are no longer articulated and hence correspond more directly to the internal vision. In the face of death, the sharp slender Florentine accent flowered once more.

The biological phases of the development and unfolding of Michelangelo's personality and art are seen most clearly only at the two ends of his life's journey: in his youth and advanced old age. During his maturity his genius, tending to liberate itself from the biological determinism, stamps the cyclical works with the mark of his spiritual travail.

[11] Cf. Jacques Maritain, *L'intuition créatrice dans l'art de la poésie* (in press). The English edition has already been published by the Bollingen Foundation.

[12] Cf. Paola Barocchi and Giorgio Chiarini, *Catalogo dei manoscritti michelangioleschi*, Biblioteca Laurenziana, Florence 1964.

[13] Cf. Fanti, *Triompho di Fortuna*, Venice 1527.

45

Michelangelo's fame

IN LITERATURE AND CRITICISM

While Michelangelo was still alive, he was considered to be a supreme modern artistic genius. The enormous success of his works produced two opposite images of his personality in his contemporaries. His friends, admirers and followers made a mythical figure of him, as artist and as man. They called him " divine." Adversaries and detractors fabricated an image of him as a misanthrope, gloomy, haughty, miserly, even a heretic. Diderot called him " hard, vicious, envious." It was only in 1863, when his poems were first published in their true form, and in 1875, with the publication of his letters, that this image was seen to be false, and the nobility of the Master's generous heart emerged.

The first signs of a Michelangelo " cult " date from a period after 1540, starting with the *Dialoghi* of Donato Giannotti (abt. 1545). Francisco de Hollanda (1548) and Anton Francesco Doni contributed their share to the formation of this cult. A further contribution was made by Varchi, whose lectures on two poems of Michelangelo (1549) are likewise the first book written

63 David-Apollo (front view).

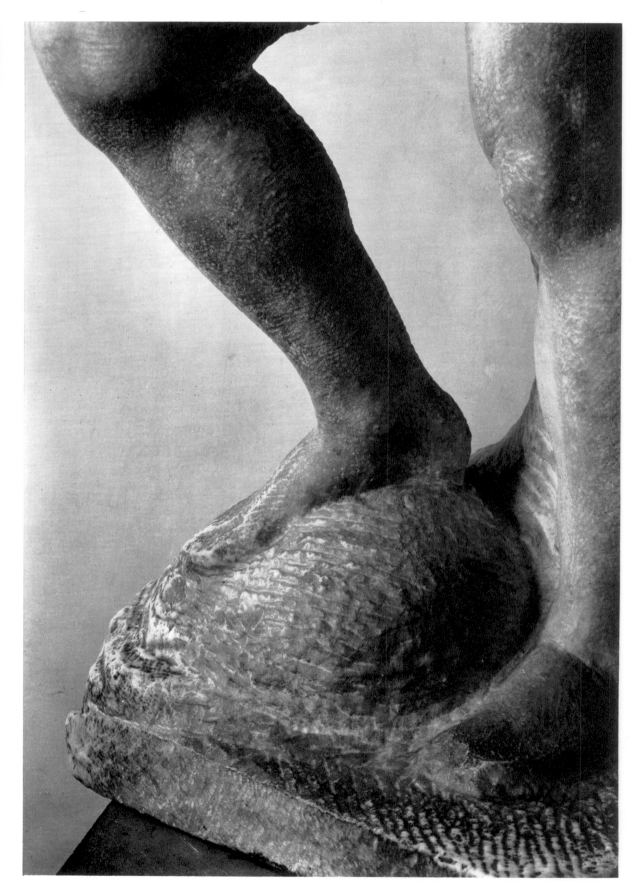

46   64 Legs of David-Apollo (right side-front view).

67 Head and torso of the Medici Virgin. Florence, San Lorenzo, New Sacristy.

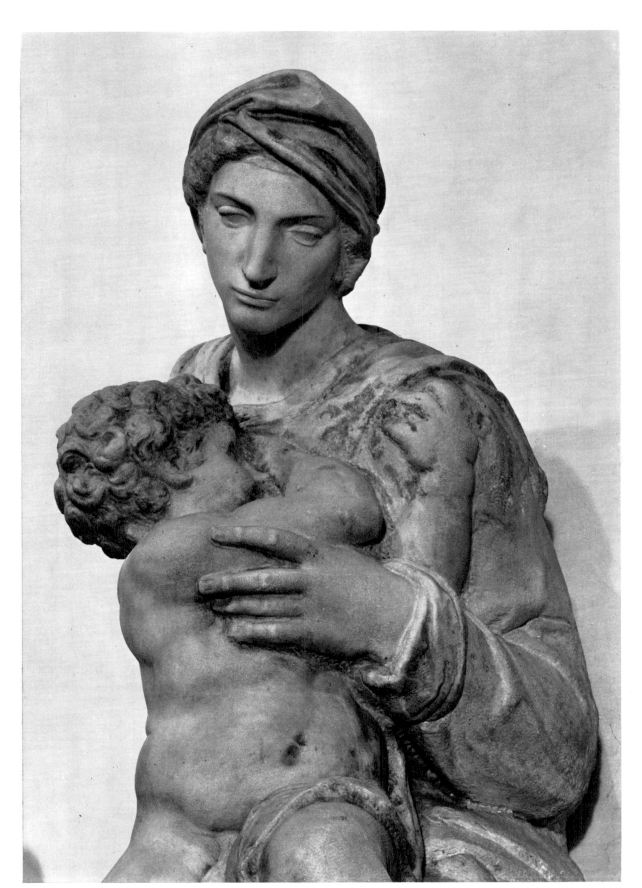

65-66 Legs of the Medici Virgin (right and left side-front views).

on the Master. In 1550 came Vasari's biography, based in part on the Anonimo Magliabechiano (1535-40), and the biography by Condivi in 1553. In 1568 came the second edition of Vasari's biography, which included data taken from Condivi, and other information. Another short biography was contained in the funeral oration delivered by Varchi in 1564. For Vasari, the history of Italian art culminates in Michelangelo, of whom he gives the most vivid portrait drawn by a contemporary, although the one by Condivi, written in part at the dictation of the Master himself, is more reliable. From Vasari and Condivi comes the "heroic" characterization of Michelangelo that has been handed down to the present.

Michelangelo's artistic work drew admiration early; he was only twenty-nine when Pomponio Gaurico (*De Sculptura*, Florence, 1504) called him one of the best of Tuscan sculptors, "etiam pictor." Vasari, as we have seen, sets him above all artists ancient and modern, and above nature itself; Buonarroti is compared to a god and his works are not merely creations of a genius, but represent the very canon of perfect art. In the Preface to the third part of his *Lives* the historian asserts: "But the man that bears off the palm among the dead and the living and surpasses and overshadows all is the divine Michelangelo Buonarroti, who is the prince not of one of these arts alone but of all three together. He goes beyond and conquers not only all those who have virtually conquered nature, but those same most renowned an-

68 Legs of Twilight (front view). Florence, San Lorenzo, New Sacristy.

cients, who with so much fame beyond any doubt went beyond her; and by himself triumphs over the former, the latter and her; nature imagining hardly anything so strange and so difficult that he, with the power [*virtù*] of his most divine genius, by means of industry, design, art, judgment and grace, does not go far beyond her..."

Not dissimilar was the judgment of other contemporaries, beginning with Cavalieri and Vittoria Colonna and ending with Condivi and Varchi. They likewise exalt the human qualities of Michelangelo. Condivi puts him on a level with the reigning pontiff, Julius III; Vittoria Colonna compares him, for goodness, with the Redeemer Himself.

The reaction began to set in with the short biography of Paolo Giovio (abt. 1515), reflecting the reservations of the court of Leo X concerning Michelangelo's "savage" nature.

The real attacks were launched from about 1540 on, and were based on the Master's alleged irreligiosity and his departure from traditional sacred iconography. The first accuser was the cynical irreligious Aretino, in a 1545 letter, which is nothing more than a piece of blackmail intended to obtain drawings from Michelangelo. Aretino's allegations were: impiety, license in iconography, regarding art as higher than faith itself. These accusations were used later during the Counter Reformation period. Don Giglio da Fabriano, in his *Dialoghi... degli errori dei pittori* (Camerino, 1564), condemns the *Last Judgment* of Michelangelo and his frescoes in the Cappella Paolina as arbitrary interpretations of the Biblical texts, contrary to the principles of "propriety." It is interesting to note that just at that time, during the action against Ve-

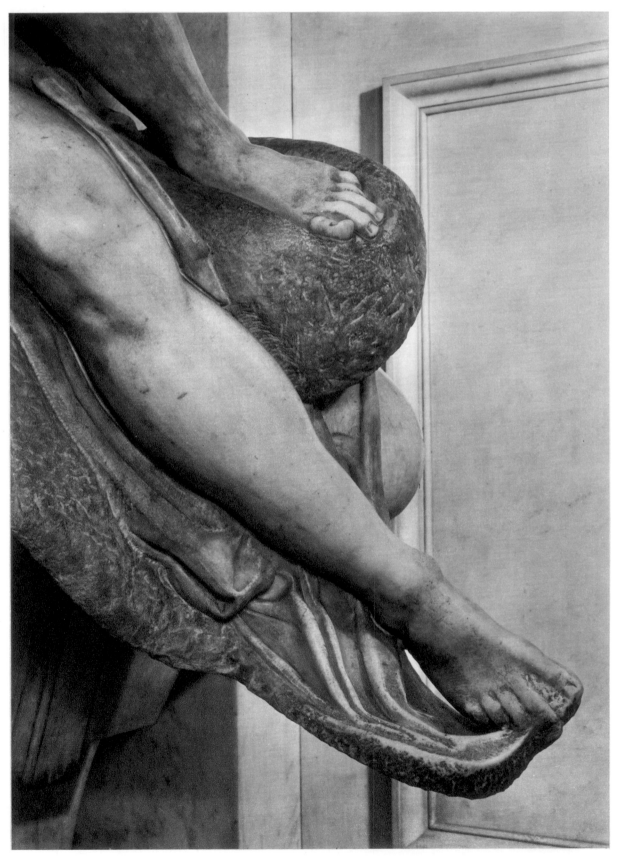

69 Legs of Dawn (right side-front view). Florence, San Lorenzo, New Sacristy.

ronese in Venice, the inquisitor held the nudes of Michelangelo's *Judgment* to be correct, inasmuch as humanity will have to appear naked before Christ the Judge.

In 1557 Lodovico Dolce declared Michelangelo's nudes to be "monotonous" as compared with the many-formed beauty of Raphael, a comparison that became the custom in academic circles from the seventeenth to the nineteenth centuries.

The originality of Michelangelo's architecture was likewise attacked, as violating the rules of Vitruvius, by the "Sangallo sect," that is, the followers of Antonio da Sangallo the younger, who hoped, after the death of their master in 1546, to fall heirs to the great architectural commissions that the pope intended instead to give to Buonarroti.

In the second half of the seventeenth century and the first half of the eighteenth, admiration for Michelangelo was on the wane. Except for classical antiquity, Raphael had become the almost exclusive artistic ideal during this period. An exception was made for Michelangelo as architect, as is shown by Bernini's statement, "Michelangelo was great as a sculptor and painter, but truly divine as an architect," a judgment repeated in Dufresnoy's *De arte grafica*, where he says, "He was the greatest architect we know of, having surpassed even the ancients." The classicist Milizia (1725-1798), although critical of the profiles as too much accentuated and the design of the Master's architectural forms as "arbitrary," clearly realized the beauty of the cornice of Palazzo Farnese and the dome of St. Peter's (*Vite*, Vol. I, p. 319; *Memorie*, Vol. I, p. 247 ff.).

70 Legs of Night (left side-front view). Florence, San Lorenzo, New Sacristy.

71 Legs of Day (right side-front view). Florence, San Lorenzo, New Sacristy.

7

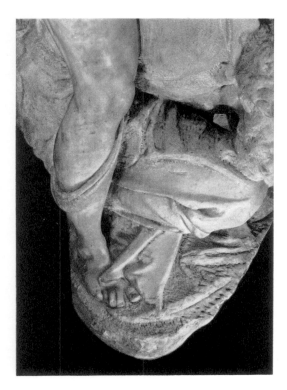

72 Leg of Genius of Victory and slave (left side-front view from above). Florence, Palazzo Vecchio.

In Italy, Michelangelo was further criticized in the second half of the seventeenth century and the first half of the eighteenth under the influence of the doctrines of the church. His works were said not to correspond exactly to the prescriptions of the Council of Trent nor to the text of the Bible. The treatise in which these opinions were laid down was written by Ottonelli and by Berrettini da Cortona, and published anonymously in 1649. Other Italian writers said that Michelangelo's style lacked the grace and beauty of ancient statuary and Raphael's works. The argument is found in Giovanni Baglioni, Carlo Ridolfi, Luigi Scaramucci (1674) and above all in G. P. Bellori. The last named author wrote a monograph on Raphael, published in 1695, in which the comparison is constantly to the disadvantage of Michelangelo.

A little before the middle of the eighteenth century, however (earlier than in other countries —except for France), the first signs of a new cult of Michelangelo appear. One of the most important motives of this revival of Michelangelo's reputation was Florentine local patriotism. Anton Francesco Gori, in his sumptuous new critical edition of the life by Condivi (Florence, 1746), declares that he had published Condivi's text " to refresh the glories of Florence, his [Michelangelo's] homeland." The other reason that Gori gives for his publication is his desire to revive, in the minds of the lovers, and especially of students, of the art of drawing, admiration for that " generous spirit."

Condivi's text is supplemented in this volume by a life of the last ten years of Michelangelo (of necessity absent from Condivi) by Girolamo Ticciati. In it are also published the valuable

73 Torso and head of the Genius of Victory (left side-front view from below).

observations of Pierre Jean Mariette, a great French connoisseur and collector who owned a number of drawings by Michelangelo (now in the Louvre, the École des Beaux-Arts and the Albertina in Vienna). Mariette's contribution is important not only because of his great erudition but also because of his favorable judgment of Michelangelo. Expressly opposing Bellori, he declares that Raphael studied Michelangelo's works (especially the *Battle of Cascina*), that is, that his art was influenced by them. He defends Michelangelo's alleged " license " in the *Last Judgment* by arguing that Dante had used similar classical motifs, for example, Charon. Mariette was one of the first to see that " the genius of Dante recurs in Michelangelo's *Judgment*." The only criticism of Buonarroti that he advances (taken, by the way, from the critics of the past) is that Michelangelo shows so many nudes in the *Last Judgment*, an argument that was presented two centuries earlier in the letters of Pietro Aretino and the treatise of Lodovico Dolce. Mariette is perhaps the first Frenchman of the eighteenth century whose writings show a change in attitude towards the Florentine. The notes of D. M. Manni supplementing this edition of Condivi are pure erudition, without judgments.

74 Torso of the Genius of Victory (right side view).

75 Genius of Victory (left side view).

The new critical edition of Vasari's *Lives* by Bottari, published in Rome in 1759 and Vasari's life of Michelangelo, published separately in 1760, are typographically more modest than Gori's edition but have other merits because of the abbé's vast erudition.

When young Joshua Reynolds came to Italy for the first time in this same year of 1760, he certainly consulted these two recent Italian editions of Condivi and Vasari, and was probably influenced by them in his change of opinion which became favorable to Michelangelo during his Italian sojourn.

In the second half of the eighteenth century, so far as we know, no important essay on Michelangelo was published. We may mention the sonnets on Michelangelo's *Moses* and on the dome of St. Peter's by Vittorio Alfieri, written in 1781. At the end of the century we find once more, in the works of Milizia and Lanzi, the classicist verdict of the seventeenth century, to wit, that Michelangelo lacked grace. We note, as an interesting point, that Lanzi compares Michelangelo with Leonardo rather than Raphael.

From the middle of the seventeenth century to the middle of the eighteenth, France was keenly aware of its own greatness, regarding its culture as the pinnacle of civilization. The French thought of the period was essentially determined by Descartes' rationalism. Empirical

51

76-77 Young Prisoner (right side view and left side-front view of legs). Florence, Academy of Fine Arts.

78 Head and torso of Young Prisoner (right side-front view).

observation of esthetics was put aside; instead, a priori rules were sought for perfect art. The idea of the " perfection of art " became the principal topic of French esthetics. Writers deduced these rules from the works of classical antiquity and of Raphael. As a result, the French writers of this era show an almost total lack of understanding of the qualities of Michelangelo's art. One of the most violent attacks on Buonarroti is contained in the book of Fréart de Chambray (1662); Michelangelo's art violates classical rules, " les convenances." Because of its audacity, he calls Michelangelo's art " infâme libertinage " and speaks of " the boldness of the libertine." According to Fréart de Chambray, Raphael is the good angel and Michelangelo the evil angel of painting. In Michelangelo's mighty figures he can see nothing but " heavy rustic stolidity."

Many of these arguments are not original but had already been expressed in other words in the Cinquecento by Italians, for example, by the Venetian Lodovico Dolce. Félibien, in his *Entretiens sur la vie des peintres* (1672), is already less violent than Chambray, but for him, too, Raphael is superior to Buonarroti because he expressed himself " with sweetness." He conceded, however, that Michelangelo had " grandeur in drawing." Roger de Piles, whose esthetics stressed, for the first time in France, the importance of color as opposed to drawing, which the French academicians regarded as the higher quality, was a great admirer of Titian and Rubens. Although for him, too, Michelangelo lacked " the elegance of the antique," he grants that " whatever the nature of his thoughts, they were always grand..."

One of the reasons for the shift in esthetic taste after the death of Louis XIV was the influence of the English sensualistic philosophy of Locke and Hume (Gantner). Instead of objective a priori rules aiming at a perfect art, French esthetics began to stress the subjec-

79-80 Bearded Prisoner (left side-front views). Florence, Academy of Fine Arts.

tive behavior of the spectator and to describe the impression he received from the work of art. They began to recognize that the most important virtue of a work of art is to be moving. This point of view seems to have been introduced into France by Fénelon (1651-1715) and the Abbé du Bos (1670-1742). By 1719 the latter was writing, " The first purpose of painting and poetry is to touch us." Although for them, too, the work of Raphael was still the height of artistic creation, they called Michelangelo " the Corneille of painting." D'Argenville, the follower of De Piles, in his *Abrégé de la vie des peintres* (1745), gives high praise to Michelangelo's *Last Judgment* because it moves us. The first French biography of Michelangelo is by the Abbé Hauchecorne, *Vie de Michel-Ange* (1763), based on the Gori edition of Condivi's biography.

In the meantime, in 1755 the German J. J. Winckelmann published his fundamental work on ancient sculpture, *Über die Nachahmung der Antiken Skulptur.* In this work we find the judgment that Michelangelo was the only sculptor " who has attained the greatness of those of antiquity." For him, Michelangelo was the greatest artist since the Greeks and before Canova. But Winckelmann later changed his opinion, probably under the influence of his friend, the painter Raphael Mengs, and in his *Von der Grazie in den Werken der Kunst* (1756-59) put Raphael higher than Michelangelo. Towards the end of his life he once more placed Michelangelo among the three greatest artists of modern times, along with Ariosto and Raphael. We note further that Winckelmann considered St. Peter's to be the most perfect edifice since antiquity. The judgment of the young Goethe in his *Italienische Reise* (1786-1787-1805) is already free of classicist prejudices, and the greatness of Buonarroti's genius is clearly felt. In the late Goethe, however, there was a shift, as von Einem has observed, and he now preferred Raphael. Goethe's friends in Rome, Karl Philip Moritz and Karl Ludwig Fernow, appreciated the subjective expression of Michelangelo which corresponded to the artistic tendencies of the *Sturm und Drang.*

53

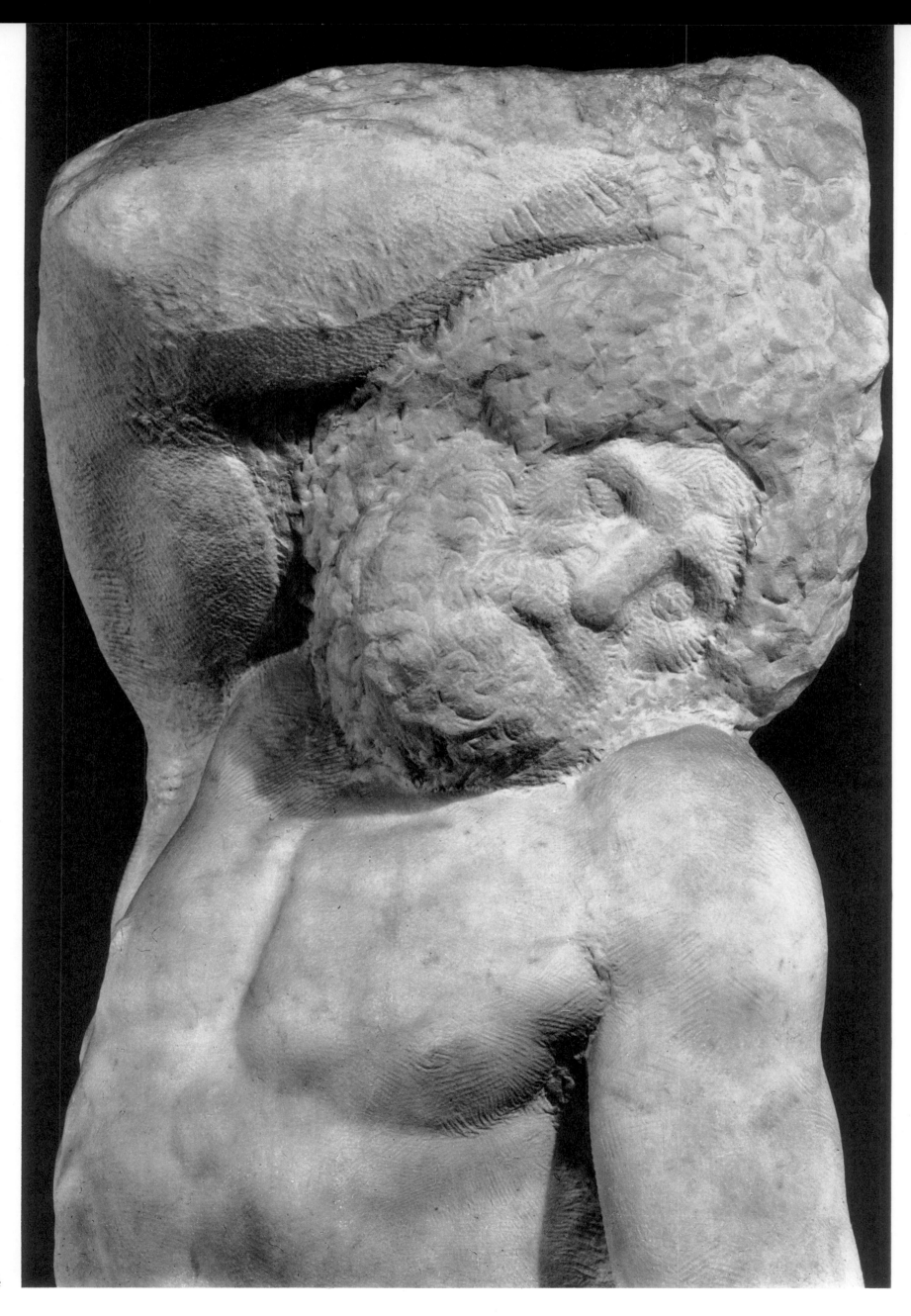

81 Head and torso of bearded Prisoner (front view).

82 Head of reawakening Prisoner (left side-front view). Florence, Academy of Fine Arts.

The image of Michelangelo in the minds of the French Romantics is not a mere continuation of this shift in esthetic valuation in the second half of the eighteenth century, but seems to be an authentic and spontaneous rediscovery of the greatness of his genius, based on an internal affinity. Stendhal (1817), Géricault (1819) and Delacroix (1830 and 1837) were the first to identify completely with the genius of the Florentine, whom they see in all his greatness but not yet in his relationship to history. The exaltation of the genius of Michelangelo in Stendhal, and the portrait of the solitary passionate Artist drawn by Delacroix were born from their personal experience and ardent identification with the Master. The French Romantic historians, Edgar Quinet, Henri Martin and Jules Michelet, integrated the figure of Michelangelo into their own historical world. Michelet sees, already prefigured in Michelangelo, his own ideal of universal justice (but is nonetheless able to analyze the vault of the Sistine with keen sensitivity). In Quinet, Buonarroti becomes " the conscience of the human race " (*Allemagne et Italie*, Paris, 1839), an idea that recurs in M. Dvořák (1928). Quinet (*Révolution d'Italie*, Paris, 1848) later saw in Michelangelo the synthesis of the two " Italian revolutions ": the pagan Renaissance and the Catholic one. From that time on almost all biographers were to follow this Romantic pattern.

But from about 1860 on the historical material becomes richer and richer. The biographies of Grimm (1860-63), Gotti (1875), Symonds (1893), Justi (1900), Thode (1902-13), Rolland (1907) are better documented than previous ones, although with the exception of Rolland's, the figure of Michelangelo comes out weaker in these studies. This would be the result of a bourgeois conception. The figure of the artist, although retaining its artistic prestige, now appears humanly weak, fragile and suffering.

A new phase in interpretation began with deeper researches into the relationships between Michelangelo's works and the historical context. Wölfflin (1891) followed an accurate monographich method for the youthful works; and likewise, for the other periods, Justi (1900) for the tomb of Julius II, Steinmann (1905) for the Sistine vault and the *Last Judgment*, E. A. Popp (1922) for the Medici Chapel, and Baumgart and Biagetti (1934) for the Cappella Paolina.

With the reawakening of historical consciousness in the second half of the nineteenth century there also came the tendency to integrate the artistic figure of Michelangelo into his time; that is, the attempt was made to consider his forms in order to discover the play of influences within them. The contours of his original genius began to grow fainter. Shrewd inquiries were conducted into the relationship of his art with the past and his own time, but it was no longer asked what the reasons were for the affinities with the artists that influenced him, nor what personal experiences might have dictated Michelangelo's inventions to him.

The latest criticism, while granting that even so humanly and artistically gigantic a personality as Michelangelo's is bound up with his time, sees his works, however, as formulation of an original force that makes use of traditions in sovereign fashion, that breaks the classical figurative unities and that by combining previously separate elements into new organic forms, succeeds in expressing a feeling of life or a personal experience of existence itself. The effort

83-84 Reawakening Prisoner (left side-front view, and left side-front view of the legs).

is made in this way to bring out the internal dynamic structure of his works, which reveals itself in and of itself as the expression of a message that is vital and spiritual, conscious and subconscious at the same time. In point of fact, the works of Michelangelo, although idealized, are more personal than those of any other Tuscan master. In the faces of *Proclus*, *David*, *Moses* and *Brutus* are reflected the pride and haughty morality of the artist; the Prophets and Sibyls of the Sistine vault express his spiritual ecstasy; in the Eternal, the unbounded creative force that he felt surging within him. The suffering of imprisonment of the *Slaves* of the tomb of Julius II; the weighing down, the melancholy, the disdain of the figures of the Medici Chapel; all express feelings that were the Master's own. The spiritualization of the figures of the Captains has a parallel in the ideal aspiration that lives in his poems, written a little later, for Cavalieri. His yearning for liberation from terrestrial limits is manifested movingly in the *Slaves* and in three drawings for the *Resurrection* (Louvre, Windsor, British Museum); the Conversion of St. Paul is his own "conversion,, and the Crucifixion of St. Peter is nothing other than the objective representation of his own intolerance of the human condition. In this light, Michelangelo's work could be regarded as a self-portrait, whether conscious or unconscious. Both in the *Last Judgment* and in the *Pietà* of Santa Maria del Fiore the autobiographical allusions are more direct, even though veiled. In the *Judgment* he portrayed himself as damned in the skin of St. Bartholomew (La Cava); in the Florentine *Pietà*, which according to Vasari was intended for his tomb, he carved his ideal portrait in *Joseph of Arimathea*.

Not since the Hellenistic era had feeling and the state of mind of inspiration been expressed with such intensity. But in Michelangelo the subjectivity of the sentiment, we repeat, rises to universal value, finding systematic expression in a philosophical or religious doctrine. He never speaks in the first person, nor does he wish to express individual experiences, but only universal truths, in absolute forms; that is, he wants his work to be objective even if those universal truths actually are born out of profound personal motivations.

MICHELANGELO'S INFLUENCE IN ART: MICHELANGELISM

Although the personality and the art of Michelangelo dominated the sixteenth century and part of the seventeenth, and found new vigor in the Romantic age, his message (at least so far as representational art is concerned) was not understood in its entirety. Each artist drew his inspiration from a single aspect of the Master's art, transforming it and integrating it within the scope of his own tendencies.

Among Michelangelo's contemporaries, his innovations had prompt repercussions. This took form in the reinforcement of the plastic modeling of the figures, in the new majesty of their carriage, in the drama and dignity of their gestures. Examples of this are to be found in the late drawings of Leonardo, in Raphael's works of the Roman period, in the panels of the mature Fra Bartolomeo, in Andrea del Sarto and Correggio and a little later in the canvases of Titian.

After the inauguration of the Sistine vault in 1512, it was virtually impossible any longer to continue to paint, in Rome, by the standards of the traditional style. This is shown, for example, by the development of the artistic personality of Sebastiano del Piombo. He had learned the art in Venice, in the *bottega* of Giovanni Bellini and Giorgione. From 1515-16 on, the time when he became acquainted with Michelangelo, he changed, taking isolated themes of Michelangelo's and setting them in the background of his compositions (as, for example, in the Leningrad *Lamentation*), or giving a Michelangelesque character to entire compositions (from the *Flagellation of Christ*, 1515, in San Pietro in Montorio, on). In addition, his drawing and modeling become more precise, under Michelangelo's influence. We know that at the time of preparing more than one of his pictures, Sebastiano del Piombo asked Michelangelo for " a little light... as to the invention, since *sine tuo lumine nihil est in homine* " (March 25, 1532).

After the death of Leonardo (1519) and Raphael (1520), Michelangelo remained the unopposed ruler of the artistic scene. In the opinion of the painters born in the last decade of the Quattrocento, art had attained its peak of perfection in Leonardo, Michelangelo and Raphael, an opinion that was likewise expressed in the Preface to Vasari's *Lives*. But this could not prevent the young artists from desiring to show their own talents. They sought to free themselves from the tyranny of the canons of classical art, since that evoked a normative image of nature; that is, an ideal world expressing the essence of reality. With the help of Michelangelism, they tended to express a sort of anti-reality, an irrational and artificial world made up of equally fabulous and arbitrary elements, created in part by transforming nature according to the subjective caprices of their imaginations. The proportions of the figures became arbitrary; rational space disappeared, to be replaced by an indeterminate spatiality filled with figurative elements, often fragmentary and in levitation.

The classic artists, Leonardo and Raphael, worked by the selective principle of beauty in nature. Michelangelo constructed his creations on an inward image of beauty, an image that he made more concrete " *a posteriori* " by means of profound study of the natural model.

The first Mannerists worked on the basis of subjectively interpreted studies, and were stimulated more by other works of art than by the study of nature, and especially the works of such northern masters as Dürer and Van Leyden, and by the vault of the Sistine Chapel.

Michelangelo's new decorative conception of the nude in movement, of rhythmic outlines freely arranged in space and no longer tied to earth, encouraged an entire group of young artists to liberate themselves from the classical Renaissance canons. The range of clear and opaque colors in Michelangelo's frescoes had great success and was widely used in the works of these young men.

Pontormo, perhaps the most important of these first Mannerists, was already influenced by Buonarroti about 1518, as is shown by his lunette at Poggio a Caiano, in which we can recognize the pose of Jonah and that of one of Michelangelo's nudes, converted into slim elegant figures. In his altarpiece of San Michele Visdomini (1518) and the *Descent from the Cross* of Santa Felicita (1524-26), the ground no longer determines the position of the figures, which instead remain suspended in three superposed zones, filling the entire surface of the pictures and giving the illusion of a certain distance, as though they were swimming in an aquarium. At the end of his life, in his projects for the fresco decoration of the choirs of San Lorenzo in Florence, he assimilated and developed (especially in the drawings for the *Flood*) the principle of intertwined grouping of the nude figures of Michelangelo's *Last Judgment*, composing complexes of flexible nudes in a manner unheard of up to that time.

Rosso Fiorentino, on the other hand, was inspired by those of Michelangelo's compositions that had the nature of a bas-relief, such as the *Sacrifice of Noah* in the Sistine Chapel. Instead of Michelangelo's solid figures, he preferred empty phantoms, with which he obtained

85 Atlas Prisoner (left side-front view). Florence, Academy of Fine Arts.

86 Torso of the Atlas Prisoner (left side-front view).

87-88 Rachel and Lia. Rome, San Pietro in Vincoli.

a freakish eccentric effect as if we were viewing "pattern" in light, empty geometrical forms.

After the inauguration of Michelangelo's *Last Judgment* (1541), all of Europe was seized by the taste for a "serious art" and "gigantic" form, in both structure and figures. One of the first representatives of this second Mannerism was Bronzino. The group also included Daniele da Volterra, Vasari, Salviati, Battista Franco, Pellegrino Tibaldi and Allori, in Italy; and Scorel, Heemskerk and Floris in the Low Countries. The new canon of the powerful muscular nudes of the *Judgment* took the place of the more refined and slender canon of the figures of the first Mannerism, in the Sistine vault and the Medici Chapel. In his fresco of the *Martyrdom of St. Lawrence* (1565-69), Bronzino used these heavier types of Michelangelo's models, grouping them in a sort of wreath around the center. In the large historical frescoes of Vasari, Salviati or Battista Franco, on the other hand, the sculptural style of Michelangelo's figures is supplemented with frequent quotations from Roman antiquity, presented against an architectural scene to the sixteenth century taste inspired by Raphael's backgrounds. The fact is that in representing incidents it was impossible to follow exclusively the abstract concept of space. Thus in a sense the second Mannerism marks a return to the classical Renaissance style. In this phase the imaginative boldness of the first Mannerism loses its vigor and the style becomes rather dry, almost "academic."

Towards 1570, however, a reaction sets in against this second Mannerism, and there is a return to the eccentric imagination of the first Manner, as can be seen in the works of the artists that decorated the cabinet of the Palazzo Vecchio in Florence. This tendency appeared outside of Italy as well; for example in the school of Utrecht and in a group of German and Dutch painters working at the court of Rudolph II in Prague. They have a refined style, by means of which they evoked the world of the ancient fables or the Bible stories.

Meanwhile at Bologna, such masters as the Caracci, Domenichino and Guido Reni were making an eclectic fusion of Michelangelo's sculptural style and dynamism with classical elements derived from Raphael, Correggio and Titian.

The Mannerist trend became more abstract. A reaction against this enfeeblement had begun as early as the third decade of the century in northern Italy, especially in the region of Venice. It is not surprising, therefore, that the two masters who made the most originally creative use of the message of Michelangelo came from those regions. Tintoretto succeeded in achieving a synthesis of the luminous Venetian color and the rigor of Michelangelo's dynamic sculptural drawing, as well as transforming the "antireal" and arbitrary world of Mannerism (as in Parmigianino) into an image of the macrocosm sanctified by a divine light, by virtue of his genuine religious ardor. His canvases seem to reveal cosmic visions, alive with planet-like motions, that break suddenly into an everyday domestic scene.

The origins of Caravaggio's style have been traced back to Lombard local tradition (in Bergamo, Cremona and Brescia), and in particular to the milieu of Antonio and Vincenzo Campi (Longhi). These circles already manifest a reaction not only against the ideal style of Michelangelo but against Mannerism as well; these artists prefer to depict genre scenes in a realistic style, with deep shadow effects. Similar tendencies are found in the work of the Bassano family, Girolamo Savoldo and partially, as has been said, in Tintoretto.

The origin of the esthetic doctrines of this stream leading to Caravaggio may be traced to Aristotle's distinction (*Poetics*, IV) between serious poets, who treat of sublime themes and are understood only by the initiate, and poets of trivial mind, who prefer to treat of vulgar themes dealing with everyday life, and who address themselves to the common people. Artists belong-

89 Lia's head and torso.

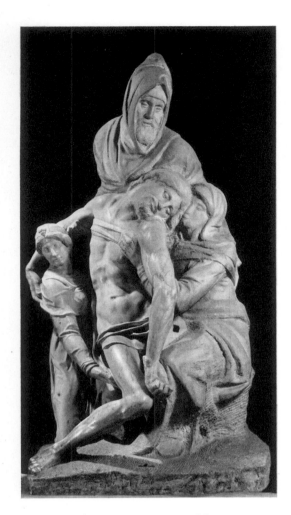

90 Pietà. Florence, Santa Maria del Fiore.

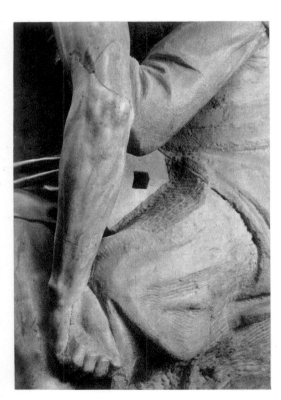

91-92 Christ's arm (front view) and Christ and Mary (right side-front view), in the Pietà in Santa Maria del Fiore.

ing to the first group have a style based on a selective principle of beauty in nature; the style of the second group imitates natural things " as they appear to the eye."

These two styles existed side by side in the Middle Ages, as can be seen from the codices of the thirteenth and fourteenth centuries, in whose miniatures the Biblican scenes are represented in the " sublime " style, and the marginal scenes, the " drôleries," in " vulgar " style. During the Renaissance, and especially after 1500, the " vulgar style " began to be highly appreciated, first in the northern countries and a little later in Italy. The greatest masters of the Low Countries in the first half of the Cinquecento, like H. Bosch, G. Metsys, H. met de Bles and Peter Bruegel the Older, regarded themselves as belonging to this tendency. In Germany the so-called " Nürenberger Kleinmeister," and in Italy Dosso Dossi, G. Savoldo and the Bassani are representatives of the trend which has a counterpart in the history of literature, in the style of Sebastian Brandt and Kaiser von Kaisersperg in Germany; Erasmus of Rotterdam in Holland; in Spain, the beginnings of the picaresque novel, like Lazarillo de Tormes, and later the Cervantes of the " *entremeses*;" in France, Rabelais and in Italy, Merlin Coccaio. Thus, Caravaggio's " revolution " in painting was a long time preparing. But he was the greatest exponent of this trend in painting, and showed in his works that the lowly themes of " still life " and the genre scenes have as much artistic value as the sublime themes of the " stories;" that even religious subjects can, in fact should, be treated by the standards or accents of the vulgar idiom, as if the events of the Bible were a part of daily life; and that these tendencies could be given artistic embodiment and high pictural quality by means of a solid honest technique based on direct study of nature. Caravaggio was thus the bearer of a message of simplicity and truth in the artificial and sophisticated artistic milieu of Rome at the end of the sixteenth century.

It would be hard to accept the recent opinion to the effect that " Caravaggio worked out art from the ground up." On the contrary, his point of departure was a conventional structure that he derived from the Lombard and Roman Mannerists, whose ideal style he brought down to earth, immersing it as it were in nature. In his pictures we find the customary triangular grouping of the figures, surrounded by *repoussoir* figures, and some motifs derived directly from Michelangelo or the Mannerists. He has, however, simplified the conventional Mannerist structure, which thereby loses its tapestry decorative character, and done away with the architectural setting, replacing it by a simple space that is almost empty and dark.

Today it is common to define Caravaggio's relationship to Michelangelo as an " anti-Michelangelo polemic," as a " parody " (persiflage) aimed at Michelangelo. Actually, the use of Michelangelesque figures had already been established as a convention by the Mannerists and was intended as an admiring tribute to the Master. When artists like Pontormo, Rosso or Dosso Dossi introduce the motifs of the Sistine nudes into their own works, they do so because they are captivated by the beauty and clarity of the shapes. These practices were carried over into the seventeenth-century Bologna school; for example, in the works of Guido Reni, who in his *Sacred and Profane Love* (in Pisa) converted Michelangelo's *Rebel Slave* (Louvre) into a *Cupid* and, on another occasion, into a *St. Sebastian* (Louvre). When Caravaggio converts a Michelangelo nude into a *St. John the Baptist* (Toledo), for example, he follows the same principle and makes sure that it remains monumental, despite his realistic treatment of the surface and the chiaroscuro. He must have seen the Michelangelesque prototype as the best solution he could find without falling into a trite fragmentation. Very likely the other insertions of motifs from Michelangelo are to be interpreted as signs of admiring homage to the Master, including the free borrowings (for example, the theme of San Matteo inspired by an angel-spirit, in San Luigi dei Francesi, as the prophets and sibyls of the Sistine vault are inspired by little spirits).

Caravaggio's arrangement of the *Conversion of St. Paul* and the *Crucifixion of St. Peter* on the side walls of the relatively small and dark Cappella Cerasi in Santa Maria del Popolo in Rome follows the arrangement of the corresponding frescoes of Michelangelo in the Cappella Paolina. The two canvases of Caravaggio are framed in a rich molded stucco ornamental setting. They are in oil, and come out warm and tactile in their vivid colors and intense sculptural modeling, thanks to the effects of chiaroscuro; and in that way they dominate the heavy ornament enclosing them. On the other hand, the relatively flat and pale aspect of the traditional frescoes in Roman chapels subordinates them to their sculptural stucco frames. The contrast between light and shade, often breaking up the shapes, was used by Caravaggio to make the details more palpable and to counteract the darkness of the chapel. His chiaroscuro can hardly be interpreted as " supernatural light," for it is clear (for example, in the *Conversion of St. Paul*) that Caravaggio rejected supernatural light even where it had always been depicted and gave the scene a profoundly human dimension.

Despite the basic difference in their tendencies, Michelangelo and Caravaggio are linked by their constant intention of using their works to evoke, not the Mannerists' artificial universe of subjective inventions, but their respective conceptions of " true reality," archetypal and transcendent in Michelangelo, particular and immanent in Caravaggio. The former proceeded by first evoking his internal vision, which he then embodied by means of empirical observation. Caravaggio seems to lack the initial vision; his method consists of giving life to a borrowed structure by means of intense evocation of materials and faces. Both rejuvenated religious experience, albeit in diametrically opposite manners: Michelangelo wanted to rouse humanity

94 Christ's head in the Rondanini Pietà (left side view). Milan, Sforza Castle Civic Museums.

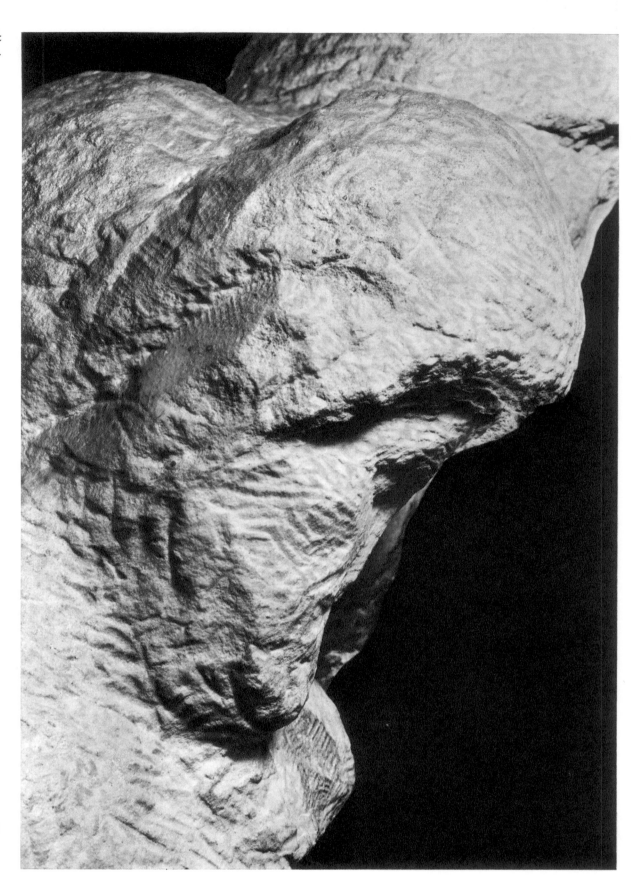

93 Mutilated arm in the Rondanini Pietà (left side view).

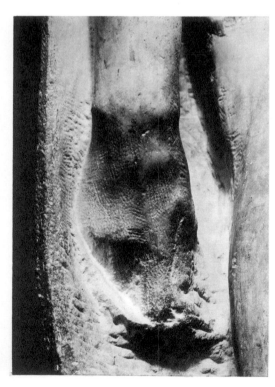

by revealing in his works the cosmic fatality to which man is subject; Caravaggio seems to console the poor and lowly by means of a new "*biblia pauperum.*"

The style and themes of Caravaggio's art seem to be directed to the people, even though his admirers were members of the aristocracy (e. g. the Cardinal Del Monte or Marquis Vincenzo Giustiniani). In point of fact, only cultured and refined connoisseurs could appreciate the high quality of his painting and the artistic beauty of the familiar and humble elements of his art. The same had been true a little earlier in the Low Countries, in the peasant scenes of Peter Bruegel the Older, whose greatest admirer was not found among the peasants but in Granvelle, the humanistically educated cardinal.

At the beginning of the seventeenth century the " realism " and "darkness" of Caravaggio dominated Europe; virtually all the geniuses that appeared in the early years of the century started in the Caravaggian style. Nevertheless, the prestige of Michelangelo was still high. There are frequent citations from him in the work of Greco and Velazquez, in Spain; in Rembrandt, in Holland; and even in classicist France, in Poussin, especially when he came to depict God the Father. The borrowings are always of movements and gestures of Michelangelo, as had been the case for Caravaggio.

The only great artist of the early seventeenth century who assimilated an essential aspect of Michelangelo's cosmos and immediately transformed it according to his own requirements

96 Christ's torso and arm in the Rondanini Pietà (left rear-side view).

95 Mary's leg and Christ's side in the Rondanini Pietà (right side view).

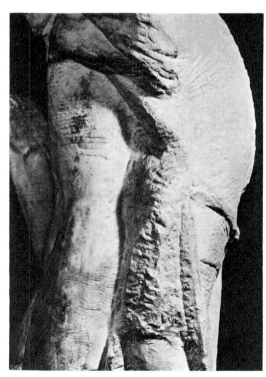

was Rubens. It is true that his personality and world view were the opposite of Michelangelo's; he was an optimist who throughout his entire life and enormous production expressed a single message—a hymn to the fertility and abundance of creative nature. Rubens was perhaps the greatest pantheist in the world of figurative art. He lived in a country and age that suited his optimistic nature. It was the period of the triumph of the Counter Reformation in Flanders, and this harmony between the man and the times gave his art a certain aura. Rubens, who felt the pulsing of the sap in every living thing, was well able to realize the fluctuation of the forces contained in Michelangelo's bodies, as well as the dynamic conception of space in the later compositions of the Florentine Master.

During his first stay in Italy, Rubens copied various works by Michelangelo (for example, the *Battle of the Centaurs*, figures from the *Battle of Cascina*, as well as prophets, sibyls and incidents from the vault of the Sistine). Obviously, the work of Michelangelo was for him, as for previous artists, a vast treasury of postures and actions; in a way essentially the same as the models of antiquity, a sort of encyclopedia of heroic figures in movement. Later, he was attracted by the vital force within the ideal forms of Michelangelo's figures, which he transformed by making the skin and drapery softer and enveloping them in the vibrant light of the natural atmosphere.

After his return to Antwerp, Rubens also assimilated, as no one else had done before him, the new compositional standards and dynamic conception of space in Michelangelo's late frescoes.

As in the compositions of Buonarroti, a great curve passes through his groups of figures, unifying heaven and earth. In his two *Last Judgments* (Munich) and his *Fall of the Damned* (Munich), Rubens eliminated the traditional superposed zones, replacing them by vertical currents, as Michelangelo had done before him. The beauty and freshness of the skin of the nudes gives a triumphal spring aspect even to these compositions with a tragic content. Rubens' " contribution " was that he succeeded in liberating the vital currents that he felt in Buonarroti's figures from their ideal solitude and bringing them back to nature.

During the seventeenth century in France, and the first half of the eighteenth in the rest of Europe, this veneration for Michelangelo began to decline, as we have seen from the art criticism of the period, and was replaced by veneration for Raphael. Buonarroti's art was regarded as too " violent " and contrary to the classicistic taste of the times. In England, it was only towards 1770 that taste changed in favor of Michelangelo.

Sir Joshua Reynolds, following a spiritual trend whose source was the new cult of the " genius," conceived of an emotional and passionate art. In his lecture at the Royal Academy, Reynolds, the first advocate of Michelangelo in England, showed little originality in his theoretical appreciation of the Florentine's art. Many of his judgments are paraphrases of those by Condivi and Vasari, which he could read in the new editions by Anton Francesco Gori and Bottari, respectively, that had appeared shortly before his arrival in Italy. As a painter, Reynolds was a portraitist, and hence the influence of Michelangelo on his art could be only a limited one. However, by introducing certain actions and movements of the master into his portraits of English lords and ladies, he hoped to give them increased dignity, in contrast with the style of his rival Gainsborough, who preferred the "simple style " in his portraits, confining himself to expressing only social respectability.

Füseli, who had come to England from Switzerland, was Reynolds' successor as president of the Royal Academy (1799). He sometimes took as his inspiration entire compositions of Michelangelo's, and made free paraphrases of the vault of the Sistine Chapel (for example, in a series of drawings on subjects from Shakespeare). He identifies the concept of the " sublime " with that of " terror." For him, the concept of " emotion " is essentially theatrical; that is, the emotions are presented with a view to their effect on the public and not as ex-

97-99 Sketch for Hercules. Florence, Casa Buonarroti.

100-102 Sketch for David. Florence, Casa Buonarroti.

pressions of an internal movement of the soul. Füseli also wrote interesting observations on the compositions and coloring of Michelangelo.

William Blake reacted violently against the rhetorical image of Michelangelo that Reynolds had made popular. For example, he rejected the cliché that Michelangelo was not a great colorist. Blake was above all a master in evoking fantastic apparitions and dream images, and although his artistic language was inspired by Raphael rather than by Michelangelo, the fact that his figures do not have the theatricality of Füseli's shows that he must have felt a closer affinity to Buonarroti.

These three English masters represent three phases of Michelangelo's influence in England, beginning with Reynolds' borrowings and culminating in the more genuine affinities of Blake.

The reevaluation of Michelangelo in eighteenth-century England was an indirect prelude to a more definite rediscovery of his art on the part of the French Romantic painters.

French Romanticism was a revolt against the tyranny of the canons of classicism; a proclamation of artistic freedom from academic prescriptions; in other words, the emancipation of passion from the control of reason. The *fons et origo* of this revolt was, in literature, Stendhal. In his *Histoire de la peinture italienne* (1817) he pays a warm tribute to Michelangelo, affirming the authentic quality of his works as against the "*false grandeur*" of the academicians. For Stendhal, Michelangelo's work represents the clearest manifestation of artistic freedom; the passionate quality of his style is in contrast with the "Philistine pettiness" of the academy. Stendhal declares prophetically: "The taste for Michelangelo will be reborn." It is the taste for "grandeur." He identifies his own artistic genius with that of Buonarroti; and it is in virtue of this identification that the writer became the model for the two greatest French Romantic painters, Géricault and Delacroix.

Géricault, in his *Radeau de la Méduse* (1819), not only takes over the idea of the bark of the Flood in the Sistine vault and certain figures of the *Last Judgment*, but makes up his mind to create painting that is enormous in dimensions and grand in its forms, fit to express the grandeur of man's drama in his battle against the elements, a battle in which he gets no help from Transcendence. This picture is a manifesto of man's condition, by means of which Géricault wants to arouse the spectator, just as Michelangelo had done in the *Last Judgment*.

Delacroix too, like Stendhal, identified with the genius of Buonarroti. In fact, the image he had of Michelangelo was formed in essence through Stendhal, as can be seen by reading the two penetrating studies on Michelangelo that he wrote in 1830 and 1837. The Florentine Master was his idol throughout his youth and maturity (but around 1850 was replaced by Titian). His *Liberty Leading the People* (1831) is itself a manifesto, painted in the conviction that he could arouse the passions of the people towards the ideals of liberty. The most evident document of Delacroix's self-identification with Michelangelo is the small canvas entitled *Michelangelo in his Studio* (1849-50, in Montpellier). Undoubtedly, in the figure of Michelangelo, Delacroix wanted as well to present his own moral self-portrait, as the contemporary critic Silvestre observed. The theme of the canvas is the disappointment and suffering of the genius during creation; the sculptor has thrown his chisel to the ground in front of him and seems overwhelmed with discouragement. In back of him, like white phantoms, appear the *Moses* and the *Medici Madonna*. This is the first time in the figurative arts that the doubt and discouragement of creative genius are represented.

The French Romantics were thus the first artists for whom Michelangelo's genius as such was to be reincarnate. And this was the first time that Buonarroti's genius was seen in its true grandeur. But all this had no sequel in the era of Positivism. The realism of the Barbizon school and impressionism had more modest aims: coming closer to empirical nature, accompanied by the internal delight in the state of mind produced. Of the impressionists and post-impressionists, mainly Degas and Cézanne drew in the manner of Michelangelo, although their studies remained episodic. The official school of the academicians imitated only the externals of Michelangelo's art.

The last important revival of Michelangelo's art is linked to the name of Rodin; that he admired and deeply understood the art of the Master is proved by the magnificent pages he wrote on Michelangelo in his books *L'Art* and *Les Cathédrales de France*. He was struck by the "unfinished" aspect of Buonarroti's sculpture, which reveals the genesis of the final form even in the raw material, and the process by which the latter arises out of the former.

In France, appreciation of the "unfinished" was furthered by an old tradition, influenced by what Vasari, Condivi or Bocchi had written on the subject, and beginning as early as the middle of the seventeenth century, with the poem "*Promenade de Richelieu ou Les vertues chrétiennes*" (1653) by Desmarets de St. Sorlin. Lafontaine, too, speaks of this matter in a letter to his wife dated September 12, 1663 (Dörken, 1936). The tradition was resumed toward the middle of the nineteenth century by Delacroix, whose *Journal* discusses the "unfinished" effects of Michelangelo, declaring that "the unfinished portions enhance the importance of the completed portions." Elsewhere, however, he states: "It is probable that his conception was vague..."

Thus, Michelangelo's art circulated as a vital fluid in the veins of all the artistic schools of Europe, beginning with the middle of the sixteenth century, having a continually operative function, transforming and unifying the language of national and local schools: a phenomenon that had been unknown in Europe since the Gothic period.

It was Buonarroti's achievement to have awakened in the artists of the early sixteenth century boldness and the need for the gigantic; that is, for monumental composition and mighty form, in both dimensions and in attitudes.

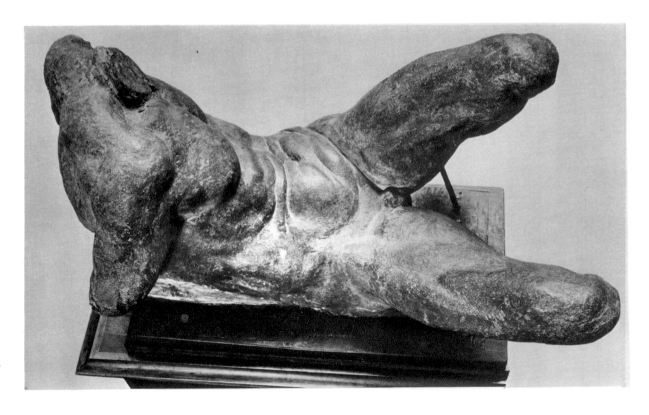

103 Model of a river god. Florence, Academy of Fine Arts.

104-105 Hercules and Cacus. Florence, Casa Buonarroti.

Michelangelo freed art from its dependence on the visible world, revealing a more universal world, one that better corresponded to its "idea." It can be said that he inaugurated the European "ideal style" of the Cinquecento. This language, freed of the forms of the contingent, had been created by the Master to express the loftiest themes of humanity, but later came to lose its internal justification; it became hollow in the hands of imitators, who used it on conventional or even banal themes; Michelangelo's Platonic spiritualism found no true successor in figurative art.

A different aspect of Michelangelo's art, however, the vital inner current that animates his nudes, but now without its idealistic premises, found an original interpreter in Rubens, as we have seen.

The aim and function of Buonarroti's art, namely, to make the spectator tremble at the sight of his own destiny, was understood by Géricault in his *Radeau de la Méduse*; the relationship between the shape of the block and the movement of the figure was taken up again and given a new interpretation by Rodin. These great artists, however, always remained within the confines of the natural world, and did not try to set forth a transcendental reality following the message of Michelangelo. Down to the present, no artist in the figurative art has revived this message in its entirety, whereas in literature the pages of Goethe, Stendhal, Delacroix, Rodin, Barrès evoke this aspect, at once transcendent and real, of Michelangelo's world. The discrepancy between discursive penetration and artistic interpretation seems to be characteristic of the intellectualism of the nineteenth century. It was a century in which, in point of fact, literature held the place of pride.

While the most diverse stylistic currents, from the classical Renaissance to Mannerism, the Baroque and Romanticism, can be seen in relation to Michelangelo, the art of the Master goes beyond any attempt to classify it. The starting point and foundation of his language is the monumental Tuscan art of the late Middle Ages; he makes use of its elements with an   67 independent spirit, combining them in a new manner, imbuing them with a dynamic quality hitherto unknown, in order to create symbol-images that express an internal reality, objectivizing the torment of his spirit. Accordingly, the message of Michelangelo, in its entirety, could not find successors.

As at the time of the fourth centennial of Michelangelo's birth (1875), the fourth centennial of his death (1964) has brought a revival of interest in the Master, which has resulted in a veritable flowering of Michelangelo studies.

We should like here to indicate only the most important contributions. There have been two new attributions of works that had been thought to be lost: Margrit Lisner has found the *Crucifix of Santo Spirito*, a finding that fills a painful gap in our knowledge of the works of 1494. Lisner has published an acute study on the *Crucifix* in an Italian brochure, as well as in German in the *Münchner Jahrbuch der bildenden Kunst* (1964, p. 7 ff.). We personally have pointed to a wood model in Casa Buonarroti, which had not previously been expressly attributed to the Master, as the model of a large wooden crucifix that Michelangelo intended to begin in August 1562, as is evidenced by two letters preserved in the Archivio Buonarroti, addressed to Leonardo Buonarroti, the artist's nephew. These letters have already been cited in this chapter. A study of ours on this model is being published in the *Commentari* and in the *Atti del XXI Congresso Internazionale della Storia dell'Arte* held in Bonn in 1964. The third attribution is that of the choir of the Cathedral of Padua, the design and model for which were by Michelangelo, as is documented; this fact was known in the eighteenth century but was forgotten for a long time and the work has now been reintroduced by us into the Buonarroti corpus (C. de Tolnay, " A Forgotten Architectural Project by Michelangelo: The Choir of the Cathedral of Padua," in *Festschrift H. von Einem*, Berlin, pp. 247 ff.).

Other recent, but less certain attributions are: Fernanda De' Maffei, in a recent book, has tried to identify a marble statue in New York (Tozzi Gallery) as the *Infant St. John*, a lost youthful work by Michelangelo. De' Maffei's study, although serious and rigorous, does not convince us that the statue belongs to Michelangelo rather than to Pierino da Vinci, as the effeminate character of the type suggests. A. Parronchi has sought to identify a wooden Crucifix, larger than life, in the church of San Rocco at Massa Carrara, as the true Crucifix of Santo Spirito by Michelangelo: apart from reservations as to the stylistic elements of this work, which put it at least thirty years later, Parronchi has not succeeded in explaining how a figure of these dimensions (we know from Condivi that the Christ by Michelangelo was smaller than life size) ended up at Massa Carrara. There is also another Crucifix, this one painted on a small panel, that D. Redig de Campos has hypothetically identified, in a communication presented at the Bonn Congress, with the Crucifix that Michelangelo presented to Vittoria Colonna. Even granting that this little picture has the finest technical qualities of all the many painted copies of Michelangelo's celebrated Crucifix, the delicate execution and sentimental expression of the face of Christ are foreign to the Master's style and indicate rather that its author must have had a feminine temperament. We know from a letter by Amilcare Anguissola, dated May 7, 1557, that his daughter, the painter Sofonisba, was in the habit of copying Michelangelo drawings and making oil paintings of them. It is not out of the question, therefore, that the work in question (in a private collection in Rome) is a work by Sofonisba Anguissola.

Finally, A. Parronchi in *Arte Antica e Moderna*, 1964, believes that he can reconstruct Michelangelo's lost *Cupid* on the basis of the ancient *Hermaphrodite*, and points out the interesting fact that one of the hovering angels in the *Conversion of St. Paul* (Cappella Paolina) was inspired by the *Hermaphrodite*.

The most important of the new attributions of drawings is that of the Amsterdam sheet showing ink drawings of nudes, which can be dated as of the period from 1501 to 1505, discovered by J. Q. Van Regteren-Altena and presented at the Bonn Congress. Less convincing to us is his attribution of a drawing representing St. Catherine, on Venetian paper, in his private collection. A drawing of an ideal woman's head, in red chalk, in the Louvre, has been attributed to Michelangelo by A. B. Sutherland and appeared in *Burlington Magazine* (December 1964).

There have been two further attempts to reconstruct lost works, e. g. *The Sleeping Cupids*. One is by A. Parronchi (see *Arte Antica e Moderna*, 1964, Florence, pp. 281 ff.); the other is the *Fontainebleau Hercules*, a drawing by Rubens kept in the Louvre (Lugt, 1073), on the basis of a model in Casa Buonarroti, believed to be a model for the *David* and brought forward by ourselves (cf. *Gazette des Beaux Arts*, 1964, pp. 125 ff.).

During the celebration of the Michelangelo year new contemporary documents were brought forward. Ugo Procacci has discovered marginal notes in a copy of Condivi that he owns, written by a contemporary who must certainly have had direct contact with Michelangelo, since in a number of annotations he corrects and criticizes the text of the author, referring to oral statements made directly by the Master. These facts are primarily of biographical value. A. Parronchi has presented a document recently found in a private collection in Florence by the archivist Corti, containing the memoirs of G. B. Figiovanni, prior of San Lorenzo, who from March 1520 on was supervisor of works on the New Sacristy, and for many years in charge of the works for which Michelangelo was commissioned. These memoirs shed new light on Michelangelo's attitude in 1529, when he fled from Florence shortly before the siege; they establish November 4, 1519, as the day on which work was begun on the Sacristy.

The Exhibition of Autographs held at the Laurentian Library contained several unpublished letters addressed to Michelangelo, printed in the exhibition catalogue edited by Paola Barocchi and G. Chiarini. The most important publication, however, which Giovanni Poggi prepared for many years, is the critical edition of Michelangelo's correspondence, with the letters by and to him, published under the auspices of the Istituto Nazionale di Studi sul Rinascimento, by G. Nencioni, R. Ristori and supplemented by critical notes by P. Barocchi.

Among the new researches on Michelangelo's activity as an architect, we should stress here the monumental volume edited by Zevi and Portoghesi, who obtained the collaboration of distinguished Italian scholars (for example, Argan, Bertini, Bettini, etc.). It has a new and very rich photographic documentation. These studies likewise include the researches on the subject conducted by foreign scholars during the last forty years. In addition, a useful short manual on Michelangelo's architecture has been published by F. Barbieri and L. Puppi (Rizzoli). The magazine *Capitolium* has published an interesting number on the history of the Campidoglio, in prelude to publication of a luxurious volume on the same subject edited by De Angelis d'Ossat and C. Pietrangeli, soon to appear.

W. Lotz has analyzed architectural drawings in Casa Buonarroti and in London, copies taken from the Coner codex (Ashley) that Lotz regards as being from the hand of the Master. We personally are unable to see the hand of Michelangelo in the drawings; it seems more likely to us that he had one of his apprentices copy the drawings of Giuliano da Sangallo relating to ancient buildings for study purposes.

106-108 Michelangelo: wooden model for a Crucifix (1562). Florence, Casa Buonarroti.

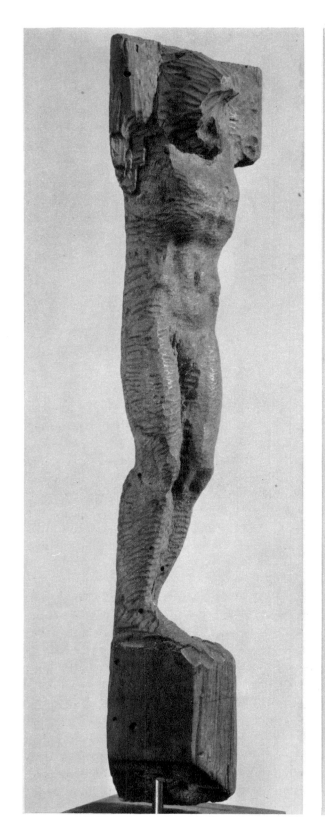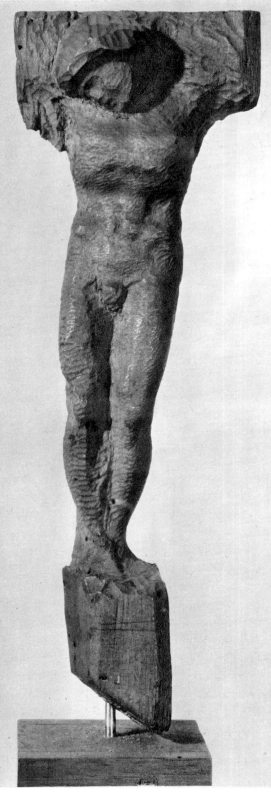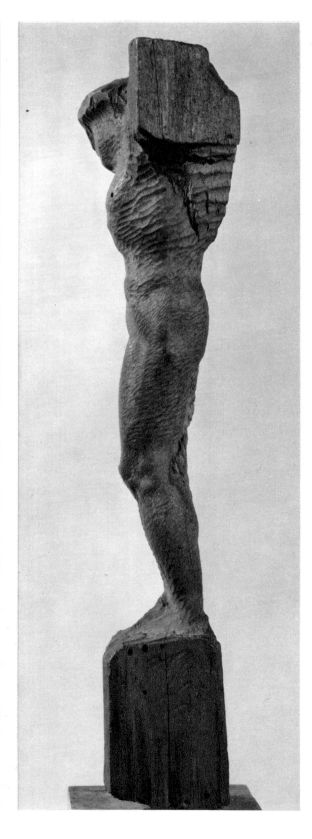

Frommel published an article on the architecture of the Cappella Paolina (in *Zeitschrift für Kunstgeschichte*, 1964); he also presented a communication at the Bonn Congress, in which he tried to prove that the dome of the Medici Chapel is modeled on the dome of Sant'Eligio degli Orefici, designed by Raphael. We ourselves presented at the same Congress a selection from a group of over one hundred drawings of architectural work by Michelangelo in Florence and Rome after 1556, collected in a roll, which we identified in 1947; it is now in the Metropolitan Museum, New York. The drawings from Florentine works are by an Italian artist; those on works in Rome are by a Frenchman, as can be seen from the captions. It is not impossible that they should be attributed to Giovanni Franzese, a cabinetmaker who was commissioned to make the wood model of the dome of St. Peter's; one series of these drawings refers precisely to the wood model of that dome. All this new material, which enriches our knowledge of the architectural works of the master, will be included in our book on *Michelangelo Architect and Poet*, Volume VI of our major work on Michelangelo.

The history of the dome of St. Peter's and the problem of reconstructing its original aspect have been dealt with in two important publications. The first is Wittkower's volume (*La Cupola di S. Pietro*, Florence 1964), which brings up to date an article of his that appeared as early as 1933. His thesis is that the exterior shape of Michelangelo's dome was hemispherical and produced an effect of heaviness. He thinks that the dome of Giacomo della Porta's final version was a radical alteration of Michelangelo's idea, to suit the taste of the end of the century. The second publication is Roberto Di Stefano's study (*La Cupola di San Pietro*, Naples, 1963), in which the author, on the basis of keen and original observation, proves that the shape of Giacomo della Porta's dome is identical, or almost identical, with that of Michelangelo, the difference being that it was raised by about five meters as compared with the original project. But, Di Stefano adds, Michelangelo himself would most probably have decided in favor of raising the level so that the dome would be plainly visible to a spectator viewing it from a point opposite the façade. We see, therefore, that researches on Michelangelo as architect have had important results.

On the other hand, the recent literature on Michelangelo as sculptor has not been nearly so rich. The most important contributions here relate to the period of his youth, which is not surprising in view of the fact that this is the phase for which the gaps in our knowledge are largest. The study by Stefano Bottari (*L'Arca di San Domenico in Bologna*, Bologna, 1964) contains new and interesting observations on Michelangelo's statuettes, especially the one at San Petronio, which would appear to have been begun by Niccolò dell'Arca (see the back) and finished by Michelangelo. Interesting observations on the Bologna statuettes, and in particular on the original appearance of San Procolo before its ruin, were presented by Lisner at the Bonn Congress. She gave convincing stylistic arguments for attributing to Baccio da Montelupo the heads of the frame of the *Doni Madonna*. Charles Seymour Junior has tried (at the Bonn Congress) to integrate Michelangelo's *David* into the series for decorating the buttresses of the cathedral at Florence of which the block was originally a part. A volume on *Michelangelo Scultore* (Rome, 1964) edited by Eugenio Battisti, and with the collaboration of R. J. Clements, G. C. Argan, F. Negri Arnoldi, S. Casartelli-Novelli, is the first study containing color illustrations of all the statues of Michelangelo, a technique that in a number of cases succeeds in bringing out the quality of the marble and the chisel work; unfortunately, not all the illustrations are equally successful.

John Pope-Hennessy presented new and convincing arguments at the Bonn Congress against attributing the *Palestrina Pietà* to Michelangelo and suggested that it might have been done by Mellini about 1635 (we are inclined to think it the work of a different artist in the second half of the sixteenth century).

Interest in the essence of Michelangelo's sculptural form, and in particular the problem of the " unfinished," seems to be attracting more attention from scholars today than does the schematic assignment of his works into stylistic categories that was popular from the end of the nineteenth century on (e. g. Late Renaissance, or Mannerism, or Baroque). The problem of the " unfinished " was the topic of three communications (Sanpaolesi at the Florence Congress, Bonelli at the Rome Congress and Brandi, with keen and original arguments, at the Bonn Congress).

Today, we realize more and more that Michelangelo gave a specific character to his style by seeking inspiration in the intrinsic requirements of his material, marble, which he handled better than any other artist of the time.

There have been few important contributions on Michelangelo as painter. Among them, mention should be made of Salmi's communication at the Florence Congress, which showed that in the Pandolfo Malatesta altarpiece (Museo Comunale, Rimini) the figure of *San Rocco*, done by Francesco Granacci, a friend of young Michelangelo, shows a reflection of Buonarroti's art; and the same can be noted in the resemblance of the face of the saint to that of the new Santo Spirito Crucifix. We mention an erudite study on the technique of the *Manchester Madonna* in London, published in *Burlington Magazine* 1964 by Ruhemann and Plesters. A large volume by Valerio Mariani on Michelangelo as a painter has also been published (Milan, 1964). Finally, mention should be made of the new edition of D. Redig de Campos' work on the *Last Judgment* (Milan, 1964), with color photographs. Unfortunately, the author does not go into the problem of the drawings Michelangelo made for the *Last Judgment*.

Interest in Michelangelo's drawings has increased. Two anthologies were published during the Michelangelo year. One was edited by Maria Vittoria Brugnoli, under the title *Michelangelo*, in the series " *I grandi maestri del disegno*," (Milan, 1964), with a selection of drawings and an intelligent introduction. The other anthology is entitled *Disegni di Michelangelo* and contains one hundred and three facsimiles of representative drawings by the Master, with a preface by Mario Salmi, an introduction by us and notes by Paola Barocchi. She also edited the third volume of the *Catalogo dei Disegni di Michelangelo a Firenze*, under the title *Michelangelo e la sua Scuola* (Florence, 1964), containing the drawings of the Master in the Archivio Buonarroti, first published by us in 1928. We published the drawings of the *Resurrection of Christ* in a new grouping and a new chronology in an article entitled " *Morte e Resurrezione in Michelangelo*," in *Commentari* (1964, fasc. 1 and 2), and in German in the volume *Michelangelo Buonarroti*, published by the Società Dantesca, Würzburg, 1964.

Under the auspices of a steering committee made up of Mario Salmi, Ugo Procacci and ourselves, a beginning has been made on preparing the *Corpus* of all of the drawings of Michelangelo and his school, which will be published in facsimile, under the auspices of the Associazione delle Casse di Risparmio italiane.

There have been few publications on Michelangelo as poet and writer, but they have been of great value. Among them we should like to indicate Girardi's book (*Studi sulle rime di Michelangelo*, Milan, 1964) and Walter Binni's communication on *Michelangelo scrittore* (read at the Florence Congress), as well as a reprint of the critical edition of the poems by C. Frey (*Die Dichtungen des Michelangelo Buonarroti*, Berlin, 1964), with an introduction by Hugo Friedrich and a few additions by H. W. Frey. Hugo Friedrich has also written an essay on Michelangelo as poet, published in the volume *Epochen der Italienischen Lyrik* (1964).

With reference to Buonarroti's life and political personality, a graceful short biography of Michelangelo has been published by B. Samminiatelli (Rome, 1964). Giorgio Spini has produced a valuable article on " Michelangelo's Politics " (*Rivista Storica Italiana*, 1964, pp. 557 ff.), the text of which had previously been given by Spini at the Florence Congress.

A useful little volume (*Michelangelo—a self-portrait*, Englewood Cliffs, 1963), bringing together statements by Michelangelo and contemporaries, is due to Robert J. Clements. Finally, with reference to the spiritual and artistic personality of the Master, we have published in an English translation, under the title *The Art and Thought of Michelangelo* (New York, 1964), four lectures originally given at the Collège de France, Paris.

It is to be hoped that this burgeoning of Michelangelo studies will continue in the future and bear fruit in a profounder interpretation of his genius. This is one of the hopes and tasks that the recently founded Center of Michelangelo Studies, headed by myself, has set for itself at its headquarters in the Casa Buonarroti, restored to its ancient splendor on the occasion of the fourth centennial of the death of the Master.

PLATE I " Madonna della Scala." Florence, Casa Buonarroti.

II

SCULPTURE

by Umberto Baldini

The beginning

Michelangelo as a sculptor must have been born early in 1489. That is the traditional date of his separation—enforced or not—from the studio of Ghirlandaio, who had accepted him a year before as an apprentice " to learn painting and to practice that art " on the high scaffolding of the main choir of Santa Maria Novella; it was the date of his transfer to that garden of San Marco that the sources describe as a regular school, created under the sign of the most cultivated and academic humanism by Lorenzo the Magnificent and directed by Bertoldo.

Francesco Granacci would seem to have been the *deus ex machina* of Michelangelo's first steps in sculpture, as in painting.

To tell the truth, there is not much that we know about that garden, formerly located on Piazza San Marco, on Via Larga, facing the Monastery of San Marco.[1]

But Vasari's text, which is still our major source on the subject, although it gives us no concrete data concerning a real situation that seems to have been polished up in courtier fashion—not to say invented—in order to give antiquity to the scholastic patronage and artistic intelligence of the Medici princes, is, we feel, the only plausible account we have of Michelangelo's beginnings.

It provides a first element that, although limited in its terms, cannot but be historic truth, and a second one that, if not historical, takes on historical value by the solid critical identification it makes of Michelangelo's youthful activity.

The first relates to the presence of " good ancient marble statues " in the garden;[2] the second relates to the reference to Bertoldo, Donatello's old disciple.

We no longer possess (if they ever existed) the first sculptures that Michelangelo may have made in the garden of San Marco (" certain figures in the round, of clay " made in competition with Torrigiano, and a " faun's head " copied from the antique);[3] we do have two works, both in Casa Buonarroti in Florence which, if not of this period, are not much later. These works, which we agree in placing as the beginning of his known activity as sculptor,[4] support our belief in the historical validity of Vasari's story.

In both of them the ancient and the modern reflect and interpenetrate each other on planes of a new conception. So much so that we really think, in spite of the references, that the personality of the artist had already fully developed; that the technical exercises had soon been mastered, revealing a well-defined and critical attitude with respect to both antiquity and to his most recent contemporaries.

And, it seems to us, this explains and justifies what Michelangelo was to say to Vasari one day, referring to these first independent steps: " George, if I have nothing good in my spirit, that comes from being born in the thinness of the air of your Arezzo country; just as I got from my nurse's milk the chisels and mallets with which I make my statues." "Jestingly," as Vasari says. But, we should add, with every appearance of wanting to stress, even in jest, the little or nothing that he got *directly* from Florentine art towards his formation. The school of the garden of San Marco is never mentioned as a school in the true sense of the word. It was at his own sweet will that he could study the " antiquities " there; for him they were not merely occasions for exercises but sources of new messages, full-blown motifs for the stylistic

and moral themes of his poetics. With this he must have mingled, with equal freedom of interpretation, the teachings of Donatello and the valid substance of Giotto and Pisano, meditation on Christian themes and pagan myths and, within the cult of antiquity, on the solemn anthropomorphism of humanism.

The *Madonna della Scala*, although as a type it follows Donatello's pattern in the *Madonna del Latte* and may recall ancient images that appear on Roman sarcophagi of fourth-century Greek reliefs, goes beyond any and all aspects of imitation (the antique and Donatello become two veritable " tests of mastery "), taking from his models only partial and external technical data (Fig. 2 and Figs. 1 and 2 chap. I).

Here the *flattening* does not have the slightest pictural accent nor does it register linear rhythms: it serves only to bring out the powerful drive of the forms. The great squared block on which the Virgin sits (a motif of blocking by dynamic contraposition that will be seen again, for example, in the Pitti Tondo), the high steps, the child shown climbing up them, certain hard unfinished planes, are all motifs that serve to define a situation in contrast rather than in modulation, energy in restraint rather than in expansion, plastic in evidence. All are given strength by the quick but sharp vibration of the light, which does not immerse the forms in the cosmic infinitude, but works powerfully to isolate the great sheath of the Virgin, from whose tormented draperies emerge, in accentuated striving for sculptural definition, an extremely firm and individual profile, the big hands framing the Herculean back of the Son (already modelled in conformity with a formal invention that will recur in the *Day* and with the arm falling and reversed, as in the several *Pietà*) in a circle of violent energy, the two strong feet.

We have left the orbit of Donatello; the Virgin with her eyes fixed on the distance has nothing of the humanly heroic quality of the Quattrocento: not the rapid terrible glance of Masaccio's men nor the calm dominating glance of Donatello's St. George. " Archetype of woman as creator of life and at the same time guardian of death," the *Virgin* already has within it those meanings of Life and Death that constitute one of the most dramatic aspects

3-4 Santo Spirito Crucifix. Florence, Casa Buonarroti.

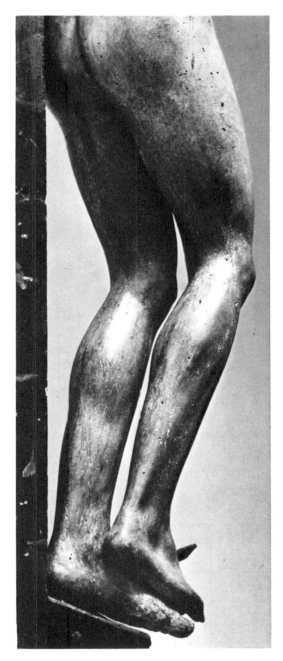

of Michelangelo's poetics, and that seem here to have a precise reference in the theme of the putti holding the winding-sheet on high. In this way, too, any citation of the antique is surpassed; the pagan goddess Demeter gives way to the *Mater Dei*.

The work, mentioned in Vasari, as has been said, is a marble bas-relief. It measures 55.5 cm in height and 40 cm in width, and is in Casa Buonarroti in Florence, where it was held by Michelangelo's nephew Leonardo, who presented it to Duke Cosimo in 1566. Restored to the Buonarroti family in 1617, it has remained ever since where it now is. An attempt by E. Benkard (*Michelangelo's Madonna an der Treppe*, Berlin, 1933, p. 11 ff.) to shift the work to the milieu of the school of Bandinelli, denying its authenticity, which had already been questioned by C. Holroyd (*Michael Angelo Buonarroti*, London, 1903, p. 104) has been completely unsuccessful.

By now Michelangelo had already given a new dimension to human ideas on antique form, and in a short time was to make his thinking still more precise in the *Crucifix* of Santo Spirito and the Rome *Pietà*, while continuing his exercises on and for the antique with the *Hercules* (a work that has been lost, but whose general nature we can surmise, thanks chiefly to the researches of de Tolnay) and the *Bacchus*. This was before he turned, as Vasari puts it, to " give perfection to the great design he later had."

Some would have it that Politian suggested the theme of the *Centauromachia*, perhaps on the basis of a passage in Ovid describing the carrying of Hippodamia by the centaur Eurytion (Fig. 1 and Figs. 3-11 chap. I).

Whether or not the reference is true, it gives an acceptable date, along with a cultural fact concerning the garden of San Marco. In it were seen from time to time the works of Donatello, Bertoldo (with his relief of the *Battle of the Bargello*), Nicola and Giovanni Pisano (with their pulpit reliefs), Pollaiolo (for dynamism), antiquities Greek and Greco-Roman and even Etrus-

75

6 Head of Santo Spirito Crucifix.

5 Santo Spirito Crucifix (left side view).

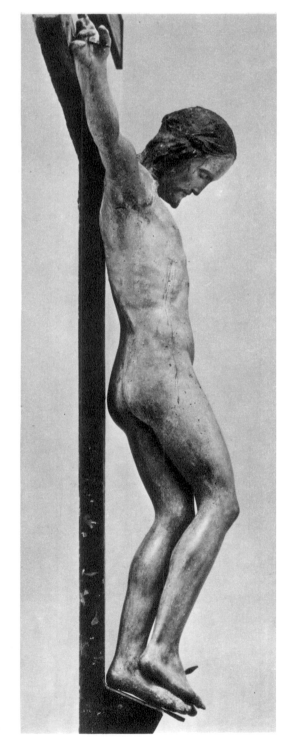

76

can (and there are precise indications of sarcophagi); but all these are antecedents that Michelangelo goes beyond, fully free, with a poetic imagination rejecting cultural fetters to create an entirely new epic quality pulsing with extraordinary and continuous vitality. Once again light is the primordial element for bringing out the forms. Struggle, as von Einem said, is seen as exaltation and manifestation of life. In a wild tangle, like the *Laocoön*, the figures are picked out and defined by their powerful muscles and limbs, in a battle to the death which for the instant seems to be dominated by the central figure with raised arm (as if in anticipation of the *Christ* in the Sistine Chapel): many of the figures are turned toward him and look in his direction as if in expectation, in the brief pause in the struggle; but it is a passing moment and everything goes back to dramatic movement in the varied whirl, full of shouts and chaos.

The human pyramid, after the fashion of Leonardo, seems to link the figures in a triangle going from the figure seated sadly at the lower left corner, up to the head and raised arm of the central figure above, and ending in the right corner. But it is continually broken up by the knotted intersections running around and binding the upper corners, and scales off in the gradated depth of the three principal planes in which the figures are set, and thereby enters into relationship with the world around it, heavily laden and yet given measure merely by the power and keenness of the bodily forms.

This work may be the first manifestation of decided opposition to the theorizing doctrine of Leonardo; in the full absolute liberty given the subject, it is also the first and most decided affirmation of Michelangelo's type of vision.

PLATE II   Santo Spirito Crucifix.   Florence, Casa Buonarroti.

7-8 S. Proclus. Bologna, San Domenico.

Others have seen pictural quality that brings out the masses and the forms; we do not.

The bas-relief is a remarkable collection of physical situations: a regular dictionary that contains in germ all the possible developments of Michelangelo in the future. We have noted the figure in the center at the top; but there are any number of other hints. This is why the work is considered as basic, in its first free complete self-expression, with virtually no interference from the subject. This Michelangelo himself must have realized, for Condivi recalls hearing him " say that, when he looks at it again, he recognizes how much he went against nature in not following the art of sculpture at once, judging from this work how much he could do."

Completion of the work must have taken place shortly before the death of Lorenzo the Magnificent on April 8, 1492.

The work, which is mentioned in the sources, is preserved in Casa Buonarroti, where it has always been. It is a high relief in marble: 84.5 cm in height and 90.5 cm in width. There has been much discussion on the subject, which it is hard to put into definite terms; it was early given varying descriptions, " the Battle of Hercules with the Centaurs " according to Vasari, " the carrying off of Deianira and the scuffle of the Centaurs " according to Condivi. In addition to the reference to Ovid that we have spoken of (*Metamorphoses*, Book XII), the fables of Hyginus have been mentioned, the Theseus of Dante, Theseus doing battle with the Centaurs. Without arriving at any excessively precise reference, it seems more logical to think of an exercise by Michelangelo, only in part suggested by mythology. Most scholars place the execution of the work between 1492 and 1494, a little later, that is, than the *Madonna della Scala* (but cf. in Note 4 the hypothesis of Longhi). No doubts have ever been expressed as to its authenticity.

9 Angel. Bologna, San Domenico.

10-11 S. Petronius. Bologna, San Domenico.

The death of Lorenzo the Magnificent removed Michelangelo temporarily from the Medici house. Before his return to the court of Piero de' Medici, he stayed either at home or at the monastery of Santo Spirito.

There he made the wooden *Crucifix*, today in Casa Buonarroti (Figs. 3-6).

The work marks a step forward in Michelangelo's development, another interpretation of classical antiquity, but one now defined by new contextual requirements. Outside of the "grand high manner" that was to come later, it represents the first precise approach to the subject that involves the human form in an absolutely new dialogue. The religious theme, and its solution with reference to the human physique, brings Michelangelo to a much more committed position than in the more discursive *Madonna della Scala*.

His conception is already close to the one we are soon to see fully applied in the Virgin in the Rome *Pietà* that he was to carve soon thereafter. Just as there, to bring out the purity of the Virgin, he was to embody a sublime theology of his own (faithfully reported by Condivi), making "Our Lady too young." In designing the human shape of his first non-heroic Christ he gave Him an almost boyish body, as if to exalt an extreme chastity, an absolute and un-corrupted purity—despite the seemingly hermaphroditic beauty. For us, that is rather a cultural theme that we should be surprised not to find; it is so necessarily involved in his observation. But note how it is basically something on the surface, a thing of softness, complete-ly submerged in the extreme mystical purity of the whole, concentrated in the adult face, large as compared with the body, with its big forehead that even at a distance (and the raised position of the crucifix would bring this out from below in its strong inclination) appears as the only dramatic note in its strong resistance to corruptibility and death, with the sharp profile of its nose, with the broad cut of the eye-sockets and closed lids, with the mouth hold-

12 Bacchus. Florence, Bargello National Museum.

13 Head and bust of Bacchus.

ing back all the bitterness and resignation, in an attitude that we shall find many times in his works. And once more the iconography brings us something new, in the special posture of the body, already twisted in the serpentine form that is a basic motif and one that is all Michelangelo's, suggested and resolved in the angle of the right leg (as if in torsion) leading to a new plastic tension among the knees, the body torsion, and the development of the movement towards the face. This modifies and renews the late Florentine tradition as seen in the models of a Benedetto da Maiano or a Giuliano da San Gallo.[5]

Something else that could be regarded as an innovation (not entirely so, since decisive instances of the same trend can already be seen in the *Centauromachia*) is the anatomical render-

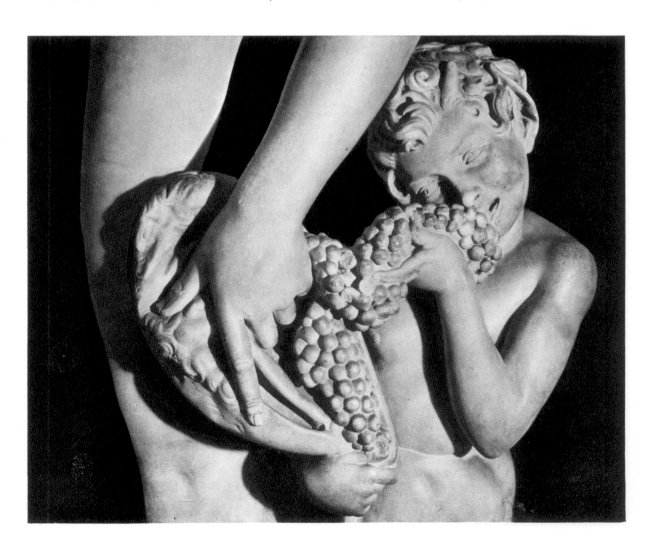

14 Little Satyr of Bacchus.

15 Torso of Bacchus (rear view).

ing of the body, which for the first time follows a unit modulus that goes beyond the accustomed rules of Quattrocento anatomy and brings into unison all the factors of the surface. This is certainly a precise application of his first practical anatomy studies, begun now in the Monastery of Santo Spirito and followed out in his later activity.

The polychromy is likewise remarkably acute and subtle; very fine in its least detail. It is a sign that Michelangelo was still engaged in work as a painter (as can be seen as well from the context in Condivi cited in connection with the *Centauromachia*). Here, in the *Crucifix*, painting and sculpture are integrated in a continuous relationship: a faint olive tint, suggestive of death, covers the body; over it, from the side and forehead, run trickles of blood that get thicker and thinner, sensitively flowing over the modelling with so subtle and continuous attention that they become elements of definition and accompaniment possessing great plastic power. With the same subtle sensibility, the hair on the shoulder and upper chest continues the relief of the hair on the head; and so with the tufts on the chest, armpits and groin.

The *Crucifix* was done for the Prior of Santo Spirito, Niccolò di Giovanni di Lapo Bichiellini. It was believed lost, after its disappearance at the time of the French occupation and the suppression of the monastery at the same time, but was recently recovered (1962) in the monastery, under a thick coating of paint that completely masked its form and character. It was identified by M. Lisner (*Kunstchronik*, January, 1963, p. 1 ff.; and *id., Il Crocifisso di Michelangelo in Santo Spirito in Firenze,* Munich, 1964, the original text of which is in *Münchener Jahrbuch der bildenden Kunst,* Band XV, 1964). Many previous attempts at identification had been made by critics who dwelt on two crucifixes in Santo Spirito, one in the sacristy and one at the high altar, but they could only find motifs reflecting

17 Head of Bacchus (right side view).

16 Lion's Mask of Bacchus.

18 Pietà. Rome, St. Peter's.

19 Head and torso of Mary and Christ, in the Pietà.

the original crucifix by Michelangelo. More recently, but with little success, A. Parronchi (*Studi Urbinati, XXXV*, 1, 1961), proposed to identify it with a wooden crucifix (traditionally attributed to Felice Palma and having some characteristics, of late date, of Giambolognese), formerly at San Rocco di Massa Carrara and now in the Museo San Matteo, Pisa.

The *Crucifix* is mentioned in the two principal sources, Vasari and Condivi, and before that, by Albertini (*Memoriale di molte statue, etc.*, Florence, 1510, 2nd. ed., 1863, p. 16), who states that it is in the choir " on the high relief of the high altar." It measures 1.35 meters in height and 1.35 meters in width, and hence in consonance with Condivi's statement that it is " a little smaller than lifesize " and the measurements given by Bottari (Vasari, ed. Bottari, III, Rome 1759-60, p. 196 No. 1 and p. 358 No. 3), who says that it is " about two ells and a half high." It is preserved in Casa Buonarroti. The cross on which it is hung is not original but was added at the time of its repainting, which may have taken place between the end of the eighteenth century and the middle of the nineteenth. On the other hand, the superscription is original, although it had been hung upside down on the new cross; in its correct position now given it in the exhibition it has the three legends in Hebrew, Greek and Latin in an analogical transcription as can be seen, although in fragmentary form, in the relic of the superscription that was found in Rome in 1491 in the Church of Santa Croce in Gerusalemme, word of which reached Florence (for this cf. A. Parronchi in *La Nazione*, November 4, 1964; but on this and the restoration of the *Crucifix*, cf. also the article by U. Procacci and U. Baldini appended to Lisner, *op. cit.*, Munich, 1964).

Also on the superscription, cf. U. Baldini, in *La Nazione*, July 26, 1964. On the rediscovered *Crucifix*, see also F. Russoli in *Pirelli*, XVIII, No. 1, 1965, p. 95.

A. Parronchi (*La Nazione*, Feb. 21, 1964) insists on the defects in anatomy that can be found in the Santo Spirito *Crucifix*. It is not a very convincing argument, to tell the truth; on the contrary, the body obviously shows continuous subtle anatomical observation in every smallest part. There is no detailed stress on the musculature, but this is closely related to the intended effect; an extremely boyish body. It is unlikely that there would be any such conception of anatomy in view of the fact that at that time Michelangelo was taking the skin off corpses and would have his attention directed towards a more robust and complex conception of anatomy. It should be noted that the passages in both Vasari and Condivi speak first of the execution of the *Crucifix* and then of his entering Santo Spirito, where he " was given a room and bodies so that he could make dissections," and this would suggest that this was the actual sequence in time. Further, in accord with de Tolnay's thesis that the lost *Hercules* was done by Michelangelo in unusual form and size, but without any commission, in order to establish his position after the death of Lorenzo the Magnificent and win commissions,

it seems logical to suppose that Michelangelo himself made the offer to the Prior of Santo Spirito in order to get another chance to do work and thereby gain official entry into ecclesiastical circles.

We have no notice of other sculpture from this period and the brief period of his return to the court of the Medici. The *Hercules* has disappeared; it must have been an extremely important stage, as the first effort in sculpture in marble in the round, and must certainly have

20-21 Bruges Madonna. Bruges, Notre-Dame.

reflected the deeper studies in anatomy at Santo Spirito, being, as it were, a prelude to the *David*.

A number of attempts have been made to trace or find data that would make possible an iconographical reconstruction of the *Hercules*. Michelangelo carved the statue of marble for his own account in 1494, before his flight to Bologna in October of that year. We know its measurements from Condivi, who says the statue is "four ells" high, or about 2.4 meters. It was bought by the Strozzi, who sold it to Giovan Battista Palla, by whom it was transferred to France, sold to Henry II and placed in the Jardin de l'Etang; it was destroyed in 1713. Tolnay has just announced further documents (*Gazette des Beaux-Arts*, 1965). Condivi tells us of a marginal activity in this fresh period at the Medici court: a snow statue that Piero de' Medici had him make "in the middle of his courtyard."

[1] The garden was bought by Lorenzo for his wife, Clarice Orsini, in 1480, and only after her death, in 1488, would it become a "school of artists." A. Chastel ("Vasari and the Medici Legend: the School in St. Mark's Garden," *Studi Vasariani*, 1952, p. 162 ff.) regards the School of S. Marco as a myth of Vasari's. Along these lines, M. Lisner (*Zeitschrift für Bildende Kunst*, XII, Leipzig, 1958, p. 141-156) denies it any share in the formation of Michelangelo as a sculptor; she suggests that Michelangelo was formed in the milieu of Benedetto da Maiano. According to her, testimony to this and Michelangelo's first work, would be a cherub above and on the right of the marble altar of Sant'Anna dei Lombardi in Naples, done by Benedetto da Maiano.

[2] Other sources, too, mention these statues: Albertini (*Memoriale di molte statue et picture, etc.*, Florentia, 1510, ed. G. Milanesi, C. Guasti, C. Milanesi, Florence, 1863, p. 12) speaks of "a number of ancient statues brought from Rome"; Condivi (*Vita di Michelangelo Buonarroti raccolta per Ascanio Condivi de la Ripa Transone*, Rome, 1553, ed. Frey, Berlin, 1887 p. 20) speaks of the garden as "decorated with various ancient statues and figures."

22 Bruges Madonna (right side view).

23 Head of Bruges Madonna (right side-front view).

24-26 Bruges Madonna (rear view; front view of
Child and body of Madonna; front view
of head of Madonna).

[3] Michelangelo's copy of the ancient Faun was identified with the mask of the Faun formerly in the Bargello (the piece was one of those carried off by the German troops during the war and since then lost track of) by the Richardsons in 1728 (*Traité de la peinture et de la sculpture* par Richardson, père et fils, Amsterdam, 1728, III, p. 94 ff.); but criticism, both modern and of the time, rejects any possible identification, including the one proposed by A. Venturi (*L'Arte*, XXV, 1922, p. 177 ff.) with the Cyclops' head, likewise in the Bargello.

[4] Held to have been executed in 1490-1492, the *Centauromachia* being prior to the *Madonna della Scala* (in this following Vasari and Condivi) and the *Madonna della Scala* being universally accepted as earlier. This dating is opposed by R. Longhi ("Two Proposals for the Young Michelangelo," *Paragone*, 1958, 101, p. 61 ff.) who proposes a later date for the two sculptures, toward the end of the century, after execution of the works in Bologna and even after the *Pietà* in St. Peter's; A. E. Brinckmann (*Barockskulptur*, etc., Berlin, 1919, I, p. 18), who regards the *Madonna della Scala* as of 1494; and E. Arslan (*Michelangelo*, Pavia, 1943-44, p. 5 ff.), who dates the *Madonna della Scala* 1495-1496.

[5] Lisner (*op. cit.*, p. 14) insists on contacts, and even apprenticeship in the milieu of the studio, between Michelangelo and Benedetto da Maiano at this time, and the beginning of his activity as sculptor; she relates the *Santo Spirito Crucifix* to Benedetto's wooden *Crucifix* formerly in Sant'Onofrio and now in the Educatorio di Fuligno in Florence.

The sojourn in Bologna

But Piero's court was no longer the same as that of Lorenzo, and Michelangelo felt ill at ease and discontented, to such a point that with extreme foresight and impressed by obscure visions that disturbed his mind, he left Florence suddenly in October 1494, went to Venice for a few days and then came down towards Tuscany again, stopping at Bologna, where he shortly received word of the expulsion of the Medici.

For Francesco Aldovrandi in Bologna, between the autumn of 1494 and the end of 1495, 85 he completed the Tomb of St. Dominic, carving three marble statues: an *Angel* and two saints: *S. Petronio* and *S. Procolo* (Figs. 7-11).

They show a great cultural growth, ranging from study of Jacopo della Quercia to the Ferrarese painters. One obvious piece of evidence for this is the Quercesque arrangement of the *S. Petronio*, where the drapery has noticeable references to the obsessive curling of the garments of Cosmè Tura's saints; another is the organized violent movement of the *S. Procolo*, possibly not alien to Ercole de' Roberti; and yet another in the echo of Donatello's *St. George* and of David Martelli, not foreign to resonance of Verrocchio's *Colleoni*.

The *Angel* holding a candelabrum (making a pendant to the one by Niccolò dell'Arca) resumes a typical motif of Quattrocento Tuscan sculpture but endows it with a new dynamic organization, gives it substance and monumental boldness, going beyond the cultural heritage of Jacopo della Quercia and Donatello, and transforms into severe meditation the "refined and minute subtlety" of Niccolò dell'Arca, while equalling it in technique. We have again, now worked out in the round, the motifs of dynamic materialization of the drapery as they were seen in the *Madonna della Scala*. The *S. Procolo* and *S. Petronio* manifest a profound spirituality; the former is already laden with the "terribleness" of a *David*, the second is awesomely fixed, as in a slow majestic ingression.

The three works are first referred to as works of Michelangelo by Leandro Alberti, *De divi Dominici Galaguritani obitu et sepultura*, Bononiae, 1535, f. 9). Vasari and Condivi, who are unaware of this source, speak only of the *Angel* and the *S. Petronio*. Today most scholars regard all three as authentic, despite some reworking and restoration that has been done on the statuettes of the two saints. All

27 Head of Bruges Madonna (rear view).

86   28 Head and bust of Child, Bruges Madonna.

29 Hands of Child and of Madonna, Bruges Madonna.

30-31 Left hand of Madonna and feet of Child, Bruges Madonna.

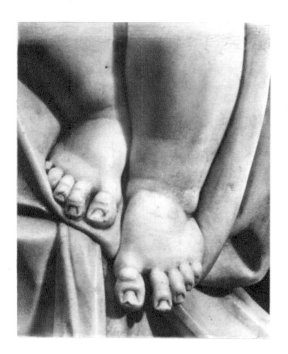

are in marble, in the round, and all are in San Domenico, Bologna. The *Angel* is 51.5 cm high, with the base; the *S. Petronio*, 64 cm; the *S. Procolo*, 58.5 cm.

The references to Jacopo della Quercia were first noted by F. Wickhoff (*Mitteilungen des Instituts für österreichische Geschichtsforschung*, III, Innsbruck, 1882, p. 430); the links with Ferrarese painting were brought out mainly by Longhi for Tura (R. Longhi, *Ampliamenti nell'Officina ferrarese*, Florence, 1956, p. 136 ff.) and more generally by C. J. Holmes (*The Burlington Magazine*, XI, 1907, p. 235 ff.) and G. Fiocco (*La Critica d'Arte*, II, 1937, p. 173 and *Le Arti*, IV, 1941, p. 17). For the *S. Procolo*, F. Kriegbaum finds references to the *S. Giovanni Battista* of Benedetto da Maiano (*Michelangelo Buonarroti*, Berlin, 1940); Tolnay brings out the relations to Donatello (*Michelangelo*, I, Princeton, 1943, p. 137 ff.); recently Lisner (*op. cit.*, p. 10) indicates an echo, in the face, of Verrocchio's *Colleoni*, which Michelangelo saw in Venice during his brief stay there just previously.

The stay in Bologna was short, "little more than a year," Condivi says. At the end of 1495, therefore, we find Michelangelo at Florence once more. There, at the end of spring 1496, he carved two works now lost: a *Youthful St. John* and a *Sleeping Cupid*.

About six months was the length of his stay in Florence. In connection with the *Youthful St. John*, some have thought it a commission from the Medici suggested by Savonarola (cf. W. R. Valentiner, *Art Quarterly*, I, 1938, p. 30) or even that the work was begun at Bologna (J. Wilde, *Mitteilungen des Kunsthistorischen Instituts in Florenz*, IV, Burg b. M., Florenz, 1932-34, p. 52 ff.; Valentiner in *Art Quarterly*, V, 1942, p. 44, No. 14).

There are no detailed data on the *Youthful St. John* in the sources and we do not know the measurements; on the other hand, the *Cupid*, who "is lying asleep on one hand," is said to be about 80 cm high.

Many attempts have been made to identify the two works. In the case of the *Youthful St. John*, consideration was given, at the turn of the century, to a sculpture in the Kaiser Friedrich Museum in Berlin, formerly in the Rosselmini house in Pisa. This thesis was advanced by S. Salvini (*La Nazione*, Jan. 10, 1875) and W. Bode (*Jahrbuch der Preussischen Kunstsammlungen*, II, Berlin, 1881, p. 72 ff.), but has been invalidated by recent criticism since; as Tolnay points out (*op. cit.*, I, p. 200), the Berlin work dates from the end of the sixteenth century, in the manner of the school of Francavilla. More recently, other references have been sought: to a sculpture in the Chapel del Salvador in Úbeba, Spain (M. Gomez-Moreno, *La escultura del Renacimiento en España*, Barcelona, 1931, Plate IX), with little success; to a *St. John* in the Pierpont Morgan Library in New York (Valentiner, *op. cit.*), attributed to Rustici by Middeldorf and Ragghianti and to Silvio Cosini by Tolnay; to the *Youthful St. John* on the door of the sacristy of San Giovanni dei Fiorentini in Rome (Longhi in *Paragone*, 1958, 101, p. 59); to the charming *St. John* in the Bargello in Florence, formerly attributed to Donatello (Parronchi, *Studi Urbinati*, XXXIV, 1960, p. 68 ff.) and assigned by Kauffmann (*Donatello*, Berlin, 1936, p. 211, No. 137) to Francesco da Sangallo.

Critics have become interested in a *Youthful St. John* in the Tozzi Collection, New York. F. De Maffei (*Michelangelo's Lost St. John: the Story of a Discovery*, New York, 1964) has published it in an accurate and detailed volume, with full photographic and other documentation, establishing a number of connections with original works by Michelangelo and, in the end, holding it to be authentic. Although it has been worn by drastic polishing, the work would not seem identifiable with the lost original, despite the high quality of some of its parts; it would rather seem to be derived from works by Michelangelo, in the manner of a Pierino da Vinci. But on this see also J. V. Lombardo, *Michelangelo: The Pietà and Other Masterpieces*, New York, 1965.

More precise data exist for the sleeping *Cupid*. It was bought from Baldassare Milanese by Cesare Borgia in Rome in 1496, as a *cosa antica*. Borgia presented it to Guidobaldo da Montefeltro, but took it back in 1502 and gave it to Isabella d'Este. It is cited in a Mantuan inventory dated 1542. Its traces have been lost since 1632, when it was sent to King Charles I of England. Attempts to identify it with a *Cupid* in the Accademia Virgiliana of Mantua (Ch. Clément, *Michel-Ange etc.*, Paris, 1861, p. 380; J. A. Symonds, *The Life of Michelangelo etc.*, I, London, 1893, p. 52 No. 1) or with a *Cupid* of the Turin Museo Archeologico (K. Lange, *Zeitschrift für Bildende Kunst*, XVIII, Leipzig, 1883, p. 233 ff.; C. Justi, *Michelangelo*, Berlin, 1909, p. 68; Valentiner, *Commentari*, VII, 1956, p. 242 ff.) have not had the slightest success; nor have any of the hypotheses formulated as to its possible iconography led to significant results.

Rome and the ancient world

Almost the only conclusion that can be drawn from these two works is that Michelangelo was still greatly interested in classical antiquity at that time, whether or not the story be true that the *Cupid* was buried, apparently without Michelangelo's knowledge, and faked up to look like something that had been dug up. It was sold as an ancient piece to Cardinal di San Giorgio, and then by Baldassare Milanesi to Cesare Borgia. We must consider it as being an exercise in the antique, for this was a period in the artist's career in which he returned to virtuoso classicist variations in a complex Hellenistic program, as if desiring to drill away any technical uncertainty, in order to perfect his idiom and at the same time test his strength against Roman antiquity, as it were, in a most civilized kind of falsification.[6] His stay in Rome (his departure from Florence is noted on June 20) revived this colloquy with the ancient world and sent Michelangelo deeper into these exercises. A convincing proof of this is the *Bacchus* in the Bargello, and further proof of it would have been another *Cupid* that Michelangelo carved in Rome for Jacopo Galli, which has been lost (Figs. 12-17).

32-33 St. Paul. Siena, Cathedral.

The extreme, and extremely pure, sensibility of the young man which he had expressed in the *Crucifix* of Santo Spirito returns in the Bargello sculpture. Some attitudes are repeated, such as the serpentine and very light contraposition of the limbs, the foreshortening of the buttocks by the half-turn of the torso on the legs, which here have the instability of a rhythmical canon; but the spiritual content is dominated by the theme, renewing the ancient myth of the young drunken god, not only evoked by his attributes (the grapes, the little satyr and the cup) but expressed by the turbid softness of the modelling—a sort of equivocal physical sensuality. For an instant Michelangelo forgets the deep moral and human intensity of his characters and lets himself go in an external cult. It has often been pointed out, and with truth, that the work is only episodic in the body of the artist's production. So much so that if we had discovered it today, it would be difficult *a posteriori* to be sure about its belonging to Michelangelo. But it should not be forgotten that we do not today have the cultural supporting documents constituted by the two lost cupids, by which we could have gotten a better overall picture of that moment when, in the thrill of a more immediate and direct naturalism, the artist turned to interpreting the antique. It is an extremely positive fact; a decisive one not only as an extreme instance of technical training, but also as a demonstration, half polemic and half delight, for the humanistic public of Rome, feverishly engaging in the enchantment of classic excavation.

The *Bacchus* was bought by Francesco de' Medici in 1571-1572, for two hundred forty ducats and went from the Galleries of the Grand Duke to the Bargello, where it has been since 1873. It is of marble, in the round, 2.03 meters in height with the base. The work was commissioned by Cardinal Riario. Done in Rome some time later than June 1496, it was refused by the cardinal and

34-35 St. Gregory. Siena, Cathedral.

bought by the banker Jacopo Galli, who put it among a collection of antique pieces in the garden of his house near San Lorenzo in Damaso. A drawing (1532-1535) by Martin Van Heemskerk and a print by Cornelis Bos show it in the garden, with the right hand missing. Before it was purchased by the Medici it must have been restored, perhaps by Michelangelo himself, but in any case with great fidelity to the original.

It is generally held to be earlier than the *Pietà*, i.e. 1496-1497, with the exception of H. Wölfflin (*Die Jugendwerke des Michelangelo*, Munich, 1891, p. 26 ff.), who gives it a later date.

The lost *Apollo* or *Cupid*, "large as life," was commissioned by Jacopo Galli; it may be that Michelangelo used the marble bought for an earlier commission from Piero de' Medici, later cancelled, of which we have word in a letter from the artist to his father Ludovico, dated August 19, 1497. It is described by U. Aldovrandi (*Delle Statue antiche che per tutta Roma in diversi luoghi e case si veggono*, appendaged to L. Manzo, *Le antichità de la città di Roma*, Venice 1556, p. 173): "a nude Apollo, full-length, with quiver and arrows on his side: and he has a vase at his feet." It stayed with Galli until the middle of the sixteenth century; then it went into the Medici collection (probably in 1572, at the same time the *Bacchus* was acquired). Since that time, it has dropped out of sight. Attempts at identification have been made, unsuccessfully, in the past and more recently; from the *Cupid* or *Eros* of the Victoria and Albert Museum in London, which had great credit with most scholars from Clément to Venturi, Berenson and Toesca, but has been strongly opposed more recently by Kriegbaum, Tolnay, Wittkover and Bertini, to the *David Apollo* of the Bargello (Valentiner, *Art Quarterly*, XXI, 1958, p. 257 ff.), which is an authentic work of Michelangelo's but is to be dated at least as late as the third decade of the century and, therefore, has no connection with this early period of creativity (cf. Figs. 99-101).

In connection with the *Bacchus*, reference has been made to the absence, or at least weakness, of fusion between the element of imagination and the stylistic research, because the descriptive intent

prevails at the expense of the figurative values (A. Bertini, *Michelangelo fino alla Sistina*, Turin, 1942, p. 33 ff.; E. Carli, *Michelangelo*, Bergamo, 1942, p. 33 ff.; Tolnay, *op. cit.*, I, 1943, p. 90; E. W. Arslan, *Michelangelo*, Pavia, 1943-44, p. 12 ff.). Attempts have also been made to define this work in terms of a mythological symbolism, complex and in fact possibly alien to its externally manifested emotion. Thus, Wind finds in it a direct reference to the myths of Life (the vine) and Death (the leopard skin); Tolnay (*op. cit.*, p. 89) reads in it the incarnation of the cosmic cycles of Death (lion mask), Life in renewal (in the face of the satyr) and the end of Life (in Bacchus himself).

And moreover, against the background of this polemic and this pleasure, we can also place the execution of the *Pietà*, even though on an entirely different plane. It is the only signed work, signed to be sure because he was content with the result attained with loving " toil " (as Vasari tells us), but also, perhaps, because of his combative pride in putting before the eyes of even occasional viewers the exceptional and elevated reality of his art (Figs. 18, 19).

The dialogue we have referred to in the wooden crucifix of Santo Spirito is brought to its first great conclusion in this work. But here the plastic quality given the forms is even more strongly idealized, to a point at which the reality, pursued in the extreme refinement and perfection of the polish of the marble, is transformed into a high poetical reality, constant in lyrical intensity.

It is the reaction of his modernity to the tendencies towards intoxication with the antique. In it he reaffirms his Florentine origin and with it all the essential values of the equilibrium that his Quattrocento education meant for him. The human pyramid merging pictorially in space among the manifold incidents of the vast drapery, in which no sinuous crevice, no fold

36-37 St. Pius. Siena, Cathedral.

is allowed to escape the rigorous return of a higher "academy," seems to relate, not so much to a context of Leonardo, as rather to the highly sophisticated chiaroscural emphasis of a Verrocchio.[7]

Rhythm, pictorial quality, tranquil light and dramatic emotion, all concur to fuse the Renaissance ideal of naturalistic illusion with the most exquisite and abstract formal research. They make the group one of Michelangelo's recaptures, earthly and spiritual at once, in which the reality of the material is sublimated by the spirit in the renewed rethinking of death.

The contract for the *Pietà* is dated August 26 or 27, 1498. It stipulates, under the guarantee of Jacopo Galli, that the work will be completed within a year; the parties are Michelangelo and Cardinal Jean Bilhères de Lagraulas, Abbot of St. Denis and ambassador of Charles VIII to Alexander VI. But the commission goes back at least to November 1497, since we have correspondence from that period relating to obtaining marble in Carrara, where Michelangelo was in December 1497 (cf. Vasari, *La Vita di Michelangelo etc.*, Paola Barocchi ed., Milan and Naples, 1962, II, p. 171 No. 145).

The work is in St. Peter's in Rome. It is in marble, in the round. It is 1.74 meters high; the base is 1.95 meters wide. On the band that crosses the breast of the Madonna, in interlocking Roman letters is inscribed: MICHAEL.AGELUS.BONAROTUS.FLORENT. FACIEBAT. It was first erected in 1499, the date of its completion, in the church of Santa Petronilla, where the cardinal who commissioned it was also buried (H. von Einem, *Michelangelo*, Stuttgart, 1959, regards it as commissioned by Bilhères as a monument for his tomb). A little before 1517 it was moved to the old Sacristy of St. Peter's, and in 1568 to the old Sistine choir; then to the altar of SS. Simone and Giuda, and in 1626 to the present choir. Since 1749 it is in its present location, in the first chapel on the north side of St. Peter's.

38-39 St. Peter. Siena, Cathedral.

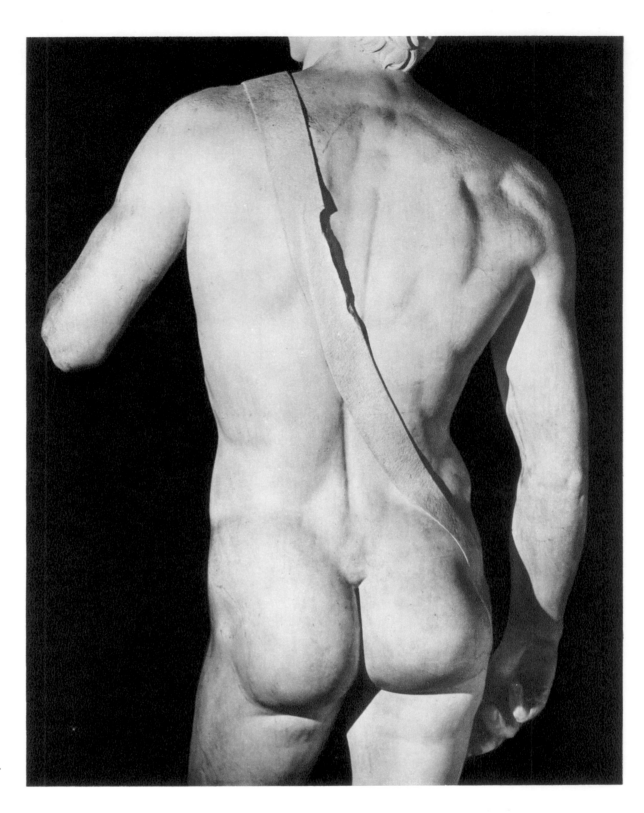

40 Torso of David (rear view). Florence, Academy of Fine Arts.

Except by Wölfflin (*op. cit.*, p. 22 ff.), it is unanimously held to have been executed after the *Bacchus*. In 1736 Giuseppe Lironi restored four fingers of the right hand.

The theological explanation of the Virgin's youth as compared with the Son is given in Vasari and Condivi; more recently, there have been attempts to regard it as a religious inspiration linked to Savonarola (E. Guillaume, *Gazette des Beaux-Arts*, I, 1876, p. 62; Bode, *Denkmäler der Renaissance—Skulptur Toscanas*, Munich, 1892-1905, p. 171; M. Brion, *Michel-Ange*, Paris, 1939, p. 105), or an idealization based on Greek models (Justi, *op. cit.*, Berlin, 1909, p. 86 ff.) or a symbolism in Biblical key (M. Ferbach, *Das Chaos in der Michelangelo-Forschung*, Vienna, 1957, p. 43 ff.). Tolnay (*op. cit.*, p. 92) sees the Virgin as resigned to the Divine Will rather than as compassionate over Her dead Son; von Einem (*op. cit.*) sees not only the Christ of the Story but the Corpus Domini, and Mary not only as the mother mourning her Son but also the *Mater Dei* enthroned.

Iconographical sources have been found in ancient pagan representations (e. g. Eos and Memnon on the David cup, according to von Einem, *op. cit.*; the myth of Meleager on the sarcophagus of Palazzo Barberini in Rome, according to A. von Salis, *Antike und Renaissance*, Zurich, 1947) or in painted or carved Byzantine and North and Central European medieval pictures, or closer to home, and with more logical consequence and historical filiation, in the painted descents from the cross of the fifteenth century. More particular influences have been seen: Ferrarese (*Pietà* of Liverpool by Ercole de' Roberti) by Longhi (*Officina Ferrarese*, Florence, 1956); Donatello (*Judith*); della Quercia (*Madonna* on the portal of S. Petronio) by von Einem (*op. cit.*); Leonardo (drapery) by Wilde (*Burlington Magazine*, XCV, 1953, pp. 65-77).

[6] C. L. Ragghianti, *Miscellanea Minore di Critica d'Arte*, Bari, 1946, p. 153 ff.

[7] The observation is F. Russoli's (*Tutta la scultura di Michelangelo*, Milan, 1953, p. 15); he sees in Verrocchio the possibility, for Michelangelo, of finding some solutions (but how partial, and how alien to his spirit!) to the problems that his stay in Bologna and acquaintance with the Ferrarese painters had raised.

41 Head of David (front view).

42-44 Hair (left side-front view) and right hand (rear and front view) of David.

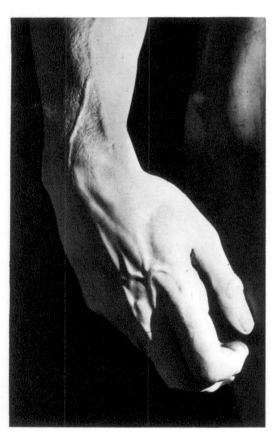

Return to Tuscany: Florence and Siena

Back in Florence (perhaps in spring 1501), Michelangelo was immediately overwhelmed with work and commitments.

The work that came next in time after the *Pietà* in St. Peter's was the *Madonna and Child* in the church of Notre-Dame in Bruges, which carries over from the Roman work the chiaroscuro pattern and the movement of the drapery. But the result is different. In it the openness to the light of the *Pietà* is replaced by a more solemn architecture that locks the form in a pattern of heightened plastic solemnity (Figs. 20-31).

The verticality of the long oval face, supreme in its thoughtful beauty (Tolnay correctly sees in it an anticipation of the Delphic Sibyl) and made even more ample and solemn in the tremendous counterpoint of its large planes with the great swelling of the veil on the hair, finds its rhythmic and architectonic counterpart in the big clasp of the garment, high on the chest, and continues from there in the fall of the dress to the waist: the very breath of the Virgin seems to halt suspended in that static silence.

The rest of Her actions seem to have no will, as if in a moment of absorption: the movement of the right hand, held back as if more to avoid its falling than to hold the book; the left hand does not press the Son to Her nor communicate in mutual vitality, but is only like a hook fastener to hold Him; and so the posture of the legs. This is a way of parting, dividing, almost contrasting the differing physical and moral essence of the two personages, given autonomy of actions because of antinomy of thought. It is the same antinomy that had

94

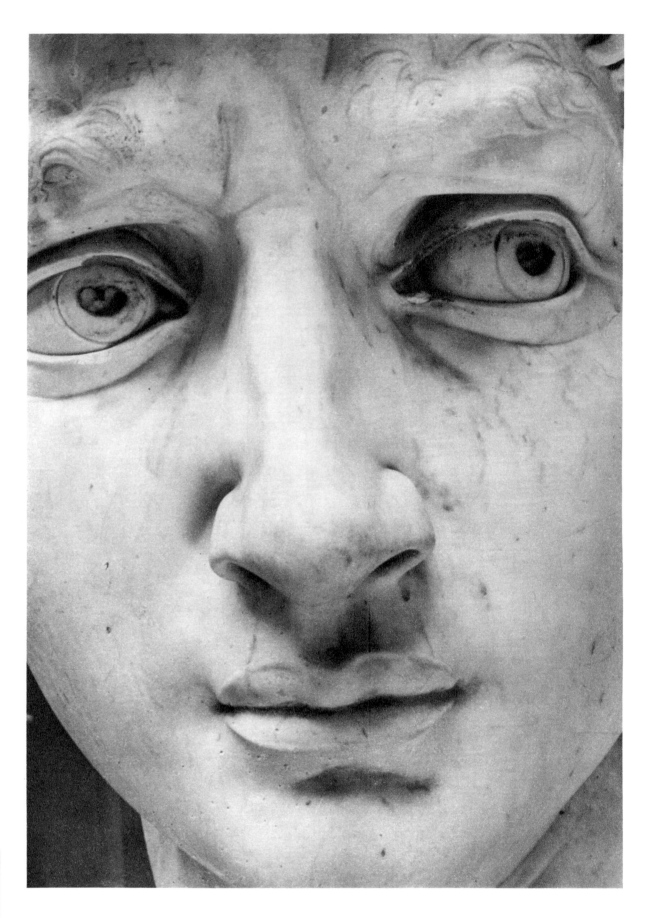

46-47 Details of head of David.

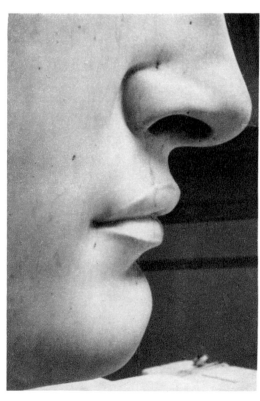

placed Mother and Son in an entirely new relationship in the *Madonna della Scala*, the same that we shall find later in the Sacristy of San Lorenzo: the Mother withdrawn in the presentiment of sorrow and death, the Son dynamic, material, insurgent physical force.

This is the way that Michelangelo interprets the mystery of the incarnation; but at the same time that he removes from the Mother of God any apparent sign of human affection (compare the traditional conversations, on the model of the delicate modesty of Luca della Robbia, which were to bring Raphael to his most familiar poetry), he doubles Her intensity, bringing it to the highest drama on the historical plane.

The *Madonna* is in marble, in the round, and is 1.28 meters high with the base.

The inaccuracies of the sources in their references to this work (in Condivi and Varchi it is said to be a " bronze," in Vasari a " tondo ") can be explained by the fact that the work was seen by few people before being shipped to Bruges, by Michelangelo's wishes, as seems to be shown by a letter to his father dated from Rome on January 31: " that marble Notre Dame, I wish you would have it taken to your house and not let anyone see it."

Further information comes from a letter of Giovanni Balducci dated August 14, 1506, telling Michelangelo of the possibility of shipping the statue " to Flanders, that is to Bruges, to the office of Giovanni and Alessandro Moscheroni *e comp.*, as their property" (cf. A. Gotti, *Vita di Michelangelo etc.*, Florence, 1875, p. 51). It is also known that the work was sold for 4000 florins (M. Van Waer-

48 Pitti Tondo. Florence, Bargello National
Museum.

newyck, *Storia del Belgio*, 1560); it was put up in the family chapel in the cathedral, where it was seen
by Dürer in April 1521 (K. Lange and F. Fuhse. *A. Dürer's schriftlichen Nachlass*, Halle, 1893, p. 156).
Transferred to France during the time of Napoleon, it was restored to Bruges in 1815. In 1952 the
work was exhibited in Florence in the Salone delle Armi of the Bargello, in an exchange of loans
with Van der Goes' Portinari triptych from the Uffizi.

Iconographical analogies have been sought with the Byzantine motif of the Virgin *Platitera*, or
Virgin bearing the Child on Her breast; and with Donatello's conception of the Virgin on the
altar of the Saint [St. Anthony of Padua?-Tr] (Tolnay, *op. cit.*), with Tuscan sculptures of the early
Quattrocento, with works by Jacopo della Quercia, and with the *Carità* of the Pisan pulpit of Nicola
Pisano (F. Russoli, *Tutta la Scultura di Michelangelo*, Milan, 1953, p. 16).

The thesis has been advanced that the statue may have been designed for the group of the Piccolomini altar (J. Hess, *The Burlington Magazine*, LXXXII, 1943, p. 62; Valentiner, *op. cit.*, 1950,

p. 214; von Einem, *op. cit.*, 1959), but it is not accepted by other critics, who for the most part think that its execution dates from a period between the Roman *Pietà* and the *David*. It was held to be contemporaneous with the *David* by H. Grimm (*Leben Michelangelos*, I, 1860-63, p. 213 ff.), Wölfflin (*Die Jugendwerke des Michelangelo*, Munich, 1891, p. 38 ff.), K. Frey (*Die Handzeichnungen Michelagniolos Buonarroti*, Berlin, 1909-11, p. 35), and more recently by Bertini (*op. cit.*, p. 415) and E. Carli (*Michelangelo e Siena*, Rome, 1964, p. 21), who thinks of a 1503 date; H. Thode (*Michelangelo Kritische Unters*, etc., 1908-13, p. 59 ff.), with others, dates it 1497, that is, during the first Roman period.

This high dramatic quality is repeated in the two round bas-reliefs in the Bargello and the Royal Academy, works done in the lee of the Bruges group, very probably in 1503 (Figs. 48-49).

In them, and especially in the London *Taddei Tondo*, some have seen Michelangelo as concentrating on a space conceived as an " atmosphere " vibrating to the light, in connection with meditation on Leonardo's researches. The two works would signify another transition (after the experiments with the classics) in the formation of Michelangelo; a test and at the same time a passing experience, another version of culture.

But we find it difficult to assign the motive of this version, which Michelangelo did not need, especially at a time when events looked fortuitous and were taking him in the opposite direction, to raise the anti-Leonardo standard in Florence.

Even the *Battle of the Centaurs*, we feel, may have been a polemic against the new pyramidal conception heralded by the *Adorazione degli Scopeti*, just as the Roman *Pietà* is at bottom anti-Leonardo, entering into space more by means of formal contrapositions than by fusions of lights. The same is true of the *Madonna* of Bruges, which glorifies the form in its architectural potency of a clear-cut envelope contained and defined by the contours without cropped margins toward the outside; but occupying and forcing the space. Also, that is the time of his most lofty expression in painting, the Doni Tondo, which gives a bold summary of his way of understanding and defining form and space, light and color.

As we see it, only external technical aspects can lead us to interpret the two bas-reliefs in the key of Leonardo. They are suggested by the " unfinished quality " that enters expressively into the treatment of the marble. But the vibrations of the atmosphere and the chiaroscuro portions suggested are means that serve only to glorify the form, which is given its character and brought by a contraposition of the light to a deeper plastic power.

Thus, instead of the form's being immersed in the light and inserted into the substance of the cosmos, we have its mighty emergence; its isolation as the final point of a terrible creative travail.

49 Taddei Tondo. London, Royal Academy.

50-51 St. Matthew. Florence, Academy of Fine Arts.

The great dynamic whirl of the *Pitti Tondo* has two decisive stops in its vibration: the great cubic seat of the Virgin and her head are like the fixed spheres of a quadrant that for a moment halt the course of time and life, violently breaking into the frame around the edge, encroaching on the plane, bringing together and glorifying the supreme sculptural quality and reality of the forms. Once again the dialogue between the Mother and the Son is put aside; and the presence of the Youthful St. John is only one more theme in the statuary glorification of the great visage of the Virgin, made heroic and prophetic. The pyramidal outer line of the group is constantly broken by horizontals, by oblique lines and by frequent cuts in the space, in an incessant relationship of sculptural feeling.

The *Pitti Tondo*, a marble relief (horizontal diam. 82 cm; vertical, 85.5 cm), has been in the Bargello in Florence since 1873. According to Vasari, it was made for Bartolomeo Pitti and presented to Luigi Guicciardini by Fra Miniato Pitti, the son of Bartolomeo. Varchi reports it in the Guicciardini house (belonging to Pietro Guicciardini, Luigi's grandson) in 1564 (Benedetto Varchi, *op. cit.* p. 28). It was acquired by the Florence Galleries in 1823.

53 Head and torso of St. Matthew, horizontal
light.

52 St. Matthew (left side-front view).

Criticism has found many iconographic references to the antique (for the Child, precise relationships
have been cited with funerary genii, as on the Phedra sarcophagus in the Pisa Camposanto: Wilde,
op. cit.), to the Quattrocento style of Jacopo della Quercia (Tolnay, *op. cit.*, 1943, p. 101, relates the
Virgin to the Prudence of the Fonte Gaia in Siena), and Donatello (Tolnay, *op. cit.*: the cherub on
the forehead of the Virgin, symbolizing the gift of prophecy, resembling the Madonna on the altar
of St. Anthony in Padua).

Some recent scholars who consider it to be later than the *Taddei Tondo* following Vasari include
M. Hauptmann (*Der Tondo*, Frankfurt, 1936, p. 163 ff.), F. Kriegbaum (*Centenario del Giudizio*, 1942,
p. 111), Bertini (*op. cit.* p. 53), M. Weinberger (*Art Bulletin*, XXVIII, 1945, p. 71) and von Einem
(*op. cit.*). It is held to be earlier, and to be dated 1503-1504, by Justi (*op. cit.*, p. 184 ff.), Thode (*op.
cit.*), Carli (*op. cit.*, p. 21 ff.), Valentiner (*Art Quarterly*, V, 1942, p. 14) and Tolnay (*op. cit.*, I, 1943,
p. 162 ff.).

In the *Taddei Tondo* all the definitions are sharper; it is a dynamic, pulsating, "focussing,"
exalting the power and solidity of the form, in a chiaroscuro that brings out the finished aspect
thanks to, and in contrast to, the unfinished. Apparently taken from Leonardo's theoretical
esthetics, it employs the same means, only carrying them to absolutely opposite consequences.

The *Taddei Tondo*, a marble relief (1.09 meters in diameter), is in the Royal Academy of Fine
Arts in London, coming there after Sir George Beaumont had bought it in Rome from the Wicar
Collection.

Vasari mentions it, stating that it was done for Taddeo Taddei. For it, too, derivations from the
antique have been suggested, e.g. the Medea sarcophagus of the Berlin Museum (E. Panofsky, *Study
in Iconology, etc.*, New York and Oxford, 1939). Other comparisons relate the type of the Child
to the traditional Tuscan iconography (with the goldfinch in his hand to symbolize the soul) and
the type of the Virgin (modelled on the Sibyl) to the one by Giovanni Pisano on the pulpit of S.
Andrea in Pistoia.

99

For ist date, reference should be made to what has been said about the Tondo Pitti; but it is added that A. Venturi (*Michelangelo*, 1926, p. 47 ff.) considers it as contemporaneous with the Sistine Chapel paintings.

That Michelangelo executed the work has been called into question by R. Wittkover (*The Burlington Magazine*, 1941, p. 133), who believes that the relief was worked over by a pupil, by Tolnay (*op. cit.*, I, 1943, p. 162 ff.), who accepts Wittkover's thesis, and by Arslan (*op. cit.*, p. 49 ff.), who denies authorship by Michelangelo, considering the tondo as the work of a follower, perhaps an important artist in his youthful period, still under the Master's influence.

The influence of Leonardo has been noted by H. Mackowsky (*Michelangelo*, Berlin, 1908, p. 52) and by P. Toesca (*Enc. Italiana*, XXIII, 1934), C. Gamba (*La scultura di Michelangelo*, Novara, 1943), Bertini (*op. cit.*, p. 52), Wilde (*op. cit.*, p. 69) and Russoli (*op. cit.*, p. 19-20).

On the anti-Leonardo position of Michelangelo at this time, cf. U. Baldini, *Il Rinascimento nell'Italia Centrale*, Bergamo, 1962, p. 28-32.

It is at this period, between late spring or early summer of 1503 and October 1504, that the execution of the Piccolomini statues in Siena is to be placed. These are four statues inserted in the niches of the Piccolomini altar of Siena Cathedral. For at least three of them, the *St. Paul*, *St. Peter* and *St. Pius*, we can be confident of their authenticity; the uncertain features of the *St. Gregory* may be attributed to the hand of someone in the studio. The relationships with the Doni Tondo (although only for the face in the case of the *St. Pius*), with the Bruges *Madonna* and with the Vatican *Pietà*, three works close together in time but also three different positions in the development of Michelangelo, may perhaps be explained by

54 Dying Slave. Paris, Louvre.

55 Head and torso of Dying Slave.

56 Rebellious Slave. Paris, Louvre.

57-58 Moses. Rome, San Pietro in Vincoli.

intermittent work on them, often abandoned for larger tasks and then resumed at odd moments and under pressure from the patrons (Figs. 32-39).

Imagination, richness of drapery, modulated balance between lights and shadows, elegant development of line, monumentality, meditative aristocratic melancholy, balance between intensity of psychological penetration and formal purity, both arising out of a refined intellectualization of the plastic means: such are the terms most frequently employed in the analysis of these works which, although not always accepted by all critics, seem to us by all means to merit inclusion in this catalogue of Michelangelo.

The four statues are in the round, in marble; at the back, which was up against the back of the niche, the marble is only roughed out. They represent St. Paul, St. Peter, St. Pius and St. Gregory. In that order, their heights are 1.27, 1.24, 1.34 and 1.36 meters. Two are in niches in the first order and two in the second, in an arrangement by pairs, two apostles and two saints, made by E. Carli after the statues had been brought back from the place of safety they had been removed to during the last conflict (cf. Carli, *op. cit.*, p. 11). They are on the Piccolomini altar done by Andrea Bregno between 1483 and 1485. Pietro Torrigiani had begun a *St. Francis* for it (which Michelangelo had to complete in order to have it match his own statues) when on June 5, 1501, Michelangelo made his contract with Cardinal Francesco Tedeschini Piccolomini (Michelangelo signed it on June 19 and Jacopo Galli on June 25) to " make fifteen figures of new, clear, white, unveined Carrara marble " for 500 gold ducats, at the rate of 33 and a third ducats per statue. A new contract dated October 11, 1504 relates to the execution of the four statues. Michelangelo did no more work on the others, despite a new request by Antonmaria Piccolomini in December 1537; in 1561, after further fruitless entreaties, the contract was cancelled by Francesco Bandini Piccolomini, Archbishop of Siena.

By and large, the four statues have not been much admired by the critics, who have often denied they were Michelangelo's: from Wölfflin (*op. cit.*, p. 77 ff.) to Mackowsky (*op. cit.*, p. 395 ff.), and recently Longhi (*Ampliamenti nell'Officina ferrarese*, Florence, 1956, p. 137).

Thode (*op. cit.*, p. 67 ff.), reevaluating the documents, held the works to have been done by Michelangelo; Thode's opinion, supported by new aspects of interpretation, was supported by Toesca (*op. cit., ad vocem*), Kriegbaum (*Centenario del Giudizio*, 1942, p. 94 ff.), Valentiner (*Art Quarterly*, V, 1942, p. 42 ff.), E. Hanfstaengl (*Pantheon*, XXXI, 1943, p. 77 ff.), Gamba (*op. cit.*, 1943), Arslan (*op. cit.*, 1943, p. 21 ff.), and, recently, Carli (*op. cit.*, 1964), who feels that the *St. Gregory* was done by assistants. Wilde (*Mitteilungen des Kunsthist. Inst. in Florenz*, IV, 1932-1934, p. 56 ff.) considers it as having been done by assistants after a design by Michelangelo; Tolnay (*op. cit.*, I, 1943, p. 229; id. *The Art Bulletin*, XXVII, 1945, p. 144; id. *Michelangelo*, Florence, 1951, p. 243), on the basis of a letter from Ludovico Buonarroti, dated June 28, 1510, to Michelangelo in Rome, holds that the statue was done by Baccio da Montelupo and sees the hand of Michelangelo only in the *St. Paul* and *St. Peter*; but cf. Carli (*op. cit.*, p. 12), who more correctly holds the letter to refer to what still remained to be done.

Longhi (*op. cit.*) has seen iconographical and stylistic relationships of Ferrarese origin in the *St. Paul*; Tolnay (*loc. cit.*) sees memories of Donatello in it, and Russoli (*op. cit.*) the influence of Nanni di Banco. Carli (*op. cit.*, p. 23), taking up an idea of Kriegbaum (*loc. cit.*), sees the face of the *St. Paul*, as Michelangelo's first portrait, or rather self-portrait. The date of the group is put between 1501 and 1504; Hanfstaengl (*loc. cit.*) gives late 1501 for the *St. Paul*, 1502 for the *St. Peter*, 1503 and 1504 for the *St. Gregory* and *St. Pius*.

On August 16, 1501 Michelangelo signed a contract for the *David* with the Opera del Duomo in Florence, and went to work on it on September 13 (Figs. 40-47).

More than any other of Michelangelo's works, the *David*, in its dimensions and mere physical nature, expresses the plastic aims of the artist, the final point of his long and passionate cogitations on form and man. Without descending to the romantic classifications that define it as a first document in the passage from the "sweet" to the "terrible," we must regard

59 Head and bust of Moses.

60 Christ Risen. Rome, Santa Maria sopra Minerva.

it as a turning point in his course. So precisely does the work sum up his researches that we are almost tempted to say that if he had not had such a gigantic block of marble fall into his hands to carve, he would have sought one out at that moment. It is a final point and at the same time a starting point, an essential crossing, an imperious assertion of his way of understanding and seeing. All the positive values that he had gathered in observing the antique and practicing it, all his exercises and direct studies on the human body, all the internal spiritual forces that he had thrown into interpreting the world both in myth and in reality: all come into play here. The incommensurable becomes measurable and measured; man is set down in his physical and moral reality, without being glorified but without being put down or violated. All the blandishments of illustration are put aside in order to state and corroborate the reality of a body that vibrates with its twofold power, physical and moral.

The *David*, in marble and in the round, is 4.10 meters high. Since 1873 it has been in the gallery of the Accademia of Florence, after having stood at the gate of Palazzo Vecchio in Piazza della Signoria, where a copy now stands.

For his statue Michelangelo used a marble block that had been given, in 1463-64 to Agostino di Duccio to make a giant, perhaps a David (as Tolnay believes) but more likely a prophet, as the relevant document of the Opera dated August 18, 1464 tells us (cf. G. Poggi, *Il Duomo di Firenze*, Berlin, 1909, p. 81 ff., No. 441), to go on one of the buttresses of the Cathedral. Agostino did not finish the work and the block was then turned over to Antonio Rossellino on May 6, 1476, but without results (cf. Poggi, *op. cit.*, p. 83, No. 446).

And so the block was left in the courtyard of the Opera, " *male abbozzatum et sculptum* " (Poggi, *op. cit.*, p. 83 ff., No. 448), and entrusted to Michelangelo on August 16, 1501. After giving it a few blows of the chisel on September 9 to test its hardness, "*firmiter et fortiter* " (cf. Poggi, *op. cit.*, p. 84, No. 449), on October 14 he made a " *turata*," a shed of boards, so that he could work under cover (cf. Thode, *op. cit.*, p. 76). The work was *quasi finita* on January 25, 1504, when a commission was named to choose a site for it.

Among the members of the commission were such artists as Andrea della Robbia, Cosimo Rosselli, Francesco Granacci, Piero di Cosimo, Davide Ghirlandaio, Simone del Pollaiolo, Filippino Lippi, Sandro Botticelli, Antonio and Giuliano da Sangallo, Andrea Sansovino, Leonardo da Vinci, Pietro Perugino and Lorenzo di Credi. A majority favored putting the work in Orcagna's Loggia (dei Lanzi), but were overruled by the Signori dell'Opera who decided (May 28-29, 1504) to set it up at the side of the doorway of Palazzo Vecchio, and this was done June 8, 1504, in place of Donatello's *Judith*, which was shifted to the Loggia. Execution of the base was entrusted (June 11, 1504) to Simone del Pollaiolo and Antonio da Sangallo. On September 8 the *David* was in place, with its base "*fornito e scoperto di tutto* " (L. Landucci, *Diario fiorentino, etc.*, Florence, 1883, p. 268 ff.).

We hear of a lightning stroke that hit the base in 1512, without damaging the statue, and of the left arm's being broken into three pieces in 1527 during the conflicts in the city at the time of the expulsion of the Medici; the damage was later restored by Vasari and Francesco Salviati.

References have been made to ancient statues (G. Kleiner, *Die Begegnungen M.s mit der Antike*, Berlin, 1950, p. 18 ff.), more precisely to the Dioscuri of Montecavallo (Bertini, *op. cit.*, p. 39 ff.) and to statues of Hercules, on Roman sarcophagi or on the pulpit of the Baptistery of Pisa (Tolnay, *op. cit.*). Tolnay (*ibid.*) gives the most convincing iconological interpretation of the statue: a Hercules-David synthesis, personifying the two main civic virtues of the Renaissance: Wrath and Strength. But references have also been proposed to Dante (K. Borinski, *Die Rätsel Michelangelos*, Munich, 1908, p. 72) and to Savonarola (H. Brockhaus, *Michelangelo und die Medici Kapelle*, Leipzig, 1901, p. 12 ff.).

These first years of Michelangelo's new stay in Florence after his Roman experience were a time of great involvement. In addition to producing the works we have already described, he was engaged in two other tasks: the marble statue of *Matthew the Apostle* for Santa Maria del Fiore and a *David* in bronze for Pierre de Rohan.

The *St. Matthew*, the only one of these two that has come down to us, although unfinished, has the aspect of a large bas-relief of great dynamic quality, which breaks with the restrained and composed impulse of the *David* and carries the action to heroic heights, depicted with extreme vibrations of struggle and travail. It comes to us as one of the most sublime expressions of Michelangelo's art, as a genuine representation of primordial suffering (to use Tolnay's words), of a moment at which the soul is prey to superhuman cosmic forces that destroy its individuality. Rather than anthropomorphic glorification in and of itself, it is a glorification of the eternal struggle between the powers of the spirit and the blindness of matter. The form surges out of the surface, chipped and striated by the chisel blows; once more it is a total departure from Leonardo's chiaroscuro poetics, once more the potent embodiment of the form. Within that shell taking form, and already disclosed to a great extent, there pulses the physical and moral life of man: victorious over the chaos and cosmos surrounding him, champion and not indifferent actor, center and sole truth of the universe. It is through this that the apparent infinite is defined; it is through this that we see no contradiction with the creative aspect that in other cases (for example, in the painting of the *Doni Tondo*) leads to total definition of form. That definition appears here too; it only seems to be potential, while in fact it is already achieved in the content and expressive value (Figs. 50-53).

The unfinished *St. Matthew* (height 2.61 meters) is in the gallery of the Accademia in Florence; down to 1834 it was in the premises of the Opera del Duomo.

The contract between the consuls of the Arte della Lana and the members of the Opera of Santa

61 Head and torso of Dawn. Florence, San Lorenzo, New Sacristy.

62 Legs of Dawn (right rear-side view).

Maria del Fiore, on the one hand, and Michelangelo on the other, was signed on April 24, 1503. The artist undertook to make twelve statues of the Apostles to go in the positions where Bicci di Lorenzo later painted the Apostles. But the only thing accomplished, and left incomplete at that, was this *St. Matthew*. Actually the contract was cancelled on December 18, 1505, although Michelangelo, who left for Bologna the following year and returned to Florence in March 1508, may have intended to resume the work. But once again nothing came of it, for in April or so he was called to Rome for the Sistine Chapel, and the commission for the Apostles was given to other sculptors: Andrea and Jacopo Sansovino, Benedetto da Rovezzano, Baccio Bandinelli and Andrea Ferrucci. Michelangelo must have done the *St. Matthew* between 1505 and 1506.

Sources of inspiration have been sought for this work as well, and particular reference has been made to the *Laocoön*, rediscovered in Rome in 1506 (O. Ollendorf, *Repertorium für Kunstwissenschaft*, XXI, Berlin and Leipzig, 1898, p. 114 ff.) and the *Pasquino* (A. Grünwald, *Jahrbuch der Sammlungen*, XXVII, Vienna, 1907-9, p. 130 ff.). Suggestions relating to less remote works have also been given: the insistent frontality has been linked to the representational principles of the Middle Ages (von Einem, *op. cit.*) and comparisons have been drawn with Donatello's sculpture of the type of the *Abraham* for the campanile of the Duomo (G. de Francovich in *Bollettino d'Arte*, IX, 1929-30, p. 145 ff.).

The *David* in bronze has been lost. Michelangelo signed a contract for doing it, on August 12, 1502, with the Signoria of Florence, acting for Pierre de Rohan, Marshal of France, a well-known art lover who had come into Italy with Charles VIII and had requested a David in bronze through the ambassadors of Florence in Lyons, Pier Tosinghi and Lorenzo de' Medici. It is known that Michelangelo went to work on it at once, but later, for one reason and another, the execution of the commission dragged, so that many inquiries and requests came from France to the Signoria, who finally intervened vigorously and obtained the help of Benedetto da Rovezzano in finishing the work and shipping it after the casting, in October 1508. Once finished, it was packed for shipping by November 6 of that year and transported down the Arno to Leghorn, from which it had already left on December 26. On its arrival in France it was installed in the Hôtel d'Alluye and then in the Château de Bury. Before 1650 it was transferred to the Château de Villeroy, near Mennecy; there all trace of it is lost.

Attempts at identifying the work have not led to any positive result. Among the suggestions are the little *David* formerly belonging to Pulszky, now in the Louvre (L. Courajod, *Gazette Archéologique*, X, Paris, 1885, p. 77), which is probably a copy of Donatello's Martelli *David* (Tolnay, *op. cit.*, I, p. 208 ff.); a David in the Amsterdam Rijksmuseum (A. Pit, *Revue de l'Art ancien et moderne*, II, 1897,

63 Head of Dawn.

p. 455 ff.), which may very well be a copy but is insignificant (Bertini, *op. cit.*, p. 55 ff.); a terracotta sketch in Casa Buonarroti, Florence (proposed by Bayersdorfer, *Leben und Schriften*, Munich, 1902, p. 84 ff.), which has nothing to do with Michelangelo; and a bronze *David* in the Museo di Capodimonte, Naples, attributed to Pollaiolo and referred to Michelangelo by Parronchi (*Studi Urbinati*, XXXVI, 1962, p. 208).

As we know, the most important testimony concerning it is the original drawing in the Louvre, 714 r; the engravings of Ducerceau in 1576 on the Château de Bury (Ducerceau, *Les plus excellents bâtiments de France*, 1576, p. 124 ff.) and a drawing of Michelangelo's catafalque in the Ambrosiana, noted by Tolnay (*loc. cit.*), give no indications.

By this time we have come to the first negotiations for the Tomb of Julius II. But first Michelangelo brought to completion a bronze statue that was placed on the façade of San Petronio in Bologna.

The statue represented *Pope Julius II* in pontifical robes, seated on his throne with his right hand raised to give a blessing and his left hand, holding the keys, resting on his knee. It was about 2.92 meters in height, according to Vasari; 3.30, according to the chroniclers; and 3.53 or 4.12, according to Michelangelo, who gives its height sometimes as 6 and sometimes as 7 ells. Michelangelo received the commission from Julius II himself toward the end of the year in Bologna, where the artist had gone to get pardon for his flight from Rome arising out of the delay in the work on the tomb. We know of the difficulties in the casting (there were two, the first not having turned out well) and of the final satisfaction felt by Michelangelo. The statue was put into place on the façade of San Petronio on February 21, 1508, in a niche over the main portal. On December 30, 1511, after the return of the Bentivoglio to Bologna, the people tore it down and demolished it. The pieces were taken to Ferrara, where Duke Alfonso d'Este had them used to make a culverin, which was given the name "Giuliana." Attempts at reconstructing the iconography of the statue have not yielded any satisfactory results.

64 Legs of Dawn (right side view).

65 Lorenzo de' Medici. Florence, San Lorenzo, New Sacristy.

The tragedy of the tomb

After this sojourn in Bologna, Michelangelo came back to Florence and then moved to Rome, and his activity as a sculptor came to a halt: he was totally engaged on the Sistine vault, and not until the year after its completion do we find Michelangelo undertaking to begin on the *Tomb of Julius II*, after having come to an agreement with the Pope's heirs on the new arrangement and form of the mausoleum.

Letters of Michelangelo, for the most part bitter and tormented, copies of lost designs, more or less fragmentary designs, notices and descriptions, not always consonant with one another, in Vasari and Condivi, tell us of what even at that time was called "the tragedy of the tomb" (the phrase is in Condivi). For forty years after the initial negotiations in 1505, various projects were drawn up, some works were done and others commenced, until in 1545 there came the conclusion and definitive installation of the *Tomb of Julius II* in San Pietro in Vincoli, where we see it today. But this is a solution that, with the exception of the *Moses*, retains nothing of the original ideas and the much grander first project. It is a patched-up solution, as it were, that Michelangelo arrived at in order to get it done after so much suffering; that is, after the initial project had already been altered five times.

107

68 Head and bust of Lorenzo de' Medici (front view).

67 Lorenzo de' Medici (rear view).

It was in 1505 that Pope Julius II called Michelangelo to Rome and commissioned him to make a funeral monument for himself, to be erected in the apse of the new basilica of St. Peter's. Condivi and Vasari are our only sources on this *first project*, on which Michelangelo began work at once, travelling to Carrara to choose the marble for it. But it was abandoned, for all practical purposes, after his flight from Rome on August 17, 1506 because the Pope, angered by the delays and possibly instigated by Michelangelo's competitors, had him put out of the Vatican. However, despite considerable discrepancies in the descriptions given, we can get a fairly clear idea at least of its general outlines. It was to have been an isolated monument, that is, one standing clear of the walls—a true mausoleum—rectangular in shape, about 10.8 meters long and 7.2 wide, rising in three orders or zones, tapering off into a pyramid at the top. The lowest region was divided into three parts architecturally: two large lateral niches for statues of Victories, marked off by *termae* or *hermae* against which were backed up, on dado pedestals, statues of Prisons or Slaves, and a middle part into which opened (perhaps on two opposite sides of the monument or perhaps on only one) a door into the funeral chamber, an oval shrine with the Pope's sepulcher. The middle zone, introduced by architraves and cornice, concluded the upward thrust of the two niches with Victories, showing two seated figures on the front of the monument and two at the back (Moses, St. Paul, the Active Life and the Contemplative Life). The uppermost zone, rising as a roof in the form of a truncated pyramid with reliefs in bronze and other sculptures, presented two allegorical figures (Angels for Condivi; Heaven and Earth for Vasari) supporting a catafalque or bier with the figure of Julius II.

After Julius II's death in February 1513, Michelangelo, pursuant to the Pope's will, resumed work on the project which, however, was amended by agreement with the heirs, in a contract for a *second project*, signed in May of that year.

Fundamental changes, carrying over later into the 1542 solution that was to be the definitive one, were the elimination of the mortuary chamber and the backing of the tomb up against the wall. The tomb was thus no longer conceived of as an isolated monument. As a result, the statues were crowded closer together; those that in the first project were to have been on two sides, near the corners, were transferred to the front. There was a similar effect of perspective interpretation for the lowermost zone, which, however, lost its central grill, but a plastic intensification in the middle zone, which now had not two but four statues (in pairs); and the sarcophagus in the uppermost zone was surrounded by four statues; still higher, within an arch and pilaster enclosure, a Madonna and Child within an almond and five other figures.

But by July 1516 a contract for a *third project* was signed.

The mausoleum, which in the second project still projected deeply from the wall, now took on the aspect of an architectural entity of the type of a façade enlivened with sculptural decorations. The lowest zone is still unchanged, but at the center there would have been a bronze relief replacing the door of the first version. Above, there are again two large seated figures, with the Pope in the center as in a two-figured Pietà and surmounted by the Virgin and Child, within a niche.

In October 1526 Michelangelo prepared a *fourth project* for the heirs of Julius II, who since 1522 had been asking for the return of the money they had advanced on the tomb and in 1524 had threatened him with a lawsuit. But the project was not acceptable. The new version is not known to us. However, it may be a reduction of the preceding project, perhaps (as Tolnay supposes) a façade with niches, the central one containing the seated figure of the Pope.

And so on April 29, 1532 Michelangelo signed a new contract in which he bound himself to execute the work within three years. The only thing we know precisely about this *fifth project* is that the site of the tomb was now to be the basilica of San Pietro in Vincoli, and that the marble pieces already worked up would be used for it. This suggests that the new version would be a variant of the type of the third project of 1516.

Years after the term of the 1532 obligation had expired, yet another contract was signed, on August 20, 1542. This was the *sixth project* for the tomb and was finally executed, as we see it today, in 1545.

Many assistants worked with Michelangelo on his designs and under his direction. The architecture of the uppermost story of the tomb was done by Giovanni Marchesi and Francesco da Urbino. Other sculpture work was executed by Donato Benti and Jacopo del Duca. The figures of the Virgin, the Prophet and the Sibyl (already roughed out by Michelangelo in 1537) were executed by Domenico Fancelli and Raffaello da Montelupo; the figure of the Pope, by Tommaso Boscoli.

69 Head of Lorenzo de' Medici (rear view, from above).

70 Head and bust of Lorenzo de' Medici (left side-front view).

71 Head of Twilight (right side view). Florence, San Lorenzo, New Sacristy.

During Michelangelo's work on the Sistine, his only sculptural activity was on a task imposed on him by the Signoria of Florence, the elaboration of a sketch for the statue that Pier Soderini wanted to have erected on the Piazza della Signoria, to match the *David*.

And now, after slaving on the painting for four years, he took up work on the tomb of Julius II once more, producing the two *Slaves* in the Louvre. But now, in taking up an argu-

72 Twilight.

73 Head and shoulder of Day (front view). Florence, San Lorenzo, New Sacristy.

ment already begun with the *St. Matthew* and left unfinished, he shifts it in the direction of fluid design sensibilities, giving the forms enhanced pictural quality in a formal beauty, at once disturbing and spiritual, more stressed in the *Dying Slave*, which sinks toward the light in the pattern of its contrary (Figs. 54-55). The figure (for which a source has been seen in Leonardo) finds a hedonistic immersion in the drama itself, becomes purer and falls into a dream,

74 Day.

76 Day (left side-front view).

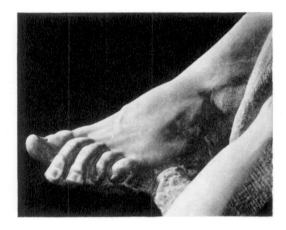

75 Left foot of Day (rear view).

77 Head and torso of Twilight.

as if weary. It is, as it were, the reply to what Longhi calls the "titanic superorganism of fettered slaves, of high-girdled Sibyls, of immemorial old ages" of the Sistine. It is something like a pause, an instant of sublime abandon to the search for the utmost limits of total pulsation of the form, in its soft beauty; something to enjoy and possess in the most relaxed of occasions. But suddenly the heroic countenance, the countenance of struggle, as if in a dramatic resurgence of dynamic violence, regains the upper hand with the other *Rebellious Slave*, ready to break loose. The muscles swell and the body twists in sharp contrapositions, taking on sculptural vigor in the dramatic individuality of the face: a tormented mask enveloped in a mobility concentrated and intensified in the light, which does not play over it but halts to search out vibrations of a titanic, savage physicality (Fig. 56).

The two statues, marble and in the round, are usually identified by the titles of the *Dying Slave* and the *Rebellious Slave*. They are shown to have been done in 1513 by a letter of Michelangelo, which speaks of a visit of Luca Signorelli to his house in Rome in the Macello dei Corvi as he was working "on a marble figure, upright, four ells high, with its hands behind its back." This puts the figures in direct relationship with the work on the second version of the *Tomb of Julius II*, on which they were to be placed on the lower zone of the monument, against the pilasters with *herme* flanking the niches with *Victories*. They were eliminated from the last of the designs for the tomb, as provided in the contract dated August 20, 1542. Some time after 1546, Michelangelo presented the two statues to Roberto Strozzi in gratitude for his hospitable reception in Strozzi's house in Rome when he was sick in July 1544 and January 1546. Roberto Strozzi, exiled in Lyons, had the two works shipped to France at his expense in April 1550. We find them there in 1578, in niches in the courtyard of the Constable de Montmorency, in his château at Écouen near Paris (cf. the view by Ducerceau [*op. cit.*]). In 1632 Henri II de Montmorency presented them to Cardinal Richelieu, who set them up in his château in Poitou, where they were seen by a number of travellers who mention and draw them, including G. L. Bernini (*Journal du Voyage, etc.*, 1665, Paris, 1885, p. 198). In 1749 the Duc de Richelieu had them brought to Paris, in the Pavillon de Hanovre. They were sequestered in 1793 when the widow of the last of the Marshals de Richelieu had put them up for sale and A. Lenoir (cf. P. J. Mariette, *Abecedario*, I, 1851-53, p. 221 ff.) had them taken over by the French Government. Since then they have been in the Louvre collections.

For these statues, too, iconographic references to antiquity have been made, particularly to the influence of the *Laocoön* and late Hellenistic sculpture in general (Ollendorf, *op. cit.*, and von Einem, *op. cit.*). Reference has also been made to the figures of prisoners carved on triumphal arches (Justi, *op. cit.*, Leipzig, 1900).

Especially for the *Rebellious Slave*, von Einem (*loc. cit.*) lays stress on a fusion of classical and

78 Giuliano de' Medici. Florence, San Lorenzo, New Sacristy.

79 Tomb of Giuliano de' Medici.

113

15

80 Head of Giuliano de' Medici (left rear-side view).

81-82 Right hand and forearm with left hand of Giuliano de' Medici.

Christian elements, such as the representations of St. Sebastian, a drawing of whom (by Leonardo) is cited by Tolnay (*op. cit.*, 1963); for the *Dying Slave* (or sleeping slave, as Tolnay, Thode, Kriegbaum and others would have it) citation to Antonio Rossellino's *St. Sebastian* in the Tabernacle of the Museo della Collegiata of Empoli, and Benedetto da Maiano's in the Misericordia in Florence (cf. von Einem, *loc. cit.*).

Vasari gives an historical interpretation of the iconological significance of the *Slaves*, considering the figures to be representations of the provinces subjected by Julius II and brought into obedience to the Church of Rome; Condivi sees in them an allegorical reference to the Liberal Arts.

But interpretation of the meanings has not stopped at this point; some who have accepted Condivi's ideas (Thode, *op. cit.*, p. 206 ff.; Kriegbaum, M. Buonarroti, pp. 11, 36; H. W. Janson, *Apes and Ape*, London, 1952, p. 295 ff.) have seen the *Dying Slave* as the symbol of painting (because of the ape *ars simia naturae* sketched at the feet of the statue) and the *Rebel* as a symbol of architecture (Kriegbaum) or sculpture (Janson); among those agreeing with Vasari (Justi, *op. cit.*, p. 226 ff.; J. Lange, *Studien über Michelangelo*, Strassburg, 1910, p. 3 ff.; A. Rodin, *La Revue*, LXXXVI, 1910, p. 14; W. Weisbach, *Trionfi*, 1919, p. 122) some, like Tolnay (*op. cit.*, 1951-1954), have amended in Neoplatonic terms, seeing in it a " representation of the triumph of the apostolic church in line with the pattern of the *Trionfi* but, overcoming the antinomy between Christian and pagan ... the *Slaves* change from trophies to symbols of the desperate struggle of the human soul against the chains of the body." Still others have educed interpretations of their own, stressing the contrast in the postures of the two statues and giving autobiographical reasons for this (O. Ollendorf in *Zeitschrift für Bildende Kunst*, IX, Leipzig, 1898, p. 278 ff.; Brion, *op. cit.*, p. 233 ff.; K. A. Laux, *Michelangelos Juliusmonument*, Berlin, 1943, p. 38 ff.), or reasons of a psychological nature (Grimm, *op. cit.*, p. 384 ff.; A. Springer, *Raffael und Michelangelo*, II, Leipzig, 1883, p. 26 ff.; E. Müntz, *Revue des Deux Mondes*, CXIV, Paris, 1892, p. 892; Wölfflin, *Die Klass. Kunst*, 1899, p. 71 ff.), or the incarnation of universal sorrow (M. Carrière, *Die Kunst in Zusammenhang etc.*, IV, Leipzig, 1884, p. 145), or the sculptural embodiment of architectonic forces (A. Schmarsow, *Jahrbuch der Preussischen Kunstsammlungen*, V, Berlin, 1884, p. 75), or the titanic power of conception (A. Farinelli, *Michelangelo e Dante etc.*,

◁ 83 Head of Giuliano de' Medici (right side view).

Torino, 1918, p. 96), or the very law of life (G. Delogu, *Michelangelo*, Bergamo, 1934, p. 7), or sensing universal meanings in them (H. Brockhaus, *Medici Kap.*, 1909, p. 20 ff.; Justi, *op. cit.*, p. 232 ff.), or Platonic meanings (Ollendorf, *Zeitschrift für Bildende Kunst*, IX, Leipzig, 1898, p. 276 ff.; Panofsky, *Study in Iconology, etc.*, p. 194 ff.; F. Hartt, *The Art Bulletin*, XXXII, 1950, p. 137; von Einem, *Festschrift Jantzen*, 1951, p. 159; Tolnay, *op. cit.*, 1951, p. 107).

It is the same power that inspires Michelangelo in the *Moses*, the only one of the sculptures conceived and executed for the first versions of the tomb of Julius II that was to be left in the last and definitive form of the monument. Here the factor of delight in form has disappeared; the individuality is decisive; and only the volume expresses the enormous strength, in a continuous examination of the surfaces, a continuous alternation of plains and voids, a robust fluctuating play of lights and shadows. Continuous carving of the huge marble block, pushed to its final finish, enormously magnifies the symbolic glorification of the character. And a further purpose is to add completeness to the spiritual scrutiny, the stormy moral conception, the human potency of the figure: a supreme reality embodying a symbol of absolute spirituality. This giant of history has none of the striking calm, balanced nobility of the *David*: here the power has turned into the extreme of dynamism (Figs. 57-59).

84 Rear mask on cuirass of Giuliano de' Medici.

The statue of *Moses* is at the base and center of the façade of the Tomb of Julius II in San Pietro in Vincoli. It is of marble, in the round, 2.35 meters high. With the exception of Wölfflin (*Die Klass. Kunst*, p. 72), B. Berenson (*The Drawings of the Florentine Painters*, I, London, 1903, 2nd ed., 1938, p. 209) and Thode (*Michelangelo, Kritische Unters. etc.*, p. 194 ff.), who assign the execution of the

85 Giuliano de' Medici (rear view).

86 Night. Florence, San Lorenzo, New Sacristy.

87 Night (right side-front view).

work to the time of the first design for the tomb, in 1505, most scholars relate it to the 1513 design, in which the statue was to have been located in the middle zone, perhaps in the right niche (according to von Einem, *loc. cit.*, in the left niche); that is, in an elevated position (cf. E. Rosenthal, *The Art Bulletin*, XLVI, 1964, p. 544 ff.). On the basis of a letter of Michelangelo's dated 1515, it has been argued that at that time the work, begun in 1513, was still in process.

It is thus the only statue that persisted throughout all the changing projects and designs; but from being but one element in the whole, it has grown in importance to become the dominant figure in the final arrangement—so much so that it has been held to be a genuine idealized portrait of Julius II (Stendhal, *Histoire de la peinture en Italie*, II, Paris, 1817, p. 328) or at any rate a symbolic personification of him (L. Cicognara, *Storia della Scultura, etc.*, V, Venice, 1813-18, pp. 138-140; F. Gregorovius, *Die Grabmäler der Römischen Päpste*, Leipzig, 1857, p. 184 ff.; Grimm, *op. cit.*, p. 382 ff.;

88 Head and torso of Night (front view).

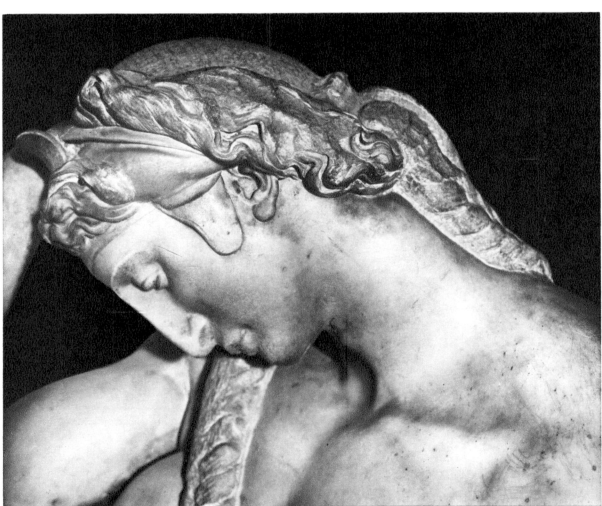

89 Head of Night (right side-front view).

Thode, *op. cit.*, p. 206; S. Freud, "Michelangelo's Moses," 1914, in *Gesammelte Schriften*, X, Leipzig-Vienna-Zurich, 1924, p. 283 ff.; G. Parroni, *L'Illustrazione Vaticana*, IV, 1933, 3, p. 890; A. Venturi, *Storia dell'Arte Italiana*, X, 2, 1936, p. 52; F. Kriegbaum, *Michelangelo Buonarroti*, p. 12).

Varying interpretations of the statue have been given over the years, both by itself and in relationship to those that were to have been grouped around it. The *Moses* has been seen as the Vicar of Christ (A. Borboni, *Delle Statue, etc.*, Rome, 1661, p. 139), as the genesis of political power (E. Montégut, *Revue des Deux Mondes*, LXXXV, Paris, 1870, p. 949 ff.), as a Savonarolian document (J. Michelet, *Histoire de France*, I, Paris, 1876, p. 331 ff.; Thode, *loc. cit.*), as a self-portrait (Grimm, *loc. cit.*) or at any rate autobiographical (M. Carrière, *op. cit.*, p. 136; G. Parroni, *op. cit.*, p. 890 ff.; Brion, *Michel-Ange*, p. 239 ff.).

Further, psychological significations have been found, with *Moses* said to be depicted in the act of   **117**

90 Abdomen of Night.

contemplating the apostasy of the Hebrew people (J. Burckhardt, *Beiträge zur Kunstgeschichte etc.*, Basel, 1885, p. 634; W. Lübke, *Geschichte der Plastik etc.*, II, Leipzig, 1863, p. 1840; A. Tari, *Saggi e Critica*, Trani, 1886, p. 474 ff.; A. Michel-J. de Foville, *La Sculpture italienne etc.*, IV, I, 1909, p. 233 ff.; F. Avenarius, *Michelangelo Mappendes Kunstwart*, IV, Munich, 1911-14, p. A), or in an effort at self-control and inhibition (Grimm, *op. cit.*, p. 383; C. H. Wilson, *Life and Works of M. B.*, London, 1876, p. 450; Wölfflin, *Die Klass. Kunst etc.*, p. 72).

Finally, the character of the *Moses* has been discussed in its logical relationship to the Active Life and the Contemplative Life; following the description given in the sources (W. Watkiss-Lloyd, *The Moses of Michelangelo*, London, 1863, p. 10 ff.; Thode, *loc. cit.*, p. 204 ff.; Freud, *loc. cit.*, p. 27 ff.; D. Frey, *Michelangelo Buonarroti*, Rome, 1923, p. 9 ff.; Toesca, *Enc. Italiana*, p. 19) recourse has been had to allegorical representation of a cosmic being (Tolnay, *op. cit.*, 1951, p. 114) with attributes corresponding to a precise symbolism: the hair as flames, the beard as water, the limbs and garments as rocks, representing the composition of man according to ancient ideas; or to symbolic meanings such as force or order in the infinite (A. Quatremère de Quincy, *Histoire de la vie et des ouvrages de Michel-Ange Buonarroti*, Paris, 1835, p. 221; A. de Lamartine, *Vie de Michel-Ange*, Paris, 1868, p. 315 ff.; G. Capponi, *Storia della Repubblica di Firenze*, II, 1875, p. 378).

For the *Moses*, too, iconographic references have been found in ancient civilization and in times closer to its own. In particular, emphasis has been laid on the flowing robes of Roman type, as in the figures on Trajan's column, for example (Justi, *loc. cit.*), or on suggestions of the *Belvedere Torso* (von Einem, *loc. cit.*), or on ancient river deities (Lalande, *Voyage en Italie*, III, Paris, 1768, p. 348 ff.; J. J. Volkmann, *Historisch-Kritische Nachrichten von Italien etc.*, Leipzig, 1777, p. 226 ff.). But relationships with the Quattrocento have been stressed even more, with references to the posture of the *St. John the Evangelist* of Donatello now in the Opera del Duomo in Florence (Bode, Tolnay and von Einem, *loc. cit.*). There must have been connections with the demolished statue of Julius II in Bologna, as Tolnay has seen; he also makes connections with the *Prophets* in the Sistine. Russoli (*op. cit.*, p. 56), also makes a connection with the later *Giuliano dei Medici* in the New Sacristy of San Lorenzo.

Other important jobs, especially in the architectural field, engaged Michelangelo in this second decade of the century. His work as a sculptor came to a halt, despite the new project for the Tomb, and was confined to marginal works.

Pier Soderini, the gonfaloniere of the Signoria of Florence, had already thought towards the end of the previous decade of having Michelangelo do a statue to stand in front of Palazzo Vecchio, matching the *David*. The work was never executed by Michelangelo, although he made at least two sketches for it, the second of which, dating from 1525 or later, has *Hercules and Cacus* as its subject, and perhaps relates to the model in Casa Buonarroti.

Pier Soderini's intention is gathered from a letter dated May 10, 1508, in which he asks Alberigo Malaspina to save a large block of marble at Carrara. But since Michelangelo was detained in Rome in the Sistine Chapel, the project was abandoned. The work was to represent a *Hercules and Antaeus;*

Michelangelo himself may have made a model for this, which was later given to Leone Leoni, and lost. In 1525 Pope Clement VII entrusted the block of marble to Baccio Bandinelli, who prepared a sketch in wax for the *Hercules and Cacus*. But the Signoria of Florence did not give up the idea of having the statue made by Michelangelo, and Michelangelo himself may have made a model that may perhaps be identified with the clay sketch in Casa Buonarroti, as Thode thought (*Michelangelo Kritische, etc.,*) and Tolnay (*Michelangelo*, I, 1943). The sketch is 41 cm high. It is mentioned by Vasari, who describes it as *Samson and the Philistines;* he is followed in this by W. Bode (*Italienische Bildhauer der Renaissance*, Berlin, 1887) and K. Frey (*Michelangelo Buonarroti*, Berlin, 1907). Springer (*loc. cit.*) and Wilde (*Michelangelo's Victory*, London, 1954) consider it as a pendant to the *Victory* on the Tomb of Julius II.

After the Medici were expelled from Florence, the block of marble, which Bandinelli had already started to rough out, was recovered by the Signoria, who gave it to Michelangelo again in 1528; he was thinking in terms of a group with Samson and the Philistines. After the fall of the republic, Clement VII had the block restored to Bandinelli, who finally completed it in 1534. His *Hercules and Cacus* is still in Piazza Signoria, to the right of the front portal of Palazzo Vecchio.

91 Owl of Night.

Between 1518 and 1520 Michelangelo did the *Christ Risen* for the church of Santa Maria sopra Minerva in Rome. It was a second version of an idea that had already been translated into marble in great part, between 1514 and 1516, and interrupted for reasons connected with defects in the marble (Fig. 60).

This second version, although considerably enfeebled by damage and, above all, by the retouchings of two artists whom Michelangelo, from Florence, had commissioned to refinish the work before it was set up in Rome, is still a piece of great formal harmony. Once again, the spiral is the dominant form of the composition, entering into space with its sculptural envelope. Once again, a solemn rhythm obtained by constant contrapositions organizes marked classical motifs. But all physical hedonism is given up for naturalness of gesture and the gentle, thoughtful remoteness of the face. With its simple gesture, fastened to the cross and with the symbols of his martyrdom in his hands, the figure has shaken off any hints of Hellenism and all pagan subtleties, rising to its high witness to faith. It is the nude as eternal symbol of nobility and purity, the nude without sculptural stimulation, the nude with its limbs free from any anthropomorphic distortion.

The statue is of marble, in the round. It is 2.05 meters high and stands in the church of Santa Maria sopra Minerva in Rome. Michelangelo carved it between 1518 and 1520; it is the second version of a subject he had begun work on for the same patrons: Bernardo Cencio, Canon of St.

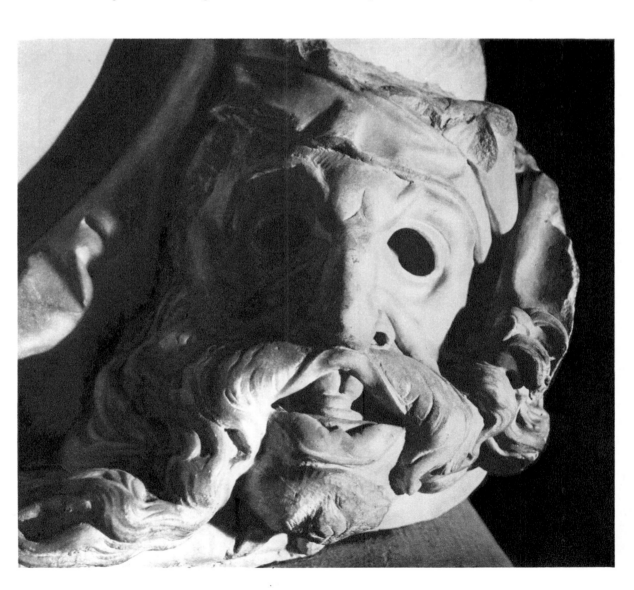

92 Mask of Night.

119

93-95 Madonna and Child (front view; rear view; right side-front view of Child and head and bust of Madonna). Florence, San Lorenzo, New Sacristy.

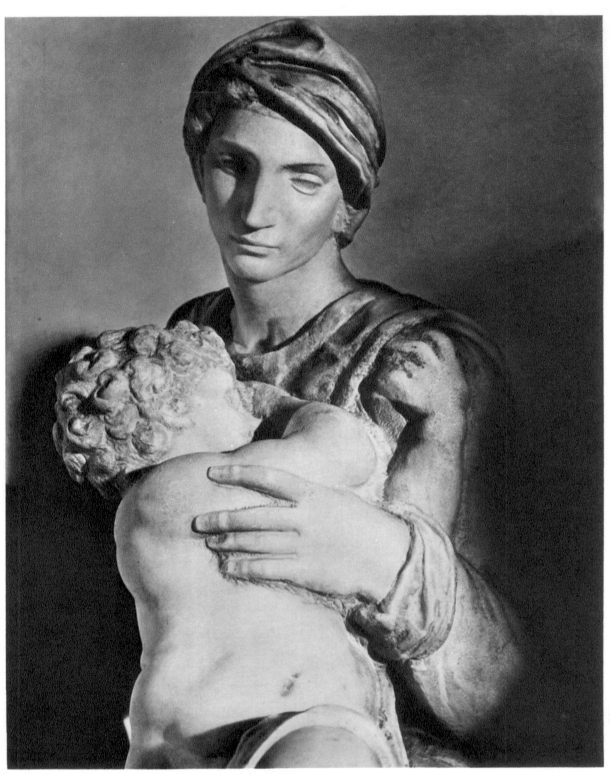

Peter's; Mario Scappucci; Pietro Paolo Castellano and Metello Vari, who intended it for the church of the Minerva, as appears from a contract signed on June 14, 1514. Michelangelo worked on the first version from 1514 to 1516 but had to stop work, although it was already far advanced, because of a black vein in the marble on the face. After work had been suspended for a couple of years, the four-year term stipulated in the contract ran out and the orderers called for its execution anew; meanwhile Michelangelo had left Rome. Michelangelo worked on a new block of marble in Florence between the second half of 1519 and April 1520. In March 1521 the statue was taken to Rome, and there was worked on by Pietro Urbano, an apprentice of Michelangelo's. However, he was doing it so clumsily that Sebastiano del Piombo wrote Michelangelo in September to take Pietro off the job and give it to Federico Frizzi to repair the harm done and see to its erection. This was done, and the statue was finally put in place in the church on December 27, 1521. However, Michelangelo was not entirely satisfied with the way it had turned out, and was ready to do another Christ, from the beginning; but Vari was not willing and was content to get as a gift the unfinished marble of the first version; this he put in his garden. It is mentioned as being there in 1556 by Aldovrandi (*op. cit.*, p. 247); and this is the only mention we have of this work, now lost.

In its existing version, the work in Santa Maria sopra Minerva shows the work of the assistants, especially in the face, hair, beard, feet, hands, instruments of the Passion, and drapery; in general, the knees, arms and torso are more decidedly Michelangelesque and purer in execution.

Remarkable similarities with classic art have been seen in the Praxitelean posture of the nude (cf. V. Mariani, *Michelangelo*, Turin, 1942, p. 127 ff.).

From the iconological point of view, the work has been seen as expressing the spirit of antiquity (Lübke, *op. cit.*, p. 842 ff.); or the meeting of Greece and Christianity (Holroyd, *op. cit.*, p. 189); or an intrinsic dissension in that meeting (Thode, *Michelangelo und das Ende der Renaissance*, III, Berlin, 1902-13, p. 536 ff.); or a polemical austerity in the sense of Savonarola and the Reformation (Tolnay, *op. cit.*, III, p. 91 ff.), supported by the fact that the church of Santa Maria sopra Minerva is attached to the Dominican order.

97 Child and bust of Madonna and Child (front view).

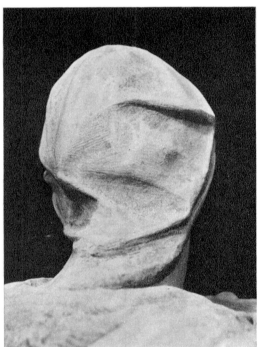

96 Head of Madonna and Child (rear view).

The New Sacristy of San Lorenzo

We have come by now to what may be considered the most sublime of Michelangelo's labors, the New Sacristy of San Lorenzo, which with extraordinary power sums up the highest of poetical meditations on Man and his Eternity, in a highly spiritual theme to which the most diverse contents have been attributed, but which presents a remarkably elevated and solid expression of his art as a sculptor. This appears in the continuous coincidence and coexistence of opposites, in the architectonic structure, in the concentration on the human body as a means of plumbing not so much heroism as psychic force, spiritual energy taken in the Christian way as the ultimate and only true framework of the world.

Every compositional device is brought to bear in a rediscovery of the naturalistic datum that seems to surge from the spiritual impulse and movement.

This is why, for all that the sculptures are indissolubly linked, in the course of time and in the course of a spiritual reality that tends towards unity, each of them lives a life of its own. Here the reminiscences of the ancient world do not apply—as has rightly been written [8]— nor the prehistory of the attitudes; as with the *Moses*, which contains within itself the entire weight of a new potent reality, every figure comprises and guards its own reality. Whether the statue stands in contrast or in harmony with the others, it is thereby even a vaster and more sublime sign of the artist's greatness, the matchless mark of his ability to keep in hand the guide lines of an entire universe; most important of all, each of them goes beyond all rational dialectics, fusing into the severe gravity, the sublime immediacy of a poetical sentiment that puts out of mind any stylistic calculation, any cultural elaboration. And every subtlest techni-

121

cal means is brought to bear with a mastery never surpassed even by himself: now turning and polishing, to give lunar gleams to the chill *Night*; now giving supreme physical beauty to the *Dawn*; now giving a distant gentleness to the fixed gaze of the *Virgin*; now binding the faces of the *Day* and the *Twilight* in a climax of opposition or drama; now dwelling on the external attributes of the two dukes; and all in continuous excitement, in sudden cadences and unexpected contrasts, in a deep motion of planes and forms that brings out every more immediate and deeper reality.

We do not have any regular contracts, but it can be seen from various documents that work had been begun by March 1520. Cardinal Giulio de' Medici and Pope Leo X proposed to Michelangelo the erection of a chapel that would be a pendant to Brunelleschi's, contain the tombs of Lorenzo the Magnificent and his brother Giuliano, Lorenzo Duke of Urbino (the son of Piero, Lorenzo the Magnificent's oldest son) and Giuliano Duke of Nemours (third son of Lorenzo the Magnificent). In the light of closer study of the letters and drawings that have come down to us, and thanks above all to the work of Popp (A. E. Popp, *Die Medici-Kapelle Michelangelos*, Munich, 1922) and Tolnay (*Michelangelo, III, The Medici Chapel*, Princeton, 1948), we are able today to reconstruct the various phases of the projects. These designs did not emerge in the formal order that critics formerly listed (tombs standing free of the walls, combined in a structure in the center of the chapel; wall tombs in pairs for the four persons; single wall tombs); they were changed in the course of the work, in relation to the wall structures. Thus, it is stated (Popp, *op. cit.*, p. 126 ff.) that the plans for the double and single tombs were contemporaneous, and we can retrace the laborious creative process in detail by means of drawings and documents (Tolnay, *op. cit.*, p. 33 ff.).

The first idea was related to the first architectural project, conceived in Brunelleschian vein in March 1520 (J. Wilde, in *Journal of the Warburg and Courtauld Institutes*, London, XVIII, 1955, p. 54 ff.); it contemplated wall tombs at the corners (see also Tolnay, *op. cit.*, p. 37).

On October 23 of the same year Michelangelo presented to Cardinal Giulio the idea of independent tombs in the center of a four-walled shrine. The cardinal liked the idea and, despite some doubts as to the proportions between the shrine and the space of the chapel, left the artist completely free to choose between a free-standing emplacement and one against the wall: he only wanted to have a drawing showing him a wall of the tomb (letter from Rome, Cardinal Giulio to Michelangelo, dated November 28, 1520, in K. Frey, *Sammlung ausgewählter Briefe an Michelagniolo Buonarroti*, Berlin, 1899, p. 161; letters from D. Buoninsegni to Michelangelo dated December 14 and 17, 1520, in Tolnay, *op. cit.*, p. 225 ff.). This was done on December 21, and as a result the cardinal himself proposed a solution with a four-armed arch (letter from Buoninsegni to Michelangelo dated December 28, 1520, in Tolnay, *op. cit.*, p. 226). This persuaded Michelangelo to look for a wall solution, with single or double tombs, until the idea took shape of single tombs for the dukes and double ones for the Magnificent's heirs.

Models for the tombs of the dukes, the only ones that were finally executed, were begun in January 1524. Cardinal Giulio's election to the papal throne as Clement VII must have given the work a new stimulus.

In spring 1524 Michelangelo worked on clay models for the statues, and in the fall the marble quarried at Carrara arrived. In 1525 and 1526 four figures were all but completed (including the *Night* and the *Dawn*) and models of four others had been done.

The first tomb, that of Lorenzo, was built in 1526, but that of Giuliano was far from completed as late as 1531. On June 17, 1526 Michelangelo wrote to Rome: " I am working as hard as I can, and within two weeks I will have the other Captain started, and then the only major thing

98   Model of a River God (front view). Florence, Casa Buonarroti.

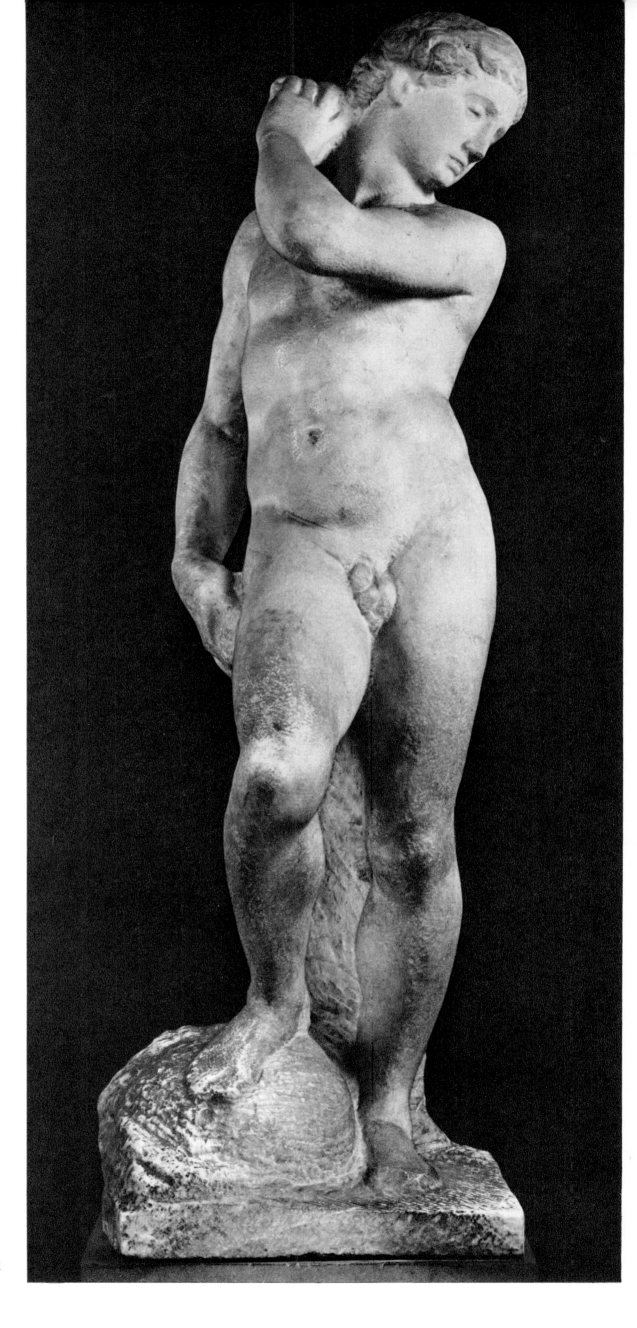

99 David Apollo. Florence, Bargello National Museum.

100-101 David Apollo (left side and right rear-side views).

left for me to do will be the four Rivers. The four figures on the caskets, the four figures on the ground, which are the Rivers, and two Captains, and Our Lady, going in the top tomb, are the statues I should like to do with my own hand: and of these six have been commenced. I feel strong enough to do them on time and have the others done in part, which are less important."

Then came the episode of the siege, and after it work was begun, in April 1531. At least two statues were finished that summer and a third one begun. The *Duke Lorenzo* was executed between 1531 and 1534; in July 1533 the *Duke Giuliano* was given to Montorsoli for finishing, while Michelangelo made two models for the allegories (*Heaven* and *Earth*) intended for the niches at the sides of the tomb of Giuliano, which allegories Tribolo was to have translated into marble. It is reasonable to assume, as has been done, that two matching allegories were to have been on the wall of Lorenzo's tomb, perhaps *Knowledge* and *Will*, as Tolnay would have it.

In 1534 Michelangelo left Florence for good, and the work was ended.

Features of the definitive project that are lacking in the existing structure are the statues in the niches at the sides of the figures of the two dukes, the allegorical statues of the four Rivers (the Rivers of Hades) which were to go at the base of the sarcophagi, and stuccos and frescoes that were to have further decorated walls and cupola. We learn of an ornament in stucco and decorations for the cupola commissioned in 1526 from Giovanni da Udine, who was to work there in 1532 and 1533 (but in 1556 Vasari covered the cupola over again with plain stucco).

In 1524-1525 Michelangelo had also designed the tombs of the Medici popes, Leo X and Clement VII, to go in the chapel; but then the idea occurred of placing these tombs in the chorus of San Lorenzo. This was never carried out.

More has been written about the general iconographical significance of the chapel than on any other of Michelangelo's works. It would be impossible here to refer completely to all the interpretations that have been advanced, either for the whole or for the individual statues. The four times of day and the statues of the two dukes have led to interpretations of every kind, often with the most directly opposite contents; an obvious and marvelous sign of the sublime idealization performed by the artist.

Resuming the motif expressed in the text of Condivi ("All-consuming Time"), it has been seen as a personification of human life, caught in a sorrowful and dramatic moment in face of the relentless passage of Time, the emblem of the continuous change of earthly things and the brevity of human life, its tragic quality, the personification of the elements of the earth and the various temperaments of man; following the panegyrics of the text in Vasari, as a veritable apotheosis of the Medici, or as rebellion against them; or the period of divine illumination, or the resurrection of the flesh.

But Tolnay (*op. cit.*) has given us the most convincing interpretation of the whole. For him the chapel, conforming to a Platonic interpretation derived from the *Phaedo*, is conceived as a summary image of the Universe with its three superposed spheres; Hades below, then the intermediate zone with its rational architecture representing the terrestrial sphere, and the lunettes and cupola signifying the vault of Heaven. The composition of the tombs would represent the liberation of the soul after the death of the earthly prison of the flesh, while the four allegorical statues of Time (and those of the Rivers that were to have been at the base of the tombs) personify the inexorable destiny of mortal life, as though their weight brought about the break in the center of the tops, and through the opening thus made the immortal soul of the deceased was freed to rise in a region inaccessible to the blind forces of Time. Here the soul is in its true essence once more, by means of the eternal contemplation of the idea of life, symbolized by the Virgin and the Child.

Night is a marble statue in the round, on the left side of the sarcophagus of Giuliano de' Medici. It is 1.94 meters long and was done between 1526 and 1531. It was one of the first on which work was started, and one of the first completed. It was made famous at once by the celebrated verses of Giovanni di Carlo Strozzi, to which Michelangelo replied immediately (reported by Vasari). Other significations were added in a variety of interpretations, with symbolic amplifications: political; psychoanalytic or psychologistic; and, in connection with the other statues of the Sacristy, as a symbol of the element of air and water, or a cosmic symbol of the fecundity of the night; and also as personification of nature and death. It is the only one of the statues to have attributes: the moon, the star in the diadem, the owl, the poppy and the mask (dream, incubus or sensuality).

102 Victory. Florence, Palazzo Vecchio.

103 Head of Victory.

Iconographically, reference has been made to the old representations of Leda and of the sleeping Ariadne. Tolnay has seen in its profile a reflection of profiles of Maenads on antique gems (Figs. 86-92).

Day is a marble statue in the round, on the right side of the sarcophagus of Giuliano de' Medici. It is 2.85 meters long and was done between 1526 and 1531. *Day*, with its powerful anatomical structure, has been seen as a symbol of rebellion against slavery and hence autobiographical motifs as well have been found in it. When related with the other statues, it has been regarded as the incarnation of revolt, the personification of life, the symbol of the light of Christ, of the element of fire, of liberty, the personification of action, of sorrow, of wrath, of scorn and of revenge.

Iconographically, a reflection has been seen in it of study on the *Belvedere Torso* (Figs. 73-76).

The *Dawn* is in marble, in the round, on the right side of the sarcophagus of Lorenzo de' Medici. It is 2.05 meters long and was done between 1524 and 1526 (at which date it is reproduced in an engraving of the *Triumph of Fortune* by Sigismondo Fanti, Venice, 1527, fol. 38). Like the *Twilight* on the other side of the sarcophagus, it has been related iconographically to the mountain and river deities on the reliefs on the arch of Septimius Severus in Rome, by Tolnay (*Michelangelo*, III, 1948); E. Steinmann (*Das Geheimnis der Medicigräber Michelangelos*, Leipzig, 1907, p. 88 ff.) finds iconographic anticipations of them as early as the Sistine Chapel, in the lunettes of the vault.

In the various interpretations of the chapel, the *Dawn* has been taken to be the emblem and theme of " bitterness "; of the sorrow of the world seen through the " melancholy temperament "; as the symbol of the divine light driving away darkness; brought into relation with the element of the air and with the sanguine temperament, or with the element of earth; but it has also been linked to tyranny and political events in Florence, destined as it was to a sad historical fate (Figs. 61-64).

Twilight is of marble, in the round, to the left of the sarcophagus of Lorenzo de' Medici. Length 1.95 meters and was done between 1524 and 1531.

The work has been interpreted in relation and contrast to the *Dawn*, with the same meanings. But autobiographical or religious significations have also been attributed (Figs. 71, 72, 77).

126   104 Head of slave of Victory (right side view).

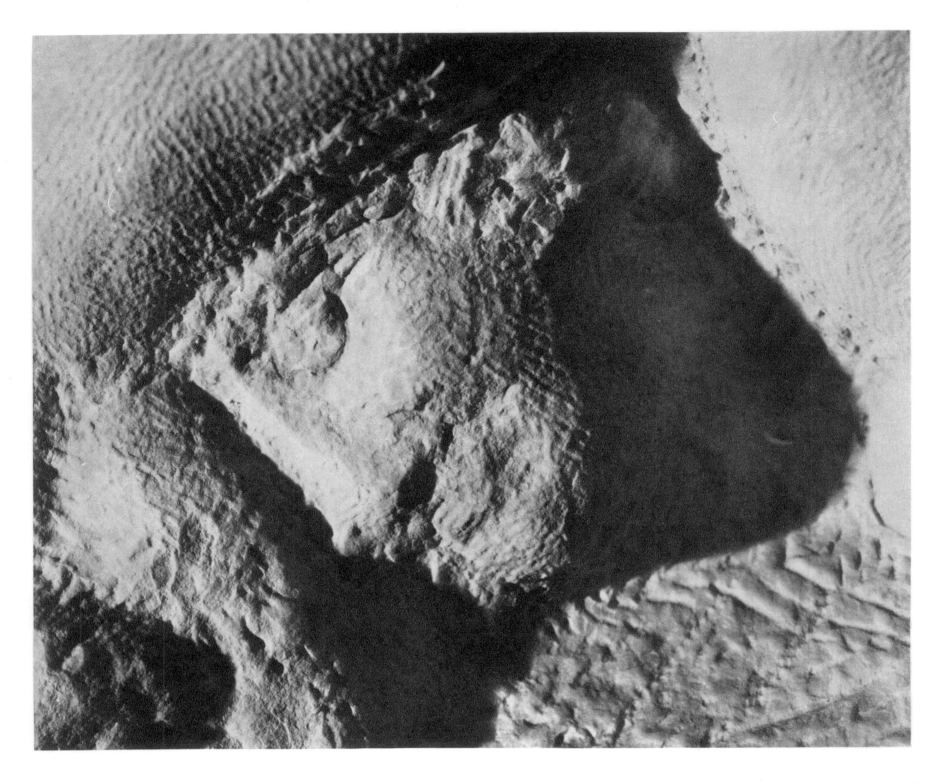

106 Head of Young Slave.

◁ 105 Head and torso of Young Slave. Florence,
Academy of Fine Arts.

107 Left leg of Young Slave (right side view).

Lorenzo de' Medici is a statue in the round, in the center in a niche above the sarcophagus with the *Twilight* and the *Dawn* on the south wall of the chapel. Under way or begun in 1525.

Vasari was the first to designate it as the Thinker. F. Bocchi and G. Cinelli (*Le bellezze della città di Firenze, etc.*, Florence, 1677, p. 534 ff.) regarded it as a conventional portrait of thought. The Richardsons (*Traité de la peinture et de la sculpture*, III, Amsterdam, 1728, p. 136 ff.) saw it as an image of the Contemplative Life, introducing a Neoplatonizing interpretation that was advanced, in particular, by Borinsky (*op. cit.*, p. 104 ff.), Panofsky (*op. cit., Studies in Iconology*, p. 209 ff.) and Tolnay (*op. cit.*, p. 68). But while relationships with the historical truth were made, incongruences and inconsistencies were also noted, and it was regarded by some as expressing the tyrant's meditation (G. B. Niccolini, *Del Sublime di Michelangelo*, Florence, 1825, p. 22 ff.; and others later). The meditation has also been considered on the level of psychological autobiography (C. H. Perkins, *Historical Handbook of Italian Sculpture*, London, 1883, p. 29 ff.; and others later), while for Steinmann its significance would be the union of two "temperaments," the phlegmatic and the melancholy (E. Steinmann, *op. cit.*, p. 120).

With respect to the attributes, the helmet with the lion mask, a theme already present in Etruscan art, has been seen as a symbol of Fortitude; the casket for coins has been taken to be a symbol of parsimony (Panofsky and Steinmann), or a symbol of death (Tolnay); for Mackowsky (*op. cit.*) the object in his left hand is a small purse, for Panofsky (*op. cit.*) a scarf.

From the iconographic point of view, a relationship has been seen with the seated figures of the Sistine; but it has also been linked to the *Moses* and the demolished statue of Julius II in Bologna. Tolnay has seen a classical motif in the armor, which is typical of Roman statues of the Empire (Figs. 65-70).

Giuliano de' Medici is a marble statue in the round, 1.73 meters high. It is in the center, in a niche above the sarcophagus with the *Night* and the *Day*, on the north wall of the chapel. Possibly under way as early as 1526, it was far from having been finished in 1531. For both this work and the *Lorenzo*, documents show that in 1533 and 1534 Montorsoli did final refinishing touches, which however did not affect the substance of the works.

Vasari regarded it as depicting pride; compared and contrasted with the statue of *Lorenzo*, it has been seen as personifying Vigilance (Bocchi and Cinelli, *loc. cit.*), the Active Life (Richardson, Thode,

108 Legs of Young Slave (front view).

Panofsky), the "choleric" and "sanguine" temperaments (Steinmann, *loc. cit.*), the principle of anti-Machiavellianism (V. Kaiser, *Zeitschrift für Völkerpsychologie und Sprachwiss.*, XVI, 1886, p. 220 ff.), or as the strong-willed violent despot (F. Burger, *Geschichte des florentinischen etc.*, Strassburg, 1904, p. 374), or as contemplation of the Divine vision by way of desire (Tolnay, *loc. cit.*).

As for the attributes, Bocchi and Cinelli saw the baton of command as the baton of the Church (*loc. cit.*); the coin in his hand has been seen (Steinmann and Panofsky) as a symbol of generosity (Figs. 78-85).

The *Virgin with the Child* is a statue in the round 2.26 meters high, including the base. It is on the right wall as one enters and has at its sides the statues of Saints Cosma and Damiano. It was begun in 1521, still in process in 1526 and in 1534 left in that incomplete state. Tolnay has seen it as a second, reworked version of the first, on the same block. Iconographically, it repeats the type of the *Madonna del Latte* or *Humility*. References to the funeral service have been made by Brockhaus, and to a representation of the Mater Ecclesia by Hartt. Varchi cited the verses of Dante, " and like the child stretching its arms to its mother, after taking the milk," and others have followed him in this reference to Dante. It has also been regarded as reflecting Michelangelo's sad personality, or the anguish of Fate; but it has always been treated as the spiritual center of the entire complex, as an incarnation of life (Figs. 93-97).

The executants of the two statues at the sides of the *Virgin*, models for which were done by Michelangelo about 1532, were Raffaele da Montelupo for the *S. Damiano*, in 1534, and G. A. Montorsoli for the *S. Cosma*, about 1536-37.

109 Legs of Young Slave (left side view).

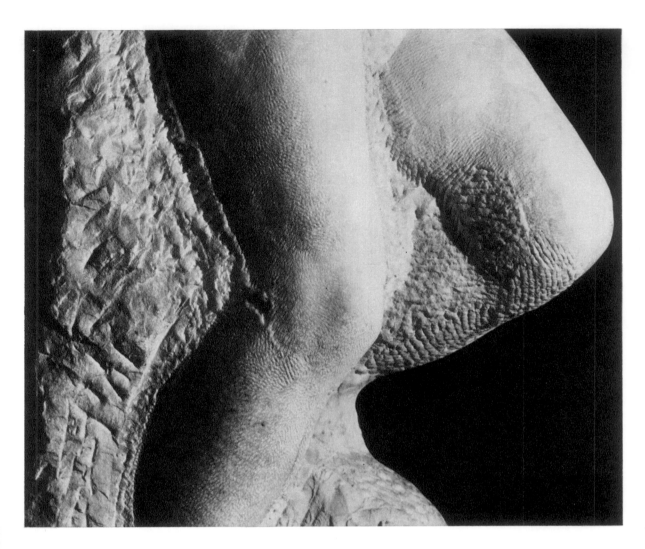

110 Left leg of Young Slave (right side view, horizontal light).

In 1906 the sketch for a river god, in wood, clay, wool and tow, in the gallery of the Accademia in Florence was linked to the Medici tombs by A. Gottschewsky (*Rivista d'Arte*, IV, 1906, p. 73 ff.) and Poggi (*ibid.*, p. 104 ff.). It is 1.80 meters long. It was presented by Cosimo I to Bartolommeo Ammannati, and given to the Accademia on April 28, 1583.

The execution of this sketch must date from March-April 1524; it may be one of those that in 1552 were at the base of the sarcophagi in the chapel (cf. *I marmi del Doni Academico Peregrino*, Venice, 1552).

Acceptance of the attribution to Michelangelo is not unanimous; it is rejected by Wölfflin, Frey and Popp, among others; Popp holds it to be a work of Ammannati.

In support of its authenticity there are, in addition to documents in the archives of the Accademia, Cinquecento paintings in which the model is depicted, as well as a number of drawings. From the drawings, however, at least three versions of these sculptures can be identified. According to Wilde (*Belvedere*, XI, 1927, p. 143 ff.), followed by Kriegbaum and Tolnay, the present position of the sketch is not the original one; the outside of the right leg and the right elbow must have been resting on the ground.

A different posture, and a different version, is proposed here for a wax sketch in Casa Buonarroti (Fig. 98). The sketch, formerly placed upright, had been related to the *Slaves* of the Academy; but its true posture identifies it, in our opinion beyond a doubt, as a river god.

The Leningrad *Crouching Youth* (Fig. 140) has likewise been seen as linked to the Medici chapels. This is a marble statue in the round, 54 cm high. It is not mentioned in any of the literary sources or any document. Formerly in the Medici collection, it was acquired by the Lyde Brown collection, and from there reached the Academy of Fine Arts in Leningrad; it was mounted in the Hermitage of that city in 1851, where it still is. Popp (*op. cit.*, p. 136) relates this work to a letter to Michelangelo from Leonardo Sellajo in 1526, and to a British Museum drawing concerning a first design for the New Sacristy. Before then and afterwards, the work had been considered independently (Wölfflin, *Die Klassische Kunst, etc.*, p. 1805; Justi, *Michelangelo*, Leipzig, 1900, p. 289; Thode, *Michelangelo, Kritische, etc.*, p. 2843; Venturi, *op. cit.*, p. 93; Wittkower, *op. cit.*, p. 133; Mariani, *op. cit.*, p. 125 ff.; O. Kurz in *The Burlington Magazine*, XCIII, 1951, p. 172) or in relation to the *Victory* for the tomb of Julius II (Springer, *op. cit.*, p. 30).

Proposed dates oscillate around 1524. Only F. Knapp (*Michelangelo*, Stuttgart and Leipzig, 1906, p. XXXVII) put it as of 1530, and K. Frey (*Michelagniolo Buonarroti, sein Leben und seine Werke*, I, Berlin, 1907, p. 314 ff.) assigns it to the youth of the artist, between 1497 and 1500.

Justi (*Michelangelo*, Berlin, 1909) has found affinities with the classical motif of the boy removing the thorn from his foot. Allegorically, an explanation of the statue has been offered as a symbol of the unborn souls, destined for the lower regions (cf. Panofsky, *op. cit.*, p. 212), or more simply as a funerary genius (Tolnay, *loc. cit.*) or a young warrior (Kriegbaum, *loc. cit.*) or a prisoner, in reference to the military enterprises of the Dukes of the Sacristy (F. Hartt, in *Beiträge für George Swarzenski*, Berlin, 1951, p. 154 ff.).

Many doubts have been expressed as to the authorship by Michelangelo; the work has been held to have been done by pupils (Tolnay, *loc. cit.*), specifically by Tribolo (Kriegbaum, *loc. cit.*) and Pierino da Vinci (Wittkower, *loc. cit.*).

112-113 Bearded Slave. Florence, Academy of
Fine Arts.

Other works of uncertain destination and date may be assigned to the decade 1525-1535.
Among them is the *David Apollo* of the Bargello, which takes up a theme already adumbrated
in the *Christ* of Santa Maria sopra Minerva and gives it a new form; a soft and exciting
sublimation of languid beauty. As compared with the physical reality of its predecessor, here
we have the tense harmonious fading of a gesture and movement in suspension, in continuous
vibration, with a form that is completed and yet incomplete, in a vitality no longer passive but
ready to soar into the reality that already invests it, which is intensified in the continuous
contraposition of the parts going to make up its envelope: a dawn of creation that yet has
but a trembling pleasure in the beauty that is arising. It is an unfinished finish, a fully achieved
unity and absoluteness (Figs. 99-101).

It is a marble statue in the round, 1.46 meters high, in the Museo del Bargello, Florence, coming from
the Uffizi and before that the Boboli amphitheater, after having been in Casa Medici up to the end of
the sixteenth century. Borghini cites it in the Medici collection, in the chamber of Grand Duke Francesco, but the work is already listed in a Medici inventory dated 1553, although not as an Apollo
(as Vasari states) but as a David. Done by Michelangelo for Baccio Valori, it is also linked to the lost
Apollo for Jacopo Galli (about 1516; Valentiner in *The Art Quarterly*, XXI, 1958, p. 257 ff.). The
reference to Valori being correct, its most probable date of execution would be little before 1530, perhaps 1525-1526, a date accepted by S. Bottari (*Michelangelo*, Catania, 1941, p. 106 ff.), Carli (*op.
cit.*, p. 34) and Tolnay (*Michelangelo*, III, Princeton, 1948, p. 96 ff.). Tolnay accepts a similar date
first proposed by Popp (*op. cit.*, p. 172), in opposition to the thesis of Popp herself, who believes the
work to be related to the tomb of the Magnificent in the New Sacristy; Tolnay proposes a connection,
a more logical step, with the *Christ* of Santa Maria sopra Minerva and thinks that the work was
conceived as a David and then transformed into an Apollo by Michelangelo himself.
Stylistic comparisons with the *Victory* have been made by Guillaume (*op. cit.*, p. 95) and L. Roger-
Milès (*Michel-Ange, etc.*, Paris, 1893, p. 80 ff.); with the *Slaves* of the tomb of Julius II by Symonds
(*op. cit.*, p. 445 ff.), by Springer (*op. cit.*, p. 235), and Roger-Milès (*loc. cit.*).

The same contrapuntal motif of the action is found in the *Victory* in Palazzo Vecchio. But
the work, which may have been conceived and executed for the fifth version of the tomb of
Julius II in 1532, is more related to the figures in San Lorenzo, at least in virtue of the proportion it achieves within its almost incredibly dynamic rhythm and the contrast of its free and
open form with the entwinement of the vanquished (Figs. 102-104).

The group is in marble, in the round, 2.61 meters high, in the Salone dei Cinquecento, on the
south wall, within a modern niche.
Vasari relates the statue to the first design for the tomb of Julius II, which would make the date
of its execution 1505-1506. But in Michelangelo's design (and in the one of 1513 as well), the Victories

131

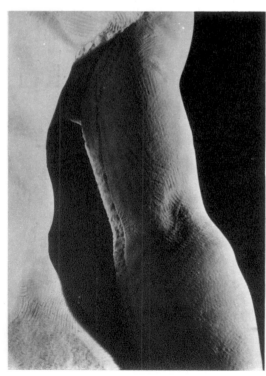

132

were shown draped, not nude. However, Vasari's chronology has not been without supporters, even in recent times, from Kriegbaum (*Michelangelo Buonarroti, etc.*, p. 35 ff.) to von Einem (*Festschrift Jantzen*, 1951, p. 158). It was dated 1513, that is, contemporaneous with the *Slaves* of the Louvre, by Berenson (*op. cit.*, p. 202) and Michel and de Foville (*op. cit.*, p. 229 ff.). It has been related to the *Slaves* of the Accademia, that is 1519-1525, by Mackowsky (*op. cit.*, p. 150 ff.), Thode (*Michelangelo, Kritische, etc.*, p. 216 ff.), Laux (*op. cit.*, p. 96 ff.). Burger assigns it to 1524 (*op. cit.*, p. 327); Popp to 1527 (*The Burlington Magazine*, LXIX, p. 207); Wilde and Clark to 1527-1530 (K. Clark, *The Nude, etc.*, New York, 1956, p. 211), along with Barocchi (*Giorgio Vasari: La Vita di Michelangelo*, II, Milan and Naples, 1942, p. 324); it is dated 1532-1534 by Russoli (*op. cit.*, 1953, p. 61), Tolnay (*Michelangelo*, 1954, p. 50 ff.) and L. Grassi (*Problemi intorno a Michelangelo e il concetto di maniera*, Rome, 1955, p. 161).

Almost all criticism accepts the relationship with the tomb of Julius II, with the exception of the doubts expressed by Holroyd (*op. cit.*, p. 228) and Toesca (*Enc. Italiana, ad vocem*).

The statue remained in Michelangelo's studio in Via Mozza; it is mentioned in a letter from Vasari dated March 10, 1564 in reply to Leonardo Buonarroti who, with Daniele da Volterra, had thought to use it to adorn the tomb of Michelangelo in Santa Croce. Vasari is against this and convinces Leonardo to present the statue to Duke Cosimo on March 22, 1564. It was taken to Palazzo Vecchio in December 1565, along with Bandinelli's statue of Leo X, and adorned the Salone dei Cinquecento, from which it was transferred to the Bargello in 1868 and brought back on November 6, 1921.

All the critics agree on Michelangelo's authorship of the work, although Wittkover (*The Burlington Magazine*, LXXVIII, 1941, p. 133) attributes the execution of the head to Vincenzo Danti. Holroyd (*op. cit.*, 1903, p. 129 ff.) and Mackowsky (*loc. cit.*) had already thought that assistants had helped on the work.

116 Awakening Slave. Florence, Academy of Fine
Arts.

117 Head of Awakening Slave (horizontal light).

Iconographic connections have been seen with the type of the Hercules and the Hydra of classical antiquity (Kriegbaum, *loc. cit.*, and von Einem, *loc. cit.*); the group has also been taken to be a variation on the theme of David and Goliath (Tolnay).

Vasari interpreted the statue as an allegory of the provinces brought into submission by Julius II; this markedly political version has been generally abandoned for various other interpretations. A glorification of force has been seen in the contrast between the body of the victorious youth over the bearded old man at his feet (Stendhal, *op. cit.*); patriotic morals have been drawn (G. D'Annunzio, *Canti della guerra latina*, 1914-1918, p. 140); a situation of conquered-conqueror has been envisaged (R. Rolland, *Vie de Michel-Ange*, Paris, 1905, p. 9), or the victor awaiting one who will overcome him (R. De Campos, *Raffaello e Michelangelo*, Rome, 1946, p. 143). Some critics have also traced, in the inevitable victory of fate, of youth over old age (Tolnay, *op. cit.*, IV, p. 59 ff.), autobiographical allusions related to Michelangelo's love for the young Tommaso de' Cavalieri (Symonds, *op. cit.*, p. 85; A. E. Brinckmann, *Barockskulptur, etc.*, Berlin, 1919, I, p. 85; Brion, *op. cit.*, p. 295; Panofsky, *op. cit.*, p. 218; L. Goldscheider, *Michelangelo Drawings*, London, 1951, p. 17), or Christian-Platonic meanings (Ollendorf, *Zeitschrift für Bildende Kunst*, IX, Leipzig, 1898, p. 279 No. 2; A. Mackowsky, *op. cit.*, p. 140 ff.; Brockhaus, *op. cit.*, p. 21).

Wilde (*Michelangelo's Victory*, London, 1954) has seen Fortune and Justice in it as counterparts of a Virtue and Vice (a relic of which would be the sketch by Buonarroti that others have referred to the Hercules and Cacus).

The set of four colossal sketches for the *Slaves*, now in the Accademia in Florence, must be only slightly later in date. Although they are not finished, the originality of the composition and the power of the idea that moves them are striking, with a superb suggestion of emerging life, of liberation from the matter that still retains them, that dominates them or against which they are in rebellion. We do not believe that Michelangelo consciously wished to leave these sculptures as they are because he felt they were completed. But, in the long run, this occasional unfinished quality must have given him thought. Keeping them in his Florentine studio in Via Mozza for so long must have brought out their full value and the full scope of his researches into form. These researches were to bring him to increasing interiorization of the dynamic relationships impressed on the figures; they " would be summed up in rapid essential notes, pure exhalations of life emerging from the destruction of the matter." [9]

The four unfinished sculptures are in the gallery of the Accademia of Florence. Left in Michelangelo's studio in Via Mozza, they were presented to Cosimo I by Michelangelo's nephew Leonardo in 1564, along with the *Victory*. They were placed at the four corners of the Grotta del Buontalenti in Boboli Gardens and remained there until 1908, when they were removed to the Accademia. They have been given names to distinguish them: the young slave (Figs. 105-111), the bearded slave (Figs. 112-115), the " Atlas " slave (Figs. 118-122), the slave awakening (Figs. 116, 117). Their heights are 2.56, 2.63, 2.77 and 2.67 meters, respectively.

Their chronology is a matter of dispute, because of variously conceived stylistic comparisons and, particularly, because of the varying relationships to the tomb of Julius II that have been seen. In addition, the relevant documents, notices and letters do not yield any single unequivocal conclusion. Hence, the dates assigned run from 1519 to 1534-1536. The vicinity of 1519 is given by Justi (Justi, *Michelangelo*, Leipzig, 1900, p. 287), Burger (*loc. cit.*), Thode (*Michelangelo, Kritische, etc.*, p. 213 ff.), Kriegbaum (*Michelangelo Buonarroti. Die Bildwerke*, Berlin, 1940, p. 36 ff.), Laux (*op. cit.*, p. 96); 1520-1522 is given by Toesca (*Enc. Italiana, ad vocem*), S. Bottari (*Michelangelo*, Catania, 1941, p. 92 ff.) and Carli (*op. cit.*, p. 30 ff.); 1527-1530 by Popp (*The Burlington Magazine*, LXIX, 1936, p. 207); 1530-1534 by Tolnay (*Michelangelo*, IV, p. 114), who had previously (*Michelangelo*, Florence, 1951, p. 121) proposed as late a date as 1534-1536, pursuant to Vasari's description, which indicated four *Slaves* still in Michelangelo's house in Rome. But since it is more probable that the statues were executed in Florence, the more logical date would be 1530-1534, which would put them in relationship with the fifth version of the tomb of Julius II.

The theme of suffering as aspiration to emerge from the formless has suggested a number of interpretations, including some in an autobiographical vein.

The authenticity of these works is universally granted beyond question, although E. Hildebrandt (*Michelangelo*, Leipzig and Berlin 1913, p. 119 ff.) and Kriegbaum (*Buonarroti*, Berlin, 1940) believed they could detect the hand of pupils in the young slave and the bearded slave.

Back in Rome, Michelangelo carved the bust of *Brutus* for his friend Donato Giannotti. It is a work, stately and powerful, raised to grandeur and moral rigor precisely by the unfinished aspects, the essential quality of a face and a conscience emerging unexpectedly, as it were, from the cold envelope of the great drapery, finely finished in obvious contrast. The *Brutus*, one of the highest expressions of Michelangelo's art, comprises in complete and absolute form the values of a moral reality, decisive and unfeigning, with a heroic content under the surface of the face starting from the neck with its taut muscles. Roman portraiture is only the faintest of iconographic starting points; external glorification is forgotten, submerged in the glorification of the idea, which alone makes the character absolutely alive. Here in truth thought and action interpenetrate in an absolute moral indissolubility; by comparison, the portraits of the two dukes, although idealized beyond any physical resemblance, seem like puppets, mere negative symbols of thought and action (Figs. 123, 124).

The statue is of marble, in the round, 74 cm high, without base. It was carved for Cardinal Niccolò Ridolfi at the suggestion of Donato Giannotti. Between 1574 and 1584 the sculpture was acquired by Grand Duke Francesco de' Medici and a bronze tablet was affixed to the pedestal, with the Latin verse, *Dum Bruti effigiem sculptor de marmore ducit—in mentem sceleris venit et abstinuit* (As the sculptor draws the image of Brutus from the marble—he came to the thought of the crime and abstained). The verse, which might well emphasize the political undercurrent of glorification of tyrannicide, was erroneously believed to be by Bembo, Politian or Giannotti himself.

The work is mentioned by Vasari, who also speaks of a large part in it by Tiberio Calcagni; today we know that he only helped with part.

Iconographical links to the antique were first suggested by Vasari (" from an ancient carnelian in the house of Signor Giuliano Cesarino ") and are substantially correct, even if he stated them in order to prevent any possible connection of the work with the history of the time (slaying of Duke Alessandro in 1537; destiny of anti-Medicean patrons). Direct derivations from the classical have been stressed by Thode (*Michelangelo, Kritische, etc.* p. 288), Brinckmann (*op. cit.*, p. 90 ff.), Kriegbaum (*Michelangelo Buonarroti*, p. 44), Kleiner (*op. cit.*, p. 38), Russoli (*op. cit.*, p. 62) and Tolnay (*Michelangelo*, IV, pp. 76 ff., 233): these critics related the work to Roman busts of the period of Caracalla (in particular, a bust of Caracalla in the Naples Museum). Another link with the antique has been identified by Tolnay (*op. cit.*) in the *fibula*, which has a profile (possibly the portrait of Donato Giannotti himself) like those found on ancient coins of the time of Brutus. Most scholars date the work 1539-1540, but it has also been regarded as dating from the time of the siege (Lamartine, *op. cit.*, p. 329) or prior to the *Last Judgment* (Carli, *op. cit.*, p. 40 ff.; Kriegbaum (*loc. cit.*), or 1537-1538 (A. M. Brizio, *Vite scelte di Giorgio Vasari*, Turin, 1948, p. 470, No. 187).

Finally, in 1545, and not till then, the work was finished that had given him so much torment: the tomb of Julius II that is only a pale image of what he had planned at first, although still powerful even in its simplified structure. Nor are the statues his that are on it today, except for the *Moses*, executed long since, and the figures of *Leah* and *Rachel*, in which, however, the great surge of mystic contemplation, that now engages Michelangelo in his renewed spiritual adhesion to Christ, comes through rather blunted.

118-119 Atlas Slave (front and left side-front views). Florence, Academy of Fine Arts.

135

Leah and Rachel are two marble statues in the round. The Rachel is 1.97 meters high, the Leah 2.09. They are on the tomb of Julius II in San Pietro in Vincoli (and have been since February 1545) to the left and right, respectively, of the Moses, in the niches previously intended for the Slaves in earlier versions of the Tomb. It appears from documents (request of Michelangelo to Paul III dated July 20) that both statues were well along in 1542. A month later Michelangelo himself draws up a contract with Raffaello da Montelupo for finishing the five statues of the Tomb, including the Leah and the Rachel, later again reserving for himself the execution of these two statues. However, the part played by Montelupo is generally conceded today, even if only within the limits of polishing and refinishing. The works were completed before the end of 1542.

Vasari and Condivi call the Rachel the Active Life. The allegory is said to have its origin in Dante. Condivi's thesis has been taken up recently by von Einem (Antike und Abendland, I, 1945, p. 73 ff.), Laux (op. cit., pp. 326, 380 ff.) and Tolnay (Michelangelo, IV, pp. 72, 122), who, however, presumes a direct derivation as well from Landino's text on the Disputationes Camaldulenses.

Iconographically, the two statues have been linked to the Middle Ages and the Gothic (reference to statues of the Virtues), as well as to the antique.

The "mirror," as Vasari calls it, that Leah is holding in her right hand is now, following the allegory in Dante (Purgatorio, XXVII, 100 ff.), held to be a "diadem" (as Condivi wrote), by Thode (Michelangelo, Kritische, etc., p. 220 ff.), Kriegbaum (Michelangelo Buonarroti, p. 35) and Tolnay (loc. cit.).

[8] L. Berti, Michelangelo: Le Tombe Medicee, Florence, 1965.
[9] E. Carli, Michelangelo, Bergamo, 1942.

120 Legs of Atlas Slave (front view).

The last works

In the last two decades of his life, it was the new importance of his religious conscience that gave the measure of his new idiom, beginning with the Pietà of Florence Cathedral and concluding, on the brink of the grave, with the Rondanini Pietà in the Sforza Castle in Milan.

The Pietà del Duomo (Figs. 125-128), in all probability done between 1550 and 1555, shows in its pyramidal pattern a return to a figurative composition of stricter Florentine character. But it is a return that is an advancing and a going beyond; the sudden, shooting, contrapuntal movements that break it up are calmed only in the spiral that starts from the sharp point of the Nicodemus and descends lyrically to support Christ on the ground.

The marble group, in the round, is 2.26 meters high. Vasari and Condivi inform us of an idea Michelangelo had of wanting to be buried at the feet of this sculpture in Santa Maria Maggiore in Rome. The idea was changed later, for in 1561 the artist sold the group to Francesco Bandini for

137

◁ 122 Legs of Atlas Slave (left side-front view).

123-124 Bust of Brutus. Florence, Bargello National Museum.

two hundred scudi; the first desire, to be buried in Rome, was soon replaced by the thought of reposing in Florence. Bandini placed the group in his Roman gardens at Montecavallo, and presumably it remained there until 1674 (Bandini died in 1564), when it was transported to Florence at the desire of Cosimo III, who intended it for San Lorenzo. It stayed in the church basement and was moved to Santa Maria del Fiore in 1722, behind the high altar. It is only since 1933 that it has been in the first chapel to the right in the north apse.

As for its date, the group must have been started in 1550; according to Condivi, Michelangelo was still working on it in 1553. Most critics place it between 1550 and 1555, and set in the same period the execution of a first version, documented by a copy by Lorenzo Sabatini, now in the Sacristy of St. Peter's in Rome, a print by Cherubino Alberti and a model in wax (once thought to be the original but actually a copy) owned by the heirs of O. Gigli in Florence (cf. O. Gigli, *Documenti relativi al bozzetto de cera etc.*, Florence, 1873; A. de Angelis, *Capitolium*, XXVIII, 1953, p. 347 ff.).

In an attempt to change the legs of the Christ, the statue broke along a vein in the marble. As we look at it today, we can trace a number of accidents, voluntary and involuntary, to the work which Michelangelo abandoned unfinished: the left arm broken above the elbow; the left leg of the Christ

125 Pietà. Florence, Santa Maria del Fiore.

128 Head of Virgin in Pietà of Santa Maria del Fiore.

126-127 Pietà of Santa Maria del Fiore (left side-front view, and head of Nicodemus).

incomplete (a part of the leg is described in the inventory of Daniele da Volterra's property); a break on the chest of the Christ, to the left, and on the fingers of the hand of the Virgin.

Bandini got the sculpture through Tiberio Calcagni, who tried to finish it, especially the Magdalene, also working on other parts, listed in different ways by different critics. The figure of Nicodemus has been thought to be a self-portrait of Michelangelo.

From the point of view of iconography, it has been pointed out that the work picks up a traditional theme of the fourteenth and fifteenth centuries, mainly linked to the Florentine ambience. The group has also been linked to the pattern of the lost *Pietà* for Vittoria Colonna, done about 1538. Echoes of antiquity have also been alleged, and reference has been made to a scene on an Etruscan vase depicting the carrying away of the corpse of Patroclus, now in the Archeological Museum in Florence and formerly in Casa Buonarroti.

Tolnay alone has given the group an allegorical interpretation (*Michelangiolo*, Florence, 1951, p. 158): "Once more the symbolism of the two sides is seen: the right side, towards Magdalene, is the side of Life, and the right side, towards Mary, is the side of Death. Personifying Divine Providence, Nicodemus, like the priest at a wedding, with deep emotion performs the reunion of the Mother and the Son, so much desired by Mary. Sorrow for death is overcome: the living personages are imbued with the same feeling of beatitude that is to be read in the serene features of the dead Christ. The individual bodies merge into one another, interpenetrating as do the feelings of the persons. Each figure is but a gradation of this beatitude, which is the result of the common participation in the Divine Love. This new conception of the Pietà proves that Michelangiolo had come to terms with the idea of death, which now appears to him as the supreme liberation of the soul."

Less intense in the second Pietà, the *Palestrina Pietà*, now in the Accademia and formerly at Palestrina. Its rather forced and theatrical quality strongly suggests doubts as to its authenticity (Figs. 129-134).

The *Palestrina Pietà* is the only work of major importance for which we find no mention in the sources nor in any old document. The group is of marble, in the round, 2.53 meters high. It was carved out of a fragment of an old Roman structure and a piece of an architrave, traces of whose ornamental decoration can still be seen on the back of the statue. It is in the gallery of the Accademia in Florence, for which it was purchased by the Italian Government in 1939 from a chapel of the Palazzo Barberini in Palestrina. It is first mentioned as being there by E. Cecconi in 1756 (*Storia di Palestrina, città del Prisco Lazio*, Ascoli, 1756, p. 111), as a " sketch by the celebrated Buonarroti." In modern times A. Grenier (*Gazette des Beaux-Arts*, I, 1907, pp. 182 ff., 293 ff.) has repeated the attri-bution to Michelangelo, dating it about 1550. The attribution is accepted by most scholars, from Wölfflin to Vasnier, Wallerstein, Bertini, Brion, Gengaro, Clark, Venturi, Cecchi, Bottari, Carli, Toesca and Mariani, who regard the work as having been executed between 1550 and 1559, between

129 Palestrina Pietà (left side view). Florence, Academy of Fine Arts.

130 Palestrina Pietà.

131 Head of Magdalene in Palestrina Pietà (right side-front view).

the first and second versions of the *Rondanini Pietà*. Toesca, however (*Le Arti*, I, 1938-1939, p. 109 ff.), assigns a date between 1547 and 1555, and Carli (*op. cit.*, p. 39 ff.) gives c. 1540. Despite so much assent, the work presents a number of dubious points, to which particular attention has been given by Thode (*Michelangelo: Krit. etc.*, p. 281 ff.), Berenson, Steinmann, Popp, von Einem (*Jahrbuch der Preussischen, etc.*, p. 82 No. 1), Wittkower (*The Burlington Magazine*, LXXVIII, 1941, p. 133), Tolnay (*Michelangelo*, Florence, 1951, p. 265 ff.), E. Sestieri (*L'ultima Pietà di Michelangelo*, Rome, 1952): these critics regard the work as having been done by a pupil. Others, such as M. Guerrisi (*Il Giudizio di Michelangelo*, Rome, 1947, p. 130 ff.), Russoli (*op. cit.*, p. 44), L. Goldscheider (*Michelangelo*, London and Florence, 1953, p. 22 ff.) and Grassi (*op. cit.*, p. 205 ff.) think in terms of a work conceived by Michelangelo but executed by an assistant; this is our opinion as well.

In contrast, the *Rondanini Pietà*, which Michelangelo embarked on as if to translate an idea that he had been unable to carry to completion in the *Pietà* of the Duomo in Florence, is sublime. It is the consummation of his idiom and the creation of a new sculptural idiom (Figs. 135-139).

Under the blows of the chisel the great block constantly gives way; the broad grand form disappears; every outcropping of the excessively physical is broken up; the form itself becomes " concept," spirit, in the earthly consummation of the body. Every principle of bodily beauty is abandoned for the expression of a pure feeling. In the idiom of the *Slaves* of the Academy, in the genesis of his own sculptural operation, Michelangelo found his highest sublimation; but here it is no longer the struggle to free himself from matter, it is the matter itself that has become spirit.

132 Head and torso of Christ in Palestrina Pietà.

133 Head and bust of Magdalene in Palestrina Pietà (left side-front view).

The *Rondanini Pietà* is a marble group in the round, unfinished. It is 1.95 meters high.

While the work was still in process, it was given to Antonio del Francese by Michelangelo himself, in August 1561. It is cited by Vasari, in two letters of Daniele da Volterra written to Vasari and Leonardo Buonarroti, respectively, in March and June 1564, after the death of Michelangelo (letters that attest how the artist had worked on it down to the brink of death) and in the inventory of Michelangelo's house in Rome, where it is described as follows: " another statue, with the Christ as the main figure and another figure above it, the two attached to each other, roughed-out and not finished." A century later, in 1652, it was in a Roman studio, where Ottonelli and Berrettini saw it (G. D. Ottonelli and P. Berrettini, *Trattato della pittura e scultura, etc.*, Florence, 1652, p. 210). From here, perhaps, it went to Palazzo Rondanini, where it stood for centuries in the courtyard. From there it went to the Counts of Vimercati-Sanseverino, and was bought in 1952 by the Commune of Milan for the Museum of the Sforza Castle, where it is now.

It is generally believed that Michelangelo began work on the group immediately after having abandoned the group that is now in the cathedral at Florence. It remained incomplete and bears witness to the continual changes made by the artist, obviously over an extended period of time. The group as it now appears is made up of parts entirely finished and not destroyed or reworked from a first version (such as the right arm, detached from the body, traces of a different expression on the face of the Virgin, the legs of the Christ), and parts in the process of being reworked (new face of the Virgin, polished portions on the legs of the Christ) in a second version. The dates of execution are usually set as 1552-1553 for the first version, and some time between 1554 and 1564 for the second. According to Tolnay (*The Burlington Magazine*, LXV, 1934, p. 146 ff.), a free copy of the first version is to be found in Taddeo Zuccari's *Descent from the Cross*, dating from about 1560, now in the Galleria Borghese, Rome, and can be reconstructed from some drawings in Oxford.

Iconographically, the work has been related to medieval compositions in general. Particular references to works by Giovanni da Milano and the Flémalle Master have been made by Panofsky (*Festschrift Friedländer*, 1927, p. 270); to German sculpture by F. Baumgart (*Jahrbuch der Preuss. Kunstsamml.*, LXI, Berlin, 1935, p. 44 ff.); to the Scandinavian Gothic by von Einem (*Jahrbuch der Preuss. Kunstsamml.*, p. 88 ff.); D. Frey (*Kunstgeschichtliche Studien für H. Kauffmann*, Berlin, 1956, p. 213) and Clark (*op. cit.*, p. 259); to the Pietà type of the late Middle Ages in which God the Father, standing, holds the corpse of Christ, by Tolnay (*Michelangelo*, Florence, 1951, p. 257).

From the literary point of view, the work has been related to the Reformist culture of the Roman

143

144   135-136 Rondanini Pietà (left side-front and right side views). Milan, Sforza Castle Civic Museums.

PLATE III   Rondanini Pietà.   Milan, Sforza Castle Civic Museums.

137 Rondanini Pietà (front view). Milan, Sforza
Castle Civic Museums.

139 Heads of Christ and Virgin in Rondanini Pietà (left side-front view).

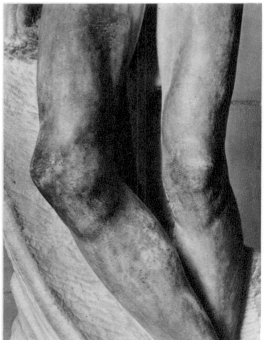

138 Legs of Christ in Rondanini Pietà.

milieu surrounding Vittoria Colonna, Juan de Valdès, etc. (Tolnay, *The Burlington Magazine*, LXV, 1934, p. 152 ff.) in the cult of the Trinity here united in the theme of the Pietà, and with Plotinus (M. L. Gengaro in *Acme*, VI, 1952, p. 134 ff.) in the sense of " breaking with the body " to attain the " form." Von Einem sees in it an accentuation of the theme of the intimate union between Mother and Son (*loc. cit.*).

In order to understand Michelangelo's " unfinished " quality, or to be able to form substantiated interpretative hypotheses on it, a distinction must be drawn between those of his works that were " not finished," that is, not brought to completion because of accidental reasons, and those that are " unfinished " but are to be regarded as brought to completion by the artist, who did them in that way and so concluded them poetically, in a manner that for him was definitive.

Hence, we shall omit such works as the *Slaves* in the Accademia, the *St. Matthew* in the same gallery, and the *Rondanini Pietà* in the Museum of the Sforza Castle in Milan, even though in a sense they will come back under discussion in another way, as exceptional protagonists in the genesis of Michelangelo's work. For these six works we have historical proofs that work was abandoned on them for external causes (as was the case for the *Slaves* and the *St. Matthew*) or that total completion was impossible, likewise because of external circumstances (as with the *Rondanini Pietà*, on which Michelangelo was still working only a short time before his death).

In the case of the other sculptures (excluding those few examples for which the finish is completely carried out and definite, technically speaking), finished zones alternate and are mingled in various ways and varying effects with unfinished ones. It is precisely the plurality of manners and variety of effects that lend credence to the idea that the unfinished must have a figurative effect varying in relation to the esthetics, the intellectual aspiration of the artist, the development of the internal chronology of his operation; and, therefore, must be evaluated separately in each case.

It is clear, in the first case, that the unfinished is to be regarded as a technical means that the artist employs in order better to elucidate and bring out his conceptions, adapting it with the greatest freedom and mastery to the most varied, disparate and often antithetical effects, even when it originates or participates in or defines higher and deeper moral and psychological conditions of the artist himself.

These conditions had already been pointed out by Vasari, who went beyond explanations more material in nature (defects in the marble, excessive number of commitments taken on, changes of patrons,

140 Crouching Youth. Leningrad, Hermitage.

obstacles raised by the envy of colleagues) and accepted the thesis of Condivi, first, that the artist could never be content with his work, and then, his awareness of his own subjective limitations and his constant effort to overcome them.

Cellini finds in this situation factors of deficiency on the part of the sculptor, to be remedied by means of admixture of pictural elements.

These two essential aspects, the psychological and the figurative, have been the basis of critical interpretations, which in general fall under two heads: dissatisfaction and satisfaction.

We repeat, in explanation of this, Aru's now classical summary:

" Some critics have dwelt upon a state of dissatisfaction, said to have prevented Michelangelo from carrying his vision to complete embodiment and caused him to abandon work, either because of the tragic discouragement aroused in him by the eternal dissension between spirit and matter [Mariani] or the impossibility of giving a mystic-Christian content to the plastic-pagan form [Thode].

" Others have made the contrary conjecture, that the sudden halting of work was caused by satisfaction over having completed the embodiment of his vision: by reason of the emphasis that the unfinished gives the sculptural relief when compared with the finished [Venturi, Bertini]; or the heightened emotional expression given by a very rapid and daring synthesis [Bertini]; or the accentuation of movement arising out of a form striving to liberate itself from the block [Bertini]; or love of ancient sculptures, more powerful and expressive when worn and truncated [Toesca]; or the suggestive power of figures that emerge from the rough marble, in which the activity of the human spirit seems to be associated with the forces of the cosmos and, therefore, has an infinite ideal background instead of the limited background of a personality or an epoch."

Aru, for his part, gave new support to Cellini's thesis of the singlemindedness of vision which led Michelangelo to adhere unchangingly to his practice of carving " by virtue of removing," while sculpture was gradually taking to other pathways and attenuating its plastic qualities.

It is a pleasure to express my thanks to the Azienda Autonoma di Turismo of Florence and to its President, Avv. Raffaello Torricelli, for permission to publish, in this section of the text, photographs of works of Michelangelo by Alfredo Garuti of Florence, who has magnificently interpreted the spirit and the technique of Michelangelo's art, with precision and deep effectiveness.

III

PAINTING

by Roberto Salvini

Michelangelo as painter

Any discussion of Michelangelo as a painter must first consider the rôle that painting played in the master's career. Obviously, there are disadvantages in concentrating on any single aspect of Michelangelo's art and it is especially difficult to trace its internal development when, as in the occasion, one is restricted to painting alone. Of course, we know that he always considered sculpture rather than painting as his real vocation. It is well known how reluctantly he mounted the scaffolding in the Sistine Chapel and started to paint the frescoes of the vaulted ceiling. His bad humor was not entirely due to the fact that he was being forced to break off his work on the tomb for Pope Julius on which he had already expended so much labor. There was also his conviction that he was faced with a task that was beyond his powers, or at any rate too far removed from what he felt was his calling. The documents are familiar, but it will do no harm to recall them: in a letter to his father, dated from Rome, he apologizes for not being able for the moment to send him any money, because, he adds, " it has been a year since I got a cent from this Pope, and I don't ask him for any, because my work isn't going ahead well enough for me to feel I deserve it. And this is the trouble with the work, *and also that it is not my profession.* And so I am wasting my time without any results." [1]

The letter is dated January 27, 1509, about eight months after his work in the chapel was begun. In the same year, according to Guasti (or the following year, according to Frey), came the famous sonnet to Giovanni da Pistoia, ending with the sarcastic description of the hardships of working in the Sistine scaffolding: " not being in the right place, nor I a painter." [2]

Such aversion to the art of painting, just at the moment when the master was creating one of the world's supreme masterpieces, might seem strange and hard to understand if we did not know that it had deep roots in Michelangelo's thinking. In the celebrated dispute overt he relative merits of the various arts (the earliest skirmishes antedate Varchi's debate by at least a century), Michelangelo took the side of sculpture. In his reply to Varchi's questionnaire he contemptuously referred to " the man that wrote that painting was nobler than sculpture " ("if he understood the other things he has written as well as he did that, my servant would have written them better."). This bitter comment may reflect Michelangelo's heated discussion of the subject with Leonardo earlier in the century. The scene for this famous quarrel was either in the Annunziata in front of Leonardo's cartoon for the St. Anne, or in the Palazzo Vecchio where each artist had submitted a great cartoon for a battle scene. " I say," Michelangelo wrote to Varchi in 1547, " that painting is regarded as being better the more it approaches relief, and relief is regarded as being worse the more it approaches painting; and therefore I used to think that sculpture was the lantern of painting, and that the difference between the two is that between the sun and the moon. Now that I have read in your little book the part where you say that, philosophically speaking, those things that have the same end are one and the same thing, I have changed my mind; and I say, that if greater judgment and difficulty, hindrance and labor do not make greater nobility, then painting and sculpture are one and the same thing; and for that to be so, every painter should not fail to do sculpture as well as painting; and likewise the sculptor should do painting as well as sculpture. I mean by sculpture, that which is done by taking away; that which is done by adding, is like painting. Well then, since both of them come from the same understanding, sculpture and painting that is, peace can well be made between them, and all these disputes can be dropped, because more time goes into them than into making works of art." [3]

Comments on this famous passage have often emphasized Michelangelo's impatience with

149

theoretical discussions and his possible early advocacy for unity, rather than diversity, among the arts. It seems to me, on the other hand, that the real point here is Michelangelo's insistence on the superiority of sculpture. Although he said he was ready to abandon this claim, this was more in deference to the philosophical arguments of his learned correspondent than to his own inner conviction. After all, he was in his element creating works of art and not in rhetorical debate. Michelangelo was probably led to his preference for sculpture by the Platonic idea that plastic art because it produces an image that is existentially concrete, like the very human body that it aims at reproducing, is in a similar position, as compared to painting, to that of the Idea as compared to reality [4]—it is the incorruptible model of innumerable imperfect embodiments (so much so that painting has to feign the relief that sculpture has by its very nature). This view is also evident from his statement that sculpture is the lantern of painting and from his moral conviction that a work requiring greater dedication and physical effort has an ethical superiority. This is a position diametrically opposed to that of Leonardo who had declared that " sculpture is not a science but a most mechanical art because it causes sweat and weariness." In contrast to the proud Renaissance intellectualism of Leonardo, who asserted that " the sculptor brings to his work greater physical effort than the painter, while the painter brings to his [medium] greater intellectual effort," in Michelangelo there is once again a medieval pride in the sweat which goes into a work of art. In the lofty realm where art appears as the expression of thought, an awareness of the supreme nobility of technique was reborn in Michelangelo.

Once the figurative arts acquired the unquestioned dignity of an academic discipline, Michelangelo reclaims as co-essential with the very notion of art the old conception of *ars mechanica*, which was represented better by sculpture than by its sister art. At the very moment that he was exploiting to the very fullest the secular content of classical civilization, the same spiritual process led him to a recovery of a religious intensity that can be matched by only a few of the greatest medieval artists—such as Cimabue for example. Altogether, this enthusiastic regard for the ethical value embodied in the manual labour of the artist is paralleled by another phenomenon in Michelangelo's art. His boundless admiration for the Antique was permeated with a renewed and profound Christianity the forms of which were drawn as the final consequences of the ideals of heroic classic beauty. [5]

After thus tracing, at least hypothetically, the reasons for Michelangelo's preference for sculpture, it should be said at once that this is not in any way intended as an attempt to belittle his tremendous achievement as a painter, an achievement that has been confirmed by a tradition of unanimous criticism dating from the artist's own time. Save in the strictly biographical sense, there is not a trace either in Condivi or in Vasari of the discontent which we know accompanied all Michelangelo's great efforts—a discontent all too familiar from his own writings. On the contrary, it is certain that the discontent was always resolved in a dramatic determination to overcome the difficulties of the work, and in high expressive tension. Still another argument could be made in favor of the pictorial work of Michelangelo. When we consider, on the one hand, the artist's great groups of sculpture and, on the other, his three great cycles of paintings, we see at once that the latter exist today as completely and perfectly finished works, whereas the former remained in the state of great sketches. It is an irony of fate—and we know all too well how much the master suffered from it—that it was precisely his greatest undertakings in sculpture that never came to completion despite the prodigious efforts of his will. Even in the New Sacristy—within the most suitable of architectural settings and, in fact of his own design, Michelangelo succeeded in giving form to the representation of the eternal flow of time through a continuous series of colossal figures of Day and Night, Evening and Morning, but was unable to complete the scheme with the figures planned for the rivers and for the third wall where only the Virgin is by his own hand. And of course the work that was to have been his largest and most perfect achievement, the tomb of Julius II, with its forty statues, could never be brought even close to completion. The Moses, the Prisons, and the Slaves are grand creations and each of them, whether finished or unfinished, is a powerful and integrated work of art. But the whole monument that was to unite into an organic and meaningful group all the individual parts that the artist had or would have created, could never be brought into being. However, the vault of the Sistine Chapel, the Last Judgment and the two frescoes in the Pauline Chapel are great works and great cycles which fortunately, despite the artist's discontent, achieved ultimate perfection. Therefore they can be judged and interpreted both as to their formal structure and their basis in thought. Hence the road that leads to Michelangelo by way of painting is not a narrow path, and there is no danger that it may lead us into a peripheral region of the great personality. On the contrary, a study of the great pictorial cycles can reveal to us, along with much of his formal world, the nature of his thought. Perhaps by taking this route, criticism—hitherto too one-sided in its devotion to formal analysis and the search for hidden significance—may set about to discover the meaning with which Michelangelo undoubtedly intended to imbue each of his works (and especially those of greater complexity and size). It is in the forms themselves that the necessary and sufficient language is to be found which Michelangelo used for expressing the poetic insight nourished by his intellect.

[1] G. Milanesi, *Le Lettere di Michelangelo Buonarroti, pubblicate coi ricordi ed i contratti artistici*, Florence, 1875, p. 17; *Lettere di Michelangelo Buonarroti*, with introduction by Giovanni Papini, I, Lanciano, n. d., No. LII, p. 47.

[2] Michelangelo Buonarroti, *Le Rime, Introduzione e note* by Valentino Piccoli, Turin, 1930, p. 7-8 (No. IX); ed. by E. N. Girardi, Bari, 1960 (Scrittori d'Italia, No. 217) p. 4 ff. (No. 5).

[3] In addition to the well-known editions of Michelangelo's letters, the famous reply to Varchi can be read, with a sober commentary, in *Trattati d'Arte del Cinquecento fra Manierismo e Controriforma*, edited by Paola Barocchi, I, Bari, 1960, p. 82.

[4] R. J. Clements, *Michelangelo*, I, *Le Idee sull'Arte*, translated by E. Battisti, Milan, 1964, p. 374, ascribes " Michelangelo's preference for carving over modelling " to the " Neoplatonic theory of the concept inherent in the material." In part, I think, Michelangelo's tenacious conviction that sculpture is superior to painting is to be attributed to similar Neoplatonic reasoning.

[5] In sharp contrast to Leonardo's idea of the superiority of painting, as an " intellectual " art, over the " manual " art of sculpture, critics have often stressed (cf. esp. A. Blunt, *Artistic Theory in Italy*, Oxford, 1940, p. 54 and passim) Michelangelo's firm intention of claiming no less a degree of " intellectuality " for sculpture than is accorded its sister art. This is undoubtedly correct, but does not exclude Buonarroti's recovery, alone among the artists of his time, of the Christian and medieval conception of the nobility of labor and manual work, a point to which it seems critics have not given attention. But see a collection, with accurate commentary, of passages from Michelangelo and the sources on the problem of the comparison in R. J. Clements, *op. cit.*, p. 360-88.

1 Francesco Granacci: Madonna and Child with Youthful St. John. Dublin, National Gallery.

2 Master of the Manchester Madonna: Madonna and Child with Youthful St. John. Vienna, Academy of Fine Arts.

The early works

In April 1488, the thirteen year old Michelangelo was introduced by his older friend, Francesco Granacci, to the studio of the famous painter, Domenico Ghirlandaio. Although Michelangelo's father had agreed to a three year contract with Domenico and his brother, Davide, the boy soon broke off his first apprenticeship with them and went off to the school that Bertoldo had in the gardens of San Marco. There he threw himself passionately into the study of antiquity and sculpture. It is uncertain how long Michelangelo remained with Ghirlandaio; his two biographers, Condivi and Vasari, are inexact and they disagree. If we accept Condivi's statement that the young Buonarroti was with Lorenzo for two years (Vasari says four, evidently in error), it would follow that Michelangelo left Ghirlandaio in the spring of 1490, after working with him for precisely two years (Lorenzo died in April 1492). This hypothesis seems likely because the boy would have needed at least two years to become proficient in fresco technique. We know that he became a master in this medium and there was no better place to learn it then than in the Ghirlandaio shop. If Michelangelo's apprenticeship with Ghirlandaio lasted two full years, there is the further possibility that he may have had a hand in the frescoes in Santa Maria Novella. This is of considerable importance with regard to the problem of his early activity as a painter.

This problem centers around the Doni *tondo*. As is well known, the picture is Michelangelo's earliest surviving painting. However, it dates from a fairly advanced period, 1503-1504—or even later.

Since the *tondo* is an apparently mature work, the question arises as to what Michelangelo painted in the years of adolescence and early youth. Aside from a few drawings, it will be impossible to obtain any notion of his early paintings unless two legendary pictures of his youth are discovered. One of these is said to have been a copy of Martin Schongauer's print of the *Temptation of St. Anthony*. The other picture was the copy of a head, the patina of which was so marvelously rendered that it was mistaken for the original.[6] It may be helpful to consider first those few surviving sketches in pen and ink which Michelangelo made after certain figures by Giotto and Masaccio.

It is highly significant that Michelangelo copied Giotto and Masaccio rather than Ghirlandaio, Filippino, Verrocchio, Botticelli or Pollaiuolo. Even if we imagine him to have made drawings (since lost) after works by these older contemporaries as well, the fact remains that he felt the need to study the great masters of earlier generations too. In any case, the drawings made from the murals in Santa Croce and the Carmine show his rejection of the subtle and nervous sensibility of late Quattrocento Florentine art and his return to the majestic and synthetic spirit of the Early Renaissance. These drawings are something more than mere exercises in copying. The oldest of them is in all probability the Munich sheet reproducing Masaccio's Peter Receiving the Tribute Money (Fig. 2 ch. V). It is no masterpiece, to be sure; the treatment has something timid and uncertain about it that betrays the hand of the beginner.[7] Yet, when compared with the original, this figure reveals a search for something new. Michelangelo has drawn the loop of cloth falling from the shoulder broader and more clearly detached from the body and he has added a small fold at the bottom of the figure. Intensifying and developing what was only a slight accent in the original, he has converted the lowermost fold into a junction of two separate folds. In Masaccio's figure, the drapery follows the lines of the body more docilely; in Michelangelo, there is an attempt to give the drapery a plastic life of its own. Similar remarks could be made concerning the drawing in the Louvre that copies two figures in the Ascension of St. John the Evangelist in the Peruzzi Chapel (Fig. 3 ch. V). Here a vitality is introduced which tends to enrich and dynamically mold the relief of the figures. A further step in the same direction is represented by the drawing in the Albertina, likewise a copy from Masaccio (Fig. 4 ch. V). We cannot refer to the original, a detail in the scene commemorating the Carmine's consecration in 1422, which has since disappeared. However, our knowledge of Masaccio helps us to imagine, or rather to calculate, the distance

3 Master of the Manchester Madonna: Manchester Madonna. London, National Gallery.

153

20

between the copy and the lost original. Michelangelo must certainly have been faithful to his model. But the powerful thrust of the great fold hanging from the arm, with the shadow thickening in the hollow, the powerful rumpling of the cloth, and further elements that would take too long to list, are all features that were surely less prominent in Masaccio's figure. In this way the figure assumes a more robust character; the cloak no longer suggests merely the plastic quality of the body it covers, but also a new spiritual force. Masaccio's simple heroic austerity is heightened and expanded into a new dramatic intensity. Finally we come to the impressive drawing of a Sage or Astrologer, in the British Museum, which is not a copy, but still belongs to this group of drawings (Fig. 7 ch. V). By way of interpretative imitation of Giotto, and especially of Masaccio, Michelangelo by now had achieved the mighty solemnity that emanates from every line of this stupendous sheet. The fact that reflection on the principles of Masaccio's art went hand in hand with interest in Antiquity is likewise shown by the drawing at Chantilly which is a little later in date. Along with a strong female nude (of undoubtedly Masaccian inspiration) there are three more studies—two of which are undoubtedly based on classical statuary (Fig. 9 ch. V).

Although it would be going too far to say that these precocious fruits of Michelangelo's genius have not received the attention they deserve, these drawings are usually associated with his first works in sculpture rather than with the more closely related medium of painting. The drawings have been universally admired and Bertini has justly said that " even in his copies, Michelangelo reveals his personality through powerful simplification, formal rigor, clarity of stroke, and the universality he achieves."[8] Mariani has also noted that we need only " a copy in pen and ink, a simple (and certainly unacademic) study after Giotto to show us the emerging artist, master of what was most essential to him which consisted in the manner of proceding from an intimate knowledge of plasticity to its expressive formulation—moving from an austere morality towards a monumental interpretation of form itself."[9] Had the profound importance of these drawings in the formation of the painter been recognized, criticism could have spared itself the doubtless courageous attempts of hypothetically reconstructing the master's earliest activities. Such attempts involved contradictions with the style of the first undoubted works and is an approach which today is gradually being abandoned.[10]

The effort has been made to attribute a series of Madonnas to Michelangelo's first essays in painting. Of these, only the Virgin in Dublin and the Vienna *tondo* (Figs. 1, 2) will be mentioned. The Dublin Madonna had been attributed to Granacci until Fiocco considered

154   4   Master of the Manchester Madonna: Descent
          from the Cross. London, National Gallery.

5 Domenico Ghirlandaio and workshop (Michelangelo ?): detail of the Baptism of Christ. Florence, Santa Maria Novella.

it as a possible Michelangelo of the earliest years. The figure of Mary has a majesty and the composition of the masses has a power which are inconceivable without some kind of contact with Michelangelo. On the other hand, the landscape has a pictorial richness bordering on the picturesque and a descriptive gusto which always were foreign to Buonarroti. Further, the composition of the main group, the posture and actions of the two children, as well as the soft treatment of the surfaces of the flesh, recall Leonardo and the Florentine Madonnas of Raphael. All this is hard to reconcile with the possibility of the picture being a youthful essay by Michelangelo, a work, that would have to be earlier than 1500 and probably earlier than 1495. It should be noted that although the prototype for the Christ Child is to be found in 155

7 Domenico Ghirlandaio and workshop (Michelangelo ?): detail of the Dormitio Virginis. Florence, Santa Maria Novella.

6 Michelangelo (?): St. John the Evangelist (fragment). Switzerland, private collection.

Leonardo's Milanese Madonnas (which Michelangelo could hardly have seen), the infant Baptist is dependant upon Leonardo's London cartoon for the St. Anne. This cartoon was made in Milan but its elements may have reappeared in the lost cartoon exhibited in the Annunziata in 1501 because the motif became popular in Florence only through the Raphael-esque variations of 1505-1507. The two trees framing the figure of the Madonna could not have been painted earlier than those of the *Madonna del Cardellino* and other Florentine paintings by Raphael. Although Granacci was six years older than his great friend, it may very well be that he painted the Dublin picture under Michelangelo's influence, perhaps using a study or drawing by Buonarroti around 1505 or later and during Raphael's stay in Florence.

As for the Vienna *tondo* and others of the same series, it has been thought that a confirmation of Michelangelo's authorship may be seen in the relationships they show with Ferrarese paintings of the turn of the century in the circle of Francesco Cossa, Ercole de' Roberti and Lorenzo Costa. Michelangelo was, in fact, in Bologna between 1494 and 1495 where it has been said that he admired the lost frescoes in the Garganelli Chapel of San Pietro by Cossa and de' Roberti. Actually there is little or nothing to be found of a Ferrarese factor in the master's authentic paintings, even if Fiocco is justified in relating the *Pietà* of St. Peter's to Roberti's *Pietà* in Liverpool. Moreover, what the great Ferrarese painters could offer Michelangelo was precisely what he was not interested in. For Ferrarese painting, though dramatic, is also subtle and nervous, and charged with a skittish anxiety the young Buonarroti would have rejected,

156

8*a*   Nude men in the Doni tondo.   Florence, Uffizi.

8*b*   Nude men and Youthful St. John in the Doni tondo.   Florence, Uffizi.

attracted as he was to the grand simplicity of Masaccio and the controlled dramatic spirit of Hellenistic-Roman sculpture.

The surprising affinity of single features, such as the Virgin's face, testifies that the Vienna *tondo* belongs to the same group which includes the Manchester Madonna in the London Na-

9   Aristotele da Sangallo: copy of the Battle of Cascina.   Holkham Hall, Earl of Leicester collection.

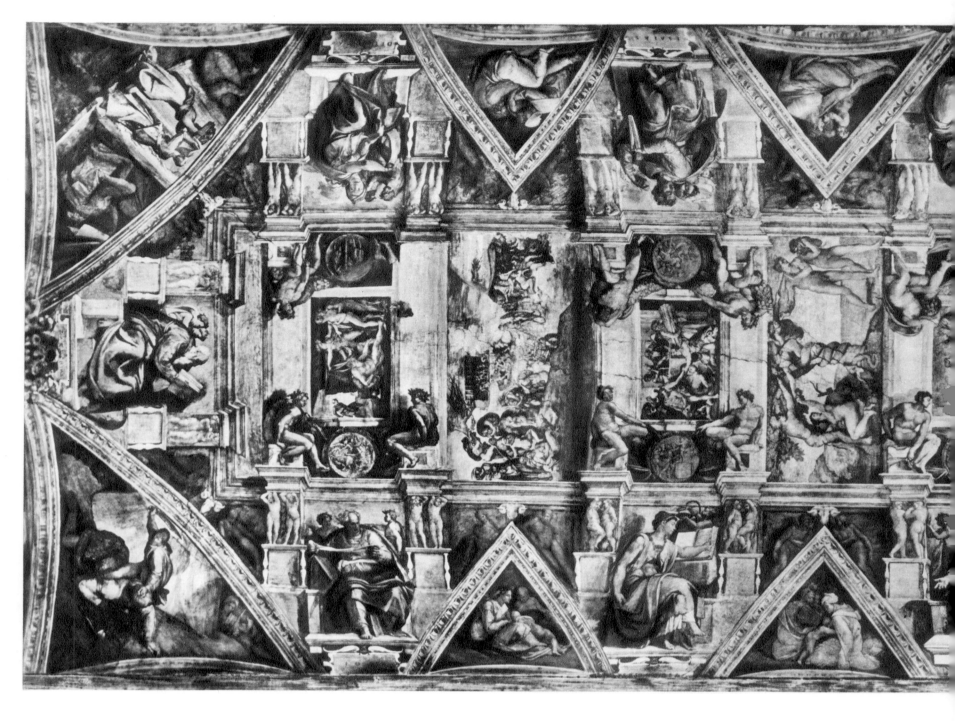

10 Vault of the Sistine Chapel. Rome, Vatican

tional Gallery—certainly a more beautiful picture (Fig. 3). Here too, the charm of the unfinished has its share in creating the illusion of being face to face with a work by Michelangelo.
The problem has been convincingly solved, I believe, by Zeri in an article ten years ago
reconstructing the activity of the " Master of the Manchester Madonna."[11] This painting is
the work of an unknown painter, a friend of Michelangelo's, living in Rome about 1510, who
must have made use of some drawings which Michelangelo himself placed at his disposal. It
is also possible that the master helped him with advice and even, here and there, with the
brush. The two angels to the right are undoubtedly the most beautiful figures in the picture
and they are derived from the *putti* of the Sistine Chapel. The Madonna and the Child,
however, which are strongly reminiscent of the marble Madonna that Michelangelo had made
some years earlier for Moucheron and sent to Bruges, seem to be a translation into painting
of a drawing intended as a study for sculpture: the form of the marble block may even be
recognized in the chipped base. In Zeri's hypothesis, the author of these and the other paintings
of the group might be sought among the members of the team of Umbro-Bolognese painters
who in those years were frescoing the Borgia apartment in the Vatican. This would explain
the presence of Emilian stylistic themes traceable in these pictures as has been mentioned
earlier. Mariani has just written a passionate defense of this picture in which he sees, as others
do, the earliest example of Michelangelo's painting that has come down to us. Among other
things, he has I think rightly noted that " the idea of pairs of angels may have emerged from
Michelangelo's fantasy from a distant memory of the figures of Luca della Robbia's choir loft,
while there appears to be a much closer relation, to the point of seeming to be a direct contact,
with Desiderio da Settignano's relief of *Jesus and the Infant Baptist* in the Mellon Collection of
the National Gallery in Washington." And it is clear that such a reference to the ambience
of the early Quattrocento can be credited to none other than the young Buonarroti. Mariani
has also drawn attention to " the beautiful passage disclosing the virginal breast of the Madonna," an idea that " seems to be the fruit of an adolescent's infatuation with the ancient
theme of the *Madonna del latte*." It is not our intention here to deny the presence of Michel-

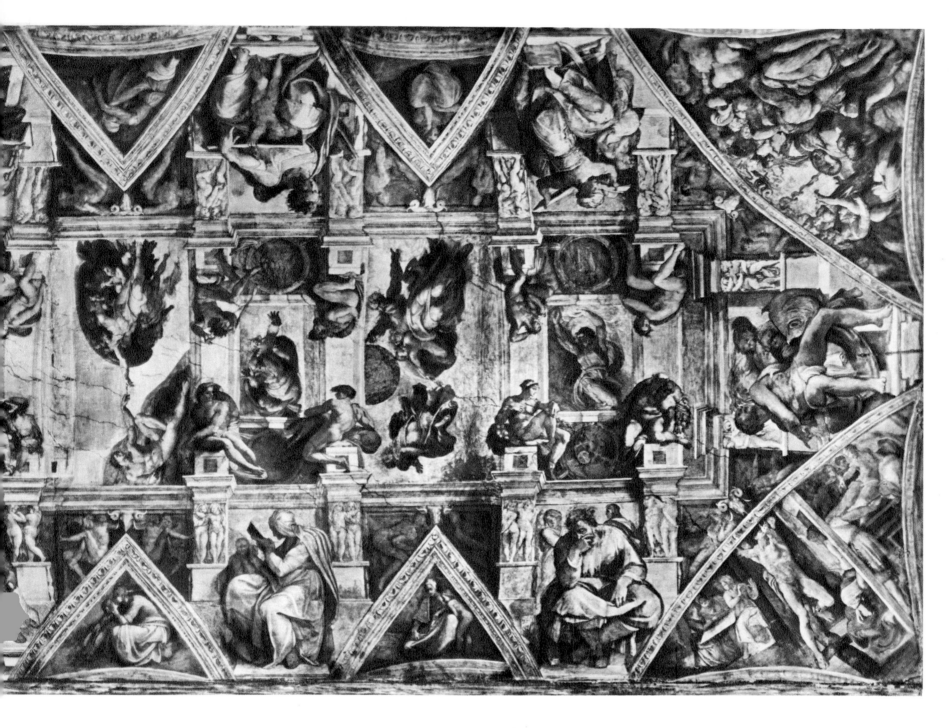

angelesque ideas in this work. The matter is another: whether it is necessary to postulate the actual presence of his hand, or rather if these and other Michelangelesque elements are not better explained (in view of the picture's mannered and precious aspects) by the anonymous painter's use of Michelangelo's graphic models and by the master's occasional intervention in the generous capacity of rescuing a friend in trouble.

Following the always useful method of Morelli, we can compare the Manchester Madonna to the Vienna *tondo* and the Contini picture to the Zürich painting—all are clearly works by the same hand (excepting those passages in the London picture in which Michelangelo himself may have had a share). How can one ignore in the faces of the Madonnas of Vienna, Zurich and London the same typological ensemble and even the smallest details which usually are the hallmarks of identical authorship? And how can we help assigning also the little Contini Madonna to the same hand if for no other reason than for the identical drawing of the veils covering the head in each picture? Therefore, it seems to me that in spite of the superior quality of the Manchester Madonna, one must accept or reject *en bloc* the entire group of these supposed *juvenilia* of Michelangelo. That rejection rather than acceptance is the case here seems to me demonstrated by the taste of these paintings which is incongruous with the stylistic and, I would venture to say, ethical orientation of the young genius known to us from the first drawings.

Those who accept as well as those who reject the Manchester Madonna agree in attributing it to the same hand responsible for the *Descent from the Cross* in the National Gallery (Fig. 4), whether it be by Buonarroti or not. Zeri also assigns it to the Master of the Manchester Madonna. Here, in any case, one must admit that Michelangelo's participation was greater. To him is certainly due the general design of the composition. During his first years in Rome, Michelangelo more than once looked at Northern art. Here, as has been noted, the idea for the composition vaguely reflects Roger van der Weyden's *Pietà* in the Uffizi. Similarly, the scheme for Michelangelo's *Pietà* in St. Peter's was inspired by the tradition of the German *Vesperbild*. The great figure of Christ was certainly designed by Michelangelo and in part 159 executed by him, at least in the lower portion, where the plastic emergence of the legs is extremely powerful, and the tension is harsh and sorrowful. Also the figure of St. John is so forceful and so true in its relation to that of Christ that it leads us to believe that it was designed and partly executed by Michelangelo. But the obvious weakness of the lateral figures cannot be explained merely by the incomplete state in which they were left: the figure of the woman supporting the Saviour's body is certainly superb in conception, but its soft and fragile aspect cannot be attributed to the master, nor can the figure beside it which is so flat and clumsy. As for the Maria Salomè on the left, the existence of a drawing by Michelangelo (that preserved in the Louvre is so hard that it is often considered to be a copy) only shows that the painter of the minor figures of the London *Deposition* resorted to studies furnished by the master. And as for the head of Joseph of Arimathea, the facial similarity to the St. Joseph of the Doni *tondo* is no proof of Michelangelo's authorship either, in view of the general nature of the painting.

In all these works, Michelangelo's share appears at best to have been only partial and often indirect. If he provided drawn models and sometimes lent the aid of his own hand and brush, it was only because of the great master's notorious generosity and readiness to help his friends. Moreover, the most important of these works, the Manchester Madonna and the Descent from the Cross, cannot be earlier than 1508-1510. They can by no means fill the gap in Michelangelo's *œuvre* due to the absence of paintings prior to the Florentine *tondo*. The entire group seems to be the product of a temperament that was mannerist before mannerism, or rather, the work of an artisan who grafted forms and motifs taken from Michelangelo on to a culture imbued with " late Quattrocento decadence," and thus assumed the guise of precocious mannerism. An old essay of Antal's comes to mind which re-

160   11 Sistine Chapel. Rome, Vatican.

PLATE VI   Universal Flood.   Vault of the Sistine Chapel.

PLATE VII   Noah's Sacrifice.   Vault of the Sistine Chapel.

PLATE XI   Separation of the Earth from the Waters.   Vault of the Sistine Chapel.

PLATE XIII   Separation of the Light from the Darkness.   Vault of the Sistine Chapel.

12 Noah's Drunkenness. Vault of the Sistine
Chapel.

ferred to a singular phenomenon. The essay found little response in its time but its theme
may be worth going into more deeply. Antal tried to point out a continuity of development
between the 15th century mannerism centered around Filippino and the Florentine Mannerism of the second and third decades of the *Cinquecento*.[12] What should be stressed here is that
although Michelangelo's mature art supplied the broad basis and the vast formal vocabulary
for the first as well as the second Mannerism of the *Cinquecento*, his early drawings and sculpture show that his initial development occurred in the spirit of a reaction against the subtleties
and decadent preciousness of Florentine painting at the end of the century, and returned to
the purer sources of the early Renaissance.

Excepting Fineschi's and Holroyd's timid suggestions made in 1836 and 1903 [13] which had
no following, it is only very recent that criticism has started down a different and apparently
more promising path. When the young Buonarroti entered into the three year contract as
an apprentice in Domenico Ghirlandaio's shop, this prolific and respected painter was busy
with his students decorating the choir of Santa Maria Novella with frescoes. The contract states
specifically that Michelangelo was not only to learn but also to paint. Thus the question
arises which 19th and 20th century literature has hardly touched upon: that of the possibility of Michelangelo's participation in Ghirlandaio's greatest project of those years—even
if he only served in the very subordinate capacity of an apprentice. Recently, Marchini has
maintained that Michelangelo's youthful hand can be recognized in some of the figures in
the *Dormition of the Virgin* and in the *Baptism of Christ*.[14] In the Dormition, Marchini cites the
third and fourth figures as possibly being Michelangelo's work, as well as the figure of the
young angel in the group at the extreme left (Fig. 7). The most convincing of these is the
man in the toga seen from the back. The simple grandeur of the drapery and the vigorous
way the toga is flung give to the image the solidity of statuary. Further, one can discern
beneath the robes not only corporeal plasticity but also a secret spiritual energy. Compared
to Ghirlandaio's descriptive style, this figure seems to be inspired by Masaccio's austere simplicity animated by a new dramatic note. This is also characteristic of the drawings presumably made during the same years when Michelangelo was studying the solemn frescoes in
the Carmine. Even stronger are the three figures in the Baptism scene which Marchini refers
to, namely the nude neophyte on his knees and the two prophet-like personages behind him
(Fig. 5). The nude boy is constructed with such simplicity and grandeur, and his movement
is rendered with such mastery by the sustained tension of the contours following the solid
plastic forms, that the whole is invested with a new spiritual force. The measured, yet slightly
antagonistic relationship between the masses of the two standing figures strongly suggests a
mute dialogue of dense moral significance. If one then turns to the figure viewed from the
back with its drapery of almost stoney hardness and thickly wrinkled folds, one cannot help

161

remembering the way in which the young Buonarroti translated Masaccio's drapery into something quite new and intensely dramatic by means of the vigorous stroke of his drawing. It seems to me that this figure, and particularly its drapery, occupies an intermediate position between the study from Masaccio in the Albertina and the Astrologer of the British Museum. As for the figure of the person about to be baptized, one can note further that its conception and the way the left foot is set on the ground recalls the figure of Theophilus' son returned to life painted only a few years earlier, when Filippino Lippi used the young Francesco Granacci as his model for this episode in Masaccio's unfinished fresco in the Carmine. It is not difficult to imagine that during Michelangelo's many visits to the Brancacci Chapel, occasionally in company of his mentor Granacci, the older man with a touch of vanity drew the boy's attention to the solemn little nude for which he had posed. These few observations, together with references to the drawn studies, should confirm Marchini's attributions which seem to me sufficiently convincing. Attention should also be drawn to his judicious remarks concerning the color of these small sections in the Santa Maria Novella frescoes: bright and luminous color tending to create dissonant effects which were later to become even more violent in the Doni *tondo*. In the figure of the Baptism, cited earlier, Marchini notes that " Here the form tends to be simplified almost to the point of an intellectual solution in order to obtain grandeur of volume, as, for example, in the knot of drapery on the flank of the frontal, standing figure in the Baptism, and moreover—and this is very important—it is rendered in a colouring which emphasizes this effect, isolating the separate volumes by the strong opposition of tints." In the Baptism, the figure shown from the rear has a scarlet cloak, a green tunic, and orange shoes, while the shoes of the neophyte are virtually black. The other standing figure shows a juxtaposition of blue and yellow, with a marked chromatic contrast closely resembling the Holy Family of the Uffizi. According to Marchini's reckoning, the presumable date of execution of those portions of the frescoes containing work attributed to Michelangelo would correspond with the period of his apprenticeship in Ghirlandaio's studio. The contract for the choir of Santa Maria Novella was made on September 1, 1485, and it is unlikely that Ghirlandaio began the work before 1487, because until December 15th, 1486 he was busy with the frescoes in the Sassetti Chapel of Santa Trinita. After a certain period of preparation, which would have included the making of working drawings and the raising of the scaffolding, the painting according to conventional practise must have been begun in the vault. Remembering that the entire cycle was finished in December 1490, the lunette with the Dormition of the Virgin (which appears to have been done last) would have been reached by the Autumn of 1488 while the zone below, containing the Baptism, would have been painted by the Spring of 1489. That insertions attributable to the same hand we have been speaking of are no longer to be found at a level lower than the Baptism agrees perfectly with our knowledge of Michelangelo's departure from the Ghirlandaio studio for the gardens of San Marco.

No matter how modest and unnoticed was the young Michelangelo's debut in the choir of Santa Maria Novella, it was nevertheless of great historical importance. With these few figures which he was allowed to carry out there—following the main outlines of Ghirlandaio's drawings or *sinopie*—Michelangelo initiated his polemic against an entire generation of Florentine artists. Against Ghirlandaio's superficial illustration and descriptive extravagance, against Filippino's fastidious and dainty narrative style, Michelangelo asserted the need for a return to the simple, heroic grandeur of Masaccio; and in his drive towards the conquest of largely seen forms, he demonstrated what the imitation of Nature really was.

So far, Marchini's proposal has had little critical response. Longhi has recently suggested that we may have in the fragmentary St. John, in a Swiss private collection (Fig. 6), " the only possible sample of Michelangelo's activity as a painter during the period of his apprenticeship with Granacci under Ghirlandaio." This attribution will appear more convincing if we consider the picture as the conclusion of a development which was represented in its initial phases by the studies drawn from Masaccio and Giotto, and by his share (limited though it may have been) in the frescoes in Santa Maria Novella's choir.[15] In the drawing made in the Peruzzi Chapel, the reenforcement of the " plastic block by the swelling of the tunic over the belt," a detail already noted, *went beyond a merely literal copy of the model.* " The fullness of a hem in the mantle " appears, apart from some of the graphic exercises based on Masaccio already mentioned, also in the loop of the mantle belonging to the *repoussoir* figure in the Dormition at Santa Maria Novella and, lower down, along the arm of the old man watching the Baptism who, similarly, almost turns his back on us. The strong sculptural sweep of the folds on the left arm is a new idea, preluding the much freer twisting and massing of cloth around the athletic limbs of the figures of the Uffizi *tondo*, while " in the unheard of foreshortening of the face... the artist anticipates... the contracted elasticity of the face of the Doni Madonna." The clawed crumplings of the cloak and the corded folds converging toward the bottom of the tunic are already found, in a different syntax, in the figures already referred to in the Dormition and the Baptism of Santa Maria Novella.

[6] Vasari mentions, even in the first edition of the *Vite* (1550), the copy young Buonarroti made, during his apprenticeship under Ghirlandaio, of the famous engraving of Martin Schongauer (erroneously attributed to Dürer by Vasari). This would have been an ink drawing, later colored (" he drew it in ink...and painted the same in colors "). According to Condivi (1553), who seems to get the information from Vasari, correcting the name of the print's author to " Martino d'Olanda," it would have been an easel painting. But in his second edition Vasari repeats the version in the first, giving

15 Fleeing man and woman, in the Universal
Flood. Vault of the Sistine Chapel.

◁ 13 Fleeing mother and child, in the Universal
Flood. Vault of the Sistine Chapel.

14 Fleeing people with household goods, in the
Universal Flood. Vault of the Sistine Chapel.

the name of " Martino Tedesco " in correction of his own mistake and Condivi's inexactness. As for the copy of a head,
so well done and given so good a patina as to pass in jest for an original, the statement comes from Condivi, with no
indication of the technique. It was repeated by Varchi (1564), who states that it was a painting, while Vasari (1568)
spoke in a general way of many forgeries of " papers from the hands of many old masters."

7 In dating and giving the chronological order of these drawings from Giotto and Masaccio, critics range from 1488 to 1493.
8 A. Bertini, *Michelangelo fino alla Sistina*, Turin, 1942, p. 26.
9 V. Mariani, *Michelangelo*, Turin, 1942, p. 9 (new ed., Naples, 1964, p. 6).
10 G. Fiocco "Francesco Granacci's Date of Birth and an Hypothesis on Michelangelo," in *Rivista d'Arte*, XII, 1930,
p. 193, and XIII, 1931, p. 109), on the basis of patient and acute research in the documents, made a correct reevaluation
of Granacci's date of birth, showing that he was six years older than Michelangelo. From that Fiocco went on to attribute
to Michelangelo's early youth the *Madonna* in the National Gallery of Dublin, formerly attributed to Granacci; to confirm
as Michelangelo's the *tondo* in the Academy of Fine Arts in Vienna, already accepted by A. Venturi (*Michelangelo*, Rome,
n. d.); and then to the attribution of a *Madonna* in a private collection in Baden, Switzerland, near Zurich, and another
formerly in England and now in the Contini collection in Florence (" Another Painting of Michelangelo's Youth," in *La Critica
d'Arte*, II, 1937, p. 172; " Michelangelo's First Steps as a Painter," in *Le Arti*, 1941-42, p. 5; " Michelangelo's First Fruits,"
in *Rivista d'Arte*, XXVI, 1950, p. 149), naturally reasserting Michelangelo's authorship of the *Manchester Madonna* and the
Descent from the Cross, both in the National Gallery in London.
11 F. Zeri, " The Master of the Manchester Madonna," in *Paragone*, IV, 1954, No. 43, p. 15.
12 F. Antal, " Studies on the Gothic in the Quattrocento," in *Jahrbuch der preussischen Kunstsammlungen*, 1925.
13 R. V. Fineschi, *Il Forestiere istruito in Santa Maria Novella*, Florence, 1836, p. 25; C. Holroyd, *Michel Angelo Buonarroti*,
London, 1903, p. 99. And cf., on the entire question of the relations between Michelangelo and Ghirlandaio, G. Vasari,
La Vita di Michelangelo etc., edited and commented by Paola Barocchi, II, p. 68 ff.
14 G. Marchini, " The Frescoes in the Choir of Santa Maria Novella," in *Burlington Magazine*, XCV, 1953, p. 320.
15 R. Longhi, " Two Proposals for Young Michelangelo," in *Paragone*, IX, 1959, No. 101, p. 59.

17 Old man and young man fainted, in the Universal Flood. Vault of the Sistine Chapel.

16 Survivors on a rock, in the Universal Flood. Vault of the Sistine Chapel.

The Doni tondo

There is a broad gap in the activity of Michelangelo as a painter between these first efforts and the oldest documented work, whether this dates from 1503-1504 or from a year or two later. In any case, it is probable that Michelangelo did little or no painting after his brief apprenticeship in Ghirlandaio's *bottega* until he resumed with the Doni *tondo*, the cartoon for the Battle of Cascina, and the vault of the Sistine Chapel. Condivi's phrase, following his reference to the Bruges Madonna, seems to imply that for some time the artist had not put his hand to painting: "and so as not to abandon painting altogether, he made Our Lady on a round panel for Messer Agnol Doni." It was as if he had waited with considerable impatience for an occasion which would test his mettle in what had been the medium of his early youth. The premature departure from the apprenticeship with Ghirlandaio cannot be explained just by difficult relations between pupil and master. This idea even led Condivi to deny that Michelangelo had actually been a disciple in Domenico's shop (later disproved by Vasari who had a document to hand) and to accuse Ghirlandaio of having been jealous of the gifted boy. Clearly, Michelangelo soon began to find sculpture more congenial to him. Through his acquaintance with Bertoldo, he was attracted to the powerful art of Donatello

165

and the shining example of ancient sculpture. In this medium, he was able to explore Antiquity more directly and it facilitated his conquest of the grand and austere manner which he had already begun to rediscover on his own in his meditations on Giotto and Masaccio. The only Florentine painter of his time to whom he might have turned with some profit was Antonio del Pollaiuolo. But in November 1489, Pollaiuolo had moved to Rome to work on the tomb of Sixtus IV, and it is not impossible that he had left Florence several years earlier. Michelangelo's stay in Bologna from 1494 to 1495 could only have confirmed his preference for sculpture by introducing to him Jacopo della Quercia's dramatic reliefs and the tormented figures of Niccolò dell'Arca. Another factor that may have contributed to his aversion to painting may have been the preaching of Fra Girolamo Savonarola, who used to reproach the painters of the day for the luxurious clothes they put on sacred personages and their habit of showing the Madonna and female saints in the guise of charming Florentine ladies. On grounds of moral strictness, those aspects of gay *reportage*, portraiture, and love of episode were condemned which also aroused the distaste of the austere youth for the same as well as esthetic reasons. That Michelangelo felt the fascination of Savonarola's personality and that he was among the audience who listened to his sermons is attested to by Condivi: "for whom he always had great affection, *the memory of the sound of his (Savonarola's) voice still remains in his mind.*" In a recent and very incisive account of the difficult problem of Michelangelo's political views (Congress of Michelangelo Studies, Florence, June 16th, 1964), Spini has observed that despite the well documented connections between the Buonarroti family and the Dominican order on the one hand, and between Savonarola and the Neoplatonic circle in which the young artist grew up on the other, "when we come to define concretely what relation Michelangelo had to Savonarola's preaching, we find ourselves, as usual, on very shifty ground." There is no work by Michelangelo that can be called Savonarolian as unequivocally as the Botticelli Crucifixion in the Fogg Museum which is so full of the apocalyptic terror of the punishments menacing Florence.[16] The hypothesis, offered by Spini with much caution, is very attractive. It suggests that the Bargello Bacchus may be understood not, as Condivi explains, as a mere warning against drunkenness, but as a celebration of the " triumph of the mysterious and orgiastic power of divinity over attempts to imprison it." This is a reference to the myth of Bacchus enchained by Tyrrhenian pirates, who was freed by transforming himself into a lion, the ship's mast into a vine, and the pirates into dolphins, and may allude to Pope Alexander VI's attempts to silence Savonarola. It was, in fact, in July 1496 (when in all probability the Bacchus was commissioned in Rome by the Florentine Jacopo Galli), that Savonarola's preaching was interrupted a second time only to be resumed a little later that Autumn. Unfortunately, as Spini himself notes, this suggestive hypothesis is " based only

18 Noah's Sacrifice. Vault of the Sistine Chapel.

on inferences, rather than on incontrovertible facts." It should be said that this interpretation in sympathy with the austere Dominican should not be rejected just because we are faced with a nude Bacchus accompanied by a little satyr.

This supposition does not have to be rejected because it comes as something of a surprise to see a nude Bacchus, and what is more with a little satyr accompanying him, embodying a stand in favor of the austere Dominican. Condivi's reminder of Michelangelo's "affection" for Savonarola is followed immediately by the statement that Michelangelo "also loved the beauty of the body," and understood love in Platonic terms. This succeeded by his passionate defense against the gossip of those "carnal men who can only understand love of beauty as lascivious and dishonorable." I do not think it too farfetched to suppose that the old Michelangelo, as he sketched his spiritual self-portrait in conversation with Condivi, relived in memory the learned, philosophical milieu in which he had grown up in Lorenzo the Magnificent's house, the same atmosphere that had enabled Ficino to apply to Fra Girolamo's preaching "the Platonic theory of prophecy as divine madness" (Spini). Thus, it would be natural for his biographer to place the passage on beauty and Platonic love directly following the recollection of Savonarola and his preaching. Neither in his youth nor in his old age did he feel any contradiction between his ethical and religious convictions (which drove him to listen to Savonarola's sermons, to study the Bible and its commentaries) and his passion for antiquity, for the nude, and his immersion in that sphere of Neoplatonic thought which is later reflected in the formal and iconographical structure of his major works and is echoed in his poems. Botticelli was also nourished on Neoplatonic philosophy, but in his sensitive and restless temperament this intellectual substratum was translated into imagery through the creation of nostalgic myths of a golden age in which contemplative purity and subtle sensuality could coexist as two sides of a single fabulous reality.[17] This is why the impression of the friar's fierce preaching, and the tragic events that brought it to an end, were such a shock to him that it brought about a break and reaction in his stylistic development. Not so for Michelangelo, for whom Platonic themes and meditations were never occasions for escape, but constituted a central concept —(this he could have also found in his Dante)—involving the notion of the beauty of the universe and man as a reflection of the divine idea of beauty and light. Hence he had no qualms about using the heroic nude of classical antiquity to embody his own severe religious fervour and his hope for moral renewal in man.

Whatever their iconographical justification, it is therefore not surprising to find that superb series of nudes in his first great pictorial enterprise based on a religious theme (Figs. 8a, 8b and Plate IV). Without any specific points of reference it is difficult, and probably impossible, to solve the problem of the exact date of the Doni *tondo* in the Uffizi.[18] In any case, it is, in the last analysis, a problem of secondary importance whether it was painted for the occasion of the marriage of Agnolo Doni and Maddalena Strozzi (which took place at the end of 1503 or early in 1504), or whether it was done for the Strozzi in anticipation of the event (as Poggi supposed when he found the Strozzi arms on the frame). It might just as well have been painted later, at the same time, or after the cartoon for the Battle of Cascina as the full maturity of the picture's style and its affinity with the figures of the Sistine Chapel lead one to suspect. What is more important is the recognition by modern criticism that this painting could not have been made without its author having given serious consideration to the significance of Leonardo's art. In the spring of 1501, that is a few weeks before Buonarroti returned from Rome, Leonardo da Vinci, who had just come home from Milan, had exhibited the cartoon for the Saint Anne in the Annunziata, causing a great stir in artistic circles. This cartoon, as is well known, cannot be identified with the one in London, for the description that Pietro da Novellara gives of it indicates that the composition had already reached a form very close to the definitive version achieved in the Louvre picture. Freedberg has recently suggested that the St. Anne by Brescianino, formerly in the Kaiser Friedrich Museum in Berlin, may be a faithful reflection of the lost cartoon.[19] If this is the case, the Florentine cartoon differed from the final version in that it still retained in part the pyramidal design, while already moving towards the spherical arrangement of the definitive composition. Two drawings of Michelangelo have been preserved that seem to have been done under the direct impact of Leonardo's cartoon (Figs. 19, 23 ch. V). The older one, in the Ashmolean Museum in Oxford, is almost a polemic reaction to its model. Everything soft and rounded that had been present in Leonardo's composition is here decisively rejected. Instead, Michelangelo seeks to get a contrast between the predominantly vertical posture of the two figures and the meeting of their thighs, between the general statuesque design of the whole and the twist of the two bodies. In this way a strong dynamic tension is created between the block-like unity of the group and a tendency toward a spiral articulation. Out of this sketch, incidentally, a sculptural group could have been made, but not a painting. On the other hand, the later drawing in the Louvre could have been developed either into a plastic group or an easel painting. But the most important point is that the figures have now become full and powerful masses penetrating obliquely into the sheet conquering space. Here Michelangelo perfectly understood the relationship between figures and space in Leonardo's cartoon, and has thoroughly grasped the significance of his model as an expression of a total unity, almost as a mirror of the universe, even though the main emphasis is on contrast and dramatic tension rather than on the calm, static existence of the images. Buonarroti must have considered this drawing as an exercise in the manner of Leonardo for, as Mariani has recently observed, he noted on the margin: "who would ever say that this was by my hand". **167**

19 Eve's head, in Original Sin. Vault of the Sistine Chapel.

Yet, in its impressive distribution of broad masses in space, it can be regarded as a prelude, if not a preparatory study, for the Doni *tondo*. Accordingly, as Wilde in particular has brought out, the round picture may be taken as the final and definitive variant of a compositional conception formed in Michelangelo's imagination after a thorough meditation on Leonardo's cartoon for the St. Anne.[20]

It is not in any way our intention to belittle the originality of this youthful masterpiece of Michelangelo's when we say that the painting developed out of the deep and considered reworking of an idea of Leonardo's. On the contrary, it is to assert its central position in the " classical style " of the High Renaissance. In a very different way from Leonardo, but no less decisively, Michelangelo here departs from the perspective tradition of the Florentine Quattrocento. The space no longer extends back of the figures in a series of horizontal strata, but is at once created and limited by the semicircular wall of rock on which the nude youths easily lean. Much of the landscape in the background is hidden by these figures, and where it is still visible it consists only of compact, summary masses of color. The semi-circular rock wall, in accord with the circular form of picture and frame, molds the space spherically. Thus, the space of the picture is no longer, as in the Quattrocento, felt as a measurable section cut out of terrestrial space, but is given as a synthesis of universal space. In fact, Tolnay interprets the painting as a crystal sphere, a sort of transparent globe: the pagan images of the nude youths would represent humanity before the Law; the Madonna and St. Joseph humanity of the Old Testament, or mankind under the Law; and the Child Jesus, who, raised from the support of his parents, embodies the humanity of the New Testament, or mankind under Grace. Here Michelangelo follows and surpasses a medieval iconographical tradition. The Youthful St. John, set slightly apart behind the low wall surrounding the area of the three principal figures but in front of the group of nudes, would represent the link between paganism and the Judeo-Christian world.[21] It is hard to say whether this interpretation hits the target

20 Adam and Eve, in Original Sin. Vault of the Sistine Chapel.

22

21 Adam and Eve, in the Driving out of Eden.
    Vault of the Sistine Chapel.

exactly. Reasonable objections could easily be made. Why, for example, should the Baptist (even though he is presented with a plumpness and an open smile that make him resemble a childish Bacchus), being of Jewish stock, act as the link (as his position in the picture would suggest) between paganism and Christianity? There would seem to be merit in Mariani's proposal to see the nudes (who seem to be helping each other disrobe) as neophytes preparing to immerse themselves in an unseen pool. The Youthful St. John's presence would then be readily explained as an allusion to the sacrament of Baptism.[22] This is not to say that the classic beauty of the nudes need necessarily evoke the idea of the pagan world. Michelangelo, who had grown up in the house of Lorenzo de' Medici, in a milieu deeply imbued with Neoplatonic ideas, had certainly adopted the syncretism of that philosophy. Moreover, as a man of the Renaissance, he would not have been able to imagine beauty, including the beauty of the spirit, in forms diverging from those of classical antiquity. On the other hand, I do not believe that it is legitimate, as some scholars would have it, to deny any symbolic significance to these and other works of the master. I do not see how we can deny that Michelangelo intended to impart an ethical-religious significance to his most complex works of sculpture and painting; that there must also have been a travail of thought accompanying the profound travail of the spirit that nourished his art. Otherwise, we exclude any possibility of understanding all its grandeur. All the great artists of the early Cinquecento intended their works to express theological or philosophical concepts stated in programmes prepared by thinkers and men of learning—either by themselves, or in collaboration with the artist. This is demonstrated by Fra Pietro da Novellara's interpretative description of Leonardo's cartoon for the St. Anne and by what is known, or can be reconstructed, of Raphael's *Stanze*. This is where modern criticism should concentrate its efforts in order to avoid the dangers of mere formalism—no matter how refined or ingenious, as well as the opposite extreme of abstractly considering the work of art only for its content—a common failing of the iconographers, their great merit notwithstanding.

But to return to the *tondo* in the Uffizi: whether it is intended to represent a synthesis of the story of mankind in its three great epochs, or more simply a synthesis of Christianity by the depiction of the three personages and an allusion to Baptism; in either case, the traditional subject of the Holy Family is here raised from the status of a devotional motif (or one alluding to an historical event) to that of a universal symbol of human existence under the sign of Faith. To this totality of the content, there corresponds the universality of the form. Nonetheless, within this self-contained composition, embracing a space that is not merely earthly but universal, there prevails a continuous tension which in the artist's mind expressed the dramatic feeling accompanying man's religious renewal. In a way, the main group is isolated from its surroundings as if it was carved out of a heavy marble block. The masses, articulated in a rich system of antitheses, are aligned along a developing spiral which confers upon the images and the entire group a restless movement full of contrasts. Even the arrangement of the group around a vertical axis is in opposition to the circular form of the picture. Here Michelangelo created a new conception of the *tondo* which was in sharp contrast with the traditional Quattrocento formula. The earlier masterpieces in this genre are the *tondi* by Filippo Lippi in the Pitti Palace and by Domenico Veneziano in Berlin. They conceived this type of picture as an oculus through which the viewer was invited to look at what was taking place inside a shaded room or in a brilliant landscape. Of course, the painter did not add anything to the edges to indicate the existence of this large window; in fact, from the representational point of view, it was not even suggested. Nevertheless, according to the perspective vision of the early Quattrocento, the space appears cut and organized as if seen from behind a large round window. This conception was just the same in the rectangular panels and frescoes. Here too the section of space reproduced was cut off just as it would appear if viewed from a window corresponding to the size of the picture frame. During the second half of the Quattrocento, this mode of vision was mitigated though not directly discarded. Especially in Botticelli's *tondi*, the figures are gathered into the frontmost planes and, taking up the circular motif of the frame, are involved in an essentially rhythmic relationship—whether contrapuntal in nature as in the Berlin *tondo* and the Florence *Melagrana*, or melodic as is in the exemplary instance of the *Magnificat*. In Botticelli's pictures, the sense of the historical reality of an event or person, fades or disappears; the image is removed from time and space; history is transfigured into myth or into a spectacle rather than into narrative. All appear like fables of

22 Creation of Eve. Vault of the Sistine Chapel.

the remote past and hence are timeless allusions to truths of a moral order; images that substitute for history a beauty that is Platonically identified with reality. Although Botticelli seems almost archaic in his means of expression, he foreshadows the a-historic universality of classical Renaissance art and, therefore, also anticipates Michelangelo. Yet his cadences were so contemplative and ecstatic that they found no echo in Buonarroti's tormented spirit.

Instead, Michelangelo might have found Luca Signorelli's *tondi* useful and, up to a point, congenial premises: both in specific compositional motifs, and in that pathos of high melancholy and potential drama with which the Cortonese painter set forth his detached, virtually mythic, visions. The compositional idea of the Virgin's figure rendered in *contrapposto* already exists in the *tondo* of the Madonna with two Prophets in the Uffizi. On stylistic grounds, it is thought that Signorelli painted it around 1490 for Lorenzo di Pierfrancesco de' Medici. Therefore, Buonarroti may easily have known it in 1495, on his return from his flight to Bologna, when it will be remembered that Lorenzo di Pierfrancesco had commissioned Michelangelo to make for him a statue of the Youthful St. John. Signorelli's picture may also be the source for the idea of the nudes in the background, especially since the nude youths in the *tondo* (who represent the shepherds who have been miraculously informed of the Saviour's birth) had already assumed the noble, classical forms of ancient heroes.

In another well-known *tondo* in the Uffizi, somewhat later in date, painted for the *Capitani di Parte Guelfa* (and therefore accessible to the public), we already find fully stated the overwhelming domination of the group of sacred personages in the foreground and the composition of large masses in tension and conflict. One could also cite the Ginori *tondo* in the Munich Alte Pinakothek (judged by Salmi [23] to be close to the Bichi altarpiece of 1498) for its mighty structure, its *contrapposto*, for its Madonna and its statuesque nude in the background (which is certainly a neophyte removing his sandals before immersion in the river—possible evidence favouring the baptismal interpretation of the nudes in the Doni *tondo*). An attempt has been made to reverse the order of these works by dating the Parte Guelfa *tondo* later and making the Signorelli dependent on the Doni *tondo*. This has been recently refuted by Mariani who observed the stylistic impossibility of dating Luca's Holy Family later than 1503:

" when the artist no longer expressed that vigor and conciseness of composition and, instead, everything reminds us of the earlier frescoes of the San Brizio Chapel in Orvieto. Similar is the bold structure of the bodies, the mastery of broad pictorial effects, and even the type of Virgin which has so much in common with the female figures in the more peaceful areas of these murals. Then there is the similar importance given to effects of perspective and foreshortening which assume an almost symbolic significance in, for example, the half-opened book. This is a reflection of the formal investigations of Piero della Francesca and of late Quattrocento Florence. All these elements bring us back to Orvieto—especially to the celebrated portrait of Dante there. Thus, Signorelli's picture seems certainly to antedate Michelangelo's tondo and is the closest Quattrocento prototype for the formation of Buonarroti's heroic style." [24]

If we accept the above analysis and apply it to other *tondi* by Signorelli, the alleged reversal of the relationship between the two works becomes even harder to maintain since it would involve upsetting much of the chronology of Signorelli's career. It is clear that in the Doni picture something absolutely new springs from the traditional motif of the *tondo*. This consists in representing a theme which goes beyond the limits of a specific subject and is set forth as a symbol and expression of the supreme fulfillment of human destiny in a Christianity which includes and exalts the perfection of Antiquity. Only in Michelangelo's great intellect could this have taken form.

The bright, harsh colour brings out the plastic organization of the masses and intones a slow, solemn rhythm which full and loud heightens the heroic pitch of everything. For this reason too, despite the intensity of its plastic values, this picture cannot be considered a mere translation of sculptural relief into painting. On the contrary, comparison with the slightly earlier Pitti and Taddei *tondi* reliefs (Florence and London) shows that only in this picture, and for the first time, the artist succeeded in stating an absolutely new thought with full expressive power. It is true, however, that already in the reliefs there exists a tension between the calmness of the round frame and the grandiose dynamism of the composition of the group. In fact, the Florentine marble already decisively states the harsh contrast between the vertical axis around which the Virgin accompanied by the two children painfully turn, on the one hand, and the circular boundary of the picture, on the other. But the mastery of the space, or rather the creation of it as an image of universal space, is fully established only in the painted tondo. Thus it seems advisable to date the Uffizi picture a few years later than the two marble *tondi*. It would then just precede, or be contemporary with, the cartoon for the Battle of Cascina. The structure of space and mass is subordinated to the figures which are the vehicles for expressing a universal and a-historic content signifying the regeneration of mankind through

⊲ 23 Head of Adam asleep, in the Creation of Eve. Vault of the Sistine Chapel.

173

24 Adam, in the Creation of Adam. Vault of
the Sistine Chapel.

Christianity. The idea of such a regeneration of faith was the fruit of a hard victory achieved
through a very harsh and continuous spiritual struggle. The heroic accent and dramatic tone
characteristic of the formal language is expressed with such poetic clarity that no illustrative
support was needed at all. In the power and hardness of its masses, the main group calls to
mind the impassioned labour of its maker to extract it, as it were, from a granite block. At
the same time, a sense of sad, unresolvable anxiety, destined to endure for eternity, is expressed
by the lines of force which, like a web, enmesh the block. The plastic articulations reflect the
same spirit: conflict and complexity, the play of opposing twists in the unearthly figures of the
Madonna and St. Joseph, and in the way the perfect plastic unity of the whole is at once
respected yet animated by the dynamic contrasts of movement into the midst of which the
Child is set. The very presence of the Infant Baptist, which some critics have regarded as a
trivial or even discordant element, has an exact and indispensable function in the dynamics
of the composition. He forms an asymmetrical accent which functions as a spring triggering
the movement of the upper parts of the main figures towards the left; this is a linking motif
that inexorably brings the eye back to the central group after it has reluctantly passed along
the semi-circle of nudes. The nudes serve not only to close off the background with a curve
essential to the conception of the picture's design as a globe, but also constitute a play of
movement consisting of elasticity and counterpoise, of an interrelation of correspondence and
contrast, which altogether form a highly effective foil to the closed tension of the group of
protagonists. Considering the four nudes which are entirely visible (the fifth on the right is half
hidden by his neighbour and is but a plastic reenforcement for the Infant Baptist), one notices
how they are composed with respect to each other—at once chiastic and symmetrical. The seated
figure at the outer left corresponds to the figure standing at the opposite end, and one sitting
just to the right of the group is paired with another standing just to the left (distribution in
chiasmus). Nevertheless, the outer figures with their crossed legs, cramped movement, and compact posture form a contrast with those between them who have their legs apart in a leisurely
pose and introduce a clear note of symmetry to the entire group (Figs. 8a, 8b and Plate IV).

174

26 God, in the Separation of the Earth from the Waters. Vault of the Sistine Chapel.

In this way, these secondary figures develop a complex dialectic relationship of opposites which basically repeats in minor key the fundamental contrast between the static unity of the single block and the tormented movement within it. By means of a continuous play of tension and release, the series of nudes thus reflects the static-dynamic dialectic of the large figures which from their central block generate in the world around them a contraction of force and distension of anxiety. Whether the nudes represent the Gentiles or neophytes preparing for the baptism, or whether (according to Carli's theory [25]) they are angels or genies spreading a cloth of honour behind the sacred personages (as, for instance, the *putti* do in the Madonna della Scala), they have cast aside the bucolic melancholy of Signorelli's youths and seem to exist in an atmosphere of anxious exaltation spreading a mood of joyous expectation in anticipation of the drama which accompanies the opening of a new era.

[16] G. Spini, *Michelangelo as a Citizen of Florence*, a lecture given at the Congress of Michelangelo Studies in Florence, June 1964.

[17] R. Salvini, "Notes on Botticelli. 3. Political and Philosophical Interpretations of Some Botticellian Allegories," in *Scritti di Storia dell'Arte in onore di Mario Salmi*, II, Rome, 1962, p. 315, esp. p. 325 ff.

[18] G. Poggi, "Michelangelo's Doni Madonna in the Uffizi," in *Jahresberichte des Kunsthistorischen Instituts in Florenz*, 1906-1907, p. 10, and in *Kunstchronik*, N. F. XVIII, 1907, p. 299, having discovered the arms of the Strozzi on the frame, supposed that the *tondo*, which is referred to by the Anonimo Magliabechiano, ed. Frey, p. 290, and by A. F. Doni (M. G. Bottari, *Raccolta di lettere sulla pittura, scultura ed architettura* etc., Milan, 1825, III, p. 347) in the house of Agnolo Doni in 1549, was done on the occasion of the marriage of Agnolo Doni to Maddalena Strozzi, which took place at the end of 1503 or the beginning of 1504. But see, in Vasari-Barocchi, *op. cit.*, p. 239 ff., a survey of critical opinions as to this date.

[19] S. J. Freedberg, *Painting of the High Renaissance in Rome and Florence*, Cambridge, Mass., 1961, I, p. 40, II, Fig. 23.

[20] J. Wilde, "Michelangelo and Leonardo," in *Burlington Magazine*, XCV, 1953, p. 65; V. Mariani, *Michelangelo Pittore*, Milan, 1964, p. 26.

[21] C. de Tolnay, *The Youth of Michelangelo*, Princeton, 1941, 2nd ed., 1947; C. de Tolnay, *Michelangelo*, Florence, 1951, p. 34 ff.

[22] V. Mariani, *Michelangelo*, Turin, 1942, p. 57, and new ed., Naples, 1964, p. 51.

[23] M. Salmi, *Luca Signorelli*, Novara, 1953, pp. 49, 55 ff. and *passim*.

[24] V. Mariani, *op. cit.*, Milan, 1964, p. 26.

[25] E. Carli, *Michelangelo*, Bergamo, 1942, p. 21; E. Carli, *Tutta la Pittura di Michelangelo*, Milan, 1951, p. 23.

The Battle of Cascina

In the Autumn of 1503, the Signoria had commissioned Leonardo da Vinci to execute a fresco in the *Sala del Gran Consiglio*, the great assembly hall built in 1495 by Cronaca to house the officials of the Savonarolian republic. The mural was to depict one of the great victories of the Florentine commune—the Battle of Anghiari fought on June 20th, 1440, in which the army of the republic defeated the mercenaries of the Duke of Milan captained by the famous Niccolò Piccinino. Vasari informs us that "while Leonardo da Vinci, (the) most excellent

◁ 25 God's head, in the Creation of Adam. Vault of the Sistine Chapel.

28 God, in the Creation of the Worlds. Vault
of the Sistine Chapel.

painter, was painting in the great council hall it happened (that)... Piero Soderini, who was
then *gonfaloniere*, alloted a part of the hall to Michelangelo because of his great regard for
him; this, then, caused him to compete with Leonardo on the opposite wall where he took
as his theme the War against Pisa," or to be more exact, the decisive skirmish of the war,
the Battle of Cascina, where, on July 30th, 1364, the Florentines defeated the Pisan army
commanded by John Hawkwood. Just at this time, the subject had great topical interest and
augured well for Florence, because during the Summer of 1504, although the end of the current
(and final) war with Pisa was not yet in sight, the prospects were so poor that the city council
resolved to approve Leonardo's utopian project for obtaining the long-hoped for outlet to the
sea by diverting the Arno away from the rival city.

The problem of the Battle of Cascina is, just as much as the Battle of Anghiari, full of
difficulties and is fraught with a series of philological questions which cannot be adequately
discussed here. The cartoons executed by the two masters were studied and admired by hordes
of artists, but were soon dismembered and lost. The last surviving fragment of Michelangelo's
cartoon was last reported in Turin in 1635, after which it disappeared without trace. Of
Leonardo's cartoon there is a fragment in Oxford, but it has been completely gone over by a
later hand. Leonardo began to carry out his composition into painting, but the artist, as is
well known, escogitated new methods of painting based on Pliny which did not entail the
rapidity and regularity essential to true fresco technique. From Bandello's precious eye-witness
account of the master at work in the Cenacolo, we know how impatient and sensitive he was
—sometimes working from dawn to dark, but at others rushing off to Santa Maria delle Grazie
at noon to make a brush stroke or two only to depart again. The practical results were so
disastrous that the work on the battle piece was abandoned at the summons of the French
governor in Milan, and eventually it was left to Vasari to erase the last traces. As for Michelangelo, it is certain that he began his cartoon in the Autumn of 1504. It is not known exactly
when it was finished. He himself said in a letter to Fattucci in 1524 that it was already done
in March 1505 when he obeyed Julius II's call to Rome where he received the commission for
the pope's tomb. According to Condivi, he finished it only after his sudden return to Florence
in April 1506. The biographer is probably right. When Michelangelo wrote to Fattucci in
1524 he was full of the bitterness and pent up indignation of a man who sees his labours ill
repaid and feels himself tossed about, a leaf in the wind, by the caprices of the mighty. It is
a splendid letter aiming to show his heavy financial losses and the trials he had to suffer in
keeping up with the pope's capricious wishes and having to defend himself from the charge of

◁ 27 God's head, in the Separation of the Earth
from the Waters. Vault of the Sistine Chapel.

30 God, in the Separation of the Light from the Darkness. Vault of the Sistine Chapel.

◁ 29 God's head, in the Creation of the Worlds. Vault of the Sistine Chapel.

being a swindler. Therefore, he was probably inadvertently led to say that the work begun twenty years before was already finished when it was, in fact, only near completion:

"You ask me in one of your letters how my affairs stand with Pope Julius. I tell you that if one could claim damages and recompensation *I would sooner make an estimate of 'credit-credit' than credit-debit*. Because when he sent for me in Florence, which I believe was in the second year of his pontificate, I had undertaken to do half of the Council Hall of Florence—that is to paint it; I already had 3000 ducats *and the cartoon* was already made as everyone in Florence knows; this, it seemed to me was (money) earned. *And ever since Pope Julius took me away from there I have not had anything of either or one or the other.*"

Moreover, it seems unlikely that in 1506 Michelangelo had begun to realize the fresco from the cartoon, as some have wished to infer from a letter of Soderini's to the Cardinal of Volterra who was in Bologna when the artist "was forced to go there with a leash at his neck to beg [the pope's] pardon" and where one reads further that he "has begun a scene for the populace which will be admirable." This general statement does not prove at all that Michelangelo had progressed beyond the cartoon.[26]

Of greater importance are the problems concerning the exact location of the two projected frescoes and their content. As for the latter, biographers and copyists are agreed in considering chiefly, in fact, almost exclusively, two themes which in neither case could have occupied the entire composition. In Leonardo's work this was the battle around the standard, and in Michelangelo's it was the soldiers surprised while bathing in the Arno. The latter episode took place the day before the battle which occurred on July 29th, 1364, when, Villani informs us, the Florentine army was encamped near Cascina:

" during the day, because of the excessive heat, three parts and more of the host... had taken off their armor; some were bathing in the Arno, some were airing their clothes in shady spots, and some were disarming, taking their rest in various ways. [Since] the brave knight, Messer Manno Donati... knew the great peril the camp was in... moved by fervent zeal he began to rouse the camp, saying ' We are lost.'..."

33 Head of "Ignudo". Vault of the Sistine Chapel.

32 "Ignudo". Vault of the Sistine Chapel.

The substance of the event, therefore, was a false alarm used as a pretext to call the troops and their captain (who was aged and suffering from a tertian fever) back to duty, and once the camp was fortified, to prepare for the victory on the following day. Clearly the representation of the two battles could not have been limited to only these two episodes. Michelangelo's did not even belong to the actual battle itself. And in fact, from the few sketches and studies which have come down to us by the two artists, it seems that we can deduce that other episodes in these battles must have been contained in these two compositions as well. We lack an important, in fact, indispensable element in the solution of this problem; namely, the size of the wall which each artist had at his disposal, and this matter is still under discussion. Vasari says that "this... caused him to compete with Leonardo on the opposite wall ("*l'altra facciata*"), it seems clear, therefore, that the two frescoes were destined to cover the two main walls of the hall (the smaller walls were known in Buonarroti's time as the "*testate*" or "*teste*," meaning heads). This is not contradicted by the expression "half of the hall" used by Michelangelo in the letter to Fattucci cited earlier. Recent criticism, worried by the enormous area that each painter would have had to cover with a single incident, has tended to favour the thesis that the two spaces to be frescoed were both on the same wall. This would have been the eastern side of the hall flanking the "most eminent residence" of the *Gonfaloniere* and the *Signoria* which, like the government bench in modern parliaments, occupied a place at its centre. On the opposite, or western wall, an altar for saying Mass occupied the central position.[27] Other factors contributing to our uncertainty arises from our ignorance of the dimensions and locations of the windows which were opened in various numbers on both walls after the hall's construction was finished. Recently a very careful and shrewd study of the problem, based on the literary sources, archival material, and the painted copies has been made by Isermeyer (who has kindly allowed me to see the proofs) which resolves the knotty problem in a very satisfactory way. The reader is referred to Isermeyer's article contained in *Festschrift für Ludwig Heydenreich;* I shall confine myself here to stating its conclusions.[28] Each artist was commissioned to paint one of the two long walls, not with a single subject but with three large pictures exactly as Vasari later did when he modernized the hall.

The frames must have been set high up, like a frieze, beneath the ceiling which at that time was considerably lower than the present one by Vasari in the *Salone dei Cinquecento*. The original idea of those giving the commission was that the two painters should first do the complete cartoon for all three phases of the subject. But at a certain point, as an agreement with Leonardo made on May 4th 1504 shows, the master was allowed to begin painting on the wall whenever he saw fit—before having finished the entire cartoon: " and it might be that it should suit the said Lionardo to begin to paint and color on the wall of the said hall that part that he had designed and delivered in the said cartoon; however when this comes to pass, the aforesaid *Magnificent Signori* are content to give him each month the salary that will be suitable for making the said painting... And so, the said Lionardo spending time on painting on the said wall, the said Magnificent Signori are content to extend and lengthen the above mentioned time, in which the said Lionardo has to supply the cartoon..." Evidently Leonardo took advantage of the permission granted him and as soon as he had finished the cartoon for the central episode, the skirmish around the standard, undertook to translate the cartoon into a painting, at first on the " experimental " panel (of which the Anonimo Magliabechiano speaks and which is reproduced in the engraving by Zacchia) and then, with unhappier results, on the wall itself. Long after Leonardo had begun his own work, Michelangelo received his commission. This was probably due to the fact that it came to be realized that

34 " Ignudo ". Vault of the Sistine Chapel.

35 Head of " Ignudo ". Vault of the Sistine Chapel.

183

the task of decorating the two walls was too great for one master. Michelangelo began his cartoon with the earlier episode in time, the false alarm, and brought this part to completion—a copy of which was later made by Aristotele da Sangallo. As for the second episode, the Pisans' Attack, probably Michelangelo managed to start it before abandoning the work forever, because Vasari also mentions the presence of mounted combatants who, moreover, are to be seen in some of the master's own sketches. However, all that is known of Leonardo's and Michelangelo's cartoons is based on copies which do not show fragments of the entire scenes but are complete and self-contained compositions to which others would have been added if the huge programme could have been carried out.

Some observations may be made on Michelangelo's lost cartoon on the basis of the Holkham Hall copy (**Fig. 9**) and his own drawn studies. Confronted with this new work by his older rival, it was only natural that Michelangelo should take up again the problem of his relationship to Leonardo's art which had already weighed upon him during the preparatory period for the Doni *tondo* when he had admired and examined with a critical eye the cartoon for the St. Anne. For the central composition for his wall, Leonardo, in Vasari's happy phrase, conceived of that " knot of horses which fought for a standard." The central accent, therefore, was placed on a tangle of forms overlapping and merging into one another with the greatest pictorial fluidity giving expression to that poetry of continuous transmutation, of the irresistible course of life through which the artist viewed all earthly objects and events. By comparison, Michelangelo's cartoons, as we know them from descriptions, drawings, and copies, appeared often to be episodic virtuoso pieces. One can read in any handbook that Buonarroti chose the surprise of the bathing soldiers as the subject for his composition because it allowed him to use his fa-

184   36 " Ignudo ".   Vault of the Sistine Chapel.

vourite theme, that of the heroic nude, or because it gave him the opportunity to make complex studies of anatomy and *contrapposto*. One of the leading students of Leonardo, Heydenreich, concludes his comparison of these two parallel works by saying that "in its content, Michelangelo's picture remains an anecdotal description though of overpowering presence and of admirable richness of motif, while Leonardo's surpasses the limits of a history picture attaining the character of a symbol." [29] More recently, Freedberg has argued that contrary to what one can say of Leonardo:

"For Michelangelo, however, the subject 'battle' was not a datum of human experience of which the essential nature required to be summarized in terms of art; it was rather a pretext from which he could extract the main matter of real interest to him, the human anatomy in action: the sculptor takes the given problem on his own terms. The conception of the theme in this exclusively anthropocentric sense implies a kind of ideality, but one narrower and more exclusive than Leonardo's, and less synthetic; instead of a meeting, as in Leonardo's case, between artist and subject there is a constraint of the subject to the artist's interests and will."

And further on:

"The alarm of the arriving enemy is more pretext than true motivation of the actions of the soldiery; they are moved by the artist, not by their situation. In spite of a development of classicizing structure in the figures, there is a disparity between bodily forms and their humanly expressive content which, by the Leonardesque paradigm, is not wholly classical." [30]

37 "Ignudo". Vault of the Sistine Chapel.

38 Head of "Ignudo". Vault of the Sistine Chapel.

40 Head of "Ignudo". Vault of the Sistine Chapel.

39 "Ignudo". Vault of the Sistine Chapel.

Although it is not our intention to differ completely with these opinions, Mariani's recent effort to attribute the same degree of universality to both cartoons seems very attractive. He maintains that if Leonardo expressed:

" the furious turbulence of humanity dragged by the demon of war into a struggle which, in the artist's vision, assumed the vaster significance of a quasi-cosmic drama ... Michelangelo articulated the language of plastic forms into the nude as a vigorous, imperative celebration of man's priority—developing his movements into a concatenation of feelings provoked by the vital drive of the action. [Thus] as different as the two great masters were when they approached the new century, they were aroused by the same idealistic urge which via their study of reality they succeeded in surpassing its infinitesimal character." [31]

This view, inspired by a knowledge of Michelangelo's entire work, probably does more justice to the qualities of the lost original than do Sangallo's copy and the studies for individual figures. Drawings like the famous ones in the British Museum for the central nude in the foreground, or the one in Casa Buonarroti (73 F) on which the first figure on the left of the cartoon was to be based, can only confirm the common interpretation of the work as academicism of the highest type (Fig. 52 ch. V). In other cases, however, comparison of the first sketch of an image to its embodiment in the cartoon results entirely to the advantage of the sketch, even when allowances for the hardness due to the copyist are made. Two pencil sketches for the second figure on the upper left are known. The one in the British Museum is Leonardesque, even

186

to the technical detail of the strokes following the curves of the forms to which Wilde has drawn attention. But the fluidity and ease sought for in this way are in conflict with the sharp *contrapposto* into which Michelangelo resolves the twist of the body (Fig. 47 ch. V). On a sheet in the Uffizi, there is a pencil sketch which looms like a giant amidst the smaller pen drawings around it. It still has something of Leonardo in the smoky density of the shading, but the vibrant intensity of the contours (which is already that of the Sistine nudes) has the potential plastic energy which easily seems to generate the subdued twist of the bust. We thus witness the emergence of a figure highly expressive of painful, tenacious effort overcoming inertia through a heroic, yet calm tension of the will (Fig. 34 ch. V). But in the final version, this figure differs sharply from the initial conception. It is an already manneristic, and also mannered, image of a man self-consciously twisting himself about to lace his breeches. Other battle sketches (to which especially Wilde has drawn attention in the above mentioned essay on the relations with Leonardo) are studies for sections of the cartoon which do not appear in Sangallo's copy and which probably never reached the stage of being incorporated into the cartoon. Among these, the equestrian scene in the British Museum is so strongly in the style of Leonardo that Clark takes it to be a copy of a sketch by da Vinci himself [32] (Fig. 35 ch. V). It seems more likely that this is an interpretation, to a great extent original, of themes from Leonardo. It is a drawing full of intense vitality, revealing that nascent search for a synthesis

41 " Ignudo ". Vault of the Sistine Chapel.

42 " Ignudo ". Vault of the Sistine Chapel.

between the unleashed and uncontrollable force of cosmic motion, characteristic of Leonardo, and the brusque effort to halt this outpouring by means of a dramatic play of contrasts. Although the da Vincian aspect still prevails, and despite a certain brevity of line, this rapid sketch already promises a vision which, though different, is as equally pervaded with cosmic overtones as Leonardo's. This prospect becomes surer in the drawing in the Ashmolean Museum at Oxford, in which, apart from the inspiration of Leonardo's motif of the " knot of horses," there is a search for sculptural definition of the forms and a closely packed series of *contrapposti* (Fig. 42 ch. V). But these prospects were neither fulfilled nor further developed in the detailed studies for individual figures and for the compositional scheme of the cartoon.

What took place in the elaborations for the Battle of Cascina was, in a sense, the opposite of what happened in the imaginative process leading up to the Doni *tondo* as we have tried to reconstruct it. While Michelangelo continued his meditations of the St. Anne cartoon in his graphic sketches and exercises, he advanced towards an ever more solid comprehension of the universal significance of Leonardo's example, at the same time increasingly asserting his own vigorous originality. It can truly be said that rarely has there been so fertile a meeting between two great artists who, though of profoundly different character, were each other's equal. In the case of the Battle of Cascina, no matter how far Leonardo may have gotten with his cartoon for the Battle of Anghiari and the studies for it, the impression made upon Michelangelo was very strong. Buonarroti must have seen at least some of these drawings during the inevitable contact with Leonardo while both were engaged on the same decorative project. So great was this impression on Michelangelo that some of his sketches either tend to imitate Leonardo's drawing technique or appear to be interpretative copies of his sketches. In turn, this overpowering experience did not fail to stimulate new ideas in the young man's imagination —directing him in his search for a means of charging the Leonardesque sense of universal transmutation with dramatic human accents. But at some point, this process of imaginative ripening underwent a sharp change of direction. What the psychological motivation may have been is, of course, hard to say. Perhaps the theme, which the artist himself had chosen, induced him to go beyond the limits of expressive necessity in his investigation of the formal problems of the nude in action. Once again he turned to the example of classical sculpture from which he made specific as well as general borrowings for various figures in the cartoon. This may also have been a sporadic burst whereby Michelangelo deliberately wanted to differentiate himself, in the most radical possible way, from the style of his rival whose greatness he acknowledged in spite of himself. In time, this must roughly coincide with the meeting between the two artists in Piazza Santa Trinita which the Anonimo Magliabechiano describes in an anecdote but which may very well have taken place. To a certain extent, the competitive spirit may have driven Michelangelo to resume the study of the Antique with greater intensity than ever before, and to make use of his earlier studies of classical motifs if, for no other reason, than "to show," as Varchi was to say, "how much having been in Rome had done for him." What the final result would have been, if, for one cause or another, the course of Michelangelo's development had not shifted, can be imagined from a ruined but very beautiful sketch in the Uffizi collection (Fig. 43 ch. V). The drawing's attribution has often been questioned, but its many variations from the Sangallo copy and its superlative quality confirm its authenticity as has recently been shown by Barocchi and Mariani.[33] I am convinced that this drawing occupies a clearly determinable, key position in the process of the cartoon's preparation. In time, it comes after the most Leonardesque of the rough sketches, but precedes the more finished, and more classicizing anatomical studies of the type represented by 73 F in the Casa Buonarroti and by 1887-5-2-116 in

43 "Ignudo". Vault of the Sistine Chapel.

44 Head of "Ignudo". Vault of the Sistine Chapel.

189

45 "Ignudo". Vault of the Sistine Chapel.

the British Museum (Figs. 52, 53 ch. V, and Plate XXIX). Among the few graphic documents which have come down to us, it shows more clearly than any other, Michelangelo's original use of what he had absorbed from Leonardo. It represents the pitch of his fully developed fantasy just before it was inverted towards the more classicizing manneristic style. The proof of this is, that it is precisely those figures echoing classical motifs which are absent from the sketch... The figure, so much admired by Vasari, of the old man pulling on his hose with great effort (a motif, which Hekler has shown was derived from an Hellenistic gem [34]) had not yet made its appearance. Similarly absent, is the nude running from the right with his clothes wrapped around an arm—a figure, Wilde believes, based upon one of the Dioscuri on the Quirinal·hill for which there is a preliminary study in the British Museum (No. 1887-5-2-117). Tolnay maintains that this drawing was, in turn, a translation of the static motif of the Apollo Belvedere into terms of movement.[35] Already present, on the left, is the figure of the man scaling the cliff. But his appearance is very different from that shown in the Leicester copy where the same figure, now on the extreme left, presupposes (as the corresponding portion of the Uffizi sketch does not) the 73 F drawing in Casa Buonarroti which, Wilde has pointed out, is unquestionable based upon a sarcophagus fragment in the Lateran Museum. Another figure, still absent, is that which appears on the upper left in the Sangallo copy. It repeats a motif drawn from one of the master's youthful works, the Battle of the Centaurs, which was also dependant upon classical models. He borrowed the posture of the bust from one figure and the gesture of covering the head with an arm from another. All the literal references to the Antique, therefore, appearing in the cartoon were inserted at some time after the Casa Buonarroti sketch was made. In a broader sense, the latter drawing precedes

46 Head of "Ignudo". Vault of the Sistine Chapel.

the shift towards the "academic." This is clearly seen by a comparison of the same iconographic motifs present in the sketch and in the copy of the cartoon, as well as in some other drawings. In the sketch, the torso of the nude seated on the rocks in the foreground turning towards the rear, is treated with much greater fluidity and with much more rapidity of movement than is the corresponding figure in the cartoon. This is the only figure preceded by the "finished" drawing in the British Museum which, by comparison, seems inhibited by the studious articulation of the individual parts seen in *contrapposto*. Similar observations can be made by a comparison of the two versions of the captain lacing his breeches, noting, however, that in this case the rough design is to be recognized again in a pencil sketch in the Uffizi which also precedes the overall plan. Here the motif is more Leonardesque and has not yet been included in the dynamics of the composition.

From this remarkable graphic document, it is possible to see how Michelangelo, in a certain phase of his meditation on the theme, came to conceive the composition in a profoundly different way than the definitive version which is reflected by the Holkham Hall copy. In the Florentine drawing, the chain of movement achieved by arranging pairs of figures in *contrapposto* and the construction of the individual figures themselves also conceived in terms of *contrapposto*, are of marginal importance and far removed from the absolute dominion they enjoy in the final version. In the composition, they serve as nodes anchoring the explosive motion of the figures to a space equivalent to their plastic capacity which has not yet become a stylistic expedient for dramatizing the nude. Even though the right side of the drawing shows the composition to be still in an incomplete state due to the fact that the artist's idea for it was not yet quite clear, undoubtedly the basic design consisted of a rapid swirling movement descending from the impressive figure with staring eyes to the seated nude about to leap

49 "Ignudo". Vault of the Sistine Chapel.

up from the bank. The vortex then moves upwards toward the right, in an oblique direction, beginning at the bottom with the figure scaling the cliff and going on to the rest of the compact group articulated, as it were, *in crescendo*. The movement is, of course, rendered more dramatic by the insertion of various contrapuntal elements, such as the vertical figure toward the lower center and the couple seen in *contrapposto* at the extreme left of the sheet. At the centre, the captain, already on his feet and lacing his breeches, is the pivot for the entire composition. Here the complex twist of the body is, in its incompleteness, considerably more effective than its counterpart in the final version which is excessively defined and belaboured. His movement partakes of the dynamics of the whole, while the isolated position of eminence removed from the main flow of action makes him a point of reference and firm anchor. The continuity characteristic of the compositional scheme is matched by the rapid flow of stroke, conferring upon the left portion of the drawing (the better defined and more finished section) a solidity and plastic continuity which, I believe, must be interpreted as a perfect translation into completely Michelangelesque terms of the dynamic pictorial unity exemplified by Leonardo. The result is that the masses, instead of being disposed in a stratified succession of planes (as in the cartoon), carve out the space for themselves—a space, although still indeterminate in the sketch, is already suggestive of the overpowering, convulsive sense of that in the Flood in the Sistine Chapel.

Reference to the Flood is a recurrent theme in the literature on the Battle of Cascina. This reference, however, acquires greater significance if applied, not, as is usually the case, to the cartoon reflected in the Leicester copy, but to the germinal concept contained in the Florentine sketch which was subsequently abandoned. Furthermore, I am certain, as will be shown later,

50 "Ignudo". Vault of the Sistine Chapel.

that the Flood is to be appreciated not solely, or principally, for the power of its statue-like groups which is the well known view of Berenson: above all, it is to be praised for its total composition and the renewal of its concept of space. But this unreal and apocalyptic vision of space as a projection of the pathos of the human images was already implicit in the drawing in question and would have been nobly developed in the final version of the work, had the master himself not, for the moment, cut short its already promising solution and given his researches a different orientation. In the phase of imaginative exploration, such as is represented by our sketch, the Flood, like the Battle of Cascina, shows, in fact, the utter, desperate anxiety involved in salvation.

It is of no importance that in Villani's account of the episode, the soldiers surprised while at ease rush with dramatic haste to their arms in hopes of repelling the attack and reversing the fate of the battle. That which inspired Michelangelo's imagination was the sudden, fearful effort made to escape from a force driven by absolute terror before which no alternative remains but flight. The sense of utter route is the psychological theme he has isolated from the many other possibilities that the episode chosen as the subject might have suggested. From several well known facts of his life, it is easy to find the seeds for this theme in Michelangelo's mind. However, this choice is not to be understood in an exclusively psychological sense. Probably it was rooted in the social position of the Buonarroti, who, although belonging to the rank of citizens, had for two generations been impoverished. They were always on the brink of complete economic ruin and risked losing even the modest privileges which their rank otherwise entitled them to in public affairs. This family situation, as well as the effect made by Savonarola's dire prophecies of frightful disasters in his early youth, must have made a profound impression on him since Condivi was able to report in 1553 that Michelangelo had " still in his mind the memory of the sound of his voice." At the recent Congress in Florence, Giorgio Spini made reference to this Savonarolian component in the motivation of Michelangelo's famous " escapes ": the flight to Bologna in 1494 following the account of Cardiere's

51 Head of "Ignudo". Vault of the Sistine Chapel.

52 "Ignudo". Vault of the Sistine Chapel.

dream, the flight from Rome in 1506, his abandonment of Florence during the siege of 1529, and his later retreat to the mountain refuge near Spoleto.[36] Walter Binni has shown that in Michelangelo's letters a poetic motive is frequently made of:

"that frightening and dramatic sense of hostile times looming as an oppressive incubus of impending, apocalyptic catastrophe... which provoked the recurring need for disordered flight in the face of overpowering elements beyond man's ability to cope with... A need for escape... which above all else must be viewed in the light of an upbringing dominated by Savonarolian prophecy colored by a certain factor of magic and superstition, and by a tragic vision of the world and its crises in which the merits of the *homo faber* were no longer sufficient. The harmonious values of Renaissance conception were succeeded by a profound sense of insecurity, a sense of the infinite human capacity to err." [37]

Binni has pointed out the theme of flight in the cartoon for the Battle of Cascina, the *sauve qui peut* in the face of an irresistible enemy. But this is to be seen even more clearly in the Uffizi drawing than in the copy of the cartoon. Here the theme is raised to the highest level, in spite of the fact that its poetry is not yet entirely defined. The stupendous group of figures in flight on the left almost seems to take wing—a motif which will be found infinitely multiplied and developed to the fullest on the gigantic wall of the Last Judgment.

This first great idea for the Battle, therefore, contains a universality that is not inferior to that which can be seen in Leonardo's sketches and the copies of his Battle of Anghiari. In this work too, Leonardo's poetry was born of contemplation of the irresistible forces of nature which,

194

as a scientist, he studied with such passion. The same spirit is to be found on a famous page of the so-called Treatise on Painting where, in his account of how to paint a battle, he creates an image of the universal transmutation of things by stressing with great poetic force the change of dust into blood and of the mingling of water, dust and air. Michelangelo's poetry flows from an equally universal feeling for the tragic solitude of man, whose inclination to sin exposes him to the most devastating punishments. But the artist was still reluctant to allow this feeling to be brought to its ultimate poetic solution in a finished work. Instead, he turned towards complex formal studies which, as far as can be judged from the copy of the cartoon and the series of his own separate sketches for it, never reached the same poetic heights. Nevertheless, it must be recognized that these studies were very useful in that they provided a vast repertoire of formal themes for the further development of his art, themes which he later used to enrich the expressive wealth of his language, beginning with the vault of the Sistine Chapel.

The Battle of Cascina, therefore, was not merely an academy piece of very high quality for its study of the nude, nor was it just a pretext for the technical excercises of a virtuoso. To Michelangelo's contemporaries, the piece represented a kind of manual of manneristic formal recipes, and to later generations it served as the authoritative dictionary for the language of the *Maniera*. But these are not the only reasons for its eminent position in the history of Cinquecento art. In the history of Michelangelo's own development, the famous cartoon must be viewed as a work of indispensable technical as well as expressive apprenticeship. As a result of the experiences endured while working on this commission, the artist must have acquired a clearer awareness of the relations existing between the search for means of expression and the investigation of form. In the working out of the Battle, the very emphasis on the poetic possibilities of the heroic nude (which he used as the repository for the most dramatic universal forces) had run aground on the rock of formal virtuosity, and on that rock much of the *virtus poëtica* of the master was wrecked. But once warned of this previously unsuspected

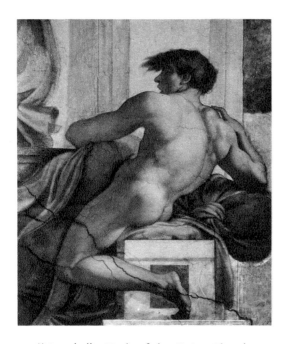

54 " Ignudo ". Vault of the Sistine Chapel.

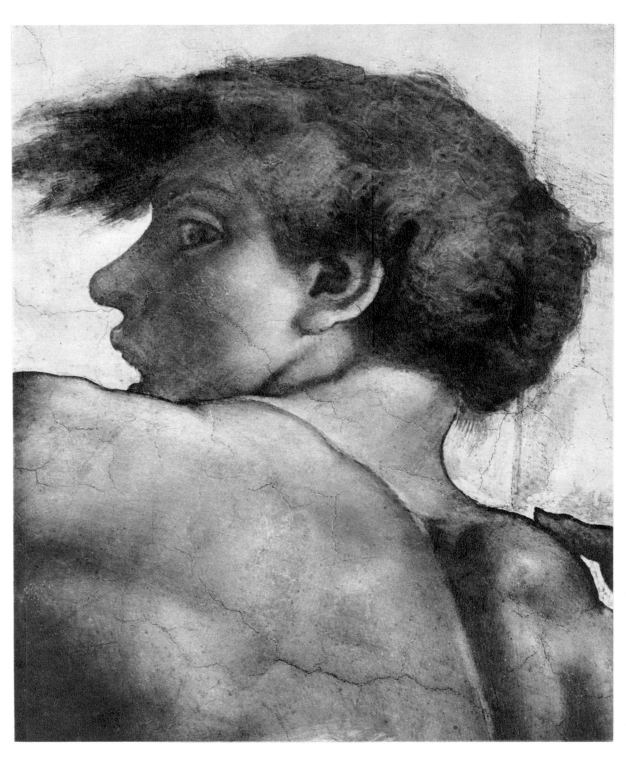

55 Head of " Ignudo ". Vault of the Sistine Chapel.

risk, it was easier for him to avoid similar situations in the future. For he had become aware of the limits beyond which insistence on technical elaboration no longer was suited to the requisites of expression.

[26] For a clear and complete review of the questions concerning the cartoon for the Battle and the various opinions of critics, see the rich commentary of Paola Barocchi on Vasari's *Life, op. cit.*, II, p. 248 ff.

[27] This is the thesis worked out and maintained by J. Wilde, " The Hall of the Great Council of Florence," in *Journal of the Warburg and Courtauld Institutes*, VII, 1944, p. 65; it is repeated by the same scholar in *Burlington Magazine, loc. cit.*, and frequently accepted, among others by Barocchi, *op. cit.*, II, p. 253, to whom reference is made for a survey of other opinions (p. 252 ff.).

[28] C. A. Isermeyer, " The Works by Leonardo and Michelangelo for the Great Hall of the Council in Florence," in *Studien zur Toskanischen Kunst. Festschrift für Ludwig Heinrich Heydenreich*, Munich, 1964, p. 83.

[29] L. H. Heydenreich, *Leonardo da Vinci*, Basel, 1954, p. 53.

[30] S. J. Freedberg, *op. cit.*, pp. 46, 47.

[31] V. Mariani, *Michelangelo Pittore, cit.*, p. 40 ff.

[32] K. Clark, *Catalogue of Drawings of Leonardo da Vinci at Windsor Castle*, Cambridge, 1935, I, p. xliii; and cf. K. Clark, *Leonardo da Vinci*, Cambridge, 1939, 2nd ed. 1952, p. 137.

[33] P. Barocchi, *Michelangelo e la sua Scuola. I Disegni di Casa Buonarroti e degli Uffizi*, I, Florence, 1962, p. 8 ff.; V. Mariani, *Michelangelo Pittore, op. cit.*, p. 40.

[34] A. Hekler, " Michelangelo and Antiquity," in *Wiener Jahrbuch für Kunstgeschichte*, VII, 1930, p. 204.

[35] J. Wilde, " A Study from the Antique by Michelangelo," in *Mitteilungen des kunsthistorischen Institutes in Florenz*, IV, 1932-34, p. 41, followed by L. Dussler, *Die Zeichnungen des Michelangelo*, Berlin, 1959, No. 56, but opposed by P. Barocchi, *op. cit.*, 1962, p. 13, and C. de Tolnay, *op. cit.*, 1951, p. 292 (and in other writings). Tolnay is right in accepting Wilde's reference of the Florentine drawing to a motif of classical sarcophagi.

[36] G. Spini, *loc. cit.*

[37] W. Binni, *Michelangelo Scrittore*, an address at the Congress of Michelangelo Studies in Florence, June, 1964.

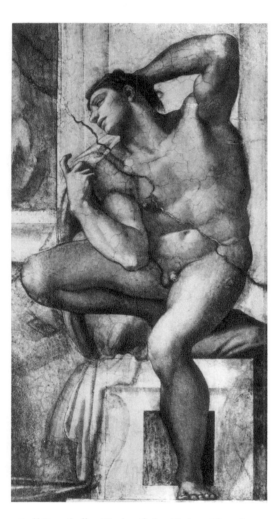

56 " Ignudo ". Vault of the Sistine Chapel.

57 Head of " Ignudo ". Vault of the Sistine Chapel.

59 Head of "Ignudo". Vault of the Sistine Chapel.

58 "Ignudo". Vault of the Sistine Chapel.

The Sistine vault

In the Spring of 1506, a brief from Pope Julius II summoned Michelangelo to Rome charging him to fresco the walls of Pope Sixtus' chapel. From a note in his diary, we know that on May 10th Michelangelo received an advance payment and began work. This consisted, not of painting, but of drawings and cartoons, because we know from other documents that on May 11th the scaffolding was being raised and the first rough layer of plaster was being applied to the wall. By the eve of Pentecost, we know from Paride de Grassis' journal that " *in altis cornicibus cappellae fabricabatur cum maximis pulveribus* " and that the workmen did not want to stop for the singing of vespers until the Pope had to send his emissaries twice with orders to cease. On July 27th a payment was made for the balance due for the scaffolding and the preparation of the ceiling. This indicates that by then the preparatory work had been finished and perhaps the artist began work on the vault between the end of July and the first days of August. The murals were completed in October 1512, since, as De Grassis notes, the chapel cleared of scaffolding was reopened on All Hallows' Eve (Figs. 10, 11).

The chronology of the various parts of the cycle between these two dates is a matter of some controversy. The sources establish that work began on the side over the entrance and proceded towards the altar. Condivi cites the Flood as the first fresco to be finished, which would correspond to the second scene from the entrance. It is equally certain that after approximately half of the vault had been done, there was a brief interruption while the scaffolding was taken down and set up again beneath the other half. The most uncertain point concerns the time when the first portion was unveiled, since there are two witnesses who contradict each other. If we follow De Grassis, this would be August 1511, for he records that on Assumption Day of that year the Pope entered the chapel during the services, "either to see the new pictures recently uncovered there, or because he was impelled by devotion;" but in two letters from Michelangelo to his father dated November 5 and 7, 1510, we read: "I am letting you know that the Pope owes me here 500 ducats which I've earned, and he owes me as much again for making the scaffolding and carrying out the rest of my work; and he has gone away without leaving any order for me whatever." It would follow from this that by the Fall of 1510, the artist had finished the first part and was waiting for funds in order to be able to put the scaffolding up under the other half, and continue the work. The interruption was not a short one, for in a letter of 1524 to Fattucci, in which Buonarroti summarizes his dealings with Julius II, one reads:

"just when the vault was almost finished, the Pope returned to Bologna. I went there twice for the money due me, I got nothing, and lost all that time until he returned to Rome. Back in Rome I set about making cartoons for this project, that is for the end walls and sides of the said Sisto's chapel, hoping to get the money in order to finish it. But I was never able to obtain anything..."

until finally, at the end, 2000 ducats were paid him.

Pope Julius' return to Rome was in January 1511, therefore this is the period when Michelangelo began preparing the cartoons for the lunettes at the tops of the narrow walls (*teste*) and along the side walls (*faccie*) of the chapel, while waiting for a payment on account that would

60 "Ignudo". Vault of the Sistine Chapel.

61 Head of "Ignudo". Vault of the Sistine Chapel.

63-66 Death of Joram, son of Ahab; Joab kills
Abner; Destruction of Baal's image; Death
of Urias. Vault of the Sistine Chapel.

◁ 62 "Ignudo". Vault of the Sistine Chapel.

enable him to put up the scaffolding for the second part of the vault. All this adds up to the following: from August 1508 to late Summer or early Autumn 1510, the artist did the first half of the vault, but waited until Assumption Day, August 15th 1511, before uncovering it because he had not received the payment due him and the advance for the scaffolding. Then he carried out all the rest, including the lunettes, between August 1511 and October 1512. Or, after having finished the first half of the work during the Summer or Autumn of 1510, he uncovered it and, after an interruption of several months, he did the second half of the vault between the Spring 1511 and August of the same year and uncovered this too. Then, at the very end, he would have painted the lunettes on the walls beneath, between September 1511 and October 1512. It is hard to decide which of the two hypotheses is likely to be closer to the truth. The first phase of the work, occupying two years, must, in any case, have involved more than half of the vault up to and including the Creation of Eve with the *ignudi*, sibyls and prophets beneath it.[38]

According to the original plan, which was certainly worked out in agreement with the Pope's wishes, the decoration was to have been confined to figures of the twelve Apostles in the lunettes, while the middle of the vault would have had, the artist informs Fattucci, "a kind of compartment full of the usual adornments." We have an idea of how this first project looked from two well known sketches in the British Museum (a third drawing in Detroit is of doubtful authenticity). It consisted, just as the artist wrote, of "the usual adornments." But here the fact is that these framed medaillions and rhombs are already firmly engaged to strong plastic units, namely the architectonic thrones of the Apostles. The idea of superimposing upon the vault a complex scheme of fictive architecture, a complex plastic armature in which the figures were to be inserted, is already present in this initial plan. However, Buonarroti continues, "having begun said work, it seemed to me that it would turn out poorly. [The Pope] asked me why [I thought so]. I told him it was because they too [the Apostles] were poor. At which he then gave me a new contract so that I could make it as I wanted and [do] what would satisfy me and that I should paint down to the scenes below." Another letter of almost the same date to Fattucci shows that the work had not yet got beyond the stage of planning: "after I had made some drawings, it seemed to me it would come out poorly, so he gave me a different allocation down to the scenes below, and that I could do as I wished in the vault."[39]

The fact that the Pope gave Michelangelo the fullest liberty with respect to choosing the subject is of great importance in the history of the relationship between artist and client; it marks an importance step forwards in the process of liberating the artist and raising the visual arts to the level of the liberal arts. It was not by any means the custom of the time for a patron, and a Pope at that, calmly to leave the choice of subject to the painter. That this could happen was undoubtedly due to the exceptional reputation the young Michelangelo had by then attained and to the faith placed, not only in his artistic abilities but also on his widespread knowledge and his qualities as a thinker. It is to these factors that modern criticism should give its attention too. It is out of the question that the artist resorted to theological texts for guidance or to the voice of some learned cleric or other. The invention of the general scheme and the decisive choices were however all left to him. Moreover, these inventions and choices had to be based on his own philosophical convictions viewed in relation to the possibility of their being translated pictorially. A basic unity of thought and form, of content and language had to preside over the invention of the great project. Acknowledging this, criticism is faced with a big problem. Admittedly, the Sistine ceiling as a work of art is only of value to us for its expressive content realized in its own clear, formal language. But can we avoid asking ourselves what message Michelangelo wanted to communicate to his contemporaries and to posterity in this work? Does formal analysis suffice to render an account of this masterpiece, or must we not rather make the effort to penetrate into the deeper intentions of its author and evaluate the form as the expression of a spiritual content that the artist had meditated deeply upon?

Unfortunately, neither Michelangelo himself, nor his biographers or the earliest commentators give us any information that would make our task easier. This leaves the way open to the most diverse interpretations. Putting aside the many unfounded or fantastic hypotheses that have accumulated over the centuries, it suffices to point out that recent criticism, in particular Hartt,[40] has been oriented toward theological schemes medieval in stamp, or else has leaned in the direction of Neoplatonism, so dear to the Florentine Quattrocento, with its *emanatio* and *remanatio*—or the divine origin of the soul and its ultimate return to God. The culmination of this type of interpretation is that of Tolnay.[41] Considered on their merits, both approaches appear equally tenable. In his youth, Michelangelo had been associated with Fra Gerolamo Savonarola's circle as well as with the Neoplatonic environment of the humanists who gravitated towards Lorenzo the Magnificent. However, if one considers Michelangelo's own frequent statements of his veneration for the Antique, the painful profundity of thought expressed in the *Rime*, and, in general, if one remembers the master's modernity of spirit in spite of his complex and contradictory personality—all this makes the Neoplatonic interpretation appear to be the more likely one. At this point, a note of caution seems advisable. Many allusions which to us seem obscure, or become clear only after lengthy investigations, very probably were immediately understood by the cultivated public of those times. The fact that Michelangelo left behind no hint concerning the content of his greatest work, either

ZACHERIAS

PLATE XV   The Prophet Zacharias.   Vault of the Sistine Chapel.

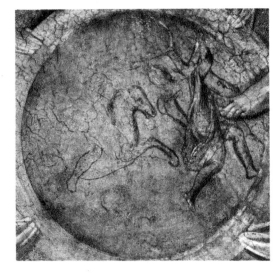

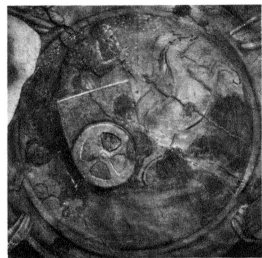

67-70 Massacre of the tribe of Ahab; Nathan and David; Death of Absalom; Elias on the chariot of fire. Vault of the Sistine Chapel.

directly or in the accounts of his biographers, may in part be due to the aloofness and abruptness characteristic of his temperament. In any case, it seems to me that this also signifies that in the master's pictorial conception the meaning of his thought must have been much clearer and notably simpler than his modern interpreters usually imagine. He must have thought that the philosophical significance of his pictures, in the luminous evidence of their form, would easily have revealed itself to any cultivated visitor to the sacred place. Michelangelo would have formulated a thought that was clear and simple in its greatness, organizing it in harmony with the distribution and articulation of the areas to be frescoed in the vault. The walls of the chapel already were painted with scenes from the Old and New Testaments arranged in typological parallels, as Tolnay observes, according to the story of humanity under the Law and in the reign of Grace. Once the idea of reinforcing the New Testament theme by adding the Apostles was abandoned, it was natural that the vault, or crown of the entire ensemble, should be devoted to the story of humanity prior to the Law. Thus, the scenes chosen were the Creation and the earliest events of human history down to the appearance of the first great legislator, Moses, with whose deeds the Old Testament stories on the walls below began. But on these walls there was for every event occurring under the ancient law, a corresponding one from the new evangelical era.

In order to be consistent with the general theme of the advent of Christianity as the culmination of the spiritual history of man, also the ceiling had to emphasize the connections between Creation and the *re*-creation of man and the world through Christianity, and between original sin and redemption. The powerful images of the great seers were used to serve this purpose. The Hebrew prophets foresaw redemption as well as the sibyls of Antiquity who, though imprisoned in the darkness of paganism, were also far-seeing spirits, divinely inspired with the as yet obscure presentiment of rebirth. By means of the Sibyls, Michelangelo was able to include the classical world in his summary of the history of human destiny. Thereby he at once enobled Antiquity in the Renaissance spirit and included the whole of mankind prior to and anticipating the advent of Christianity. While the Prophets and Sibyls represent the preparation for the new spiritual era, the series of Christ's ancestors refer to his reincarnation.

Tolnay observes that in the vault, the subjects are arranged in three tiers. In the highest zone at the center is set God's revelation and the first men. The next tier is occupied by those endowed with a spiritual power making them divine instruments: the Prophets and Sibyls. In the third and lowermost zone, are the ancestors of Christ who unconsciously were involved in his incarnation. It seems highly probable that behind all this was the neoplatonic idea that God's image is reflected in man in different degrees. Also neoplatonic is the triumph of beauty embodied in the stupendous *ignudi* which probably are connected in some way with the platonic conceptions of the Beautiful and of Eros. In any case, it seems pointless to make a laboured search for the exact meaning of all the details. Even the famous *ignudi* defy precise definition. They have been interpreted as symbols of sensual joy or despairing enslavement; Christian angels or Platonic Eroses have been discovered in them; they have been interpreted as Platonic symbols of beauty and love, and as incarnations of the far-seeing spirit of the Prophets and the Sibyls. And this is but a meager sampling of the explanations that have been proposed for these enigmatic figures. For those wishing to discover all the reasons behind the iconographical choices for the major and minor figures of the scheme, an endless field of erudite research is open among the theological and philosophical texts which would have been accessible to the artist or his learned councillors.[42]

In the last analysis, however, all this is irrelevant to the artistic expression even though it is related to the fundamental idea which the painter intended to bring out in the work as a whole. It seems less probable that a direct link exists between this and all the separate aspects of the content. During the refining of each detail, all the erudite notions which might at some point have caught the artist's mind would not have been simply "tacked on," as it were. Instead, once the lines of the general concept for the whole had been worked out, keeping the pictorial scheme always in mind, the artist let himself be guided in the details by a formal logic (in the sense of the logic of artistic forms) rather than by discursive reasoning. This is why so many of the iconographical features cannot be explained "iconologically," simply because they were born from considerations foreign to the subject matter, the prime function of which was that of a general frame and armature.

In conclusion, it is necessary to recognize the presence of a theological concept which operated as the basis of the work. This consists of the fateful story of man from his original innocence to his sin and punishment, from there to his reconciliation with God and then once more to sin, awaiting final redemption from the hands of Christ. This basic conception is not expressed with ecclesiastical rigor, but with sovereign, open-minded freedom, in a grandiose vision of history in which the religious and moral ideas of Judaism and Christianity coincide with the aesthetic-moral values of classical antiquity. Keeping in view this interpretation, summary though it be, and realizing that in Michelangelo's mind there was this coincidence of the Judeo-Christian moral values with the aesthetic values of the classical world (something that the master could find prefigured, more or less, in the entire civilization and culture of the Quattrocento Renaissance), we shall be in a position to understand the evident contrast, the dialectical stress that strikes the observer's first view of the Sistine vault: on the one hand, the dramatic excitement, the extraordinary animation of all the forms and all the images; and on the other, the elevated, serene beauty, the solid and, after all, tranquil order that holds the gigantic work together—the anticlassical and the classical aspects of the art of Michelangelo.

The development and ripening of this fundamental idea went step by step with the formation of the decorative structure of the ceiling—that is with its division. Michelangelo found the Sistine ceiling as a starry sky painted by Pier Matteo d'Amelia. In some quarters it is held that this conception of the barrel vault as the vault of heaven remained operative in the new decoration, so that it would be a sort of Biblical Olympus populated by seers and that the stories were conceived " as visions of the Prophets and Sibyls the results of which are extended to the *ignudi*." [43] The contrary, however, seems to have been the case. From the outset, the artist apparently discarded the idea of the sky image; since the sketches related to the first project had the enthroned Apostles set at the springing of the vault and the upper area was to have been treated as a coffered system with squares and medallions (probably adorned with simulated reliefs) according to an illusionistic conception which respected the actual nature of the vault. In fact, as soon as the artist had got permission from the Pope to paint what he pleased in the vault and to extend the decoration down to the region around the windows bordering on the Quattrocento frescoes, the ideas that had been maturing during his long meditation on the tomb of Pope Julius came forth again. As Justi has remarked, there was a projection, as it were, on the vault surface of the principal motifs contained in the project for the tomb. But there was nothing in the conception of the tomb either that suggested the idea of the heavens. Moreover, to attribute to the Prophets and Sibyls visions retrospective of Creation and man's earliest history, instead of seeing them as forecasts of the grim and glorious events of mankind, really seems most improbable. Even though Condivi,

71 The Prophet Zacharias. Vault of the Sistine Chapel.

72 Head of the Prophet Zacharias. Vault of the Sistine Chapel.

202

73 Accolytes of the Prophet Zacharias. Vault of
the Sistine Chapel.

in his conscientious description of the general decorative structure, saw opening above him
" in the middle ot the vault like an open sky from top to bottom," in reality, it is at most
a number of skies: one for each scene. Because, the perspective is not illusionistic, that is,
with one fixed point of view for the entire surface (as was the case in Baroque ceilings); each
compartment has its own perspective with its own point of view. Tolnay has justly remarked
that Michelangelo conceived his decoration " as a sort of high relief carved out of a monolith,"
organized in such a way that " the impression of balance remains complete even when the vault
is considered apart from the walls supporting it. It seems to bend under its own weight and
appears to be held up by the internal tension of its surface: an autonomous and sovereign
world." [44] Vasari had already seen clearly that " in the compartments he did not use foreshortened systems of perspective, nor is there a fixed point of view, but he proceeded by
adjusting the compartments to the figures rather than the figures to the compartments, it suf-
ficing to draw the nudes and the dressed figures with perfection..." Thus, Vasari attributed
the absence of illusionism to the artist's overriding interest in plastic form. Undoubtedly, this
signified an advance to have understood the metaphysical merit which the decoration assumed
by virtue of its divisions. Perhaps it is in order to accentuate the autonomy of the figures that
Tolnay seeks to interpret the scenes of the Creation and the Fall as vision. But there is no
need to go so far. The Sistine Ceiling loses nothing either in autonomy or detachment if the
same degree of " reality " is accorded to the scenes as to the images of the seers. Furthermore,
in the context of the entire ceiling, all the figures must be understood as simulated sculpture.
Even the colors (which originally were much stronger, richer, and more varied than is generally recognized today) allude to the tones of marble, bronze, or other metals. Taken by themselves, these figures acquired such a high degree of reality that they encroach upon the boundary between reality and fiction. Even the putti-caryatids of the thrones, which in their capacity
as ornaments of the chair ought to be seen as fictive sculpture, seem just as alive as the
large *ignudi*. The fact is that if the figures are understood in relation to the chapel architecture as fictive statues and reliefs, in their plasticity and relief the artist happily contradicts himself and thus involves reality as a whole. So, in the end it becomes futile to inquire if one
figure or another is supposed to be alive or carved. The vitality, after all, is to be identified   203

74 Head of an accolyte of the Prophet Joel. Vault of the Sistine Chapel.

with its sculptural quality. The same is true of the color if Freedberg is right: " even the painter's coloring of this design remains dependent on the sculptural conception of its forms: the dominant tone is that of the fictive stone of its architecture and of the population of nude figures that inhabit it, whose flesh is muted toward the tones of ancient marble. Where the figures are clothed, as are the Seers, their colors—though they become, as painting proceeds, increasingly fluid and harmonious—seem often like the varied patinas of old bronze; the draperies evoke the memory of metal." [45] However, a perfect illusion of reality is never sought after, nor is there any effort to counterfeit the stuff of which a figure, real or imagined, is made. In both the form and the color there is an *allusion* to the world of sculpture, rather than a simulation. Thus the images remain suspended in an ambiguous sphere bordering on reality and simulation, and on this is based the expression of that sense of autonomy and detachment, and that metaphysical aura which coincides with a conception which is allegorical and philosophical rather than historical.

As we know, the painter began on the side near the entrance, that is with those episodes which come latest in the legend's chronology. It seems certain from Condivi's testimony (" nor was he without troubles here for, after he had begun and had made the picture of the Flood, the work began to get mildy ") that the first scene to be painted was the Flood, that's to say, that which is the middle and largest episode of the first group of three (Figs. 13-17 and Plate VI). Moreover, memories of the Battle of Cascina are stronger here than elsewhere. In fact, as evidence of the artist's relative immaturity in the new task, it has recently been pointed out that a certain unsureness exists between the pictorial vision of the space and the effort to loosen the groups of figures; as well as the persistent, fundamentally sculptural nature of these groups for which the painter, due to the indeterminate character of the space, was left without any structure capable of giving unity to the volumes set in space. Therefore, the Flood remained " in a limbo between a painter's and a sculptor's aesthetic." [46] Actually, despite the persistence of

76 Head of the Delphic Sibyl. Vault of the Sistine Chapel.

that taste for separate pre-Manneristic formal solutions characteristic of the final version of the Battle, one must admit that a new vision already prevails in the Flood—by virtue moreover, of the revised notion of space. Michelangelo withdraws from the traditional perspective of the Quattrocento and from the special structure which he imposes upon the scene there arises the dominant impression of an endless, distraught space. The diminution of the figures by stages into the distance no longer corresponds to any system of measurement, but is attained by a 'rule of thumb' perspective. The impression of depth is obtained by means of a plastic play of the masses and by the imbalance of the composition due to the two asymmetric groups of mountains on the sides with the centre opening out on an empty stretch of water. It is in the figures that the composition frees itself through fits and starts from group to group, along a gigantic " S " spread out from the men entering the ark in the background to those savagely struggling for possession of the boat in the middle, on to the people who save themselves on the mountain on the right, and then continuing with a sudden swerve along the coastline to the crowd laboriously climbing up the rise on the left, to exhaust itself at last in the desperately outstretched branches of the dry tree beyond the stupendous group with the mother. This is, therefore, a dynamic space in which everything is accomplished by the plastic structure of the composition and by the movement of the volumes. It is a space which is not simply deputized, as it were, as the site for action, as is a theatre for a play, but is itself a drama in that it arises from and grows with the development of the figure composition itself. From this comes the feeling of desperate tragedy which inspires the whole composition as well as pervades the details such as the painful disengagement of one figure from another, the contortions of the powerful bodies, and in the intensely tragic bundling together of the limbs. Here Michelangelo deliberately opposes a plastic conception to the pictorial unity of the whole. The connection between plastic and pictorial vision is thus perfectly adjusted to the expressive requirements of this fresco, and, in this sense, it is impossible to speak of the artist's immaturity. The only weakness is, rather, of a pictorial nature. As has often been noted, Michelangelo was unable to check the effect from a distance because the scaffolding was in the way; there-

77 The Delphic Sibyl. Vault of the Sistine Chapel.

ERITHRAEA

78 The Erythraean Sibyl. Vault of the Sistine
Chapel.

fore, he painted many of the figures in too small a size for them to be clearly seen and appreciated from the ground. But apart from this, the nude everywhere already has the greatest possible plastic clarity. Even the tonality of the color runs from terracotta to a warm marble patina broken here and there by brighter accents which heighten the plastic neatness of the forms.

The Sacrifice of Noah is one of the least popular of the Sistine frescoes and has sometimes been criticized as a learned but empty academy piece (Fig. 18 and Plate VII). It can be conceded that Michelangelo's primary interest here was the solution of a formal problem. But the beautiful series of plastic forms which is emphasized by a larger variety of tints turns out so logically and gives way to a rhythm at once lively and solemn filling the picture of this ritual act with a profound seriousness and moral grandeur. The spacial composition here is kept rigorously in perspective and is clarified by the angle at which the altar is turned. The figures, however, are arranged along an oval course which is completely closed in upon itself thereby nullifying their perspective relation to the observer and assuming the appearance of a classic relief with its usual sense of lofty detachment. The allusion to Antiquity, far from rendering the subject generic, strengthens its splendid isolation as well as the vivid sense of its symbolic significance. The scene as a whole possesses so much power that the major restorations made after Michelangelo's death by Domenico Carnevali (who was responsible for repainting the youth and the woman in the left foreground) do not immediately interfere with its effect.

Also in the Drunkenness of Noah, it seems that the artist's chief, if not exclusive, concern was to resolve the compositional problem in terms of a classical relief (Fig. 12 and Plate V). It is just by means of the great simplicity of this compositional scheme that Michelangelo was able to charge

206

◁ 79 Head of the Erythraean Sibyl. Vault of the Sistine Chapel.

the scene with an exact moral significance. The surprising feature of the nude sons deriding their father's nudity has sometimes been explained by the idea current in Antiquity that nudity was only blameworthy and improper for the aged but not for the young (E. Wind). But there is another interpretation that seems more convincing, namely, that the sons are not scandalized by their father's nakedness but by his drunkenness, which is interpreted Platonically as a symbol of the imprisonment of the soul in the body (Tolnay) or, more simply, in the light of common sense, if we wish to avoid this kind of symbology which overloads the scene with multiple meanings, it is to be understood as a darkening of the spirit.[47] Such an interpretation seems to have a clearer relation to the formal aspects of the picture consisting of a space seen in a perspective determined by the foreshortening of the ceiling, and the vigorous, explosive elasticity of the figures of the sons which is contrasted with the father's heavy, inert body inspired by ancient representations of rivers. This figure anticipates the Adam in the Creation of Man, save that in the latter it acquired a full elastic tension. It was only after having painted these three episodes that the artist proceded with the three Prophets, the two Sibyls, and the eight *ignudi* of the first zone. He had by then developed sufficient maturity and skill that these figures differ much less among themselves and from those he did later than the first scenes do from the subsequent ones. Yet, the Delphic Sibyl, which recalls the Doni

80 The Prophet Isaias. Vault of the Sistine Chapel.

81 Head of the Prophet Isaias. Vault of the Sistine Chapel.

DELPHICA

PLATE XVI   The Delphic Sibyl.   Vault of the Sistine Chapel.

84 The Prophet Ezekiel. Vault of the Sistine Chapel.

82-83 Hand of the Prophet Ezekiel; head of an accolyte of the Prophet Ezekiel. Vault of the Sistine Chapel.

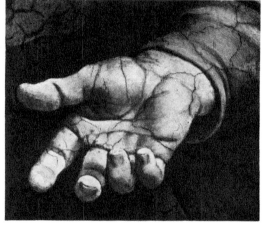

Madonna, is isolated even from the throne containing her; she encloses herself in a sphere which is clearly indicated by the curvature of the forms in the *contrapposto* composition. As in the Sacrifice of Noah, the figures are isolated from their perspective environment and are enclosed in an oval scheme (Figs. 76, 77 and Plate XVI). The self-sufficiency of the figure is thus exalted in the earliest of these Sibyls; she is removed from the earthly perspective space and is, instead, freed by virtue of the composition in a spherical space of universal character. It would be superfluous here to dwell once more upon the perfect unity shown in this figure between the compact, plastic realization of the form and the continuity of the vital tension which pervades it, or the imposing beauty of the face seen frontally in its lofty almost emblematic, geometric regularity. Possibly, the Delphic Sibyl was executed after the Prophet Zacharias (Figs. 71-73 and Plate XV), undoubtedly a grandiose figure, but one for which Bertini has expressed reservations with which we concur; he " suspects that too much of the figure's suggestiveness comes from the dimensions, that is, from the incompletely spiritualized material." [48] If we accept the criterion of a constant increase in quality, then the Joel too (Figs. 74, 75) must have been done before the Delphic Sibyl; it is a solemn figure, not without typological reminiscences of Signorelli, and it may be, as Freedberg would have it, that it shows a greater power and virility than the figure of the Sibyl. Yet it is equally true that " its scanning the unrolled scroll alludes to the practical intelligence of an experienced technician rather than to prophetic inspiration " (Bertini), lending credibility to its tentative identification as a portrait of Bramante, just as the Zacharias is thought to be the likeness of Julius II.[49]

Only the Isaiah is comparable in quality to the Delphic Sibyl. Criticism has long seen him as the personification of the birth of prophetic inspiration. This is to be seen not only in the illustrative feature of the book which the Prophet closes while turning to listen to a voice, or take cognizance of a vision almost as if obeying its call, but also in the figure's formal structure in which once again a spherical enclosure isolates it from the earthly space of the throne. With this spherical space is allied a strong, continuous, rotary movement further emphasized by the various patches of bright color which intensify its isolation. Also the Erythraean Sibyl, which is given such dynamic unity by the right arm hanging down in a curve reminiscent of that in Michelangelo's marble David, is a superb figure who, moved by a sudden and mysterious impulse, is entirely absorbed in the act of looking for the prophetic text in the great book.

As for the *ignudi*, it is generally agreed that there is a certain difference between the first four around the Drunkenness of Noah and the others surrounding the Sacrifice. The first figures are already constructed with a perfect sculptural amplitude in view of fulfilling their function of supporting the bronze-like medallions, and are arranged symmetrically in pairs curving forward or stretched backward (one of the latter was almost completely destroyed, except for the head and feet, by an explosion during the eighteenth century); they are also very beautiful for the potential energy concentrated there (Figs. 31-35 and Plate V). The other four are more complex in posture and structure, freer in symmetry, and now appear animated by an inspired vitality, so much so that there has been long and inconclusive argument as to whether they reflect the sacred fury of the seers or comment upon the content of the scene (which actually

85　The Cuman Sibyl. Vault of the Sistine Chapel.

86　Head of the Cuman Sibyl. Vault of the Sistine Chapel.

210

87 The Persian Sibyl. Vault of the Sistine Chapel.

is of a ritualistic rather than exciting nature) they frame or the bronze-like medallion which they strive to hold in balance for the spectator's attention (Figs. 36-41 and Plate VII).

To this first phase of work also belong the two spandrels containing Judith and David who represent two of the four miraculous «salvations of Israel», clearly anticipating Christian salvation, which complete the biblical cycle. The first picture has a more directly narrative composition largely inspired by Signorellian motifs; while in the second, the artist without negating the pictorial unity of the space, plastically isolates the group of David and Goliath in a pyramidal scheme which tends to remove them from the context of Quattrocentesque perspective space (Figs. 97, 98 and Plate XVII).

Starting from the area containing the Creation of Eve and, preceding it, the Fall and Expulsion, the proportions of the figures increase, the composition becomes more sculptural, and the optic connection with the spectator becomes established with much greater certainty. Here, therefore, one is faced with the second phase of work after the scaffolding for the first section had been demolished and Michelangelo had the opportunity to examine from a distance what he had painted thus far. The importance of this change should not be underestimated. The compositional rhythm broadens into a stronger beat focusing upon the objective circumstance of the subjects themselves: to the narration of the solitary doings of the first men and thereby requiring fewer figures. There is a happy coincidence between the stylistic

88 Head of the Persian Sibyl. Vault of the Sistine Chapel.

90 The Prophet Daniel. Vault of the Sistine
Chapel.

DANIEL

89 Putti-caryatids supporting the Prophet Daniel's
throne. Vault of the Sistine Chapel.

212

exigencies imposed by the master and illustrative necessity which Michelangelo knew how to
exploit to the maximum. The Fall and Expulsion perfectly correspond to both sides of the
same composition (Figs. 19-21 and Plate VIII). It is, however, a dynamic balance full of
tension because the *contrapposto* twist and plastic structure of the blocks of figures in the Fall
dissolve, so to speak, in the broader and freer development of the bodies in the scene of the Expulsion. The two episodes, therefore, are thus brought into a tight formal relationship and the
tragedy does not appear suddenly in the Expulsion but is already potentially present in the left
portion of the composition; from this comes the pregnant sense of doom that pervades the entire
picture. In the Expulsion Michelangelo returns to pay tribute to Masaccio, both in the foreshortening of the angel and in the elastic step of the two figures. Yet he organizes the two nudes
differently, giving the relief more roundness and the contours a more powerful sinuousness;
thereby the drama becomes more portentous and the sorrow more harrowing. By comparison, the
despair of Masaccio's Adam and Eve has a note of heroic acceptance of their fate. Freedberg
has observed that the background in the Expulsion has less the effect of a plane in relief than
that in the Fall, so that the figures are now treated as fully three-dimensional.[50] For this
reason he maintains, probably correctly, that the scene was executed later than the Creation
of Eve in which the feeling for composition in relief is stronger (Figs. 22, 23 and Plate IX).
There is also the memory of Masaccio in the Creation of Eve. One might say that when a
lofty simplicity was called for, Michelangelo felt the need of referring to the master who had
inspired him at the beginning of his career with the sense of high moral austerity. The figure
of the Creator is enclosed in stony drapery like the Apostles of the Tribute Money. Here,
obviously, Michelangelo resorted to his youthful drawing made from the Carmine frescoes
(Fig. 4 ch. V), but Masaccio's heroic humanity is now raised to a pitch of superhuman " *terri-*

91 The Prophet Jeremias. Vault of the Sistine Chapel.

bilità." The tremendous power of the solid, energetic mass of this image is so irresistible that Eve seems truly to be called forth by the magnetic force of the Creator's gesture. Firm and solid as a gravitational field, the composition appears in a quadrilateral structure; it expresses in simple, imperative language the feeling of dramatic destiny inherent in the very act of creation.

In the Creation of Adam the composition is based on the *contrapposto* relationship between the bare earth on which the man is lying and the wind-filled cloak enveloping the Lord (Figs. 24, 25 and Plates X, XIV). No other artist has realized so poetically as Michelangelo the terrible solemnity of the freshly created world and the idea of God as vital energy. The illustrative conception is basically so simple here that the happy idea of having the vital spark jump at the contact of the fingers, as if across an electrical contact, takes on the highest significance.

In the dialectical contrast between the spherical structure of the cloak harboring the restless troop of angels and the extended line of His body, the image of the Lord assumes human grandeur and at the same time conveys the feeling of the instantaneousness of the flight. The balanced composition of Adam's robust body gives the figure of the first man a superb beauty, the harmony of the form coinciding with the harmony of the slow and hesitant movement of his limbs.

92 Torso of the Prophet Jeremias. Vault of the Sistine Chapel.

93 The Libyan Sibyl. Vault of the Sistine Chapel.

Prior to Michelangelo, the Creation of Man had been conceived as the work of a skillful artisan, or as the miraculous act of a divine but anthropomorphic being. In some Romanesque reliefs, for example, the Creator models, like a sculptor, the first man from the mud of the earth, *ex limo terrae*, or infuses the spirit into the already formed Adam by placing an omnipotent hand on his head—not very differently from the way in which a saint performs the miracle of healing a cripple or a blind man. It is only Michelangelo who represents the Creator, without bringing his anthropomorphic appearance into question, as a primeval force of nature. Of course, this image of the living God was not intended as an abstract conception. Yet Michelangelo did not intend merely to represent a robust old man, but also meant to embody in this terrible and revered image the idea of pure and absolute power. Precisely by virtue of the fact that this unquestionably and completely human figure evokes the idea of an irresistible force, the incident of the Creation is not only a symbolic allusion, as was usual, but is a true, actual representation. Thus, in the next picture, the lightning flight of the powerful old man is performed by the eloquent gesture of the two outstretched hands, by means of which he sets the cosmos in order, separating the earth from the waters (Figs. 26, 27 and Plate XI). In the next composition He creates the sun and moon (Figs. 28, 29 and Plate XII), spreading out both arms with an imperious gesture, and on the left he needs only to extend a hand with open fingers, as he flies over the land, for the vegetation to grow. The complexity of the *contrapposto* in the scene's composition and the marvelous foreshortening of the figure on the left brings dynamically before our eyes the impression of the infinity of space. These final scenes of the Creation (or, the first ones in the chronological order of events)—and especially the last episode of the separation of light from darkness (Fig. 30 and Plate XIII)

—have often aroused criticism. For example, Bertini says, in connection with the last scene:

" Despite the originality of the foreshortening and the very daring suggestion of mass in motion, a certain abstractness remains in the representation which does not come only from the formal facility...Involuntarily one is reminded of Dante's phrase, ' *a l'alta fantasia qui mancò possa* ' (here ability fell short of the lofty imagination, Par. 33). The progressive elevation and transfiguration of the material could not be matched by a simultaneously gradual spirituali-

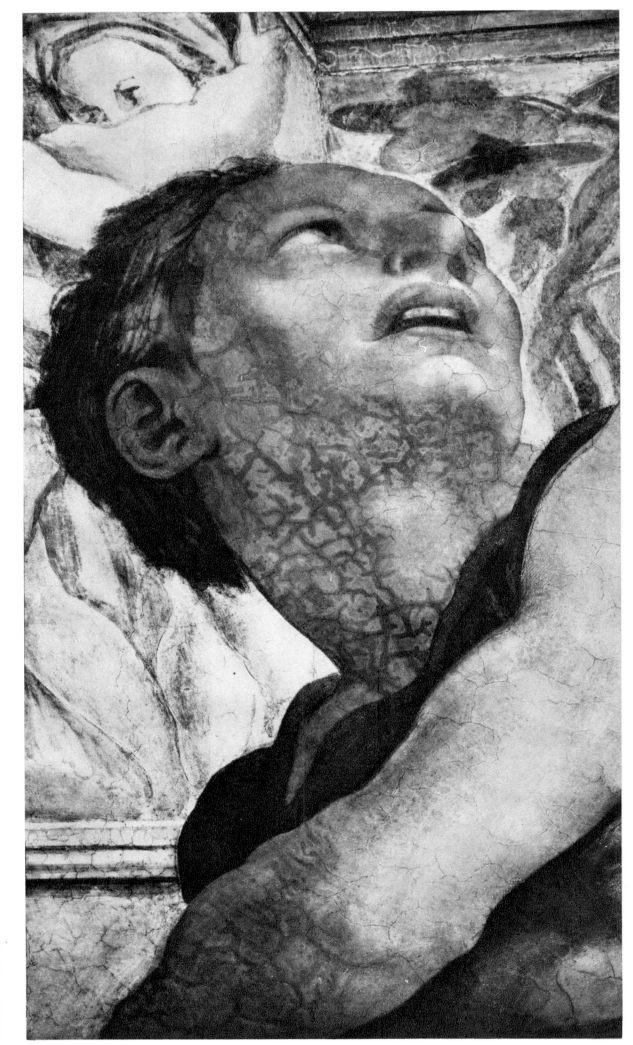

96 Head of the Prophet Jonah. Vault of the Sistine Chapel.

95 The Prophet Jonah. Vault of the Sistine Chapel.

97 David and Goliath. Vault of the Sistine Chapel.

zation of the poetic tone which, however capable of renewal, suffered from an overly rarefied atmosphere for the senses." [51]

The favourable evaluation of an Anglo-Saxon scholar does not share the Italian taste for the supreme concreteness of the image which stems from the thought and criticism of the great De Sanctis. In fact Freedberg expresses himself thus:

" But the last panel of the Ceiling, the first act of Genesis, is conceived by Michelangelo in an image still more remote, and at the same time intellectually and spiritually yet more profound. The beginning of creation is reduced to an essence which reaches as if above and through the first bald sentence of the Bible to a vision of a hardly apprehensible God, seemingly newly self-formed from the surrounding chaos. He turns in chaos—and again a cosmic simile suggests itself, unknown to Michelangelo, of a solar body in its process of formation—seeking to shape the dark reaches where there is as yet no form and no direction. The idea of this image, so exalted and so nearly abstract, is given us in a corresponding language, so general as to border on abstraction." [52]

Clearly, the opposite views of these two critics (apart from the fact that they start from two different conceptions of criticism, one being based on the sharpest kind of distinction between thought and image, the other on a tendency, if not to confuse these two terms, at least to have one shade into the other) can be reconciled by considering the individual scenes in the larger context of the entire work. Let us concede, with Bertini, that the idea here is not thoroughly clarified in the image. But if we consider these last scenes as a rhythmic ensemble, then the poetic image emerges with limpid clarity. This consists of the vivid and immediate impression of the enormous expenditure of force that the act of creation called for on the part of the Creator, a huge effort on the superhuman and cosmic scale which dramatically illumines the birth of the world and of man. The anthropomorphic element animating Michelangelo's conception of the creation of the world is derived from the Bible account, but is certainly reinforced by experience of the Antique. It is just this Biblical and classical anthropomorphism that makes it possible for the artist to attain the powerful, incredible drama of his representation. The Creator is not only a gigantic man endowed with insuperable prowess. Through the energy of the plastic and dynamic structure of God's figure, the Creator is also conceived as the primeval force of nature: he seems really to incarnate the irresistible, primeval forces

216

PLATE XVII Judith and Holophernes. Vault of the Sistine Chapel.

of the cosmos. In this way, Michelangelo (certainly without realizing it conceptually) created a new myth of the Creation by spontaneous divination which, anticipating science, seems to embody a modern secular concept of the formation of the universe.

After the picture of the Creation of Eve, the *ignudi* increase in size and grandeur; their actions and violent bodily strain go ever further beyond the modest illustrative requirements of their poses. They are disposed in couples which become increasingly antithetical almost as if beating out an alternating rhythm. Around the Creation of Eve, two are arranged in a restrained, ordered posture; while in the opposite pair, the power stored up in them seems to burst forth and overcome their powerful bodies turning them round to an almost frontal position where the movement is arrested in the stunned wide-open eyes (Figs. 42-48 and Plate IX). Around the Creator Separating the Waters, the two *ignudi* on the same side as those last mentioned, again restrain their power in block-like masses seen in fixed profile while the opposite pair have the most dramatic movements which avoid the profile by turning the chest or the back (Figs. 49-55 and Plate XI). Finally, around the last picture, the rhythm accelerates because here the contrast is no longer between the two members of each pair (Figs. 56-62 and Plate XIII). One of the *ignudi* sets the *contrapposto* of his plastic structure into a classic harmony seen in the purest of profile views that foreshadows the mighty figures of the New Sacristy. His partner, however, painfully adjusts the weight on his shoulders in a more dramatic *contrapposto* achieved by his turning to a frontal view which, in its three-dimensional character, required powerful fore-shortenings. On the other side, the two figures repeat in front view and profile the postures of the other pair setting up a relationship between the two couples that is at once a direct clash and a crossed, or chiastic, correspondence. Beyond what has already been said of those in the zone painted first, this is the way the function of these figures is defined within the terms of the entire arrangement. These images alone now suggest a convincing interpretation: they are the incarnation of the prodigious energies released by the acts of creation and the dramatic incidents in the lives of the first human beings. Within the series of their *contrapposto* movements, they seem to intone a rhythm for the great events shown by the episodes and provide a symphonic accompaniment for these happenings. But the artist has placed emphasis not only on the dynamic release of these forces, but also on the purest, most luminous beauty. Therefore, one spontaneously sees in these mysterious figures the incarnation and symbol of the dramatic significance of creation, and at the same time an allusion to the Neoplatonic idea that creation is beauty and beauty creation. That the same pictures can be given diverse, or rather multivalent significances is due to the fact that these are not by any means ingeniously thought-up allegories; what we see before us are images that give poetical form to complex

98 Judith and Holofernes. Vault of the Sistine Chapel.

states of mind fed by wide knowledge and by philosophical meditations.[53] In the Sibyls and Prophets, too, we see, between the first and the second phase of the execution, a crescendo of dimension and grandeur, of power and profundity.

Freedberg observes that "the ancient crone *Cumea* (Figs. 85, 86), almost clumsy in her heavy-muscled compact shape, contrasts with the grave, suave, slow-unfolding power of the grander *Persica* (Figs. 87, 88). The mood and movement of *Ezekiel* are almost blunt by comparison with that of *Daniel*, whose state of spiritual possession electrifies the swift and subtle action of his form" (Figs. 82, 84, 90). The Libyan Sibyl is the seer that "most of all resembles, in kind of ideal meaning, one of the aspects of the Ignudi... Among the Seers she is the one who most intends an archetypal beauty of physical presence and of formal attitude... She may be regarded as a development in a special sense of one of the ideas, that of formal beauty, which elsewhere in the Ceiling... had appeared only as one among the complex of elements that composed the synthetic whole of a mature classical image." The Jonah (Figs. 95, 96), however, represents another culmination—that of the intensity of expressive action: "more terribly inspired and possessed than any other figure on the Ceiling, Jonah moves with a vehemence that strains the limits of a classical constraint. His energy of action, like his implication of content, expands beyond the bounds of his allotted place." The Jeremiah (Figs. 91, 92), finally, the prophet of lamentations, attains a third archetype, that of concentration of thought: his "great, compact, gathered form expresses the dimension of his thought and its concentration." [54]

We have quoted these remarks because they seem to us to contribute toward clarifying the variations of tone that lend so much richness to the context of the Sistine ceiling and attest to the continual tension of Michelangelo's thought and imagination in a marvelous crescendo of profundity and expressive intensity. But more generally, as for the Prophets and Sibyls, attention should be drawn to their structure consisting of masses in *contrapposto* held in tension. The plastic value of the bodies is reinforced by the weight of the drapery, which is further obtained by means of the density of the colors, and by the powerful simplicity of the folds. A further element contributing to the power of these images is their relationship to the marble-like thrones on which they are seated. In fact, the perspective of the thrones is precisely drawn, each from its own point of view, but the effect of depth is deliberately limited: there is only enough to allow the plastic potential of the figure to distinguish itself. The space is even made deliberately insufficient so as better to set off the contrast between the vital and painful effort of these divinely possessed beings. The spirit of the great seers radiates a secret energy embodied not only by the children moving about in various ways behind them (Figs. 73, 74, 83), but is also reflected in the *putti* decorating the thrones (Fig. 89). It is interesting to see how these figures, even though they were primarily conceived as plastic ornament, never-

99 Hanging of Haman. Vault of the Sistine Chapel.

100 Brazen Serpent. Vault of the Sistine Chapel.

theless have an intense and full dramatic vitality which makes them approach the threshold separating fiction from reality.

A different tribe inhabits the triangular spaces between the Prophets and Sibyls and the lunettes around the windows below. These are the ancestors of Christ, or generations of Israel. They are twilight images distributed in family groups seated or, rather, encamped, on the ground—weary, pensive and exhausted, as if pausing for a rest during the interminable march of a centuries-long voyage in search of repose (Figs. 101-130 and Plate XVIII). Probably, the artist here wanted to compare the long wait for salvation with an endless march of generation upon generation. Wrongly, these figures are much less admired than others in the Sistine Chapel. At first glance, they may not seem very Michelangelesque, but actually they are among the greatest creations of the master's imagination. Their composition is no less complex than that of the seers and the *ignudi*. The *contrapposto* of the masses in the single figures and their interlocked relationship have their usual effectiveness. Only the tension is looser and the whole rhythm has become slower. The plastic modelling of the volumes and the rendering of the draperies has once more the simple grandeur reminiscent of Masaccio. Compared to the super-human images in the central zone of the vault, Michelangelo here at the edges of the grandiose decoration gave form to a sadder, more modest type of man, who, untouched by the rays of divinity, leads an obtuse and shadowy existence, hardly aware of the Saviour's coming.

To achieve this new expressive inflection, he resorted to Masaccio's archaic austerity on the one hand, while on the other, he so amplified the register of his formal inventions that just these less famous figures became one of the prime sources for a flock of Mannerists. To mistake the reduction of the formal tension of the figures with a slackening in the artist's powers of imagination, as has been frequently maintained (and most recently by Freedberg[55]), seems unjust. The reverse is true despite certain statements concerning his weariness made by the master himself in a letter of July 1512 which is cited by Freedberg: "I'm more tired than any man ever was, sick and with very great effort; yet, I've the patience to come to the desired goal." Of course, a careful analysis might disclose some instances of weariness, but on the whole, the exasperated simplification of the forms which has been interpreted as a

219

flight into indeterminate abstraction does not appear to have been a pretext for evasion. Rather, from the compressed energy of the reduced and often flattened forms comes a new *terribilità* which is manifested in the heavy silence of the imagery—the glance sometimes hidden, sometimes astonished with a hallucinatory fixedness, or with a fierce, surly gleam in the eyes.

From the expressive point of view, therefore, the Generations of Israel are at the opposite pole from the final episodes of the Creation and the two spandrels with the Brazen Serpent and the Hanging of Haman (Figs. 99, 100) with which the work in the decoration of the vault proper was concluded, and before the master climbed down to start painting the lunettes. This opinion has been put forward on several occasions because in the Brazen Serpent and the Hanging of Haman (which faintly echo the impression made by the discovery of the Laocoön in 1506), Michelangelo seems to have reached a peak of exaltation in the dynamic structure of the composition which convulses the space and breaks all the bonds of classical decorum. At this point, it would have been impossible to go further save by altering the scale of the figures—making them gigantic—as he later did in the Last Judgment.

Although this chronological explanation is psychologically plausible since it would consider the lunettes as a relaxation following extreme tension, we prefer a different interpretation taking account of other factors. For one, there is the enormous complexity of Michelangelo's

mind and imagination with the potential antinomies inherent in every example of his art. Then there is the fact that the master did not consider art to be a purely formal exercise, but rather as an effective vehicle to communicate a thought or a moral conviction. He set great importance on the subject as a complex of ideological and ethical material, the formulation of which he assumed full responsibility for, nothwithstanding any collaboration he might have had. In short, he had to devise a gradation of intensity going from the middle to the edges of the great system which, from the very start, had to be in accord with the themes of the various representations.

The Creation and man's first acts, comprising the very origins of mankind's spiritual history as told in the Old Testament, demanded the highest formal tension and the most supreme evocation of power. This is as true of the *ignudi* (who are used to comment upon the events in a kind of ritual dance) as of all the other figures alluding to the anxious wait for Redemption, such as the precursors of Israel's Salvation and the images of the great seers. But in the ancestors, who were only Christ's precursors in a physical sense, the waiting for His coming is confused and obscure. Once the argument was so fixed in the artist's own mind, its rendering required more reserved accents, a subdued drama turned in upon itself. These tones of expression were well within the grasp of the artist's imagination which spanned a very broad arc. Similar elements were already visible in the obscure agitation of the St. Matthew in his stony shell, and later in the exhausted and resigned figures of the Slaves and in the meditat-

103 Forefathers of Christ: Ozias. Vault of the Sistine Chapel.

ing Dawn of the Medici Chapel. It is true, of course, that the substance of artistic expression resides in the form and that even the most elaborate and intellectually most valid content is still neutral and open to every possibility, until it has been translated into form. Examples of artists are not lacking for whom the subject was but a pretext; in such cases, the form arises from lyrical situations which are determined quite independently of the subject prescribed. But in Michelangelo's case, who was able to impose his own conception of the work on he Pope, the subject and its ideological meanings were from the outset included in the imaginative elaboration of the image. Taking this into account does not mean ignoring that art is a language and language is form; what it does do is to put us in a better position for understanding the significance of the form in all its density and for penetrating the artist's spirituality.

[38] For the exact dating and chronology of the frescoes of the vault, see P. Barocchi's commentary on Vasari's *Life*, II, p. 411 ff.
[39] E. Wind, " Sante Pagnini and Michelangelo," in *Gazette des Beaux-Arts*, 1944, II, p. 211, and " Typology in the Sistine Ceiling," in *Art Bulletin*, XXXIII, 1951, p. 41, has proposed interpreting the pattern of the first project as allusive to the tree of Jesse, while F. Hartt, " Lignum Vitae in medio Paradisi," in *Art Bulletin*, XXXII, 1950, pp. 115, 181, has seen an allusion to the tree of life. In either event, the definitive program that was actually carried out would have brought to full development the idea contained in germ in the first sketch. Thus, the liberty that the pontiff left the artist would have related (as H. von Einem points out, *Michelangelo*, Stuttgart, 1959, p. 55) not to the theme of the representation, but only to its formal embodiment. It seems clear to me, however, from the testimony of Michelangelo himself, that the pope, yielding to the insistence of the master, gave up the initial idea of the Apostles, allowing the artist to paint the ceiling as he saw fit.
[40] Cf. the preceding note and: E. Wind, "The Ark of Noah: A Study in the Symbolism of Michelangelo " in *Measure*, I, 1950, p. 411.

Forefathers of Christ: Ezechias. Vault of the Sistine Chapel.

[41] C. de Tolnay, *Michelangelo. II: The Sistine Ceiling*, Princeton, 1945, 2nd ed., 1949; *Werk und Weltbild des Michelangelo*, Zurich, 1949, *op. cit.*, 1951; "Michelangelo" in *Enciclopedia Universale dell'Arte*, IX, Venice and Rome, 1963.

[42] A rich sampling of interpretations and hypotheses on the literary sources of the various figures of the Sistine is in P. Barocchi's commentary on Vasari, *op. cit.*, II, p. 462 to 622.

[43] C. de Tolnay, in *Enciclopedia, loc. cit.*

[44] C. de Tolnay, *op. cit.*, 1945, p. 16 ff. Later, *op. cit.*, 1951, p. 41, Tolnay states: "Michelangelo finally finds the plastic symbol that gives an explanation, on the artistic plane, of the curvature of the entire framework, interpreting it as a consequence of the weight of the Prophets and the Sibyls, whose heavy masses draw the gigantic structure down.

105 Heads of the family of Ezechias. Vault of the Sistine Chapel.

Thus his system expresses the forces latent in the vault, which appears as curved by its own weight and supported by its own tension."

[45] S. J. Freedberg, *op. cit.*, p. 93.
[46] S. J. Freedberg, *op. cit.*, p. 98.
[47] E. Wind, 1950, *op. cit.* and 1951, *op. cit.*; C. de Tolnay, *op. cit.*, 1945, p. 25 ff.
[48] A. Bertini, *op. cit.*, p. 81.
[49] Freedberg, *op. cit.*, p. 100; Bertini, *op. cit.*, p. 81.
[50] Freedberg, *op. cit.*, p. 103.
[51] Bertini, *op. cit.*, p. 74.
[52] Freedberg, *op. cit.*, p. 105.
[53] For the greatly varying interpretations, cf. Vasari-Barocchi, *op. cit.*, II, p. 499 ff.
[54] Freedberg, *op. cit.*, p. 107 ff.
[55] Freedberg, *op. cit.*, p. 111 ff.

The Last Judgment

If, therefore, the changing accent of the figures of Christ's forbears can be plausibly explained as a gradation of the vital and dramatic tension among the various parts of the ceiling according to a higher expressive unity for the whole scheme, rather than as a change in the artist's mood of inspiration during the course of time, this does not mean that the poetic note of gloom, withdrawn sadness, and existential melancholy were not destined to play a major rôle and that they did not develop and deepen in the ever more complex modulations of the works directly following the completion of the Sistine ceiling. In the Moses, conceived and in large part executed in 1513 (although it was finished much later), Michelangelo again resumed the drama and terrible vitality of the Sistine prophets in terms of marble. Already in the Bound Slave in the Louvre there is a tendency towards a supreme effort: the complexity of the *contrapposto*, infinitely rich in internal contrasts and in the external play of converging and diverging planes, presages not the triumph of a superhuman force of liberation but an energy falling back on itself in impotence. Thus, this figure anticipates its companion, the Exhausted Slave, where the forms are elongated into a marked torsion which becomes ever more accentuated but is never resolved in a chiastic play of *contrapposti* which dissolves itself in the flow of the contours expressing a torment gradually extinguishing itself in weakening langour. These figures, however, radiate an Apollonian beauty that was not achieved in the sorrowing figures of Christ's forbears; these young giants stretch out their limbs in a free space that they themselves have delimited. Nevertheless they live in an atmosphere of restrained meditation and melancholy. Much the same could be said of the Slaves in Florence which were done shortly afterwards. The master was working on the Medici tombs, which were executed between about 1520 and 1534, down to the time of his conception of the Last Judgment. Here the theme of Time standing still in the face of Death is realized in a dramatic cosmic elegy—in a vision of life which is appropriately sorrowful and darkly melancholic. Contrary to all appearances, this vision further developed the fundamental theme of Christ's forbears with a new cosmic breadth and energy.

This cursory glance at some of Michelangelo's most important works dating from the interval between the completion of the ceiling and the conception of the Last Judgment, cannot

106 Forefathers of Christ: Roboam. Vault of the Sistine Chapel.

107 Forefathers of Christ: Asa. Vault of the Sistine Chapel.

108 Forefathers of Christ: Salmon. Vault of the Sistine Chapel.

224 109 Forefathers of Christ: Jesse. Vault of the Sistine Chapel.

pretend to describe the inexhaustible richness of content and expression in these masterpieces. Our intention here is merely to designate, in the summary and imprecise character of a sketch, the inner vicissitudes which led the artist from the final figures in the vault to those very different images on the gigantic wall. The distance between these two great pictorial projects seems almost insurmountably great if measured from the images of the Creation (intensely and sorrowfully dramatic, yet animated by a vitality that is, after all, joyous) to the gloomy despair of the Last Judgment. But a consistent thread, tenuous though it may seem, is to be found if we start from the existential melancholy of the groups and figures of the Generations of Israel at the springing of the vault. Always against a closed background of painful meditation, there is from these figures onwards a gradual recovery of beauty and vitality with an ever greater openness which is to be seen in the monumental rhythm of form as well as in the ideological complexity of the great plastic cycles, moving towards visions of cosmic vitality in the Slaves of the ever changing, but never realized plan for Pope Julius' monument and in the Medici tombs.

111 Forefathers of Christ: Aminadab. Vault of the Sistine Chapel.

110 Aminadab. Vault of the Sistine Chapel.

Thus, the Last Judgment can be seen not as an unexpected and almost unmotivated explosion, except for the secret places of its creator's genius, but rather as the full maturity and culminating expression of a long process of development. But certainly this extraordinary ignition of the imagination found fuel in the troubled and often painful experiences Michelangelo had endured in those years in both his private and public affairs. His letters tell of his fear for the lives of members of his family during the plague of 1527 and we know that in every event of this kind Michelangelo's mind re-echoed with the obscure threats of Divine punishment heard in his youth from Savonarola. The year afterwards, Buonarroto, his beloved brother died. He had been Michelangelo's sole support in his efforts to relieve the economic difficulties of the unfortunate family whom he supported at great personal sacrifice. In 1530, the artist lost his father whom despite his honest but mediocre stature, he respected as an eminent example of the moral solidity of the " good old days." Then he was troubled by the varying fortunes of the Florentine republic. Despite years and even decades of voluntary exile, Michelangelo never ceased to feel himself a citizen of Florence. In 1512 Soderini's government fell; it had largely corresponded to Buonarroti's ideals of republican moderatism. The government fell beneath the pressure of Spanish troops who sacked Prato and reinstalled Medici rule.

Michelangelo in Rome sympathized with the Florentine exiles and, while seeking to deny that he had spoken ill of the new regime, did not conceal his indignation at the " case of Prato: if the stones could speak, they would have spoken," and advised his family against putting themselves on the side of the victors.[56] Later on, he was to work for Leo X and Clement VII, while his family once more had access to public office and his brother Buonarroto was among those nominated as priors of the guilds. But even in this period of relative calm, there were outbursts of ill humour on the part of the artist and expressions of profound pessimism based on religious grounds. And when in 1527, as a consequence of the sack of Rome, Medici rule fell and the final neo-Savonarolan Republic was born, Michelangelo enthusiastically supported the new regime and put himself at its service.

When the government of the new-born Republic, in turn, passed from the oligarchy into the hands of the *popolani*, Michelangelo assumed the responsibility of supervising the city's de-

112 Forefathers of Christ: Booz and Obed. Vault of the Sistine Chapel.

fenses. All this could not have occurred without dramatic internal conflict in the artist's mind. For, as Spini has recently shown, in these affairs he was aware of the ambiguous aspects of the oligarchical factions, to which he really belonged, and yet he had to collaborate with the *popolani* even though he knew that they opposed his own party (all this doubtlessly contributed to his famous flight in September 1529). Nevertheless the *popolani* were the only group determined and brave enough to defend Florentine liberty down to the last man.[57] Then came the betrayal of Baglioni, foreseen by Michelangelo, but in vain; the surrender of the city to the imperial army; the fears of the victors' revenge; the pardon by Clement VII—and the return to papal servitude. All these events must have deeply troubled the sensitive and apprehensive mind of Michelangelo. Still more important, as Giorgio Spini notes, is that Michelangelo understood all the turns of fate and misfortune which befell his city as a divine punishment. His ears still rang with Savonarola's fierce prophesies:

" One must be patient and commend oneself to God and mend one's ways; because these adversities come from nothing else, and most especially, from pride and ingratitude; and never were there more ungrateful or prouder people than the Florentines. Thus if judgment comes, it is well deserved."

Certain drafts for religious poems of these years, cited by Spini, show how the artist viewed the trouble and uncertain times as a sign of Divine wrath and was increasingly led to see

113 Forefathers of Christ: Abia. Vault of the Sistine Chapel.

114 Forefathers of Christ: Joatham and Achaz.
Vault of the Sistine Chapel.

115 Achaz. Vault of the Sistine Chapel.

227

116 Forefathers of Christ: Abiud and Eliacim.
Vault of the Sistine Chapel.

228 117 Eliacim. Vault of the Sistine Chapel.

the world around him as in the toils of sin from which man's liberation could in the end come not from feeble " works," but only from Grace. Among the spiritual premises and antecedents for the tremendous sense of the inexorable which emerges from the fresco of the Last Judgment may well be this obsessive idea of divine punishment and the tormented search for salvation in the mystical ascent to God, or, God's descent into his soul:

> " despoil me of myself and with thy shield
> with the stone and your arms true and sweet
> protect me from myself, for all other things
> are as if not, taken away in brief.
>
> While from the body, the soul is not removed,
> Lord, the entire universe can do nothing.
> Maker, Ruler, Monarch of every thing,
> little room is left in me for Thee."

The first commission for the Last Judgment goes back to the Fall of 1533, while the artist in Florence was engaged in completing the Medici tombs in S. Lorenzo. It is probable that Pope Clement spoke to him of it for the first time on September 22. On that day, a " memorandum " of Michelangelo tells us, " I went to Santo Miniato al Tedesco to speak to Pope Clement, who was going to Nice; and on that day frate Sebastiano del Piombo lent me a horse of his." The intention of the pontiff seems to have been not only to have the Last Judgment painted on the altar wall, but also the Fall of the Rebel Angels on the entrance wall; it is true that we have no evidence beyond the detailed account by Vasari, unsupported by Condivi and the other sources. At any rate, the artist, who had gone to Rome in October, must soon have started thinking about the theme of the Last Judgment and making the first sketches for it, although the pressure was still on him to go ahead with Pope Julius' tomb first.

Condivi is explicit on this point: " Michelangelo, who knew the obligation he was under to the Duke of Urbino, avoided this thing (namely the commission to paint the Last Judgment) as long as he could; but since he could not liberate himself, he drew the matter out; and pretending to be busy on the cartoon, *as he was to some extent*, he secretly worked on those statues that were to go on the tomb." By February of the following year a *tavolato* had been put up in the chapel; in all probability, this was a provisional scaffolding for studying and preparing the wall. Michelangelo went again—for the last time in his life—to Florence to superintend the work on the Laurentian Library, and had hardly returned to Rome in Sep-

118-119 Forefathers of Christ: Achim; Eliud. Vault of the Sistine Chapel.

120 Forefathers of Christ: Eliazar and Nathan. Vault of the Sistine Chapel.

tember, when the pope died. The next pope, Paul III Farnese, confirmed the artist's commission, and Michelangelo, although reluctant, as usual, went to work and completed it, without any interruption of importance, between 1536 and 1541. It appears from Paul's brief dated November 1536 that Michelangelo had already sketched designs and made cartoons during the reign of Clement VII; the brief notes that Pope Clement had invited the artist to paint the fresco in conformity with the design of the cartoons he himself had executed.[58]

The conception for the great mural therefore goes back to the years between 1534 and 1536, but, obviously, during the six laborious years spent on the scaffoldings in the chapel, the separate figures took on a more precise shape in the artist's imagination than they had reached in the cartoon. We can see from the few drawings for the composition as a whole that have come down to us that the artist had at first tried to respect the *status quo* of the wall, leaving on it both his own lunettes and the simulated panel in fresco by Perugino over the altar. That in the end he broke all bounds, even destroying work from his own brush, has a profound reason. This can be summed up in the new conception of space that has been best defined, perhaps, by Max Dvořák: "space is no longer something definite and corporeal as in previous Florentine and Roman art, and still less a merely optical impression as with the Venetians but is only a principle opposed to the volume, something that eludes measurement and any artistic structuring and that can be recognized exclusively by means of the volumetric extension of the masses and their movement."[59] A space of this kind cannot endure any limit; and we may take as the hallmark of the different spatial conception dividing the Last Judgment from the vault frescoes the contrast with the solid set of frames enclosing the figures on

230   121 Forefathers of Christ: Azor and Sadoc. Vault of the Sistine Chapel.

the ceiling and the fact that there is no frame at all around the Last Judgment, the only boundaries of which are the corners of the wall (Fig. 131). Doing away with the frame was an absolute pictorial necessity, derived directly from the fact that, here as in the vault, Michelangelo abandoned perspective construction from a single point of view, in the Quattrocento tradition. On the vault there were a series of distinct pictures, each having its own point of view, while the end wall was to be covered entirely with a single scene. The presence of a frame would have brought with it the need for a synthetic view seen from a definite distance and from a fixed point. But this would have given rise to an illusionist effect, suggesting a space, necessarily limited, no matter how vast, to be seen through a window, no matter how large. This would have destroyed the effect of dynamic opening-up of the void, the creation of an endless and convulsed space that was obviously the artist's intention. What was necessary, on the contrary, was that open unlimited spatiality should inundate the entire immense wall, abandoning any attempt at measurable relationships with the figures. The figures, in isolated

122-123 Forefathers of Christ: Jechonias and Salathiel. Vault of the Sistine Chapel.

plastic groups, swim in desperate solitude amidst the tremendous infinity of space. Around Christ, there is a maelstrom of figures comprising the celestial court. The Damned fall in torrents on the right as the Blessed ascend on the left. All are seen against a background consisting of a spacial abyss evoked by the bold and complex foreshortening of the figures as if they were caught in a cosmic cataclysm. A truly cosmic force breaks forth from the Judge's gesture of terrible finality which seems to unhinge the universe. Despite the mural's far from brilliant state of preservation and the many heavy repaintings imposed by the petty moralistic scruples of the Counter Reformation, the impact of the hundreds of figures remains virtually intact (Figs. 132-176 and Plates XIX-XXII). We may consider them as isolated images and groups, as Wölfflin did when he wrote that " here Michelangelo abandons himself to the Promethean joy of summoning to reality all the possibilities of movement, situation, foreshortening, and composition of the nude human figure." And we might even go so far as to say, with Voss, that " they all have in common the elastic self-sufficiency that abstracts from any spacial ambience, contenting itself with the fullness of movement within the scope of the volume," " The specific inclination of the great painter and sculptor," Voss continues, " is expressed precisely in this: that he transfers to the composition of a fresco inhabited by a multiplicity of figures

231

124 Forefathers of Christ: Manasses and Amon.
     Vault of the Sistine Chapel.

a vision that is born, basically, from the sculpture of statues." [60] Wölfflin's approach sees Michelangelo too much as the father of the Baroque, while Voss considers him too strictly from the point of view of Mannerism. It was just this isolation of the sculptural mass that appealed to the Mannerists, above all else, in the Sistine Last Judgment. However, in Michelangelo's profoundly unified vision, the plastic isolation of form was placed in a deliberately dialectical relation to the concept of a limitless space. Therefore, we must take into equal consideration both the plastic thesis and the spacial antithesis if we truly wish to understand the grandiose synthesis of the Last Judgment.

But as we proceed in our attempt to give a coherent interpretation of this bewildering masterpiece, we cannot avoid the question that we tried to answer before in reference to the figures of the ceiling: as to whether the artist intended to add a further figurative and anagogical significance to the composition's obvious literal meaning. Tolnay, on the basis of the Apollonian aspect of Christ's face, found a symbol of the sun in the figure of the Judge (in Antiquity, Apollo was identified with the Sun, while Christianity identified Christ with the Sun; thereby transforming the *Sol invictus* into the *Sol justitiae*). Around Him " move the constellations of spirits, magically attracted and at once repelled in the infinite space of the universe," and finally embodying in the stormy composition of the Last Judgment a heliocentric conception of the universe " that corresponds strangely to that of his contemporary, Copernicus." Similarly, " in his conception of unlimited space he anticipates the infinite universe of Giordano Bruno." This conception, however, is said to have interested the artist not " in the scientific sense, as would have been the case with Leonardo, but inasmuch as it makes manifest the destiny of humanity." Actually, " man, son of the earth and molded of its slime, is governed by new

125 Forefathers of Christ: Josaphat and Joram.
     Vault of the Sistine Chapel.

127-128 Forefathers of Christ: David; Solomon. Vault of the Chapel.

◁ 126 Josaphat. Vault of the Sistine Chapel.

forces after death. A new era begins for him: freed from matter and weight, he comes under the dominion of the sun. It is the end of the Telluric realm and the coming of the Uranian realm, the pure and direct revelation of cosmic fatality." [61]

Although this hermeneutic hypothesis is based, in Tolnay's reasoning, which we have summarized very briefly, on vast erudition and a great number of references to Pythagorean myths and other astral fables of Antiquity, it is hardly convincing. For one thing, it would require us to suppose that Michelangelo had a wealth of well-organized mythological-philosophical notions, of which not the slightest trace can be found in his writings, not even in the *Rime*, which are so interwoven with Neoplatonic themes. Furthermore, unlike the Neoplatonic interpretations of the figures in the vault (which, if stripped of excess foliage and reduced to a simple and general idea, can, as we have seen, contribute to the comprehension of the expressive tone of the work of art), the fundamental idea implicit in any such cosmological vision seems to be more in contrast than in harmony with the dominant expressive accent of the work. If the composition really were intended to signify the life of souls under the empire of the "sun of justice," the rotation of the figures around the Apollonian gesture of Christ should evolve in a regular and serene rhythm according to the ordered movement of the heavenly bodies, and not in that frightening whirl evoking Dante's "never ceasing infernal storm." It hardly seems possible to reconcile the dark and desperate atmosphere of this scene in any way with an allusion to a solar myth.

Unfortunately, the paucity of the surviving drawings does not allow us to follow the course of the artist's imagination in concretizing, developing and refining the details for the grandiose image. But down to the overall sketch in the Casa Buonarroti (Fig. 194 ch. V), it is clear that Michelangelo after the first attempts to partially dynamize the traditional schemes (as is still to be seen in the Bayonne sketch for the upper portion), conceived the vision of the culminating event of human history as the unleashing of a tremendous, irresistible force. This force impresses upon the universe an unarrestable rotary movement which has not the calm regularity of a universal phenomenon such as gravitation, but the uncontrollable fury of a cosmic

129-130 Forefathers of Christ: Naasson. Vault of the Sistine Chapel.

catastrophe. In the Casa Buonarroti drawing, Tolnay followed by von Einem has discerned "the battle of a race of Titans to scale the clouds of the heavens," as in the classical myth of the giants' assault on Olympus.[62] Actually, only an isolated figure or two, such as the lowest of the Blessed at our left, is in a posture suggestive of a scaling operation. Most of them clearly appear to be carried aloft towards the heavens by blasts of a tempestuous wind, rather than by the attraction of a heavenly body, even if all of the figures are drawn towards Christ in a current that culminates in the Virgin's buoyant gesture of supplication. The major difference between the drawing and the final version in the finished work consists in the predominance of the ascending movement over its opposite, of the motif of rise over that of fall. The fall of the damned is still conceived as a struggle between the angels and the damned, rather in the manner of the scheme used for the rebel angels. Although the struggle motif does not disappear entirely in the fresco, it is absorbed into the overwhelming fall of souls into Hell. The compositional scheme of the sketch is not to be read (as does von Einem) as a giant " S " starting from the lower right among the damned, rising in a bend towards Christ at the left, and continuing beyond toward the bottom of the group of saints on the right. Rather, it is to be seen as an ogival arch culminating in Christ, with the descending arch of the damned, rejected and hurled downwards forming a counterpoint. It is a still imperfect compositional idea because there is no clear link or transition between the two main lines of direction. Nevertheless, it is already full of force and *terribilità* which are centered around the vision of an irresistible vortex born of the feeling of cosmic tragedy. According to von Einem, the Florentine sketch, in its renunciation of the traditional division into three tiers, in its abandonment of symmetry, its stress of the median vertical axis, and Christ's dynamic gesture, marks the most advanced point that the artist reached in overcoming the traditional type of symbolic representation. In the fresco, according to von Einem, he tried to recover the old symbolic content by means of " the abandonment of the asymmetrical movement, by the reintroduction of zones and groups, and the re-establishment of balance." Our different reading of the Casa Buonarroti drawing makes this interpretation less feasible. Of course, we must

235

131 Last Judgment. Sistine Chapel.

also take into account the fact that the sketch, even though it is a project for the entire composition (which still observed the *status quo* of the chapel's existing pictorial decoration) was not yet a complete one in the sense that it does specify all the parts of the composition—but confines itself to putting down only some of the salient ideas. The truly fundamental difference between the drawing and the fresco is one of degree. In the definitive composition, we find the dominant ideas of the Florentine sketch detailed, clarified, and, above all, developed and multiplied. The Casa Buonarroti drawing caught all the elements in an early stage when they were still in ferment, pressing on the artist's imagination. From the idea of the ogival arch pointed towards Christ, there was then developed the idea of an eliptical movement of the Saints and Patriarchs around the Judge, as well as a second elipse longer and further out, formed at the top among the furthest of the figures in the celestial court who hasten towards Christ, and at the bottom among the blessed who rise and among the damned who fall. But in the second elipse there is no gap between the two zones. From the contrapuntal motif of the struggle of the angels with the hurling down of the rebels obliquely from the center towards the right, is born the new theme of the group of trumpeting angels at the bottom center of the composition. From these two oblique lines marked by the trumpets, the link is established with the lower horizontal zone which, judging from Venusti's copy in Naples, was somewhat cut off at the bottom by later alterations. These oblique passages contain the resurrection of the dead, the bark of Charon and the mouths of Hell which form the base of the entire composition. But in this very zone, some of the resurrected on the left and the damned

132 Christ the Judge and Mary, in the Last Judgment. Sistine Chapel.

237

134-135 Heads of angels supporting the Cross, in the Last Judgment. Sistine Chapel.

on the right act, in their turn, to establish the link with the vertical motion of descent and ascent of the Blessed and the Damned in the zone above, thereby creating an interweaving and interaction of guidelines and forces that is resolved in the extraordinary dynamics of the entire composition. All the more so in that (a point hitherto unnoticed) the groups of angels in the two lunettes, dramatically engaged in holding up while in flight the cross and the column, initiate two diagonals at the top of the fresco which are broken off at once by the vortex of figures beneath and are then resumed by the two oblique lines, cited above, that pass from the trumpeting angels and reach the bottom of the resurrection of the dead and the bark of Charon.

The groups in the lunettes have often seemed specially awkward to ancient and modern interpreters of the Last Judgment. We do not refer to the centuries old theological-iconographical dispute concerning the impropriety of these wingless angels in attitudes that make them look like " acrobats and jugglers," as Gilio wrote; or as Fréart said a hundred years later, " as if [the artist] in derision delighted in rendering them uglier and more deformed than the devils themselves." [63] What we refer to are the many misunderstood explanations given for their beauty by writers who meant to give warm approval and high praise. Who would be led to imagine anything even remotely resembling Michelangelo's passionate, athletic figures struggling with the weight of the huge column and gigantic cross, when one reads Condivi's almost idyllic description: " at the right and left sides in the upper portion of the wall are seen groups of little angels in lovely, unusual attitudes bringing up to Heaven the cross of the Son of God, the sponge, the crown of thorns, the nails and the column where He was scourged, so as to reproach the wicked with God's blessings towards which they were most ungrateful and ignorant; and to comfort and give faith to the good "? Vasari does better even in the first edition where he evokes, at least indirectly, the dramatic atmosphere in which the presentation of the symbols of the Passion takes place: " having depicted the terror of those days, where he knew how to represent, to increase the pain of those who had not lived well, all of his passion making the various nude figures carrying in the air the cross, the column, the lance, the sponge, the nails and the crown with diverse and varied attitudes which in their facility were brought to completion with much difficulty." In modern literature, the two lunettes have provoked some criticism. It has been felt that, pictorially, they do not fit well into the total composition, there being " between them and the zone beneath... a brusque separation " (De Campos-Biagetti) and they have even been considered an " intrusion " impairing the fresco's unity (Mariani). Sometimes they have been passed over in silence, or have not received the attention due them. [64] In this respect it is well to recall von Einem's recent and very just observation that the insertion of the two lunettes into the vast field of the fresco serves to accentuate more strongly the absolute predominance of Christ's figure, since " all the lines of the architecture converge on it, restoring that which might have seemed to have been taken

238

away from it." Von Einem further remarks with pertinence that the movement and postures of these angels:

" have no other point of support aside from the banks of clouds, and are like swimmers constrained to cling to the cross and the column. Complete masters of their power, they are, nevertheless, limited in their movements by the element supporting them. It is just this restriction on their otherwise apparently complete freedom that explains the almost inexhaustible richness of motifs of movement that we find in this fresco. This is also true of the expression which never has anything torrential about it, but is severe, restrained, charged with tension." [65]

If we add to this our observation, noted above, concerning the close compositional relationship that, in an unexpected and strong way, connects the top of the immense fresco with

136   Angels supporting the Cross, in the Last Judgment.   Sistine Chapel.

137   Flying angels, in the Last Judgment.   Sistine Chapel.

138 Glory of the instruments of the Passion, in the Last Judgment. Sistine Chapel.

its base, it will be clear that the insertion of the two lunettes not only corresponds with the legitimate need to enlarge the painted field (given the monumental scale of the figures and their actions), but also is appropriate to the more complex search for a general compositional tension, to the unprecedented counterpoint of straight, darting and crossed trajectories involved in the turbolent rotation of the central and principal part of the composition. In fact, this counterpoint enters into a more general dialectic between uncontrolled movement and elements of control and arrest—among which should be noted the discrete return to the division of the scene into three zones (celestial glory, the Blessed and the Damned, and the terrestrial sphere with the resurrection of the flesh) according to the traditional iconography. Then there is the singular classical beauty of the Apollonian Christ, the virtually motionless mover of so much movement. It is no accident that only here (few other instances, such as the well-known figure inspired by a Niobe, are far less outstanding in the view of the whole) does the inspiration from Antiquity emerge bright and clear in an anticlassical context. Christ's image is dynamic, and if it were not for the utter lack of any actual borrowing on Michelangelo's part, one might say it was more Scopaic than Phidian. The figure is extremely well balanced in its position between a sitting and a standing posture caught in the act, which the power of the forms fixes for eternity, of bracing itself in the very moment of raising the right arm in damnation while the left arm summons or attracts the elect. It is precisely the circle described by the motion of the two arms that holds the figure in balance giving it a majesty greater than any enormous nimbus could. The equilibrium is established, calmly and discreetly, by the understated *contrapposto* of the arms and legs. Thus, in this figure of restrained tension, is concentrated all the terrible power displayed in the universe of the hundreds upon hundreds of figures. This, however, has not always been taken for granted. Vasari, to begin with, places the accent on the fierceness of the expression and the cursing gesture: "Behold Christ, seated with horrible, fierce face, turning towards the damned and cursing them." On the contrary, it is precisely the fact that the gesture of damnation is balanced not only in content but also visually by the gesture of the summoning of the elect and that both are caught in a single circular motion that stylistically justifies the movement of universal rotation which is the major principle of the fresco and accentuates the function of Christ the Judge as the unmoved mover. This explains the interpretation of those who, like Tolnay, have seen in the Judgment an allusion to a solar myth and regarded the rotation of the superhuman figures in the immense space as

PLATE XIX   Christ the Judge and Mary, in the Last Judgment.   Sistine Chapel.

139-140 Heads of angels, in the Last Judgment. Sistine Chapel.

similar to the heavenly bodies moving around the sun. As we have said before, this superposition of an anagogical meaning seems entirely superfluous in the face of the density of implications of the literal significance. Furthermore, it encounters difficulties with the compositional elements of counterpoint and contrast, and in the dizzying velocity of movement, in the vivid sense of the unexpected explosion of a tempest. All this is difficult to reconcile with the idea of the eternal rotation of the heavenly bodies which is incredibly fast but fatally regular.

But the dialectic referred to above, between bursts of unrestrained movement and elements of arrest and balance, are to be found everywhere—among the single figures and groups as well as in the relationship of opposite parts of the composition. To return to the lunettes, they undoubtedly constitute two of the most dramatic and forceful episodes of the scene. The effort made by the athletic angels (visually expressed by the exceptional complexity of the foreshortenings and the *contrapposti*) is so great that, were it not for our knowledge of the iconographic tradition, it might seem that they were trying to uproot and demolish the column and the cross instead of erecting them. Actually, in the very act of trying to raise them, they seem to be seriously impeded by the weakness of their cloud support and by the blast of a stormy wind that carries them with it, sweeping away the two huge instruments of martyrdom. If we then consider the compositions of the two lunettes in their reciprocal relationship, we see that they belong to the firm architecture of the whole. This is achieved through the loose symmetry that links them, by the opposition of the angle of the Cross in one and that of the column in the other, in the *contrapposto* between the youth with his arms around the column and that of his comrade with his arms about the Cross, in the inverse correspondence of the two groups of angels in flight who, at the right, occupy the outer margin of the fresco, while at the left they tend toward the center. As has been pointed out, this convergent symmetry not only accentuates the domination of Christ's figure over the picture, but also binds these two fields to the lower part of the composition. The separation that is, in fact, observed and that does not emerge from Venusti's copy, appears to be due primarily to the changes in the blue of the sky and the warm terracotta tones of the small figures in the heavenly host—tones that have darkened until they create the impression of a slightly arched and neatly drawn line of demarcation which was certainly not in the artist's intentions. The group of the Apostles massed on the right and the Patriarchs on the left are aligned in a circle around Christ and the Virgin. Although they consist of figures hastening in flight or treading a cloudy path in attitudes of emotional excitement, they are, on the whole, rather reserved and composed. This is due either to the relative moderation of the *contrapposto* effects of the individual figures, or because of the largely symmetrical correspondences between the figures on either side, culminating in the two martyrs, Lawrence and Bartholomew. But just at this point, when the dialectic of the two opposing elements is revived, the figure of the Virgin intervenes. She turns in upon herself not as a supplicant, but moved and " a bit timorous in aspect " (Condivi). Her presence breaks the symmetry, introducing a secondary center beside the principal one. While her strongly serpentine figure and the harsh colors of her garments create a sharp dissonance as if to stress the dynamic at the expense of the static element in the nearby figure of Christ. The movement and postures of the figures populating the outermost circle (the

142 Angel supporting the column of the Passion, in the Last Judgment. Sistine Chapel.

143 Head of one of the elect, in the Last Judgment. Sistine Chapel.

prophets, confessors, and martyrs on the right; and the Old Testament heroines, sibyls, and virgin saints on the left), are freer, more explicitly agitated in the complexity of their *contrapposti* and their foreshortening. But here too the tissue of correspondences across a distance between the two opposing groups, and the rhythmic relationship binding the figures of the outermost groups to those in the circle around Christ, are clear despite the numerous exceptions. As hardly needs to be said, there is never a lapse into exact, pedantic symmetry.

The lower section of the fresco, with the ascent of the elect and the fall of the damned, has the greatest variety of arrangements, yet this does not interrupt the play of reciprocals between the two opposite zones even though these are often inverted or occasionally shifted in level. For that matter, this is in harmony with the fact that the rise of the blessed on the left overlaps the region which, on the opposite side, is solidly held by the troop of martyrs weighing heavily upon the fall of the damned. It has not been, I believe, hitherto noticed that the rise of the Blessed and the fall of the Damned owes its clarity to this felicitous unbalance. Were it not for this shift of weight in the composition towards the right, the direction of the movement would have relied solely upon the presence on the right of a few figures turned upside down. We would not have remarked that the upright figures are also being thrown down, until the entire group had been analyzed and the presence of the fierce warrior angels chasing the damned downwards had been discerned. This would have destroyed the immediacy of impression that, after all, is the real impetus for the superhuman forces let loose across the entire surface of this immense fresco. All the more effective is the powerful surge of movement coming from the left edge of the composition in that it is prepared by the actions of the figures rising from the dead which, at first, are laboured and slow and then become progressively easier and quicker. It is a spread out composition, the final vehemence of which is left to the oblique course of action and on the foreshortenings of the embracing couples rising from the dead. In one instance, the member already revived by the Divine summons painfully pulls up his partner who still lies inert in the sleep of death; in another, at the right, the couple repels a demon. In their more limited compositional function, these figures closely anticipate the central groups of the Cappella Paolina frescoes. The sense of the progressive liberation of the forces of ascension is rendered more clearly by the contrast with the corresponding region on the right. This is occupied by the disembarkation of the damned

144 Group of Patriarchs, Sibyls and Virgins, in the Last Judgment. Sistine Chapel.

under the blows of Charon's oar and the judgment of Minos. It is a crowded, compact scene, particularly heavy because of the modelling of the nudes and the intense and largely uniform color.

Incidentally, it is pedantic to deny, as has been attempted, that Dante inspired this episode on the pretext that Charon "beats with his oar" the disembarking souls and not, as in Dante, at embarkation; and that Minos judges and dispenses winding around his body a serpent's tail instead of one of human flesh. These are variants or departures that are easily explained. The first variant was obviously due to the artist's intention to use the blows of Charon's oar as a starting point for the crescendo accompanying the fall of the damned into Hell, dragged to the depths by devils. Unquestionably, Michelangelo was a passionate reader of Dante. It seems equally evident that a Dante-like spirit hovers over the entire fresco, over and beyond any literal reference. The very idea of the flight of the elect, attracted by the power of Divine love, had no precedent in art other than in one of the four pictures of the Last Judgment by Hieronymous Bosch in the Doge's Palace in Venice and Michelangelo could hardly have known it even though it may have been in Cardinal Grimani's collection since 1521. Perhaps the point of departure for this iconographically new solution may have been a combination of two themes from the Divine Comedy: Dante and Beatrice flying from sphere to sphere in Paradise by divine attraction, and the image of "those two that go together—and seem to be so light in the wind" from Canto V of the Inferno. Of especially Dantesque flavour are the inexorable representational power of the imagery, the naked conciseness of the language, and the absence of moralistic scruples in the lofty morality of the conception (the "great stew of nudes" was condemned by its detractors who found fault with some of the damned whom devils hold by the genitals).

On the whole, the lower half of the fresco is less crowded with figures, the bodies being more spread out revealing more of the sky. This affords an opportunity to discuss the relationship between the figures and the background, the spacial structure of the composition and the plastic structure of the figures. It has frequently been observed that the figures, although so numerous and so densely intertwined, still have the isolation characteristic of a sculptural block. Each of them is like a statue, perfectly defined by its own contours retaining the sense of the marble block from which it has been ideally carved. Among the various individual figures it is not hard to recognize a reflection or a prefiguration of statues already realized in the artist's fantasy or actually carved by his chisel. Sometimes the sense of the compact block is so strong that it brings to mind rock-like images. This is the case with the famous group of the damned soul seated on a crag of clouds, shrinking within himself and covering half his face while two demons seize him by the legs and feet dragging him down into the abyss. But even in the more active figures, the *contrapposti* and spiral movements observe the same canons as do the unfinished Slaves, straining to free themselves from their material envelope. Then there is a motif in the group on the left with the woman supporting a man by holding him under

146-148 Head of a woman among the Patriarchs; Mary Magdalen; Patriarchs, in the Last Judgment. Sistine Chapel.

149 Saints, in the Last Judgment. Sistine Chapel.

150 Sibyl, in the Last Judgment. Sistine Chapel.

the armpits which already prefigures the later Pietà of marble. From a technical-formal point of view, each of these figures might seem to be enclosed within the paradigm of a formal problem's solution, furnishing new stimuli to the intellectualistic formal researches of the Mannerists. But in Michelangelo's great work they are always seen in their reciprocal correspondence, linked together by the expressive requirements of the drama. But this bond, and the very plastic development of the masses, no longer occurs in the plane but in the third dimension and in space via the foreshortenings and the entire network of oblique lines of direction in depth as well as on the surface. Therefore, it seems to me that a correction must be made to the common critical view which sees the fresco of the Last Judgment as a sort of enormous tapestry, or an imitation in painting of a high relief—as if, after the abandonment of Quattrocento perspective, and before the advent of Baroque illusionism, no other solution could be found than the neo-medieval one of a planimetric vision or of fictive relief. One can even read that the painter applied a sort of inverse perspective, making the more distant figures appear larger. But this interpretation is derived from considering the composition of the Last Judgment in terms of Quattrocento perspective; that is, from the three-dimensional view everything is set higher up on the surface of the painting and thus seems to be more distant, thereby forgetting that here the imaginary story is unfolded on various levels, from the earth below to the highest regions of Heaven. Within the range of each zone—terrestrial, intermediate and empyrean—the figures that are furthest away in depth are represented smaller in size even though there is no clear unit of measurement due to the absence of any measurable feature of architecture or landscape. The occasional exceptions to the rule are due to the expressive requirements of the drama. The fact that Michelangelo represented the figures of Christ and the celestial personages larger and more dominant than those of humanity rising from its grave or the damned driven into Hell by Charon's oar, is due to his intention to abstract them completely from any reference to an earthly observer. Thus he chose his observation point in a very remote, ideal region from which it would be possible to span the universe. At the same time, he saw the need of augmenting the weight of the heavenly persons and events, of accentuating the downward force of the masses in the upper section in order to get a more inevitable and imperative effect of universal ruin. Perhaps this is the moment to restate something that has already been referred to in passing: despite all the elements of balance that hold the enormous, agitated composition together in a comprehensible whole, the power of the forces unleashed is so great that no observer can avoid the impression of being witness to the collapse of a world, of the unhinging of universal order. To be sure, the liberation of the elect in flight balances the casting down of the damned. But a sense of universal terror arises from the realization that everything occurs by virtue of mysterious irresistible forces, beyond any possibility of human control. To obtain this, the artist could not have confined himself to negating Quattrocento space, while ignoring the spherical, universal space of Bramante and Raphael. He had to accentuate those effects of a space infinite and convulsed, no longer measurable in its immensity. He had already evoked this within narrower limits, in the scene of the Deluge painted on the vault. Here he had to populate it with tormented giants like those in the spandrels of the Brazen Serpent and the Hanging of Haman, which in their supreme intensification of sculptural plasticity, the amazing intensity of their forms, and the daring foreshortenings, prefigure the great images of the Judgment.

It is just in this union between a vision of unlimited space and images of a sorrowing humanity that the tragic pessimism of Michelangelo finds expression: the grotesque self-portrait stamped on the skin of St. Bartholomew is its emblem. Returning for a moment to the obvious illustrative level, it should be noted that despite Vasari's claim, the work is not "full of all possible human emotions." Even less can we see with the Romantics "stupendous expressions of beatitude, of joy, of contentment in the elect." Apart from the vehement embraces of a few couples in the celestial court, the elect flying towards Paradise seem full of amazement or involved in painful efforts rather than to be radiant with joy. It is as if they had been suddenly swept into beatitude by a tremendous, obscure force while still in a semiconscious state. Thus, there is some support for the hypothesis of those who discern in the con-

151 Heads of some of the elect, in the Last Judgment. Sistine Chapel.

153 St. Laurence, in the Last Judgment. Sistine Chapel.

152 Woman's head, in the Last Judgment. Sistine Chapel.

ception of the scene an influence of the Protestant idea of justification by faith rather than by works. An argument to the contrary advocated by a Catholic scholar is invalid; he claims that " many of the blessed show, or even display the instruments of their martyrdom, as the signs of how much they have suffered and of the deeds they have accomplished—without which faith is dead." [66] However martyrdom actually appears as the supreme proof of faith inflicted upon these saints not for whatever good work they performed, but because of their refusal to deny their faith. Even the presence of Mary beside her Son is not in itself proof of the orthodox character of the conception, because she is not shown in the act of intercession. Even the saints in Paradise do not intercede, although Catholic doctrine generally considers them advocates of men. But it is hard to believe that Michelangelo wanted to refer to the contemporary disputes concerning justification by faith alone or by works. When he conceived the Last Judgment, Michelangelo did not yet know Vittoria Colonna and had not come in contact with the group of Catholic reformers with whom she was connected. The fact remains that the terrible sense of fatality that breathes throughout the great work, and the entire gigantic vision of humanity as the victim of irresistible forces, agree better with a conception of the Pauline or Augustinian type centering around the idea of Grace, rather than with the prevailing official conception of free will. Probably, Michelangelo (who must have heard echoes of the current theological dispute and of Luther's rebellion) did not put the problem in conceptual terms. Still less would he have intended to make polemical statements in the great fresco he was painting for the Pope's residence. But that his nature was inclined to protest, if not to Protestantism, is apparent from every expression that he confided to verbal or figurative speech. That the behavior of the papal court aroused in him feelings of revolt is attested to

154 The elect and the Resurrection of the Flesh, in the Last Judgment. Sistine Chapel.

155 Angel raising the elect with the rosary, in the Last Judgment. Sistine Chapel.

156 Elect, in the Last Judgment. Sistine Chapel.

by the famous sonnet written long before: " here helmets are made of chalices, and swords— and the blood of Christ is sold by the handful." It is anything but unlikely that he might have been inclined to the theory of justification *sola fide*, even before being aware of its theological motivations. At least it was a polemic outburst in a milieu where the " works " most acceptable to the hierarchy were ostentatious donations to monasteries, splendid foundations, and the purchase of indulgences. From all that we know of Michelangelo's personality and remembering his youthful education with Savonarola's stern sermons which instilled in him the fear of divine punishment, it seems entirely credible that the artist's high morality should have rejected the opportunism that was concealed under the doctrine of " works," and that he should anxiously have sought for active means for making faith personal. Such an inclination may have found some response in the reforming spirit of Pope Paul III. However, there is no need to postulate a religious " conversion," as is often done, for this time or immediately afterwards. This is the period marked by the friendship with Vittoria Colonna and the frescoes of the *Cappella Paolina* and some have seen it as a transition in Michelangelo's life from a pagan conception to a Christian vision. Actually, as we have tried to show in the earlier pages of this essay, it is clear that even in his youth, Michelangelo's Neoplatonism of Medicean origin, coexisted with a deep Savonarolan religiosity, just as he was able to reconcile gratitude and affection for Lorenzo the Magnificent and other members of the Medici household with austere republican ideals.

The attention that has been given in these pages, with all due discretion, to the spiritual antecedents of Michelangelo's artistic creations does not seem misguided. Not that there is any intention to deny, or even to cast doubt on, the fact that in the last analysis art consists entirely of form. But it must equally be evident that form, if it is to be understood as language and expression, can not find its explanation exclusively within itself, as if born out of nothing. Proof of this is the repeatedly demonstrated inability of formalist criticism to do justice to Michelangelo's late work. To confine ourselves to the most brilliant instance in this field, let us recall Berenson's criticism of the *Last Judgment* and the frescoes in the Cappella Paolina, and his conclusion: that Michelangelo's masterpiece would have been the lost cartoon for the *Battle*. Not that the great critic failed to take note of the discontent and solitude of the artists's old age. But he looked for an exclusively formal explanation in the con-

157 Dead arising, in the Last Judgment. Sistine Chapel.

158 Head of a risen man, in the Last Judgment. Sistine Chapel.

159 Risen and elect, in the Last Judgment.   Sistine Chapel.

tradiction between the master's inclination toward glorification of life in the nude and the subjects of sorrow and death that were imposed on him:

" He lived on in a world he could not but despise, in a world which really could no more employ him than it could understand him. He was not allowed, therefore, to busy himself where he felt most drawn by his genius, and, much against his own strongest impulses, he was obliged to expend his energy upon such subjects as the ' Last Judgment.' His later works all show signs of the altered conditions, first in an overflow into the figures he was creating of the scorn and bitterness he was feeling, then in the lack of harmony between his genius and what he was compelled to execute. His passion was the nude, his ideal power. But what outlet for such a passion, what expression for such an ideal could there be in subjects like the ' Last Judgment,' or the ' Crucifixion of Peter'—subjects which the Christian world imperatively demanded should incarnate the fear of the humble and the self-sacrifice of the patient? Now humility and patience were feelings as unknown to Michelangelo as to Dante before him, or, for that matter, to any other of the world's creative geniuses at any time. Even had he felt them, he had no means of expressing them, for his nudes could convey a sense of power, not of weakness; of terror, not of dread; of despair, but not of submission. And terror the giant nudes of the ' Last Judgment ' do feel, but it is not terror of the Judge, who, being in no wise different from the others, in spite of his omnipotent gesture, seems to be *announcing* rather than *willing* what the bystanders, his fellows, could not *unwill*. As the representation of the moment before the universe disappears in chaos—Gods huddling together for the *Götterdämmerung*—the ' Last Judgment ' is as grandly conceived as possible: but when the crash comes, none will survive it, no, not even God. Michelangelo therefore failed in his conception of the subject, and could not but fail. But where else in the whole world

160 Head of St. John the Evangelist, in the Last Judgment. Sistine Chapel.

162 St. Peter and Apostles, in the Last Judgment. Sistine Chapel.

161 Head of an Apostle, in the Last Judgment. Sistine Chapel.

of art shall we receive such blasts of energy as from this giant's dream, or, if you will, nightmare? For kindred reason, the 'Crucifixion of Peter' is a failure. Art can be only life-communicating and life-enhancing. If it treats of pain and death, these must always appear as manifestations and as results only of living resolutely and energetically. What chance is there, I ask, for this, artistically the only possible treatment, in the representation of a man crucified with his head downwards? Michelangelo could do nothing but make the bystanders, the executioners, all the more life-communicating, and therefore inevitably more sympathetic! No wonder he failed here! What a tragedy, by the way, that the one subject perfectly cut out for his genius, the one subject which required none but genuinely artistic treatment, his 'Bathers,' executed forty years before these last works, has disappeared, leaving but scant traces! Yet even these suffice to enable the competent student to recognise that this composition must have been the greatest masterpiece in figure art of modern times."

[56] Undated letter (No. LXXXIX), ed. Papini, cit., I, p. 69. The warning to his family not to get involved in factions is in the letter, probably a little earlier, dated September 18, 1512 and received by Buonarroto on the 23rd. The advice corresponds to the line of absolute prudence constantly urged on his people and on himself, but there is also implicit the feeling of dignity of one who does not wish to hasten to get on the side of the victors, and probably also conceals a political position more hostile than favorable to the Medici party, as well as secret hope of a change in the near future: " I gathered from your last letter that the world was in great danger; which put me into a state. Now it is said once more that the House of the Medici has entered Florence and that now everything is settled: from which I believe that the danger is over, that is, from the Spaniards, and I do not believe that there is any more need to leave; but remain in peace and do not make friends or acquaintances with anyone, except God; and do not speak good nor evil of anyone, because one does not know how things will turn out in the end: just mind your own business."
[57] G. Spini, op. cit.
[58] The brief is dated November 17, 1536; text in Vasari-Barocchi, op. cit., III, p. 1193 ff.

[59] M. Dvořák, *Geschichte der Italienischen Kunst im Zeitalter der Renaissance*, Munich, 1927-28, p. 128.

[60] H. Voss, *Die Malerei der Spätrenaissance in Rom und Florenz*, Berlin, 1920, p. 115; H. Wölfflin, *Die klassische Kunst*, Munich, 1899, p. 183.

[61] C. de Tolnay, *op. cit.*, 1951, p. 83 ff., and in *Enciclopedia, op. cit.* But see also de Tolnay, " Michelangelo's Last Judgment," in *Art Quarterly*, III, 1940, p. 125, and esp. *Michelangelo. V. The Last Judgment*, Princeton, 1960.

[62] Tolnay, *op. cit.*, 1940, and in other places; H. von Einem, " Michelangelo's Last Judgment in the Pictural Tradition," in *Kunstchronik*, VIII, 1955, p. 89 and *op. cit.*, p. 117 ff.

[63] Citations taken from Vasari-Barocchi, III, p. 1312, 1314 f. *Ibid.*, p. 1254-1402, an enormous documentation on the fate of the *Judgment* in criticism, old and new.

[64] D. Redig De Campos and B. Biagetti, *Il Giudizio Universale di Michelangelo*, Rome, 1944, I, p. 32; V. Mariani, *op. cit.*, 1942, p. 181; but he abandons all reservations in *Michelangelo Pittore, op. cit.*, 1964, p. 114.

[65] Von Einem, *op. cit.*, p. 119.

[66] D. Redig De Campos, *The Sistine Chapel*, New York, 1963.

The Cappella Paolina

The Last Judgment, which was completed and open to view at the end of October 1541, was immediately followed by the two frescoes in the *Cappella Paolina*. The first of them was begun in November 1542 (Fig. 177). Meanwhile, the artist had set about executing the statues of Rachel and Leah which were to be placed beside the Moses of the Julius tomb in the church of San Pietro in Vincoli. The two frescoes were to adorn the chapel recently built

163 Apostles and Saints, in the Last Judgment. Sistine Chapel.

164 Prophets, in the Last Judgment.   Sistine
Chapel.

for Paul III by Antonio da Sangallo the Younger " in imitation of the chapel of Nicholas V "
which had been frescoed by Fra Angelico. Michelangelo's murals were executed approximately between late 1542 and 1550. Although the artist continued to work feverishly on completing Julius II's tomb, the first of the frescoes was already finished in July 1545 when the
Pope came to visit the chapel and the paintings that Michelangelo had completed (as the
source, the diary of Firmano, tells us: " *ad videndum capellam seu picturas factas per dominum
Michaelem Angelum* "). On August 10th of the same year, payment was made for the expenses
incurred in laying the rough layer of plaster (the *arriccio*) on the other wall. After a fire in
1544 or 1545, however, repairs to the chapel roof along with a serious illness of the artist,
delayed the beginning on the second fresco until Spring 1546 (it was only in late March that
the scaffolding was raised and the paints bought). Sad events such as the death of his friend
Luigi del Riccio in November 1546 and of Vittoria Colonna on February 25th 1547, and illness (between the end of 1548 and April 1549) further slowed down progress on the work.
It was not yet finished in October 1549 when the Pope, by then in advanced years, had to
climb " a ladder with ten or twelve rungs " to see the paintings. From the documents, it is
not clear which of the two frescoes was done first; they only refer in a general way to the
" painting " that Buonarroti was doing in the chapel. Opinion, however, is virtually unanimous in giving precedence to the Conversion of St. Paul which appears to be closer in style
to the Last Judgment. Vasari, who published the first edition of his *Vite* in 1550, refers to the
two pictures using the verb in the present tense as if they had not yet been finished (" he
is painting two scenes, one of St. Peter, the other of St. Paul "). He cites one of the frescoes
with the title of the Delivery of the Keys (" the one where Christ gives the keys to Peter, the

Plate XXII   Charon's boat, in the Last Judgment.   Sistine Chapel.

other the terrible Conversion of Paul ''). Whether this was an oversight on Vasari's part, or whether a change in the programme had taken place in the meantime, the fact that the subject of one of the paintings is referred to incorrectly, very probably means that it had not been painted yet, or had only been begun when the author was writting the Life of Michelangelo presumably a year or two before publication.[67]

In the Conversion of Saul, that which most clearly recalls the Last Judgment is the apparition in the sky of the Lord, dashing down, headlong in the act of stopping His lightning descent with an arm on a cloud bank surrounded by breathless troops of angels. Both the velocity of the motion and the variety of foreshortenings recall the swirl of the Blessed and the Damned and the passionate gathering of the patriarchs and saints around the Judge. More generally, the state of mind out of which the Last Judgment arose is recalled by the extreme agitation and the irresistible release of movement (Figs. 178-185 and Plates XXIII-XXIV). The dynamic quality is curbed in the composition of the Crucifixion of Peter, passionate yet compact and solemn. Therefore it may reasonably be supposed to have been done at a greater distance of time from the great fresco in the Sistine Chapel. But there is a third aspect, a more strictly stylistic one, linking the Conversion to the Last Judgment. There is a repetition here, considerably altered in proportions, but identical in relationship, of the juxtaposition of a terrestrial scene with a celestial event. As in the lower zone of the enormous Sistine mural, the terrestrial space here disappears into a perspective slipping towards unexplained distances, while the celestial host is lowered compactly on a plane behind which only the foreshortenings and the chromatic transparency suggest the sky's indefinite spacial immensity. As in the Last Judgment, where the link is established by two couples of the saved whose flight from earth takes an oblique

165-167 Heads of Saints; Martyrs, in the Last Judgment. Sistine Chapel.

168 Some of the Damned, in the Last Judgment.
Sistine Chapel.

course; here too the dynamic bond is represented by the fleeing great horse whose gallop urges him into the distance and, at the same time, drives him upwards. It can, in fact, be said that here a compositional motif comes to maturity and full development which had only been hinted at in the earlier fresco where it had constituted but one of the many links between earthly and celestial events. Given the marginal significance of the resurrection of the flesh in the episode of the Last Judgment, and the absolute predominance of the heavenly events, there was no need of a single obvious connection between the two areas—one of which, by the attraction of its mass, finally absorbs the other minor one. Here Michelangelo repeats and heightens the effect of a tragically limitless space by the power of the foreshortenings and by constructing the composition by means of a system of oblique lines of direction. The effect is enhanced by the bare and undefined landscape rendered with a few broad undulations which at most might suggest the image of a stormy sea. The city in the background, confined to a corner at the right, is as compact and schematic as the symbolic views of medieval painting. "Michelangelo aimed only... at perfection of art, because there are neither country, trees, houses nor certain artistic variations and pleasantries, for he never aimed at these." In these words Vasari, implicitly polemicized against those who even then complained of the artist's austerity. He perfectly understood the expressive value of this rigorous simplicity, even though, in tribute to the poetics of the time, he tried to explain it by the superiority of figure painting: "for he never aimed at these, as one who may not have wished to debase his great genius in such things."

Recent criticism, especially von Einem, has retraced the path that led from the older iconographic conceptions of the scene of the Conversion of Saul to Michelangelo's innovating version of the subject.[68] The motif of the stumbling horse, which is not in the Biblical account, had already become part of the scene's iconography through the influence of Prudentius' illustrations for the struggle between Humility and Pride which, in turn, were derived from the ancient composition of Philoxenus of Eretria's Battle of Alexander. The motif of the man trying to control the runaway horse, similarly goes back (probably by way of Raphael's tapestry) to the classical figure of the horse tamer; while the type of prostrate Saul, also of ancient origin, is influenced by the interpretation of Raphael's fallen Heliodorus based on the

169 Head of angel of the Damnation, in the Last Judgment. Sistine Chapel.

170-171 Head of angel of the Damnation; head of one of the Damned, in the Last Judgment. Sistine Chapel.

172 Angel blowing horn, in the Last Judgment. Sistine Chapel.

same ancient model. Other figures, including the one of the soldier with the shield, derive from Signorelli's fresco in the sacristy of Loreto. But no research among the sources could ever account sufficiently for the novelty and grandeur of Michelangelo's vision. The episode of Saul's conversion as he falls dazzled by the supernatural light, listening to the call of the Lord, is not represented as an historical event determined in space and time, but as a mystical experience of contact between Man and God. Moreover, it is shown not as an experience exclusive to the apostle but as a possibility for every faithful Christian. The spectator is lured into the space of the picture through the virtual abolition of the lower edge of the picture which is cut off by the two soldiers seen from the back climbing up to reach the scene of action (of which they do not as yet seem to be aware). The spectator is put into the position of an observing participant and is placed in direct contact with the emotion of the aroused bystanders. The thunderous immediacy and lightening-like power of the miracle find a most effective expression in the centrifugal composition realized by the two groups going off in an arc across the surface and at the same time into space, and by the runaway horse which darts from the central axis obliquely upwards towards the left. Here the incipient divergence between the animal and the man who tries to hold him underlines the divergence between the two major lines of direction. A tight play of *contrapposti* contrasts and thereby accentuates the effect, enriching the dynamic quality of the composition. The centrifugal movement of the lower portion corresponds inversely with the centripetal motion of the celestial scene in which the nude angels (some of the drapery are later additions) converge in a circle toward Christ. There are strong connections between the two zones by means of *contrapposto*. First of all, one

259

173 Damned and devils, in the Last Judgment. Sistine Chapel.

should note the not irreverent relationship that the painter has established between the horse and Christ which was dictated by expressive as well as formal factors. The horse is launched upwards obliquely towards the left, while Christ moves downwards towards the right. But there are other corresponding figures, above and below, which stress the connection: the soldier stopping his ears at the lower right and the great angel flying a little above the horse's head. Sometimes it has seemed even to critics of great sensitivity that this fresco was somewhat disordered in its spate of energy (D'Ancona), that it tends towards Manneristic tastes (Toesca), or that it contains various incongruences such as " deep breaks between one group and another "—a " contrast between unattained spaciality and strong sculptural tendencies in the foreground figures " and should, therefore, be judged to be " a work with great power but to a great extent dispersed in various incoherent directions " (Mariani).[69] The analysis we have attempted, however, points in the direction of a substantial coherence and unity in the work, despite the fact that it is composed of two parts—each of which could stand by itself. For example, if we imagine the entire upper region to be removed, we would find that the scene of the Saint's fall and his companions' terror is complete and self-contained. Nonetheless, the presence of the action in the sky fits perfectly with and accentuates the effect of the action on the ground. Baumgart was right in saying that " in the Conversion of Saul, the composition, violently broken up and yet held together, the intensity of sentiment that is attained and the dramatic nature of the gestures are the last echo of a particular period of Michelangelo's art which found its monumental expression in the great fresco of the Sistine Chapel." [70]

The artist's state of mind when he painted this first picture of the Pauline Chapel must still have been very much like that which gave rise to the Last Judgment. Beyond all the stylistic correspondences of detail, there is still the deep note of pessimism that we encountered in the Last Judgment and the vision of boundless empty space and an awestruck humanity. In addition, there is a strengthening of the mystical element in the more specific inclusion of the spectator within the radius of the event represented. While in place of the feeling of tragic sorrow, there enters an expression of anxiety and trouble. A factor contributing to this is the fact that, whereas in the Judgment the maelstrom of masses was substantially aligned on a single plane beyond which is only endless space; here, as in the Martyrdom of St. Peter, the figures are realized in powerful sculptural masses and turn about well inside the desolate open space. This new note of anxiety here added to the high tragic quality of the Last Judgment may, perhaps, be related to the new religious experience that Michelangelo might have had in the circle of Catholic reformers around the Marchioness of Pescara, Vittoria Colonna. The meeting with her occurred in 1536 or, more probably, in 1538. Although the noble woman's ideas and religious sentiment may have had no sensible influence upon the Last Judgment (which by then had already been conceived in its general structure and was well towards completion), it seems likely that Buonarroti's already existing tendency towards a more profound and more personal religiosity in the spirit of the reformers found stimulus in his conversations with the Marchioness and with her spiritual director Bernardino Ochino, or with Cardinal Pole, both of whom were followers of Juan de Valdès. Allusions to the weakness of human virtue and human works as compared with the omnipotence of Grace are frequent in the letters and poems that Michelangelo sent to Vittoria Colonna. In a letter which has been variously dated between 1540 and 1545, he wrote:

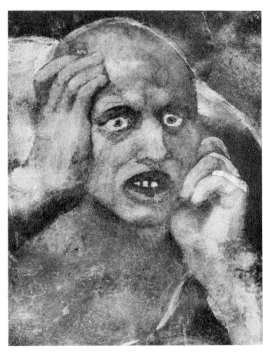

174-176 Heads of some of the Damned, in the Last Judgment. Sistine Chapel.

261

177 Pauline Chapel. Rome, Vatican.

"having realized and seen that the grace of God is incomparable [that is, with one's own works] ..."; and in the madrigal *Per fido esemplo:* " to which Ascent without grace is a vain thought "; and in the same vein, his question which, by pure coincidence, recalls Luther's *pecca fortiter:*

> " if there is a lower place in Heaven
> for humble sin than for excessive good."

In Michelangelo's late poems there are frequent invocations to God to remedy his own impotence for good:

> " Thee alone call I and invoke
> Against my useless blind torment... "
> . . . .
> " All good without Thee, Lord, I lack;
> Changing of fate is only in Divine power; "
> . . . .
> " I love Thee in my words and then I sorrow
> Love comes not to the heart;
> I know not where
> The door of grace is open "
> . . . .
> " I speak to Thee, O Lord, for all may trials
> Apart from thy Blood does not make man happy."

How deeply the problem of grace was felt by Michelangelo is shown by the unfinished sonnet, somewhat Dante-like in inspiration, on the various modes of grace:

> " Though there is only One that moves the sun
> . . . .
> Not always do we see it as the same
> But more or less, as His grace doth rain down."

262

The thought of the weakness of human actions and of the need for grace which cannot be purchased but only achieved by an intimate union of the soul with God, besets the artist's mind and fills his spirit with anxiety:

> " I wish to wish, O Lord, what I wish not
> Between the fire and the heat of ice a veil is hidden
> That the fire doth quench..."

Fearing that his devotion might remain formal and insincere, he wrote:

> " whence do not match
> The brush and the work, and makes the paper false."

Here is the same anguished fear that comes through the turbulent fright of the men in the disconsolate land of the Conversion of Saul. The greater vivacity of color compared to the earthy and largely uniform tones of the Last Judgment cannot be adduced as proof of an alleged serenity of spirit dominating this fresco and its companion piece in the Cappella Paolina. It may be that the fine gradations of color indicate contact with Venetian painters whom Michelangelo might have known through his association with Fra Sebastiano del Piombo. Certain sunset and twilight effects in the skies, far from setting a quiet, contemplative mood, are rather of a " Romantic " nature intensifying the pathos of the whole.

Critics have sometimes been perplexed by the pairing of the two subjects, the Conversion of Saul and the Martyrdom of Peter. Of course, it is no wonder that scenes concerning these two saints should have been chosen. These were the two " principal Apostles " and, what is more, the two frescoes were intended for the private chapel of a pope—a successor of Peter who had taken the name of Paul. But it would have been more conventional to have the Martyrdom of St. Peter matched by the Martyrdom of St. Paul, or the Conversion of Paul paired with the Delivery of the Keys to Peter. In this way, either the supreme proof of the faith of the two apostles would have been shown, or the two outstanding events of their earthly labors. It has been pointed out that Vasari's Torrentino edition mentions the Delivery of the Keys to St. Peter being beside the Conversion of St. Paul. It is very likely that what is involved here is not merely an oversight on the biographer's part, duly corrected in the Giunti edition, but that the Pope actually intended the pictures to depict the Conversion of Paul and the Delivery of the Symbols of Authority to St. Peter—especially, since the latter episode would serve as an historical justification for the Pope's own power. The reason for the change can only be sought in Michelangelo who had already succeeded in totally changing the programme

180 Heads, in the Conversion of St. Paul. Pauline Chapel.

180 Heads, in the Conversion of St. Paul. Pauline Chapel.

179 Head, in the Conversion of St. Paul. Pauline Chapel.

of the Sistine ceiling and getting Julius II to accept it. By his choice of the subjects, Michelangelo evidently wished to express the power of grace and faith: conversion by unexpected descent of grace and martyrdom as the supreme proof of faith. Together with the refusal to paint the Delivery of the Keys (that is the act constituting the Church), this brings us back to the cycle of thoughts and feelings that must have nourished the artist during those years spent among the reformers.

The Crucifixion of St. Peter has been more uniformly praised by modern critics for its high quality (Figs. 186-195 and Plates XXV-XXVI). Here there is a total renunciation of an objective vision of space in favor of a subjective formation of it (Dvořák, Neumeyer); the universal expression of human suffering in silent solemnity (Baumgart); the solid, heroic firmness of the composition (Mariani); the balanced compositional rhythm as compared with the disorder of the Conversion of Saul (D'Ancona).[71] Actually, both the harmony and the dissonance of this composition match those of the other fresco. There is the same conception of space, deep, and boundless but unrelated to the observer because of the absence of a fixed view point. But, it does, in fact, include the spectator by means of the intersection of groups of figures in the foreground near the lower edge. There is an identically broad rhythm of the desert landscape in a few vast

Plate XXIV   Detail of the Conversion of St. Paul.   Cappella Paolina.

PLATE XXVI   Detail of the Crucifixion of St. Peter.   Cappella Paolina.

◁ 181 Detail of the Conversion of St. Paul. Pauline Chapel.

undulations. There is the similar oblique pattern of the main lines of direction in the composition: in one, represented by the horse; in the other, by the cross. They are different and opposite in the organization of the bystanders around the fulcrum: in one case, divergent and centrifugal; in the other, centripetal and circular. A broad, strong rotary motion is given the figures of the soldiers and the groups of mourners which all describe a wide arc around the center, consisting of the Saint's head, and the convergence is picked up by the group of mounted soldiers coming in from the left and the crowd running in from the right. A smaller circle is described in the movement of the figures of the two executioners at the arms of the cross. To the movement of rotation in the plane, is added the suggestion of a vertical rotation in the cross's position which is shown in the act of being raised and thus proposes a spherical and universal vision of space. This is Michelangelo's great iconographical innovation from which all the stylistic novelties follow; the traditional representations of this scene presented the cross already upright and Peter head downward. Here the cross is aslant, raised from the earth by the executioners' arms at one end, while the crucifix turns with the body as if under the pressure of the movement it is being subjected to. In this way, the artist was able to make Peter's head and proud eyes the fulcrum of the entire composition and to show the scene dynamically during the course of the tragedy without sacrificing the fixed point of the martyr's spiritual triumph. In the picture of the Conversion, the sense of the miraculous springs from the lightening rapidity of the event. Here a sense of equally miraculous fatality emerges from the slow regularity of the many rotating movements. It has been acutely observed that here

" humanity is made once more earthy and rough. However, these colossal men and women, who seem to have been driven out of distant lands by a cataclysm, pass beside the crucified

182 Horse, in the Conversion of St. Paul. Pauline Chapel.

183 St. Paul, in the Conversion of St. Paul. Pauline Chapel.

apostle, commenting on his torment with broad gestures and enclosing themselves in mute sorrow. Yet, they do not stop; they run through the shallow space between the horizon and our eye with great strides pursued by a Nemesis that we cannot sense " (Mariani).

Another critic has noted:

" the personages of the fresco do not directly participate in the action. They are there like unintentional witnesses who have come from every point on the horizon, and go past, moved and resigned before the committed crime. The boundaries of space and time disappear, the scene is transformed into a locus that synthesizes the universe, in which the whirl of humanity goes on forever " (Tolnay).[72]

Here, more than in the other picture, the masses merge in compact sculptural formations, almost metaphysical in nature, matched by the fixity of the facial expressions which bespeak an hallucinatory, inhuman disturbance. The visionary tone and expressionistic accent have reached a further peak of intensity while, as has been pointed out, the greater variety and delicacy of the color increases the resonance of the silence.

The apocalyptic spirit aside, and remembering that Michelangelo was averse to take any active part in the great spiritual battles of his time, nevertheless he felt in his morose solitude the deep impact of the great crisis, and in his later years he felt more uneasy and discontent. The optimistic vision born of humanism and Neoplatonic ideas that had induced him in the Sistine ceiling to identify morality and beauty in a Renaissance equation of classicism and Christianity, had now left him. Reformation and Counter Reformation were now in full swing. His personal faith could not be content either with the laxness of the Roman Church

184 View of Damascus, in the Conversion of St. Paul. Pauline Chapel.

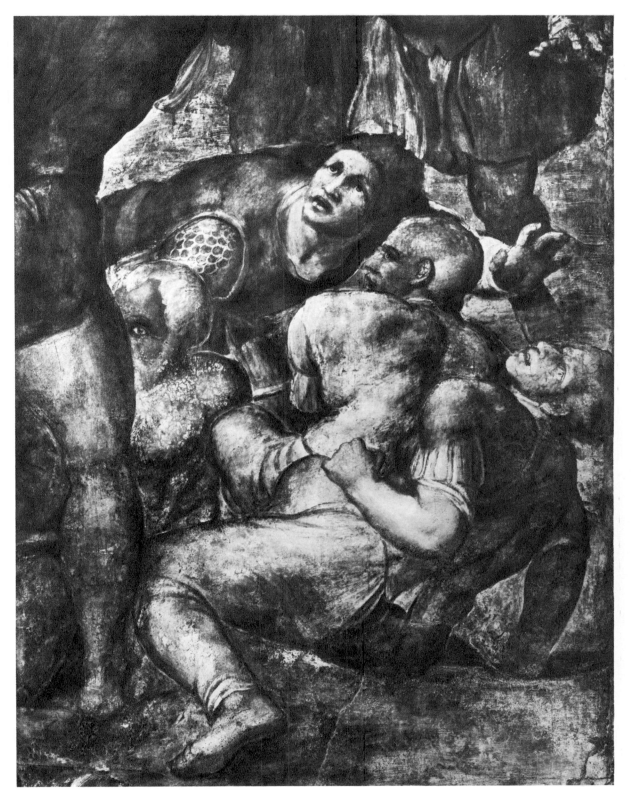

185 Detail of the Conversion of St. Paul. Pauline Chapel.

267

of his youth, nor with the superficiality and power politics of the Church of those years which was then veering towards the Counter Reformation. Just about 1545, when the artist was putting his hand to the second fresco, Vittoria Colonna, intimidated by the threats of the Inquisition, broke with her reforming friends some of whom, including Ochino, had become Protestants. Michelangelo had to remain alone clinging to the idea of salvation by faith alone, and this may partly explain the atmosphere of mystery and anguish that breathes through the two frescoes of the Cappella Paolina—especially the second one, in which humanity seems to have lost all faith in itself and with fear and trembling to await salvation from an arduous, mystic unification with God.

We have not discussed the lost paintings in this essay, save for the extremely important cartoon for the Battle of Cascina as it is known to us from prints and copies. Thus, nothing has been said of the Leda painted for Alfonso d'Este, Duke of Ferrara, during the siege of Florence, which was never delivered and, instead, presented to Antonio Mini, who sold it to the King of France. Nor have we dealt with the *Noli me tangere* cartoon for the Marchese del Vasto, about 1530. But a word is essential on the pictures the artist made, or intended to make, for Vittoria Colonna. Partly echoing Condivi, Vasari reports: " And for her Michelangelo drew a marvelous Pietà in Our Lady's lap with two cherubs, and a Christ crucified on the Cross raising His head and recommending his soul to the Father, a thing divine; as well as a Christ with the Samaritan woman at the well." The Pietà was never made into a picture by Michelangelo. Nor is there any information to indicate that the Samaritan Woman, which we know from a print by Beatrizet, ever became a painting. Our interest in it lies primarily in the sonnet that Vittoria Colonna wrote about it in which the Gospel incident alluding to charity and the equality of men and races was given an interpretation favouring intimate prayer as the direct conversation between the believer and God aside from the Church's mediation. This constitutes further evidence of the reformist attitude of the circle that Buonarroti frequented in those years. On the other hand, the Crucifix seems to have been made into a painting by Michelangelo himself, although both Condivi and Vasari mention only a drawing. In two letters that can be dated 1539 or 1540, Vittoria first asks the artist to send her the Crucifix to see, even though it was unfinished:

" Because I should like to show it to gentlemen of the Most Reverend Cardinal of Mantua."

Then she praises the Crucifix that the painter had sent her and asks whether it belonged to him, in which cashe se would like to buy it:

187 Warriors, in the Crucifixion of St. Peter.
Pauline Chapel.

" I have had your letter and seen the Crucifix, which certainly has crucified in my memory any other pictures I ever saw, and no better made, more vivid and more perfect an image can be seen; and certainly I could never explain how cleverly and wonderfully it is done so that I have resolved that I do not want it to be in other hands, and so tell me, if it is [intended] for others, then patience. If it is yours, I will take it from you by all means, but in case it is not yours and you want to have it done by your man [that is, have a copy made by ' that

188 Heads, in the Crucifixion of St. Peter. Pauline Chapel.

269

189-190 Head of warrior, in the Crucifixion of St. Peter; detail of the Crucifixion of St. Peter. Pauline Chapel.

painter of yours,' which was probably Venusti], we will discuss the matter first, since I know how hard it is to imitate it, I think I had rather have him do something else [that is, copy a different work by Michelangelo] than this; but if you own this one, prepare yourself for my not returning it anymore. I have looked at it carefully in the light and with the glass and with the mirror and I never saw a more perfect thing.''

Various painted copies of this Crucifix have been preserved, including one by Venusti which has, besides the two cherubs in the sky, the figures of two mourners. There is also an engraving by Bonasone without the mourners, and three drawings in Oxford, Paris, and London. The latter, in charcoal, is held by some to be an original, by others and a copy. Leaving the authorship of the sketch to the writer who discusses the drawings in this volume, all the iconographical evidence indicates that the crucifix was flanked by two cherubs. De Campos, at the recent Michelangelo conference in Rome, presented a little picture as probably an original by the master in which the Crucifix stands alone without angels. The absence of the cherubs has been taken as an argument favouring the authenticity of the panel—engravers and copyists are said to have reproduced the London drawing and not the painting—for only Michelangelo himself could have decided to eliminate the two angels. But in another letter which seems to have been written by the Marchioness after she had definitely received the Crucifix (it appears from the letter that she made some suggestions to the artist concerning the work's completion) the two angels are mentioned:

" Your effects forcibly arouse the judgments of one who sees them and by having more experience of them I spoke of adding goodness to perfect things. And I have seen that *omnia*

192 Head, in the Crucifixion of St. Peter. Pauline Chapel.

193-195 Details of the Crucifixion of St. Peter. Pauline Chapel.

possibilia sunt credenti. I had very great faith in God that he would give you supernatural grace to make this Christ. Then I saw it so admirable that it was better in every way than any expectation. Then, emboldened by your miracles, I wished for that which I now see marvelously fulfilled, namely that it is of the highest perfection in every part, and more could not be desired, nor could one manage to desire so much. And I tell you that I am very glad that the *right-hand angel is much more beautiful,* because Michael will set you, Michelangelo, at the right hand of the Lord on the last day. And at this point I do not know how otherwise to serve you than to pray for you to that gentle Christ that you have painted so well and perfectly, and pray you to command me as your servant in everything and for everything." [73]

The Crucifix painted by Michelangelo thus had the two angels. To judge from the color reproduction in a weekly magazine, the newly discovered painting seems to be of the finest 271 quality, but not on the same level of power—in fact, it is too faithfully exact to the charcoal drawing in London which would be more characteristic of a copy than of a version of the original by the artist himself. The harsh and almost surly expression of the face in the drawing is transferred to the painting with a certain softening of timbre that is slightly pietistic, and not in consonance with Michelangelo's conception.

The frescoes in the Cappella Paolina are Michelangelo's last works of painting. In 1547 Vittoria Colonna died, in 1549 Pope Paul III, and the next pope struck out decisively on the road of Counter Reformation reaction. The friends of the Marchioness of Pescara, followers of Valdès, were now openly persecuted; anonymous accusations of heresy touched Buonarroti himself, although the ecclesiastical authorities ignored them out of respect to the greatness of the artist, and preferred instead to make use of his talent. Michelangelo felt himself more and more alone, more and more a stranger to the world around him. It is a mistake on the part of critics to maintain that he felt himself liberated from alleged requirements of formal finesse according to the tastes of Vittoria Colonna. The "*finitezza*" that recurs in the lady's letters is a synonym for perfection in the artistic sense, of completeness of expression, not of technical refinement. The advice she sometimes took it upon herself to suggest to the artist, probably related to themes of iconography and content in connection with the religious doctrines of her circle, and not to the technique of art. The reasons for the failure to finish his last works of sculpture are another matter. Disheartened, and fearful of the "second death," Michelangelo now sought refuge in the more rational activity of architecture (which furthermore spared his old age the most wearisome of physical tasks). Moreover, architecture enabled him to give expression to his grand vision of dynamics and cosmic drama. He had always regarded painting not as his art. The clear and sharply defined language of sculpture now appeared inadequate to his anxious desire to express direct union with God in faith and grace. Thus, his last works in sculpture all remained unfinished, even though perfect in the fullness of their expression: "Nor painting nor carving now be more than quiet/The soul turned to that love divine/that opened its arms to take us on the cross."

[67] On the chronology of the frescoes of the Paolina, see Vasari-Barocchi, III, p. 1408 ff.

[68] H. von Einem, "Michelangelo's Frescoes in the Pauline Chapel," in *Festschrift K. Bauch*, Munich, 1957, p. 193; and more briefly, *op. cit.*, p. 143 ff.

[69] P. Toesca, article "Michelangelo" in *Enciclopedia Italiana*, XXIII, 1934; V. Mariani, *op. cit.*, 1942, p. 203 ff. (but all reservations have disappeared in *Michelangelo Pittore, op. cit.*, p. 126 ff.); P. D'Ancona, A. Pinna and I. Cardellini, *Michelangelo Architetto Pittore Scultore*, Milan, 1964, p. xiii. On the two frescoes of the Paolina, D'Ancona states that "while not denying the presence of magnificent bits of painting ... these jumbled and strained compositions, largely done by assistants, do not show the intense from-creating spirituality that is characteristic of Michelangelo."

[70] F. Baumgart and B. Biagetti, *Gli Affreschi di Michelangelo e di L. Sabbatini e F. Zuccari nella Cappella Paolina in Vaticano*, Vatican City, 1934, p. 34.

[71] M. Dvořák, *op. cit.*, II, p. 131; A. Neumeyer in *Zeitschrift für bildende Kunst*, LXIII, 1929-30, p. 176 ff.; Baumgart-Biagetti, *op. cit.*, p. 27 ff.; Mariani, *op. cit.*, 1942, p. 204; P. D'Ancona, *Michelangelo. Affreschi della Cappella Paolina in Vaticano*, Milan, 1952.

[72] Mariani, *op. cit.*, 1942, p. 206; Tolnay, *op. cit.*, 1951, p. 93.

[73] Text of the letter in Vasari-Barocchi, IV, p. 2004.

Bibliographical Note

The enormous literature on Michelangelo, most of which deals with his painting as well, is listed, up to 1926, in E. Steinmann and R. Wittkower, *Michelangelo-Bibliographie*, Leipzig, 1927; from 1927 to 1930 in E. Steinmann, *Michelangelo im Spiegel seiner Zeit* (appendix to H. W. Schmidt, *Nachtrag und Fortsetzung der Michelangelo Bibliographie von Steinmann-Wittkower bis 1930*), Leipzig, 1930; from 1931 to 1942 in *Michelangelo Buonarroti nel IV Centenario del Giudizio Universale* (P. Cherubelli, *Supplemento alla Bibliografia Michelangiolesca*), Florence, 1942; from 1942 to 1961 (with supplements to the earlier bibliographies) in G. Vasari, *La Vita di Michelangelo nelle redazioni del 1550 e del 1568*, edited and commented by Paola Barocchi, Milan and Naples, 1962, I, p. 341 ff. We have made large use of the exhaustive and exemplary documentation of this commentary, for all Michelangelesque problems. We therefore confine ourselves to listing below a few publications on Michelangelo's painting that have appeared since 1961 and that we have used.

C. de Tolnay, "Michelangelo Buonarroti", in *Enciclopedia Universale dell'Arte*, IX, col. 263, Venice and Rome, 1963.

P. D'Ancona, A. Pinna and I. Cardellini, *Michelangelo Architetto Pittore Scultore*, Milan, 1964.

D. Redig De Campos, *Il Giudizio Universale di Michelangelo*, Rome, 1964.

C. A. Isermeyer, "The Works of Leonardo and Michelangelo for the Hall of the Grand Council in Florence", in *Studien zur Toskanischen Kunst. Festschrift für L. H. Heydenreich*, Munich, 1964, p. 83.

V. Mariani, *Michelangelo*, Naples, 1964.

V. Mariani, *Michelangelo Pittore*, Milan, 1964.

P. Hartt, *Michelangelo*, Milan, 1964.

IV

ARCHITECTURE

by Guglielmo De Angelis d'Ossat

Introduction

The evaluation of Michelangelo's architectural works has been, up to our own times, delayed for various reasons. Only recently has the lack of development in this specific field of study been realised, which has remained extraneous and almost absent from the continuous and vast flux of Buonarroti's contributions, and an important, hitherto ignored, " corpus " of works has finally been brought to the eyes of the critics. These works assure ample margin for exact historical research and fruitful discussion, urgently desirable.

The similar profession of sculptor, which the Master was long pleased to affirm, is at its historic origins of deviating prejudices and forgetful silences; all incomprehensions which have clouded his other exceptional artistic manifestations and have, above all, impeded the configuration of the autonomy of his architectural conceptions and the recognition of the high conscious message. The prevailing qualification of sculptor is easily extended to and superimposed on the architecture of Michelangelo, mortgaging and distorting all evaluation; thus the thoughts, impulses, experiences and architectural masterpieces of the Master have escaped methodic analysis and measured criticism.

To this, substantially subordinate, are added the other reasons—as a whole, more common and generic—which are derived from the difficulty of reading architectural documents and works and from the consequent laboriousness of the related studies. All these contribute to making appear remote, dim and vague, a panorama which instead is clean and vivid.

Only in an estranged and depressed atmosphere can so many unconstrained and conformed opinions, even the incredible denials of Charles Garnier and, nearer to us, the unjustified condemnation expressed by Frank Lloyd Wright, can be explained.

Such a wide problem of such crucial importance could not remain entirely without echo and intention of evaluation in the general reawakening of historic-artistic interests in the last few decades. Apart from sporadic, partial contributions, only in these past few years have specific studies been made, fruit of the German school of historians.

To Charles de Tolnay, we owe a notable group of fundamental interventions and penetrating essays which await collection in a forthcoming volume. Recently, James Ackerman has completed a fine work on the entire range of the Master's architectural activities, also those presumed, by means of a large precious collection of historical sources.

Shortly afterwards, and on the occasion of the Centenary of Michelangelo, the imposing publication of Bruno Zevi, assisted by Paolo Portoghesi, appeared; composed of a series of essays by various authors on all the most important works, the episodic and unequal character of the work finds a common denominator in a burning critical will and in the desire to effect the realisation of the architectural phenomenon. This solid volume is recommended for its fine and useful documentation of the works and drawings of Michelangelo.

Though the Master's works have at last been submitted to methodical study, it is not through this that the complete, complex figure of Michelangelo, architect, has come forth, from the formative process to the final accomplishments, through linguistic research, compositive methods and formal predilections. Nor has the reconstruction of the contemporary ambient and dialectics always succeeded in clarifying important circumstances or fundamental components of his spatial conquests.

1 Madonna della Scala (research for the exterior front setup and volumetric connections). Florence, Casa Buonarroti.

2 Drawing reconstruction of the first plan for the Mausoleum of Julius II. (The drawings 2, 6 and 7 are drawn from the work of C. Tolnay).

3 Giacomo Rocchetti: drawing of the second plan for the Mausoleum of Julius II (1513). Berlin, Kupferstichkabinett.

274

The whole of his architectural production, even if vigorously estimated, has not always been considered at its true value; the difference between the estimation of the Florentine works and the Roman of his old age has not been balanced and has suffered from old, incomplete literature and obligatory, laudatory translations.

Finally, the analysis of the drawings, object generally of exemplary studies and publications, appears other than dispensing in this field. Their often just importance is basic and illuminating for a true interpretation of his works. Profound researches into Michelangelo's architectural drawings are indispensable.

Approach to architecture

MADONNA DELLA SCALA

Precise architectonic values emerge even from the first work of the young Michelangelo. In the *Madonna della Scala* (in which the tradition of the " Florentine flattening " is refreshed in the imposing volumes of the figures) the background is deepened by a bold illuminant perspective (Fig. 1).

Apart from the determining tectonic value of the Madonna, other elements and precise compositional relationships contribute to give a deliberate architectonic framework, announced at once by the squareness of the chair.

The emerging episode of the staircase (which distinguishes the relief and gives it its name) operates with the simplest of planes and volumes, without any formal definition but expressive by virtue of their precise mass values: the massive parapet would suffice to characterize the staircase and set it apart from similar basreliefs by Donatello. The background, like the entire work, is brought out by the sharp perspective below: a bit of simple popular architecture, redeemed and made unmistakable by the unconventional and highly significant carving. In the little external staircase, the choice of the point of view does not even show the probable line of the parapet; the immanence of a modest rustic house is suggested, but is felt to be transfigured by a powerful magic. The perspective runs off towards regions out of view but not beyond the imagination, leaving the finale of the episode open; and there might even be the suggestion of a more important theme of a staircase with two wings—anticipating the mature creations of Michelangelo—if consistent with the hidden indication of a wall, placed frontally to close off the scene and inhibit stray visions.

The bold perspective announces new demands of taste, going beyond the spirit of Renaissance experience and foreshadowing new researches, deriving from rigorous but merely suggested connection between the descending parapet and the positioning of the solid terminal block on which the Madonna is seated. The solemn figure connected with this base thus stands out from the childish episodes, and makes the staircase monumental, seeming to form with it a single body, by virtue of a high compositional logic, in an atmosphere of giant and peremptory prospective effects. Michelangelo certainly imagined the scene as viewed with the amazed wide eyes of a child, one of the little *putti* who had already descended the staircase and could view it from below and take in its surprising effects.

By the insistent bold *fugato* of the steps, tending always upwards, the usual representation is avoided, that of short horizontal planes, and the steps are suggested as an invisible source of elastic impulse for the unquiet feet of the *putti*. Their receding slope was to return as a characteristic of the Master's drawing in many a staircase design, as if to mark its sharp ascent or hinder the downward trend (Fig. 127).

All the tension of the foreshortened perspective is summed up here in the expressive downward plunge of the parapet, an oblique element of force from which a perfect concluding central whirl of limbs and drapery seems to have its beginning: like a shield for the heart of the Mother and a sure dynamic seal to the composition.

TOMB OF JULIUS II

Although the enterprise of the tomb of Julius II caused Michelangelo so many bitter experiences, it also gave him a varied approach to architectural studies. The " tragedy of the tomb " was placed against the shifting background of a spectacular undertaking that was always in the process of changing, if only by reason of the sites chosen—or only imagined—for the unending labor.

Designed in 1505 as a tomb standing free on all sides, it was not placed in the center of the church but in the choir of old St. Peter's basilica, whose renovation had been begun by Rossellino. The great length of the axial plan and the absence of a great altar, as well as the limited dimensions of the edifice, spoke against locating the tomb above the sepulcher of the Apostle, admitted and accredited with too great facility. The monumental theme

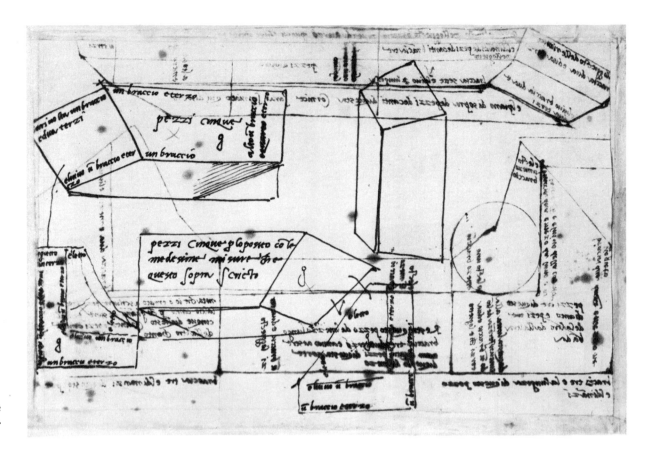

4 Sketches for the cutting of marble for the Mausoleum of Julius II. Florence, Casa Buonarroti, 67 A v.

appears in the plan and measurements, and is solved with a conception that is more sculptural than architectonic: an unprecedented, vital marble mass carved within the hollow of a chapel.

To judge from what data have come down to us, the architectural lines were not used to frame, and perhaps not even to organize, the remarkable complex of sculptures carved out on a number of stepped-back planes, culminating in the group of the pontifical cenotaph at the summit of a remarkable pyramid (Fig. 2). They were used only to provide base and background planes, volumes and surfaces in assonance or contrast with sculptural representations of human feelings and passions, still alive in the cold rock, even after death. One feels that Michelangelo employs architectonic material but does not find it his major interest, does not dominate it. He borrows divisions, forms and ornaments, but does not yet animate them and form them with genius. Treated in this way, the architecture serves here merely as a support and frame for his sculptures.

Possibly, a clear and compelling architectural definition may have been reserved for the innermost cella, planned as a funerary chamber with an elliptical plan; if built, it would have been the firts Renaissance chapel of such a shape. We have a better idea of the original exterior. On the floor level, projecting pilaster hermae alternated with deep niches. On the pilasters were the varied torments of the *Slaves;* in the niches, *Victories* and *Virtues.*

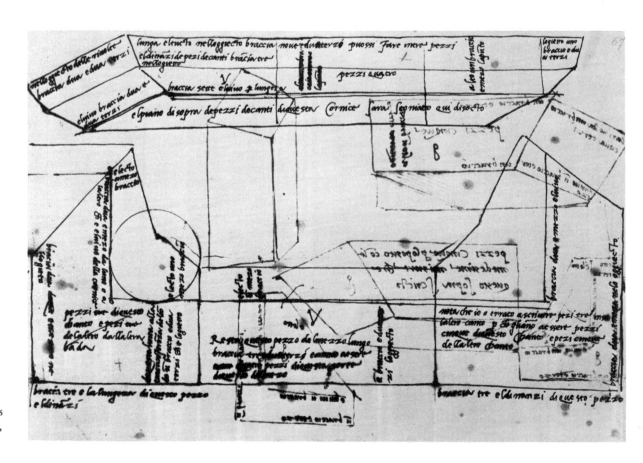

5 Sketches for the cutting of the marble ashlars for the Mausoleum of Julius II. Florence, Casa Buonarroti 67 A r.

6 Drawing reconstruction of the third plan (1516) for the Mausoleum of Julius II.

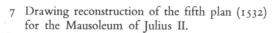

8 Antonio Salamanca: engraving of the final arrangement (1545) of the Mausoleum of Julius II.

7 Drawing reconstruction of the fifth plan (1532) for the Mausoleum of Julius II.

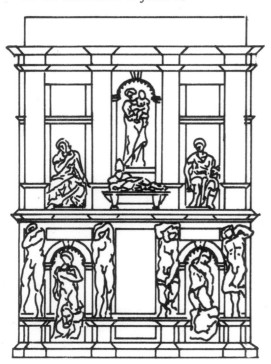

All the works of the chisel, the first things to be seen by the visitor, would have their dramatic expressions enhanced by the ingenuous flowered decorative frame of the background, but not architectural evidence. The reconstruction of the upper portion is less secure; there, the attenuated architectural values served to give a vital dialectic to the ascent of the compositional pattern.

Some other sketches by the Master, suggesting complex triumphal arches, are to be referred to this phase of the project (Florence, Archivio Buonarroti, Vol. IX, 539 v. and London, British Museum, Wilde 22 r.). This reference is unlikely, not only because of the absence of any funerary character but also because of the great divergence between the two conceptions. In fact, the difficulty of fitting such arches inside a church would, in my opinion, exclude all other sepulchral relationship.

Different, and architecturally bolder and more dynamic, was the second project, dated 1513, in which the short side of the mausoleum was joined to a wall of the church. The new composition, while making use of the previous studies and traditional iconographic motifs, was originally designed, rising enormous against the wall, with a religious image projecting from the rest of the tomb design, guarding it and in intentional contrast (Fig. 3). In the geomet-

ric design, the dissimilarity of the two parts emerges: it is the peal of refusal to the traditional superimposition of the orders.

To move the composition almost to make it leave the vertical plane on which development takes place, the Master appears to have had the idea of an outward-facing orientation for the corner statues above the architectural platform, so as to suggest diagonal lines of expansion.

If our reference is to be to Bramante's basilica, I think that a mausoleum of this kind could have found a place only in one of the apsidal solutions of the new St. Peter's; this would also justify the extent of protrusion, since it would not be subject to side views at a distance. The composition develops along two guide lines; on the lower level, the world of human changes and struggles centers around the papal vestments; above, the Divine presence is announced at once, like a detached celestial vision. This was the Master's first dramatic architectural design, based on the sharp incidence of a longitudinal development upon a perpendicular one, closed by a free arched motif, a calming rainbow for the spirit.

Perhaps some sculptural lacerto of this project could be recognised in several puttini then reutilised and inserted—with motifs and forms presumed of the Sistine—in the pillaring of the balustrade in Cappella del Monte in San Pietro in Montorio. Michelangelo supervised the foundations and the decoration of the noble tomb of the forebears of Julius III.

This was followed in 1516 by a third project, reduced merely to the front of the great work that had been under design for so long, but all but incapable of execution because of the superhuman demands on the sculptor (Fig. 6). Actually, the 1516 contract, in addition to a second order of " half columns," called for *rivolte*, i. e. the side faces on the flanks, equal in size to the niches on the sides of the front, and likewise embellished with statues. At that time there was no willingness to give up the plastic and volumetric protrusion of the work from the rear wall, but this was not destined to be put into execution, in spite of the care taken by Michelangelo in personally defining the stereotomy of the marble blocks (Figs. 4 and 5). Subsequent vicissitudes no longer involved the essence of the now confined architectural project.

From being a remarkable sculptural vision fully in the round, the theme had sunk to being an organized wall solution; instead of ennobling the Vatican temple, it was to fit on a side wall of S. Pietro in Vincoli, where the last act of the " tragedy " ended only in 1545. The Master's interest had gradually decreased (Fig. 7) until by that time it had all but disappeared. Through a series of variants, none of which changed the basic architectural organization, the dreamed-of mausoleum had been reduced to the mere emplacement of ready-made pieces of sculpture; renouncing all plastic effects, it was now only the ordinary wall type that so many efforts had been made to avoid.

In S. Pietro in Vincoli we see only the front of the original mausoleum, taken out of its old context and framed on the wall without any relief. On this is superposed a distant reminiscence of the bold vertical motif of 1513, fitting, however, into a different and expanded architectural arrangement. It frames, without prestige, the group of the Madonna and the Child, which had originally been conceived of as under a lofty projecting tabernacle. If this genetic history were not taken into consideration, the oldest architectural portions would seem even more incoherent than they are; deprived of the exalting presence of the *Slaves*, they got as makeshift replacement inverted consoles and crude images of hermae (Fig. 8). Above the old ornate base there now rise simple stone volumes, projecting from sharp rectilinear frames; an order and vestment that the sole Atlas heads do not succeed in joining with the sculptural world underneath.

The two aspects are not formally compatible; certainly, forty years had not passed in vain for Michelangelo and for the development of his architectural conceptions. The two variants of his arrangement (tripartite with projecting elements, and a differentiated solution in the center) are here frankly superimposed, not so much to indict a belated embodiment with its anachronistic floral decorations still in the fifteenth-century taste, as to attest the ever-renewed validity of an idea and unswerving loyalty to a favorite theme. And, above all, to reaffirm his independence in the proportioning of structures and superimposed orders.

We are therefore led to take into isolated consideration the polite elegance of the upper order, the clean edges and the smart details: rigorous architecture, with no further concessions to tradition and now polemically refuses the curved lines.

The statues, set within unconnected frames, end up by appearing an independent of one another. The papal cenotaph in the center is reduced in its modest, almost ridiculous posture compressed inside the narrow frame.

Of greater interest is the original pontifical coat of arms between candelabra. No longer applied to the wall, but strangely detached, it rises boldly at the end of the frieze, as if symbolically to redeem the work, that the Master wished to immerse in a luminous ambient.

A large simple arch, suitably carved at the top of the wall, covers the entire facade, leaving a high space on the axis of the transept, ready to suggest illusory but not improbable depths for the papal monument. A glass enclosure now deprives us of the original effect (Fig. 8), but still permits the text to be read.

Under the protection of this wide sweep of the authoritative arch of the second project, the hoped-for third dimension seems to find an image, if not substance, in the small windows that

Buonarroti opened in the upper order; unusual openings indicating internal uses and functions, and giving new unexpected aspects.

Although Michelangelo was forced to make considerable revisions and sorrowful renunciations, he cannot be said to have been altogether resigned to defeat. The wall, cut by a decisive curve, which seems to better invigorate image of the rainbow, breaks a traditional lack of spatial communication between the church and the convent. Against the unexpected void, and once lifted by the light, we see the crown of the tomb, organized and emphasized by the candelabras and by the beautiful coat of arms, certainly not unobserved by a Borromini; just below blink the lighted, and nowadays, mysteriously shaded little apertures.

THE SISTINE CHAPEL

After his first plastic experiments, aiming at a new perspective organization of space or at the composition of unprecedented sculptural groups, Michelangelo was called upon to decorate the *vault of the Sistine Chapel*. This led him to pose, and to solve in the pictural plane, the difficult problem of an illusionistic architecture, nonetheless valid and personal.

At the outset, the great subject, commissioned in 1506 by Julius II, did not seem to involve architectural difficulties and searchings. He himself states the nature of " the first design of the said work: twelve apostles in the lunettes and the rest a certain compartmentation filled with ornament, as is the custom." Here, " lunettes " obviously must mean the initial portions of the facetted vault between the sixteen lunettes properly so called: they formed twelve spaces that were well suited to depictions of the Apostles. The iconographic subject entrusted to him thus was grafted on a Christian symbolism that even in architecture often linked with the number twelve the memory and the composition of the college of Apostles.

The figures were to have been placed five on each side, while the two similar spaces on the end walls were to have been reserved for depicting Saints Peter and Paul. It was in these twelve spaces, which Condivi calls, less elegantly but more clearly, " horns of the lunettes," that there appeared Michelangelo's thrones, on which, instead of the Apostles, were seated Prophets and Sibyls.

On this basis, it is not hard to reconstruct the stages of Michelangelo's thinking for organizing the vault of the Sistine, based on the designs handed down to us. The simple " compartmentation " suggested to him would have come out too minute, and certainly appeared banal to Michelangelo, as he pointed out to the pontiff. From the essays along these lines, however, an informative drawing has come down to us from which I have taken (Fig. 9).

Buonarroti's intentions in dealing with the theme come out clearly on the basis of the practical " custom." He breaks the Renaissance unity of the " compartments " with a free alternation of effects and forms, among which there already appear precious indications of oblique lines. The division thus accentuated is stated without diminishing the preeminence of the thrones and their essential value as fulcra. It is a first manful interpretation that respects the theme set him; but it is also an honest denunciation of the bonds imposed and an implicit suggestion for future developments.

This critical position is the starting point for a second sketch by Michelangelo, which shows that greater freedom of action has been conquered (Fig. 10). The creative anxiety not only tries finally to reduce and clarify the frame, but above all tends to make it take on the character of a mere ornament with another that is more ordering and structural, by searching for new lines of force between the essential nodes. Accordingly, the opposite thrones are linked, two by two, by continuous motifs that boldly leap over the space, cutting out broad free frames, which Michelangelo geometrizes in prominent octagons. It must not be argued from the drawing that these fields might have alternated with simpler broad rectangular spaces; this deduction should be rejected in view of the even number of compartments that would have resulted. The alternation sought for, however, was soon to prove to be productive of the final determinations.

In this intermediate study, the Master already showed that he wanted to place the accent on the bands going across the vault, incorporating them with a dense sequence of elliptical and rectangular scrolls. The desire for simplification appears more in the dividing of the surfaces and identification of the ideal structures than in the details and ornaments.

The final solution hinges on the later developments, with as starting point the thicker little pilasters at the sides of the chairs, which are spaced and prolonged in a strong partition. As these isolated bonds were doubled across the top of the vault and their essential architectural value was realized, the final pattern was arrived at, based on the rhythmic division of the entire central portion of the vault into large alternate fields, which Michelangelo dreamed of as inhabited by free titanic visions. All that was left of the old " compartmentation " were the monochrome medallions to recall the close bond between the two pilasters of each throne and bring out the binary motif of the ribbing on the thrones which had by now become broader and more solemn. The studies are followed by the fresco work begun at the end of 1508 and carried out practically single handed, with infinite labour (Fig. 11).

The final embodiment (echoed in another much-discussed drawing that is difficult to interpret) thus appears as a logical elaboration; the result of the two preceding studies. The theme that has prevailed and become dominant is the united motif of the large arches across the vault of heaven, a division that brings out the structural will and daring and already seems to aspire to concrete embodiments, with the anticipation of the boldest visions for the St. John of the Florentines.

Michelangelo's vast solitary labor was completed, as he tells us himself, on October 31, 1512, after he had unfolded, on the preordained plan, an entire figurative poem of unmatched sweep and power. In summing up Michelangelo's labors, so noble and so new, Vasari did not overlook the dynamics of the architectural process: " he proceeded, fitting the compartmentation to the figures rather than the figures to the compartmentation." And in point of fact, such was the final outcome of the work, if not its program.

We cannot but recognize the full originality of the architectonic design; so much so that it has sometimes been judged in isolation from the representations that justify it and give it substance. This cannot be done; it must be seen in its connections, also for the intentional absence of concrete imitations, not having used order and prospectives which may represent.

The studied contrapuntal relations between the figurative and architectural aspects have been brought out by Tolnay and referred to the origin of the resultant effects, which ring in our mind's ear, multiple and sonorous, as if preluding the new polyphonic music.

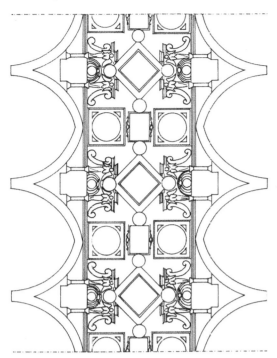

9 Diagram of a study for the architectural distribution of the Sistine Chapel vault, from a drawing in the British Museum, London. Wilde, 72.

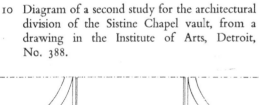

11 Sistine Chapel. Rome, Vatican Palaces.

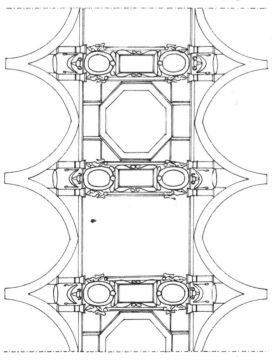

10 Diagram of a second study for the architectural division of the Sistine Chapel vault, from a drawing in the Institute of Arts, Detroit, No. 388.

Within the large frames, the figures are gigantic and the architectural episodes appear as rare and minor. Only Noah's Ark emerges in geometrical and abstract elegance, in a static block form, certainly not motivated by functional requirements nor in conformity with the traditional Biblical measurements. In this representation, however, we are struck by a native simplicity, a formal purism, that was in the future to have sporadic developments in the Master's work.

In choosing and composing the framings of his Sistine organism, Michelangelo appears as a trained and masterful worker, free and joyous in expressing himself in the painted mouldings. It is here that he begins to try a new language; without embarking on theatrical effects, he brings out every element in perspective (as he had already proposed to do in his quick sketches), infusing it with a life of its own. In this way, he defines a base plane of reference of his architectural structures, and out of it leap the incidents. Michelangelo dominates this painted interpretation of the architecture, creating a set of variations in formal research. He is truly a genius in opposing slim balusters to square blocks and softening the points with sinuous and energetic lines.

Each of these painted architectural episodes seems to have a perspicuous individuality of its own, to be aware of its own real life, which was to be instilled into the mural works.

FAÇADE IN CASTEL SANT'ANGELO

Vivid in fantasy, and undoubtedly Michelangelesque in origin, appears the marble façade on the side of the Cappella in Castel S. Angelo, dedicated by Leo X to the Medici Saints Cosma and Damiano, protectors of his family. New themes, tried out by genius, coexist whith gentle traditional forms. The contrast of the two, in a first dialectic of Buonarroti, heightens the interest of the work and brings out the feeling of subtle ambiguity impressed on youthful forms that was already announced in his first Roman sculptures. It seems to me that, in this atmosphere, we have his first completed work as architect, dated 1514.

The three-part projecting façade, the two-part form of the central motif, the juxtaposition

12 Giambattista da Sangallo: drawing of a plan for the Chapel of Leo X in Castel Sant'Angelo. Lille, Museum des Beaux Arts, 733.

13-14 Details of the side exterior view of the Chapel of Leo X. Rome, Castel Sant'Angelo.

15 Lateral marble façade of the Chapel of Leo X. Rome, Castel Sant'Angelo. (Before the so-called restoration).

of the windows and small apertures above: all are elements characteristic of the artist's language, which can easily find parallels in drawings of the Master and in his future works.

The curious and original solution of the central motif, embodied in the marble of its statues, may have its roots in the set of crossed windows but is free from natural preliminaries and rich in new elaboration in a Mannerist key. Accessible to the view, it emerges as new and appropriate: a poetic escape from the military atmosphere of the Castle, dimensioned to the limited space surrounding it.

The well-known Lille drawing, attributed to G. B. da Sangallo (Fig. 12), gives us another

version of the façade: perhaps the original one, with tighter proportions and more strikingly marked by the central console. Especially disquieting is the presence of great " glazed " eyes above the square windows, a juxtaposition that recurs in autograph studies by the Master. However, the round windows in the drawing were replaced from the outset by elongated rectangular openings (Fig. 15). It is not impossible that the changes from the drawing, presented by the finished work, were made by the Master himself for reasons of solemnity and neatness and to eliminate ornate and chromatic episodes. This is not to state that the execution was directly supervised by Buonarroti: it seems instead to have been entrusted to a traditional stonecutter, as shown by the ingenuous simplicity and inexpressive combinations of the moldings, where the execution attributed to young Antonio da Sangallo cannot even be recognised.

The changes intended as restorations, violently inserting inadequate little circular apertures in place of the elongated upper windows (Fig. 14), succeeded only in bastardising the essence of the work and lowering its quality, which it is a pleasure to see as it appears in old photo-

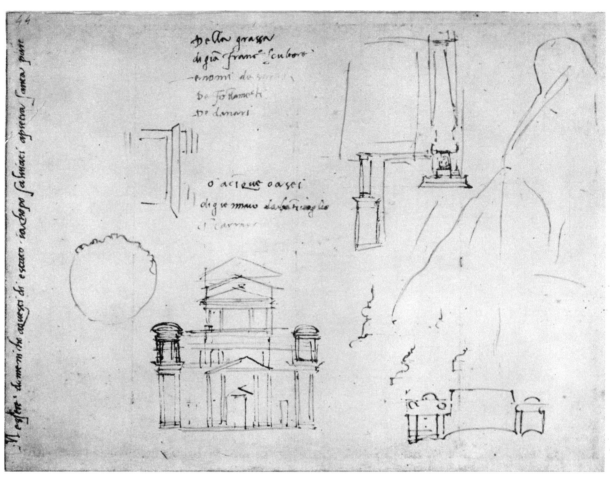

16 Drawing for the façade of San Lorenzo, in Florence. Florence, Casa Buonarroti, 44 A r.

17 Drawing for the façade of San Lorenzo, Florence. Florence, Casa Buonarroti, 47 A r.

18 Final wooden model of the façade of San Lorenzo, Florence (the wax reliefs have been lost). Florence, Casa Buonarroti.

graphs (Fig. 15). Prior to the alleged restorations there was a more severe and clear-cut secondary framework within the order, which Michelangelo often broke up into superimposed fields, like those obtained with the rectilinear windows.

In the absence of explanatory documents, we must take as principal element the compilation of the work as it has come down to us before modification. One cannot, at the moment, give details or expound hypotheses on the aspects of this great episode. Only the architectural thought must strike us. It appears well defined and indicative in its functional opening and in the terse dialectic composition. It does not, however, seem possible also to see the Master's hand in the executive details, just as he had succeeded in representing them, with his brush, on the vault of the Sistine, and how he personally was to come later to mould them.

19 Completion of the model of the façade of San Lorenzo, Florence. Tempera by Gaetano Alibrandi.

CHURCH OF SAN LORENZO

It would appear that Leo X, as soon as he ascended the pontifical throne, invited various artists to make designs for a *facade for the Medici church of San Lorenzo in Florence*. A substantial set of drawings by Giuliano da Sangallo, who died on October 20, 1516, shows how greatly he was interested in the theme.

These drawings that have come down to us were not like entries in a competition with other architects. They are studies of only slightly differentiated solutions, clearly worked out for the choice of a patron who had already outlined his own orientation.

In the autumn of the same year we find Michelangelo engaged in studying the problem, which was to be on his mind for some years. The sequence of his ideas, carefully followed out by Tolnay, enables us to trace the genesis and development of his architectural thinking, all of which goes back to the many studies by Giuliano, so much so as suggest to us that he inherited the commission.

A first project, designed in Rome at the end of the year, was put into the form of a wooden model by Baccio d'Agnolo: "a thing for children," Michelangelo called it; he had no use for the artist associated with him for San Lorenzo and soon managed to get rid of him. We do not know its exact nature, but it was probably inspired by the strongly classicist solutions of Giuliano da Sangallo, into which Michelangelo infused a new spirit. The façade was to be decorated by ten statues and have an Attic story. It seems likely that it can be identified with a documented sketch.

It is certain that these were the premises that Michelangelo developed more fully in his solution, for which we have studies in two drawings in Casa Buonarroti (91 A and 44 A, Fig. 16), which clearly converge towards drawing 47 A. The latter may be considered to sum up an entire phase, which some scholars define as intermediate (Fig. 17).

The idea comes out clearly in the simple purposeful drawing. The second order is grafted precisely onto the first; the organisation of the façade is obtained not only by the great central body but also by the two high lateral projections, closed off by the accentuated motif of the shrines: the five bodies vaguely hint at the internal basilica partition. Michelangelo's starting point was Uffizi Drawing 277 by Giuliano; but while repeating all its elements, he has given them quite another vitality.

In his treatment of the lower order he has broken the continual servile replica of the rhythmic framework of Bramante; above, he has developed the second order to the point of making it more imposing than the lower one, substituting pilasters for the columns, and thereby succeeding in loudly contradicting Giuliano's timid Quattrocento inhibitions and the rules of conformist classicism. I think that this courageous formal revolt, dared on many other occasions, will have been supported by a famous example of antiquity: that of the Colosseum, where the last pilastered order stands out, for its bolder proportions, over the lower ones interspersed with columns. The Master also gives full weight to the central and outer parts, he tones down the intermediate regions and puts them into the background, setting up a broad grand vertical rhythm. Accentuating and giving animation to classical compartmentation, he proposes and achieves grandly simple effects. In this context he even inserts the motif of high paired openings, a personal tribute to the Brunelleschi tradition.

In the first months of 1517 Michelangelo made a little clay model at Carrara, in order better to express the plastic quality of the work, mindful as he was of the way in which Baccio's flat wood model had debased his conceptions.

In the meantime, the project matured and grew to giant size in the mind of the Master. The famous Drawing 43 A (Plate XXVII) and the model preserved in Casa Buonarroti (Fig. 18) give a pale idea of Michelangelo's final and celebrating aspiration: "the façade of San Lorenzo, so that in architecture and structure it will be the mirror of all Italy." It should be pointed out that the adoption of so many statues can be noted as well in the drawings of Giuliano da Sangallo, at the express desire of the orderer. Obviously, Michelangelo took Giuliano's place after his death; this is shown by the alien origin of his starting points and the slow continuity of the transitions, both unusual in Michelangelo. Even the interruption of the orders in the corner articulations, satisfactorily based on the motif of the repeated lateral wings, is derived from the clear, numerous drawings by old Giuliano. But by now he was far from Giuliano's model, having integrated the entire second order into a compact vision: a colossal stone rectangle standing out resolutely from the gradation of the aisles and chapels. In this connection, the earlier example of the medieval churches of the Abruzzi has been recalled, which are shown with a squared "curtain" front. Here the solution is crowned by a short pediment in the center; it is more showy, but not entirely unitary because of the insertion of an intermediate horizontal zone supporting the statues. The so-called Attic story, also planned by Giuliano, is here inserted into an original anticlassical sequence which is supported by the unifying power of a compact solution.

Michelangelo makes no further reference to the volumetric conceptions of the Brunelleschian organism, now planning to set in front of it a square bulk of solid and contrasting composition densely peopled with statues. It is the first case of a Renaissance façade, understood as independent and autonomous. The January 1518 contract translated the remarkable ideas from the marbles into legal terms.

The work is complete in itself. Rather than a façade, it is a frontal unit because of the presence of the "volutes," as in the contemporaneous design for the tomb of Julius II and the later Palazzo dei Conservatori on the Capitoline.

This façade would have been a monumental "sacred conversation." The Medicean iconographic program had attained its greatest development. The marble façade was to be enlivened by an incredible number of sculptures, eighteen enormous statues, six in bronze, and nineteen panels in *mezzo rilievo*, some large, some medium-sized (Fig. 19).

From the architectural point of view, the partnership with sculpture takes on new dimensions; different, almost the reverse of the subordinate role it had had in the tomb of Julius II, that of merely providing a support for the sculptural riches. Here "Michelangelo's imagination was more engaged in the architectural problem than in the sculptural one. What might abstractly have been defined as a simple skeleton constitutes a profoundly new architectural solution" (Bertini). One proof of this would be the architectural values embodied in some of the sculptures, like the seated ones, located just where the façade began to rise and fall back, as if to mitigate the effect of retreat. They were to be in bronze, the better to define the nodal points of the composition and given chromatic emphasis to the center of the vertical elements, consisting of coupled superposed columns, above which would come the architectural frame of the façade and the "volutes." With the two lateral pilasters, the *pilamidoni* of the contract, these seated giants must have recalled the thrones of the Sistine chapel closed off by the broad lateral pilasters that likewise are prolonged in the binary motif of the supports.

The model appears highly finished with formal solutions linked to tradition, and the Master's drawings for the façade do not seem to show any personal researches in the formulation of the elements and architectural details. It is not excluded that the Master wanted to reserve the possibility of getting away, later, from the current practice that is so clearly adhered to in these projects and many have been required by the patrons of the work; the possibility of giving a more personal character to the great marble shrine that he meant to place in freedom in front of Brunelleschi's pile. An indication is given by a phrase in the contract: "inasmuch as in the said model not all the ornaments are done entirely, such as the carving of the frames and doorways and upper episodes, the aforesaid Michelangelo consents to be held to do all the said things in the manner and places that are suitable."

The work thus reveals its own limits that are partly implicitly conceded by the artist himself. They arise, from the outset, in the fact that he was working out a plan that was not his own. Michelangelo did not want to, or more likely could not, get very far away from Giuliano's design. We must admit in all frankness that the project seemed abortive, not only physically but even from the point of view of new artistic directions.

The image of Buonarroti is not impaired by this judgment; it emerges intact in the incorruptible power of his personality, rather, enriched by the founded prospects of new openings and future formal developments. In the end the Master's genius would have transcended the patterns imposed on him as he had succeeded in breaking the canons on the hierarchy and on the continuity of the orders. Also his tactical ability is the guarantee of that. We cannot imagine a Michelangelo following other people!

The task he had undertaken was of unparalleled magnitude and boldness. Realizing the practical difficulties of setting up the work site, he had at once bought an area near the city walls, near the demolished church of S. Caterina. I have identified this site by comparting Casa Buonarroti Drawing N. 32 A and 12 A r., thus removing this last from the Florentine fortifications. Further, he soon had new foundations started to support the heavy structure contemplated coming up against the inadequate foundations of an "old portico," possibly belonging to Brunelleschi's design. Michelangelo gave every appearance of being anxious to make all the preparations needed to carry out the work entrusted to him, even though we have no sculptures by him that we can say with certainty were intended for the façade, nor architectural drawings of an executive character.

The attempt to do everything by himself, rejecting assistance, was certainly a major cause for the failure of the work to be brought to completion. It did not suffice that he gave loving study to solving the difficulties of the project, to choosing marbles and carving ornaments, as can be seen from an admirable notebook in which, with the passion of the sculptor taking marble for his own works, he detailed the shapes and measurements of the blocks needed for the architectural framework.

The contract for this work, which was in fact not capable of being carried out, just as in the case of the tomb of Julius II, was annulled in March 1520, leaving damage and bitterness for the stout-hearted artist and clipping the wings of any one who might have dreamed, in later centuries, of providing the Medici basilica with a countenance.

COMPLETION OF THE CUPOLA OF SANTA MARIA DEL FIORE

It is a well-documented fact that Michelangelo had worked on a solution of his own for the circular gallery of Santa Maria del Fiore to complete the dome, on the external band linking the drum and the great vault, but all the data concerning the project and any figurative results emerging from it remain obscure.

All that we know clearly is Buonarroti's reaction to the "gallery" begun by Baccio d'Agnolo, one of the winners of the competition launched in 1507 to obtain a solution for this link. The reaction was so violent that it caused work to be broken off around Brunelleschi's dome, and so earnest that it caused the Master to take a direct part in solving the problem: "let him show what had to be done." While the effects of Michelangelo's criticism persisted, and can still be seen today (since Baccio's project could no longer be carried out and no alternative was set on foot), we do not know what positive architectural idea Michelangelo suggested.

The only portion of Baccio's gallery (labeled "a cricket cage") that was built was unveiled for the festival of St. John on June 24, 1515. Michelangelo's studies, if they cannot be attributed to the spring of that year when he was in Florence, must be only a little later in date, practically coinciding with his return to Tuscany.

Casa Buonarroti Drawings 50 A and 66 A (Fig. 21) exhibit data in common, on both sides, that have induced most scholars (excepting Frey, Berenson and in part Tolnay) to connect them with the great Florentine dome only in a general way, especially in view of the serious difficulties in interpreting them. Three drawings deal with the hypothetical face of the drum under the dome, isolated and simplified in its divisions and, above all, higher than in reality. The changed proportions cannot be explained as a mistake or other accident, since it is repeated identically in all three cases. Accordingly, the doubts that have been voiced are legitimate, just as there is support for the view of those who have regarded these drawings as intended for some modest project. Their inherent simplicity seems to indicate a diverse scale; they have been regarded as studies for an altar frontal.

The fourth drawing, on the recto of 50 A, has always been harder to interpret. Apart from the episodic motif of the pilasters bunched at a corner, the complicated sketch at the left has been referred to as a vertical cross section of the octagonal dome (Fig. 22).

Note that at one portion of the cross section of the wall, there is no corresponding internal portion of the drum. In my opinion, this is a bold juxtaposition of the view of one of the external faces, indicated by the large round window, the horizontal cornice immediately above it and, unmistakably, the presence of one of the exterior service doors. Thus, the prior repeated motif reappears once again, barely suggested and, as it were, rarefied; but as informative and outstanding as can be, because it is already framed by and inserted into the architectural context. The drawing, clarified in its nature begins to reveal its secrets in the elements that confirm its relevance to S. Maria del Fiore.

A valuable and decisive indication seems to me to be given by the double row of small quadrangles. I am sure that they can be connected with the bonding elements still in existence on the outside of the drum, the "bonds that Filippo Brunelleschi had left on the outside, not by accident," and whose loss Michelangelo had grieved over when Baccio had them taken off all along one side in order to execute the criticised project (Fig. 23).

It was to these supports that Buonarroti had wished to make a precise and important reference; it was from them that he started in developing and positioning his pellucid architectural idea. In point of fact, these two rows of projecting stones, easily visible on the structure, comprise exactly the new framing proposed by the Master. Michelangelo intended to refer back to Brunelleschi's plan, and reached a simple grand solution, better worked out with coherence and consistency in the sketches first referred to, now given a clear *raison d'être* and peremptory identification. Around a center formed by the circular windows, he conceived of a new harmonious compartmentation geometrizing the round windows by enclosing them in a square. In order to give further prominence and spacious dignity to the walls of the drum, he renews the organization of the structural elements, not even stopping at the revetment erected by Manetti in 1480 but proposing the necessary changes. Thus, the base and crown cornices are also covered, the latter being likewise indicated, as we have seen, in Drawing 50 A r.; for these he arranges new positions and formal definitions. Buonarroti gets them further apart, and the result is to emphasize the new proportion of the face of the drum revealed in the project sketches.

This is in substance Michelangelo's proposal for completing the dome of S. Maria del Fiore, in which he did not confine himself to presenting a model for another gallery, as has been suggested, against whose banality he had protested. The Master could not but go beyond the worn out theme, the modest episode, to a decisive flowing achievement: "this structure, so great, called for something bigger, done with a different design, different art and different grace." What emerged was a broad and decisive conception, marked by the higher drum and the harmonious emplacement of the great round windows. Even without redoing the base of the dome, the total effect would certainly have been more unified and imposing, exalted by the juxtaposition of the compact frame of the drum with the soaring rise of the great vault. Retaining the projection and profile of the angular cornices and adding decided shoulders, he was able to bring the accent back to the values of the framework, considering it likewise as the solid base of sharp contrast with the spring of the dome above (Fig. 24).

The unity of Michelangelo's conception comes out even better when it is compared with the proposed circular galleries. The effect of fragmentary chiaroscuro shading may have been attenuated, but it was not done away with; at most, one term of the relation would have been shifted from the gallery to the great surfaces of the drum, which Michelangelo always thought of as made of dark marble, for one thing to habituate the eye to the compact chromatic organization of the reliefs of the dome.

20 Wooden model of Michelangelo's plan for completion of the dome of Santa Maria del Fiore. Florence, Museo dell'Opera del Duomo, 144.

21 Drawing for the dome of Santa Maria del Fiore. Florence, Casa Buonarroti, 66 A r.

285

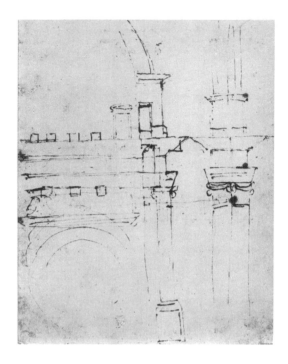

22 Drawing for the dome of Santa Maria del Fiore. Florence, Casa Buonarroti, 50 A r.

23 Detail of the dome of Santa Maria del Fiore. Florence.

24 View of the apse of Santa Maria del Fiore and, to the right, photo-montage of Michelangelo's plan for the drum of the dome.

His work would have been inserted into the preexisting structure, precious not so much for its new formal researches as for its innovating quality in the unexpected expansion of the volumes supporting the dome. It was a solution of indubitable plastic value, more open and peremptory, decisive in transcending any residues of the Gothic. The drum-dome relationship is given in immediate and final terms, harmoniously linked to bring out the effect, as if in homage to Brunelleschi, claiming the genius of his predecessor by his own action.

Buonarroti's addition would thus have been more of an innovation than a mere supplement, since it proposed to move and lower even the cornice under the round windows, without disturbing the dome-shaped covers of the arms, and perhaps hardly redoing those of the protruding chapels of Brunelleschi, the so-called « deal tribunes ».

A useful comparison could be made with the dome of the Basilica of Loreto, done in 1500 by his old friend Giuliano da Sangallo, because of the obvious points of contact arising out of the elaboration of the same Brunelleschi pattern. Giuliano worked on this Florentine problem as well, but we do not know how far his studies were carried nor what the spirit was that

25 Detail of the corbels of windows on the ground floor of Palazzo Medici-Riccardi. Florence.

26 Detail of the corbels of windows on the ground floor of Palazzo Medici-Riccardi. Florence.

inspired them. It would not appear, however, that Michelangelo assimilated any of its points, as was the case with Buonarroti's studies at the same time for the façade of San Lorenzo.

The Master's conviction of the correctness of the solution he had conceived was deep-rooted and truly personal. When he came to make his first plans for the Vatican dome, he came back to this unfinished study of his for the first ideas on the drum of St. Peter's, which show the Florentine theme of large round windows inserted between quadrangles. He had tried a similar geometrizing solution, in conjunction with Santa Maria del Fiore, in the Chapel of Castel S. Angelo and in the façade of San Lorenzo. It recurs frequently in Buonarroti's architectural researches, especially in the beginning, and can be seen already in the sketches for the compartmentation of the Sistine vault, in the studies for the Medici and papal tombs in San Lorenzo, in various lesser tombs (Drawing 114 A v. in Casa Buonarroti) and actually built in the Ricetto of the Laurentian Library.

Michelangelo's solution for the Duomo in Florence did not win the necessary approval because it called for such extensive revisions: it was very showy and called for substantial changes in the drum. Its new aspect was integrated and spacious and constituted a better introduction to the dome, but did not have much connection with the structure underneath, the decorative divisions and the scale of revetments of the entire fabric.

Michelangelo's unexpected and costly proposal remained a contender for a long time, however, but with no chances of winning. The disputes produced doubts and uncertainties in the mind of Cardinal Giovanni de' Medici, and led to a dilatory decision that later proved to be the definitive one.

One of the many models in the Museo dell'Opera del Duomo relating to the projects for the drum and its crown differs from all the others in its proportions: they are the same as those presented by the squared-off design of Michelangelo's sketches (Fig. 20).

The little wooden model also gives the same solution for the architectural order and the Attic order above it. The final cornice, with its square brackets projecting to support the decorations above it, accentuates the innovating quality of the model and helps set its date. It cannot be the oldest one, as has always been thought by reason of its bare aspect, but proves to be much later, perhaps the last of all.

This spare wood is evidently linked closely with the solution outlined for redoing the drum, and should therefore be referred to Buonarroti. In height and position, the organization fits precisely the space between the two horizontal ranges of supports still to be seen. Typical of the model is a continuous internal passage getting light from embrasures at the level of the frieze. The same solution can be seen in Drawing 50 A r., with the space for this concealed "gallery" made in the thickness of the structure. It is evident in the cross section of the drawing, below the passage present in the angular ribs, at the height of the Attic.

The definitive proof of what I have been setting forth hitherto seems to me to be provided *ad abundantiam* by Drawing 5 A v. in Casa Buonarroti. In this drawing, by common consent dated between 1515 and 1518, we see side by side a capital of a pilaster (which I readily identify with the corner one still existing on Manetti's drum) and a familiar classical cornice, frequently drawn by artists of the Renaissance and by Michelangelo himself. It belongs to the so-called Temple of the Sun, and is characterized by the projecting ribbed brackets; it was evidently Buonarroti's model for his own cornice. To find on the same sheet, at the same period of time, two decorative recalls that are otherwise so unconnected seems to me no mere coincidence. It is an intentional linking of two details, one already in existence and the other projected. It comes to a direct visual verification of the impossibility of their coexistence, which the Master solved by the proposed elimination of the Quattrocento pilaster and capital.

FOUR WINDOWS FOR THE PALAZZO MEDICI

Following the changes made "in those rooms that are at the corner," Michelangelo provided a "model" for the ground floor windows of the Palazzo Medici that Vasari was already calling "kneed," extending the anthropomorphic interpretation of architectural forces in the direction of the irrational and bizarre.

About 1517, by order of Leo X, the loggia cut out "for the convenience and assembly of the citizens" was walled up. This had been the original vigorous motif by means of which Michelozzo had meant to go beyond the severe tradition of Florentine palaces.

Apart from the interest that Buonarroti may have shown in a more compact and solid volumetric definition of the building, it seems to me that his part is less episodic than is generally believed, for the significant transformation made on the ground floor at that time.

The windows that he attached to the building that had given him hospitality as a boy were not two in number nor three. The two passages in Vasari where he speaks of "rooms" in the plural and the "two windows" refer to the only room that was decorated by Giovanni da Udine, and an especially careful reading of the details of the work lead us at once to regard as contemporaneous the symmetrical framing of the principal façade on the other ancient side of the dwelling, where a terminal arcade opened as the entrance to the original Medici palace (Fig. 28). I add that Michelangelo's must be the other window on Via de'

27 Drawing for the windows of Palazzo Medici-Riccardi. Florence, Casa Buonarroti, 101 A.

29 Front view of a ground floor window of Palazzo Medici-Riccardi. Florence.

28 Two of Michelangelo's windows in the façade of Palazzo Medici-Riccardi. Florence.

288

Ginori opening in the end of the loggia on the garden. The cornices of Buonarroti are thus exactly four.

Perhaps he supplied only the model, because not all the moldings show the influence of Michelangelo. We need only consider the curve above the sill of the window cornice, a curve that is typically Early Renaissance and recognizable at once as alien to Buonarroti.

Moreover, an autograph drawing shows a more personal original conception (Fig. 27) and brings out the differences with the work as actually executed, in particular the broader pediment due to the wider interval between the brackets which extend beyond and include, in the play of their vertical lines, the brackets under the sill. The broad insertion and over-lapping of the two pairs of consoles bring out more clearly the idea of Michelangelo, who had also attempted a curved design for the pediment, which was rejected at once because of the analogy and contiguity with the arches by Michelozzo framing the windows. The study also brings out points and preferences of the Master that are asserted in the powerful drawing, such as the marked final partition of the so emergent consoles, whose originality outdistances all precedents. One such point is the strong projection (Fig. 26), to raise the windows beyond the smooth wall, which had been kept almost in line with the Michelozzo frame (Fig. 29); the projection harmonizes with the sober rustication. A broad, secure formal simplicity is in tune with the calm grandeur of the arch, and shows to imitating posterity a new type of ground floor window, characterized, in premonitory fashion, by the dados, already adumbrated in the drawing, between the console and the terminal pediment and connected by a horizontal little cornice above the architrave of the opening (Fig. 25).

It is not quite exact to say that " crude iron bars " were added later to these windows to take the place of the fine " pierced copper blinds " by Piloto of which the memory has not been lost, assisted by other rare Florentine examples. The iron bars were essential for security reasons, particularly acute at the time, and were clearly planned by Michelangelo in the preparatory drawing, which even shows some of the round holes for the lead that secured the blinds for which space was left alongside the side pieces. Further more, it is easy to identify in Michelangelo's four windows the small housings three for each jamb, for the supports for the old blinds, which obviously were present with the bars and had different functions.

The last window of the façade, belonging to the expansion of the palace by the Riccardi, differs from the others by the greater projection of the mouldings and the absence of the usual six holes for the blinds.

STUDIES FOR PALACES

It is difficult, apart from this medicean episode, to trace other interventions or plans in the sphere of private civil building. Michelangelo fled " the profession " and had to turn his interests to other more official and difficult themes.

The Palazzo Farnese will be discussed, clearly evidencing the lively personal impulse impressed on that building; at this point we may hint, in a brief " excursus " at other lesser questions in this specific field.

We know practically nothing about the plan for the façade of Palazzo Pucci in Rome, for which, Cardinal Lorenzo Pucci, called Santiquattro, had requested of Michelangelo, in 1525, " some drawing," suggesting placing a typically Tuscan motif in the centre of the façade: a portal flanked by two windows with gratings.

Although, so far, the building has not been named, it is easily identified with the present Palazzo di S. Uffizio near St. Peter's. Cardinal Lorenzo had begun his new building—afterwards greatly changed—by buying some small houses in 1514 and then building, in post-bramantesque form, the fine courtyard.

We do not know Buonarroti's idea on the façade, which was to face St. Peter's. To Thode's proposal to consider pertinent a partial elaborated plan of the Museo di Lilla (Wicar Collection, No. 30), I add another hypothesis. It concerns the drawing 42 A r. of Casa Buonarroti,

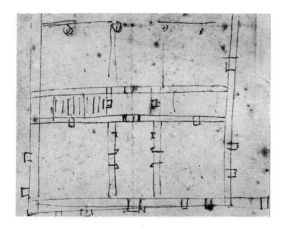

30 Plan sketch for a building. Florence, Casa Buonarroti, 33 A.

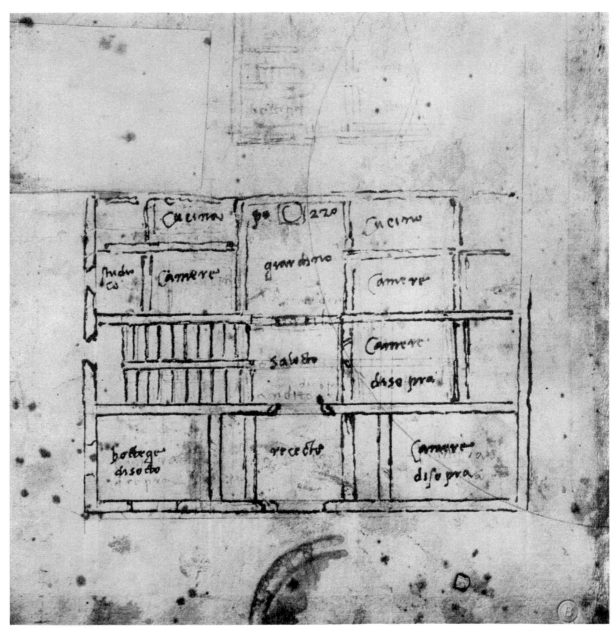

31 Plan for the Palazzo Grifoni, in Piazza della SS. Annunziata. Florence, Casa Buonarroti, 118 A.

37

289

32-34 Drawings for the Medicean tombs ideated at the center of the New Sacristy of San Lorenzo. Florence, Casa Buonarroti, 71 A r., 49 A r., 88 A r.

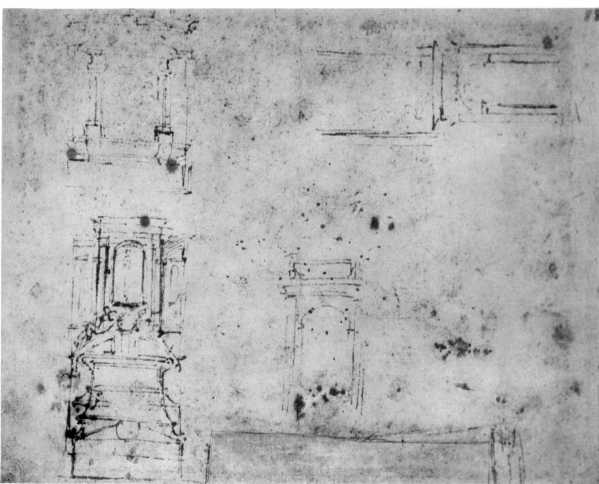

always believed to be a study for the reading room of the Laurentian. The identification is incongruous because of the complexity of three superimposed areas, two orders of windows and, particularly, because of the outline of the cornices on the corner, indicating the edge of a façade and not the interior decorations of a room.

The date of the drawing coincides practically with that of the appointment; so my hypothesis has at least a sound chronological basis. It could be likely by reason of the handwriting on the drawing and because, to our knowledge, the Master had no thoughts at that time of other palaces. The graded heights of the three superimposed registers diminish in conformity with the golden section (0,618 : 1 : 1,618). It is a fact of proportion, which will be presented as early as possible.

Concerning the intervention for the house of Baccio Valori, planned in 1532, this was not a new edifice but only a renovation—never effected—of the old Valori houses in Florence. They were those between Borgo Pinti and Via degli Albizi. For those houses, the drawings of Antonio da Sangallo il Giovane (Uffizi 763 A and 766 A) propose widening of the courtyard and other alterations which also remained undone. This was the building theme submitted to

35 Drawing for an altar with sepulchres on its flanks, for the church of San Silvestro in Capite, Rome. Florence, Casa Buonarroti, 93 A r.

36 Construction drawing for a base for the " twin sepulchres " planned in the New Sacristy of San Lorenzo. Florence, Casa Buonarroti, 59 A.

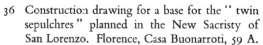

Michelangelo who retained that " no good thing can be done," as results from a letter of Valori: a theme of scarse importance.

Of the front part of a palace for Julius III at the Augusteo, consigned in 1551, a wooden model, made by Bastiano Malenotti, existed, soon taken to Florence and now lost. Fabrizio Boschi retraced, with much probability, the brief flank in the painting existing at Casa Buonarroti. If one wishes to believe this representation, it is possible to gather characters of rough, severe compactness and the rapid down-grading dimensions of the various floors, hinged on the golden section. A rare means in mid-cinquecento, but already adopted by Buonarroti in the previously mentioned drawing and not unknown in his ambient, for example, in the Palazzo Vitelli of Città di Castello. These observations may bring new credit to the reproduced model, if possible to trace the original.

There now remains only a precious set of plans for the Palace of the Altopascio, the building that Ugolino Grifoni, administrator of the Hospital of Altopascio, wanted to erect in Florence, in Piazza dell'Annunziata at the end of Via dei Servi. It was to have occupied the corner plot on which the well-known Palazzo Grifoni, now Riccardi Mannelli, was built in 1557 by Ammannati.

The plan drawings, 117 A and 118 A (Fig. 31) of Casa Buonarroti, are clear, and refer to a building of several stories, compact in form, around a small garden. It is a plan for a comfortable and refined residence, without particular functionality or brilliant innovations. Michelangelo's palace would have had its main entrance on Piazza dell'Annunziata, with rare openings only on five axes, while the front on Via dei Servi was considered less important, but was much more developed and dignified in Ammannati's structure.

At first Michelangelo planned to serve the upper floors by a scissors staircase, a sudden and grandiose motif which he later reduced to a single stairway with a double flight. Of some interest is a summary sketch of a cross section, showing the second flights shorter than the first, in order to make the " drawing-room " larger, and especially to provide a passage to the portions of the noble floor.

It should be pointed out, if for no other reason than to put an end to discussions on the matter, that Michelangelo intended to note on the same sheet, the functions of the ground-floor spaces and those above, distinguishing them summarily in his sketches, while they seem to interpenetrate in the rendering. In the plan 118 A (Fig. 31) the different distribution is indicated by the double captions (even by the less visible ones, *sala* [room] and *andito* [corridor]), in addition to the different arrangement of the divisions, whose partition walls give more space to the ground-floor shops, while above, the rooms above on the square are given equal lengths.

The compact body of the palace did not comprise extensions and outbuildings, as has been thought; all the sketches, even partial, fall within the well-defined volume of the building.

The date of the drawings is uncertain. Dussler, followed by other scholars, fixes it as about 1520, only Barocchi considers them of the late Roman period, also since Grifoni bought the previously existing houses in 1549. I agree with this last date, and place it more precisely as between 1549-1557.

In all likelihood, two other less detailed, incomplete sketches of plans—Casa Buonarroti 33 A (Fig. 30) and Archivio Buonarroti, Vol. XI, fol. 722 v.—also relate to this palace and may constitute the first studies for it. The summary way the cut of the rooms is indicated need not necessarily a different smaller overall surface.

The present Palazzo Grifoni seems to be exceptional in Ammannati's work for its solid and harsh appearance: it may be connected with the model believed for the Roman palace of Julius III and perhaps interpret Michelangelo's expression, which unfortunately we can only imagine looking at the simple and severe plans.

Finally, it is impossible not to mention the vanished " little cartoon, with drawing of a façade of a palace " included in the inventory taken at the Master's death: it might have been able to clear up any doubts of suggest matters of new interest.

The Laurentian flourish

THE NEW SACRISTY

In March 1520 Leo X had started a Medici Chapel in San Lorenzo, symmetrical to Brunelleschi's Sacristy, " to make therein the tomb of Giuliano, his brother and the Duke Lorenzo, his nephew." Without doubt this was to be a construction *ex novo*, because at this time the new structure closed off a " little door for the convenience of people going to church," which is identified with the one corresponding to the corner of the transept. We also know that work was going on in 1520 on construction of a wall of the chapel. While work was proceeding within the framework of the vision of Brunelleschi, Michelangelo entered on the scene at the end of the same year with a " design or sketch for the chapel " that Cardinal Giulio found to his liking, although pointing out " a difficulty " in the proposed location of the sepulchres " in the middle of the chapel."

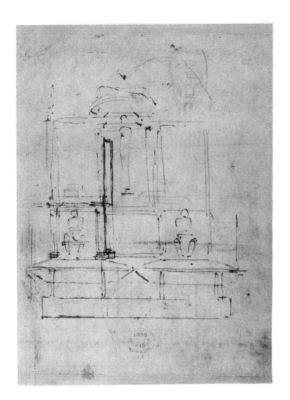

This brings us to the first conception, the tower-shaped free-standing tombs. As we gather from the sketches of Michelangelo, their lively vertical development shows how he already intended, while still respecting the assigned area of the chapel, to get away from the corresponding volumes in the Old Sacristy, the first section completed in the Laurentian complex. From the very beginning there is a freer vision of architectural volumes that was embodied in the completed work.

In the drawings (Figs. 33 and 34) the architectural imagination seems to break loose, possibly in opposition to the contemplated decrease in the dynamism of the walls. The studies for these tombs are most felicitous; the monuments are fraternally linked in a sculptural complex in which the preceding Roman experiments take form in more intense and more resounding architectonic values. There is, in substance, a resumption of the theme (which he had had to abandon under the 1516 contract) of the tomb standing free on all sides and the plastic development of the decorative elements dreamed up for the vault of the Sistine Chapel.

In all his plans for the Medici tombs, Michelangelo shows that he is eager for the utmost liberty, tending to the summit in original and imaginative compositions. This first phase of the design, exalted by nostalgia for the projected tomb of Julius II, is explained by and ends in the heightened longing for spiritual escape.

Drawing No. 93 A r. of Casa Buonarroti (Fig. 35) is usually placed in this phase of the studies, but this analogy seems to be excluded by the presence of an altar in the center of a broader

37-39 Drawings for the Medicean tombs (plans for the adjoining sepulchres). London, British Museum, 28 r., 28 v., 26 r.

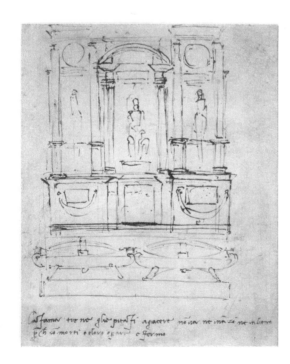

40 Drawing for the Medicean tombs (plan of parietal sepulchre). London, British Museum, Wilde 27 r.

composition, and it is also contradicted by the calmer (and in my opinion earlier) architectural plan. The two tombs outlined on the flanks of this monumental façade suggest instead the hypothesis of a study previously attempted for the new high altar in the church of S. Silvestro in Capite, in Rome. What information we have on this other unrealised work by Michelangelo, commissioned by the exile Pier Soderini in 1518, would fit in exactly with this identification, not only because of the position of the two tombs called for and incorporated into the altar complex, but also because of the squared proportions and a certain exuberance of measurements that made it impossible for Michelangelo's ideas to be put into effect. The impressive base—in the end a church, still medieval—would have shown a plan of genius which could be defined as of break, worthy of the Master and would have fitted with the choice of a modest marble altar built in the church shortly after, not unlike the central theme of Michelangelo's drawing. I hope that this new hypothesis may be considered in preference to the others vainly advanced for the complicated monument desired by Gonfaloniere.

In Florence, after the idea of the group in the center of the chapel had been abandoned, Michelangelo studied other projects for bringing the two Medici tombs together on the same side. The linking of the two monuments is intended to attest a spiritual solidarity operative even after death.

The project for the twin tombs—perhaps intended for the third side of the Cappella for the unfinished monument of the other two Medici Lorenzo il Magnifico and his brother Giuliano—

42 New Sacristy of San Lorenzo, east side (sepulchre of Giuliano). Florence.

41 Medicean tombs: comparison between the plan and the execution (by Ackerman).

43 New Sacristy of San Lorenzo, north and east sides (altar and sepulchre of Giuliano). Florence.

44 Details of the cornices of the New Sacristy of San Lorenzo. Florence.

must have been well advanced as we can see from the working drawing for the bases that Michelangelo designed for the pilasters of the " double burial " (Fig. 36).

The new unprecedented theme attracted him. His study drawings tend to provide a solution in the form of a juxtaposition; developing paired motifs that had already been tried, and using a central motif to go beyond. This leads to a triangular pattern by virtue of the prominence given to the middle shrine (Figs. 37 and 38), but one that is also careful to compose other elements in the rectangular space of the wall. In the splendid drawing of British (Fig. 39), the individuality of the two tombs is better provided for, along with a more exciting share of the sculpture.

It was in that same period of time, not being able to exclude their planned coexistence that he reached the final conception of the tombs separated on the two walls. His studies must have enabled him to focus the problem, deriving it, certainly not mechanically, from congenial experiments. A drawing in the British Museum (Fig. 40) may be regarded as the archetype of the finished work: it shows coupled pilasters spacing Michelangelesque themes—niches and shrines.

The culmination of the drawing goes beyond the limits of what was later executed, in a frothy crest that surpasses and contrasts with the terse underlying design. In contact with the reality of the wall, the final element becomes simpler and is then composed into an architectural vision that makes it possible to see the dark horizontal cornice under the motif of the arch. The sculptures resume towards the center and the architectural proportions become more delicate to echo those placed laterally at the corners of the chapel. Everything becomes more incisive and unified, and the uppermost motif enters into the architectural pattern in disciplined fashion (Figs. 41 and 42).

But the doubt arises that this careful design, by bringing out the cornice under the arch, may have deprived the central motif of the previously calculated effect of a triumphal arch. Thereby a heroic, triumphant conclusion to the Medici tombs would have been negated in the last phase of the work, coinciding with events in Florence hostile to the Medici.

The story of the tombs, which we have followed out logically, has left in the background the story of the chapel erected to hold them. What has been said up to the present agrees in considering Michelangelo's role as conditioned by a structure already irrevocably planned. A sketch by him (Archivio Buonarroti, Vol. I, fol. 98), which attempts to expand and enrich

45 Corner of the "scarsellas" with details of the wings and framework. New Sacristy of San Lorenzo. Florence.

◁ 46 Interior corner end of the New Sacristy of San Lorenzo. Florence.

the space of the chapel, would, therefore, be regarded as a personal attempt at virtually escaping from the limitations imposed on him.

We know that in April 1521 construction had got as far as the cornice of the first order and that until the election of Giulio de' Medici to the pontificate, much of the time had been spent in negotiations and discussions on the form to be given the Medici tombs. Clement VII gave new drive to the work, so that by the first months of 1524 Michelangelo could declare that the lantern too, " completely installed and unveiled... pleases every one universally."

It is clear that at the outset Buonarroti had concerned himself primarily with the tombs, on the tacit assumption that the Brunelleschian design of the new edifice could not be changed, as would necessarily follow from the choice made of the site " symmetrical with the old sacristy "

47-49 Details of the New Sacristy of San Lorenzo. Florence.

50 Drawing for the window under the dome of the New Sacristy of San Lorenzo. Florence, Casa Buonarroti, 105 A r.

and the exact repetition of the external dimensions. Later he became more and more interested in the problems of the interior architecture, as we can see in a crescendo on the monument itself: from the timid variations introduced into the Brunelleschi arrangement to the free and spirited little lantern.

The minds of Michelangelo, his patrons and the working artists were occupied with the decoration of the cupola for a long time. Giovanni da Udine, for whom they had been waiting since 1526, began to work on the stucco on October 1532, taking almost a year on the work without entirely finishing it. Nothing is left of these and other decorations, I do not know how well-viewed by Michelangelo and which we need not regret overmuch since they were certainly at variance with the design of the work today, the bare spaces freed of the colored decorations, presents much more modern interest.

We must agree that Michelangelo succeeded in interpreting the thematic cue he had been given, with respect for tradition, and at the same time with increasing expressive liberty. His architectural world is concentrated on the walls. On those planes new elements develop and intersect, in a teeming decorative life of extraordinary tension that justifies the breaking of the cornices, the overlapping of the compartments and the interpenetration of the forms.

At the top of the chapel he succeeds in molding the volumes more freely, reaching new heights without too much deviation from the exterior ties. But it is in the interior that he creates a new space, that he raises a different dome. The five rows of gradated coffers also numerically taken from the Pantheon, and an original halo, whose free structure forms (Fig. 52) the base of the little lantern, with its new advanced forms showing exactly how tremendous a distance separated Michelangelo from Brunelleschi; something that the Master had the modesty and ability to define with exactness at the end of his architectural discourse, disclosing it slowly as the construction rose from the old bases.

The lantern could look to heaven, even in the absence of a Lady Chapel and campanile; with its marble whiteness, it set on fire the square Laurentian pile.

A reading of the monument brings illuminating importance and unexpected precision to what has already been examined. The faithfulness of the brunellesque archtype, dictated the exact replica of the chapel and the adoption of the typical disposition. The only concession: the addition of the wings to the jambs of the arches and to the mouth of the "scarsella" (Fig. 43).

But it is presided by the rampant which limits the true Michelangelian space: the altar, new for its base, for the disjointed originality of the structure that raise at the extremes the flaming candelabra and, above all, because it faces the public.

In the modulations of the order, however, the hand of the Master can be seen, bringing life to the severe matter. Not certainly in the capitals, whose firm cut goes back to the classical age, for the devoted Florentine continuity, but in the refined variations of the shapes, especially of the architrave (Figs. 44 and 45). Presumed from the Temple of the Sun on the Quirinal, studied in his youthful drawings, it has often been reproduced by Michelangelo in the immediate coupling of concave "cavetto" and swollen "bastone" as in the door of the Palazzo Senatorio on Campidoglio.

The great niches (Fig. 47) originate in the interposition of the two elements of classical extraction in a bare angular linearity. The internal bent cornice is inserted in the niche with the rigour of proportion; it disassociates the softened parastades and provokes the rise of the final pediment; the deepened emptiness at the center protects the high seal of the festoon and patera and finds below the opposing pure volume of the bare base. The nearness of the niche to the door (Fig. 48) admits the ambivalence of the consoles already used to bear the supports above; the consoles, while with their cornice, modify the slender proportions of the opening, gives a contrast in finish to the smooth flank (Fig. 49) which makes them similar to those of Palazzo Medici (Figs. 25 and 26).

Higher up, the tabernacle windows of fine classical form—it is pleonastic to recall the fine S. Giovanni and Francesco di Giorgio—rejoice in the volume of the pediment (Fig. 51). The spaces extend between the parastades of the second order, also of *pietra serena*; it still shines quattrocentesco in the transcription of the brunelleschian text (Fig. 42). To their architraved cornice approaches the executive outline 60 A of Casa Buonarroti (Fig. 82), up to now retained pertinent to the Library.

Instead, the windows of the arches under the dome (Fig. 52) reveal greater liberty of expression. The jambs sloping upwards, though taken from the ancient, fulfill here, as noted by Wölfflin, the function of prospect directives.

Also in the squat preparations drawing (Fig. 50), they seem freed from the atmosphere of classicism, that appeared as though it would pervade all the elements carved in *pietra serena*.

In fact, they deliberately contrast with the replanning, now solely cultural, of the brunelleschian tondi on the crests.

Hooked forms appear from his studies for the base of the tombs (Fig. 53), while the small capitals find a renewed logic in the composition of deranged elements (Figs. 54 and 55). Deliberate reversals divide like rams' horns, like screaming masks; isolated shells instead of the rows of leaves; swollen gorgerins made of mutules upside down, of refined Michelozzian influence.

His first experience of vaulting a dome exalted him; it is logical that he resolved it with homage to Roman classicism (Figs. 52 and 57), also because he could not bring it out on the exterior practically without tambour. Referring to the dome, some bold combinations can be experi-

51 A corner window of the New Sacristy of San Lorenzo. Florence.

52 Internal view of the dome of the New Sacristy of San Lorenzo. Florence.

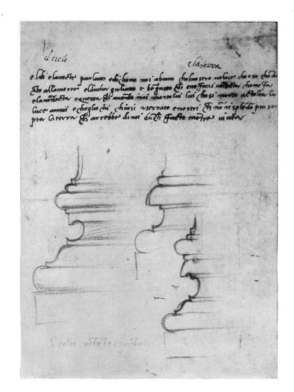

53 Studies of bases for the New Sacristy of San Lorenzo. Florence, Casa Buonarroti, 10 A r.

mented; I immediately attempt one that, on a double base, experiments the foreshortening of the perspectives of the external meniscus. One of its tercet seems to me to coincide with a sketch, never taken into consideration, traced on the sheet 114 A v. of Casa Buonarroti (Fig. 56): "The eye that underneath wanders round at ease, discovers a small part of the great sphere that least reveals its serene life."

They are annotations working towards the instinctive raising of the great Vatican dome.

The only element which indicates externally the work of Michelangelo is the lantern (Fig. 58), planned inside with the joint of the circular supporting crown with the curved convections of the ribs. Covered by contrasting shadows for the prominence of the extremely slender columns with pediments where he indulges in examples of the Quattrocento, it is surmounted by a roofing which re-establishes the composite unit. At the top, it flanks the crowning of copper, worked by the faithful Piloto: it is not a sphere, but a solid geometrical original which refracts vibratingly the light.

THE LAURENTIAN LIBRARY

Immediately after being chosen Pope in the winter of 1523, Clement VII decided to erect a library in Florence, with the main purpose of guarding there, in the noblest possible manner, the splendid collection of Medici codices that he wished to return to his city. It was an important event, which with the erection of the Laurentian Library gave Florence the prestige, contested soon after by Venice, of having the first specially designed secular library.

54-55 Capitals of the Medicean tombs, New Sacristy of San Lorenzo. Florence.

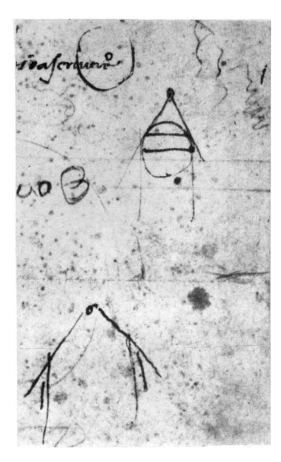

56 Sketches on the view of a sphere. Florence, Casa Buonarroti, 114 A v. (detail).

58 Lantern of the New Sacristy of San Lorenzo. Florence.

57 Axonometry of the New Sacristy of San Lorenzo. Florence.

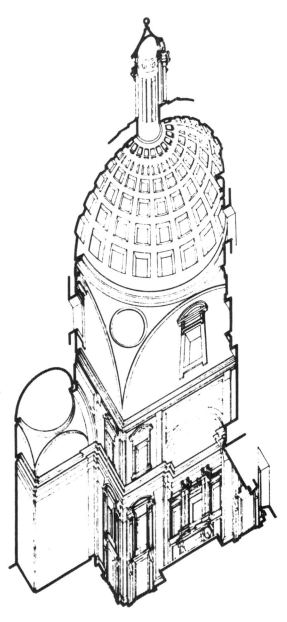

As early as the end of 1523 discussion centered on the monastery of San Lorenzo as the place to be chosen and adapted and on the name of Michelangelo, who the pope desired to see employed on this new undertaking as well.

After the first proposal, of archeological-literary suggestion, to create two different rooms, one for Greek codices and books and the other for the Latins, Buonarroti proceeded actively to look for the most suitable arrangement to give the structure.

The large floor plan drawn on Casa Buonarroti sheets 10 A and 9 A is linked to these initial researches in that it offers two alternative proposals (Fig. 60). At the outset the preference seemed to go to the one that opened solemnly at ground level right in the middle of the south side of the cloister and was most convenient for any one coming from the square or the church. In order to gain the requisite space, the new building would have had to go deeper into the next court (Fig. 59, sol. A); but because this project contemplated demolishing cells of the monastery on two floors, the pontiff decided against it.

To avoid encroaching on already existing quarters, Clement VII chose the other possibility, shown on the same drawing, which grew out of the east side of the cloister and extended to Borgo San Lorenzo, permitting greater development in length and enabling the new institution to adjoin the square. Here Michelangelo could have avoided the destruction of dwellings and shops, planning to construct the library above the existing structures and giving access to it by a new staircase (Fig. 59, sol. B).

The decision seemed now to have been made on the basis of this project, and the Pontiff came to make some suggestions, such as having two " studietti " inserted at either end of the long hall, for the most valuable books. But in spring 1524 Michelangelo proposed another solution, the one that was finally to prevail, superposed on the long wing, between the cloisters and the " garden " in the rear near the Old Sacristy. It was a bold conception that would get light from the east and the west, and would remove the new library from the sights and sounds of the square, while leaving the as yet incomplete façade of the church its due predominance (Fig. 59, sol. C).

Michelangelo conceived of the new structures as virtually independent of those already in existence; the documents inform us of the work done to insert in the old construction tall strong pilasters to support; on these pilasters he built series of arches, still solid and functioning today, on which to erect the new walls.

The suggestion of the *studioli* was repeated, but Michelangelo rejected it. The furthest he would go was to provide two expansions forming transepts (Fig. 59), and in the end he put through his unitary conception, a single long hall. In this way he broke with the tradition of the three-aisled monastery libraries that Michelozzo had initiated; but he did take from them the long shape of the large room and the arrangement of the benches for conservation and reading of the codices.

Correspondence and contracts bring out the measure and order of the entire project. The new structures are a hundred ells long, including the vestibule, named the " portico." The height of the new walls was to have been about nine meters.

The extensions projected halfway down each side of the reading room would have been square in shape, more than ten meters per side. One would have spanned the portico, pushing above the dormitory between the two cloisters; the other would have been in the free area opposite, just where the Dante tribune was later built.

We do not know why the transepts were not approved, with which it seems Michelangelo had made a tactical maneuver in order to get around the *studioli* that the pope was insisting on. But we do know that the transepts were eliminated in a decision taken August 2, 1524 and that the proposal was definitely over, for in April of the following year the pope let it be known that at the end of the reading room he " wished there to be a secret library to hold certain books more valuable than others."

The new variation, approved in November 1525, can be seen from two drawings by the Master (Figs. 64 and 65). This " secret library " would have been most original. In a stroke of genius, the strange triangular plan is based on an insuperable difficulty, a party wall with the adjacent property. The solution of the problem indicates how much importance Michelangelo attached to existing structures, in order to go beyond them, or rather, here as in so many other cases, to take the best advantage of them.

I have tried to indicate the probable elevations of the polygonal room by following the rapid notes given us by Michelangelo (Fig. 63). Lightened, like the Ricetto, only by high lights carefully planned, it would have become a to strange closed shrine; the definition was to be rich and complex and to contain, as we shall see, the framing of the niches studied on the sheet 96 A v. of Casa Buonarroti (Fig. 83). One thing certain is that he intended to continue alternating the vertical developments and the horizontal ones so clearly announced in the combination of the other two rooms (Fig. 61), resuming and concluding, at the end of the work, those upward impulses that, after leading him to build on the roofs of the monastery, " in dovecote " had persuaded him to raise again the roof of the *Ricetto*.

Many drawings studying this vestibule have come down to us; some of them have not yet been convincingly interpreted.

It seems to me that the schematic plan, traced at the top of the sheet Casa Buonarroti 89 A r. (Fig. 66), should be related to the sketches contained on Haarlem sheet A 33 v. (Fig. 68).

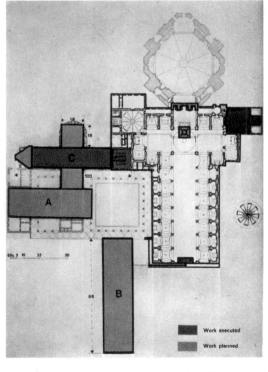

59 Planimetry of San Lorenzo, with indications of the work executed and planned by Michelangelo.

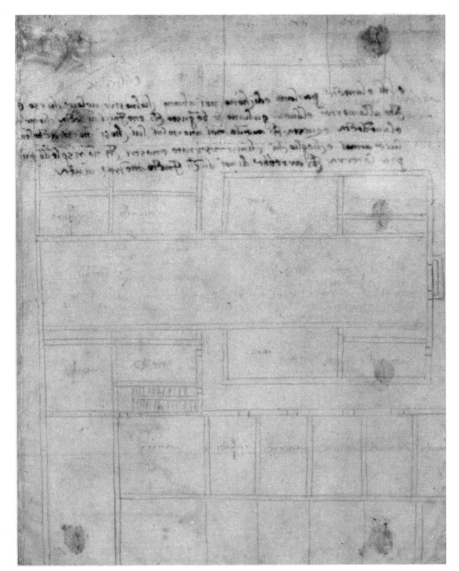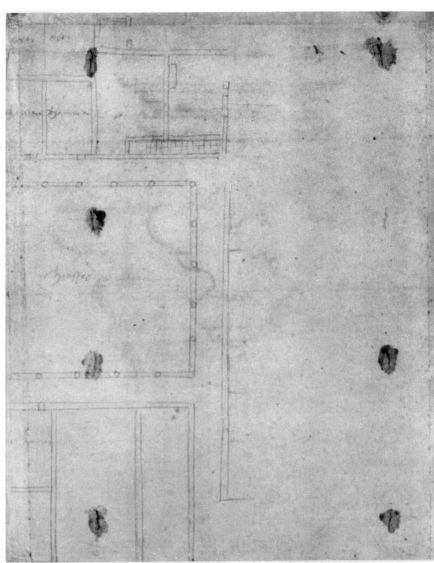

60 Plan of the Monastery of San Lorenzo, Florence, with indication of the first solutions for the Library. Florence, Casa Buonarroti, 10 A v. and 9 A v.

Here too is found a square room with a dome resting on corner supports, as in a number of studies in the elevations of the Haarlem folio. Accordingly, I deny that the Casa Buonarroti sketch refers to the chapel mentioned in the correspondence, which was never designed, for one thing because Clement VII " says that he wants no chapels there."

In connection with the problem of the vestibule are the oldest studies for the staircase that was to span the difference in level between the *Ricetto* on the upper floor of the cloister and the reading room above existing dormitories. At first the studies seem to confine themselves to a single flight on axis with the communicating door; then the steps duplicate, clinging to the side walls (the " ascent of two staircases " mentioned in Fattucci's letter dated April 29, 1524)—perhaps still in harmony with the cruciform system of one of the projected phases.

Several drawings indicate this staircase arrangement (Figs. 66 and 67). In some—Casa Buonarroti 92 A r. (Fig. 67)—the body of the staircase appears as cut within by a cylindrical surface, with interpenetrating aerial volumes that stress or perhaps only recall the circular solutions experimented with in plan and more often in the roof. In any case, the *ricetto* too

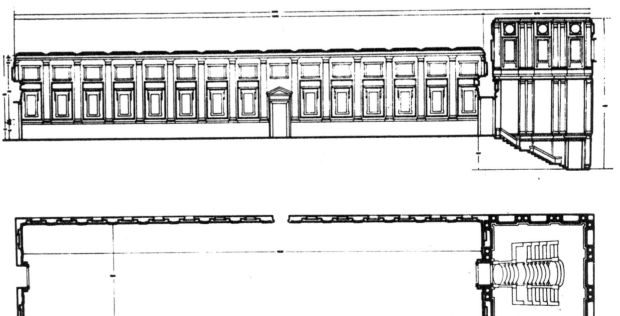

61 Longitudinal section and plan of the reading room and of the Ricetto of the Laurentian Library. Florence.

303

held fast to the solution of the unified space to which Michelangelo was so devoted that he could only make his decision very late on the dimensional shapes of the main staircase, which he had thought of doing in walnut just to bring out in greater evidence the decisive prismatic volume of his daring vestibule.

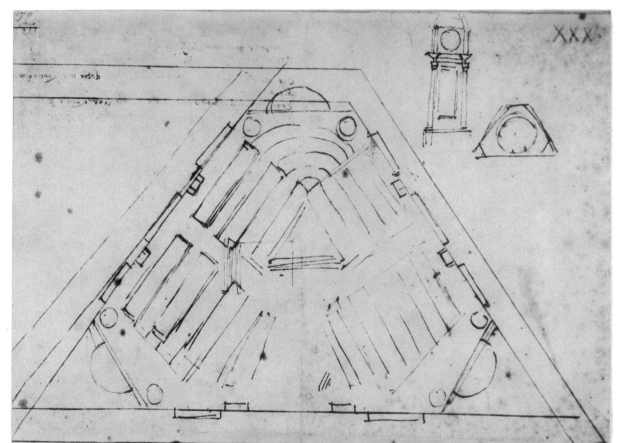

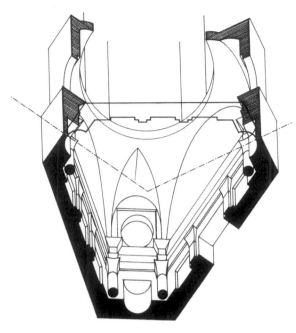

62 Axonometric study for the roofing of the " secret library " in the Laurentian Library, Florence.

64-65 Plans for the " secret library " in the Laurentian Library. Florence, Casa Buonarroti 79 A r. and 80 A.

63 Sketches for the Ricetto in the Laurentian Library. Florence, Casa Buonarroti, 92 A r.

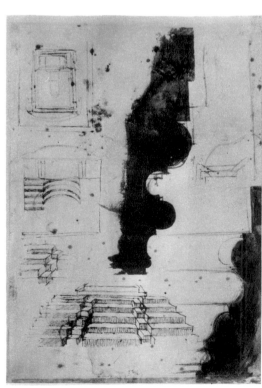

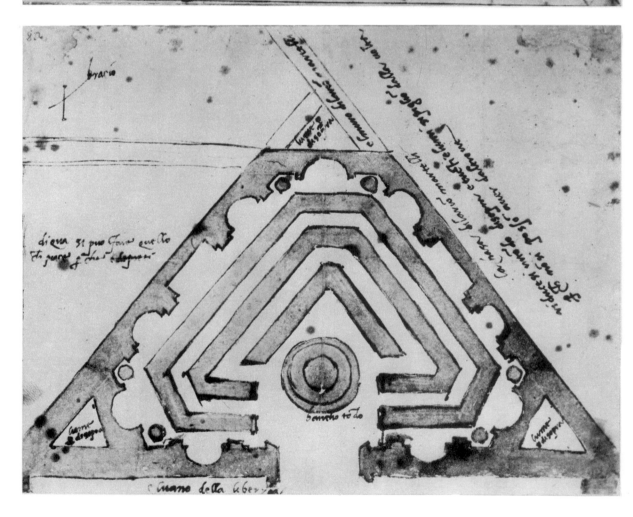

304

In August 1524 work was begun on the masonry, and carried forward briskly at first, until the general political situation collapsed; they were begun again in 1533.

Because of the light that comes only from above, the *Ricetto* immediately conveys a feeling of sterness, which proves to be a dynamic intolerant contradiction, from which the visitor, placed in contact with the bare compact base, is tempted to escape, feeling himself involved in an unexpected and wounding adventure. The urgent invitation is received to ascend to the

68 Elevation and plan studies for the Ricetto. Haarlem, Teyler Museum, 33 A v.

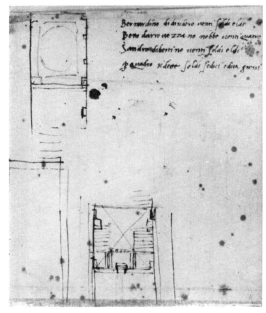

66 Studies for the Ricetto. Florence, Casa Buonarroti, 89 A r.

69 Studies for the walls of the Ricetto. Florence, Casa Buonarroti, 48 A r.

67 Studies for the Ricetto. Florence, Casa Buonarroti, 92 A r.

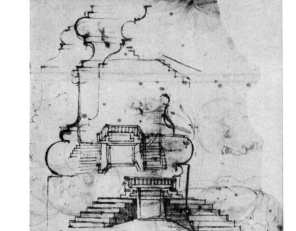

305

70 The Ricetto of the Laurentian Library. Florence.

71 Detail of the staircase of the Ricetto. Florence.
▷

reading room, to the serene luminous world of the classical manuscripts; from the high threshold of the reference room, the architecture of the Ricetto can be regarded with less visual and psychological difficulty. The axial and figurative contrast between the two rooms personifies the struggles and hopes of the outside world and the ordered development of research and soon learned leisure.

The chromatic oppositions on the walls, the contrast between the architectural elements and volumes, hinge mainly on the repeated motif of coupled fluted columns and recur in the panels that attenuate as they rise. In a known drawing (Fig. 69) is found already detailed the order on brackets with the fluted columns, even though the connection between these and the pilasters appears less arbitrary, mediated as it is by other columns. It lacks the later disposition above with the definition of the sources of light.

The whole Ricetto is now immersed in the same cold, sad luminosity. The compact foundation, with, at intervals, only gigantic brackets placed in a defensive position (Fig. 73) to provoke a sense of theoretical, unhuman perfection, contributes to accentuate the feeling of desolate depression. Thus the dados of the foundations were simplified and the curious niches planned on the drawings, were not realised; I consider these to be sites of lamps (Casa Buonarroti 92 A r., Fig. 63 and British Museum, Wilde 36 r. and v.). The visitor sees nothing pleasing, familiar or useful. After climbing the monastery stairs, one does not expect to arrive in a hostile architectural pit and to see no way out but the ornate irrational main staircase.

A heightened sense of spacing, a less decisive taste for interpenetrations seems to imbue this work as compared with the Medici Chapel, but here the architectonic spirit faces and studies an coordinated formal renewal, indication of a reforming desire that disregards the contingencies of the forms. With regard to this, are highly indicative the repeated studies for the framework of the Ricetto (Figs. 77 and 78), where unusual floor inclinations and marked *sottosquadri* accompany the profiles. Synergetic complings result which, in the abstraction of the drawing, seem to assume vital and aggressive aspects.

The pediments of the doors, less inclined for reasons of front view, are disciplined in the

72 Detail of the staircase of the Ricetto.

73 Consoles in the foundation area of the Ricetto.

74 Detail of the staircase of the Ricetto.

75 Detail of the staircase of the Ricetto.

detailed formulation of the great construction drawings (Figs. 80 and 81). With less fluid plasticity, the similar outline of another terminal, architraved cornice has been drawn, referred by me to the Medicean Chapel (Fig. 82).

From the ceiling, with elliptical and diagonal motifs (Fig. 86), from the brick floor which emphasises the central design, and from the close sequence of benches, come warm chromatic suggestions, blended by the filter of the windows. In the unfurnished room (Fig. 85), can be noted the lateral panels of the floor (1549-1554), with ostentatious and interesting geometrical patterns (Figs. 193 and 196). Michelangelo also studied the project for the benches (Fig. 87) which cover them, basing the clear functional form on a central pilaster, whose sequence approaches and renders familiar to the visitor that of the great pilasters, which undoubtedly imprint on the walls an aulic character of exterior front view.

The exterior of the Library, that with one side gives on to the open cloisters, as a massive addition but not overwhelming (Fig. 88), simplifies the internal repetitions in the continued formula of the brief fittings. A close play of proportions supports this placid, unfinished architecture also in the details of the windows, completed modernly in the second series of windows of the Ricetto. On the other hand, today hardly visible from the remains of the old vegetable garden, the series of openings directly surmounted the large structural motif of the arches made to support the Library (Fig. 89). The vestibule was without the stairs for a long time, and the upper portion was not completed until our times. Here it is not possible to retrace the long affair: the stair was infinitely varied in the mind of the Master, who successively left the question open. After all these studies and much hesitation, he managed to send Ammannati a model for the stairs, which returned to his 1533 ideas; construction was begun in February 1559 (Fig. 70), with carte blanche for deciding many details (Figs. 71, 74). In any case, the Master had the idea of the staircase as a succession of downward inclining " quantity of oval boxes."

PROJECT FOR THE HIGH ALTAR

In the fall of 1525 Clement VII commissioned Michelangelo to design the high altar, precious with porphyry and marble, for San Lorenzo in Florence, part of his intention being, at first, to be able fittingly to bring together the relics preserved in the basilica.

A clear sketch of the plan, full of data and measurements, leaves no doubts as to Buonarroti's ideas for the work, which, too, was not carried out (Fig. 90). The base was set into the steps of the choir, with a set of steps equal to those at the foot of the altar of the Medici Chapel, and bounded a rectangular space, deeper than wide, with at the corners, in conformity with tradition, four columns for supporting a baldacchino. Michelangelo wanted to bring the high altar towards the people and extend it as far forward as possible, up to the edge of the floor tomb of Cosimo de' Medici the Elder, projecting into the crossing and thus making it visible from the entire transept. Finally, by cutting down the frontal width of the structure, he must have sought not to interfere with the line of sight into the depths of the choir, so as not to diminish the effect of the planned pontifical tombs, like the frescoes that were planned later.

Although the floor plan is definite and measured in detail, we know nothing as to the aspect of the work, and in particular of the crown of the baldacchino. We may well believe that the Master would have tried to avoid encumbering the interior of the basilica, as Clement VII feared and as later happened in another church by Brunelleschi, Santo Spirito. However, the modest dimensions of the high altar are remarkable, and we do not see what solution might have been devised for housing the relics.

Emphasis should be placed on Michelangelo's choice, derived from imitation of the papal altars in Rome. And it is also a propos to stress the points of contact with the aspirations towards religious and liturgical revival, which the proposed arrangement seems to favor in the two examples at San Lorenzo, and here is clearly stated in moving the altar from the traditional location in the choir towards the people, placing it in the crossing with the transept almost under the dome.

Meanwhile, a new proposal had been put forward for housing the relics on the inner façade of the basilica, rather than under the high altar. The pope lost interest in the idea and toward

76 Niche in the walls of the Ricetto. Florence.

77-78 Outlines of cornices for the Laurentian Library. Florence, Casa Buonarroti, 62 A r. and v.

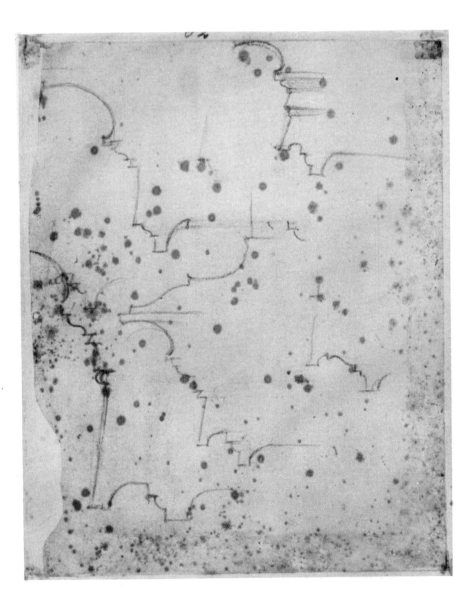

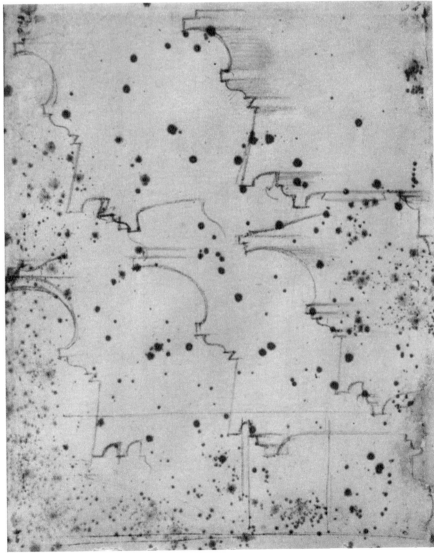

309

the end of 1526 informed Michelangelo that he wanted only a simple canopy in wood "looking like marble . . . with no cornice and painted and strong."

Michelangelo's worries, and then the change in the pontiff's attitude, were certainly not likely to inspire him to make still another design for a simple ornamental work—in imitation marble at that. The events of 1527 put an end to the project, which is attested also by the correspondence of Giovan Francesco Fattucci, secretary to Pope Clement. We are left with the example and memory of a farseeing solution, chosen and designed in a spirit that we today must still regard as bold and innovating.

PLANS FOR THE TOMBS OF THE MEDICI POPES

In May 1524 Clement VII also entrusted Michelangelo with the task of designing the Tombs of the Medici popes, that of Leo X and his own. The first idea was to locate them in the New Sacristy, but that was soon dropped because of the practical impossibility of altering the plans at the advanced stage the work had reached.

Possibly Michelangelo did not attach much weight to the theme at first, for in June of that year he thought of putting up the double funerary monument "in that washstand, where the stairs are," i.e. in a place of minor importance near the Brunelleschi Sacristy. The agent for the Roman Curia at once rejected the idea as "a little place for the Popes." It is probably to this strange and unclear solution that we should refer the Oxford drawing (Parker, II, 307 r.), whose central portion is worked out again in a drawing of the school of Michelangelo centering around the figure of a pontiff (Casa Buonarroti 52 A).

Clement VII had him asked to provide another solution in "church, in the choir or elsewhere, so long as it was a place of honor and more spacious." To this new phase of the project belong a large number of drawings intended for San Lorenzo. They had no success, perhaps because of their complexity, which clashed with the simple atmosphere of Brunelleschi's church. Thus, even before the grave events of 1527 Michelangelo's project, contemplated for the choir of San Lorenzo, had already been put aside, as is shown by the letters sent by Fattucci in 1526. After the death of Clement VII (1534), Baccio Bandinelli, in collaboration with Antonio da Sangallo the Younger, terminated the episode by erecting two separate monuments, in traditional styles, in the choir of Santa Maria sopra Minerva in Rome.

We can, therefore, do no more than try to follow the uncertain traces of the Master's thinking and activity during a period of intense intermittent preparatory studies.

The drawings can be clearly divided into two groups: the studies for the free-standing tombs and those for the "double tomb," and show Michelangelo's growing interest.

The first set must have related to the side walls of the choir. They are shown in at least two vigorous sketches, one in the British Museum (Wilde, 39 r.) and 46 A in Casa Buonarroti (Fig. 91), which seems to be later in virtue of its livelier and more elaborate rhythm, like that of other drawings for the double tombs. Both were drawn with emphasis on their "projection," and the same appears in a sketched ground plan. They must, therefore, have been less heavy in their proportions, while projecting into the choir.

The paired tombs were evidently intended for the back wall of Brunelleschi's creation. The drawings relating to them have rather similar characteristics; all refer back to Casa Buonarroti Drawing 46 A and all seem to be based on a powerful set of double pilasters, projecting fairly far out, flanked by columns that would have given an unexpected sculptural life

79 Detail before completion of the upper part of the Ricetto. Florence.

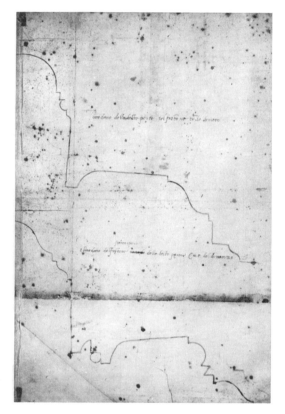

80 Outlines of cornices for the doors of the Laurentian Library. Florence, Casa Buonarroti, 53 A r.

81 Outlines of cornice and mouldings for the doors of the Laurentian Library. Florence, Casa Buonarroti, 53 A v.

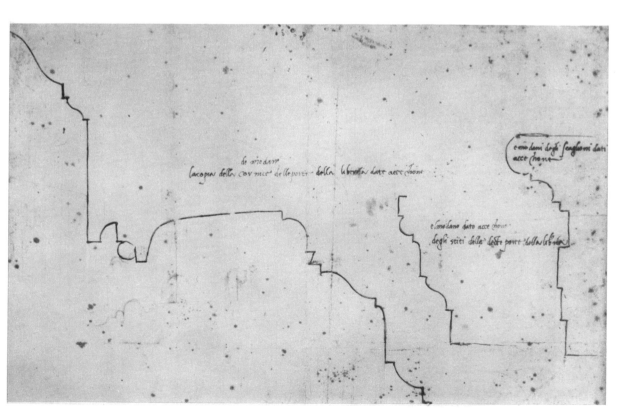

to the serene architectural ending. From the simpler sketch of the British Museum (Wilde, 38 r.) the series runs to the variants on the Oxford sheet (Fig. 92) and, finally, to the elaborate and perhaps definitive Drawing 128 A in Casa Buonarroti (Fig. 93). With this resumption of the theme, which has impressive points of contact with the British Museum drawings (Figs. 39-40) relating to the chapel, Michelangelo entered into a new phase of composition. These are the first drawings that show the intertwining of architectural orders of different heights, reaching their most exciting high point in 128 A, which is justified by the need of giving different treatment to the central portion lower, because hidden by the altar in front of it. The solutions originated here anticipated the future, with the powerful decisive motif of the pilasters linked by a lower architectural order (Fig. 92). It is already the kernel of the idea of the twin palaces on the Capitoline.

The plans for tombs and mausoleums, linked to the thought of death so familiar to the Master, fill his whole arch of life: they are infinitely repeated and re-echoed, contributing to modify the interiors of our churches, in the work of pupils and later imitators.

The signed drawings testify all the interest given to the subject and the many studies attempted, while other documents widen the sphere. Thus, for an unknown project for Dante's

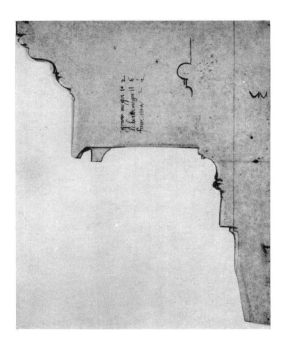

82 Study of an outline for the base cornice of the mausoleum in the Medicean Chapel. Florence, Casa Buonarroti, 60 A.

83 Studies of doorway and niches for the " secret library " of the Laurentian. Florence, Casa Buonarroti, 96 A v.

84 Relief of the door between the Ricetto and the reading room of the Laurentian Library. Florence, Casa Buonarroti, 98 A.

311

85 View, without benches, of the reading room,   86 Study for the reading room ceiling, Laurentian   87 Study for benches and lecterns, reading room of the
Laurentian Library. Florence.   Library. Florence, Casa Buonarroti, 126 A.   Laurentian Library. Florence, Casa Buonarroti, 94 A.

88 East side of the Laurentian Library and the cloisters of San Lorenzo. Florence.

89 Reconstruction of the west side of the Laurentian Library, without later superposition. Drawing of the architect Guido Morozzi.

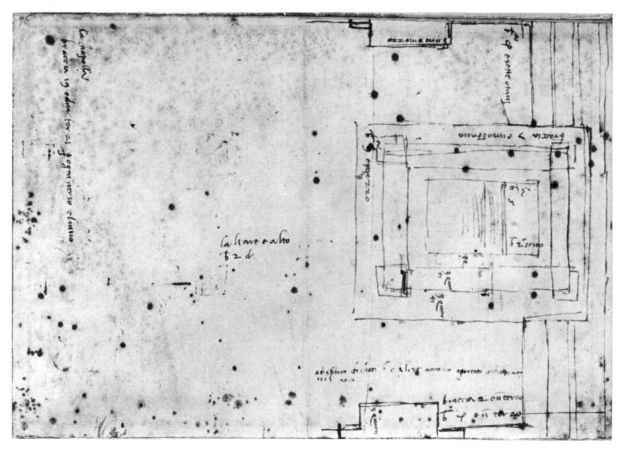

90 Plan of the high altar for San Lorenzo. Florence, Casa Buonarroti, 76 A r.

313

tomb, in 1519: " I, Michelangelo, sculptor, pray your Holiness, offering myself to the Divine Poet, to make fitting his sepulchre and in an honorable place in this city." In his verses he deals with the sepulchre of Cecchino Bracci, at Aracoeli, that interprets his thought, reproduced also in the tombs of the choir of the Santi Apostoli.

Instead, in my opinion, Michelangelo, as an artist, is extraneous to the monument of the Marchese di Marignano, in the Duomo of Milan. He only procured the commission for his pupil, Leone Leoni; this is confirmed by the latter in a frank letter " the work that, through ouy, Sire, I had from his Holiness."

LOGGIA FOR RELICS

A less-known work by Buonarroti is the design of a loggia for the exposition of relics above the main door, inside the church of San Lorenzo; it was carefully executed in 1531-32 under his personal supervision.

There are well-known drawings by Michelangelo that show the preparatory phases for such a gallery; I believe I can add to the number another autograph drawing that has not yet been correctly interpreted. This is drawings N. 89 A v. in Casa Buonarroti (Fig. 95), hith-

91 Plan of the papal tomb isolated on the side of the choir, San Lorenzo. Florence, Casa Buonarroti, 46 A.

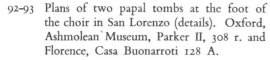

92-93 Plans of two papal tombs at the foot of the choir in San Lorenzo (details). Oxford, Ashmolean Museum, Parker II, 308 r. and Florence, Casa Buonarroti 128 A.

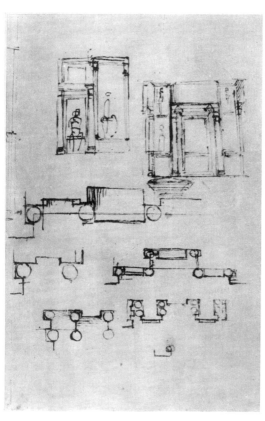

erto related to preparatory studies for the Laurentian Library, not to mention the eccentric attempt to refer it to the Chapel in Castel S. Angelo.

The sheet is characterized by a repeated paired motif of doors and openings above them, and can be dated about 1525. When the sketch is looked at with care, the idea is seen to be complete for all the brevity of the treatment. A small projecting structure is planned, the front view and one side being drawn, the side being shown detached and alongside the front, as in other Michelangelo originals, e. g. 39 r. (Wilde) of the British Museum. A note for a floor plan, sketched in underneath, clearly brings out the rectangular shape of the design; another sketch in the margin is devoted to the fourth side, opposite the front. The presence of steps shows that this solutions was intended for the outside.

Every feature exactly fits the façade wall of S. Lorenzo; the last sketch proves to be a study for the median theme of the façade, where Michelangelo had already tried paired partitions. The indications of interior vaults confirm the practicability of the loggia above the structure conceived (Fig. 94).

The corner columns, taken from those of Brunelleschi, were to frame the projecting volume within the nave and formed a dialectical composition with new panels and pilasters of lesser height, in harmony with the other contemporary studies of the Master.

Thus, this first idea for the relics loggia was incorporated by Michelangelo into something like a " listening gallery," useful as an entrance to the church; the shrine above could be reached by adopting and adapting the narrow service passage in the body of the front wall.

Nonetheless, the idea of locating the relics in a small shrine placed on the wall of the façade is a brilliant one and, so far as is known, without any exact precedents. It may be useful to refer in this connection to the location of *Westwerkes* on the fronts of Othonian churches. It is a solution that has a double function, permitting ceremonies to be performed either inside or outside the basilica, and was adopted by Michelangelo after the initial proposal relating to the high altar and after he had given up the alternative of locating a loggia of this kind over the door of the New Sacristy; it is surprising that it was not followed up, even if against the Buonarroti project not only the weight of the formal Brunelleschi tradition but even more the fear of troubling a spatial volume that was already perfect and definite was easily set.

Since the plan of locating the relics on the interior façade of the church was being considered as early as at the end of 1525, my identification fills a gap between that date and the beginning of the installation to which the previously known drawings relate, and it also leads to regarding the subsequent projects, which ended in the work actually executed, as conditioned solutions, evidently limited at the request of the orderers (Fig. 98).

After the abandonment of the project just discussed, a retreat was made to a more modest one, but still based on installing two new columns at either side of the central doorway. Michelangelo's fondness for interpenetrations was now confined to locating, within the Brunelleschi arrangement, a simple balcony resting on consoles, between the portal and the projecting framework above (Fig. 96).

The definitive solution was to take shape and vigor from this point on: the small door onto the balcony was to be repeated three times and the study for the coat of arms would be completed; it had already been begun, and here I identify it in the isolated sketch, in which hitherto the trend had been to see the profile of a console, which is actually quite different in shape, closely analogous to the doors of the Medicean Chapel.

A precise plan drawing (Oxford, 49 r., Fig. 97) shows the other step towards the final project. Here the dual function of the loggia is explicit taken and raised above the framework: the little doors would have opened outward as well, above the first order, in line with the paired columns, where the great bronze statues had been thought of.

In the " interior pulpit " the side openings were conceived of by Michelangelo as being on axis with the columns underneath, which he goes on to repeat at either side of the doorway. We know that in October 1532, Clement VII disapproved of the bold correspondence of solid form and empty space, determined by the columns and the openings above them. Michelangelo changed the arrangement, bringing the set of three doors closer to the center and giving weight and decorative value to the new pilasters designed to bind the slightly projecting upper mass. The three openings, framed in the simplest of straightmoldings, are intended to be in harmony with the Brunelleschi surroundings and seem to have essential pictural value (Fig. 99).

The extent of Michelangelo's action can be evaluated by the course of the projects in which bold personal expressions had been renounced. The adaptation called for was obtained in a frank and efficacious manner, care being taken to use the " sandstone like the other stones of the church, in order not to be discordant." It was only in details that some new device and lively grace note could be detected.

The balusters of Brunelleschian memory alternate with slender pilasters; their taut curves contrasting with the sharp corners of a central dado that seems to come from the Venetian repertory. The coat of arms, which Clement VII did not wish to be adorned with the papal insignia, buttresses the loggia with its slim sinewy lines: here, best of all, the imagination and the irony of the Master had free rein (Fig. 101). In the capitals and all the moldings Michelangelo could not depart from the pattern of Brunelleschi; only the architrave of the frame is enriched, at its lower edge, by a small finial fitting and seems to be detached from the wall: these two details prelude other capitoline applications.

94 Reconstructional sketch of Michelangelo's first plan for the Loggia delle Reliquie, San Lorenzo.

As we have stated, we here solve the much-discussed problem of the door in *pietra serena* leading from the upper loggia of the cloister of San Lorenzo to the Relics Gallery (Fig. 59), which it completes, constituting a worthy entry to the interior corridor that runs along and above the side aisle and then is cut out in the body of the façade wall. Previously, the door had been attributed to Dosio on the very feeble grounds of one of his many drawings of Michelangelo's architecture (Fig. 100), but its paternity by Michelangelo has been recognized by de Tolnay, who has recently had to restate this attribution in the face of its recent rejection by Ackerman.

The door presents clear, even if not coherent, Michelangelesque characteristics. Analysis of its various elements show an unmistakable divergence in the formation of the terminal parts as compared with the rest. As a result, the tympanum is incongruous with the tapering pilasters (recognized as similar to those of the Library), which is brought out by forced formal juxtapositions that cannot but arouse curiosity. The different spirit with which the tympanum was formed, broad in shape like the forms of the Library, suggests a stylistic caesura between the conscious purism of the Gallery and the sinewy minutiae of the Library close by. The triangular opening, protected by iron bars, within the tympanum, brings out the simple and late completion of this work.

I am convinced that material previously present had been reused; the supposition might be extended to cover the short set of elaborate steps leading into the narrow passage, for their modest function could hardly have required the use, and still less the carving for the purpose, of such elaborately worked steps, the most complex of all the many that Buonarroti did (Fig. 102).

The absolute identity of design between the pilasters of this portal and those flanking the niches of the Library leads me to put them in relation with the problem posed in the Ricetto by the blank panel, facing the other doorway, the only area that has, strangely, no shrine. The slightly larger dimensions of the two pilasters as compared with those of the library (Fig. 76) may be justified by the broader frame of the now empty panel, the only one that is wider than the others. And this might also be the reason for their not being placed in the Ricetto, just because of their slight, and perhaps unpleasing, difference in size.

Another reason for accepting this hypothesis of mine as to reuse of pieces already carved for the Library is that decisive documents assert the existence of fourteen steps all ready in 1533 for the Ricetto staircase and not installed.

The door onto the cloister, with a frame not unlike those of the loggia, should thus be regarded as a conscious adaptation by Michelangelo of pieces already in existence, surmounted by a tympanum similar to the interior one. Likewise, the design should be regarded as co-ordinated and following the arrangement of the loggia and was soon to show its compositional power in the Campidoglio design for the doors of the Consolati.

The crucial interval of the Florentine fortifications

The studies for the Florentine fortifications are linked with a period of good fortune both for the city and for Michelangelo himself. After the Medici had been driven out in May 1527, he took part in the republican life of free Florence, sharing its ideals and giving his labour to the defence of the city.

We know that he worked with dedication and enthusiasm to such an extent that " the lasting and diligent effort given to the above work, *free* and lovingly " was appreciated.

In the meantime, he was elected a member of the " Nove della Milizia." Shortly afterwards, on 6th April 1529, he was appointed " general governor and procurator for the construction and fortification of the walls and other kind of fortification and defence of the city of Florence."

The group of drawings available, exceptional from many points of view, is of previous date: it is of 1528, when he had not yet received public appointments. The drawings and the presentation of many sheets, accompanied by brief captions, recall the projects for San Giovanni dei Fiorentini: like those, disposed in different variations, they were destined to be exhibited and illustrated; they show even the trace of the elucidations given and discussions which took place.

Michelangelo has placed on paper flashes of intuition, he has searched out new techniques of active defence, and above all, has proposed bold experiments, in the burning and heroic atmosphere of that unquiet vigil. Free from exacting responsability, he was driven to more deeply examine different directives, to try ostentations solutions, to distil and extract all his knowledge, for the supreme research of the town's safety. His conscious desire to render himself as useful as possible in a serious situation that however did not seem desperate, was human and admirable.

All must admire his cleverness, his dedication and his torment: they were to bring him to

95 The first plan for the Loggia delle Reliquie, San Lorenzo. Florence, Casa Buonarroti, 89 A v.

compute actions outwith reality, incommunicable to his contemporaries and incomprehensible to posterity. His exceptional sensitivity could not fail to exalt him in that difficult atmosphere.

We know that none of his drawings attracted, even initially, nor does anything concrete remain of his other activities on fortifications in Florence.

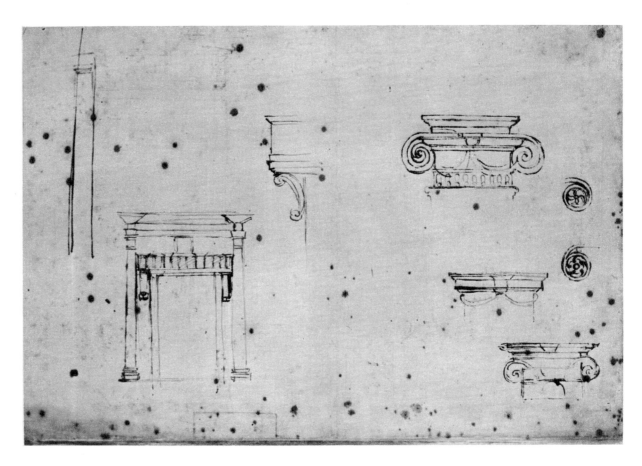

96 Later study for the Loggia delle Reliquie, San Lorenzo. Florence, Casa Buonarroti, 76 A.

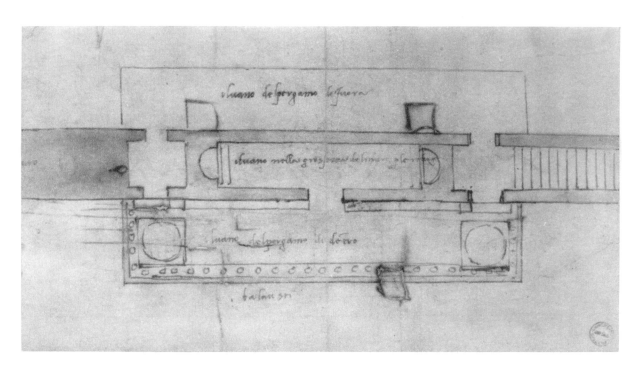

97 Plan for the Loggia delle Reliquie in San Lorenzo. Oxford, Ashmolean Museum, Parker II, 311 r.

His bold enterprises live on paper; however, one must agree with his poetic exegete that these sheets "represent the most original, tense and eversive moment of the architectural creativity of Michelangelo" (Zevi).

Since they can be considered an end in themselves, like other design productions of the

98 Loggia delle Reliquie. Florence, San Lorenzo.

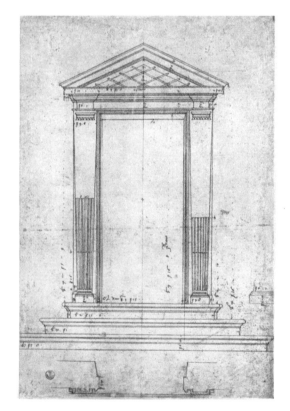

Master, in the plan of the work, their illustration has been included in the treatment of the drawings, to which reference should be made. But it is impossible to renounce some personal notes, particularly several considerations in view of an evaluation of Michelangelo as a military architect.

The similarity of certain curved dispositions with decorative motifs and designs (Figs. 103 and 104) recalls the main formal vaue of the planimetry.

The Master liked to study the strangest and most unexpected ideas, sequences of new and monstrous forms, the displayed wall sequentation, the pattern of accurate unions and elegant tangents.

The evocative force of these images has been widely tested. Why is comparison with the tense, highly strung traditional form of certain musical instruments not evoked? Shapes of double curve, certain final twists, other than such formal reminders, suggest vibrating tension, like stringed instruments; their design would seem to come from the hands of a lutemaker (Fig. 103).

Something technical, manual, is released from these shapes that, only in a summarising sense, can evoke premonitory effects of baroque ornamental scrolls and finials. But I judge still more stringent and productive some comparisons with ancient crossbows and other equipment of war studied by the Master and here cited by analogy of theme rather than function.

All the drawings are characterised by oblique and crossed structures and always followed through by lines of cross-fire. Their obsessive play accentuates, in the Master, the taste, the mental habit of diagonal planning so frequent in the course of this activity: a clear persistent heritage of this contrasted period.

100 Cloister door of San Lorenzo. Relief by
G. A. Dosio. Florence, Uffizi.

102 Detail of the Cloister door of San Lorenzo,
as access to the Loggia delle Reliquie. Florence.

The proofs of his previous fortification activities, as of these traditional and enlargening of the late Roman period, offer no secure grounds for any concrete judgement. It is surprising also in this Florentine affair, how none of his drawings considers the urgent provisional works in crude bricks and earth, which thousands were anxiously awaiting and which were the real object of his public directive action.

Substantially, remain only the preceding ideations of these extraordinary complex structures of slow, and by now impossible execution, at which his fellow townsmen had already marvelled, even if not convinced, so that he procured prominent official posts.

At this point, we must ask ourselves what practical value the stupefying plans of Casa Buonarroti could have.

I do not intend to discuss the general plan of the fortifications, nor the individual concepts of defence, treated elsewhere, and it is also useless to mention the values of the interior spaces and their relationships, already described by Zevi. I shall limit myself to a few notes on the structures proposed and on the analysis of their mural consistency, since we do not feel we should attribute secret resolutionary virtues to these drawings if the substance of the indicated works in the plan and their defensive potential is not clarified.

The fleeting and extremely rare mentions of the elevations certainly do not admit of generalisation and to the reaching of a sure vision of the resulting aspect, more since the indications of certain finishes (27 A v., 15 A and 17 A v.), cause one to think of external parameters, sometimes complex and reinforced on the surface.

It must particularly be considered that many of these plans are drawn of the level of the spaces for the cannons, somewhat limited in height, it is elementary to suppose that, above and below the loop-holes the walls are continuous.

A certain graphic confirmation of this is given in drawing 13 A v.

Buonarroti insists however in his elaborate "ricercari" of his boulevards (Figs. 103, 107) and divides and multiplies the loop-holes only to accentuate the fractioning of the external effects and experiment the geometrical play of the horizontal sections with results near to the sensitivity of the "art nouveau" a preluding abstractism (Fig. 108). By doing this, he

103 Study of fortifications for a Porta. Florence, Casa Buonarroti, 21 A.

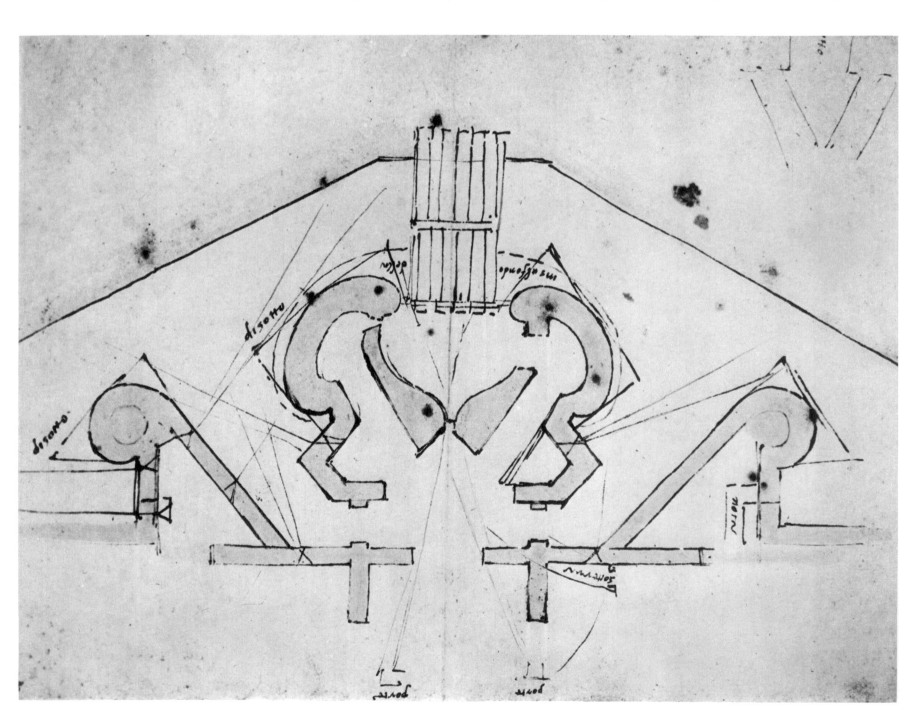

105 Study of fortifications for the Porta del Prato d'Ognissanti. Florence, Casa Buonarroti, 16 A r.

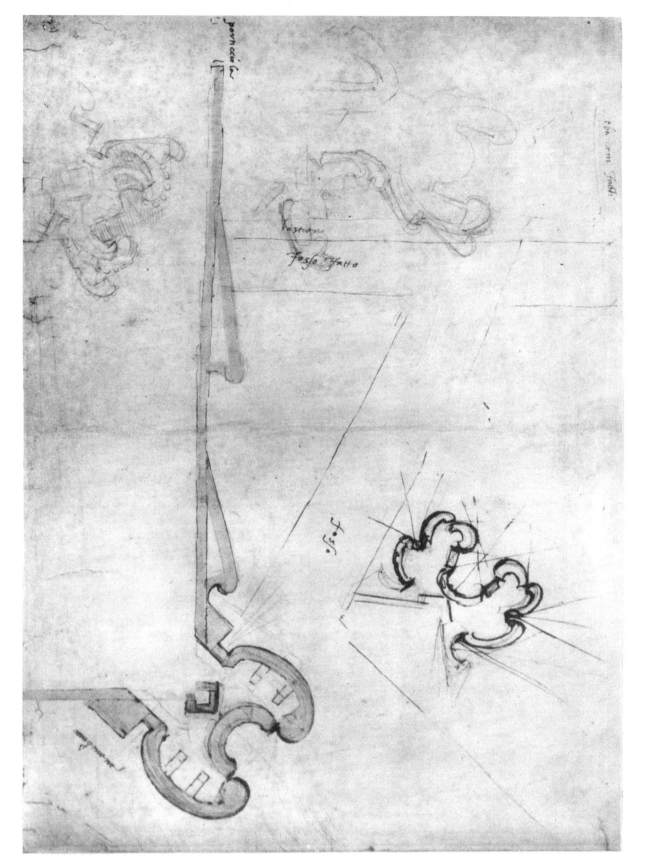

104 Study of a capital (detail). Florence, Uffizi 233 F r.

succeeds in making us almost forget that such effects are determined in the space only at certain horizontal levels, as the pyrotechnic plays live in single instants.

We must, however, clearly denounce and reject the unconstrained reconstructions that extend the so articulated external profiles, really of the *troniere*, to the whole height. But to understand these bastions, other than the problems of form, are outlined also those of structure.

Michelangelo notes—only in one salient—the quality of the material: " stone " (13 A v.). The exceptional quality of the case may be deduced, admitting rightly that the walls, in the greater part, should be of brick. And then any comparison with modern, flimsy, flexible structures of arched form, instituted in defence of Michelangelo, would fall.

In these examinations, technically objective, we must not allow ourselves to be led by the novelty and by the strong fascination of the proposals, but we should rather reflect on their practicability and efficiency. I see, for example, that the structures often appear interconnected and unified by vaults interposed " both above and below " (23 A and 22 A r.); of arches or other still suitable horizontal connections, clear trace is also seen (22 A v. and 24 A). Michelangelo had thus planned a certain collaboration of the outer walls with apparently independent structures placed behind. Wile, in some cases, the walls seem flimsy because they are dug out of solid wall masses internally lightened by spaces (15 A and 16 A r.), one cannot exclude that they are internally reinforced with wooden beams.

These considerations bring us to understand and to individuate more robust architectural 321

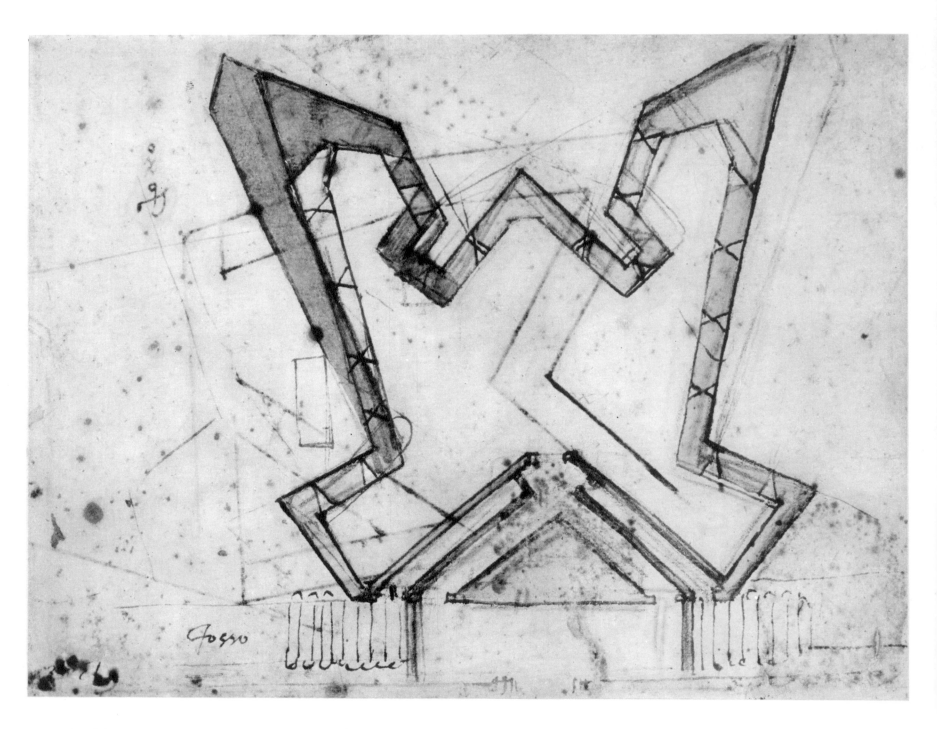

106 Study of fortification for the Porta al Prato. Florence, Casa Buonarroti, 28 A r.

components from the wide footing and united structures. The constructive problem could find more than one practicable solution as Michelangelo had doubtlessly followed. The Master was unable not to believe in the efficacy of his bastions: this is testified, if nothing else, by the limited number planned in the plain, subject of criticism made of Buonarroti on the possibility of defending these isolated boulevards.

This said, while we can absolve the Master—or at least concede all mitigations—as far as the accusation made about the eccessive thinness of the walls is concerned, we remain however impressed by the other fundamental objection made by the military technicians of the times, on the multiplicity of the sides planned and on the number and the too close position of the loop-holes.

They are fundamental criticisms that have confirmation in the generous thrust that Michelangelo's bastions make towards the enemy (Fig. 106) rather than inspiring defence. Michelangelo busied himself in watching and pushing back the enemy frontally more than considering the possibility of encirclement that many of these bastions seemed to provoke.

It has been necessary to admit, and it is fatal to recognise that the history of the fortifications, still thrust for centuries against the same arms and means of defence, has never derived any positive suggestion from Michelangelo's studies. It is a negative fact which should make prudent criticism of his projects.

It is not intended to underrate the importance of Michelangelo's drawings, but only to submit them again to a logical method of study, not to judge them with an unsuitable yardstick; that is, not regarding them more effective as projects.

We must conclude that Michelangelo was not a military architect: a letter in which he avoids expressing his exact opinion on the fortifications of Borgo, confirms this. Such a specialist activity was not congenial to him: it was alien to his own artistic education and contrary to his own neoplatonic concepts.

If he was forced to military architecture by circumstances and by the desire to be of use to his city, even he soon realised that the ambition was useless and illusory: he remains simply an architect—a great architect.

The episode of the Florentine fortifications only closed one period and opened another, but

107 Study of fortification for the Prato d'Ognissanti. Florence, Casa Buonarroti, 30 A.

it also furnished the Master with a harsh contact with military and political reality; a human experience which later was to bear fruit, not all better.

His troubles had convinced him to conclude his activities in Florence. Michelangelo was never to return to his native city and spoke of it distantly and with indifference. Attracted by more general problems and visions in a circle out of the old factions, he continued his way with new vigour, but absorbed by higher ideals and finally immersed in sublime architectural themes. It is certainly not affirmed that, after 1531, " all that follows is a slow elaboration of the unfinished."

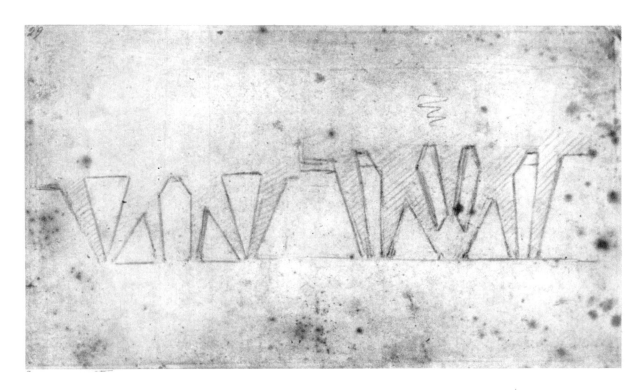

108 Plan study for multiple embrasures. Florence,
Casa Buonarroti, 28 A.

112 Capital of the Portico dei Conservatori, Campidoglio. Rome.

109-111 Studies of a capital. Florence, Casa Buonarroti, 87 A, 56 A and 83 A.

The two greatest undertakings

THE CAPITOLINE PIAZZA AND PALACES

At the beginning of the Cinquecento, the Campidoglio was still a bleak and desolate hill on the outskirts of the city. Despite the solemn nature of the environment and the prestige of its memories, only the medieval Senatorial Palace, incorporating the old structures of the Tabularium, managed to dominate with a picturesque aspect and civic dignity, although by no means rivaling the seats of the great Italian communes. The palace known as the Palazzo de' Banderesi and then de' Conservatori (put up alongside later and provided with a portico on the façade by Nicholas V), was an isolated wing towards the west. On the opposite side, the red structure of the Aracoeli loomed over the so-called Platea Capitolina, an irregular plateau dotted with carved marbles, the only reminders of past glories.

The rebuilding done in Rome in 1536 for the solemn entry of Charles V had varying, and even grandiose, aspects; but nothing could be done on that occasion to lend the new dignity planned for the Capitoline. However, the visit raised, in concrete terms, the urgent problem of renovation, of which Pope Paul III was the promoter. Among other actions, the Farnese pope had various sculptures moved to the hill, in order to increase its ideal and artistic potential. Thus, in 1537 it received the bronze equestrian statue of Marcus Aurelius, the starting point for the entire project of the Capitoline.

There is no contradicting the solid tradition that entrusts to Michelangelo the plans for the Capitoline Piazza and Palaces. Michelangelo's paternity of the work was asserted from the earliest times; it took form laboriously, not without withdrawals and variants, which were

inevitable in a work drawn out for so long by financial difficulties. Nonetheless, it arrives at luminous results of compositional coherence.

On March 22, 1539 a sum was appropriated "*in reformatione statue M. Antonii in platea Capitolij existentis secundum iudicium domini Michaelis Angeli sculptoris.*"

The indisputable intervention of the Master proves that Michelangelo had considered the new and stimulating presence of the statue and had succeeded in having a solution of his own accepted. The same resolution informs us that the decision was taken to spend the available sum in part to change the location of the Marcus Aurelius statue, "*partim circa muros fiendos in dicta platea*" (" in part for walls to be erected on the said plateau ").

In other words, the decision was made to establish the limits of the square, especially by constructing the long supporting walls flanking the church of Aracoeli (Fig. 115), as also indicated in Bufalini's plan (1551). A fundamental factor in again defining the urban space was the alignment of the wall with the central notch, the wall being so traced as to show the same slant as the Palazzo de' Conservatori with respect to the new axis defined by the center line of the Palazzo Senatorio and the statue of Marcus Aurelius. This re-echoed the arrangement of Pienza's Renaissance piazza, while preparing it for a unified compositional vista.

The 1539 decision is, therefore, of capital importance. It shows that the Conservatori had logically given precedence to preliminary works of urbanistic arrangement which defined and framed the plan of all the subsequent works. And these master guidelines, true lines of force and development, which were later to be given slow but coherent embodiment, relate to a clearly unitary project by Michelangelo, based from the outset on the dialectical interpenetration of shapes on elliptical and rectangular bases.

The present pedestal of the statue of Marcus Aurelius is the original one, whatever discredited interpretations to the contrary may have been offered. The inscribed date, the form and the character of the carved reliefs attend this beyond a doubt (Fig. 121). In 1561 Buonarroti

115 Anonymous: view of the Campidoglio (about 1554-60). Brunswick, Kupferstichkabinett.

114 E. Dupérac: planimetry of Michelangelo's plan for the Campidoglio (1567).

made a single change; into his slender base, which heightens the plastic values of the ancient work, he inserted the four vertical moldings, whose angular projections added solidity and power to the beautiful pedestal. With dynamic polyvalence, which we might almost call cubistic by anticipation, the splendid podium expressed and continued the elliptical and rectangular forms on which the entire piazza is designed.

The volumes of the buildings on the Capitoline established an aerial space, with a parallel, piped form, open at the edges, into which the broken straight lines of the base seem to expand, while the strong elliptical solution of the pavement is likewise developed in the body of the podium. Its curved shape is interrupted from the outset at the diagonals; the modulated projections seem to release radial suggestions which, echoed at the edges of the elliptical pavement, further define the diagonals of the composition.

Given the certain dating of the pedestal, it affirms its primordial value as a priceless fulcrum and fertile matrix for the entire project by Michelangelo (Figs. 114, 116).

In the years that followed, Michelangelo continued to concern himself with the Campidoglio. As Panvinio tells us, he first designed the arrangement of the fragments of the consular and triumphal Fasti, discovered in 1546, while engaged on the great staircase of the Palazzo Senatorio. 325

CAPITOLII·SCIOGRAPHIA·EX·IPSO·EXEMPLARI·MICHAELIS·ANGELI·BONAROTI·A·STEPHANO·DVPERAC·PARISIENSI·ACCVRATE·DELINEATA ET·IN·LVCEM·AEDITA·ROMAE·ANNO·SALVTIS·OODLXIX

116 E. Dupérac: perspective view of Michelangelo's plan for the Campidoglio (1568).

With the purpose of heightening the value of his exceptional discovery and of interpreting the original architectural forms that had appeared in the Forum Romanum, he collected and arranged the ancient fragments on a wall of the court of the Conservatori, surmounting the central portion of the planned façade with a triangular tympanum. Michelangelo's signature is in the choice of an arrangement that was one of his favorites; from the studies of his youth to the chapel in Castel S. Angelo from the mass of drawings and projects of every period down to the destroyed, and perhaps posthumous, theme of the entrance into the Sforza Chapel.

A sixteenth-century engraving shows us the original arrangement of the Fasti, made at the expense of Cardinal Alessandro Farnese (Fig. 113). The monument, was then reduced to its present state by cutting it off at the top and the bottom in order to allow it to fit inside one of the rooms of the palace, the room taking the name of Sala de' Fasti. This mutilation took away the character of the architectural achievement, and hence almost justifies the way in which

117 Axonometric reconstruction of Michelangelo's plan for the Campidoglio (after Ackerman).

118 The Piazza del Campidoglio seen from the
loggia of the Palazzo Senatorio. Rome.

119 The Campidoglio and Santa Maria in Aracoeli. Rome.

Michelangelo's important restoration has been completely forgotten by those who have hitherto dealt expressly with the architectural work of the Master.

The first part of the staircase by Michelangelo to be erected was the part towards the Aracoeli, as is also shown by a rare engraving by Cock, which can be relied on so far as the detailed substructures are concerned (Fig. 123). Then came the other half, to the spectator's right, as is shown by the accounts of masons and stonecutters that have come down to us. This was logical order for the work, it being possible for the first half of the stairs to be supported on existing structures while on the other side it would have been necessary first to set in place all the new outer walls of the palace, in place of the loggias still in existence. A document dated May 21, 1552 and relating to this second part of the staircase lists many stonecutting works, which have always been considered to be the last thing to be done. Actually this is not so, and the document in question does not deal with the work on the lower flight of the stairs and the landing in between, all of which is comprised in another and obviously posterior account that has come down to us. Also later is the final installation of the long bench at the front of the staircase. The new flight of steps might be located within a period running from a date not much earlier than 1547 to 1554, at which point a further piece of stonecutter's work was added: the portal at the top of the staircase.

In my opinion, the staircase, which was erected in several phases, shows some recognizable periods of construction. A first form did not have the central portion projecting forward; and the unitary design whose construction was commenced may have been flanked by broader flights of two or three approach steps, gradated frontally as well, as appears from Cock's engraving. Michelangelo's well-known sketch for the stairs, showing a single flight on each side, might well bear out this solution, including a possible ground floor entrance at the center of the

120 Francisco de Hollanda: statue of Marcus Aurelius before modification of the base (1538-39). Madrid, Prado.

121 Equestrian statue of Marcus Aurelius. Rome, Campidoglio.

122 View of the Campidoglio. Rome.

123 H. Cock: engraving of Palazzo Senatorio with Michelangelo's staircase under construction (1562; detail).

staircase, made possible by the horizontal nature of the building and suggested by Cock with the mixtilineal outline of a central entrance that seems to have been taken from the drawings for the Florentine fortifications (Fig. 127).

Onto a first project of this nature a second may have been grafted, perhaps during the course of the work. The prominence, later documented, given to the central element, further supported by the evidence of two projecting lateral landings; the organized interplay of the masses was ended off better by covering the loggia, as is seen in the engravings by Dupérac (Fig. 116).

The goal of a more complex spatial organization, called for by the dimensions and solemnity of the work, demanded a unified frontal form. This was sought by prolonging and bringing together, on the wings, the revetment of the greater flights of steps, and was finally confirmed by adding the planned continuous bench along the base (Fig. 126, 128).

The perspective engravings of Dupérac give clear and repeated indications how the high portico was to appear on the side of the square, but we cannot discover from them what solution would have been adopted on the flanks of this emergent element.

The presence, on the flanks of the initiated loggia, of ancient uprights incorporated with the pilasters of the balustrade (still in existence and shown more clearly in archive documents), and the slight extent to which they show in frontal view, led me to search for a projected solution that could be suitable to the great distances between those uprights, and not contrast with the pavement of the loggia. This, like the two lower landings, is broken up by intermediate crossing guide lines, which I have been able to show are authentic and original.

It seemed logical to me, therefore, to suppose that in order to solve the problem of the wide opening on the flanks of the loggia the idea occurred of breaking up the width by inserting a central support, which was also called for by the persistent arrangement of the guide lines right on the center line of the entrance opening thus divided. This would have been a late and unexpected elaboration of the double motifs that Michelangelo was so fond of. If the

329

126 Entrance staircase of the Palazzo Senatorio. Rome, Campidoglio.

124 Detail of the entrance staircase of Palazzo Senatorio. Rome, Campidoglio.

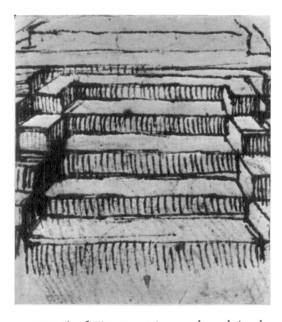

125 Detail of Fig. 63, stairway planned in the Ricetto of the Laurentian Library.

central support could be identified as a column, the elements that would have been resting against the broad smooth intrados ought to have been semicolumns, which were certainly more in keeping with the structure of the projecting vertical piers.

I have had the good fortune of finding an authentic and detailed confirmation of this original and logical solution in an autograph drawing by Michelangelo, whose subject had not previously been identifed, but which was universally accepted as dating from the late Roman period (Fig. 131).

The Capitoline accounts show that to supplement these works an entrance portal to the palace was erected, in 1554, just at the top of the staircase and hence designed to be contained within the covered loggia. Its simple appearance is handed down in the perspective views of sixteenth-century Paris and Florence. Although it was believed to have been destroyed and replaced by the existing one, I have been able to find that all its structural elements (repeatedly described and measured in the archive documents) are still *in situ*, enveloped in the richer portal designed by Giacomo della Porta in 1598, when the façade was finally completed.

There is no reason for doubting that the large door erected immediately after construction of the staircase was likewise designed by Michelangelo. The fine and originally contrasted carving of the consoles, the solemn jambs studied in youth on a Roman model, the vigour of the oak frieze and the remarkable energy of the mouldings alongside the jambs betray a sober lofty taste that aimed at emphasizing only the exterior parts of the work, which are more readiliy seen by those coming in under the covered loggia (Fig. 130).

The great staircase is an outstanding element in Michelangelo's composition. Linked to the square by its decisive sculptural and urbanistic features, and to the place by determinative

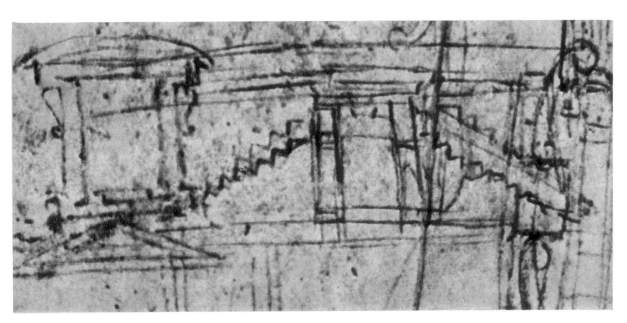

127 First study for the Capitoline steps (detail). Florence, Casa Buonarroti, 19 F r.

330

128 Details of the staircase of the Palazzo Senatorio. Rome, Campidoglio.

formal qualities, it became the vital ganglion of the entire project, even in the minds of contemporaries, and this is why its erection was put ahead of so many other urgent tasks. Imitations are frequent and endless—almost up to our own times—those of its balustrades (Figs. 124, 128), 331

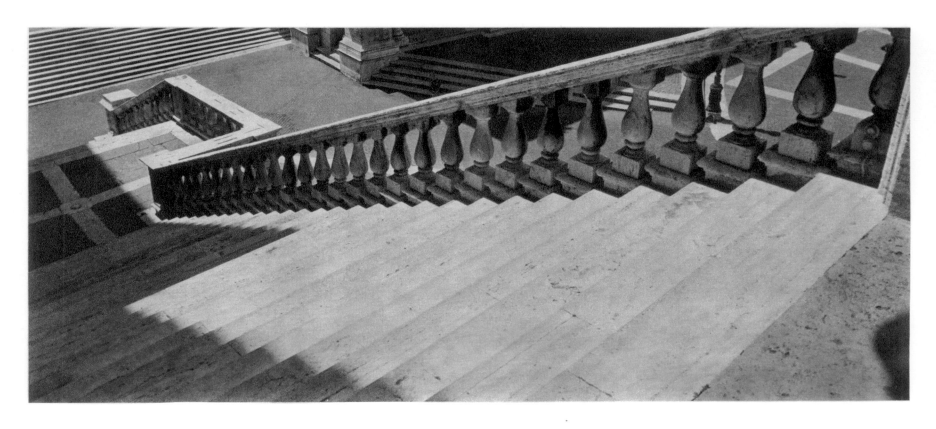

129 One of the flights of the staircase of Palazzo Senatorio. Rome, Campidoglio.

of which is given here, for the first time, a highly personal version. To be remembered is the minor reproduction of this staircase in the Nicchione di Belvedere, coinciding with the works which restricted its width excluding all theatral use. Having abolished the characteristic staircase with semi-circular steps, in 1551 " Michelangelo drew and had made the square one with balustrades of tufa " successively modified but evident in the drawings of the time. (G. A. Dosio, Uffizi, 2559 A).

The limited resources available for the Capitoline slowed up the work considerably, and even forced it to be suspended for some years.

Pius IV intervened actively in 1561 to put an end to the delays. There was first an urgent drive towards laying out the piazza, in the same year of 1561, seeing the new pavement and installation of the balustrade facing the city, later embellished with statues and trophies (Fig. 118); next came the great access steps to the square, erected in 1564 and then completed with balustrades from 1581 (Fig. 119). At the same time the pontiff took into consideration the building that was the seat of the Senator, the highest city magistrate appointed by the pope; this palace had been neglected by the Conservatori and had become virtually uninhabitable. It was rapidly and inexpensively restored during these years, perhaps only provisionally, and probably with Michelangelo having no part in the work. Mainly interior work was involved, with no architectural repercussions. It seems to me therefore, out of the question to speak of a new project for the exterior layout, due to Tommaso Cavalieri, as has been suggested by Pecchiai followed by later writers on the Campidoglio.

Leaving out of consideration the construction of the new civic tower erected by Martino Lunghi the Older in 1579–82 and the fountain in front of the grand staircase (1588–89), which go beyond Michelangelo's conception, I believe that the rearrangement of the Senatorial Palace was completed later by Giacomo della Porta in two successive phases, in 1573–77 and 1593-98. In the first, under Gregory XIII, the entire central portion of the palace was converted into a single, large very high hall, altering the basis of Michelangelo's design (Fig. 122).

After the second story had been done away with, and thereby the possibility of having it show nobly in the façade, the low windows of the mezzanine above were adapted to help the lighting of the new salon. Another important consequence of this decision was that there was no longer any point to constructing the covered loggia, which would have been out of proportion to the rest of the building and could not have been built on the upper terrace (Fig. 117).

In 1576–77, the documents tell us, the windows of the salon were carved and put in place on the façade; these were the present windows and not other ones hypothesized by Pecchiai and not mentioned in any other document.

After the publication of the perspective plan of Tempesta (1593), showing the rich new windows, the external revetment of the palace was taken up. The old loggia on the top floor was removed and the façade of the Senatorio was finally divided with the pilasters of the Michelangelo design; they were not done in travertine, however, and did not project far enough. At that time the building was given the frieze of the final balcony and was enriched with Michelangelo's portal; the stars of Clement VIII on the lateral capitals of the door confirm the date of 1598 on the scroll in memory of Senator Capelletti. Above the doorway was placed not only the inscription in eulogy of the Aldobrandini pope but also a monumental coat of arms, which was later removed to make room for the opening of the central window, which it had obstructed.

130 Photo-montage of Michelangelo's door at the top of the staircase.

332

132 Reconstruction of Michelangelo's original plan for the staircase of Palazzo Senatorio, Campidoglio. (Watercolour by Attilio Galluzzi).

131 Drawing of a twin motif for the staircase. Florence, Casa Buonarroti, 58 A.

Thus, the building forming the background of the composition, the noblest and oldest one, was the chief victim of the compromises, internal disputes and renunciations. It did not have a happy fate. Emphasis was sought in the form of the great unplanned-for salon; at the cost of the authority of the carefully studied façade; the building was even denied the travertine facing exhibited by the entire complex.

Fortunately, the powerful mass of the staircase, with its exuberant expressive force, sheds so much interest over the entire palace that it generously covers its incompleteness and mistakes. Everything becomes or seems to be Michelangelesque; the atmosphere of genius redeems and ennobles all the wretched human vicissitudes.

In the meantime, a beginning had finally been made in 1562 on Michelangelo's project for the Palazzo de' Conservatori, the renewal of which had been discussed back in the distant year of 1538. Erection of the huge façade was begun with the greatest care. Guidetto Guidetti was engaged " to carry out the orders of Michelangelo Buonarroto." After his death soon thereafter, his place in supervising the work was taken by Giacomo della Porta who for the first time took the title of Architect of the Roman People. The new façade was pushed on with vigor, but the details were finished only in 1583, a tardy and to a great extent posthumous execution of Michelangelo's design.

A drawing preserved at Oxford and published by Tolnay is the first, even though remote, document showing Michelangelo's design interest in the Palazzo de' Conservatori and shows the initial derivation from the motif of the fluted columns of the Laurentian Ricetto.

But even earlier, another drawing (42 A r. of Casa Buonarroti) erroneously referred to the reading room of the Laurentian Library has taken up and developed the same theme with such richness of detail and force of concentration that it seems impossible it could have been designed only for an interior. It is virtually a façade, that we can link with and give a prominent place to in the search for the master ideas of the Palazzo de' Conservatori (Fig. 69).

To this theme a significant transformation later suggested itself to Michelangelo's imagination. The blank geometrical wall space between the twin columns of the Ricetto, which we have seen repeated in the drawings for the papal tombs becomes animated, aware of its added

333

◁ 133 The Campidoglio seen from the steps of Aracoeli. Rome.

supporting function, organized in an architectural order. It then gains in vigor and development as compared with the twin columns, which have been relieved of the weight on them and are no longer joined by a common function, so that they can decrease in importance, lose their original close contact, spreading apart to receive between them the new deep shadows of the vivid light. This was the birth of the compartmentation of the Palazzo de' Conservatori, rising serene above the piazza with its giant order, a new and highly original invention fruitful of expressive developments. The repetition of this architectural formula, traceable " in nuce " in other Michelangelo sketches of lesser import, assumed unheard of aspects in the courtyard of the Fort of Civitavecchia (Fig. 134), that refers to an idea of the Master about 1535.

And the great engaged pilasters retain this original and perform these functions in so precise and decisive a manner that we marvel. The projecting wings attach to the flanks and make them emerge better from the composition; at the top their horizontal connection merges with that of the strengthened architectural order. The order thus comes to outline colossal bearing elements, adequate to the new aulic poetics that is also in play in the precise motif of the architraves, which are masterful ornaments in stone (Fig. 135). Thus reinforced on the flanks, the structure of the great pilasters seems to strive to penetrate, by means of the same number of wall divisions, inward into the building, crossing over the porch. On the exterior, the difference in the materials, suggesting a difference in functions, subtly indicates this organization; under the portico, the divisions differentiate showily, resuming the square simplicity of olden days, and creep in among the abutments, leaving their studied covering functions intact

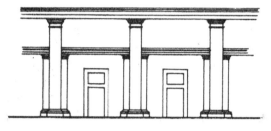

134 Diagram by Michelangelo of the exteriors in the courtyard of the Forte di Civitavecchia.

135 Detail of the front of the Palace dei Conservatori in Campidoglio. Rome.

136 Drawing for the tabernacles with dedication stones in the Palazzo dei Conservatori. Florence, Casa Buonarroti, 97 A r.

and without losing themselves therein. Rather, they accentuate an individuality that appears in the form of deep meaningful incisions, those of the bold architraves, which are travertine ornaments, carefully designed to come close and finally touch, giving a necessary unprecedented caesura in the alternation of finely decorated themes of the vaults, with the peremptory simplicity of the wall divisions (Fig. 138).

In the Conservatori, other points in common with the latest Florentine architecture are evident. The capitals of the windows (Fig. 141) are derived from the Laurentian, while the doors of the Consulats (Fig. 137) are copied from that of the loggia of the Relics (Figs. 100 and 102).

Instead, the capital of the interposed order (Figs. 112 and 138) realises, for the first time, the plan already studied by Michelangelo (Figs. 109, 110 and 111) in connecting the scrolled Ionic valutes with a frieze. It had enormous success and was named after the Master.

From the chronological point of view, as has been pointed out, Michelangelo's conception of the Palazzo de' Conservatori may be related to the general project for the Piazza del Campidoglio. But from the cogent examples of some formal solutions that can be compared with St. Peter's and Palazzo Farnese, the final design must have been reworked in the years immediately following 1546. Since it seems to me that the forms of the Conservatori are connected with the preparation of the project for the outside staircase, this dating is indirectly confirmed by the Capitoline documents for the great flight of steps.

Giacomo della Porta, in completing the building, utilised not only Buonarroti's themes but also his exact data. In this connection, are significant my identifications relating to a design belonging to Michelangelo's school (Fig. 136) for the framing of the dedicatory stones (1568), and to a sketch of the Master (Fig. 139), in which I found overlapping drawings of two sculptured elements in the Palazzo, the portal of the Archivio and the niches on the landing

137 The Porta dei Consolati in the Palazzo dei Conservatori. Rome, Campidoglio.

138 The Portico dei Conservatori. Rome, Campidoglio.

336

139 Superimposed studies of a door and tabernacle for the Palazzo dei Conservatori. Oxford, Ashmolean Museum, Parker II, 332 r.

141 Window of the Palazzo dei Conservatori.
Rome, Campidoglio.

140 Lateral top of the Palazzo dei Conservatori,
from Via del Campidoglio. Rome, Campidoglio.

of the stairs. The internal staircase, ornamented with minute stuccoes, was relieved by the
pleasant space of an open courtyard (Fig. 142 and 143).

In this atmosphere of derivation, or at least imitation of Michelangelo, one may well ask
oneself if the large window in the center of the palace, placed shortly after Buonarroti's death,
is not based on a possible idea of the Master, in successive elaborations, as happened for the
compartmentation, whose creative process we have followed through the subsequent introduction of the portico that was missing in the Tolnay design. And above all we are struck by
the fact that this last solution (once more taking tradition as its starting point, that is, the
desire to perpetuate the memory of the Quattrocento portico) was able to make use of the
porticoes to integrate the piazza on its most confined sides and fuse in the unified new architectural vision, to which it lent authentic prestige.

For in this work, too, the city-planning function was preponderant. Substantially, rather
than a palace it is a new prospect that is involved, in close correspondence and coordination
with an overall vista. It is a prospect frankly announced as such; we need only think of the
honest limitation of the walls on the flanks, consisting at that time of a single buttress—the
only one that could be seen from via dell'Aracoeli and slope opposite from the Forum (Fig. 140).
This limitation has definite urbanistic values.

In the Palazzo de' Conservatori, meanwhile, it had been decided to expand the existing hall
to adapt it for use as a council chamber, and to that end it was soon decorated pictorially by
Cavalier d'Arpino. The decision to have the great civic assemblies meet in this palace, in the

337

43

143 The second flight of stairs with the entrance to the Sala degli Orazi e Curiazi. Rome, Campidoglio.

142 The intermediate landing of the staircase, with the old courtyard, in the Palazzo dei Conservatori. Rome, Campidoglio.

room later known as the salon degli Orazi e Curiazi, was made necessary by circumstances but deprived the other building projected, symmetrical to the Palazzo de' Conservatori, of the purpose for which it had been designed.

In Michelangelo's plan it was there that the *Sala del Consiglio* should have been placed, as is clearly indicated in a perspective view of the period.

After having lost any precise function, it was to be known simply as *il Palazzo Nuovo*. Construction of this wing was decided on in 1603, but then put off until 1644. Even at that, it was not completed until 1655, while the finishing touches and the doubling of the façades on the flanks of the Palazzo de' Conservatori had to wait several more years. It was only then that the piazza could be said, after a hundred and twenty years, to have been finished (Fig. 144).

Although confined within precise dimensions and bound to conform to a consistent style and alignment, Michelangelo succeeded in creating a truly princely and original architectural atmosphere on the Campidoglio. His solution, whether in its premises or its methods, cannot be called by any means a makeshift, as has been done. Michelangelo's genius managed to draw unexpected felicitous results precisely from the difficulties; he was able to be and remain a poet even when constrained to some forced rhymes.

And thus, on the Campidoglio, too, Buonarroti conformed to the requirements with which he was faced. Fully aware of the traditional values and the meager financial resources available, he never thought of taking down the Palazzo de' Conservatori—still less the Senatorio.

He undertook to transfigure them with his forms, having drawn from them the traces of new axes at the crossing of which he wished to place the majestic Marcus Aurelius.

The architectural unity was simply and happily achieved. The main axis was directed boldly towards the city, reversing the orientation of the traditional approach, and served as a guide line to the long ramp inserted among the surrounding structures; giving a slow, solemn processional rhythm to the ascent of the hill, in order to make the visitor savor meditatively the transition from the Piazza dell'Aracoeli to the bleak hillock that Michelangelo conceived of and transformed into an Acropolis. High walls, faced with brick, were to plunge down, separating the upper piazza from the surrounding buildings, if not in scorn, at least with a meaningful contrast. Buonarroti would not permit a true street, on which carriages could pass, to lead to the citadel which he thought of as difficult of access and whose pure setting should not be encumbered. Everyone should climb the ramp, it mattered not whether on foot or on horseback, free to look around them without impediment during this carefully planned inspirational ascent.

From below, only the modest distant Capitoline tower would be visible; he did not wish its bulk and shape to be proportionate to the Palazzo Senatorio, but, as it were, relegated outside the picture. The communal struggles were now in the distant past, but their memory had to be perpetuated; and yet, under the altered conditions, it did not seem suitable, in Michelangelo's eyes, to have a proud civic tower arise in the living core of an aware modern architecture.

By rising above the plane of the city, a more precise sensation is given of detachment, including spiritual detachment, from everyday life and troubles. The ramp seems to be more airy and easy as we approach the Propylaeum sculptures; the eyes, straight ahead, little by little, get the vision of the sublime square, filtered as it were through the great sculptures aligned on the balustrade, rich in history and symbolic attributes. The wide perspective leads the eye to run easily over the straight lateral cornices and gives impressions of grandeur, yet the long way up the ramp, while giving those impressions fleetingly, does not make us regard them as unattainable. Because the ramp enforces an axis, the eyes are kept on the final goal, which is disclosed slowly: the high terrace before the portal of the Senatorial palace. But Michelangelo, foreseeing a possible covering over of the terrace at the top of the double staircase, would have agreed to an anticipation of this finale, bringing the statue of Marcus Aurelius into relief against the shadow of an imperial canopy with slim coupled columns.

The platform was to show at once the front: a citadel without defenses, with its solemn way of access established and always opened to the civic hill. The reasoned symbolic convexity of the ellipse gives the pavement a remarkable plastic life that bonds and fuses the entire incomparable architectural setting. And the aspect of the square would have been even more fused and unified if Michelangelo's plan had been followed and the pathways, like those of the ramp, had been paved with bricks laid on edge, except for the travertine steps and guide lines, the two materials of the façades which would have accentuated the luminosity and given the setting a little warm tonality.

The three buildings of the Piazza give the open space an unmistakable aura. In particular, the two symmetrical ones seem to have between them an aulic enclosed atmosphere that might almost be described as that of a great salon. If Marcus Aurelius has found his setting in the tremendous atrium of an ideal museum, that gives us an unreal impression: the joy of living in an inspiring open hall.

In reality, however, the square is designed as a terrace. We feel the circulating hill light from the long balustrade overlooking the city and the gaps left between the buildings, which reinforce the effect of height and give the feeling of living nature. Now the lengthwise view, which the eye had become accustomed to in ascending, first encounters the outpost of Marcus Aurelius, breaks against the loggia of the Palazzo Senatorio, runs diverging over the flights stairs and finally goes off into the views, once broader and more open, over the vast Forum and the swelling Palatine.

Once the visitor has emerged from the track of the ramp, he has freedom of view and movement; the very design of the pavement invites him to move about, to take possession of the surroundings, before calling him back to the staircase of the Senatorio or the radial exists. In the meantime, he drinks in a dramatic alternation of voids and fullnesses, of masses of travertine and backgrounds of sky and green, following one another and intersecting in the truemanner of Michelangelo.

The architectural unity of the square was attained rather late with the construction of the Palazzo Nuovo, known as the Museum. In Michelangelo's conception, this building not only met the need of giving the new urban setting symmetry and unity, but also had the function of separating the Capitoline Piazza from the Aracoeli and freeing it from the domination of the Franciscan church that had always loomed above it. A decisive screen was needed in order not to lose—not to contradict—the desired effect of terraced height. Otherwise, the acropolis would not have been an acropolis; it would have seen at once that the new square, no longer sublime, was on the site of the ancient " asylum," a natural depression between the two summits of the hill, and the high civic significance given the Capitoline citadel would have lost its power of conviction.

Michelangelo puts out of sight behind the two palaces the lateral flights of steps leading up to the Aracoeli monastery and to Monte Caprino while still orienting them in the civic

339

144 The Palazzo del Museo. Rome, Campidoglio.

setting. The tufa porticoes in which they end are not adorned with sacred emblems, as might have been expected at the entrance to a monastery. They were constructed between 1544 and 1553, by artists outside the orbit of Buonarroti. They are simply inconspicuous gray structures, aerial in their proportions; the contrast with Michelangelo's works makes them seem even more conventional and remote, intentionally disengaged and practically extraneous to the essence of the work like faint fresco backgrounds or marginal painted perspectives.

The square on the Capitoline would have achieved a tighter unity of composition if Buonarroti's project for the Senatorio had been carried out in the way it was designed, without diminishing the monumental quality of the second story, and done in travertine, the stone that well interprets Michelangelo's Roman architecture and was to have embodied the omitted canopy of the loggia, the outstanding sonorous episode that wolud have proclaimed itself from far, ringing with motifs and shadows.

One could speak of a metaphysical geometrical unity of the square. The elliptical resolution of a trapezoid surface, as it was conceived and carried out, seems to lend itself to a definition certainly not devoid of ideal bases and dialectical efficacy.

Although the effect produced by the two divergent edifices is by now well realized, equal emphasis has not been laid on the fact that this solution was preceded and followed by others of the kind which, by being less on the surface, are still more refined and persuasive in effect. The balustrades of the long access ramp are also a little further apart toward the top, helping to give the person walking up a slight feeling of expansion accompanying the sensation of ascent. Subtle devices bring about the same effect on all four flights of the stairs to the Palazzo Senatorio. An almost imperceptible sense of lightness and greater nobility won is slowly infused, with repeated insistence, in the end producing almost surreal convictions and effects, referrable to the metaphysical magic of Michelangelo's art.

The Piazza del Campidoglio: even if its prospects were erected after the death of the old man and do not fully reflect his thought and aspirations, it constitutes a marvelous architectural ensemble, never repeated. And, above all, it bears witness to a courageous and important urbanistic choice, made with a secure method and tenacious aspirations of civic independence. Its expansive polyphony, which only Michelangelo could supply in the mature sixteenth century, defines and leaves its imprint on the urban space, producing an atmosphere of dreams attained and ancient grandeurs, in which man recovers and glorifies the best virtues. Through this group of aulic palaces and rising to the height of a theme that demands a universal language, he realized he had to temper his unquiet dynamism to the serene light of Rome.

THE NEW ST. PETER'S

A statement of account of masonry work on the Vatican basilica gives January 1, 1547 as the day " that Michelangelo took over the work;" but the official takeover had been preceded by hard preparatory study on his part. In addition to a first chalk sketch for the new St. Peter's (mentioned in detail by Vasari and, as was Michelangelo's practice, a preliminary to the larger model to be done in wood), as early as December 11, 1546 the Fabbrica had acquired the

" wood to go into the model that Ms. Michelangelo Architect is having made," and that was completed with every care in autumn of the following year. We may conclude that after the death of Antonio da Sangallo, at the end of September 1546, there was no delay in choosing the new architect for St. Peter's, in the person of Michelangelo.

He was over seventy, and had tried to refuse being engulfed in the difficult situation of having to meet the urgent and laborious tasks that the pope wanted to load him down with, even arguing, with excessive modesty, that " architecture was not his art." But then he yielded to the wishes of Paul III and, agreed to carry the building forward, but not the structural heritage left him by Sangallo.

His projects were solemnly approved by Paul III in October 1549, with phrases of eulogy for the new architect and complete confidence in the work he was to do, a confidence later confirmed by Julius III and succeeding pontiffs.

Michelangelo held this position until his death. For seventeen years he continued to supervise the work, with daily engagement and the greatest of energy, in order to ensure faithful execution of his original projects in the essential and crucial parts of the structure, thereby succeeding in defining the nature of the entire huge work.

At this point it would be in order to bring out, by way of contrast, the venerable physical fragility of the master at that time, and the opposition of various kinds that he had to overcome laboriously: these are familiar picturesque episodes, expressions of the resentment of the milieu around the cathedral as it was shaken up by a wave of renovation.

But all the actions aimed at Buonarroti, all the intrigues and maunevers, could be explicable and are understandable in our eyes, if not exactly justified; for Michelangelo had to induce the executives of the Fabbrica, all Sangallo's men, to change their course and their standards, and even to compel them, « willfully," to tear down the parts already constructed by Antonio. In particular, a tremendous impression must have been made by the spectacular demolition of the south transept, the well-known Chapel of the King of France, which marked his strongminded and unpopular beginning on the Fabbrica of St. Peter's.

Michelangelo's conceptions clashed violently with Sangallo's project and achievements. Buonarroti could not but refuse, with scorn, the superposed orders that had been accumulating on Sangallo's wooden model, in a jumbled, almost grotesque manner, in a futile attempt to give the massive building a monumentale quality. There, the degradation of Bramante's forms had reached a paroxysm, and Michelangelo's harsh words fell bitingly on various aspects of a project that was beyond salvage.

In the course of these events, the master's personal convictions and the needs of polemics carried him at once to decided positions that were diametrically opposed. Strategy and tactics were brought into play to assert his projected innovations rapidly, to the point of an open break, and not only with what Sangallo had done. The well advertised return to Bramante, which Michelangelo advanced against his old and recent rivals, was in fact surpassed and obscured by his ideas of genius.

Naturally, the new wooden model, made with great care, must have been complete. The haste with which Michelangelo asked his nephew Leonardo for the measurements of the dome

145 St. Peter's (aerial view). Rome.

341

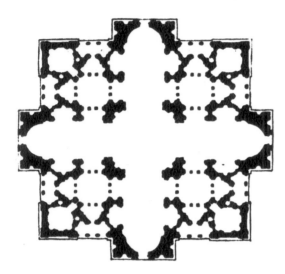

149 E. Dupérac: print of Michelangelo's plan for
St. Peter's (1569).

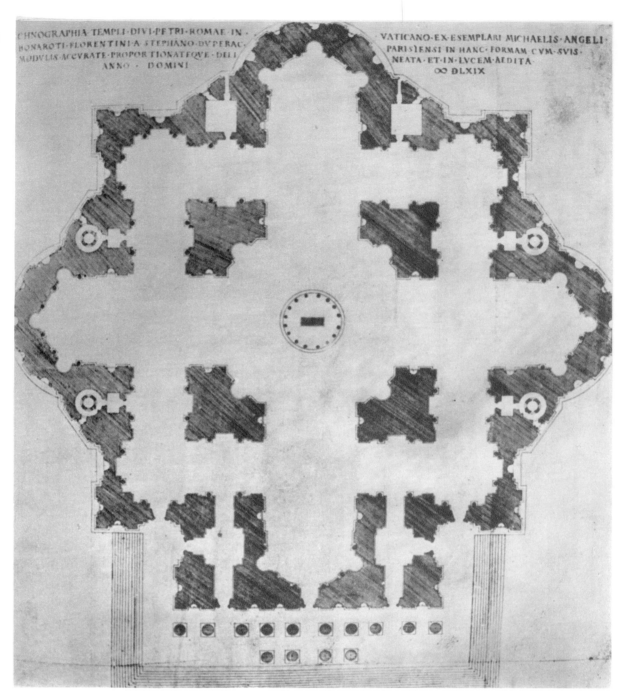

146 Plan for St. Peter's, by Bramante (1506).

147 Plan for St. Peter's, by Peruzzi (1515-20).

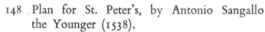
148 Plan for St. Peter's, by Antonio Sangallo
the Younger (1538).

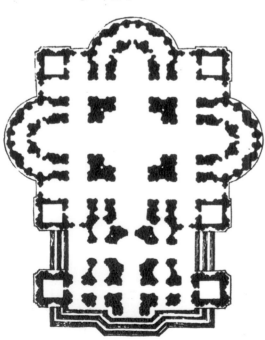

342

of S. Maria del Fiore confirms his anxiety over the crowning structure and shows where he looked for the premises for the great Roman " sister," the key to the entire composition. This sketch, which certainly must have included the great dome and the façade, has not come down to us; but it appears reproduced accurately in the geometrical drawings of Etienne Dupérac, who gives us the plan, side and internal view of Michelangelo's project. Published in 1569, they could incorporate the variants introduced also meanwhile in the external attic stories, and the drum, but not in the profile of the dome (Figs. 177 and 179).

Michelangelo did not take up Bramante's invitation to the tempting crescendo of the masses, culminating in the great central dome and the source of implicit variability, first origin of the Mannerist involutions and toilsome fragmentary quality of Sangallo's design. He did away with the basic hierarchy of the volumes, conceiving the Petrine precinct as a single mass, of maximum height, apparently subject to the gigantic order but organized in terms of the contrasting elements of the plan and the play of the animated surfaces.

The result is simple and tremendous. The interpenetration of a diagonal plan, which had been dialectically selected in order to strengthen the traditional inscribed-cross plan, seems clear and evident within the abstraction of the plan (Fig. 149), where it is justified by the insertion of the spiral service stairs rather than in the external view. But it imparts a multiplicity of aspects, an excited succession of planes and volumes, that disperses the fundamental axial relations that are manifested in the great apses.   There is a sequence of varying colossal episodes, bold and edged, in which the experience of the studies on the fortifications of Florence may have been summoned up to support the most daring juxtapositions.

The walls, thus conceived, are all animated with windows (Figs. 153 and 154) and niches. No traditional rule seems to have followed in distributing them; they are positioned in rhythms so broad and complex that one does not get a sense of imperative individual links, but rather the feeling of a new sonorous polyphony. The absence of horizontal lines feeds their free dialectic, removing all obstacles to the upward thrust toward the summit of a bold shared plateau towards which the verticals of all the pilasters aspire, corroborated by the faithful wings at their sides (Fig. 150).

The niches hollowed out between the coupled pilasters almost suggest, in their bare continuous repetition, the image of gigantic clawings made in the mass the better to bring out the firm strength of the ascending pilasters (Fig. 152). This is the first time that they are treated figuratively as regions of repose in the dramatic context of the plastic exterior (Fig. 155), instead of as superposed decorations of the walls. It was a lesson that was understood by Michelangelo's contemporaries, and soon taken over by Palladio and made his own.

Eliminating the deambulatories with which, since Peruzzi's time, it had been planned to enrich the apses, made the church less ample, reducing the inner spaces to their concise unity, that is "smaller in form but much grander," as Vasari notes. Michelangelo also took away from these endings their functions as entrances, as in the design of Bramante and Sangallo (Figs. 146 and 148). Having a single front of access justifies the differentiated solution of the façade, not known and estimable in all its details, but it was certainly based on a pronaos colonnade contrasted with the mass of the attic story above. But with all this, the axial form of the church was fixed: it was finally to turn into a building developed longitudinally.

Internally as well, where Michelangelo had taken the gigantic order, one feels the active presence of the Master in the refined variety of solutions advanced for the new chapel of the King of France. The travertine, whose value is here recognized in an unusual manner, accentuates the monumentality of the whole interior and emphasises by contrast with the priceless intaglios of the marble capitals, whose minute finesse and the curving leaves makes a strange recall of Byzantine taste.

The joining of the great pilasters with the columns of the minor order, carried out in the light of previous researches, may show hidden consonances with the façade of the palace of the Conservatori (in the Campidoglio) in that these walls aspire to the dignity of an exterior façade, even to the point of rusticated sequences (Fig. 156).

In Michelangelo's studies for the new St. Peter's, the problem of the dome must long have been the central concern of the master. From 1557 on, Michelangelo's designs deal almost exclusively with it, and his attention is concentrated on the execution of a large model of the dome that he was not to see erected (Figs. 165, 169, 171, 173 and 175). Although later altered by constructors and restorers it is still complete; it was realized of the scale of a fifteenth, between November 1558 and November 1561.

We can now all but follow the successive developments from the first ideas to the last ones adopted in the definitive model. Michelangelo undoubtedly intended to give the dome a high external profile. The questions still being debated concern measurements and precise details, as well as proposals and activites subsequent to the Master, but do not touch the definitive conception of Michelangelo.

Despite the impossibility of going into the various marginal problems, Buonarroti's ideas emerge so vividly and clearly that they overshadow the documentation and accessory studies: it is enough to think that in all his signed sketches, the Master has indicated only the lancet arch. As we see it, the drawings of the dome published in Dosio (Fig. 160) and in Dupérac's prints seem like tired and rough repetitions, which were certainly surpassed by the dominant thought and final esthetics of Michelangelo.

The first designs for the Vatican dome are directly derived from Santa Maria del Fiore, a building familiar to him and object of studies and reliefs as we have seen, especially in the course of the polemics and his proposals for the " gallery."

150 View of St. Peter's from one of the diagonal axes. Rome.

151 View of the apse of St. Peter's. Rome.

152-153 Exterior details of St. Peter's. Rome.

There was a contradiction between the essentially Gothic nature of the dome in Florence and the aspiration to a geometrical classic quality, to be inferred *inter alia* by the circular plan and the doubled number of ribs; the contradiction was resolved, in the mind of Michelangelo its conscious refusal to a generic sphericity and the adoption of a higher and tenser outside curve, meeting spiritual, or structural and perspective demands. In this respect, the Haarlem drawing is crystal clear (Fig. 163). In my opinion, this is a late drawing, but even in the Oxford drawing and in the other of Lille, which relates to a phase that is surely earlier, we see the same insistence on going beyond perfect external spherical quality.

The structure in two shells and the external ribs are permanent features, but the theme of the bull's-eye windows in the drum, characteristic of the drawing in the Wicar collection in Lille (Fig. 162), disappears in later studies and thus, too, a more complex and showy solution was given the finial lantern, which was experimented with in a number of drawings that have come down to us and that possibly have not been exhaustively studied.

344

At the outset it was conceived as without volutes to connect up with the meniscus of the dome, and is repeated in the same way down to the Dupérac prints. But the Haarlem drawing gives a different version of the lantern, shifting the volutes from the peak of the attic story to the base of the columns and focussing the new problem; the verso of that sheet details on the plan of the complex bipartite connections that were projected.

To this can perhaps be coupled another drawing, so far not precisely identified and dated (Casa Buonarroti, 70 A). In a circular plan, eight large radial structures are mentioned, with the same number of isolated elements at intervals, probably columns (Fig. 161). It might be connected with different sketches in which the lantern of St. Peter's appears with eight instead of sixteen faces, with simple instead of coupled columns, all preliminary studies of intermediate solutions concerned with the excessive fragmentary state and the formal *minutia* of the future terminal crowning.

Michelangelo intended to dot the entire exterior roofing with wide small windows, placing them at three levels; the original solution, intended to accentuate the mural life of the dome,

154 Large window in the apse of St. Peter's. Rome.

155 Pillars on the diagonal axes of St. Peter's. Rome.

158 Detail of the attic storey of St. Peter's. Rome.

156 Relief of the interior of the apses of St. Peter's. Rome.

was realised varying and making baroque the types of framing (Fig. 165 and 167). Several alterations were also made to the interior roofing, enriching the divisions planned at the ends (Figs. 175 and 178), lowering dimensions and the monumental effect, also with rich chromatic decoration (Fig. 176).

The model shows all the details of the drum beneath then in construction (Figs. 169 and 174). Clever and bold, the twin motif of the columns conceived as ideal buttresses, already from the Lille drawing. Detailed in the plan (Fig. 168), it would have had to support colossal statues; later it was also suggested to connect it with volutes (Figs. 169 and 173) to soften their powerfulness (Fig. 164).

Although the work was carried out with the building techniques of the time and under all the difficulties that were interposed, its outlines were clear from the beginning, lucid and methodical. After the detailed models, to which constant reference was to be made in the documents, since approval of the general design had been based on them, provision was made for the demolition of the discordant portions: the remaining north structures of the early Christian church and the new hemicycle of Sangallo on the south, but not yet the choir begun by Rossellino.

Buonarroti made a start on vaulting over the north transept in 1549, and the drum of the dome was erected, beginning with study (by means of a model paid for in 1549) of the great base cornice, which was completed in February 1552.

157 Attributed to B. Ammannati: view of the interior of St. Peter's with the drum of the dome under construction (about 1559-61). Hamburg, Kunsthalle, 21311.

159 Anonymous: view of St. Peter's from the north side, with the apse hemicycles and the drum of the dome in construction (about 1554-55), from Marten van Heemskerk's sketchbook. Berlin, Kupferstichkabinett.

As soon as was possible, the south transept was rebuilt on the new design (Fig. 159). In 1551 Michelangelo " has already built the King's niche," but not its difficult covering vault, which was to give him so much trouble in 1557. The mistake made there was finally corrected and on May 17, 1558 " the vault of the chapel known as the King's was finally covered over."

In the meantime, the travertine had been made ready for the columns and other parts of the drum of the dome. The drum was practically finished by 1557 (Fig. 157).

So much was done and in so organized a way, that the work completed in the previous forty years seems trifling in comparison with the substantial and definitive results achieved by Michelangelo in little more than a decade.

The work continues; Michelangelo labours hard to follow it as best he can and to study old and new problems. One concerns the completion of the external periphery above the giant order.

The Master had thought of mediating the vision between the articulated mass of the church and dome above, inserting a terminal wall area followed through only by great arches, an unadorned evocation of the Roman vault, architecture suggested to him, I believe, by the insistent vision of the bare arches of the site, of which he did not wish to cancel entirely the persistent picturesque record in the urban landscape. They are detailed in the print of Vincenzo Luchino (of 1516) where they appear already splayed from the front view (Fig. 177). Many

160 G. A. Dosio. Studies for the dome of St. Peter's, by Michelangelo. Florence, Uffizi, Arch. 94.

162 Drawing for a first study of the dome of St. Peter's. Lille, Musée des Beaux Arts, Wicar Collection, 93 r.

161 Preliminary sketch for the lantern of St. Peter's. Florence, Casa Buonarroti, 70 A.

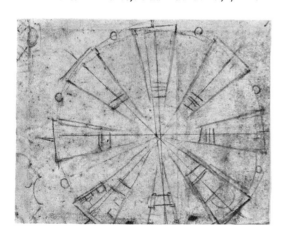

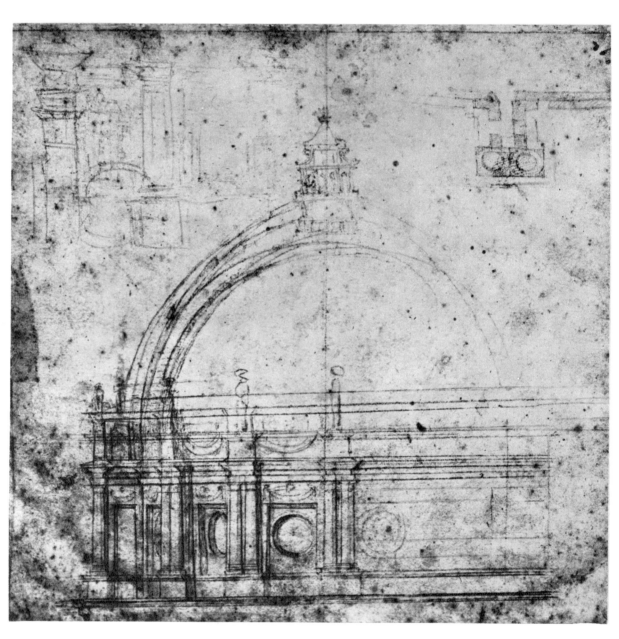

effects of contrast were determined, while the arches visibly connected the twin pilasters with a continuous and complex rhythm which we can reveal also from the representations on the south transept.

We see the solution of the attic storeys appear in a print of 1565 above the northern hemicycle (Fig. 180). The large windows are the final ones (Fig. 158) for the tangent framing of the drawings for the Porta Pia (Fig. 229). The agreement of old Michelangelo to this important change is not now exluded, but we cannot affirm that the relief decoration with the triple crown and the pontiff's keys interpret a drawing of the Master's.

The attic was continued on round the basilica, covering the area already realised according to the preceding project. A difference exists, however, between the two parts (Fig. 145) on

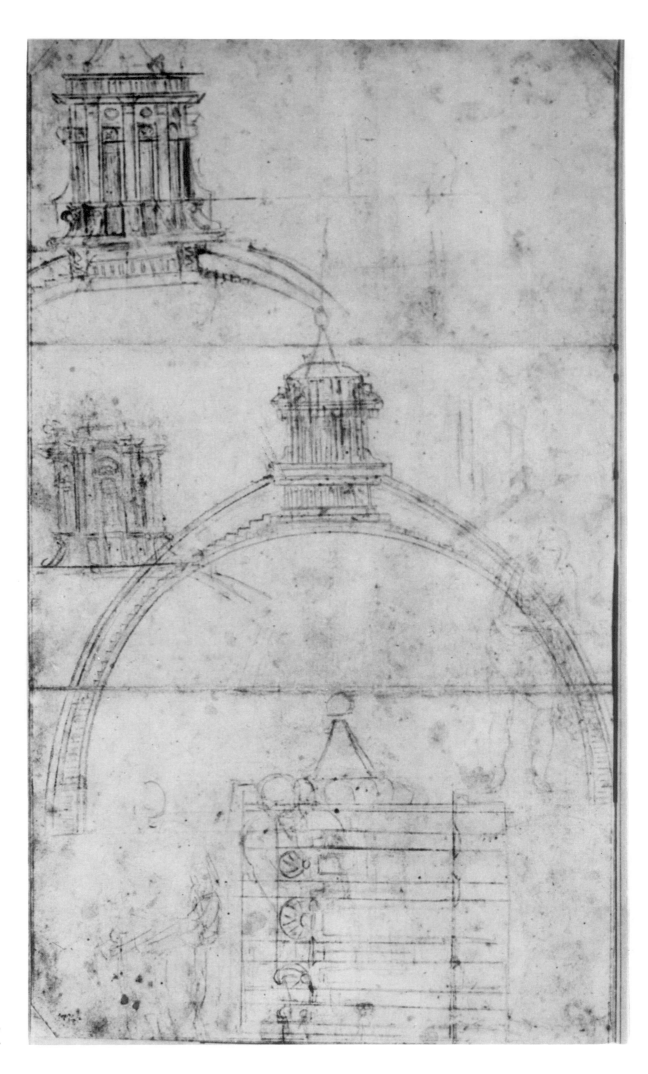

163 Studies for the dome and lantern of St. Peter's. Haarlem, Teyler Museum, A 29 r.

the north transept, the shell which surmounts the windows is larger and has a hole for the light to pass, as is indicated.

St. Peter's fills all the long ending of Michelangelo's life, in which involution and setting sun came very late.

His mystical dedication to that fabric is one of the sublime poles of his activity in Rome. Only Rome could offer him, along with the task of imparting high civic significance to the Campidoglio, the two most splendid of themes; and Buonarroti was fully aware of the supreme value and uniqueness of the symbols, and designed it and found solutions within gigantic arrangements of universal validity, expressing himself in relevant aulic language.

164 View of part of the drum with one of the minor domes of St. Peter's. Rome. ▷

348

349

165 Wooden model of the dome of St. Peter's. Palazzi Vaticani.

Never did anxiety of creation and sense of duty dominate him more than during his Vatican labors.

He stayed in Rome, ignoring all appeals: " my leaving here now would be the cause of great ruin to the Fabric of St. Peter's, a great shame and a very great sin."

Over and over again he has to repeat the same firm and final ideas in his letters of the last years, to explain that it was impossible for him to abandon his last superhuman task, fearing its practical, moral and religious consequences. And he died far from his people in order to perform the duties he had assumed towards others, towards himself, towards God.

The power of his conception transcends the earthly end of its author; those who came later could not but follow his indications. As in the case of the Campidoglio, and even more so, Michelangelo's instructions were followed faithfully for decades. Any feeble reaction against them was cancelled by the commitment to carry to conclusion a work that had been conceived as a whole and already achieved in its essential phases. The apse gallery that Rossellino had begun was built after Michelangelo's death with the same forms as the terminals in the transepts (Fig. 151); the dome, although with new vertical thrusts, was erected in close conformity with the model he had seen executed. Exact indications for the minor domes and the façade were missing; but the axial quality he had facilitated led to the basilican conclusion that surprised and submitted to revision exactly these last parts.

Here the question of the idiom of St. Peter's must be raised. It is true that in the two sublime undertakings of St. Peter's and the Campidoglio he came to express himself in a higher and more eternal meter, but it must be recognized that Michelangelo's religious drama led him to accentuate his expression more than in the Capitoline design.

The gigantic order is common to the two magnificent works, but the differences in their organ-

350 166 Dome of St. Peter's, from the Basilica roof. Rome. ▷

352

169 The drum in the model of the dome of St.
Peter's. Palazzi Vaticani.

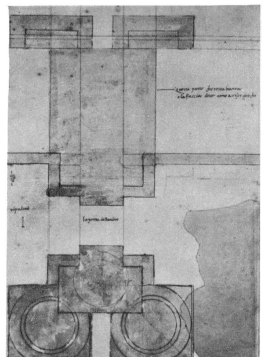

168 Plan drawing of a buttress with twin columns
for the drum of the dome of St. Peter's.
Florence, Casa Buonarroti, 31 A.

ization show specific inflections that go back to the spiritual attitude of the architect. On the
Capitoline, there was an organized composition of separated masses, corresponding to the differentiated functions of the social community; here, in contrast, there is unity of concentration on a final problem not only of architecture, revolving around and resolved in the tormented breathing unity of St. Peter's.

Other works of the twenty years of architecture

THE COMPLETION OF PALAZZO FARNESE

As for St. Peter's, in spite of his familiarity with Paolo III, Michelangelo was not able to
arrange for the completion of Palazzo Farnese before the death of Antonio da Sangallo the
Younger. For more than thirty years, he had been working at the various projects for the new

170 The drum of the dome of St. Peter's. Rome.

173 Another view of the drum in the model of
the dome of St. Peter's.

171 Interior detail of the drum in the model of
the dome of St. Peter's. Palazzi Vaticani.

residence, the plan of which, changeable and ever larger, was adjusted to the increasing fortunes of the family. The execution of the final project—which constituted the greatest glory of Sangallo—was still far from being concluded, but was now installed with classic largeness (Fig. 183), animated by a receptive variety of surveyed forms.

The decisive, energetic resumption of the work coincided with Buonarotti's appointment, and the impulse derived from the new original directives is seen; the rapidity of action stems from the enthusiasm suscitated by the Master and leads to suppose a previous elaboration of his studies. However, the historian of art seems to ignore or, at least, traditionally restrict, the organic importance of Buonarroti's efforts, limiting them almost to the episode of the final cornice (Fig. 186).

It is therefore necessary to recognise the incisive, determining presence of Michelangelo to re-establish—in the foreseen Sangallo context and with regard to the realisations effected—the real weight of his characterising work.

172 Window of the drum of the dome of St.
Peter's, from the inside. Rome.

174 Detail of the drum of the dome of St. Peter's,
from the inside. Palazzi Vaticani.

175 Detail of the model of the dome of St. Peter's, inside and section. Palazzi Vaticani.

To the work left by Sangallo, detailed by Ackerman (Fig. 184), was integrated that of Michelangelo. Between the autumn of 1546 and the spring of 1547, the third floor of the front towards the square was built; its greater height compared to that ideated by Sangallo has already been noticed. But I consider that this first intervention by Michelangelo is to be recognised as more profound and newer, giving another substantial vertical increment to the development of the palace itself; the not yet revealed height increase of the noble floor, which can be deduced from the higher and distorted ceilings compared to the courtyard behind (Fig. 189) and by the recommencement of the brickwork visible an one part of the façade. This initial arrangement, obtained by shifting the marcapiano cornice testified as of Sangallo by the drawing of the Uffizi 998 r., was indispensable to give the building the Master stroke of an impulse that gave the building a noble and detached air.

The already noted similar increase of the top floor, has its introduction in that below and is accentuated in the macroscopic development of the corner plinths, so different from those of the floor below.

Michelangelo's was not only a completing touch, but a substantial intention reforming the relationships of the façade, raising considerable the development in the wake of that same imperative direction which had already impressed cleverly Giuliano's projects for the façade of San Lorenzo and Brunelleschi's spatialness in the new sacristy. The Master also freed it from

355

176 Dome of St. Peter's, from the inside. Rome.

the dogmatic correspondence of the interior horizontality, actuating an altimetric solution, softer and more open, which was to give the possibility of inserting a secondary service floor (Fig. 189).

It has not yet been shown how the already supplied windows by Sangallo on the top floor were located on brackets, alien to the taste of Antonio the Younger. The definite hollow which divides them is a Michelangelo preference, repeated in many of his drawings of each epoch; the Master's spirit appears also in the new grace of the curves and in the strange unwinding of the spiral on the sides of the bifid brackets, positioned to set a fitting under each window. In the clear detachment which appears between the two areas of ledge, emerges the spirit of independence and of genius of the Master who wishes to affirm his own compositive requirements even working " in extremis."

I barely remember the intervention on the centre window, of which the alteration is still evident in the resumption of the mural curtain and in the horizontal section of framework inserted on the predisposed columns. The arrangement has accentuated the horizontal link, emphasising better the continuity of the series of windows and the firm value of the increased curtain, measured by the elongated crest of Michelangelo. I wish, finally, to attribute to the Master the final touch given by the addition of the bulging seat to the foot of the façade, whose outline is exactly complementary to that already meditated for the Capitoline staircase.

The print of Béatrizet, of 1549, summarises all the Michelangelian issues which have given new expression to the front views of the papal palace (Fig. 185).

The model for the interior, arranged and paid, in July 1549 to Giovampietro, joiner, has not come down to us, but it is certainly reproduced in the fine print of the front, edited by Lafreri, in 1560 (Fig. 189). The typical particulars represented in the section confirm the influence of the model of Buonarotti and value its fundamental importance.

Michelangelo tried to reform and open the closed form of the Renaissance courtyard without breaking it; in the part already planned, he wanted to pierce completely the three central arches opposite the entrance, so that one entering the palace would see the garden and the open sky. On the other hand, by closing all the archways on the flanks, at the first floor, he created contrasts and counter-positions which are repeated—in a more extended but less profound way—by leaving free the length of portico standing back from the façade.

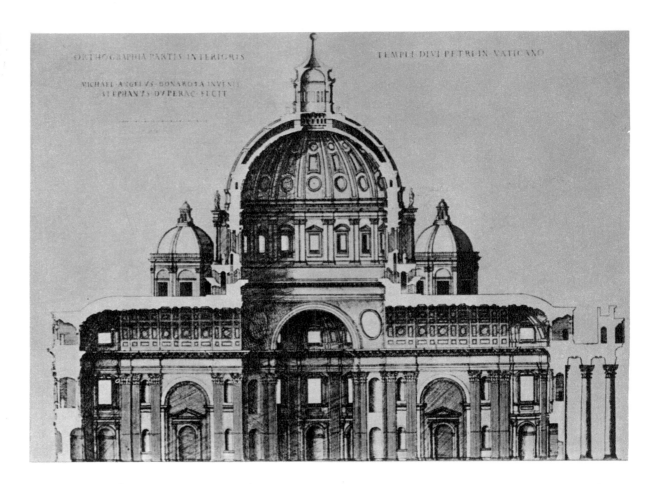

Thus, considered from the central plan, Buonarroti's intervention has imposed on the building an axial longitude which was to deeper towards the Farnese by means of the ideated bridge over the Tiber.

In completing the courtyard, classically interwoven, with the compact block of the third floor surmounting it, the position of the Master assumes firmer aspects. He reproduces here also the operation of a major vertical development of the last order, interrupted by pilasters, but realises it more freely, almost flashily: Michelangelo can set here his own seal (Fig. 190).

PROJECTS FOR THE CHURCH OF SAN GIOVANNI DEI FIORENTINI

The themes of religious architecture were often proposed to Michelangelo.

In 1551, the plans for the choir of Padua Cathedral were approved and the tender for the preliminary work to the attraction of the " modellum ipsum chori factum per longe famosissimum d. Michaelem Angelum." Although the work was quickly begun it did not proceed

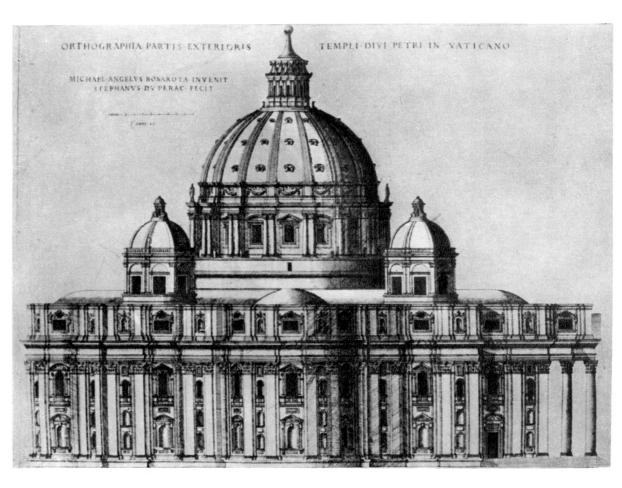

357

rapidly; the reconstruction of the choir, later reproduced in the wings of the transept, was directed and probably altered by local " proti " and does not show signs of the Master's hand. However, in the interior, the unusual adoption of the giant order, the superimposed bull's eyes cut in the vaults and the framework with the fascia of dentils underneath the modillions, may recall a Michelangelo model.

I therefore do not hesitate to recognise in the elevation sketches and in the details of a large plan, the contents of the sheet 104 A of Casa Buonarroti, the signed trace of the Master's studies for the model requested by Cardinal Francesco Pisani, with the intention of settling a long controversy. The arching of niches or windows between the capitals of the pilasters, the roundedness of the corner *pillars* and the great niche at the beginning of the transept in a recognisable assymmetrical position connect to the work executed, that seems to differ only in the terminal *apse* instead of the straight wall proposed in the drawing.

The identification of the drawing will, I trust, ease the publication of some conclusive studies on the sole Venetian work, to which a plan of Buonarroti's is now linked.

Various proofs agree on the intervention of Michelangelo in the planning of the Gesù.

S. Ignazio in 1554, a few months before the first stone was laid, testifies that the Master had promised his work " for devotion alone, without personal interest." In the absence of successive documents, it can only be asserted that the new spatiality of the Jesuitic archetype—already

185 N. Béatrizet: print of the façade of Palazzo Farnese, Rome (1549).

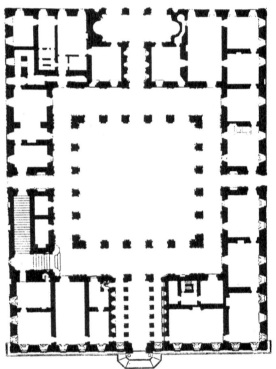

183 Plan of the ground floor of Palazzo Farnese, from Letarouilly's engraving.

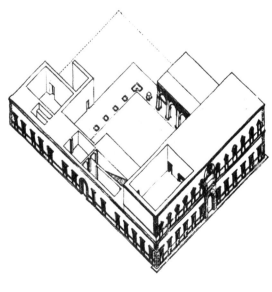

184 Axonometric indication of the parts of the Palazzo Farnese built by Antonio da Sangallo the Younger (from Ackerman).

expanded in the early drawings—must repeat its origin in Michelangelo, requested of him by Cardinal de la Cueva, rather than in other, obscure architects.

The project of constructing a church in Rome long dear to the hearts of the Florentine colony, was revived in 1559 with Michelangelo's projects for the San Giovanni dei Fiorentini.

The competition held in 1518 seemed by then to have no validity; it was in vain that Jacopo Sansovino had easily emerged the victor among a throng of great architects. Later attempts by Antonio da Sangallo the Younger to resume work had also foundered, above all because of the difficulties and expense involved in the foundations which in part had to be laid in the very bed of the Tiber. The site selected was a narrow lot between the new Via Giulia and the old Tiber, in the heart of the district inhabited by the Florentines and animated by their business.

Michelangelo, who as long ago as 1550 had tried to get Julius III to promote resumption of the work, now wrote to his nephew: " The Florentines want to put up a big building here, that is, their church, and they have all got together to put pressure on me to take care of the work, and are still putting the pressure on." But before he accepted formally, he wanted, and succeeded, to get an explicit " license and commission " from the Duke of Florence.

We have all the mannered correspondence exchanged among the Duke, the Consul and Michelangelo himself, as well as the autograph plans and designs and preparatory studies and sketches, all with a central plan. This precious documentation consoles us for the interrupted studies and the unexecuted work; there remain data, programs and indications by which we can realize the ardor and vivacity with which Michelangelo worked, and better attune ourselves to the poetics of the last period.

In a pompous letter to Cosimo I, Buonarroti states at once that among his designs (perhaps five in number) the deputies for the work " have chosen one, which in truth has seemed to me the most honorable." The Duke approved the choice, naturally, complimenting him on " this addition to your glory." The date is still 1559.

The project given the preference is indicated in the plan drawing in Casa Buonarroti, 124 A r. This shows a circular hall about twenty six meters in diameter, roofed over with a hemispherical dome on an interior peristyle of coupled columns; eight equal arches lead into peripheral chapels, alternatingly elliptical and rectangular in plan, with lateral niches (Fig. 203).

Despite Cosimo's approval, communicated directly to Michelangelo on April 30, 1560, this project never went beyond the preparation of the requisite models. Tiberio Calcagni made a large model in clay and then another in wood, which was exhibited in the rooms of the Consulate and was destroyed in 1720. From the outside the plan must have appeared compact, as if in block form on an almost quadrangular ground plan—that of the initiated foundations.

Difficulties arose at once and persisted, so that rapid neglect fell over the rapid sequence of initial steps of Michelangelo's activity; for a long time nothing was heard of the architectural program. It was only in 1583 that the Florentine made an effectual contract with Giacomo della Porta for the erection of the church in an entirely different form, a usual basilican arrangement with a crossing, later completed by Maderno. Thus ended another episode of generous proposals nurtured for so many decades by great artists of the Renaissance eager to erect a temple in the urban landscape marked by the wide bend of the Tiber.

359

186 Corner detail of the projection of Palazzo
Farnese. Rome.

187 Corner of Palazzo Farnese. Rome.

Michelangelo's sketches and projects for San Giovanni de' Fiorentini may be related to two different patterns: those with a circular plan and the others having diagonal guide lines. The former link up with the central plans already studied by Sansovino, Sangallo and Peruzzi; the others are even more original and interesting. But of the five solutions presented, the official preference went to a design with a circular plan falling within the range of traditional researches: it seemed only "the most honourable." Moreover, the project selected was greatly simplified—even changed in character—as embodied in the model, by the elimination of the characteristic interior colonnade (Figs. 205 and 206).

Those who up to the present have dealt with these ideas of Michelangelo, have made efforts to search out and establish an acceptable sequence among the various designs, in the belief that they could retrace the phases of the Master's creative thinking that culminated in the drawing selected, on which the interest of critics has been concentrated.

It has not been proved that the final ideas and preferences of Michelangelo coincide with the Calcagni model; but apart from that, such a retracing seems to be an artificial and mistaken procedure. It is a method that would bring together, in projects so different as to seem irreconcilable, the most disparate features, regarding them as successive pulses towards the final idea, whereas the scheme selected, by virtue of its evident adherence to traditional central designs, was the only one in the public domain and used as the basis of continual researches. Formulating it certainly did not call for a complex, wandering and aimless course.

Moreover, the period during which the schemes were drawn up was so short, and they all seem equally to have been so designed in a single spurt, that they cannot have been worked out in stages with pauses in between—the only possible justification for an ideal and chronological succession. On the contrary, Buonarroti's rapid grasp of the situation, his quick experi-

191 Detail of the third order of the Palazzo Farnese courtyard. Rome.

mentation with these problems, was such as to determine the presentation of intentionally independent solutions.

After the univocal target of great St. Peter's, Michelangelo, with mature experience and aims previously repressed, threw himself into the study of a considerable central structure. It must have been, for him, a vent for the stimuli he had received; the new joy of expressing himself in the boldest and most varied designs.

His fervid power of invention wanted to propose various solutions which may be classified as central and diagonal in conception, but certainly do not compromise with each other, since they posed such different problems. What interests us is seizing the various architectural ideas in their complete and genuine expression—and not only in a few special aspects—in the ambiguity of their interactions and possible contaminations.

Before embarking on any such study, we have to clear up the ambiguities produced by the

192 Terminal details of the Palazzo Farnese courtyard. Rome.

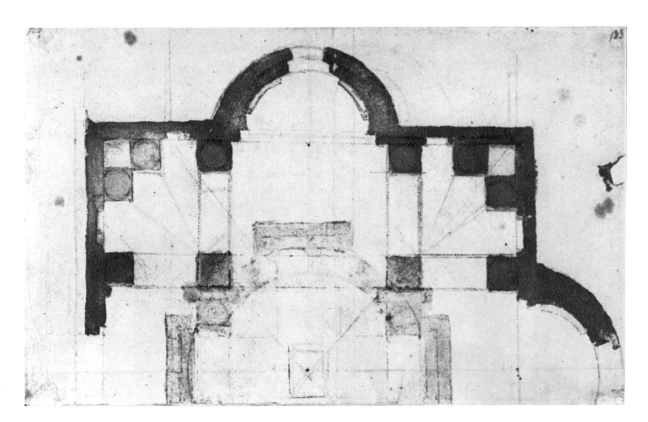

194 Plan study for San Giovanni dei Fiorentini. Florence, Casa Buonarroti, 123 A.

difficulty of reading the drawings; although not great in itself, it has not yet been overcome and has so prevented the actual composition from being evaluated exactly. The difficulty involves the indications of structures located at the center of the compositions, which have been variously interpreted as plans of crypts underneath, canopies for altars and even baptismal fonts; in any case as contemplated by Michelangelo in his interior. It seems clear to me, however, that they represent works intended to go under the dome, the various " small lanterns " that were to surmount and crown the construction, here simply projected on to the plan drawings.

It is surprising to see that studies called critical have been written without in the least taking into consideration the fact that certain encumbrances could not have been envisaged in the center of the church. They would have been in flagrant contradiction with the interior space; actually, their form as sketched was intended to pick up and develop, under the dome, the basic themes of the exterior volume.

Our examination may begin with Casa Buonarroti Drawing 123 A, whose reference is still doubtful, but whose distinctive characteristics do not allow it to go into either of the two proposed groups (Fig. 194).

However, I agree with Barocchi who, differing with other modern scholars, proposes to link the drawing to the projects for S. Giovanni de' Fiorentini. The substantially square plan and the similarity of its dimensions with those of the other solutions support this view, apart from graphic comparison and all the syntactic and stylistic analogies.

193 Floor panel in the reading room of the Laurentian Library. Florence.

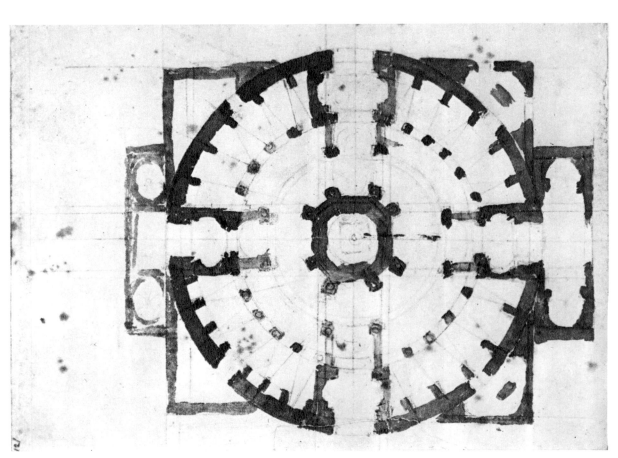

195 Plan study for San Giovanni dei Fiorentini. Florence, Casa Buonarroti, 121 A.

363

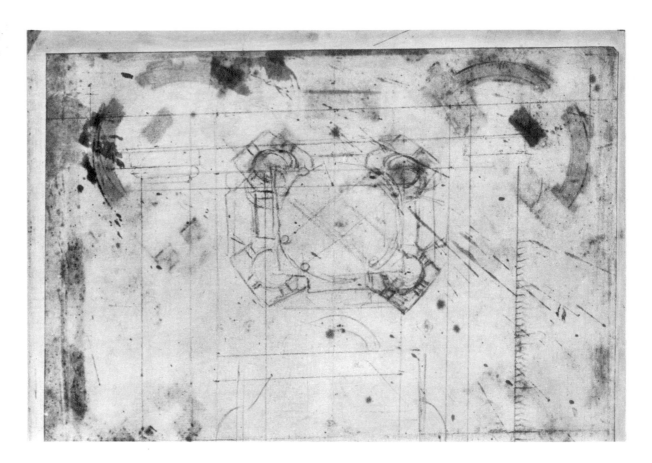

The apparent simplicity of the pattern has caused it to be regarded hitherto as a study for a religious subject of less sweep. Actually, if the drawing is read leaving out all the complex central data, a broad conception of genius emerges clearly, hinging on the unified organization of the interior spaces.

A giant order of columns stands out from the interior walls to support arches that span the space and intersect at four nodal points, on which a complex lantern was to rest and tower. This leads to the boldest and most original of solutions, which redeems the simplicity of the ground plan and renders pleonastic any kind of traditional central support, achieving a grand unitary vision, shut in by the monumentally ribbed walls and expanded only by the solemn breath of the great apses.

The lantern, cut into by four great openings like sublime portals for exterior staircases, has a bulk and organization that would provide the structure with a complex and striking configuration, so bold as to stand out vividly against the urban and river panorama. Absolutely original appears the unknown project which I deduce from this unheeded design, and such as to pledge the most excited Borrominian fantasy.

196 Floor panel in the reading room of the Laurentian Library. Florence.

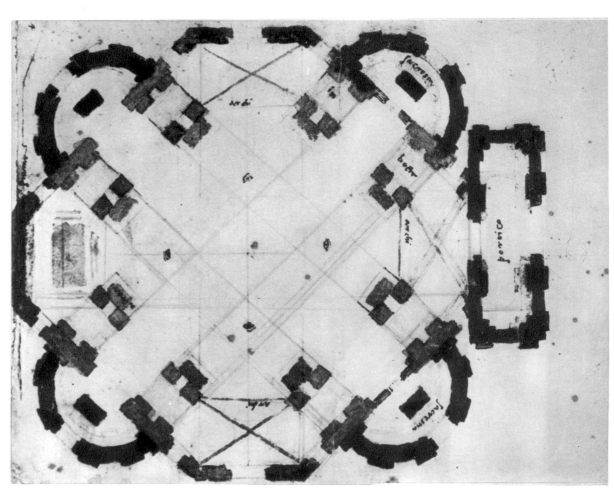

364   198 Plan study for San Giovanni dei Fiorentini. Florence, Casa Buonarroti, 120 A r.

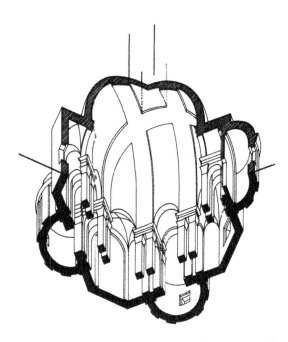

199 Axonometric reconstruction of a plan of Michelangelo's for San Giovanni dei Fiorentini, from the drawing 120 A r. at Casa Buonarroti.

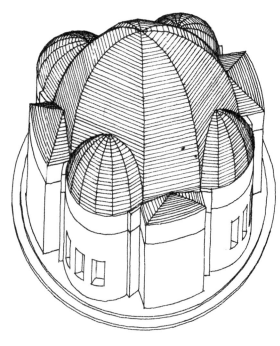

200 External axonometric reconstruction of incomplete studies referring to a plan for San Giovanni dei Fiorentini. Oxford, Ashmolean Museum, Parker II, 334 v.

201 Internal axonometric reconstruction of incomplete studies referring to a plan for San Giovanni dei Fiorentini. Oxford, Ashmolean Museum, Parker II, 334 v.

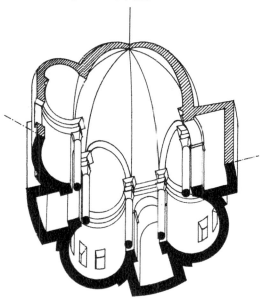

In working out the designs with a circular plan that his predecessors had already introduced, the Master followed the existing situation, which here is the square foundation slab.

Apart from the design that was to be chosen, Michelangelo's other central plan (Casa Buonarroti 121 A) tends, rather than to merge the two forms, to integrate the circular pattern with low exterior structures on a mixtilinear plan. This would include the chapels; the high altar as well would have had to be placed apart, outside the rotunda, as it were. This clears the interior space and emphasizes the unity of the effect, enriched by a circle of columns. The entire structure is traversed along the main axes by transverse designs indicating the theme of a cross (Fig. 195), whose obvious symbolism finds precedents in early Christian monuments, especially S. Stefano Rotondo.

I cannot resist drawing a connection between this contaminated representation of circles and crosses, and the intricate design of one of the late pavement panels of the Laurentian Library (Fig. 193), in which the same design of the plain is effectively geometricized.

In the interior, the plastic emphasis was carried chiefly by four projecting elements identifiable as vestibules, covered with elliptical vaults, as well as by pilasters emerging from the surrounding wall not yet collated with the colonnade in front of them. The dynamic Propylaea, protruding into the clear central area would have had so much novelty as to give its quality to the entire interior.

The lantern, with the exterior columns arranged radially on a square plan with cut-off corners, would have been a medium and summary, on the great hemispherical dome, of every starting point and base directrix.

The early Christian influence tends to shift the theme of the church towards that of a baptistery. In the absence of a central altar, and with only a few peripheral ones, this might be the explanation of the pencil notes placed at the exact center of the plan if they are not to be regarded as relating to the crown of the lantern. In that case, the two geometrical figures of the base would have come out even more sharply at the summit of the edifice.

The designs based on diagonals are to be seen in rapid sketches and carefully thought out designs. A tiny pencil sketch on the back of the large wash drawing of the plan of Casa Buonarroti 120 A v. seems to bring together unexpected experiments (Fig. 197).

From the corners of a square there emerge diagonally positioned chapels projecting very boldly with the exterior decisive prisms. The interior space, developed on a continuous curve, would be in contrast to the exterior view if provision were not made for the crossing of diagonal roof ribs springing in pairs into space and across the top to link opposite chapels.

On the recto of the same sheet, faint pencil sketches state the same theme. They go from simple geometrical arrangements to bold and precise spatial visions, all noted with geometrical rigor on the margins of the great drawing. The exterior effect now seems less clear through the presence of semicircular apses attached to the alternate sides of a simple octagon. On the other hand, the interior space is strongly characterized by the diagonal arches that we see triumphantly developed in the water-colour drawing of the same sheet (Fig. 198).

Here Michelangelo reaches the highest peak of creative genius and structural skill. The interior is most interesting and logical in the way in which it resolves the dominant diagonal plan, terminated by apses and merging with the varied aspect of the axial chapels. The visible elements placed as fulcrum of the structure would have been emphasized and enhanced by the altars almost to propitiate the destructive centrifugal impulses of the construction.

The external octagonal definition would have encircled and disciplined such an exceptional composition, crowned certainly by a " lantern " which was to rise at the intersections of the arches already indicated by Michelangelo's pen.

For such an unheard of architectural composition, it is not impossible to reconstruct the play of the roofing, at least in its essential lines (Fig. 190).

The motif of paired ribs that, with their joints, give rise to square forms, goes to execute another later panel of the Laurentian (Fig. 196). The new coincidence cannot but reinforce, also from the chronological point of view, by the essential combinations that I propose.

Instead, the project chosen by the Consulate was rendered heavily ornamented and solemn — and perhaps not without irony — for its wide use of the building materials immediately recalling Rome and the Empire (Fig. 203). While the complex articulation offers only the starting point to repeated studies of particulars (Fig. 202), the three entrances derived from Bramante's St. Peter's assume here exalted evidence in harmony with the monumental theme.

In this study that, compared to the others seems to indulge in rhetoric and a complacent conformism, could have perhaps been implanted a real dialettic contrast between such massive walls and the isolated elements planned in the internal peristasi, between the square lantern and the play of the prominent roofing. Potential qualities destined, however, to disappear with the abandoning of both opposite initial positions as results from the elaboration of the Calcagni. The new plan (Fig. 204) and the reproduction of the lost model (Fig. 206) concord in a scheme which has brought the heavy construction to a simple utilitarian disposition of the whole. Its resemblance to one of the ,, temples " shown in the V Libro del Serlio (1547) intervenes and reinforces the alien and impersonal cues of the winning plan.

365

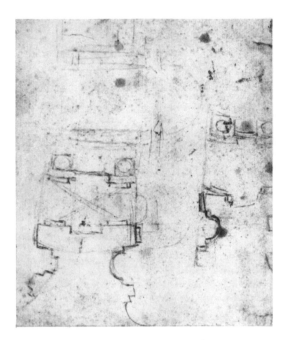

At this point, I cannot avoid uniting to these purified studies a sheet with brief later sketches of the Master (Oxford, Ashmolean Museum, Parker II, 334 v.) all relating to a similar building, of which I present an attempt at graphic reconstruction.

The theme of the eight chapels placed in a circle with alternating curved and rectangular systemation, finds here an unedited composition through the contrasted dynamism imposed by the favoured expansion of the curved spaces. The articulation of the dome was to second and summarise such premises, determining volumes punctiliously centralised, predictions of exploding tensions. A motif of a shell—shaped cap recalls a series of studies for the lantern of St. Peter's and the chronological possibility of the attribution.

SANTA MARIA DEGLI ANGELI

As early as 1560 Pius IV had begun negotiations for installing the Order of Carthusians in the Baths of Diocletian. The concession, laid down in a bull dated 1561, laid solid foundations for the planned conversion of the Diocletian " frigidarium " into a church. On the August 5, of the same year, at the laying of the first stone, the pontiff himself presided at this ceremony.

We know that a zealous Sicilian priest, Antonio Del Duca, a relative of Giacomo, the ar-

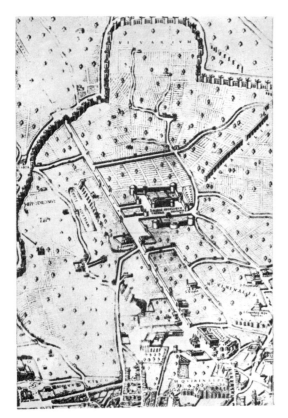

207 Mario Cartaro: engraving of the plan of Rome, detail with Santa Maria degli Angeli and Porta Pia (1576).

chitect and sculptor connected with Michelangelo, had long been insisting to consecrate to the revived cult of the Angels this unusual setting, which was employed mainly as a covered riding hall and for games of croquet (Fig. 208). In fact, in the jubilee year of 1550 he had actually made an unsuccessful attempt to provisionally adapt the church.

Now the proposal had become a possibility, with the rehabilitation of the *Alta semita* region attempted by Pius IV with the installation of the road, which he renamed, straightening it from the Quirinal to S. Agnese to the Via Nomentana (Fig. 207). Michelangelo was engaged in this projects along with construction of the Porta Pia nearby. It was certainly a theme worthy of him, because of the immense spaces involved and the possibility of various solutions.

The good Del Duca had set up no less than fourteen altars, in addition to the high altar, distributing them along the walls of the hall, seven dedicated to the Angels and the same number to the holy martyrs, after locating the high altar, at the foot of the wall opposite the entrance opened near the new Porta Pia. Although we have no definite information, and it is hard to imagine that he had used up the entire series of rooms crossing the immense baths from one side to the other, and even harder to imagine that he could have set up his high altar against some background clearly his spatial conception, in one direction in depth, was linked with a longitudinal perspective, which we can guess at from certain prints and which we may regard as traditional static. But perhaps he was mainly interested in placing a large number of altars requested for liturgical purposes.

Michelangelo, apparently not without opposition, departed from any unidirectional conception: he sought to give the spaces a more central arrangement, confining the church to the one great hall and above all giving it a number of entrances, to make the design open to unpredictable urban developments (Figs. 209 and 210). Concentrating interest on the unusual hall, and placing two entrances at its two ends—where now rise the altars of S. Brunone and Beato Albergati—he does not exclude the adjacent rooms, but rather makes it easier to visit

208 E. Dupérac: engraving of the Diocletian Baths, before being made into a church.

209 G. A. Dosio: engraving of the Diocletian Baths, with the east entrance of Santa Maria degli Angeli.

367

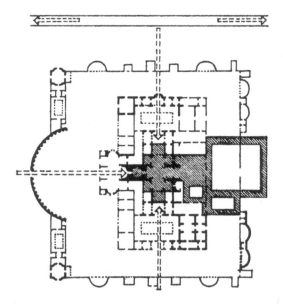

210 The Chartusian settling in the Diocletian Baths (from Zevi).

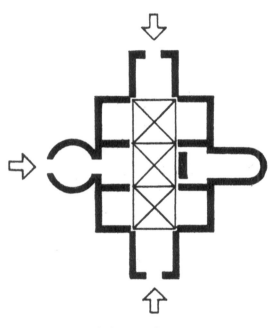

211 Diagram of the transformation worked by Michelangelo on the " frigidarium " of the Diocletian Baths (from Zevi).

212 F. Martinelli: interpretation of the choir of Santa Maria degli Angeli (engraving from " Roma ricercata nel suo sito," 1658).

368

them, as a necessary preparation for the final view. A third entrance was arranged in front of the external exedra, using the remaining rooms perpendicular to the great hall and predisposing the principal axis of the new church. This led him to put the choir for the monks at the crossing of the two axes, we hope without damaging the splendid façade on the external " natatio." It is a T-shaped arrangement with the high altar placed so as to be visible from the transepts as well (Fig. 211). The information we have as to the four columns, with bases and capitals, for this free-standing altar leads me to suppose that he intended here to repeat his previous experiments at San Lorenzo: the altar covered by a *baldacchino*, justifiable because of the enormous size of the church facing the people.

Today the hand of the Master can no longer be seen at any point of the reconsecrated baths. His work, perhaps never very extensive, was obliterated in later remodellings (Fig. 213), especially the one by Luigi Vanvitelli. It is particularly sad the destruction of a doorway on a drawing by the Master and the deepening of the choir (Fig. 212). Under these conditions it is easy to let oneself go in some bold interpretation, yielding to the suggestion of the Michelangelesque " unfinished." Actually, his work on the noted monument seems still of importance for the arrangement of the spaces and their communication with the surrounding chambers.

THE SFORZA CHAPEL

Cardinal Guido Ascanio commissioned Michelangelo to build the Sforza Chapel in Santa Maria Maggiore. In his will dated 1564—the year in which Buonarroti died—he ordered completion of the work, which was entrusted to Tiberio Calcagni and then to Giacomo della Porta, who finished it in 1573. The latter is credited with the design of the altar and tombs.

There are only a few sketches by Michelangelo that can be referred to this late conception; leaving obviously irrelevant drawings out of consideration, the most probable are those tracea-

213 F. Bianchini: engraving of the interior of Santa Maria degli Angeli (1703).

ble in the sheets of Casa Buonarroti 104 and 109. The latter, remarkably free and strong, is a note for an elongated chapel that foreshadows Borromini's design for S. Carlino at Quattro Fontane (Fig. 214).

The other drawing has a better claim to be regarded as a possible precedent for the general arrangement of spaces and sequence of interior articulations of the Sforza Chapel, although it differs in its apsidal ending and the compact aspect of the exterior walls (Fig. 215).

However, the work as erected has a much more articulated and expansive appearance, and presupposes a further decisive intervention of the Master. On the other hand, the tardy posthumous execution prevents us from making a useful reading of the form of the architectural text. However, there has been much discussion as to the decorative language and as to the travertine employed as its material, for that matter, already used by the Master for his interiors. Although the position and perspective function of the tapered windows recall those of the Medici Chapel, they can not possibly have been designed by Michelangelo's hand. Thus, while we claim for Michelangelo the entrance motif to the chapel, because of the such similar

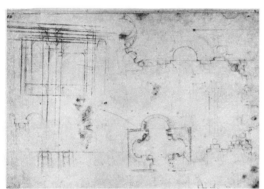

214-215 Drawings for the Sforza Chapel in Santa Maria Maggiore. Florence, Casa Buonarroti, 109 and 104.

218 L. Cruyl: drawing of Santa Maria Maggiore with the exterior of the Sforza Chapel.

cases of compartmentation retraced previously, we are unable to find confirmation for the other aspects of this structure which, incidentally, was destroyed in 1784. We cannot dwell on the execution and the formal details (Fig. 219), which are definitely an alien domain; rather than the expressions, we are concerned with Michelangelo's idea, his architectural matrix, with penetrating its essence and creative process.

Although it has not been brought into evidence, the chapel is situated exactly in the middle of one of the sides of the basilica. This precision of positional choice, now verifiable in the interior, recalls the expansion planned in the hall of the Laurentian and demands perhaps a symmetrical construction on the opposite side.

216-217 Vertical section of the Sforza Chapel in Santa Maria Maggiore, by G. G. de' Rossi, "Disegni di varii altari...", Rome.

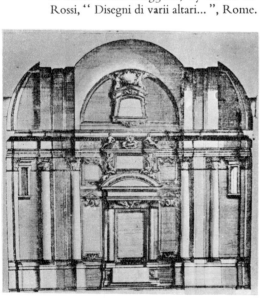

219 Detail of framework of the Sforza Chapel, in Santa Maria Maggiore, Rome.

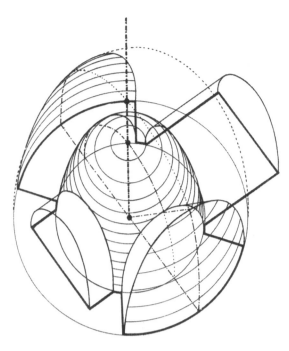

220 Axonometric sketch on the concentricity of the spherical vaults of the Sforza Chapel, in Santa Maria Maggiore. Rome.

While it explains the external mural block and the apse of the initial design, it can even suppose an eventual prolungation of the single circular vault of the chapel, above the paleochristian aisle.

The wide passage planned between the basilica and the chapel is thus almost ideated for a virtual transept, then actuated by Sisto V, by very similar methods.

Because of its plan, the Sforza Chapel may be regarded as a fusion or a rectangular region with a circular one. The crossings are vitalized as nodal points and attracted towards the center, so that the attached structures are resolved and directed along diagonal lines coinciding with the diameters of the base circle. The rooms fan out just as they do in one of the projects for San Giovanni dei Fiorentini; although they seem to be freely outlined, the outer walls fall on segments of a single circle (Fig. 221). Everything affirms the centrality of the building pervaded by a " concordia discors " which animates the articulated diagonal structures inclined towards the interior. I must admit that there—at the centre of the chapel—Michelangelo imagined the tomb of the cardinal high priest.

In the upper portions, too, the volumes carry out the original dialectic of the plan up to the roofs. A barrel vault runs along over the spaces arranged lengthwise, while the coverings of the two side chapels rise in their great curve like symmetrical portions of a single hemispherical surface, like bits of an unbuilt dome (Figs. 216 and 217).

In the center the diagonal indications of the plan rise, embodying organized vertical structures; but the median vault, instead of having transverse arches along those guide lines, turns into a clear cap. Described around the same center as the side vaults, but with a smaller radius (Fig. 222), it seems as though it were to announce the great dome suggested by the

222 Curtain vault of the Sforza Chapel, in Santa Maria Maggiore. Rome.

221 Plan of the Sforza Chapel, in Santa Maria Maggiore. Rome.

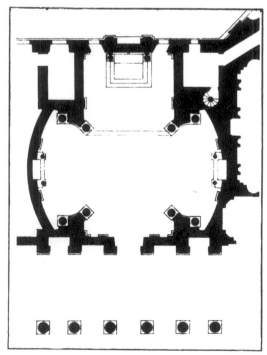

223 F. Bonzagni: medallion of Pius IV, with the plan of Porta Pia towards the countryside (1561).

224 B. Faleti: engraving with the relief of Porta Pia (1568).

225 Anonymous: engraving of Porta Pia, before it was completed by Pius IX.

coverings on the sides, which we can imagine would have been vast and serene: a final aspiration towards unattained allayed ideals (Fig. 220).

The entire spatial result is derived from a taut counterpoint of initial themes, with a solemn crescendo of effects.

Since the four windows at the sides of the altar were not there originally, light entered the chapel exclusively from above, accentuating, with its many sources, the contrasting sequence of vaults, while leaving other parts of the structure dramatically in the shade. From the bowl-shaped vaults at the sides rising above the central cap to the accompaniment of the soaring ribs, from the entire interplay of the roofs, there come suggestions of double vaults and preludes to technical solutions ready to be vivified with baroque effects of light.

Michelangelo was also fond of parallels and contrasts derived from intersections. But instead of putting these researches into effect on the surfaces, making new fine-structured broken insertions as on the walls of the Medici Chapel, he devotes his final interest exclusively to the interpenetration of the volumes, giving them young eternal life in his old age, in an essential effort, for us edged by formal contingencies, but stretched to a substantial exemplification of exasperated dilemmas.

Rome revealed and entrusted to him, the Master, spaces in which to exercise his tormented love. Here he shows that he has gone beyond the conceptions and poetics of his studies for the church of the Florentines, in the high intention of rising to other skies, hitherto unknown.

PORTA PIA

At a " diet " summoned by Paul III on February 25, 1545, Michelangelo was asked his opinion concerning the new Borgo fortifications under the supervision of Antonio da Sangallo the Younger. We may gather his attitude from the answer written the following day. While giving recommendations and counsel, he suggests above all " getting rid of the present management "; under those conditions, he would cooperate " not as helper, but as in charge of all matters." Up to that time, evidently, he could not have done anything in that sector, but we know that it was only after Sangallo's death that Buonarroti was called on to take charge of the fortifications of Rome. This position, shared with and opposed by Giacomo Meleghino, was soon left by the Master, in March 1548.

Over such a short period, hardly a year and a half, it is not easy to point out unquestioned products of Michelangelo's work and directions. It is customary to see, in the bastion known as the Belvedere, characteristics that differ slightly from the adjacent portions and some connection with a report dated March 2, 1547 on the Master's intentions; and these have facilitated an attribution. But the decisive plan of the bare corner spur and the honest use of the materials do not authorize us to propose paternity with any certainty, especially since the date carved there (1543) is prior to the intervention of the Master and the bastion is already represented in the planimetry of Antonio the Younger.

The tradition that has grown up around Michelangelo and the fortifications of Rome is undoubtedly the source of the mistaken attribution to him of Porta del Popolo, carved in the same year as Porta Pia, but a typical work by Nanni di Baccio Bigio, and of Porta di S. Giovanni, erected later (about 1580) by Giacomo del Duca.

In the case of Porta Pia, there is no doubt as to Michelangelo's authorship.

Construction of this gate was decided on early in 1561, the choice among three designs proposed going to the least costly one. The front towards the city was terminated in 1565; it must have appeared as shown in Faleti's print of 1568 (Fig. 224).

In the spring of 1561 the preliminary work was begun, while Giovanni Federico Bonzagni of Parma struck the commemorative medals. The first stone was laid on June 18. In the " pacta super confectione porte pie " dated July 2, mention is made once of the name of " mastro Michelagnilo," but he appears as the dominus of the situation. His work is carried out through an agiente of his, Pier Luigi Gaeta, who lived in the Master's house.

Construction of the gate was a result of Pius IV's improvement, by eliminating twists and grades, to the long street leading from the Quirinale, which was thereupon given the name of Via Pia. It was at this time that the straight line of the street was continued well beyond Michelangelo's gate by straightening the initial section of the Via Nomentana (Fig. 207). The new gate replaced the gate nearby, known as Porta S. Agnese or Nomentana, in order to give the Via Pia a fitting background and vista, looming over the panorama free from structures around it.

In fact, the edifice was a huge bit of urban stage-setting; the soaring structure was defined architecturally by the façade towards the city and had the function of closing off the vista. This is confirmed by the gigantic proportions of the gateway; its plan, projecting from the line of the walls inward towards the city, as if to bring the vista closer, shows how Michelangelo took advantage of this new means, so different from the measure taken on the Campidoglio, to achieve the same end.

But his work was not, and still less was to be mere theater; Porta Pia is not " surface architecture." In order to give three-dimensional quality to a design whose function was that of a background, and to save it from the all but inevitable twodimensionality determined by distance, Michelangelo did not put his gate on the previously existing walls, like the other gates of Rome. Instead, he conceived it in terms of volumes, a towering structure connected to the walls of Aurelian by two transverse wings that left a free space towards the outside. The little perspective plan by Mario Cartaro and the medals coined for the occasion show clearly that this was the original design.

It has been believed that the two variants of the medal, very much alike, refer to the internal façade and present a different project from the one actually executed. Ackermann and Gioseffi still are of this opinion; but they have not given sufficient weight to clear iconographical data, pointed out by Zanghieri, the medal (Fig. 223) instead anticipates the outer façade, logically identified by the low horizontally-cut bases and the many embrasures for defensive purposes.

Out of the contrast of the great gateway with the small apertures at its sides was to emerge the free and unusual majesty of the gate.

Michelangelo's design was not put into execution on the outside front. His death, and then the

226-228 Studies for the main doors of Porta Pia. Firenze, Casa Buonarroti, 106 A r. and Haarlem, Teyler Museum, A 29 bis.

227 Study for a door. Florence, Casa Buonarroti, 73 A bis.

372

PLATE XXVIII   Study of Porta Pia.   Florence, Casa Buonarroti, 102 A r.

election of Pius V, may be taken as valid reasons for halting the project. The solution adopted was to close in the space left open outside by means of the simplest of walls on the Aurelian trace, with an external gateway that can be seen in a perspective plan by Dupérac in 1577. This formed an atrium gate, alien to the Master's original conception but similar to examples from the classical world and the military architecture of the Italian Middle Ages.

On the side toward the city Michelangelo varied the composition by cutting down the number of openings and changing their character. They are no longer embrasures for defence, but true windows or frames and scrolls. A vertical impulse animates the central part, that curtain wall that should have been a high tower-shaped structure. The permit contemplates that the gate will be handed over at the same time as the " Turrio," a specific addition that cannot mean the wall constructed some years later; the document sounds like an echo in the Curia of the half-finished project. Dupérac's plan, to which we have referred, already shows the free-standing attic story with its triangular top, as in the Faleti print; part of this soon collapsed, strongly suggesting that it was never completed (Fig. 225).

This façade, however, employs clearly stated proportional ratios, as usual not hinging on a basic univocal value but enlivened by dialectical plurality. One is the Pythagorean golden proportion, which governs the general proportions of the volumes and the individual parts: the framing of the gateway and the scrolls. The other ratio, 1 : 2, described the openings of the gate and windows and many elements of the architecture.

Some drawings by Michelangelo, whose authenticity has sometimes been called into question, seem to relate to the outside of the portal, such as 106 A r. of Casa Buonarroti (Fig. 226). Together with Drawing A 29 bis of Haarlem (Fig. 228), this already expresses Baroque taste,

231 Detail of the main door of Porta Pia. Rome.

230 Porta Pia. Rome.

374   232 Pilaster of the main door of Porta Pia. Rome.

233 Window of Porta Pia, Rome.

anticipating goals that would be reached later, through formulations that were to become familiar first to Buontalenti. Other drawings, such as 102 A r. of Casa Buonarroti, relate to the design of the inside of the great portal where the superimposing of the images clarifies the creative process and the resultes (Plate XXVIII).

Then we have various drawings in which the interpenetration of varied themes, already evident in the studies for the Laurentian Library, take more solid and more jumbled forms (84 A r. of Casa Buonarroti). I make a few reservations about the narrow door (73 A bis of Casa Buonarroti, Fig. 227), certainly by Michelangelo and of this period, but out of keeping with the poetry of the gate. Finally, there are splendid and repeated studies for broad low frames, chronologically recalling the definitive designs for the attic story of St. Peter's (Fig. 229).

The last architecture of the Master contains lively vitality from the squared volumetry, fresh with essential episodes that the execution of Giacomo Del Duca did not succeed in contaminating (Figs. 233 and 235). It is the patronage of Pius IV that provokes from Buonarroti this appealing fruit of the rustic grain, outermost concession to military nations. His lucid inspiration becomes acute in these architectual thoughts, " extravagant and beautiful," as Vasari defines them.

Again a new personal language interprets and dominates the formal contingencies of the architectural order, reduced to brick pilasters on the façade and refined in the articulated casuistry of the monumental main door (Figs. 231 and 232), worthy of the final seal of the Master's activity, but generously open to new architectural worlds.

Two spires, not built, on the edges of the structure would have served to recall, in purely ornamental form, the planned outside design of lateral turrets, which would however also been useful for observation and defence; the spires, like the turrets, were intended to compensate the elevated central mass.

235 Ornamental scroll above the windows of Porta Pia. Rome.

234 Detail of the crowning of Porta Pia, with battlements and a base for the spire.

375

What happened later is familiar. The façade of the wall towards the country kept, for a long time, a simple gateway in a frame with an elliptical ending, which might recall touches of Michelangelo. The upper portion was completed in 1853 by Vespignani without following the indications given by Faleti, but indulging in belated Baroque reminiscences (Fig. 230). Between 1861 and 1864 the same architect erected the monumental façade towards the country and the structures, with no pretensions at interpretation and hence in neo-classicist form.

The key position of Porta Pia induces final urbanistic considerations, previously conceived in the Master's mind.

We know that, in 1558, Paolo IV asked Michelangelo to plan a road connection with three stairs from the Palazzo Venezia to the Quirinal joined to the " dirittura " of Via Pia.

Although the route and the joining points are unknown to us, the plan would certainly have caused to centre on the mobilised area of Campidoglio a large, new zone of future urban development, that was to be garrisoned, in the most prominent point, by Porta Pia. Of the three flights of stairs, the first and the last were to be covered, to give variety of view and to motivate the urban panorama.

From the Capitoline records of the same year, there is an approved project submitted by Michelangelo for the layout of the area near the Colonna Traiana, in the neighbourhood of which was the Master's house. Perhaps more than one new urbanistic plan will have been proposed to adapt the area of the diggings undertaken at the foot of the Colonna and the surroundings, as, from successive iconography, was done.

Not wishing to take up again the fine theme of the bold start and exceptional urbanistic style worked by Michelangelo on the Campidoglio, I will recall another, previous conception of Buonarroti. Layouts and views were to depart from Palazzo Farnese, coinciding with the reaffirmed axiality of the building. If Via de' Baullari was partly traced, several partial alignments barely divaricated cause one to think of the Master and of his desire to embody the exact central motif of the palace modified by him as a triforium. For the opposite part, the grandiose proposals of axial depth as far as the Farnese are known.

Axiality and a plurality of direction alternate in the plans and in Michelangelo's executions, perhaps only a pale reflection of his thoughts and urbanistic visions.

V

DRAWINGS

by Luciano Berti

Preliminary Note

As we know, the *corpus* of the drawings of Michelangelo has many gaps, but at the same time is fairly bulky and presents many difficult problems. Vasari and the documents tell us of the bonfires (the one in two installments carried out shortly before his death could not have been the only one, although perhaps it was the largest) that Buonarroti made " of drawings, sketches, and cartoons by his hand, so that no one might see the labors he had gone through and the tentative modes of his genius, not wishing to appear unless perfect." In addition, the Arezzo historian seems to inform us of the occasionally " laborious " nature (hence without that continual " perfection " that is ascribed to " genius " by an unconscious rhetorical dogmatism) of these works when he says of them that " even in seeing the greatness of that genius, we realized that when he wanted to get Minerva from the head of Jove, he needed the hammer of Vulcan." Nonetheless, despite his drastic destructions Michelangelo had made presents of various drawings (to Mini, Cavalieri, Vittoria Colonna, etc.), some others had been left at his house in Florence, and his sheets were eagerly sought after and soon copied or simply forged. Berenson's numbers (ed. 1961) for the drawings that are autographed or attributed to the school run from 1395 A to 1750 B; this is the vast field in which criticism must make its choice, a rather difficult one in most cases.

The principal groups are: in Florence, at the Casa Buonarroti (with the accession of items from the collection of the architect Buontalenti) and at the Uffizi (Medicean origin); in the British Museum (purchased last century from Cosimo Buonarroti, the last descendant; and other acquisitions, such as the Malcom Coll.); at Windsor Castle (from the Farnese Coll.); in the Ashmolean Museum at Oxford (Coll. of Sir Thomas Lawrence, and others); in Haarlem (Coll. Teyler, perhaps from the Odescalchi); in the Louvre (formerly belonging to the Kings of France, perhaps in part purchased from Antonio Mini; and acquisitions from the Jabach Père and Mariette Collections). There are smaller groups at Lille (sold by Casa Buonarroti to Wicar); in the Vienna Albertina (part of the Coll. Mariette); and various sheets at the Ecole des Beaux-Arts in Paris, in Bayonne, Chantilly, Cambridge, New York, the Vatican, etc.

Berenson was well aware of the difficulty of making decisions as to authorship, chronology, and references. He invited scholars to examine their consciences severely, almost a sort of psychoanalytic preparation, and pointed out how deceptive photographic reproductions can be. The history of the critical study of Michelangelo's drawings, in its alternatively expansionist and restrictive phases, has been well stated very recently by Tolnay in his introduction to the beautiful fresco collection published in Florence (1964). We refer to the bibliographical note at the end of this chapter for a list of the most important studies and catalogues.

One last warning. The present review of Michelangelo's drawings, although perhaps the most complete in the Italian language, with the exception of Berenson, does not of course make any pretentions to being systematic or critically exegetic, or even critical in the sense of going deeply into the basic unified value of the " drawing " that Michelangelo seems to have intuited (in the wake of antecedents) and that was picked up by the theory of Mannerism (on this topic I refer the reader particularly to the recent volume by Clements, " Michelangelo I. Le idee sull'arte," 1964, pp. 366 ff.). This subject, assuming that the present writer felt himself able to tackle it, would have called for an entirely different kind of chapter; as it is, it was to be a concise report, substantially in chronological order, on the body of the most probably authentic drawings that have come down to us. Our discussion of the drawings will deal with them primarily as graphic art, while trying not to be a merely visual

1 Figure. Lille, Musée Wicar (2).

3 Copy from Giotto. Paris, Louvre (4).

2 Copy from Masaccio. Munich, Graphische Sammlung (5).

description. Their links to works of painting, sculpture, and architecture will be taken up in the chapters on those branches, which will therefore contain the most significant drawings of this kind; the present chapter will avoid repeating the illustrations and discussions. Some small gaps may result from this treatment—our aim has not been exhaustiveness—but the reader should be able, from our chapter and its cross-references, to get an adequate idea of the body of Michelangelo's work in drawing in its various aspects. At the end of the caption of each figure that we present will be found a number referring to the note with data on catalogue number, measurements, and materials and, where needed, essential historical and bibliographical references (for this see the bibliography at the end).

The order of the illustrations, for obvious reasons, could not always be kept strictly chronological. Accordingly reference is made to the text.

378

4 Copy from Masaccio. Vienna, Albertina (5).

Youthful drawings prior to cartoon
for the Battle of Cascina
(1490 c.-1505 c.)

As a curiosity, we preface a note on the more or less fabulous prehistory of Michelangelo's drawings, starting with the putative boyish sketches on the walls of Casa Buonarroti. They are referred to by De Montfaucon in 1702 (*ibidem neque sine voluptate in muris delineata vidimus puerilia eiusdem Michaelis Angeli experimenta*) and by Gori in 1746 (" in the rooms of the top floor of his house in Florence "). The reference here is to Casa Buonarroti in via Ghibellina, which Michelangelo bought only in 1508 and which was then completely remodeled for Michelangelo Buonarroti the Younger by Pietro da Cortona, and not to the house in via Bentaccordi, which seems to have been where Michelangelo actually lived during the first years of his life. At best, these sketches could only have been done by the artist as a ma-

5 Copy (from Masaccio ?). Vienna, Albertina (5).

ture man, or by his pupils, and most likely are posthumous forgeries, or all but, to which his descendants attached a legend. In any event, no trace of them has been found, not even in the course of the recent thorough restoration of the entire house in via Ghibellina.

Gori adds that Senator Filippo Buonarroti also showed him other sketches in the rooms of the family's villa at Settignano (today, Levi) " and all around the walls of the terraces "; and there we can still see the drawing (Fig. 29) on a second-story wall, referred to by Bottari (1759-60): " In his villa at Settignano by the path is a Satyr drawn on the wall in charcoal by Michelangelo while he was warming himself. It is drawn marvelously lifelike and in his usual fierce and terrible manner. It is now enclosed in a showcase built around it to preserve it." Bottari is right in calling its clearly Michelangelesque style " fierce and terrible," but precisely this stylistic correctness leads us to reject the hypothesis, although it comes from an authoritative source, that this could be the first documented drawing that has come down to us, dating from about 1488, before he entered Ghirlandaio's *bottega*. It seems to us that the calm classicism of the work and its dynamic imagination place it a little earlier than the

◁ 6 Studies of figure. Haarlem, Teyler Museum (7).

Cascina cartoon, not earlier than the first decade of the Cinquecento, unless indeed it is a forgery done as a tribute, in the Cinquecento or even during the Baroque, with touches suggesting a self-portrait of Buonarroti.[1]

Vasari, we think, would agree in rejecting the hypothesis of a precocious manner like Pollaiolo's, and his reason would be a general principle, namely, the presence of that "grace" of the third era, the Cinquecento, which was missing in the marvelous but still rather "lean" Quattrocento anatomism.

Berenson's idea of identifying the Lille figure (Fig. 1) as drawn during his apprenticeship under Ghirlandaio (1488-89) and perhaps the very one that Granacci gave to Vasari and that Michelangelo recognized in 1550 is only a hypothesis, although it finds a sort of support in the laborious reticulate calligraphy, related to the famous copies, from Giotto to Masaccio, that we shall discuss.[2] Nor are we called on to exercise our imagination on other drawings referred to in the sources, unless indeed the imagination was not all in the pens of those historians.

One such is the drawing that depicted Ghirlandaio's scaffold and workshop in the main chapel of S. Maria Novella, "with some tables, with all the implements of the art and some of those youths at work" (Vasari); another is the "papers from the hands of various old masters" copied and counterfeited "staining them and aging them with smoke and var-

7 The Alchemist. London, British Museum (6).

8 Two figures. Haarlem, Teyler Museum (7).

9 Studies of figure and from sculptures. Chantilly, Musée Condé (10).

ious things " (and here Vasari seems to be making up a story on the basis of a single episode concerning a portrait, told by Condivi); and still another is the " hand " drawn in ink at a later time at the request of Cardinal Riario as a test of skill, like Giotto's circle (but this embellishment is in Condivi, and rejected by Vasari). Mariette fancied that he owned this sketch, now in the Albertina, but it has long been recognized as being a hand from the hand of Passarotti. [3]

This prehistory of Michelangelo's drawings does not leave much hope for discoveries in the future. It is not only that it is hard to identify trial flights that could not but be graceful and varied and impersonal, by an iron law of nature, that is, youthful nature. There is also a strong suspicion that a thoroughgoing destruction of these documents was carried out by Michelangelo himself—we know his character—and probably very early, as soon as he had passed this pre-dawn stage. But that would lend particular value to the first certain drawings, which we now discuss; Michelangelo would therefore have saved them because he felt he could leave them as his first pages, and that is the place that they now hold decently within his *œuvre*.

Only a very few sheets are involved: the copy of Giotto in S. Croce (Fig. 3); [4] those of Masaccio's Tribute and Festival (Figs. 2 and 4); [5] the so-called Alchemist of the British Museum (Fig. 7); [6] and a few more (Figs. 6 and 8).[7]

We shall not go into the details of their precise dating. For the copies, it was formerly set at 1488-89; there is now a tendency to place them later, between 1492 and 1496, but at any rate " within the limits of the experiments prior to the first trip to Rome " (Barocchi).

For that matter, the chronology of the earliest sculptures left is likewise uncertain; there may be something in Longhi's idea that both the Centauromachia and the Madonna della Scala, both in Casa Buonarroti, were reworked and perfected by Michelangelo for years after their date of origin.[8] For the Centauromachia that date would seem to be just before the death of Lorenzo the Magnificent in 1492; but what interests us here, as we shall explain, is mainly the other relief, the Madonna della Scala, which is first mentioned only in the second edition of Vasari's *Lives*. Now can this be due to the fact that Michelangelo had repudiated this work, considering it as still too much bound to the Quattrocento tradition? Actually, the

383

384   10 Apollo-Mercury. Paris, Louvre (12).

13 Studies, of Slave and other. Paris, Louvre (12).

11 Detail of Fig. 13 (12).
12 Detail of Fig. 13 (12).

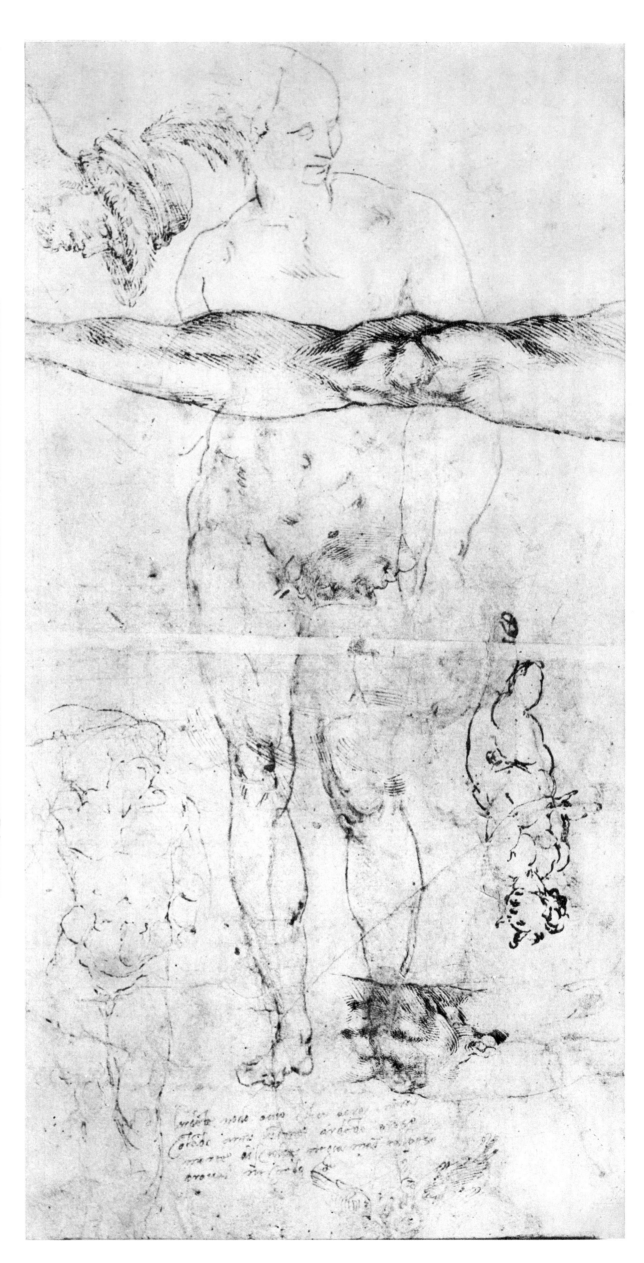

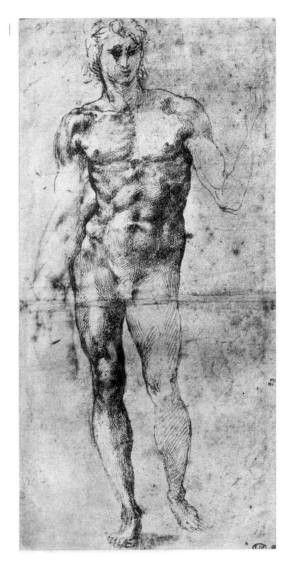

14 Nude. Paris, Louvre (13).

16 Sketches of figure. Florence, Casa Buonarroti (11).

15 Figures. Paris, Louvre (13).

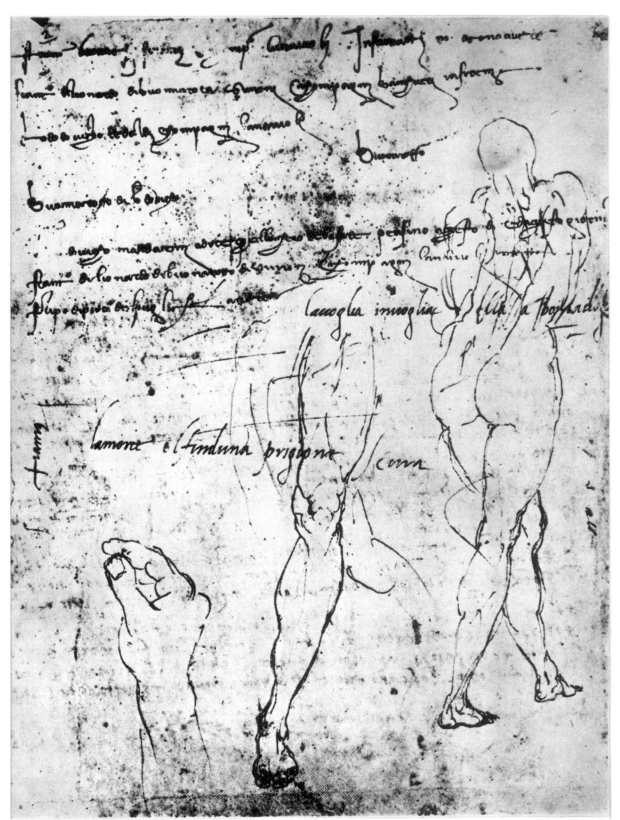

Madonna della Scala is not only a " counterfeit " of Donatello's manner, as Vasari believed, but also betrays the teachings of Bertoldo in certain refined cadences, such as the drapery at the bottom of the limbs (compare the Madonna and Angels in the Louvre) ; the work also shows links with the eurhythmic Angel of the Bologna shrine (1494-95) and, in the Herculean *putto*, with the Centauromachia. It is therefore probable, and this is the general belief, that the Madonna della Scala is the earliest surviving sculpture of Buonarroti, dating from between 1490 and 1494, perhaps early in that interval.

Now the first drawings we take up appear to be closely related to this bas-relief. One feels tempted to say that Michelangelo did them after having started work on the little marble, following certain common principles and problems of that work. The drawings seem to have been designed to fit within a similar rectangular surface. In the copy from Giotto (Fig. 3), the two figures (the only ones taken from the larger group of the old master) fill the entire sheet, in height and width, with their blunt angularity, as in its way the Virgin fully takes up the bas-relief of Casa Buonarroti. The background figure in the drawing, delineated in a different pictural abridgment, corresponds to the planar children of the Madonna della Scala and, like them, contrasts with the vertical quality of the main figure, which is more plastic and finished, a counterpoint of differently inclined forms and gradations. Something of the same sort can be said for the copy of the Festival (Fig. 4) ; in the two drawings in question, we should also note the psychological quality of the main figure, with its profile looking into the distance, much like the Virgin of the sculpture, meditative and foreboding. Indirect confirmation of a 1490-92 date would be given by Piero Torrigiani's recalling his famous punch, which broke Michelangelo's nose, given when " this Buonarroti and I were going as boys to study the [paintings] in the Masaccio chapel of the church of the Carmine "; if the copies after Masaccio that have come down to us are of that period (which need not necessarily be the case), the fact is that Torrigiani, whether or not he was banished for that assault, was out of Florence from about 1493.

There is something in these sheets, however, that already goes beyond the stage of the Madonna della Scala and its efforts at Quattrocento refinements, and reveals basic tendencies in Michelangelo, deeper and more productive. It has often been observed that they show a predominant sculptural trend, and the cross-hatching technique derived from Ghirlandaio (in whom, however, it was merely a factor in chiaroscuro) is applied here so insistently that the strong and repeated rulings of the pen really suggest the laborious chisel markings on marble. Even though in this case it is a question of " adding " and not of " removing," the first and basic conception seems here to be the one that was to be so typical of Michelangelo's genius, the painstaking evocation of the figure from the formless material (here the whiteness of the sheet of paper), with a certain pleasure in this hard and protracted but victorious labor.

17 David. Paris, Louvre (15).

18 Figures. Paris, Louvre (15).

387

19 St. Anna Metterza. Oxford, Ashmolean Museum (14).

Perhaps there is something still deeper, the intuition (though still unconscious) of a coincidence of opposites in the " concept " or idea as all but ineradicably based in the material, and consequently having the status of an archetype, since the best parts of this primary matrix will be those that are unique and even they will have the primary essential quality of the idea that is depicted. It is from this that we can realize the singular trend of Michelangelo's first drawings, his strange absolute lack of interest either in the marvelous virtuosity in drawing that the Florentine late Quattrocento had acquired in portraiture, drapery, and the organized figure (as in a Verrocchio, Leonardo, Filippino, Credi, Ghirlandaio, etc.), nor in the sketched conception of dense groups and episodes, nor in landscape, architectural settings, etc. From Masaccio's Festival Buonarroti copies three figures from an unaccustomed side, where virtually every other copyist took the denser files of the procession going in the other direction; from Giotto he isolates two figures; from the Tribute (Fig. 2) a gesture of St. Peter. The preference for Giotto and Masaccio thus must not have been merely the usual homage to the two traditional " Masters of the art "; Michelangelo's motivation must have been their special essentiality, a quest that he was more interested in than in studying the most advanced of the Quattrocentists; likewise, he was shortly, in Bologna, to read and comment on to Aldovrandi the great classics of the Trecento—Dante, Petrarch, and Boccaccio.

Archaistic and archetypal search for the essence, and laborious configuration of the form, as if with the hammer, so that in the end the form, isolated and vibrant, dominates the material of the sheet: these are the terms that characterize the first drawings in their originality, their

21 Studies of heads and torso. Oxford, Ashmolean Museum (14).

20 Detail of Fig. 21 (14).

power and, in some, their immaturity. In this connection interest attaches to the slight variants that Michelangelo introduces, for example, in the copy after Giotto (Fig. 3) the correction making the feet of the left figure more widely separated (for fear that the figure might seem about to fall), and the undersleeve eliminated with the effect of a clumsy wrist (in addition the hem of the tunic below comes out as gracefully angled); or in the copy of the Tribute (Fig. 2), greater looseness given the drapery and arm, and above all the less massive head; and similarly the special piercing typology of the faces in a transfiguring light, in which a Leonardo-like element seems to enter (cf. the Epiphany of San Donato at Scopeto). As a result, the copies from Masaccio are already of a certain strength (Figs. 2 and 4), and that of the Tribute, in its dappling, also shows a pictural sensibility that reminds us of Michelangelo in the fish market to color the wings of the two devils of Schongauer's print; the back of the drawing of the Festival (Fig. 5), if it is still from Masaccio, is of a particularly broad and powerful " execution " that goes beyond even the very vigorous model.

The Alchemist (Fig. 7), probably an attempt at original invention, is weaker; it too seems to refer vaguely to the school of Leonardo and on the other hand to recall, especially in the first figure to the left, Ghirlandaio's Baptism of Christ in S. Maria Novella, in which Marchini suspects there are parts done by Michelangelo as an apprentice.[9] Beginnings of a greater fluidity mark the Haarlem drawing (Fig. 6), in which the principal figure, with hands joined, seems inspired by a sculptured rather than a painted model, with the anatomical form appearing through the drapery, in the frontal seated pose (one feels an affinity with the statues on the

389

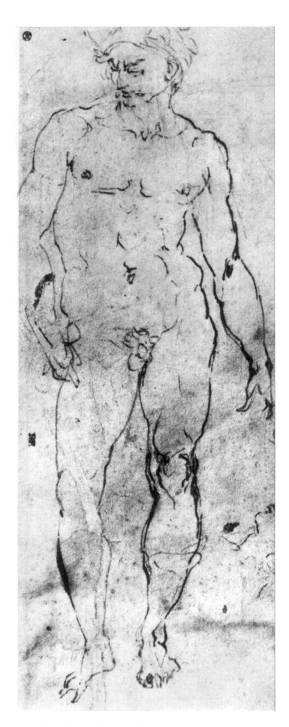

22 Detail of Fig. 23 (18).

Tombs of St. Dominic, Bologna, 1484-85), while on the reverse (Fig. 8) the increasingly summary line, with its penetrating sensibility, as compared with the other two figures on the front, becomes harsh in two possessed personages advancing to the right, as if present at a miracle.

This initial style of drawing, in which the figure is hurled by the pen and takes violent possession of the paper, with very strong chiaroscuro, was not an experiment that Michelangelo soon abandoned, but continues in a way for over a decade down to certain details for Cascina (cf. Plate **XXIX**) and even down to the study for the Christ of S. Maria sopra Minerva (1518-20).

This, along with the suggestion of a cloaked personage in vertical rear profile, as in the Quattrocento painters, explains the impression of Berenson and others that the period of Michelangelo's studies in the Medici garden, 1492 or not much later, is that of the drawing at Chantilly (Fig. 9) with five studies (three being copies of statues); on the other hand, the verso of this sheet has led Tolnay, and I believe correctly, to put it back to the first years of the Cinquecento, for a sketch drawn there corresponds to the *tondo* in the Bargello.[10]

In some respects the gaps in the documentation of Michelangelo's drawings are so complete as to support the suspicion of the deliberate destruction of certain phases. Thus, we probably have nothing from the first Roman period (1496-1501), and this really seems strange for a period that must have been devoted to extensive exercises, in the " air of Rome " and among " the ancient marble statues." By now, too, there was no longer any question of immaturity,

390   23 St. Anna Metterza. Paris, Louvre (18).

since these were the years of the Bacchus (1496-97) and the Pietà (1498-99), which Galli guaranteed in the contract "would be the finest work in marble that there is in Rome today."

To be sure, the sketches on the page in the Archivio Buonarroti (Fig. 16),[11] done perhaps in Rome early in 1501, are of great importance, bearing witness to Michelangelo's possession of a new graphic freedom—in his ability to imagine form with dynamic immediacy, as in the figure seen from the rear, in movement—but accompanied by a sure mastery of anatomy, demonstrated by the studies of legs and hands on the same sheet; and while the line accents or forms a contour, now hardly making a tentative reference, now definitive and secure, the absence of chiaroscuro seems to prefigure a final purpose of translation into the splendidly gleaming and imperishable substance of marble. We shall see this, or a similar, graphic starting point again in the studies of Michelangelo during the first decade of the Cinquecento (cf. Fig. 22) as well as later; and if we seem to find a dominant influence of Pollaiolo there, still from now on the naturalistic inspiration of Antonio is overcome by a more interior experience of anatomy, as the primary delight in the subtle modulated profiling of the functional line, which is characteristic of Pollaiolo, is overcome by interest in the entire plastic architecture.

To the present writer, however, these three sketches in the Archivio Buonarroti are more reminiscent of the Pietà (1498-99) or even of the David than of the Bacchus. At any rate, drawings that can be referred to a previous phase of research—during his first stay in Rome, even if they were done after returning to Florence—drawings that take possession of the ancient art of statuary, which also involved a certain process of assimilation: such drawings, it seems

24 Head of satyr. London, British Museum (14).

25 Herodias (?). Paris, Louvre (18).

391

27 Triton and heads. Oxford, Ashmolean Museum (16).

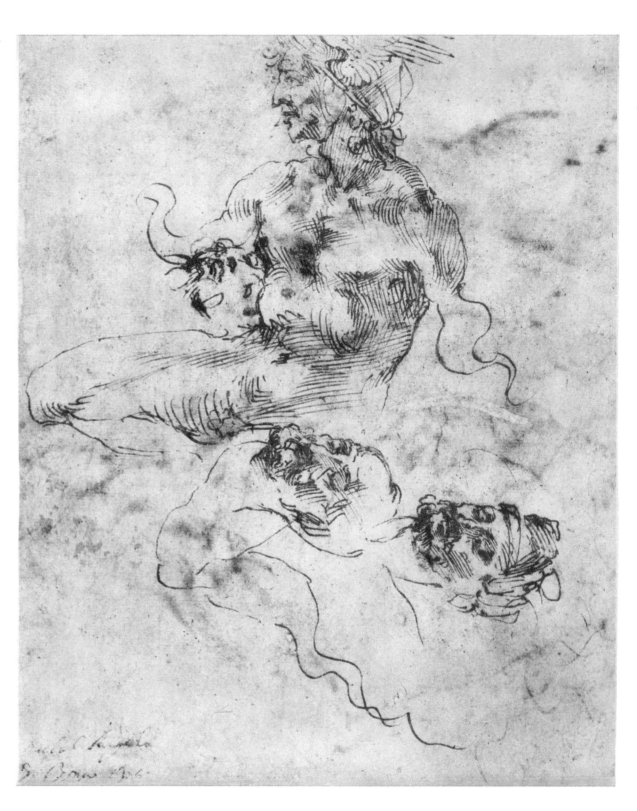

26 Detail of Fig. 27 (16).

392

to me, are the Apollo-Mercury of the Louvre (Fig. 10) [12] or the Nude of the same museum (Fig. 14) [13] that was used for the marble David; they are like others (Fig. 31), down to the unstudied Apollonian specimen in the British Museum (Fig. 56) which was to enter into the preparation of the cartoon for Cascina.

I am aware, I repeat, that for several reasons these drawings seem to date from Florence and not earlier than 1501, as historical research has decided, and I should not even venture the hypothesis that the two in the Louvre (Figs. 10 and 14) and even the one at Chantilly (Fig. 9) were sheets brought back from Rome as important preparatory studies and then used after the return to Florence; but I still retain the impression that they at least attest, and continue, a phase of Michelangelo's first work in drawing in Rome, in more direct continuity with the preceding Florentine mode. As for the Apollo-Mercury and the Nude, it seems to me that the proximate point of ideal reference should be taken to be, not the great David, since their calmly powerful anatomy lacks its greater nervous tension, but rather the sensual, carnal, and hedonistically pagan Bacchus. The image, which in these sheets is formed with antique models as the starting point, reinterprets them, nostalgically making them heroic by means of a sense of larger dimensions, but keeping the predominance of the purely physical in the small and unexpressive heads; meanwhile the pen does not aim merely at studying particular motifs of the design, but enjoys all the volumetric modeling, up to the tactile. This is quite in accord with the Bacchus, and goes beyond the experiments of the earliest Florentine period, more shut up in alignments derived from pictural models.

It has been observed several times that the sketch of S. Anna Metterza in Oxford (Fig. 19),[14] done under the influence of Leonardo's cartoon and hence dated, 1501 (Florence), recalls the

28 Torsos and arms. Oxford, Ashmolean Museum
(16).

Pietà in St. Peter's (there is also a certain alignment with the controversial Descent from the Cross in London); but one notes here especially a further step forward of Michelangelo's graphic work as if Buonarroti had suddenly extracted for himself, from Leonardo's fluid flow of forms, an accelerated presentation of the image. We recall how Stendhal thought of the contrast between the two giants: " *le génie ardent du sculpteur emportait les difficultés avec une sorte de furie qui plaisait aux amateurs; ils préféraient Michelange qui travaillait vite, à Léonard qui promettait toujours...*" It is an acceleration obtained by means of a quicker and more energetic treatment of the stroke, with some effects as it were crushed, angular, and splintered, as can be seen on the verso of the Oxford drawing (Fig. 21) and on other sheets (Figs. 17-18 and 27-28); [15-16] and from this point we cannot overlook the opening up of roads toward certain problematic

29 Satyr. Settignano, Villa Buonarroti (1).

30 Study of Madonna. Paris, Louvre (19).

regions of Michelangelo (especially in painting, because the sense of this drawing is pictural rather than sculptural), that is, the possible, in fact not improbable antecedents of the Doni *tondo*; we mean the Manchester Madonna, a reminder of which, for example, is the ephebic head on the verso of the Oxford drawing (Fig. 20); especially through the splendid page of studies in Berlin, n. 1363, Dussler Fig. 177; and likewise the London Descent from the Cross (cf. Figs. 18, 19, 31);[17] and the Taddei marble *tondo*, likewise Leonardesque, is also on a path close by.

We should expect that the maturity of Michelangelo on his return to Florence would soon lead to variant ramifications in his drawing technique. The folio in the Louvre (Figs. 23 and 25),[18] with a second study of the Madonna and St. Anne resolved into a repeating sequence, should not perhaps be put as late as has been done, after the similar study of 1501; the closest references seem to be the Bargello and Taddei *tondos*, and the conception precedes the more complexly organized one of the round Doni painting (about 1503-5?). On the back of this drawing is a nude figure (Fig. 22), which (in contrast to the stratification of the two women by the variety of plastic objects and of more or less finished treatment of the line) is formed by the course of an almost uniform, purely linear flow (a little reinforced on the right), subtle and segmented in stroke but very sure and of powerful effect, in fact almost with a component

394

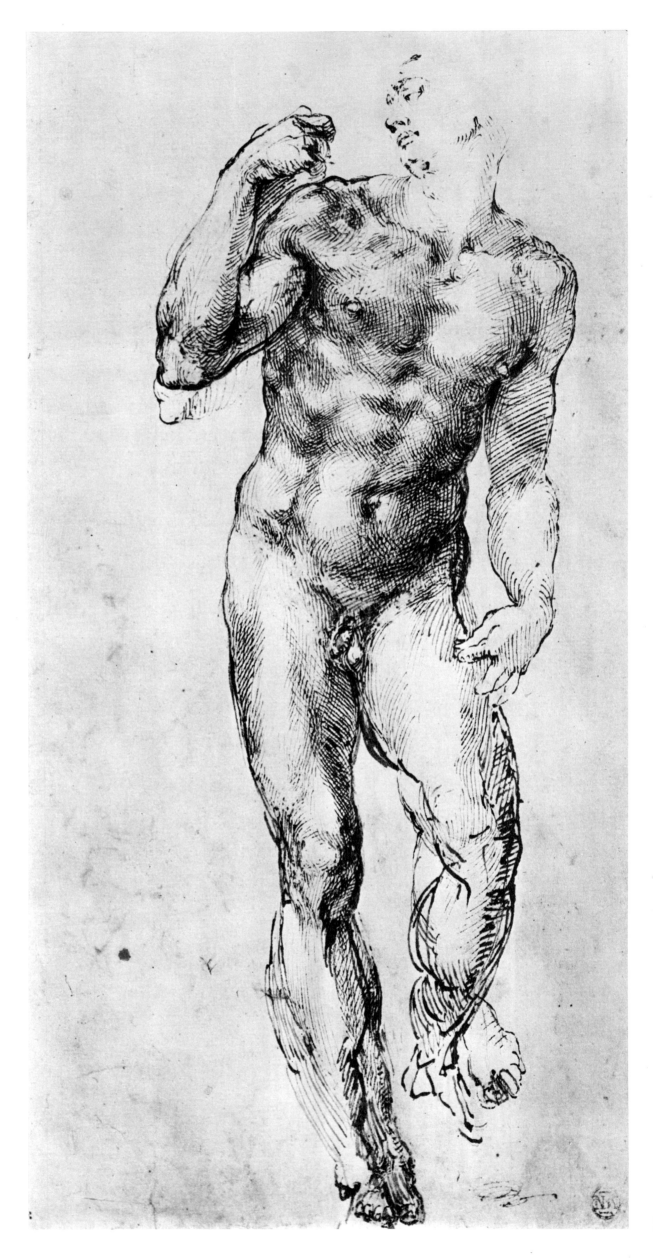

31 Figure. Paris, Louvre (19).

33 Nude man from the back. Vienna, Albertina
    (20).

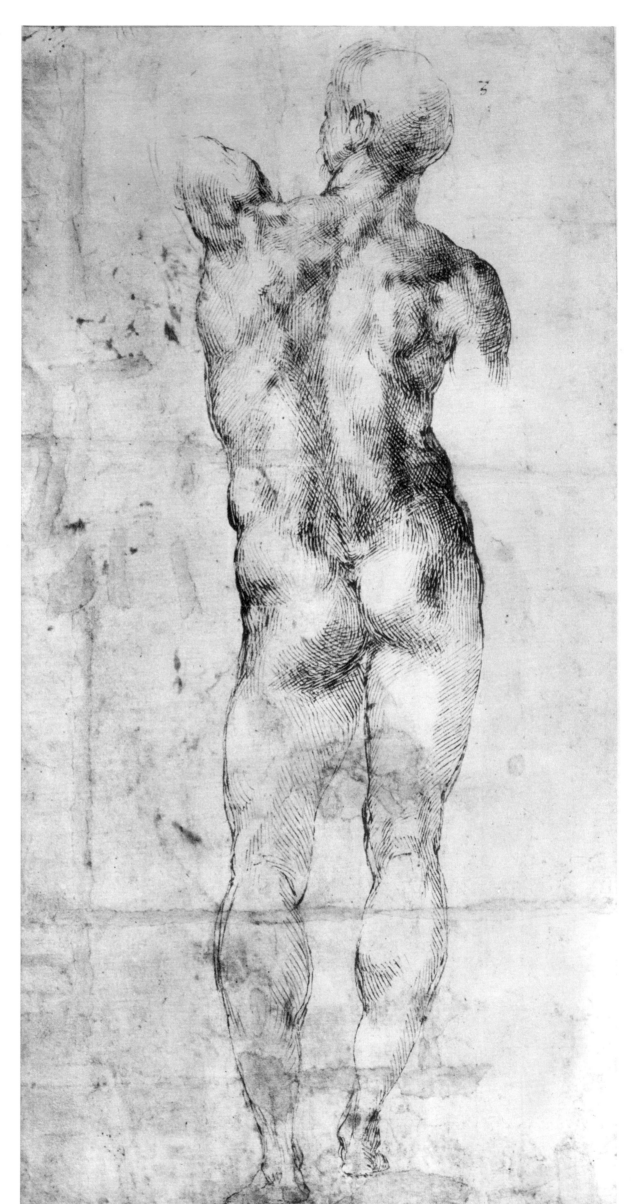

32 Madonna of the milk. Vienna, Albertina (20).

34   Various notes.   Florence, Uffizi (22).

35   Sketches of Apostle and battle.   London, British
     Museum (23).

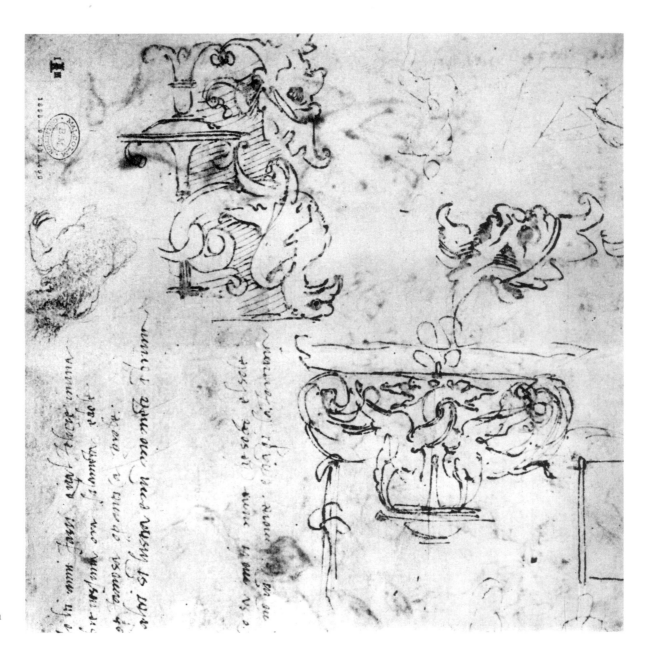

37 Decorative motifs for capitals. London, British Museum (23).

36 Study of cherub's legs. Florence, Uffizi (24).

398

of perversity. The nude, still reminiscent of Pollaiolo, may be an anticipation of those in the background of the Doni *tondo* and its touch, one might say "hooked," is the same as in the barely sketched feet of the two women on the same sheet, or the caricatured profile nearby.

Similar to this in its point of departure, but then diverging into winding curved lines, is the touch of the splendid studies (c. 1504) for a single nursing Madonna (a first stage of studies for the Doni *tondo* or for some project not too far removed in time?) on a paper in the Louvre (Fig. 30) [19] and another in the Albertina (Fig. 32): [20] there is a gradual embodiment, down to the drapery, of a sublime idea of the Madonna in an obliquely ascending version, a clear forshadowing of the future Madonna in S. Lorenzo so many years later.[21] The proof of the chronology is in a page of jottings in the Uffizi (Fig. 34),[22] which Barocchi, reasonably, dated 1503-4.

One of the small sketches concerns the same Madonna and another, the Madonna of Bruges; and still another, slightly bigger, "throws off" with similar sensibility a nude figure like those in the background of the Doni painting; and there are also the elegantly curling fantasies of a capital and, with more insistence, a figure of an Apostle for a statue worked out in tense contours.

Here since the pencil nude is to be related to the Cascina cartoon and the pen sketches were evidently put on later, on what was left of the sheet, the date is just about 1504, or a little later. Contemporary with it, incidentally, is the London sheet (Figs. 35 and 37),[23] which with more marked chiaroscuro repeats the same study for a statue, beginning it at the bottom of the page with a squirming squiggle that merges into the dynamic idea of a cavalry fray, and is, therefore, also for the background of the Battle of Cascina; on the verso are further studies of decorative motifs for capitals with facing pairs of like birds, or masks, all equally spirited.

In a study presumably for the *putto* of the Doni *tondo* (Fig. 36) [24] the anatomical thinking already manifested with such power and certainty in such drawings as the one in the Louvre already discussed (Fig. 30) reveals to us how it can rapidly take on tense muscular flesh. Here the incisive power of the pen, thickening the contours even to the point of blotting, or deepening the chiaroscuro elaboration, makes a much more violent bound, as it were increasing the density of the image.

Thus, toward 1505-6, Michelangelo's drawing was to attain all the terrible might that would soon be triumphally applied to the Sistine vault: the Florence Apostle in red (Fig. 38) [25] is so sure and masterful that it can even give rise to suspicions on the part of the experts, showing

399

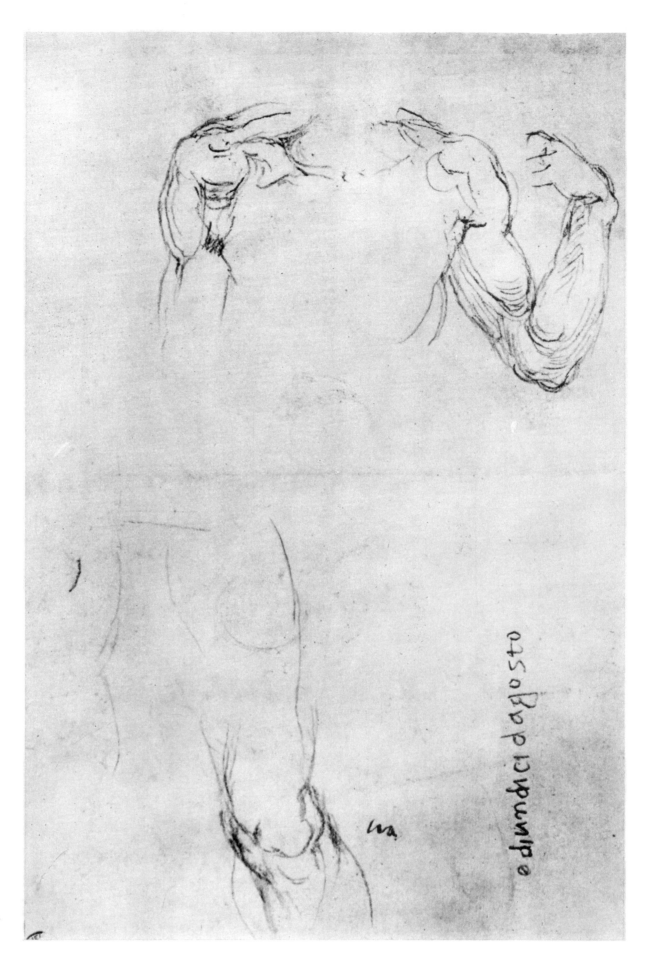

39 Anatomical studies. Oxford, Ashmolean Museum (26).

us a brother of the St. Matthew but one completely refinished, with a massiveness in which the material base is perfectly mastered and molded with a skin-like drapery so adherent to the anatomy and so transparent that we all but enter into it (" not otherwise than the skin...or indeed the waters that come up over beaches, which show by their waves what the form of the beach underneath is like: so the folds of the clothing should show the human limbs..." Doni); and the variant of the hand to the right, smaller than the hand of the David, shows how the idea of a detail can be taken up again and carried to its most complete definition, and yet with a margin that exorcizes any pettiness.

Michelangelo was now ready to meet Julius II; grand ideas met in the brief hour that was to mark the summit of Renaissance Italy. As a mere hypothesis, and an unconventional one, but in order to emphasize the by now supreme power that can be assumed in Michelangelo's drawing, I wonder whether the attested studies on a folio at Oxford (Figs. 39-40),[26] on the recto and showing certain concordances with the David, may not be of this period rather than dating from fifty years later, as is believed.

[1] On the Settignano Satyr or Triton, cf. Tolnay, pp. 69 and 175-6. The author had previously dated the drawing about 1489, when Michelangelo was in the so-called Medici Garden. Doubts as to its authenticity have been expressed in particular by Bertini (1942) and Weinberger (*Art Bulletin*, 1945, p. 70). The head has characteristics resembling those of Drawing 292 r. at Oxford.

[2] Cf. Berenson, 1475A. Berenson (who prior to 1938 had attributed it to Granacci) had failed to notice that the drawing Vasari speaks of had " some women " after Ghirlandaio, and Michelangelo re-outlined one for his fellow pupil (Granacci?), who was " astonished to see the difference in the two manners "; whereas in the Lille drawing the figure is alone; this would make the identification impossible. The drawing is in ink and white lead on pink paper, 25 × 12.5 cm. It was shown at the Exposition of old Italian painting at the Orangerie in 1956 (*Catalogo*, N. 148).

[3] On these episodes cf. Barocchi, Commento, II, Nos. 66, 74, 130.

[4] Louvre 706; pen, 31.7 × 20.4 cm. On the verso (reprod. in Tolnay I, Fig. 126), studies of arms in sanguine: Cited more recently in Barocchi, 1964 Exposition, N. 1; among the comments, V. Mariani, *M.*, 1942, pp. 7-9.

[5] The copy of St. Peter paying the tax, from the Tribute, is in ink and sanguine, 31.7 × 19.7 cm.; Munich, Graphische Sammlung 2191.
The studies of arms on the right margin, whose authorship Barocchi doubts (1964 Exposition, N. 2), may instead indicate a date that is not too early. The copy in ink of the Festival after Masaccio (Vienna, Albertina, Sc. R. 150; 29.4 × 20.1 cm.) has on the verso a solid kneeling figure (Fig. 5), which Berenson, Wilde, Tolnay, and Barocchi believe to be derived from Masaccio rather than from Pesellino (Meder). The iconographic detail of the professional cap seems to allude to SS. Cosma and Damian, that is, to an already Medicean moment. But see also Note 7.

[6] British Museum 1895-9-15-498; pen and pencil; 32.8 × 21.1 cm. The interpretation of the personage, with a pilgrim's hat and a sphere (or skull) in his hand, has ranged from sage to astrologer to alchemist (Tolnay). The head study on the verso is at least different in chronology, and later, although Berenson (N. 1522) already dates the recto as about 1500 as does Dussler (p. 21).

[7] A reproduction is also given of the recto and verso of Drawing N. 25 of the Teyler Museum in Haarlem, ink, 27 × 19.5 cm. The figure sketched kneeling, with a cap, recalls the verso of Albertina drawing N. 150, cf. Note 5 (both perhaps drawn from the same composition?). Salmi, *Masaccio*, 1947, p. 231, thinks both might be derived from a part of Masaccio's Festival in which kneeling personages appeared; Salmi feels (pp. 157-8) that the other Haarlem figures, recto and verso, might come from the putative lost fresco of Masaccio in the third order of the Brancacci Chapel with the Resurrection of the Dead.
As will be seen, we propose a date like 1494-95 for the drawing.

[8] Cf. R. Longhi in *Paragone* 101, 1958, pp. 61 ff. Longhi, it is true, leans toward a later date for the two works from the time of their conception.

[9] Cf. G. Marchini in *Burlington Magazine*, 1953, pp. 320 ff.

[10] For the drawing (N. 29 of the Musée Condé at Chantilly; 26.3 × 38.7 cm.) cf. Tolnay, I, pp. 183-4, Nos. 17 and 18 (verso). The back and profile studies of a nude female statue are probably to be referred to the Three Graces of the Piccolomini Library in Siena (the same model is seen in Drawing 28 F of Casa Buonarroti; cf. Barocchi, 1962, N. 213; and in a Cinquecento drawing in the Louvre, cf. Tolnay, Fig. 96); the male figure to the left, to an antique faun; the cloaked figure, perhaps to Masaccio's Festival; the date is put at about 1503, contrary to the earlier dates previously assigned: 1492-94 (Thode), about 1495 (Berenson), 1496-97 (Frey), about 1500 (Popp). Wilde agrees with Tolnay, and Dussler gives about 1501-3, at the beginning of the second period in Florence. The verso is reproduced in Tolnay, Fig. 97; he holds, with others, that the larger figure is by a pupil.

[11] The sheet (II-III 3 verso of the Archivio Buonarroti; ink, 27.5 × 21.5 cm.) bears on the recto, in addition to a sketch of a leg (Tolnay I, 1943, Fig. 79), reservations in Michelangelo's writing on the contract for the statues of Siena Cathedral (May 22, 1501), and is therefore to be dated just at the end of the first Roman period or just after the return to Florence in Spring 1501. According to Tolnay (1943, N. 7) the study of legs on the recto would derive from an old Dancing Silenus; but there is also a remarkable affinity with the sketches of nudes drawn by Signorelli at the same time at the tope of the *Resurrection of the Flesh* in Orvieto Cathedral (cf. Salmi, *L. Signorelli*, Novara 1953, F. 52A, especially for the nude seen from the rear). And cf. Barocchi, Exposition 1964, N. 175; the author has chosen it as the frontispiece of the catalogue.

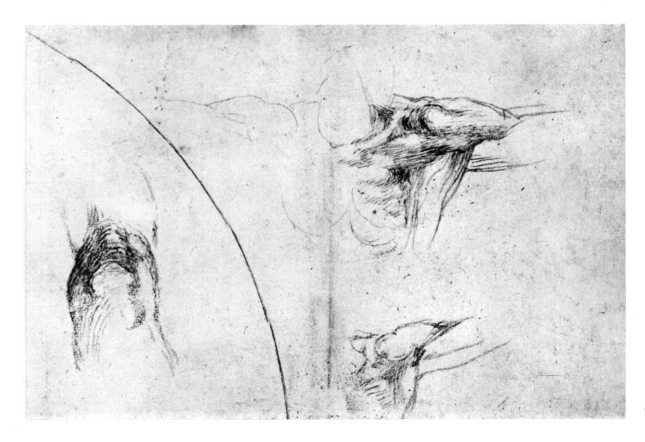

40 Studies of crucifix. Oxford, Ashmolean Museum (26).

401

42 Sketch of fray. Oxford, Ashmolean Museum (36).

41 Horses. Oxford, Ashmolean Museum (35).

[12] For this drawing (688, Louvre; ink; 39.9×21 cm.) the most recent listing is by Barocchi (Exposition 1964, N. 4) which seems to place it 1501-2, appr., upon returning from Rome. She accepts the derivation of the second figure recto from a statue of a boy for a fountain in the Giardino Cesi (reproduced in Tolnay, I, 1943, Fig. 90), but this is a solid adult nude (although Berenson, N. 1588, calls it a boy) with a wine-skin (?), which may go back to some other piece of fountain sculpture. The various sketches on the verso (Fig. 13) are undoubtedly later, as is proved by the stupendous one for a slave on the tomb of Julius II (early 1505); the verses at the bottom, in Michelangelo's handwriting, are from a sonnet by Petrarch; and it has been noted that the profile in the middle of the sheet links up with the angel to the right in the Manchester Madonna. We may agree with the dates of Tolnay, 1943, Nos. 14 and 34, about 1501 for the recto and about 1505 for the verso, at least for the latest things on it.

[13] For the nude study of the drawing (Louvre, 1068; ink; 32.5×16.8) Tolnay, I, N. 15, conceives of an inspiration derived from the Dioscuri of ancient sarcophagi and not the Apollo Belvedere; the use of the same configuration of the torso and right leg as the David, which was begun in 1501, leads the author to date the recto earlier than September of that year, when the statue was begun. It is not sure whether the date of the verso (Fig. 15) should be set much later, since the stylistic stage of the figure (formerly referred to the Haman of the Sistine, and inspired by the Laocoön) is no further advanced than the nudes in the background of the Doni *tondo* (c. 1503-4).

[14] In drawing N. 291 at Oxford (ink; 25.4×17.7 cm.) the study of St. Anna Metterza, inspired by Leonardo's cartoon exhibited in 1501 in SS. Annunziata, is set in 1501 by Tolnay (I, N. 9); the studies of heads (Fig. 21) on the verso (where the name of Leonardo appears in Michelangelo's handwriting), on the other hand, are referred to the Doni *tondo* and hence put back to 1503-4. Berenson too (N. 1561) dates the recto 1501 and the verso about 1505; and yet the two drawings may be contemporaneous. There has also been published (Fig. 24) a forceful Satyr's Head in the British Museum (1895, 9, 15, 495; ink and bister; 13×13 cm.), akin to the verso of the Oxford drawing, and dated about 1502-3 by Berenson (N. 1520).

[15] In the first drawing (Figs. 17-18) of the Louvre (N. 714; ink; 26.5×18.8 cm.) the David on the recto has been related to the bronze for Pierre de Rohan (1502) and arm to the David in marble; Tolnay (I, N. 16) therefore gives the date about 1501-2, while he links the verso stylistically to Oxford drawings 292 (following) and 291 (preceding), putting it forward to about 1501. Reproduction of recto in Berenson 1961, I, Pl. LI.

[16] Figs. 27-28. Tolnay (I, Nos. 11-12) dates the Triton and the recto 1501, while Berenson (N. 1560), linking the anatomical studies to the Cascina cartoon, made it about 1505. The drawing, Oxford 292, is in ink, 23.7×19.3 cm.

[17] The drawing in the Louvre, for the left figure in the London Descent from the Cross, is held by Tolnay not to be an autograph (I, Fig. 280).

[18] For the drawing (Louvre 685; ink; 32.5×26 cm.) it is not necessary to agree with the date of about 1505 proposed by Tolnay (I, Nos. 32-33), either for the recto, which may be a project for a marble *tondo*, or for the verso (Fig. 25) with Herodias or assistant to Judith; the sketch of her face shows instead a link with drawings such as the Louvre 714 already cited (Figs. 17-18), which can be dated about 1501-2. The date had been set variously from about 1502-3 to 1511-13 (with a reference to the Sistine: Berenson, N. 1579) and even a good deal later. Michelangelo's remark on the Madonna: "who would ever say it was by my hand" may be a later criticism by him, at least presuming that the date is not later than 1505.

[19] Cf. Barocchi (Exposition 1964, N. 7), who links to the massive nude of the verso (Fig. 31) the St. John of the London Descent from the Cross, while going along with others in dating the studies on the recto of the Madonna about 1504, that is, close to the problems of the Cascina cartoon. The drawing, Louvre 689, is in ink, 37.5×19.5 cm.

[20] In the Madonna of the recto of the drawing in the Albertina (S. R. 152; ink; 39×19.5 cm.) it is clear from the Child that this is a development of the study of Drawing 689 of the Louvre (Fig. 30, cf. preceding note). The nude on the verso (Fig. 33) is in the direction of the Cascina cartoon, but more archaic in workmanship. Berenson too (N. 1603) has arrived at the conclusion of a date about 1504. This leads to the splendid cartoon in the Casa Buonarroti, 71 F (Pl. XXXI), the authenticity of which has correctly been upheld, and the date given as the period of the Medici Sacristy (Barocchi, 1964, p. 122).

[21] The same theme is also taken up in Drawing Pp. 1-58 of the British Museum (Berenson, 1961, Fig. 620), but with consummate sensibility. Berenson (N. 1493) inclines toward dating this drawing about 1512.

[22] For Drawing 233 F of the Uffizi (black pencil and ink; 27.1×26.1 cm.) cf. Barocchi, 1962, N. 1; and 1964, N. 5. Even if we prefer to refer the sketch at the lower left to the background of the Doni *tondo* and not to one of the Apostles for the Duomo (ordered in 1503), like the other draped figure, the date still comes out approximately 1504. The sketches for the Madonna and Child are related to the Bruges group and to the studies of Louvre 689 and the Albertina 152 just referred to. The verso (Barocchi, 1962, Pl. VI) may be a study of Donatello's David in marble, for Buonarroti's bronze David for De Rohan. We note that a number of scholars call the drawing a copy or even a forgery.

[23] In the British Museum drawing (1895, 9, 15, 496; ink; 18.3×17.7 cm.) the two sketches of an apostle, perhaps the first idea for the St. Matthew, have the same aspect as in 233 F of the Uffizi; the sketch of a cavalry battle is a first idea for the Cascina cartoon, under the influence of Leonardo's Battle of Anghiari. The sketches for capitals on the verso (which are related to the capital of 233 F of the Uffizi, as Berenson, N. 1521, noted, but attributing it to a pupil) have been shown by Tolnay (I, Nos. 19 and 20) to be for the tomb of Julius II. Consequently, the date for the sheet is about 1504-5.

[24] For Drawing 23 F of the Uffizi (ink; 16.2×9.1 cm.) Barocchi too (1962, N. 9) accepts the suggestion by Wilde and Dussler of relating it to the *putto* of the Doni *tondo*. The date is thus in the neighborhood of 1503-5.

[25] Uffizi 620 E; sanguine; 43×28.2 cm. Doubted only by Dussler, the drawing is preferably referred, if not to the St. Matthew, to the studies for the Apostles of the Duomo, and dated about 1505-6, parallel to the St. Matthew (Barocchi, Exposition 1964, N. 12).

[26] Ashmolean Museum, 341 (charcoal stick; 25.2×16.1 cm.). Probably much later (Tolnay, V, Nos. 261-2, puts it after 1550; Wilde between 1555 and 1560!), but on the recto there are suggestive recalls of the David, remarked by Berenson as well, for which reason Frey ascribed it to 1503-6.

Studies for the Battle of Cascina
(1504-6)

Michelangelo's drawing came to its full unfolding and a concomitant "terribleness" through congenital psychological fierceness in the personality of the man Michelangelo that had so exclusively masculine an ideal as to run the risk of abnormality, as emerges clearly from his biography; but it found particularly propitious circumstances in the events of his career.

43 Study for the Battle of Cascina. Florence, Uffizi (28).

Incidentally, they were in all likelihood not fortuitous, if it is true that every type necessarily creates a suitable destiny for itself. What occasion could be better suited than the commission for the Battle of Cascina (1504-6): " inventing therein many naked men who, bathing in the Arno River in the heat of the day, and taking to arms at that instant to beat off the enemy assailing them, come out of the river in haste, clothing themselves in varied attitudes " (Borghini)?

We know how in Buonarroti's hands the theme took concrete form in the supreme test of the design for the cartoon and confined itself almost to a continuous and acrobatic variation on the male nude, until all its expressive possibilities under the circumstances were exhausted (" In which all the attitudes and emotions that could possibly take place in such a case are seen most naturally," Fornari, 1550). But there is here not a mere repertory of postures, but the decisive establishment of a poetics, with all its profound implications. Buonarroti's imagination concerning man is now transferred to a scale that is heroically larger than natural, totally ideal;

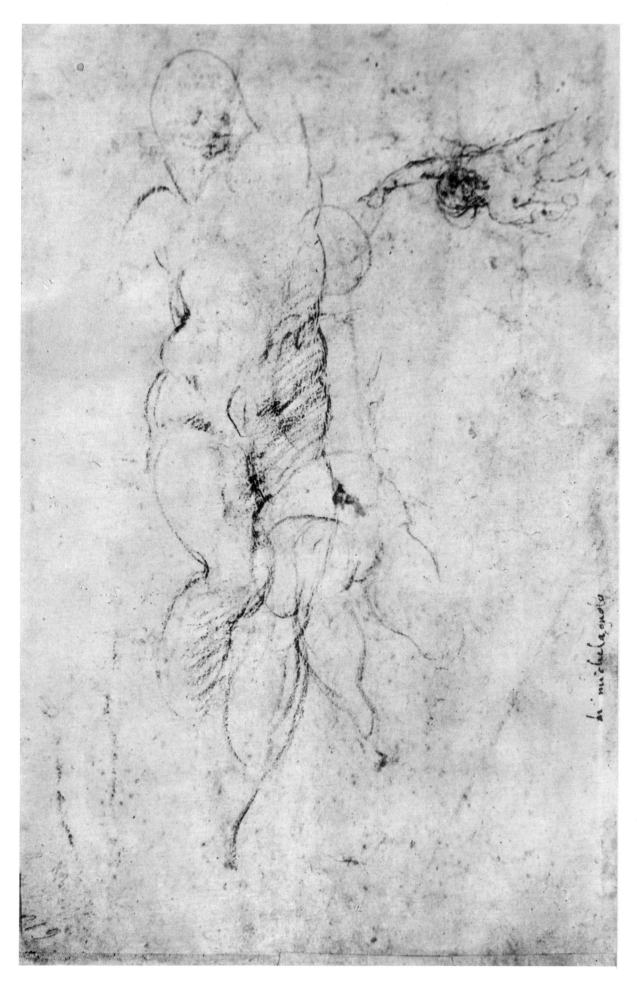

44 Study for the Battle of Cascina. Florence, Uffizi (28).

404

45 Ganymede and sketch for the Battle of Cascina. Florence, Uffizi (29).

and that titanic nude, logically in keeping with the development of the Renaissance, turns into a potentiated, hyperbolic microcosm, a mirror and measure for the measureless metaphysical macrocosm. Our reason for saying this is not to venture inadequate comments on the cartoon (that is for the historian of Michelangelo as painter and as artist in general) but that this factor touches Buonarroti's drawing as well. To understand it fully, we must now see it as charged with this teleological significance in its fixation, seemingly almost obsessive, except for the architectural studies, on a single highly concentrated set of themes: the continual stress on anatomy, with every study sounding as the tone or motif of a linked unending music, as the new combination working out the immutable set equation, as one of the infinite deductions from a spiritual metaphysics that has paradoxically taken concrete form and is immanent in an extreme physicality.

Apparently the cartoon brought out all the various technical-expressive possibilities of the drawing. " There were also many figures grouped and sketched in various ways, some outlined in charcoal, some drawn in lines, some in wash toned up with white lead, he desiring to show how much he knew of his profession. Wherefore those of the craft remained mute and dead, seeing the heights of art shown them by Michele Agnolo in this sheet " (Vasari, 1550).

But the " heights " of the cartoon are also the target hit by the arrow loosed from the bow of this strange genius from the outset. It is the boyish intuition of the Centauromachia, there a first and limited eruption of imagination and temperament, now from the enclosure of Casa Buonarroti coming to clothe the walls of the Sala Grande del Consiglio of Florence; it is the infant prodigy reared by Lorenzo the Magnificent and Politian now at thirty making a trial

405

of strength with Leonardo da Vinci; it is the nascent configuration of imprecise figures in
a dense swarm in that bas-relief that now, at the end of an entire course of apprenticeship to
the antique and to anatomy, becomes the touchstone in a supreme, taut test of skill, on a
huge scale and in a rarefied atmosphere, where every detail will have its implacable absolute
evidence.

Not much evidence in the form of drawings has come down to us concerning the Cascina
cartoon, but I should say that their interest lies in the extent to which they reveal the
process of " ontogenesis," in the conceiving and embodying of which all the necessary previous
phases of development are recapitulated.[27]

In Drawing 613 of the Uffizi (Fig. 43), recently and correctly vindicated as an autograph,[28]
the soft nude figurines, touched up with the curving pencil lines, have a supple gentleness and
a delicate generic quality of the welling image that can recall the Centauromachia; but in
another Florentine page (Fig. 45) [29] the same slender imaged material now reappears charged
more decisively with the dynamic quality learned precisely on that occasion from his rival,
Leonardo. And the fact is that, although in a different way, the softness acquired from Leonardo certainly is also found in the figurine of the abandoned and ambiguous Ganymede (or
Leda), and at the top of the same sheet Buonarroti follows, in the same mood, a quite different
imaginative strain, presaging the sensual but abysmal abandonment that was one day to prevail in him over the heroic hopes that had ended in frustration.

The charcoal sketch at Oxford, N. 296 v. (Fig. 51), with a horseman and a man dismounted,
likewise has something of the distant core of the Centauromachia; and now we see that in the
working out of the studies for this detail the torso of the dismounted man on the other side
of the sheet (Fig. 49) [30-31] probably grew on the graft of sculptural themes; but with the
further element, as shown by a related folio (Fig. 50), [32] of scientific anatomical analysis, down
to full mastery of the details, as shown in the shoulder articulation done twice in pencil with
the utmost deftness.

In any event, the image is defined by means of a much more complex and deep-reaching
process than mere inspiration developed by means of observation of nature—one that instead
takes form on the basis of a cumulative experience of culture and sense of life. This is attested
by other drawings, such as the celebrated Nude seen from the back (Plate XXIX) in

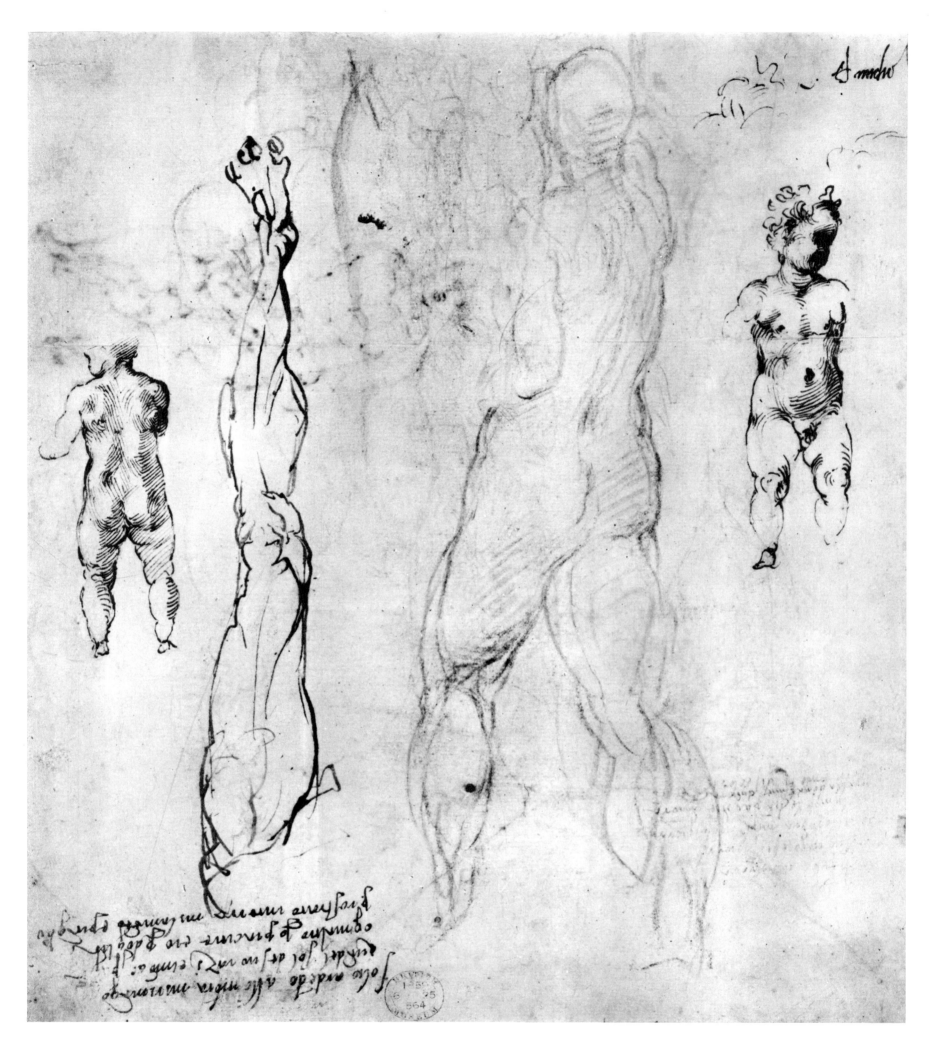

48 Studies for cherubs and for the Battle of Cascina. London, British Museum (37).

Florence [33]—a possible source for which has been seen in the Labors of Hercules on classical
sarcophagi—in which the treatment, by means of heavy contours and the line constituting a
clear continuation of the previous experiments we have discussed, envisage an evidence of the
flesh; and also the Apollonian nude in London, already referred to (Fig. 56),[34] likewise contemporaneous with the studies for the cartoon, if not related to them.

In other pages, however, the ideational aspect gushes up directly and thunderously with the
freedom of graphic expression already shown in the 1501 sketches (Fig. 16). I have even
come to wonder, in a tentative way, whether Drawing 156 of the Albertina (Berenson 1961,
Fig. 545), which is thought to be a recall from memory of the cartoon, done by someone in the
Cinquecento, might not instead be a work from Buonarroti's hand—among his earliest ideas— 407

50 Anatomical study. Florence, Uffizi (32).

49 Study of foot-soldier from the back. Oxford, Ashmolean Museum (30-31).

and whether its background, with its reference to two frescoes on sacred but still civic Florentine themes (St. John and St. George), might not be referred to the other end of the Sala, where the altar was, although doubt is cast on this hazarded idea, if by nothing else, then by the presence of too many ideas of genius all to be found in the Holkham *grisaille*. In any event, we come back to sure ground in the cavalry skirmish of the London drawing already discussed (Fig. 35), followed up by two splendid folios at Oxford (Figs. 42 and 41). The second of these sheets (Fig. 41) [35] deals vigorously with the animal subject of the horse, which as we know was one of the most celebrated themes of his rival Leonardo; the first one (Fig. 42) [36] starts with a confusion of lines and goes on to elicit from it, with strokes and spots of bister, the most inspired variety of *attitudes*, in flashing trajectory, from the first intuition in linear-pictural signs to the setting up of a connected series of tremendous sculptural ideas.

In other cases the drawing, in its insistence on a single particular, seems to have come to assimilate it so much as to slacken it into an almost Mannerist cursiveness. This is the case of the nude seen from the back for the episode of the soldier on sentry duty being relieved by two others, in a paper of the British Museum (Fig. 47), of which we find an earlier, more vigorous form, with sinuous contours, on the verso of the same drawing (Fig. 48),[37] corresponding to a more timid and accurate one on a different sheet that we have already considered (Fig. 34).

Finally, we can examine in other cases (Figs. 54-55) [38] solutions that by now are almost completely definite, and hence static in touch, for some nudes that are like prefabricated parts

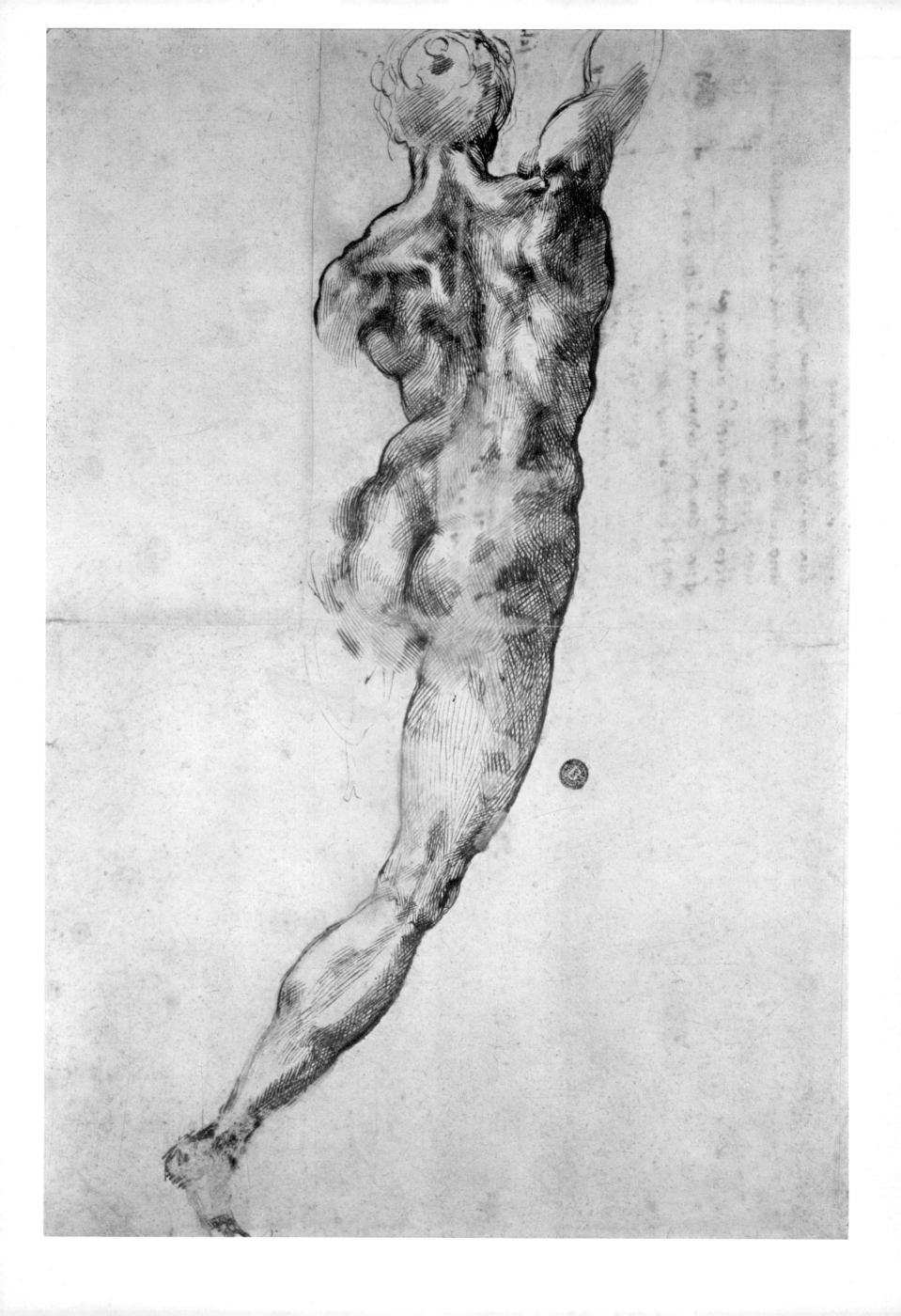

PLATE XXIX   Nude from the back.   Florence, Casa Buonarroti, 73 F.

ready to be put out on the all-over chessboard; whereas a folio like the London one for the Nude on the bank (Fig. 52),[39] although suspect and devalued today, can always give an efficacious idea of the intensity with which, on the great sheets of the cartoon, in most plastic evidence, there was played out the sounding symphony of " those nude infantrymen running to arms, and with such beautiful motions " (B. Cellini). Infantrymen, in contrast to the cavalry that were the protagonists of Leonardo's Battle: a contrast that can be attributed not only to Buonarroti's desire to be different from his rival, but also to the basic divergence of the two geniuses. In the one, the universal interest that led him, as we know, to conceive the Battle of Anghiari as a vortical shock of unloosed cosmic forces; in Buonarroti, on the other hand, an interest that was ferociously circumscribed within the narrow radius of the human subject, so that despite the first notes on cavalry set-tos (Figs. 35, 41 and 42) suggested by Vinci, later there dominates in him the anthropocentric, heroic-statuesque directive and the other ideas, if present at all, were relegated to the background. Once more, therefore, Michelangelo's drawing underwent, as it had instinctively from the very outset, the imperative of a basically closed form, whose extreme internal tension of energy was capable of being opened

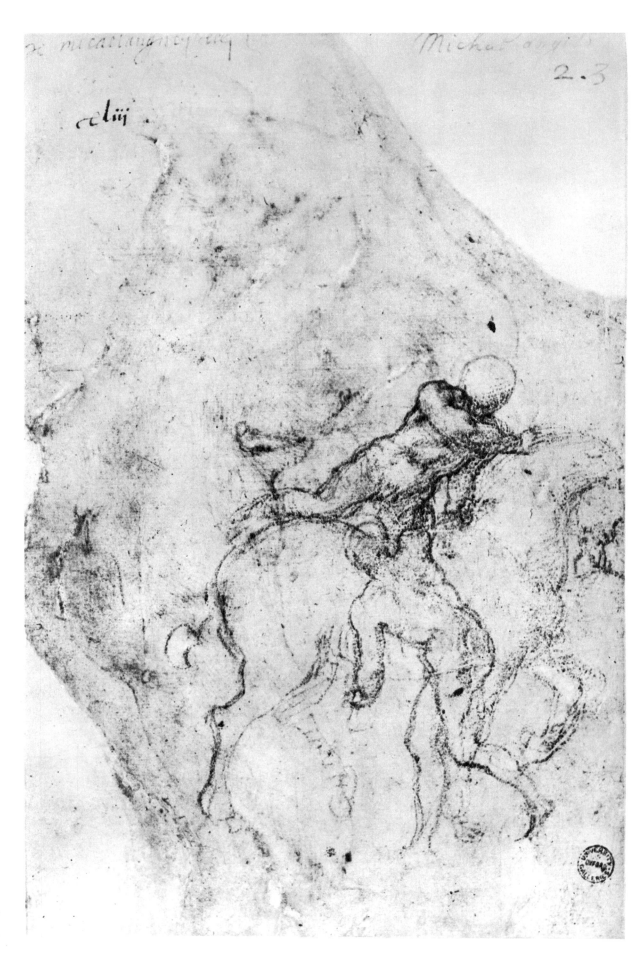

51 Horse-soldier and foot-soldier. Oxford, Ashmolean Museum (30-31).

54 Figures for the Battle of Cascina. Vienna, Albertina (38).

52 Nude man for the Battle of Cascina. London, British Museum (39).

53 Studies of legs. London, British Museum (39).

410

only transcendentally; but to create a *heroic ideal*, one that was to be followed by an entire century of art, out of a few foot soldiers hastily putting on their pants was something that was within the reach only of Buonarroti, with his secret intuition of a mysterious radical connection between the two opposites, matter and idea.

²⁷ On the cartoon for Cascina, I shall here only say that I follow the opinion that it was not limited to the composition attested by the Sangallo copy in the Holkham *grisaille*, but was extended, at least on the left, by figures of horsemen and foot soldiers in the background (as witness the drawing, formerly Fenwick and now in the British Museum; Berenson, 1961, Fig. 544); also accurate is Vasari's reference to "an infinite number fighting on horseback beginning the skirmish," and the dimensions reconstructed by Wilde. On the entire question, cf. Barocchi, Commento, II, Nos. 196 and 200; recently H. Werner Grohn in *Il Vasari*, 67-8, 1963, p. s.; and C. A. Isermeyer, *Die Arbeiten Leonardos und Michelangelos für den Grossen Ratssaal in Florenz*, in *Studien zur toskanischen Kunst* (F. Heydenreich), Munich 1964.

²⁸ The authenticity of Drawing 613 E of the Uffizi (black pencil and silver point; 23.5 × 35.6 cm.), formerly attributed to Allori or to some zealous Mannerist, has been vigorously restated by Barocchi (1962, N. 4) both for the originality of the figures on the left as compared with the definitive cartoon and for the "meditative and allusive" quality. The magnificent standing nude on the verso (Fig. 44) is clearly connected with the figure of the relieved sentry in Drawing 1859 6-25-64 in London (Fig. 47). The evident date of the drawing is 1504.

²⁹ This is Drawing 18737 F of the Uffizi (black pencil and silver point; 24.3 × 21 cm.), in which the rudimentary sketches refer to thoughts on the Cascina (and so date from 1504), while the Ganymede or Leda had already been hinted at, perhaps, in the earlier 613 E of the Uffizi, in the figurine upside down on the recto.

³⁰⁻³¹ Despite the fact that Tolnay considers them to be copies (1943, Nos. 27-8), we prefer the hypothesis of authenticity

for Drawing 296 of the Ashmolean Museum r. and v. (ink and charcoal; 27 × 18.5 cm.). Panofsky has noted the derivation of the nude seen from the back from the prototype of Myron's Discobolus.

[32] Drawing 9 of the Uffizi (ink and black pencil; 28.4 × 21 cm.) contains an analytical phase of the studies for the figure seen from the rear in Drawing 296 r. and v., Oxford; cf. preceding note.

[33] Casa Buonarroti, 73 F (ink with traces of black pencil; 40.8 × 28.4 cm.). Wilde has emphasized the relationships with the antique rather than with a model, comparing it with the Labors of Hercules in a Lateran sarcophagus (fig. in Tolnay, 1943, 111). Tolnay (N. 22) sees no direct connection with the Cascina cartoon, but contemporaneous dating, toward 1504-5 (Frey is alone in suggesting the first years of the century); but Barocchi (1962, N. 6), with others, notes the relationship of the organization to two figures sketched in 613 E r. of the Uffizi (cf. Fig. 43 and Pl. XXIX).

[34] British Museum 1887, 5, 2, 117; ink, 37.7 × 22.9 cm. For Tolnay, who dates it about 1504-5 (and so does Dussler), this is a recall of the Apollo Belvedere; the verso, with a magnificent study of putti (Tolnay, 1943, Fig. 109), with a text referring to the Bruges Madonna, is related to the Taddei tondo. The dating of the sheet as about 1504-5 is supported by the relationship of the putti to those of a drawing in the British Museum 1859-6-25-564, containing a note for the Cascina cartoon (Figs. 47-48).

[35] The studies for the hindquarters of a horse (still Leonardesque in inspiration) support the reference of this drawing (293 of the Ashmolean Museum; ink and bister; 42.7 × 28.3 cm.), also linked to N. 294 of the same museum (cf. following note), to the planning for the Battle of Cascina. The verso has poetry. Also connected with the studies of horses is Drawing 296, Oxford, for Cascina, which has already been discussed (cf. Fig. 51).

[36] From what has been said, reference to the Battle of Cascina seems the most convincing for the sketch in the Ashmolean Museum (N. 294; ink and bister; 17.9 × 25.1 cm.).

[37] The British Museum drawing (1859-6-25-564; charcoal and ink; 31.5 × 27.8 cm.) is certainly connected, on the recto, with the other superb ink sketch (Fig. 46) for the Bruges Madonna; the group of three almost acrobatic soldiers reappears in Drawing 718 of the Louvre (Berenson, 1961, N. 1598 and Fig. 552); on the verso the two putti are kin to those on the verso of British Museum drawing 1887, 5, 2, 117, already cited (cf. Berenson, 1961, Fig. 553), which is a stupendous series of varied studies of the infant figure.

[38] For this drawing in the Albertina too (N. 157; ink on recto; on verso, charcoal and white lead, Fig. 55; 27.2 × 19.9 cm.), doubts have been expressed (cf. Tolnay, 1943, Nos. 29-30) since these are figures definitely attested in the cartoon and, on the recto, completely done even in the parts that in the cartoon were covered by other figures.

[39] British Museum, 1887, 5, 2, 116; ink, with touches in water color and white lead; 41.2 × 28 cm. A rather discredited drawing; Tolnay even considers it a copy (1943, N. 31). The figure is attested in the Cascina cartoon but the left arm does not appear here. A reproduction is also given (Fig. 53) of the verso, with softer studies of legs.

55 Fighter for the Battle of Cascina. Vienna, Albertina (38).

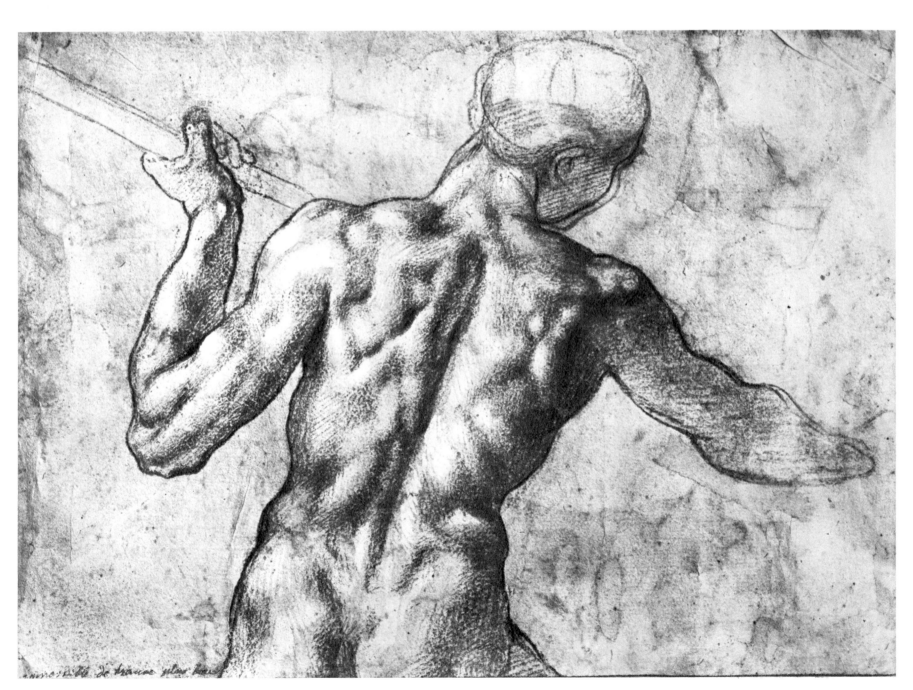

56 Nude man. London, British Museum (34).

Drawing for the vault of the Sistine Chapel
(1508-12)

In the vault of the Sistine Chapel (1508-12) Michelangelo achieved a complete realization of his *opus maximum*, in an unprecedented symphonic unfolding (compared to it, even the Cascina cartoon seems mentally a fragment); but for that titanic undertaking, lasting for years, we must admit that we have left, as usual, only a pale and very meager documentation in drawings, despite the prestige of the precious folios. This is true even if we do not confine

412

ourselves to the twelve drawings on the subject accepted by Tolnay as authentic, and accept others despite the insidious circumstances of a document so closely studied and annotated.[40]

Under examination, however, these slight remnants tell us something, even when the effort is to evaluate their intrinsic graphic qualities rather than their function as a preparation for the frescoes; above all we are interested in any new features that emerge, after having already got some experience of the variety of Michelangelo's drawing in his youth.

About the ink sketches it could be said that the concern with the decorative and architectural organization accentuates certain cubist or stenographic tendencies. In the page in the British Museum (Fig. 60), [41] relating to the " first design " with the " twelve Apostles in the lunettes, and the rest a certain compartmentation full of ornaments, as is the custom," which was later abandoned as a " poor thing," and therefore presumably dating from May 1508, there is a certain negligence in the notations for the various frames of the partitions that seems to indicate dissatisfaction; yet the little figure of an Apostle seated at the foot of the throne, although strictly speaking a manikin, is yet notable for the idea of its sculptural projection in the corbel, as it was later to be developed, although with much more imposing dimensions, in the Prophets and Sibyls. In the Detroit drawing (Fig. 57),[42] which is held to be almost contemporaneous but in which the decorative system is more unified and the bands between the various corbels are drawn in, the treatment of the sketch is if possible even more thunderous and sure-handed in indicating frames, plaques, ovate backgrounds, flanked by *putti*, garlands, hollows of thrones.

If the two Nudes with books in the Uffizi (Figs. 71, 72) [43] are really authentic and refer to the Twelve Apostles, thereby dating from 1508 (but the attribute of the books suggests rather the first ideas than the definitive project), there should be noted, despite some curvilinear starts of the pen that are later corrected, the persistence in the roughing-out of a quality of an articulated manikin on ideally cubist or geometrical moduli. In this particular form, this is a characteristic that had hitherto been absent from Michelangelo's sketches, and may be due precisely to the new system of thinking in terms of a tight symbiosis between architecture and representation (which had been also the problem in the tomb of Julius II). This may be the best way to approach acceptance of the two studies for sibyls of another well-known London

57 Sketch for the Sistine Ceiling. Detroit, Institute of Arts (42).

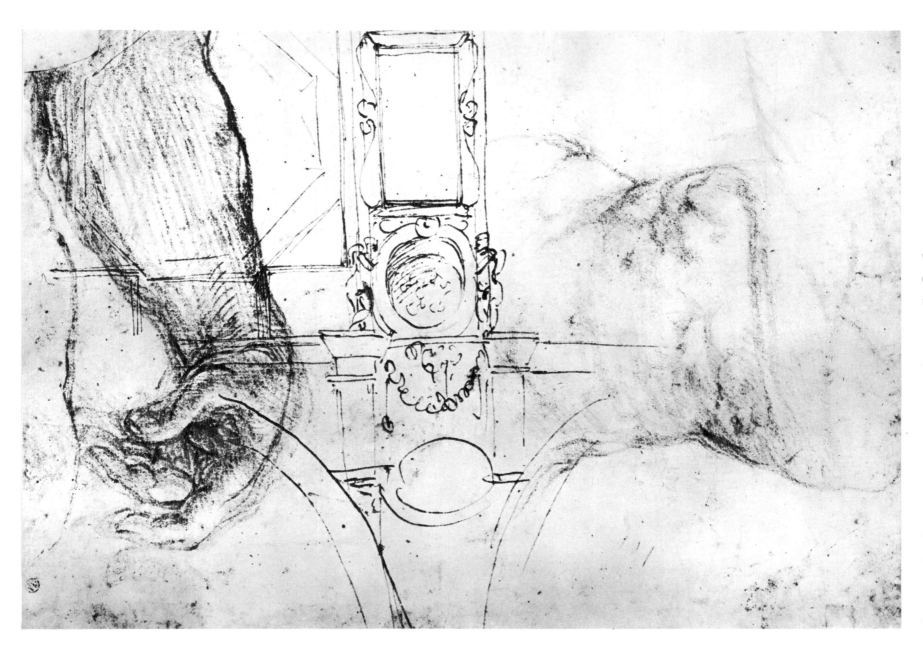

413

59 Sibyl and other studies. Detroit, Institute of Arts (42).

58 Detail of Fig. 59 (42).

sheet (Figs. 69, 70),[44] a sheet initiated early, since it has on the verso a sketch for the entire system of the vault, while the one on the recto certainly has something of a subtle suggestion of a faceted anatomy volume.[45]

Following up our annotations on the sketches, the one for the Deluge (Fig. 77),[46] if we are willing to accept Michelangelo as its author, continues the stenographic intensification but not the thinking in terms of tangles (cf. Fig. 35), in fragmentary notations. As compared with this sketch the line appears surer and straighter (that is, in accordance with the new graphic form that we wished to emphasize) in the most amusing autobiographical bit alongside the composition outburst in Casa Buonarroti (Fig. 61);[47] here the enormous and uncomfortable labor of painting the vault is concentrated as if in the most comprehensive of self-criticisms. (And what a caricature the depicted figure is, representing the huge masterpiece!)

But when the sketch is entrusted to soft, sometimes almost evanescent, pencil, as in a sheet of Casa Buonarroti concerning the Nudes (Fig. 74),[48] we get a feeling of the modellability of the image, as if it were wax or chalk, repeating and defining itself in various ways; or of a tangled manner, as at the left, keeping a wide margin of fantasy and a multiplicity of solutions.

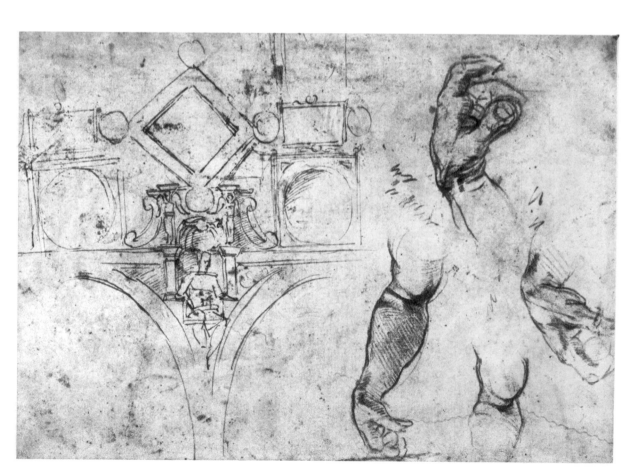

60 Sketch for the Sistine vault. London, British Museum (41).

414

63 Study of Sibyl or Prophet. London, British Museum (52).

61 Poetry and sketch. Florence, Casa Buonarroti (47).

62 Back of drawing on No. 60 (41).

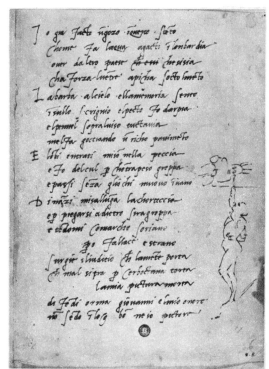

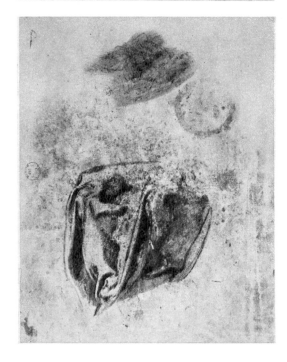

In this last aspect, and given the uncertainty of reference that is characteristic of drawings referable to the Sistine, I find that a magnificent effect is obtained with charcoal in a London drawing (Fig. 73),[49] sketching in variants, within an indeterminate halo, the idea of a potent, alluring femininity.

Finally, I cite for their rapidity, two London figures (Fig. 82),[50] which even if not authentic still seem to mirror well the most glowingly Mannerist qualities that can be found in the four corner episodes of the Sistine.

But this Mannerism is marginal to the supreme classicism of the vault of the Sistine; that is, that what we see today as pre-Mannerist had its origin at that moment in the connective tissue of the classical style, at the most cursive and accessory points of the Great Manner; in the Sistine vault we find it in the Forebears of Christ of the corbels and lunettes, in the four episodes of the large corner corbels, in the Nudes and the bronze medallions, that is, where the great classical formula is simplified into a compendium, or changes to more capricious and intimate tones. On this matter, however, the drawings tell us little;[51] it is natural that there should be no trace of research in what was achieved almost involuntarily and as a byproduct, whereas in the documentation, scarse as it is, there is abundant testimony to the maturation of the greatest classical breadth. Take as an example the sibyl in the nude on the verso of the Detroit drawing already referred to (Fig. 58). Even in this first formula-

415

65 Studies for the genius of the Libyan Sibyl and for the Slaves of the Tomb. Oxford, Ashmolean Museum (54).

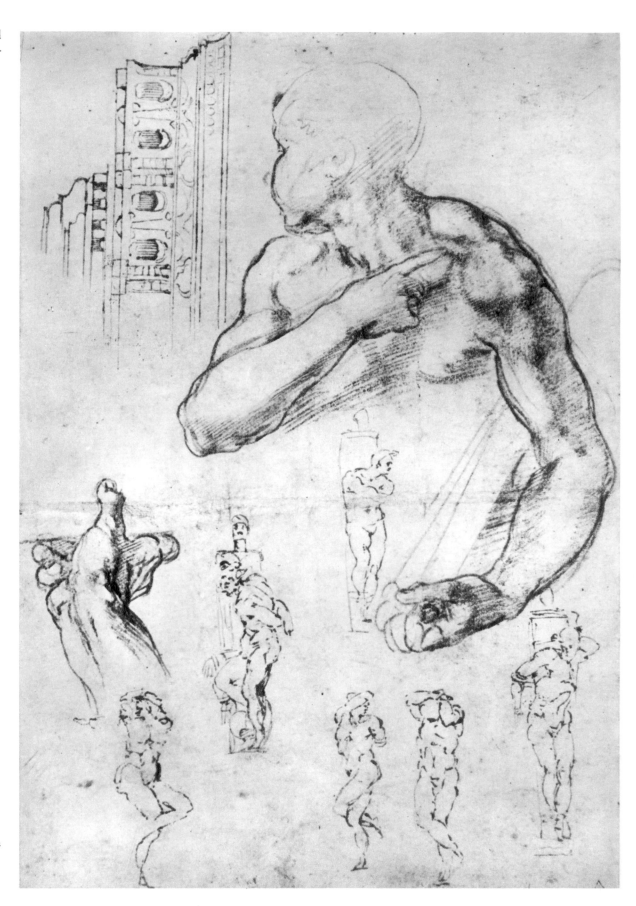

65 Studies for the genius of the Libyan Sibyl and for the Slaves of the Tomb. Oxford, Ashmolean Museum (54).

64 Study of nude man. London, British Museum (56).

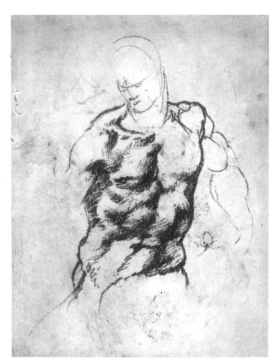

tion in ink it is conceived with a broad, rounded sense of form, recalling the perfect robustness of the marble David, while being arranged in eloquent circular rhythms (the left arm marking the course of a circle to which two other circles are tangent, one for the legs and another on which the *putto* with the book is arched; and in fact circular moduli are an active feature of the Sistine vault). And another instance is on the recto of the same Detroit drawing (Fig. 57) and the recto of the British Museum page (Fig. 60), where the theme of the arm with the hand hanging down bent (which was later to find its triumphal application in the Creation of Adam but is already found elsewhere, as in the Nudes) is worked out with a certain heaviness of touch, significant of a conception not so much in tension as of power at rest, and the studies are not of full figures but of the multivalences of a detached member. It might be the lax hand of the drunken Noah, or the hand of the created Adam, still sluggish but already having the permeating vital stream flowing through it.

Returning to the studies for the Sibyls and Prophets, the one in London relating to Isaiah (Fig. 63),[52] problematical and damaged though it is, seems to me in this sense at least hypothetically suggestive of a peak of classicism, either in that the figure is set against a solid architectural background (and in fact those figures do have an architectural background on the vault, but here we seem to see the great creature take form as it were in dialectical relationship with a world of monumental and cultural motifs) or in the resumption of the marked

416

reticulate technique of the earliest drawings—although now (the feeling of problem having deepened) without a more incisive marginal line, for example at the lower edge of the drapery—as if recovering, in this primitive technique, the tone best suited to an archaic prophetical potency, a radical timeless essence.

Well-known and much commented on are the two pages of studies for the Libyan Sibyl and the little spirit alongside her (Figs. 67, 68 and 65) in New York [53] and Oxford.[54] But just what meaning are we to attach to them? Obviously, we are at a well-advanced stage in the preparation of the figure, although not yet at the definitive cartoon. The Sibyl is nude in the drawing, although almost indeterminate in sex because the lean muscular torso has a masculine look; in the fresco the formal treatment is broader and simpler, sacrificing some of the anatomical virtuosity (Tolnay). Moreover, the left forearm, for example, is held lower than in the drawing and the torso is inclined where in the drawing it is erect; in the drawing the two arms of the Sibyl suggest a balance in almost perfect horizontal equilibrium, while in the fresco there is a perceptible inclination to the left, which perhaps incidentally emphasizes the weight of the great book that is being held up. It therefore seems clear to me that Michelangelo arrived at his final solutions only after having used his drawings to become absolute master of the figure in mind.

Accordingly, the last formulations were certainly not the most laborious, but rather natural successes, as it were, and obtainable by means of mechanical variations in the course of diligent practice on this set of ideas. In the case of the largest variant of our drawing, Michelangelo one day must have got the idea of sloping the torso more, and then we can imagine that all he had to do was to take as a basis the position of the legs to the rear (Fig. 67) and bring the torso down in front (Fig. 68), touching the line of the waist but rotating the torso downward a little, in order to obtain the actual design of the Libica. Thus, drawings like this, which as Berenson noted are hard to justify logically,[55] can have precise meaning as rehearsals in penetration. Here we have a drawing in sanguine that starts by giving a perfect

66 Study of nude men. London, British Museum (56).

68 Studies for the Libyan Sibyl. New York, Metropolitan Museum (53).

67 Studies for the Libyan Sibyl. New York, Metropolitan Museum (53).

and methodical rendering of the figure he had in mind (that is the way I feel the drawing must have begun), but a little later, as in the repetition of a chord in music, there is the trial of a gentler, more pensive facial expression, pre-Correggio, as it were, broad and general; and then, going literally from head to foot, three exercises on a foot and a great toe. *Usque ad unguem.*

And soon thereafter, in the sketch that sums up the underlying muscular situation, there comes the idea of lowering the left forearm, as it was to be in the cartoon; and then comes the left hand, done over again with more care. On the verso (Fig. 67), the charcoal is less exigent, since this part will be entirely covered by the drapery; it has a softness that is sometimes almost a presage of Piazzetta, with a restful style contrasted to the constant tension of the recto; and at the top it ends up with the jest of the formless ape, perhaps in mockery of the labored Sibyls. The same is true of the little spirit (Fig. 65), where there are more prominent corrections in the contour, already familiar in memory but not with the literalness of a copy, and capable, in the cartoon, as happens, of further changes and all in fact abbreviations (which would further guarantee that they are not copies). Then the sheet has the splendid ideas for the Prisons.

It is therefore a classicism by inclination, fully mature from the outset, whether in conceiving general designs (Figs. 57 and 60) or details (Fig. 58) or in recalling for the moment his own experience in life and culture up to that point (Fig. 63). And this is confirmed, for example, by the study for the Nudes in a London drawing (Figs. 66 and 64),[56] both on the verso, with its smooth ideas of magnificent poses, and on the recto, with a charcoal study of a torso looking like an antique fragment. And it is a classicism of full mastery of the gradually worked out individual solutions, and of certain admirable themes in reserve, as can be seen from a study for Adam driven out (Fig. 79),[57] taut in the tension between the arms spread out and the body going in the opposite direction, or the admirable arm in Casa Buonarroti (Fig. 81),[58] or a powerful torso in profile in London, a recall of Cascina (Fig. 80).[59]

Now, if conceptualization is the daughter of experience, and if the Idea distills out of intellectual mastery of things, it is certain that this aspect of Michelangelo at the time of the Sistine Chapel is no longer to be taken as classicism by instinct (as in his first drawings, which were modeled on a heroic ideal and a powerful imagination applied in studious but as yet unrealized activity) but a classicism arising out of a mature ideal synthesis, in which perfection in drawing coincides with "ideal" solutions that are no longer particular, but enclosed by meditation in reposeful absoluteness. The heads are an example, those heads of which Tolnay says accurately that they "belong in a special category which is lacking in the youthful period... They are not portraits... These heads seem turned within themselves; the external world does not seem to exist for them. This isolation permits a concentration on the essential, permanent features of the human face. They are not studies ad hoc; they form

69 Study of Sibyl and for the Sistine vault. London, British Museum (44).

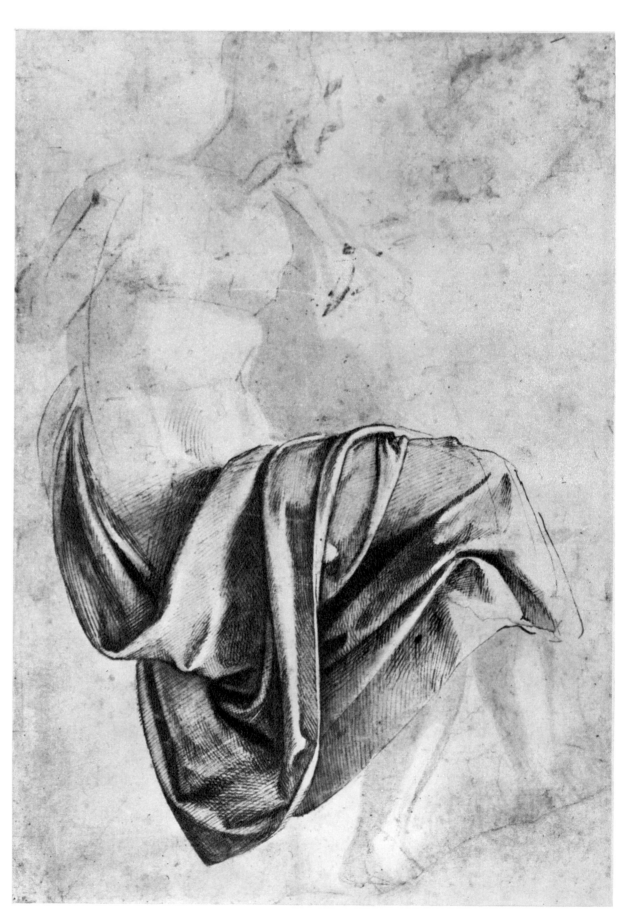

70 Study of Sibyl. London, British Museum (44).

71 Nude man with book. Florence, Uffizi (43).

72 Nude man with book. Florence, Uffizi (43).

rather a sort of repertory of heads, which Michelangelo made for himself in the manner of *exempla* to be used later in the course of his work." Now, in order to decide whether the sanguine drawing of Casa Buonarroti (Fig. 78) [60] refers to the Madonna of the Doni *tondo* or to the Jonah of the Sistine Chapel, we may do better than rely on disputable external arguments, and instead rely on an impression of atmosphere, noting that at the basis of the style of the *tondo* there is still something tense and vibrant, corresponding to the style of the drawings of that period (cf. Figs. 19-21 and 22-23), whereas here the theme of a head in inspired mood is mastered with absolute detached sureness, ideally depersonalized, raised to an Olympus above the earth.

In other respects the stylistic aspect is quite similar, in the sure lines of the diagonal hatching, in the strong pencil shading, in the barely hinted-at portions out of focus, to the superb drawing of an old man in meditation, resembling the face of Zachariah (Fig. 75).[61]

The head in sanguine should perhaps be thought of not as a study, but as a redoing (perhaps from a drawing he had kept) of the beautiful motif of the head of the Virgin in the Doni *tondo* (keeping its design, turned toward the left and only accentuating the foreshortening from below and turning it until the right eye all but disappears), but now it needed only to be turned in the opposite direction to yield the head of Jonah.

It has been said, however, that on the margin of the great manner of the Vault there flourishes along its entire edge, in the zone that is symbolically more earthly and subject to endless becoming (Tolnay), the Mannerist " caprice," as it were a useful counterweight to that sublime soaring, a necessary relief from the extreme tension, an anchorage for that extreme idealistic sublimation, in the obscure but vital and solid depths of the unconscious. Some studies of heads may allude to this: thus, as Barocchi has keenly observed, the sanguine drawing of Casa Buonarroti (Fig. 76),[62] with a bowed interiorization, tired and almost bitter, while the touch slides into greater cursiveness; and in the same context we also cite the strange, heavy profile of an Oxford folio (Fig. 83),[63] whimsical and grotesque like the profiles in the lunettes, with on the other side of the sheet a man with a pig (Fig. 84), possibly an allusion to Hercules, but in any case on the same path of unaccountable fancy. And at this point it may be well to quote the ironical angry rhyme (Fig. 61):

I have made myself a goiter in this labor
As does the water to cats in Lombardy...
My loins have now come through into my belly
I make my rump by counterweight a crupper
And make my steps in vain without my eyes.
My rind in front of me keeps stretching out,
And to bend back I tie up in a knot,
And stretch myself just like a Syrian bow.
But error-bound and strange
The judgment rises that the mind doth make
That cometh twisted in through twisted ways
And my painting dead
Defend thus, Giovanni, and my honor,
Not being in the right place, nor I a painter.

[40] Cf. Barocchi, Commento, II, N. 429, pp. 623 ff.
This list does not include (except for the sketches of the sheet of the Arch. Buonarroti Cod. XIII 145 v., Tolnay 2°, N. 40, but not relevant here) the following drawings related to the Sistine vault: 1) British Museum 1895, 9, 15, 498 v. (the r. is our Fig. 7, the Alchemist), with a head (and hand) supposed to be for the created Adam or for certain nudes (Berenson, Fig. 582), a drawing whose authenticity has been questioned; 2) the female head 7 F of Casa Buonarroti, examined elsewhere here (Pl. XXXII); the later date proposed by others (Wilde, Barocchi) is correct; it has also been linked to the Hosea triangle in the Sistine (cf. Tolnay, 2°, Figs. 141-2) and to the Manasseh lunette (*ibid.* Fig. 159), as well as to the Libyan Sibyl; 3) the sheets: N. 5 of the Teyler Museum, Haarlem (Berenson N. 1465, 569 and 584) for a Nude and the angels of the Creation of Adam; N. 7 *ibid.*, likewise for the Nudes and the Creation (Tolnay, 2°, Fig. 242); N. 1926, 10, 9, 1 of the British Museum (Berenson N. 1519 A r., Fig. 581), relating to created Adam; unnumbered Cleveland drawing (Berenson N. 1397 B-I, Fig. 567; and Tolnay, II, Figs. 244-5), still on the themes of the Nudes and the Creation; N. 860 Louvre (Berenson N. 1598 B, Figs. 575 and 571), for nudes; and N. 18720 F, Uffizi (Berenson N. 1399 D, Figs. 573 and 572); Ashmolean Museum N. 298, for the Jehosaphat (Berenson N. 1563, Fig. 580); but all these sheets are of dubious authenticity (cf. Tolnay, II, pp. 206 ff.).

[41] The study in the British Museum (1859, 6, 25, 567; ink and charcoal for the limbs; 27.5×38.6 cm.) is held by Tolnay (II, 36) to be the first idea for the vault of the Sistine. The connections that have been drawn between the studies of arms and hands with figures that were actually executed on the vault (Frey, Thode, Tolnay) seem a bit generic. On the verso (Fig. 62) the small sketch of a sibyl (?) ties up well with that of the Detroit drawing (Fig. 59) and certainly in a way anticipates the two Medici princes in San Lorenzo (Tolnay, II, N. 11 A, who, however, considers this verso to be a school piece).

[42] The drawing of the Institute of Arts, Detroit (ink and black pencil; 25×36 cm.) appears to be closely contemporaneous with the London sheet just examined (Fig. 60), that is, a very early stage of thinking for the Sistine, which was begun May 10, 1508. Berenson (N. 1624 B) and Bertini have doubted its authenticity. Wilde holds that the sturdy Sibyl

74 Study with nude men. Florence, Casa Buonarroti (48).

73 Female figure. London, British Museum (49).

on the verso (Fig. 59) may be a first idea, later changed, for the Delphic Sibyl. Tolnay (II, **N.** 37 and 12 A), who accepts only the recto as authentic, relates the torso study to the Sacrifice of Noah, and the arm to the created Adam. Shown
in the 1964 Exposition (Barocchi, *Catalogo*, N. 16).

[43] The two studies (Uffizi, 17379-80 F; ink; 10.8×6.2 cm.) have no direct referent in the Sistine vault; the idea has
therefore been suggested either of the figures of the Twelve Apostles originally planned, or the bearers of the Books of
Genealogy, formerly in the lunettes over the altar, later destroyed to make room for the Last Judgment. Cf. Barocchi,
Exposition 1964, Nos. 19-20 (and previous Nos. 13-14). For Tolnay (II, N. 14 A) they are pieces of the school.

[44] On the recto of the drawing (British Museum, 1887, 5, 2, 118; charcoal touched up with ink and water color;
38.7×26 cm.; the verso is in charcoal) the figure is sufficiently like the design of the Erythraean Sibyl (Tolnay, II,
1945, N. 38, sees it as a pupil's copy, possibly by Daniele da Volterra; for Berenson, it is authentic, except for the ink
and water color retouching). The verso too (the sketch is of the greatest importance for the general design of the Sistine
vault, marking the passage from the project with the Apostles to the definitive one) relates to a figure of the type of the
Erythraean Sibyl (Tolnay, except for this sketch, calls the figure and the hand below pupil's work).

[45] However, caution is called for in what has been said because other sketches in Oxford, copies of lunettes in the Sistine (Tolnay, II, Figs. 248-50) and attributed to a pupil by Tolnay (Silvio Falconi?), have qualities akin to Drawings
13379-80 F of the Uffizi (Figs. 71-72). However, the squared-off and generic trend seen in the Apostle in the certain

421

75 Head of old man. Florence, Uffizi (61).

76 Head. Florence, Casa Buonarroti (62).

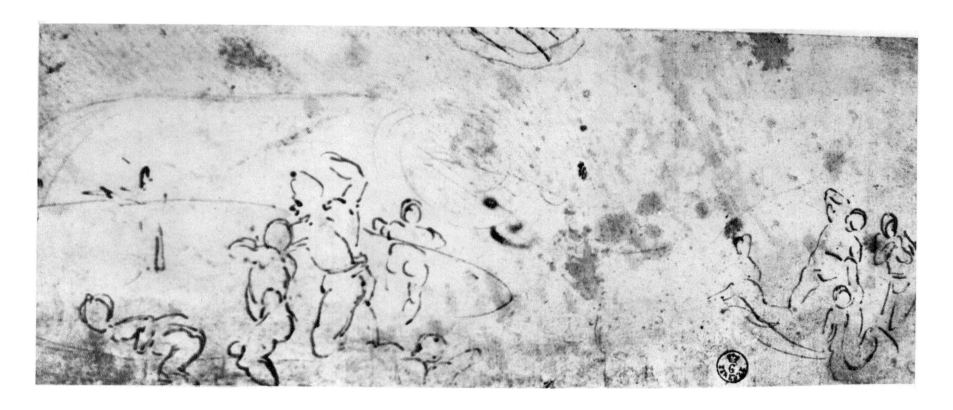

77 Sketch for the Flood. Florence, Uffizi (46).

drawing of the British Museum (Fig. 60) is worked out precisely in the figures of the lunettes, for which, according to one hypothesis, the two sketches in the Uffizi mentioned above were intended.

[46] Uffizi 17381 F; ink; 10×24.8 cm. Only Tolnay and Dussler have doubted its authenticity, but this negative judgment (it must be granted in all objectivity) is in keeping with the fact that virtually all the figures are found in the background of the fresco, making one think of a recall from memory, rather than first thoughts. Cf. to the contrary, decisively for authenticity, Barocchi, 1962, N. 12.

[47] Archivio Buonarroti XIII, 111; ink; 28.3×20 cm. Cf. Barocchi, Exposition 1964, N. 176, giving the text of the poem (cited here in part at the end of the section), and Tolnay's comment. And cf. Barocchi, Commento, II, pp. 447-8. The sheet has been dated as 1510 or 1511.

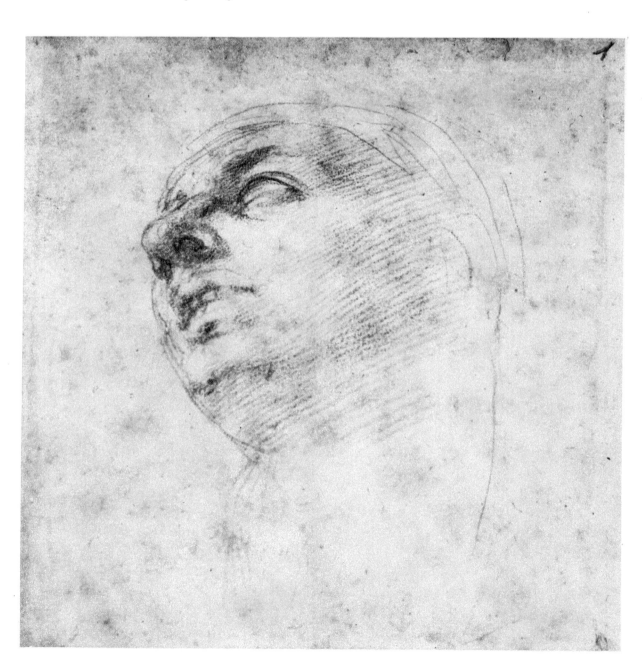

78 Head. Florence, Casa Buonarroti (60).

Folio 18 722 F of the Uffizi (Berenson, Fig. 563), in which an idea for the Eternal creating Adam seems to be combined with the picture of the painter taking his leave, would appear to be linked in whim with those moments of weariness, which however could never turn aside Buonarroti's fanatical diligence. The drawing is 25.5×35 cm. Above, in sanguine, a study for the Eternal of the Creation of Adam; the legs on the other side in the middle of the sheet (in silver point) may be referred to some Nude; but it is hard to place the small figure that seems to be scaling the rocks of a mountain (in ink), some (e. g. Berenson, N. 1399 E) seeing in it a first idea for the Sistine lunettes, others (Tolnay, II, 1945, N. 9 A, who considers it a school drawing) regarding it as a full-blown cupola. On the verso (Barocchi, 1962 Pl. XXV) other studies for the Nudes.

[48] The references of the drawing's studies for Nudes (Casa Buonarroti 75 F; black pencil and ink; 41.4×27 cm.) are for the Nude to the left of the Cumaean Sibyl, the one to the left of Ezekiel, perhaps for the one to the right of Jeremiah and for the nude to the right of Isaiah; a profile of a cornice and the inscription " *infelici* (?) *belgli* " [unfortunate (?) beauties]. Cf. Barocchi, Exposition, 1964, N. 21. For Tolnay (II, 1945, N. 16 A) and Berenson (N. 1668 A) this is a drawing of the school; for Barocchi, only the ink retouches are not autographical.

[49] For this drawing (1859, 6, 25, 558 of the British Museum; charcoal; 28×22 cm.) Berenson's definition (N. 1480), " confused scribbling " is really a bit inadequate; but the reference to the Forebears of Christ on the Sistine vault may be improved by considering the sloping bronze nudes of the corbels between the thrones.

[50] The drawing in the British Museum (1859, 6, 25, 555; ink; 24.9×16 cm.) is given a high value by Berenson (N. 1487), who relates it to the crucified Haman, while Tolnay (II, N. 24 A) denied both this connection and the authenticity. The two figures might conceivably be referred to the Deluge as well.

[51] Those that go back to these portions are in fact to be regarded as school copies, e. g. 12 F in Casa Buonarroti, of

79 Study for Adam driven out of Paradise. Florence, Casa Buonarroti (57).

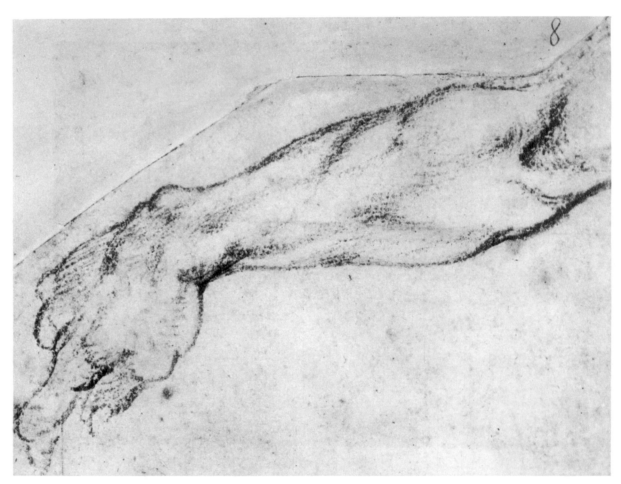

81 Study of arm. Florence, Casa Buonarroti (58).

80 Torso. London, British Museum (59).

the youth reading in the Execution of Haman (Barocchi, 1962, Pl. 284 and N. 176); or Uffizi 18721 F (Barocchi *ibid.*, N. 175), whose connection with the Sistine is in any case dubious. The link between Drawing 4112 in the Louvre (Berenson 1599, Figs. 741 and 590) and the Forebears of Christ is likewise tenuous, as is the authenticity.

[52] The drawing (sanguine, ink and bister; 42×28 cm.; 1887, 5, 2, 115 in British Museum; Berenson 1486; Wilde, *Cat.* 1959, N. 29 and Pl. LII; Dussler 323) has traditionally been referred to the Isaiah; Steinmann preferred a Sibyl. The verso (Wilde, 1953, Pl. CXL), with a church ceremony, is believed to be by a Raphaelite Florentine artist.

[53] In the superb sheet of the Metropolitan Museum of New York (recto sanguine, verso charcoal; 29×21.5 cm.), presented in detail by Bryson Burrough in *Metropolitan Museum Bulletin* 1952, pp. 6-14, Tolnay (II, N. 46 and 13 A) has seen fit to raise serious doubts as to the authenticity of the verso (and, for the recto, the replica of the head and the torso sketch); Berenson (N. 1544 D) has placed the curious apelike figure on the verso in relation with the Forebears of Christ. Tolnay, with Brinckmann, date the sheet about 1511.

[54] The drawing 297 (or 23) of the Oxford Ashmolean Museum; sanguine for the larger studies and ink; 28.8×19.9 cm.) relates to the little spirit to the right of the Libyan Sibyl, the right hand of the Sibyl, and (subsequently) six superb studies of Prisons and a cornice; on the verso, studies of legs, perhaps for a Prison (Frey). Berenson (N. 1562) tends to date the sheet from the autumn or winter of 1510, when there was a break in the work on the Sistine and Michelangelo could go back to the project for the tomb of Julius II; while Tolnay (II, N. 47) gives the date as about 1512-13, because of the relationship to the project for the tomb, which was resumed in 1513.

[55] Cf. I, pp. 289-90.

[56] The four studies on the verso of the London drawing (1859, 6, 25, 568; ink or charcoal; 19×24.5 cm.) certainly relate to the Youths on the vault of the Sistine, although more precise identification is difficult (for the larger study,

Tolnay indicates the nude above Ezekiel); the recto, with its charcoal modeled torso, probably has the same referent (cf. Steinmann) while Berenson (1484) thought of a Dead Christ. Tolnay (II, 1945, N. 41) assigns to Michelangelo only the kneeling figure on the verso, as a recall of an antique statue (Kriegbaum), and notes the *second thought* of the raised right leg; the other three sketches are school work, in his opinion. Wölfflin first pointed out the relation to the study of the kneeling *Cupid* of the Victoria and Albert Museum formerly attributed to Michelangelo and now to Danti. But could this kneeling figure be a first idea for the created Adam?

[57] The drawing (Casa Buonarroti 45 F; black pencil; 26.2×19.1 cm.) has had doubts cast on it, unjustly (from Berenson to Popp and Tolnay). The reference to Adam expelled is clear, and it is useless to substitute complicated hypotheses, like those of Goldscheider, of a late date and reference to the cartoon of *Noli me tangere* of 1531 (cf. Barocchi, 1962, N. 18). On the other hand, Drawing 64 F of Casa Buonarroti is believed to be a copy of the expelled Adam (Barocchi, 1962, N. 238).

[58] The excellent small drawing 8 F of Casa Buonarroti (black pencil; 9.8×13.1 cm.) has been condemned as a copy only by Tolnay (II, N. 23 A) and Dussler (N. 413). But Barocchi (1962, N. 20) vindicates both the authenticity and the dating at the time of the Sistine; the more definite references that have been made, to the God the Father in the Creation of Adam (Frey) or the Drunkenness of Noah (Wilde), are problematical.

82 Two in torment. London, British Museum (50).

◁ 83 Profile. Oxford, Ashmolean Museum (63).

84 Man with pig. Oxford, Ashmolean Museum
(63).

[59] The drawing (British Museum 1859, 6, 25, 563; charcoal; 22.6 × 10.7 cm.) has been referred to the cartoon for Cascina (Berenson, N. 1478) for the soldier helping a comrade to buckle on his armor, or to the Adam tempted (Tolnay II, 1945, N. 3 A: as a school copy); and even (Wilde) to the Victory (Pal. Vecchio) for the tomb of Julius II.

[60] For the sanguine drawing 1 F of Casa Buonarroti (19.9 × 17.2 cm.) there are two fundamental theses: reference to the Madonna of the Doni *tondo*, about 1505 (Berenson), and reference to the Sistine Jonah, about 1511 (Tolnay). Of the two, we prefer the second (but with an eye to compromise, as will be seen) because of the greater degree of agreement in the accentuated foreshortening as seen from below, and the pathos of the half-opened mouth. Barocchi makes the contrary evaluation (1962, N. 8). On the verso (Barocchi, Pl. CCCXLII), two crude sketches of heads, certainly the work of pupils, caricature the splendid drawing.

[61] Uffizi, 18718 F; silver point; 43.2 × 28 cm. On the verso (Barocchi, 1962, Pl. XLIII), further studies of legs. Barocchi dismisses both the usual reference to portraits of Julius II and that to Zachariah, preferring Ezekiel (but the static concentrated head leads one to prefer Zachariah).

[62] The sanguine drawing of Casa Buonarroti (47 F; 12.3 × 14.2 cm.) has been convincingly placed in the years of the Sistine, in which there is a similar typology (e. g., in a youth holding up a nude on the right in the Deluge). Barocchi (1962, N. 22) notes the special affinity with the " less idealized faces " of the Sistine triangles and lunettes. I note (not as a suspicion but because of the coincidence with seventeenth-century naturalism reacting against the abstractions of the previous century) that Commodi, a frequent visitor at Casa Buonarroti, sometimes derived his inspiration from a similar typology.

[63] The drawing in the Ashmolean Museum (N. 316; sanguine; 28.2 × 19.8 cm.) has been linked by Berenson (N. 1551) with the Forebears of Christ in the Sistine and dated about 1509; then thought to be later. The description (I, 1961, p. 286) given is: " moody young ruffian in a moment of violent negativity."

427

Architectural drawings
up to the final departure from Florence
(c. 1515-34)

The drawings (as usual, giving only partial documentation) reflect the architectural activity that Michelangelo was called on to engage in during the twenty years following the painting of the Sistine vault.

There were the famous Papal-Medicean commissions for the façade of San Lorenzo (1516-20), for the Medici Chapel in the same basilica (1520-34), for the Biblioteca Laurenziana (1524-34), and still other things there, in addition to work in connection with the tomb of Julius II; later, Michelangelo even became military architect for the defense of his republican Florence. We shall deal first with the architectural drawings of this period, and

85 Studies of Roman capitals and bases. Florence, Casa Buonarroti (64).

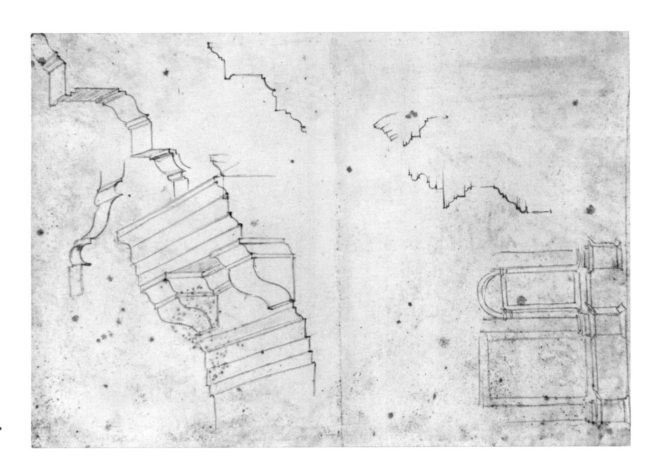

86 Studies from Roman monuments. Florence, Casa Buonarroti (65-66).

87 Studies from Roman monuments. Florence, Casa Buonarroti (65-66).

then the figure drawings, connected or not, related to his parallel activity as sculptor and painter.

The sheets of notes of Roman monuments, done in sanguine from about 1516 on, are not direct but taken from an earlier handbook, the Coner codex. They are Figs. 85,[64] 86-87,[65-66] 88-89,[67] 90,[68] and bring out Michelangelo's method as a copyist, " personal and summary, changing the point of view and eliminating the details " of the cold model of the notebook.

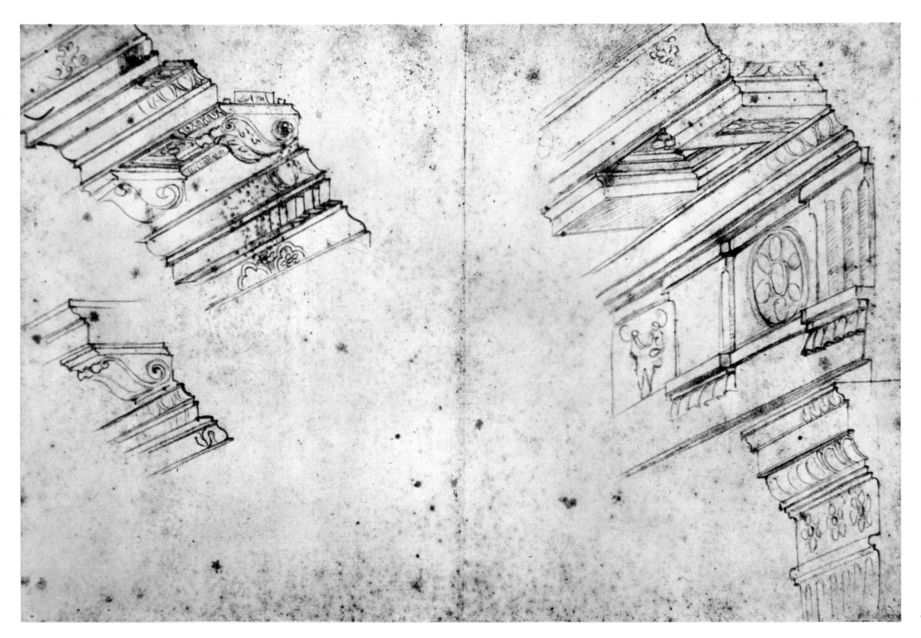

430

Although this particular circumstance, that of being copies for study, makes them unique in Michelangelo's architectural drawing, and " as it were [they] can find a worthy parallel only in the youthful drawings from Giotto to Masaccio," yet " in them Michelangelo reveals great freedom, but one restrained by ' experience '... and hence sober in aspect, although generalized and in search of new solutions..." (Barocchi). She also calls attention, in connection with Drawing Buonarroti 2 A (Figs. 86, 87), to the " powerful chiaroscuro emphases " and the " allusive detail."

Here, as compared with the youthful drawings from Giotto and Masaccio, we can see the new and different field of culture fertilized by these studies, that is the sense of the wealth and monumentality of antiquity, which the sanguine renders with a touch that is sure, discreet, calm, and serene.

These copies too soon bore fruit in the form of vigorous independent studies of architectural details, some of which will be found reproduced in th esection on Michelangelo as architect.

Here we shall merely mention them in notes, referring to the treatment by others.[69] Thus, of the documentation in drawings for the façade of San Lorenzo, referred to elsewhere, we confine ourselves to the first small note for the front elevation (Fig. 95),[70] as concise as it is breath-taking in its revolutionary conception of transferring all the weight above the first order on the active colossal scale; and we also give instances of the drawings for merely working purposes, which are still suggestive as tangible documentation (Fig. 94 [71] and Fig. 93).[72] Of

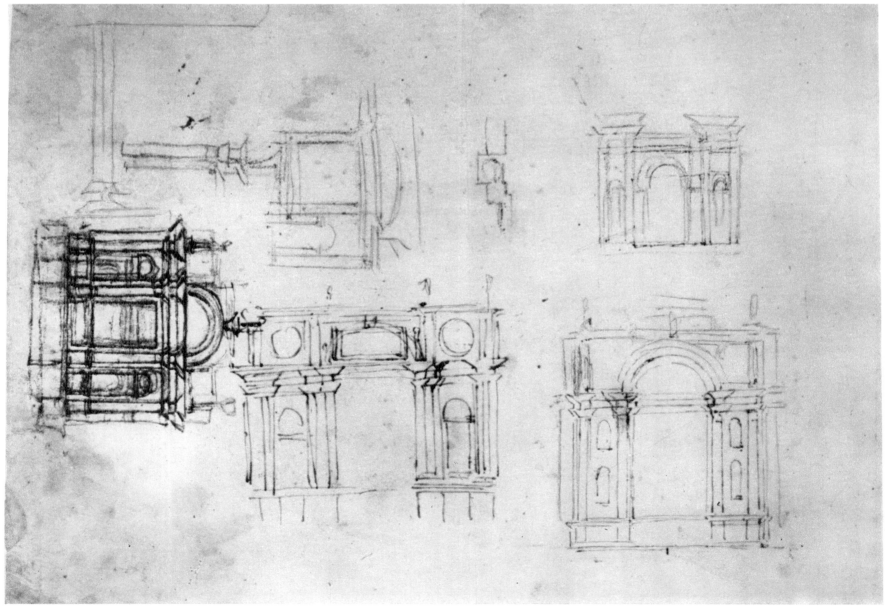

431

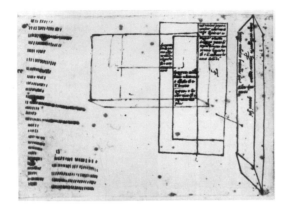

92 Marble block with calculations. Florence, Casa Buonarroti (73).

the same nature is one of the many sketches in Casa Buonarroti for blocks of marble, perhaps relating to the tomb of Julius II (c. 1516) (Fig. 92).[73]

There is richer documentation to be given for the Medici tombs of the New Sacristy, designed in 1520, although we shall not go into their special architectural-sculptural character, but deal only with their graphic side.[74] This varied evidence presents us with a powerfully suggestive mastery of touch, whether in a vertical two-ordered profile of a wall, now considered to be linked to that chapel (Fig. 96);[75] or the idea of a massive central mausoleum having sarcophagi with the highest of lids (Fig. 98);[76] or a double wall tomb for the Medici dukes (Fig. 100).[77] This last is a charcoal sketch showing a rapid increase in height and organization in sculptural motifs of the kiosk above the sarcophagi (from the left side to the right); the imagination seems not only to pursue the fragmentation and animation of the calm unity of the wall in an unceasing general vibrant dialectic of projecting structures but also, by means of various curving rhythms of the curious sarcophagi and river-type statues at the bottom, to tend toward wavy linear sculptural outcomes; and majestic breakers at the base, ending the motion of the wall, impinge upon the sensibility of the observer. In a sketch of a previous stage (Fig. 99),[78] however, we see the idea in a still germinal and rather timid form, in a broad horizontal organization; while in the last version, not too different from the actual solutions (Fig. 97),[79] the light, pictural touch seems to indulge in effects of harmonious grace and decorative projections, as in the rich panoply of the peak.

In the project for the double tomb of the Magnifici on the entrance side of the Sacristy (Figs. 101, 102),[80] which was never built, we see instead a schematic and lean graphic method, despite the warmth of the ideas, rapidly changing and amending and, as in the sarcophagi (Fig. 102), alluding to unusual modes or Baroque ideas full of conceits, like that of Fame (barely sketched) seated directly above them and cutting off the epitaphs. The remarkably vigorous and full-bodied definition of certain details, like the bases of the pilasters of the Medici Chapel (Fig. 103)[81] or the plans and front elevations of the "thrones" (Fig. 104),[82] is rendered masterfully and unconventionally by the sanguine, "with vigorous spontaneity."

Although what is presented here concerning the designing of the Laurentian Library (1524-26; 1530-34) lacks almost all the most interesting items,[83] it still will illustrate some of the gradations of the drawing, from the sketch for the two terminal appendices of the well of the

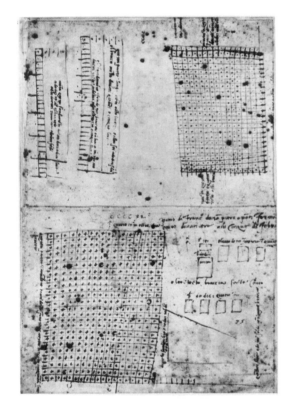

93 Calculations for wall building. Florence, Casa Buonarroti (72).

95 Sketch for the façade of S. Lorenzo. Florence, Casa Buonarroti (70).

94 Plan of column. Florence, Casa Buonarroti (71).

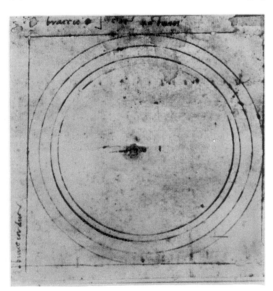

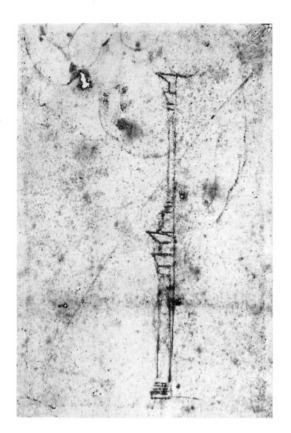

96 Wall profile. Florence, Casa Buonarroti (75).

Library (Fig. 105),[84] resolving them on one side in the staired Vestibule and on the other into a chapel with a cupola, to the other sketch, scrawled even more summarily but powerfully, for the compartmentation of the ceiling;[85] and to the elevation for the wall of the great hall, for which the pen states a rise with a more complicated and charged articulation than the one actually erected (Fig. 106);[86] and to the studies for doors and windows (Fig. 108),[87] (Fig. 110),[88] in which the touch tries and savors the new union of antitraditional solutions and a restlessness that is already Mannerist, but here without any hint of capriciousness and effort, but rather of calmly vigorous innovation; and down to the drawing (Fig. 109) in which, against the background of one, the pilasters of the Vestibule balustrade, there projects, almost surrealistically, a hand that seems to be pointing. The study is referred to the Giuliano of the Sacristy or to the cartoon for Venus and Cupid, and in it we can appreciate, one might almost say contrast, the complex sublimity that Michelangelo had attained at the same time in depicting animated form.

For the other architectural studies of various kinds that can be dated from the same period, 1524 to 1536, a presentation little more than merely visual may suffice here: a sketch for the

98 Designs for middle tomb for the Sacristy of S. Lorenzo. London, British Museum (76).

97 Study of tomb for the Sacristy of S. Lorenzo. London, British Museum (79).

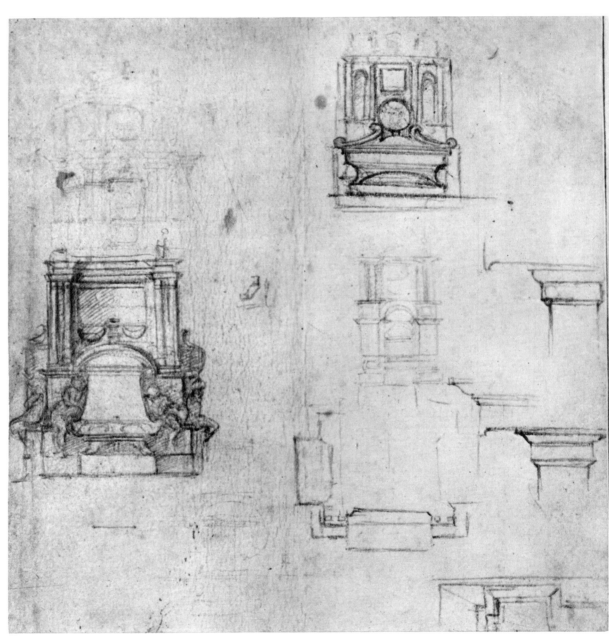

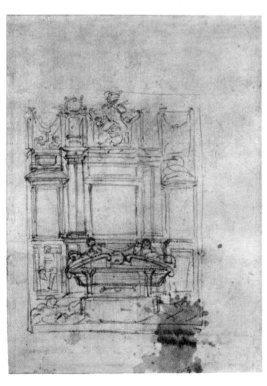

podium of the tomb of Julius II, that tormented enterprise (Fig. 112);[89] the elevation and plan of a majestic portal or altar (Fig. 111);[90] a fountain dazzlingly done in ink on white paper, with mature sureness of touch and strong shading, as if presaging the execution in marble (Fig. 113);[91] the plan of a house (Fig. 116), with on its verso the feathered wings of an eagle, for some decorative motif (Fig. 117);[92] a small shrine with a niche, of classic charm (Fig. 114);[93] an octagonal elevation (pulpit?) and figure (Figs. 118 and 115).[94]

[84] The drawing (Casa Buonarroti 1 A; sanguine; 28.2 × 42.4 cm.) is related to similar studies in sanguine (Casa Buonarroti: 2 A, cf. Figs. 86-7; 3 A, cf. Barocchi 1962, Pls. XLIX and LIV; 4 A, cf. *ibid.* Pls. LII and LVI; 8 A, cf. Fig. 90; and British Museum: 1859, 6, 25, 560-1, Figs. 88-9; 1859, 6, 25, 560-2), so that the suggestion has been advanced that this is a group, perhaps even a notebook, dated about 1516. These studies of ancient and modern monuments of Rome prove to derive from those of the Coner Codex of the Soane Museum in London, dated about 1515 and attributed to the learned Giov. Batt. Cordini da Sangallo, called il Gobbo; or perhaps from a prototype of that codex. Moreover, the attribution to Michelangelo has been called into question or limited to portions; but it has been vigorously

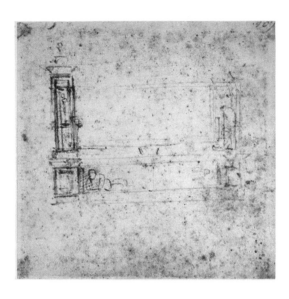

99 Sketch of double tomb for S. Lorenzo. Florence, Casa Buonarroti (78).

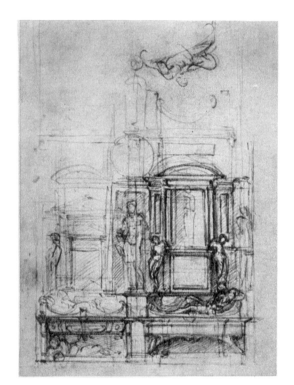

100 Design of double tomb for the Sacristy of S. Lorenzo. London, British Museum (77).

101 Sketch for the tomb of the Magnificent in S. Lorenzo. London, British Museum (80).

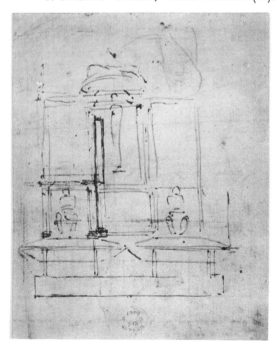

defended, in particular by Frey, Wilde, and Barocchi. For references to the Coner Codex and the precise Roman architectural details of these and other related drawing (references made possible precisely because of the information on the Coner Codex), cf. Barocchi, 1962, N. 23-27 (and also 1964, N. 29-33). Reproduction of the verso of our drawing in Barocchi, 1962, Pl. XLV, and here in the section on architecture.

[65-66] Drawing 2 A of Casa Buonarroti; sanguine; 29×42.8 cm. Cf. preceding note.

[67] Drawings 1859, 6, 25, 560-1 r. and v. of the British Museum; sanguine; 28.9×21.8 cm. Cf. esp. Wilde, 1953, N. 18; and Note 64 here. On the verso of the other similar London drawing (Wilde, N. 19, Pls. XXXIII and XXXV), there are notes on the San Lorenzo façade.

[68] Drawing 8 A, Casa Buonarroti; sanguine; 28.8×42.8 cm. Cf. Note 64. The arch is the Arch of Constantine.

[69] We refer to the following drawings: 5 A of Casa Buonarroti, entablatures, cornices, and capitals (Barocchi, 1962, N. 28); 101 A, ibid., for the windows with curved supports of Pal. Medici, 1517 (Barocchi, 1962, N. 29); the powerful studies of composite capitals of drawings 55 A, 83 A, 82 A, 56 A, 86 A, 87 A, ibid. (Barocchi, 1962, N. 31-5); 110 A ibid. with two altar canopies and a sarcophagus (Barocchi, 1962, N. 36); 114 A v. ibid. with tomb designs relating to San Silvestro in Capite, 1518 (Barocchi, 1962, N. 37); sketches for the cupola of S. Maria del Fiore of drawings 50 A and 66 A, ibid. (Barocchi, 1962, N. 38-39). In addition to Drawing 1859, 6, 25, 559 r in the British Museum (Fig. 91)—charcoal and ink; 22×29 cm.—which has been attributed either to the Tomb of Julius II (Tolnay, III, N. 67; with the date 1525-26) or to the New Sacristy, or the Tomb of Leo X in Santa Maria sopra Minerva in Rome, cf. also Berenson, N. 1499; Wilde, N. 22.

[70] For Michelangelo's design for the façade (1516-17; execution begun 1518-20), the main drawings (in addition to 91 A of Casa Buonarroti, shown here: sanguine; 8.8×8.9 cm.; cf. Barocchi, 1962, N. 42) are, still in Casa Buonarroti: 44 A, 47 A, 43 A (final project: see Pl. XXVII), which are reproduced and examined in the section on architecture; also shown at the 1964 Exposition (Barocchi, Catalogo, N. 49-51).

[71] The plan for a column and base (Casa Buonarroti 34 A; ink; 12.2×12.3 cm.) cannot with certainty be referred to the façade for San Lorenzo.

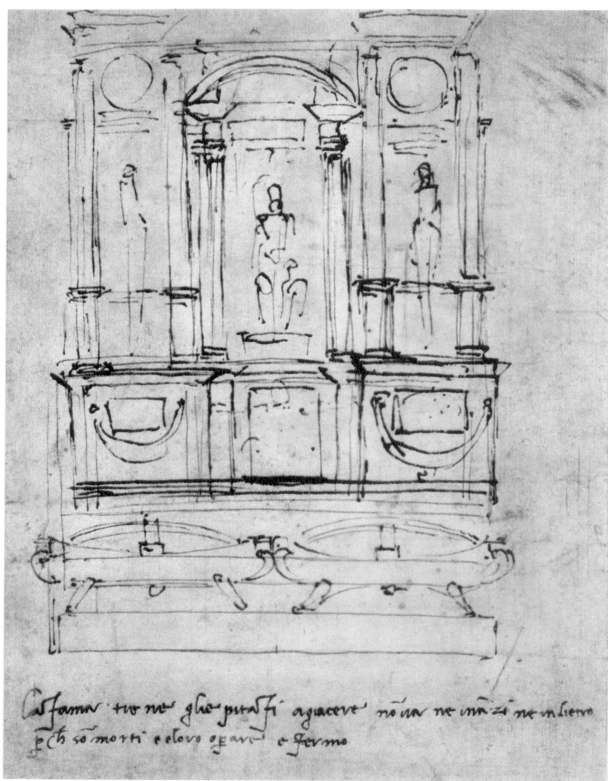

[72] The drawing has accounts for masonry work (Casa Buonarroti, 75 A v., 29.5×44.2 cm.). Cf. Barocchi, 1962, N. 50.

[73] Casa Buonarroti 68 A; ink; 20.4×30.6 cm. It has autograph instructions for the stonecutters and accounts in vertical columns (on verso).

[74] For the New Sacristy, we refer above all to Tolnay's book (III, 1948). The section in this volume on Michelangelo as architect discusses drawings 88 A, 71 A, 49 A, 93 A, various plans for the Medici tombs, in Casa Buonarroti; cf. also Barocchi 1964, N. 59-63.

[75] Drawing 57 A r. of Casa Buonarroti; sanguine; 15.6×10.1 cm. Formerly thought to be for the façade of San Lorenzo (and, I think, not without reason, since the double order, almost equal in proportions, is inconceivable in the New Sacristy). Cf. Barocchi, 1962, N. 56.

[76] Drawing 1859-6-25-545 r., British Museum; charcoal; 22.3×21.2 cm. Cf. Tolnay, III, N. 56 and p. 36; Berenson, N. 1494; Wilde, N. 25.

[77] British Museum, 1859-5-14-822 v.; charcoal; 26.4×18.8 cm. Cf. Tolnay, III, p. 37 and N. 52. The plan on the recto is also of great importance. Cf. Tolnay, *ibid.* N. 51. And cf. Berenson, N. 1495; Wilde, N. 26.

[78] Casa Buonarroti 107 A; black pencil; 14.9×15.3 cm.

[79] British Museum, 1859-5-14-823 r.; charcoal; 28.8×20.7 cm. Tolnay, III, p. 38 and N. 57; Berenson, N. 1497; Wilde, N. 27.

[80] British Museum, 1859-6-25-543 r. and v.; ink; 21.6×16.9 cm. Cf. Tolnay, III, N. 58-9 and p. 39; Berenson, N. 1496; Wilde, N. 28. About end of 1520-21.

[81] Casa Buonarroti 9 A; sanguine; 28.2×21.3 cm. Similar and related is 10 A, *ibid.*, reproduced in the section on Michelangelo as architect. Cf. Barocchi, *Catalogo* Exposition 1964, N. 63-4.

103 Bases for the Sacristy of S. Lorenzo. Florence, Casa Buonarroti (81).

◁ 102 Sketch for the tomb of the Magnificent in S. Lorenzo. London, British Museum (80).

104 Studies for the "thrones" in the Sacristy of S. Lorenzo. Florence, Casa Buonarroti (82).

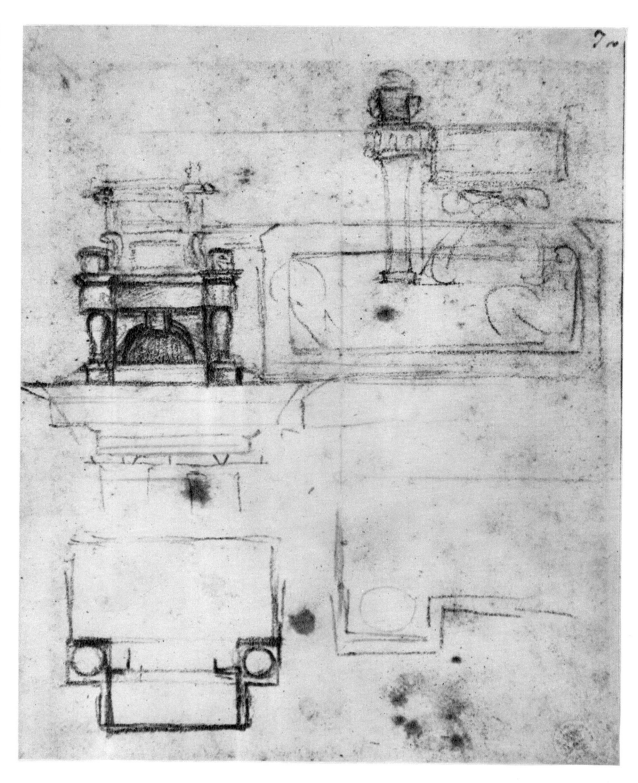

435

106 Wall design for the Laurentian Library. Florence, Casa Buonarroti (86).

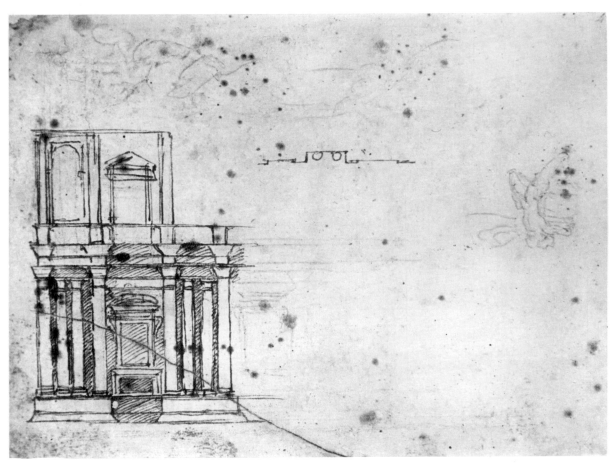

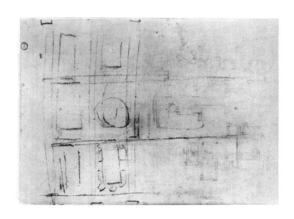

105 Sketch for the ceiling of the Laurentian Library. Oxford, Ashmolean Museum (84).

[82] Casa Buonarroti 72 A; sanguine; 16.7×13.2 cm.

[83] Of these, the following will be found in the section on Michelangelo as architect: Casa Buonarroti 48 A (study for the side elevations of the Vestibule, datable 1525); 62 A (interesting sheet of researches on cornice profiles); 79 A-80 A (studies for the Piccola Libreria, 1525); 92 A (projects for the Vestibule staircase, 1525); 94 A (study for bench with seated reader); 126 A (study of ornaments for library ceiling).

[84] Oxford, Ashmolean Museum, 40 v. (308 v.); pencil; 26.4×38.4 cm. Cf. Tolnay in *Critica d'Arte* 1955, pp. 237 ff., who publishes it, identifying it with the first "idea" for the "compartmentation of the ceiling" that Buonarroti sent to Rome prior to 3-4-1524, and that the Pope liked. The recto is our Fig. 107 relating to the New Sacristy; ink and bistre; cf. Berenson, N. 1566.

[85] Another sketch is the one in Casa Buonarroti (89 A r.), which is a study of the two terminal appendages of the well of the library, resolving them on one side into the staired vestibule, on the other into a chapel with cupola. A *terminus ante quem* is given by the Pope's rejection (letter of G. F. Fattucci to Michelangelo, dated 12-4-1525): "As for the chapel at the head of the library, he says he doesn't want chapels, but wants something like a secret library." Cf. Barocchi, 1962, N. 80 and Pl. CXXII.

[86] Casa Buonarroti 42 A r.: black pencil and pen; 20.9×29.3 cm. Datable early 1524. Cf. Barocchi, 1964, N. 79;

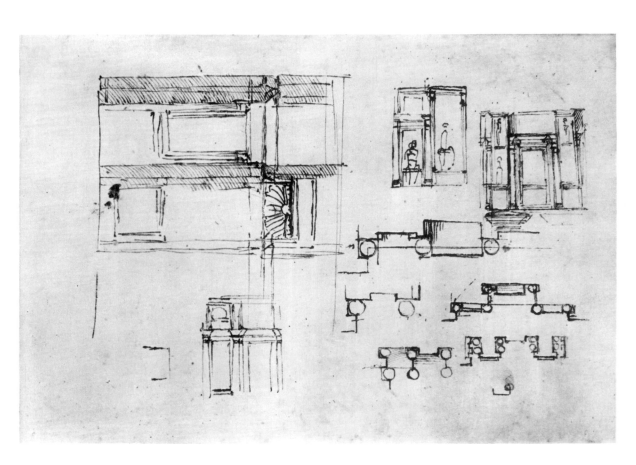

107 Plans and reliefs for the New Sacristy. Oxford, Ashmolean Museum (84).

110 Studies of windows for the Laurentian Library. London, British Museum (88).

108 Studies for doors or windows. Florence, Casa Buonarroti (87).

109 Hand and architectural framework. Florence, Casa Buonarroti (87).

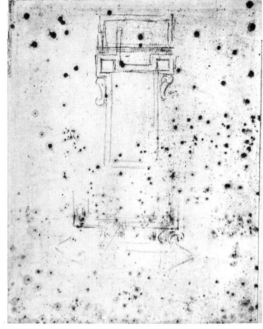

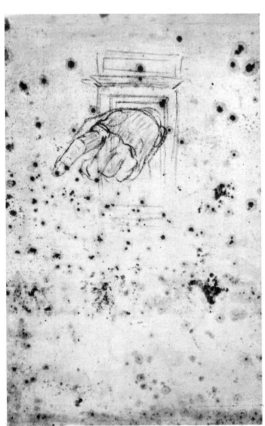

but I cannot agree with her and Dussler in denying the authenticity of the magnificent little sketch of Isaac, to the right, turned around (and cf. Barocchi, 1962, N. 78).

[87] Casa Buonarroti 37 A r.; black pencil; 37.3 × 28.2 cm. The verso is our Fig. 109 with the hand. Cf. Barocchi, 1964, N. 84.

[88] British Museum, 1859-6-25-550 v. (on recto, study of a door with the Papal coat of arms); ink; 28.4 × 20.9 cm. Cf. Dussler, 1959, N. 157; Wilde, N. 37.

[89] British Museum, 1859-5-14-824; ink; 23.6 × 14.8 cm. With autograph inscription by Michelangelo. Variously dated (1526; 1532; 1520; 1516); on this cf. Tolnay, IV, N. 127 and Wilde, N. 23.

[90] Casa Buonarroti 40 A r.; black pencil; 40 × 24.2 cm. Various suggested references (an altar for S. Apollonia or elsewhere; a wall tomb); cf. Barocchi, 1962, N. 98.

[91] Casa Buonarroti 73 A; ink; 11.7 × 16.2 cm. Another suggestion is a holy water stoup for a place nearby the New Sacristy (Tolnay).

[92] Casa Buonarroti 119 A; black pencil and sanguine; 22.3 × 35.2 cm. The reference of the plan is unidentified.

[93] Casa Buonarroti 112 A r.; sanguine and ink; 29.1 × 21.1 cm. The autograph date on the verso, 26-1-1524 gives a *terminus ante quem*. Unidentified reference of the study for the shrine. Cf. Barocchi, 1962, N. 100.

[94] Oxford, Ashmolean Museum 312; ink; 14.7 × 16.8 cm. In the same mount, the study of Fig. N. 313 (Fig. 115), ink and bister, 9.7 × 9.1 cm. Cf. Berenson N. 1567, and Dussler N. 198.

437

Studies for the fortification of Florence
(1528-30)

After April 6, 1529, Michelangelo was the governor and procurator general of the fortifications of Florence against the Imperial-Papal assault. It may not be forcing a circumstantial nexus to have this defense of political liberty coincide with the moment of Buonarroti's greatest

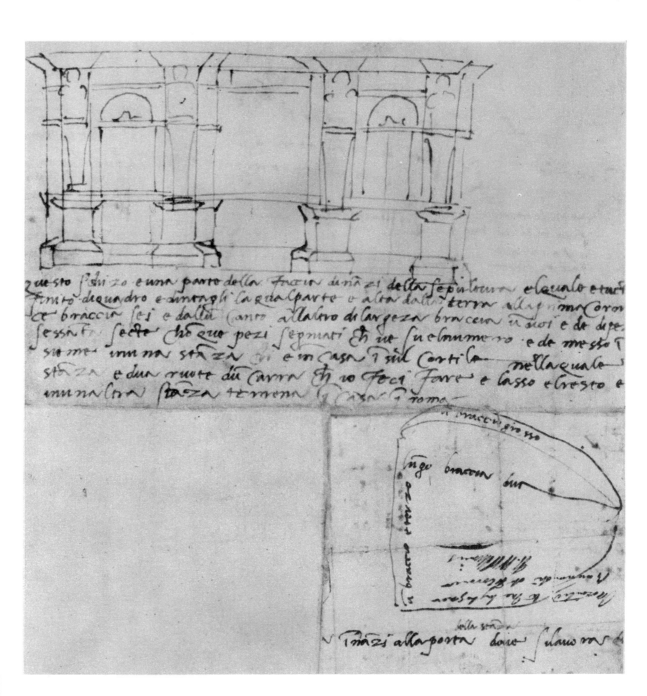

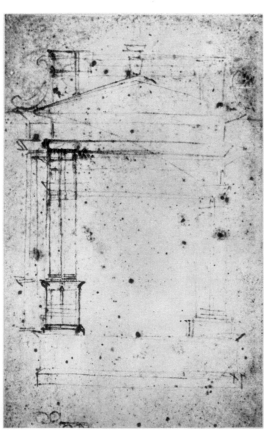

112 Sketch for the podium of Julius II's Tomb. London, British Museum (89).

111 Portal or altar. Florence, Casa Buonarroti (90).

liberty in creative imagination, as has recently been stated, with the condition that it may be realized more concretely perhaps than by means of certain analogies drawn between some remarkable designs for fortifications in Casa Buonarroti and present-day taste. Likewise, we are left a bit dubious by the references *à la page* made to Wright for the occasion, and by the elevations of extraordinary modernity deduced from faint traces on these drawings by Michelangelo.

Nonetheless, the importance given these sheets only recently (Tolnay, Wittkover, Scully) is amply justified.[95]

Here we shall confine ourselves to a preliminary indication of how the system projected by Michelangelo was to protect the entire city, concentrating the defense in the southern portion, it is true, where it was inevitable that the enemy would seize dangerous dominant positions on the hills, but also envisaging the creation of strategic strong points throughout the region this side of the Arno, on the plain, where " Michelangelo felt it was sufficient to have a few strongly fortified works before the principal paths of access or the salients of the perimeter defenses, to keep the enemy at arm's length and prevent him from setting up artillery in positions where they could effectively batter the walls; which, being high and hard to scale and to penetrate inside from, were sufficiently protected by the guard..." (Riva Palazzi).[96] Actually, the drawings relate not only to the Porta a S. Miniato and Porta a S. Pier Gattolini (or Porta Romana) and nearby points, but also to the Prato d'Ognissanti, to the Porta del Prato, to the Porta alla Giustizia (now Lungarno della Zecca), etc. These projected bastions have been imaginatively compared to armored insects planted at the outermost points of the city's plan; and in point of fact we see the projects gradually losing, in Michelangelo's imagination, the geometrical traits typical of the traditional fortifications of the Early Renaissance (and in Leonardo, as well), and instead taking on external and internal form as articulated organic structures, following a design that obeys inspirations that are no longer on the plane of geometrical-architectural abstraction and its physico-mathematical logic, but on the plane of vital naturalistic force molding its creatures in more original shapes, and obeying a more complex vitalistic logic of its own. "The bulwarks, with their zoomorphic suggestion, rush outwards psychologically assaulting and terrifying the adversary" (Zeri).

For example, compare the changes in the same project between various drawings. N. 23A (Fig. 120),[97] still of traditional structure, sets up a bastion in front of the gate, including it within the sides of an ideal triangle whose base is in the two recesses for the embrasures in the walls, and whose vertex is where the drawbridge comes down. In this case the two embrasures in question must guard the two smooth sides of the bastion, while at the base of the rampart two other pairs of flush embrasures protect the escarpment of earth in front of the walls. The ballistic and structural conceptions are therefore simply rectilinear, while the most original idea is the sharp semicircular structure guarding the approach to the bridge inside the bastion, concentrating its crossfire there. In another drawing, 21A, also shown in the section on architecture,[98] the structure begins to come alive: the moat no longer simply winds about but becomes broader around the bastion; two ramparts with spreading wings project from the walls to protect the flanks of the bastion from close up; these flanks curve out, thereby becoming stronger, but causing a further segmentation at the rear, this time angled (toward the gate), but this segmentation is protected from long shots by the culminating wings, with curving bastion, of the lateral defenses; while two tenaille buttresses bear down on anyone who might have forced the drawbridge. In Drawing 22A verso (Fig. 122),[99] the inner structure of the bastion becomes somewhat fantastic, with various imaginative stresses; one seems to glimpse toothed wheels, spear-shaped points, ribbed, polypodal structures of insects, or of many-pronged harpoons. Meanwhile, the geometrical moduli interpenetrate and split up, as the triangular pattern of the bastion goes off toward the curve of the sides until a circular conception is reached; and the lateral ramparts are thought of in two very different situa-

113 Fountain or stoup. Florence, Casa Buonarroti. (91).

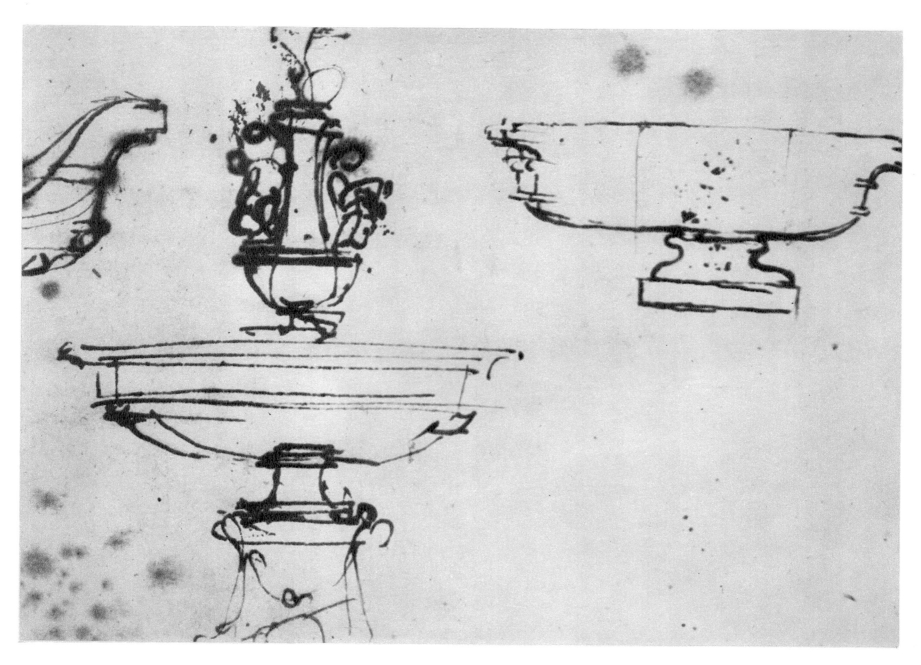

116 Plan for dwelling. Florence, Casa Buonarroti (92).

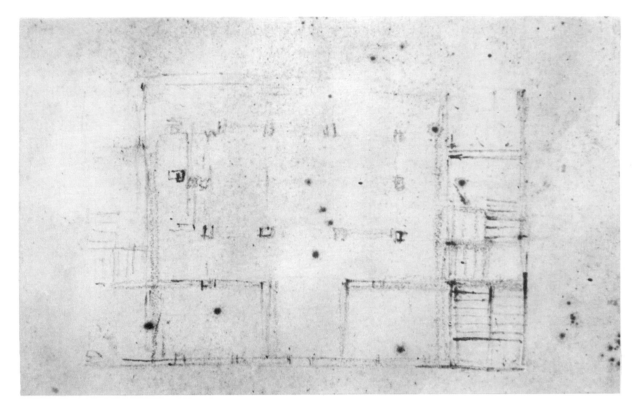

114 Tabernacle. Florence, Casa Buonarroti (93).

117 Eagle. Florence, Casa Buonarroti (92).

115 Figure. Oxford, Ashmolean Museum (94).

tions, one re-entrant and armored inside, the other extending in segmented branches. On the recto of the drawing (Fig. 121) the thought is organized, and finally is stated more clearly and practically: the bastion is in curvilinear segments, from whose junctions the embrasures spit fire; the ramparts of the wings, up hard against the bastions, form a single powerful system with it; two casemates guard the drawbridge from inside, like jaws ready to grind up foreign bodies, while a core of almost organic form suddenly divides in two and binds the entrance, which is further defended, it may be, as would seem to appear from the hatching, by stepped trenches. The drawing further emphasizes the entire defensive firepower; from the embrasures embedded in hard-to-get-at recesses the lines aggressively project and cross the lines of fire, sweeping the terrain beyond the moat. In another drawing, 24A (Fig. 123),[100] which may be for the same bastion, the pattern of organic framing is kept and the lateral ramparts are simplified, perhaps more logically, on the curvingly segmented outer front. The thought, however, seems to be concentrated on a variant of the drawbridge, which is a double one in the side sketch, at the point where the two wings converge; this is a practical error, since it nullifies the advantages of the double bridge. Since the function of the bridge is aggressive, not defensive, and in general it is clear that to increase the means of sortie is to further aggressive power,[101] Michelangelo's trend is toward aggressiveness, even when linked to an essentially defensive theme.[102]

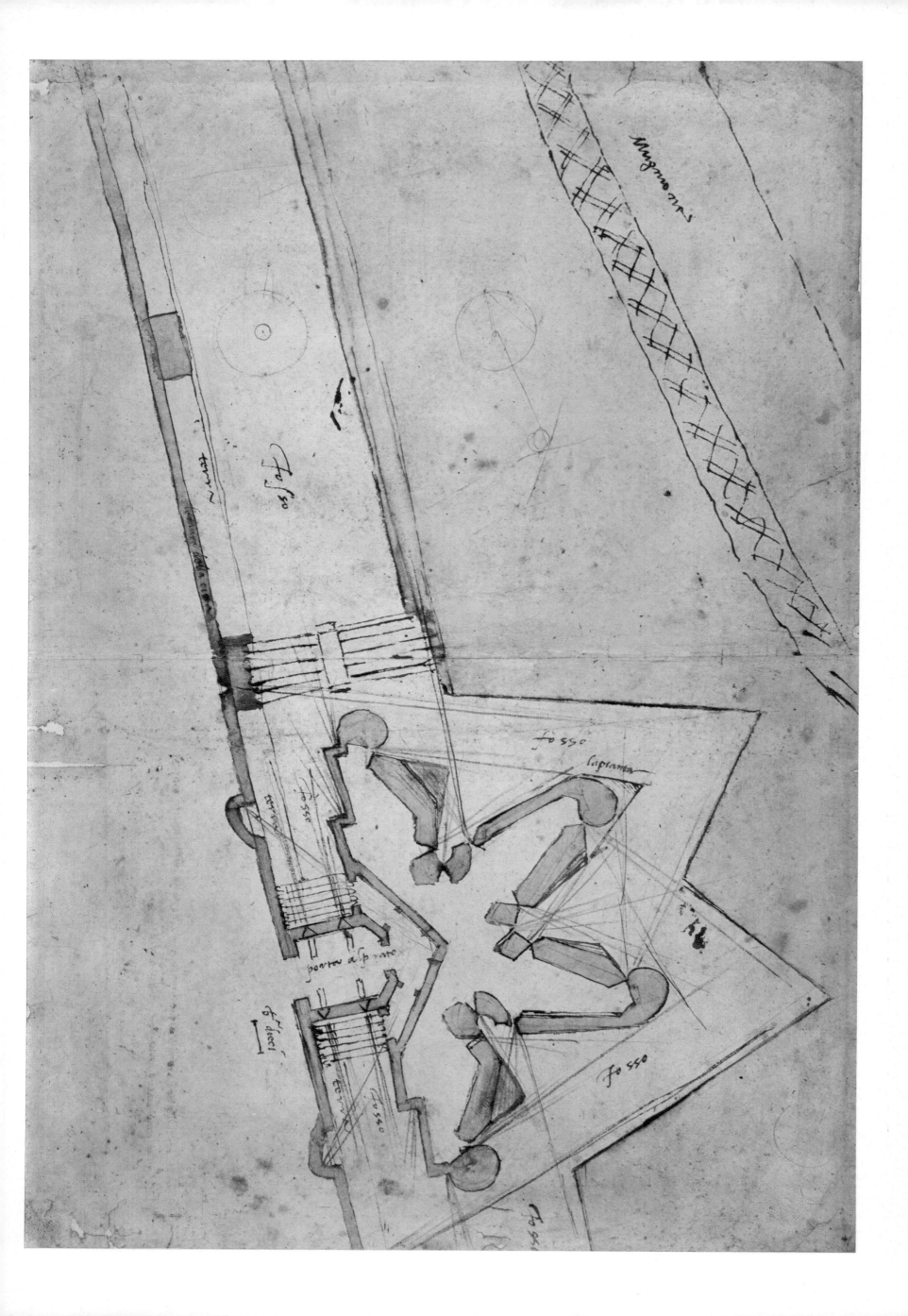

In other drawings, there is a decisive expansion, and the structures are projected onto the surrounding terrain, which receives suitable modifications. The study for the Porta alla Giustizia (Fig. 125) [103] designs a stepped-back strongpoint upstream on the Arno; the drawbridge is covered by lines of fire from the opposite bank, thanks to the bend in the bastion. In three drawings for the Prato d'Ognissanti, a bastion with two wings is inserted, by various tentative ideas, into an angle of the wall. At first the dominant idea is a bastion in the form of a menacing pincers; [104] then in Drawing 13A (Figs. 126-128) [105] it bursts forth more violently, with radiating points in the moat, while the captions indicate adaptations and changes in the configuration of the terrain, for example shifting the Mugnone. The structure is like a challenge hurled outside the *enceinte* of the walls; anyone taking it up and advancing rashly, overcoming obstacles like the Mugnone and attempting encirclement, faces the concentrated action of the lines of fire, already raging even on the paper. The form seems inspired by mechanics (cf. also Fig. 127): cogging, tenailles, metal vises.

These drawings have been said, very well, to have "a stylistic originality in keeping with Michelangelo's architectural work of the same period" (Barocchi), and Wittkower has com-

pared the drawings for the staircase of the Laurentian Library, which is likewise conceived in a key of dynamic expansiveness, with a similar process "consisting in initial meditation on abstract forms, which are later adapted to the specific purpose." Tolnay in turn has stressed the novel feature of the complex double purpose of the structures, no longer merely passively defensive but offensive as well. It might also be pointed out that another precedent is the highly original ideas for the Laurentian "little library", [106] in which the design of the benches, labyrinthine and counter to the entrance guidelines—a conception that gives such an impression of secrecy and difficulty—antecedes certain patterns of external and internal resistance in the fortifications (cf. Fig. 122). Some of the more mature fortification designs, like the one for the Prato d'Ognissanti (Fig. 126), in turn have a dynamic explosion of the spatial guidelines that anticipates later architectural ideas like the plans for San Giovanni dei Fiorentini. [107]

Although Michelangelo's fortifications were probably not erected—or only a few, at most—except for the hill of San Miniato (the celebrated Vauban admired and studied what was left of them), and although there were contemporary criticisms of the "many flanks and multiplicity of embrasures," "almost weakening each other in this way, and moreover too narrow or small, saying that heavy guns were much more effectual" (Varchi), the excessively theoretical nature of these projects is not of importance here. Rather, this excess of theoretical imagination serves to remind us of Leonardo, Michelangelo's great rival in days past, as he is also called to mind by certain imaginative principles presiding over the projects which, as has been noted, are as it were tinged with the curiosity of the physicist, engineer, and biologist, with a strong

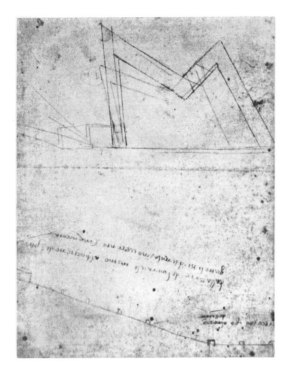

119 Section of walls and bastion. Florence, Casa Buonarroti (102).

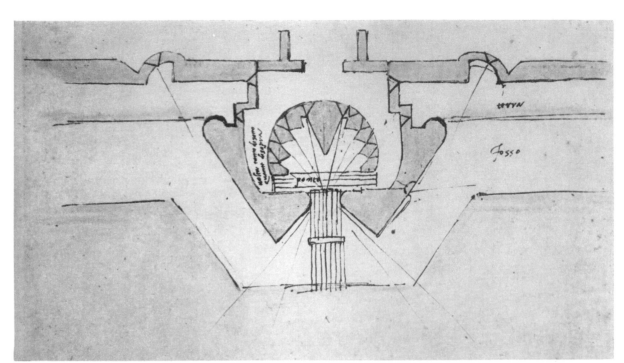

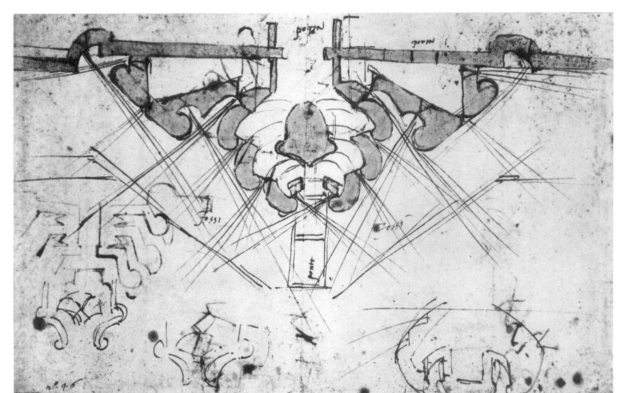

121 Walls and bastion. Florence, Casa Buonarroti (99).

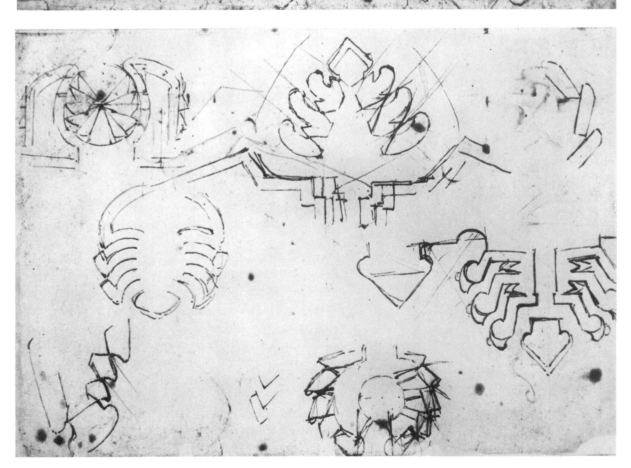

122 Sketches for a bastion. Florence, Casa Buonarroti (99).

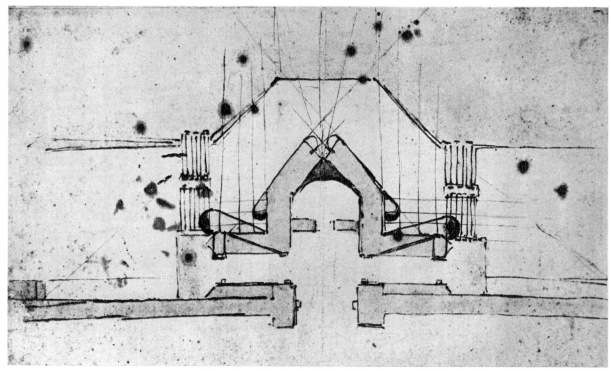

120 Defence door. Florence, Casa Buonarroti (97).

124 Bastion. Florence, Casa Buonarroti (102).

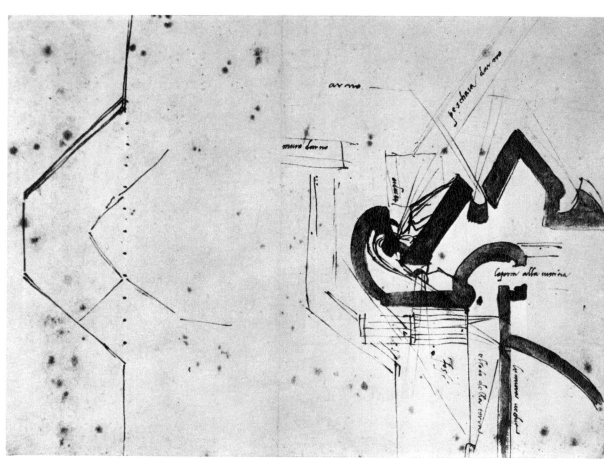

125 Defence of the Justice Door. Florence, Casa Buonarroti (103).

123 Bastion with double drawbridge. Florence, Casa Buonarroti (100).

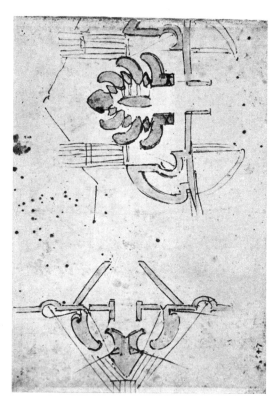

fanciful drive, rather than by the calm positive rationality of the geometer and architect. In this strange dramatic crisis that forced him to become a military architect on the spur of the moment,[108] Michelangelo could thus resort not only to the line of mathematical-Platonizing idealism that had been one of the branches of the Florentine Renaissance (and in effect the one he preferred) but also to the other branch, culminating in Leonardo, that of scientism, vitalistic and magical. In addition to a positively practical function, the fortresses he conceived in these sheets seem to seek another function as well, having a psychological value. They are unwonted and fearsome machines of war, whose unaccustomed appearance should subtly confuse and perturb the enemy; they are warning symbols, expressions of the unique power of culture, imagination, and thought of that famous city of Florence that was erecting them in its defense. Perhaps Michelangelo may never have thought of Archimedes defending Syracuse with the strength of his genius. On the other hand, these structures are clearly of "grotesque" inspiration and so accord with those well-known grotesque decorative motifs (masks, etc.) that "breathe" the feeling of a subtle religious terror into the solemn oblivious setting of the New Sacristy.

We felt it in order to recall the figure of Leonardo, and yet anyone who compares his studies for fortifications and military machines sees at once the deep-lying basic diversity of the two temperaments. In Leonardo we have the magical spirit imagining, with an imperturbably calm line, unexpected and terrifying surprises for the adversary (not only his famous armored and scythed wagons but also sprays of invisible bombards, engines for throwing down the

443

assault ladders even with the battlements devoid of defenders; or concentric circles of trenches, double moats, fortifications half under water). In Michelangelo, on the other hand, we have bastions calculated entirely on the level of abstraction, relying primarily on the proud originality of thought, of new formal principles, expressing ethical and volitional contents. The "terribility" of his fortifications has a religious, rather than a magical, savor in the sense that the new forms of walls in the drawings express an extreme tension, the flashing of unheard-of and continually self-renewing ideas from that creative and volitional center of the spirit in which man feels an analogy with the terribleness of the Divine mind. In this sense the experience of making the drawings for the fortifications may have been of the utmost value to Michelangelo, in following out his fundamental orientation toward the Divine made mental and in embodying his intuition of an absolute, tense, spiritual liberty.

[95] For an account of Michelangelo as defender of Florence I refer to Barocchi, as usual outstanding (*Commento*, 3°, N. 496, pp. 914 ff.); for the drawings, see also the same author, 1962, N. 102-118. Earlier, cf. Wittkover, in *Art Bulletin*, 1934, pp. 179 ff.; Tolnay, in *Art Bulletin*, 1940, pp. 130 ff.; Scully, in *Actes du XVII ème Congrès Intern. d'Histoire de l'Art*, The Hague, 1955, pp. 324 ff. The elevation of the fortifications, shown for example in models at the Michelangelo Exposition in Rome, 1964, were based on the notes for the elevation in Drawing 26 A of Casa Buonarroti. Cf. for this *L'architettura*, N. 99, pp. 670-5.

[96] G. Riva Palazzi, in *M. B. Ricordo al popolo italiano*, Florence 1875.

[97] Ink and water color; 25.6 × 38.5 cm. Supposed to relate to Porta a San Miniato, along with 21 A, 22 A, 24 A.

[98] Ink and water color; 27.3 × 36 cm.

[99] Ink and water color; 29.4 × 41.2 cm.

[100] Ink and water color; 28.1 × 41.5 cm.

126 Defence of the Prato d'Ognissanti. Florence, Casa Buonarroti (105).

[101] Malatesta, to excuse his passive strategy, spoke to the Signoria of the difficulty of making sorties from only a few widely separated gates.

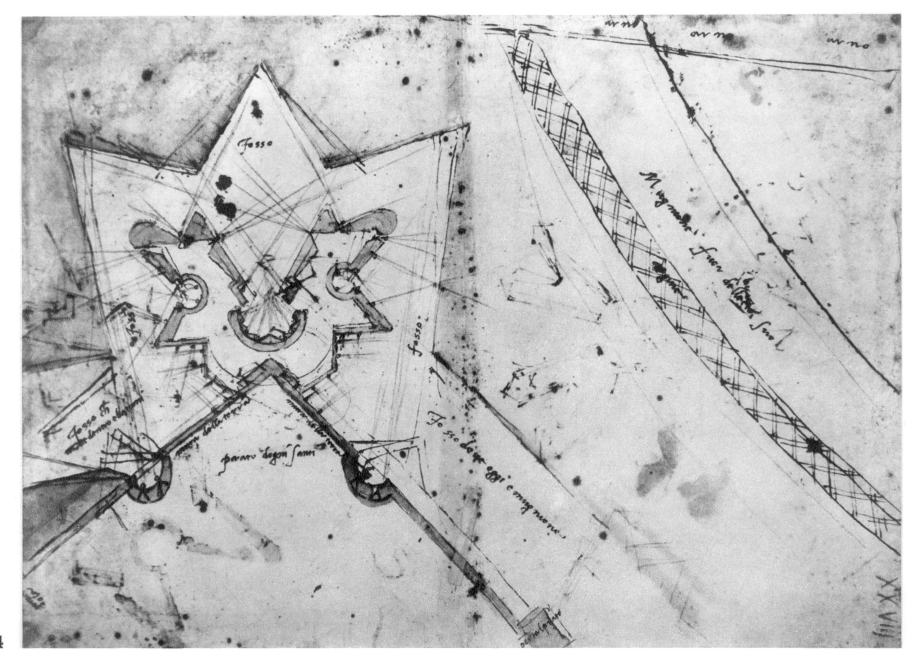

127 Sketches for the bastion of the Prato d'Ognissanti. Florence, Casa Buonarroti (105).

102 The idea of the double drawbridge also appears in Drawing 18 A (Fig. 124; ink and water color; 25.5 × 40.2 cm.) which presents a wall structure that is still fairly simple, along with some ideas for variants; it may relate to one of the southern gates. Here we also mention Drawing 25 A, which has analogies to 22 A but is "still uncertain, especially in the proportions" (Barocchi); and 26 A, which also contains the sketch for the elevation, to which attention has only recently been called (cf. Note 95 above). There is also a reproduction (Fig. 119) of Drawing 11 A (sanguine; 37.3 × 27.6 cm.), a simple note for the stretch of wall between the Torre del Miracolo and the bastion of Pier Gattolini.

103 Casa Buonarroti 19 A; ink and water color; 28.7 × 39.5 cm.

104 The reference is to Drawing 15 A, 16 A, reproduced in this volume in the section on architecture, and to 17 A.

105 Ink, water color, sanguine; 41 × 56.8 cm. Drawing 30 A (ink, water color, sanguine; 21.7 × 28 cm.; Fig. 127) is on the same project. Other drawings, 28 A, 14 A (see Pl. XXX), 20 A, relate to the fortification of Porta al Prato, with the same dynamic expansion of the spatial guidelines.

106 Especially Drawing 80 A of Casa Buonarroti; see section on architecture.

107 I refer for example to Drawing 120 A of Casa Buonarroti, reproduced in the section on architecture.

108 As Michelangelo was already under consideration in 1516 as superintendent of fortifications (letter from Argentina Malaspina to her brother the Marchese di Fosdinovo, 15-7-1516: "he is a person who knows architecture and artillery and how to fortify a site."

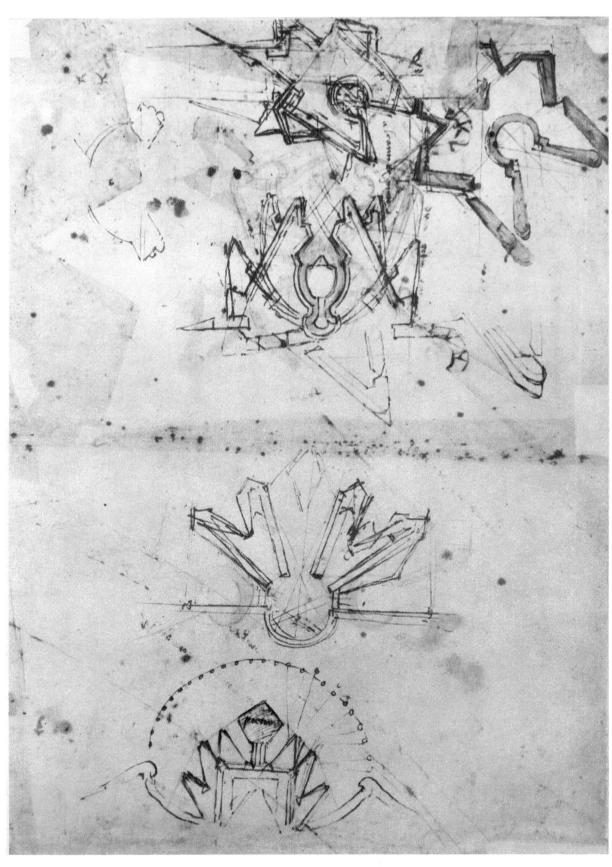

128 Sketches for the bastion of the Prato d'Ognissanti. Florence, Casa Buonarroti (105).

130 Sketch for a Pope (?). Florence, Casa Buonarroti (115).

129 Deceased prelate. Florence, Casa Buonarroti (114).

Figure studies from the vault
of the Sistine Chapel to the Last Judgment
(from about 1516 to 1534)

In connection with the tomb of Julius II, we have already had occasion to mention some drawings, such as the magnificent bound and straining Slaves of Drawing 297 in Oxford (Fig. 65),[109] linked with the two statues in the Louvre (1513). Relating to the third project for the tomb, dating from 1516, we have, in addition to Drawing 44A [110] of Casa Buonarroti, Drawing 69A of the same Casa with a side elevation,[111] perhaps the British Museum sketch for the podium (Fig. 112),[112] as well as some sketches of blocks of marbles with notations (cf. Fig. 92).[113]

On the back of a design for the façade of San Lorenzo there is likewise (Fig. 129) a sketch of a solid, dead body, mitred and nude, glidingly curvilinear in contour, being laid on a sarcophagus by a slender figure supporting him, as if anticipating the themes of the late sculptural *Pietà;* and it can be referred to the conception of the Pontiff in such a situation, and precisely for the third design: "a sort of little apse, with the figure of the deceased, that is, of Pope Julius, with two other figures laying him to rest in the middle." [114]

132 Man's head. London, British Museum (117).

131 Study of Slave (?). Florence, Uffizi (116).

One tends spontaneously to see this sketch as basically akin to another one in Casa Buonarroti (Fig. 130),[115] which too has a nude Pope, in this case seated as if alive and as it were majestically disdainful and crushing, although the treatment here is far more fragmentary, Manneristically more complex and tormented in its nervous twisted posture. It is differently oriented, but one may wonder whether, in addition to the papal tombs in the Sacristy of San Lorenzo, this proud pontiff might not possibly be referrable as well to the project of the Tomb of Julius, in an idea differently oriented and later abandoned. The idea of the forward-tending figure recalls the Virgin of the Medici Chapel; and a date about 1531-32 (at which time a further project for the tomb of Julius II was worked out), that is, subsequent to the first phase of experiments on the Chapel, seems probable.

In the page (Fig. 131) [116] with a roughed-out figure, the reference that has been preferred is to the Bearded Slave of the Accademia (about 1534-36?); but the scroll that the figure seems to hold in its left hand is an element of confusion, as is the primordial stage of the drawing, which makes dating difficult. As for the extremely pathetic head, which anticipates later sheets, of a British Museum drawing given here (Fig. 132), the reason is the head, undoubtedly recalling details of the Sistine vault, was sketched on the verso of a drawing whose recto (Fig. 98) has designs for the New Sacristy dating from about 1520; since Michelangelo had not yet, at that time, got free from the commitment of the tomb, this psychology halfway between sleep and suffering, between imprisonment in the formless and the emergent, fits well between the first pair of Slaves in the Luvaer ond the four later Slaves of the Florence Accademia.[117]

The figure studies of the period 1520-34 have a great parallel in the sculptures of the New Sacristy.

It is in this period that Barocchi places a woman's head in Casa Buonarroti (Fig. 134),[118] very direct in touch, powerful in communicating a distraught, almost hallucinatory frame of mind,[119] already somewhat in the atmosphere of the Sacristy (cf. the head of the Aurora as seen in profile); and likewise two studies of female torsos from ancient statues (Fig. 135, [120] and Fig. 136[121]), both, and in particular the second, powerfully modeled, allude to the search for an "enlarged" sculpture, tormented but fluent, as can be seen in the Medici Chapel.

In some drawings (Figs. 137 and 139,[122] Figs. 141 and 143 [123]), notes on the solution of legs for some statues (Night in particular), the research operates either on the outlined tension given the powerful limbs in their angular position, or on the chiaroscuro modeling. Details isolated in this way have a virtuoso preciosity all their own, like the knee believed to be for the

133 Sketch of Pietà. Ashmolean Museum (119).

134 Woman's head. Florence, Casa Buonarroti (118).

136 Woman's torso. Florence, Casa Buonarroti (121).

135 Woman's torso. Florence, Casa Buonarroti (120).

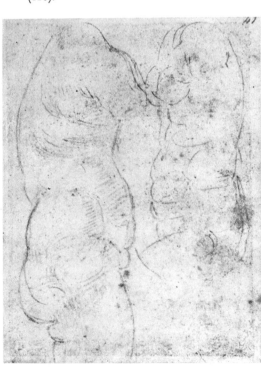

statue of Giuliano (Fig. 141), which in front view turns out to be merely a translation of the knee seen in profile that is referred instead to the Night. Uffizi drawing 10 F (Fig. 138),[124] with three rather meager studies of legs, is indeed perplexing because of the general weakness of the touch, and Berenson was not unjustified in connecting it with Bandinelli.[125]

Other drawings have been linked to decorative details of the Sacristy (cf. Fig. 148),[126] including the magnificent mask at Windsor (Fig. 140),[127] if anything too rich in particulars and of a soft refined style that suggests the fourth decade. One of the most suggestive sketches relates to the projected Rivers, conceived of dimensionally as functions of the cut of the marbles (Fig. 142).[128]

Despite the mark of the master, however, this last drawing lacks any other commitment than one of practical and summary nature; it is subsequent to the Medici Chapel that we come upon pages that give greater evidence of novelties in Michelangelo's drawing at this mature stage, whether they be direct delineations of a " rhythmic and dynamic classicism," whimsical or powerfully visionary, or a new extreme, that of consummate refinement. A set of little sketches of three nudes (Fig. 149;[129] Fig. 150;[130] Fig. 151;[131] Fig. 152;[132] Fig. 153;[133] Fig. 154;[134] Fig. 155[135]) has been thought sometimes to be connected with the Martyrdom of S. Caterina del Bugiardini, with a date of 1531-32, but actually shows us, as if in a photograph-

PLATE XXXI   Madonna and Child.   Florence,   Casa Buonarroti, 71 F.

138 Anatomical studies. Florence, Uffizi (124).

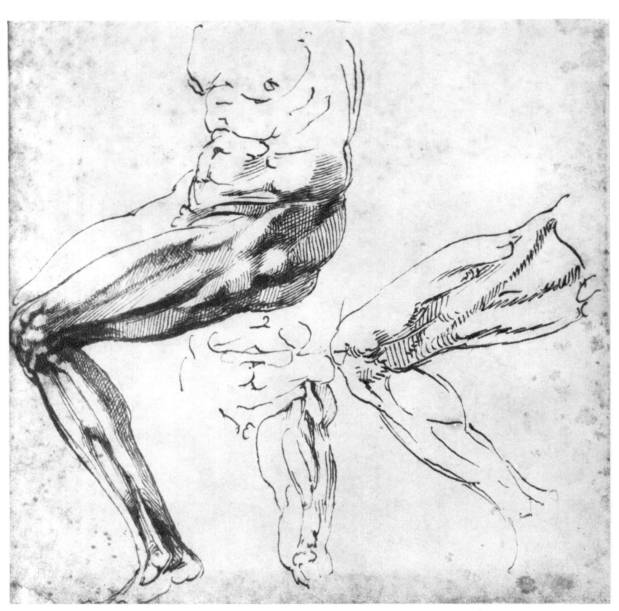

137 Studies for the legs of Night. Florence, Uffizi (122).

ic sequence, a chain of movements like that in the spirit of a ballet; a spirit that, in the sketches of the little figures with a very witty and deft touch, does not express tragic or dramatic ideas, I should say, but develops the material in a series of amusing variations. As for

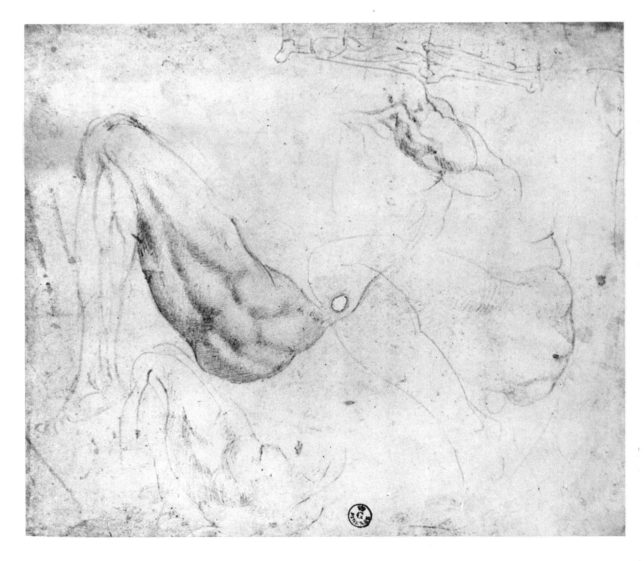

139 Studies for the legs of Night. Florence, Uffizi (122).

449

the drawing of a *putto* urinating into a cup (Fig. 156),[136] I believe it should be related to the Windsor Bacchanal of about 1533 (Fig. 181), if we compare not only the *putto* urinating in the air but the one with a similar grotesque mask turning to look at the fire to the left; and its interest is the way it shows how this drawing, with its whimsy and fantasy, akin to that in the series of three nudes, leads to the studied fabled classicism in slow poses of an invention like the one at Windsor.

When we thus observe, as in the series thought to be for the Martyrdom of St. Catherine, how Michelangelo's pattern of thinking dwells on a theme and elaborates it as a rhythmic-plastic theme, apart from its intrinsic significance, perhaps at the same time working a psychological vein of burlesque and caricature, we can explain such transitions of design as occur in the Hercules and Antaeus. In the famous London drawing with its merry lively masks, akin to the New Sacristy (in this book shown in Tolnay's Introduction),[137] a Hercules and Antaeus is sketched at the right (Fig. 157) that reappears in an Oxford page (Fig. 159)[138] which, although suspected of being by a pupil, presents once more a caricatured old woman. In truth the two Oxford studies have a pathos that in the upper one is reinforced by the strong chiaroscuro of the sanguine; but this is not to deny the authenticity of the two men wrestling in the Louvre sanguine (Fig. 160),[139] which is too lovely to be downgraded as the work of a student; it picks up themes of the earlier Hercules and Antaeus studies, now overflowing into a soft if not equivocal delight in the two entwined figures, whether in playing or tragedy we cannot say.

In the tremendous sheet of the Bronze Serpent (Fig. 176)[140] there is a different kind of line in sanguine, one of extreme finesse in which the figures seethe and proliferate like sponges in the two conglomerations, expressing a choral dramatic quality that is viewed without involvement.

140 Mask. Windsor, Royal Library (127).

141 Studies of legs for the statues of the Sacristy. Haarlem, Teyler Museum (123).

450

142 Sketches and measurements for a statue of the
River. London, British Museum (128).

143 Study of leg for the statues of the Sacristy. Haarlem, Teyler Museum (123).

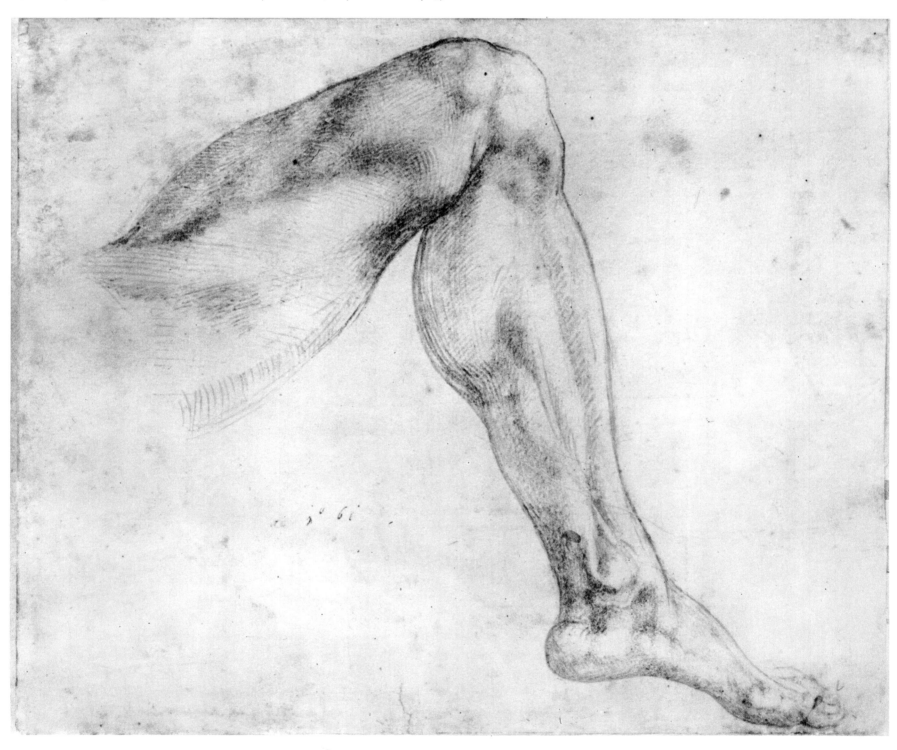

451

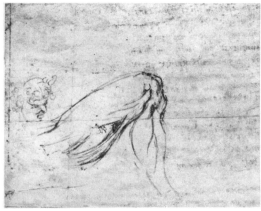

Once again there is a return to the ancient fantastic core of the Centauromachia, only that now the ingenuous contemplative classicism is replaced by a far greater capacity for orchestration in the explosively expanded or massed groups; the classicism is more precious and introverted, not without a morbid component. Other sheets from this period of transition between the New Sacristy and the Last Judgment exhibit powerful qualities of suggestion. In a small London sheet (Fig. 163) [141] there is the approach of a *putto* to a large prostrate figure; in a Florentine sanguine (Fig. 164),[142] a most forceful Christ in Limbo; and in a series of studies for a Resurrection that can be dated 1532-33 we see the image of Christ (Fig. 165; [143] Figs. 166 and 167 [144]) as a dynamic, dramatic apparition in a welter of variant ideas; the study for a soldier in the same scene (Fig. 172) [145] is likewise of great power. The whole complex of ideas then passes through various gradations (Fig. 168; [146] Fig. 171; [147] Fig. 169 [148]), but always with sublime expressive majesty, into an extreme refinement that also enters into the solution of certain details (Fig. 170; [149] Fig. 173; [150] Fig. 175 [151]) and that, as in Fig. 173, is manifested in the sinuous outlines of the long-lined powerful forms, treated with the softest of surface chiaroscuro. " *L'importanza di questa serie di disegni della Resurrezione ci par consistere nel fatto che Michelangelo è riuscito a trasformarci l'evento... in un simbolo soggettivo delle proprie aspirazioni metafisiche... Per lui la Bellezza, sia essa pagana o cristiana, è una. E poiché la Bellezza è d'origine divina, e ci riconduce al divino, Michelangelo ha potuto servirsi, come sinonimi, di motivi pagani e cristiani* " (Tolnay).

These are the years of Michelangelo's unexpected passion for the beautiful " mr. Tomaso "

144 Sonnet and sketch. London, British Museum (125).

145 Study of leg. London, British Museum (125).

148 Vase and figure. London, British Museum (126).

146 Dragon. Oxford, Ashmolean Museum (127).

147 Back of Fig. 146 (by Michelangelo's school) (127).

Cavalieri (1532-34), certainly a case of masculine Platonic love, which it is time we should no longer treat by reticently averting our faces, if only to get a full critical understanding of those " tremendous papers " that resulted from it.[152] In point of fact these drawings are nothing more nor less than equivalents of love poems, in which the *eros* is manifested and at the same time holds itself back and veils itself in the conceptual framework it has created, unfolds in formal hedonism while betraying a dark background of remorse and conflict. In psychoanalytic terms the situation is one of expression but also of sublimation and suppression and latent guilt feeling; that is, there is of necessity a " complex " here; in formal-expressive terms, the only manner of drawing in which the sentiments of the situation could find adequate represen-

149 Three nude men. Florence, Casa Buonarroti (129).

150 Three nude men. Florence, Casa Buonarroti (130).

151 Three nude men. Florence, Casa Buonarroti (131).

453

152 Three nude men. Florence, Casa Buonarroti (132).

153 Three nude men. Florence, Casa Buonarroti (133).

154 Three nude men. Oxford, Ashmolean Museum (134).

155 Three nude men. Florence, Casa Buonarroti (133).

tation is just that of these sheets, marked with extreme elaboration and classicistic academicism, whereas obviously other manners (cf. the sketch for the thundering Jove of the Fall of Phaëthon, Fig. 180 [153]) could express only more undifferentiated and germinal modes of Michelangelo's vision and would have been inadequate to the purpose. A "complex," after all, cannot but be represented "complexly," and even to some extent elusively.

We examine the three versions of the Phaëthon known to us, all three authentic, in the British Museum (Fig. 178),[154] the Accademia in Venice (Fig. 177),[155] and Windsor (Fig. 179).[156] In the London drawing there is a certain distance of view by which the scene is taken in as a whole, a certain naturalness in the description of the chariot of Phaëthon struck by lightning and in the scene by the placid Eridanus River, and of the three Heliads turning into trees; and there is also a pictural atmosphere created by the skillful touch of the line. For the present, that is, Michelangelo has simply assumed the scholarly significance of the image, suited to his young but learned friend and perhaps expressive of his sense of his inferiority in the face of the young man's divine beauty (Panofsky: Michelangelo compares his "presumption" to that of Phaëthon); but he has not gone all the way into the depths of its emotional significances (the ultimate theme being that of punishment brought about by the unleashing of instinct), nor has he yet been able to confer on it the extreme perfection behind which is his trembling (and for us pathetic) hope that his homage will find high appreciation on the part of his friend and the other participants in this rather strange episode. It makes him in fact speak of a symbol, of a "sketch" to be "finished" eventually (cf. Note 154). In the Venice drawing the quality has deteriorated but the emotional intensity of the theme has been heightened.

The view is closer and concentrated on the sudden plunge downward of the chariot, with Phaëthon in the center between the horses, who are now caught up into pairs. The lower part of the scene is reduced to dramatic masks, and Jove on high has taken on a senile aspect.

It is hardly necessary to point out how psychoanalytically revealing all these elements are of an unconscious deepening of the theme of guilt and subjective punishment. In the last version (Fig. 179) the scene is far distant, fixed and determinate in a preciosity and smoothness that take on a sensual and anxious instinctive burden, but at the same time "deter" it from any more direct and sincere manifestation. Just see the twisted posture of Phaëthon and those of the horses, making the drama tend toward the abnormal; or the highly studied depiction of the Eridanus, refined in all its attributes but psychologically closed in, in an extraneous med-

158 Various sketches. London, British Museum (137).

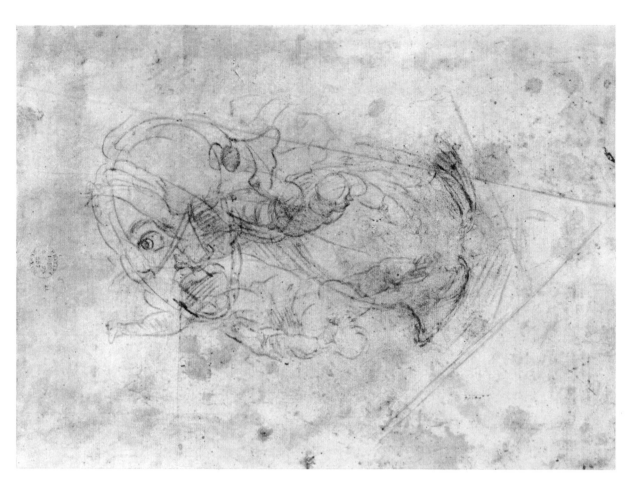

156 Cherub urinating. Florence, Uffizi (136).

157 Hercules and Antaeus (detail of a drawing) London, British Museum (137).

itation; the three Heliads resolved into the expressiveness of the nude alone, without any further metamorphosis; and also the different type of the spatiality, concentrated identically on three successive stanzas of the story arranged in a perfect triangular pattern with the vertex in Jove, a geometry that was absent in the London drawing (Fig. 178) while in the Venice folio (Fig. 177) the base was indeterminate.

In the Windsor Tityus (Fig. 162) [157] "with the vulture eating his heart," also done for Cavalieri, there is an evident allusion to the torments of love, along with the same technical virtuosity in chiaroscuro ("that the breath could not make more unified," Vasari, 1550) which, in the modeling of the nude, takes on meanings that are soft but also doleful, by virtue of some intense spots of shadow due to the vulture above; the forms of the trunk in the background, lightly drawn, seem to indicate claws and beaks.

In the same museum, the *Putti's Bacchanal* (Fig. 181), [158] likewise attested as for Cavalieri, is more complex in composition; the planes are terraced in an intersecting nexus and there is a complete impression of the figured field. Here a psychoanalyst might take note of the orgiastic significance repressed in an infantile regression, rather than "the humiliation of

159 Hercules and Antaeus (and other sketches by the school). Oxford, Ashmolean Museum (138).

455

160 Two men wrestling. Paris, Louvre (139).

161 Back of drawing of Fig. 159 (by school). Oxford, Ashmolean Museum (138).

humanity by means of sin" (Goldscheider). There is a clearly erotic meaning in the splendid Archers (Fig. 182);[159] and the period of the series for Cavalieri would also seem to be that of the Three Labors of Hercules (Fig. 183),[160] likewise at Windsor, which are similar in technique and sensibility.

The "divine heads" done so that Cavalieri "might learn to draw," and also for others, must have become famous at once, and certainly they were models of the "finished" drawing of Michelangelo. Modern scholarship, perhaps over-scrupulous, has raised doubts as to these subjects that have come down to us; their justification lies in the same sweetly refined technique with which we see basic themes of Buonarroti, such as the Sibyl, the grotesque mask, etc., treated,[161] as well in the immediate success, in the form of copies, engravings, etc., that these heads had.

The head of a man howling (Fig. 186),[162] which must certainly have gone through the hands of "his [Michelangelo's] great friend" Gherardo Perini, is in any case in accord with the grotesque ideas for the Medici Sacristy (cf. Fig. 140) and the mask of the Night and the head and neck of Giuliano; especially, I should say, they are reminiscent of Leonardo's Battle of Anghiari.[163]

Another source of inspiration, the Simonetta Vespucci of Piero di Cosimo, has justly been seen in the Cleopatra (Fig. 187),[164] where, however, the serpentine winding of the form gives a different pathos, involuted and ambiguous, between the sensually and preciously hedonistic and the mournfully tormented. But a root of the type of Piero di Cosimo also appears in that old woman's head (Fig. 188)[165] (cf. Piero's famous portrait of Francesco Giamberti in Amsterdam) given to followers to execute (so that the solutions of provost Bachiacca were to be inspired by examples from Buonarroti). Our general conclusion can be that on these occasions Michelangelo, desiring to test himself in a more communicative virtuosity, which was foreign to his solitary and absolute genius, went back more or less to cultural antecedents from the refined environment of Florence, while sounding notes of definite Mannerist resonance.

Bachiacca has also been credited with an Oxford head (Fig. 190),[166] but its meditative seriousness is not characteristic of Ubertini, who was always more superficial, and the line here models powerfully or notes peripherally, with free ease.

162 Tityus. Windsor, Royal Library (157).

163 Figure and cherub. London, British Museum (141).

164 Christ in Limbo. Florence, Casa Buonarroti (142).

In conclusion, the " divine heads " for Perini and Cavalieri, and the drawings of 1532-33 for Cavalieri, are further confirmation that the figurative phase connected with or parallel to the work on the New Sacristy marks this experience, and quite consistently so, with an extreme refinement of Michelangelo's graphic art, in both the germinal and the carefully worked-out phases, with results which are sometimes splendid but which might have been perilous, had not Buonarroti's fate and genius been oriented toward a further titanic and sorrowful achievement—an achievement realized in his last Roman period.[167]

[109] Cf. Note 55. For all the drawings connected with the tomb of Julius II, cf. Tolnay's volume (1954); but some of his opinions as to authenticity have encountered reservations.

[110] Reproduced in the architecture section; and cf. Barocchi, *Catalogo* 1964, Pl. XL. The part of the drawing that has been related to the tomb is the sketch for the herm.

[111] Reproduced in Barocchi, 1962, Pl. XC, N. 51.

[112] Cf. Note 89.

[113] Drawings 67 A and 74 A of Casa Buonarroti, plus 68 A, reproduced in Fig. 92.

[114] The recto of Drawing 43 A of Casa Buonarroti (ink with traces of sanguine; 21.2 × 14.3 cm.) is reproduced in the section on architecture. Barocchi (1962, N. 45) notes that " the alleged iconographic defects (for example, the miter instead of the tiara; cf. Frey) cannot invalidate the attribution since, as Dussler stresses, this is certainly an initial summary invention, but one with such a persuasive quality."

[115] The drawing, Casa Buonarroti 21 F, is in ink, 15.7 × 11.4 cm. The proposed connection with the tombs of the Medici popes in San Lorenzo comes from Tolnay, but Barocchi (1962, N. 124) seems to me to have been correct, with Delacre, in counting on a date of 1531-32.

[116] The drawing, 18729 F of the Uffizi (black pencil; 22.3 × 8.8 cm.), has been assigned various dates and references, from the Apostles for the Duomo in Florence to the statuette of Moses in the background of the Annunciazione del Venusti (cf. Barocchi, *Catalogo* 1964, N. 56).

[117] Drawing 1859-6-25-545 in the British Museum, already referred to (cf. Note 76), is on the verso, in black pencil with two vertical stripes in sanguine. It recalls, in addition to the created Adam, the Nudes of the Sistine vault, but there is nothing to exclude a subsequent return to these motifs (Wilde, Barocchi), to be placed at least in time with the first thoughts for the New Sacristy.

[118] Drawing 57 F; ink; 6.2 × 6.0 cm. Supposed by Frey to be a first sketch for the Erythraean Sibyl, but by others a later second thought on the Sistine.

[119] On the other hand, in Oxford Drawing 378, Fig. 133 (ink and bister; 8.3 × 7.2 cm.), to which some give the date 1524, with a dead Christ resting on the knees of a disciple, the sketch is more ruffled and dramatic. For the two

beautiful drawings in Casa Buonarroti, the Madonna and Child 71 F (see Pl. XXXI) and the study of a head 7 F (see Pl. XXXII) refer to any study of the period of the New Sacristy as we have suggested elsewhere, cf. Notes 20 and 40.

[120] Casa Buonarroti 41 F; black pencil, 20×14.7 cm.

[121] Casa Buonarroti 16 F; black pencil, 13×8 cm. Cf. Barocchi 1962, N. 69.

[122] Uffizi drawing 18719 F r. (Fig. 139) and v. (Fig. 137) is certainly referrable to the Night and is dated 1524-26, when the artist began to put his hand to model and execute the statues. Cf. Barocchi, 1962, N. 76. Silver point, 28×34.3 cm.

[123] Haarlem, Teyler Museum, N. 11 r. and in two sheets; charcoal; total 41×21.5 cm. In the sheet of Fig. 141 the knees are to be referred to the Giuliano and the rest to the left leg of the Night; on the sheet of Fig. 143 the reference is to the leg of the Day (?). Cf. Berenson, N. 1467.

[124] Ink; 26.1×26.2 cm. In favor of authenticity: Thode, Frey, Wilde and Barocchi (1962, N. 71).

[125] Reference to the New Sacristy has also been made for the British Museum drawing (Manuscripts 21907), charcoal, 15×18.5 cm. (Figs. 144, 145); the leg of the verso recalls the Day. Cf. Berenson, N. 1538.

[126] This is drawing 1859, 6, 25, 554 of the British Museum (12.2×12.4 cm.; charcoal); the vase in it is assigned to Michelangelo by Tolnay (III, N. 79a); probably for the vases on the doors of the Sacristy; the other sketches by a pupil. Berenson, N. 1488.

[127] Royal Library N. 12762; charcoal and sanguine; 24.7×12 cm. Assigned as probably Michelangelo's by Tolnay; for Berenson (N. 1610), "the finest of Michelangelo's grotesques, certainly belonging to the period of the Medici tombs."

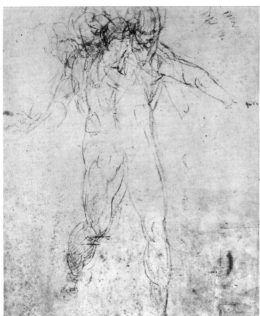

165-168 Studies for a risen Christ and Resurrection. Florence, Casa Buonarroti (143, 144, 144) and Paris, Louvre (146).

Oxford drawing 323 (Figs. 146, 147; ink and charcoal; 25.4×33.8 cm.) has had its dragon referred to the bronze candelabra on the altar of the New Sacristy; the rest is weak and has been assigned, according to the inscription, by Berenson (N. 1555) to his "Andrea di Michelangelo."

[128] British Museum, 1859, 6, 25; 544; ink; 13.7×20.9 cm. Cf. Berenson, 1491.

[129] Casa Buonarroti 38 F; ink and black pencil; 17×20.7 cm. Barocchi (1962, N. 126) regards this drawing as the first of the series discussed in the following note.

[130] Casa Buonarroti 17 F; ink; 9.5×9.1 cm. It forms a series with four others of the same Casa and one in Oxford, all shown here, referred to the Martyrdom of St. Catherine of Bugiardini, for which Michelangelo would have sketched "a line of marvelous nude figures, foreshortened in various gestures, falling some backwards and some forwards." The date is believed to be 1531-32. Cf. Barocchi, 1962, N. 125. But other references have been proposed, for example to the late Expulsion of the Moneychangers from the Temple or the Bronze Serpent.

458

171 Resurrection. Windsor, Royal Library (147).

169 Resurrection. London, British Museum (148).

170 Risen Christ. Windsor, Royal Library (149).

172 Study for a Resurrection. Florence, Casa Buonarroti (145).

¹³¹ Casa Buonarroti 18 F; ink; 8.8 × 10.6 cm.

¹³² Casa Buonarroti 67 F; ink; 11 × 11.6 cm.

¹³³ Casa Buonarroti 68 F; ink; 10.1 × 11 cm.

¹³⁴ Oxford, Ashmolean Museum 321; ink and silver point; 10.3 × 10.5 cm.

¹³⁵ Casa Buonarroti, 58 F; ink; 7 × 7.2 cm. The theme has been seen as a dance of nymphs and fauns, or as the Transfiguration of Christ; today it is linked to the preceding series (cf. Barocchi, 1962, N. 130), a reference that I find mysterious.

¹³⁶ Uffizi, 621 E; ink and black pencil; 23.8 × 21.5 cm. Cf. Barocchi, 1962, N. 131.

¹³⁷ British Museum, 1859-6-25-557; sanguine, 25 × 34 cm. The back of this drawing (Fig. 158) has, in addition to a head and a shield, two figures with lances, with a more uncertain and less successful rhythm, but yet one not too different from the rhythm of the series discussed for the Martyrdom of St. Catherine.

459

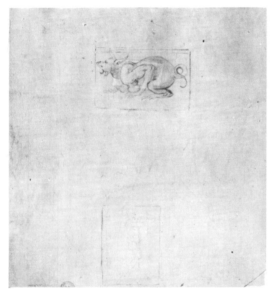

173-175 Risen Christ; back of this drawing (150);
         Risen Christ (151). British Museum.

176 The bronze serpent. Oxford, Ashmolean Mu-
     seum (140).

177-178 Fall of Phaëthon. Venice, Academy (155),
         and London, British Museum (154).

461

179 Fall of Phaëthon. Windsor, Royal Library (156).

181-182 Bacchanal of cherubs; The archers. Windsor, Royal Library (158 and 159).

[138] Ashmolean Museum 45; sanguine and ink; 28.8 × 42.7 cm. The sketches on the verso (Fig. 161) are weak indeed, and attributed to Antonio Mini, who certainly had something to do with the recto as well, but I am not sure that this applied to the caricature of the old woman.

[139] The drawing, Louvre 709, is in sanguine, 23.7 × 19 cm. The verso has an autograph poem by Michelangelo. The doubts as to attribution, arising out of notes and a sketch by Mini on the verso, should be given up in view of the quality of the recto, for which Barocchi significantly mentions its " charming chiaroscuro orchestration."

[140] Oxford, Ashmolean Museum 29; sanguine; 24.4 × 33.5 cm. Has been referred to the Sistine vault, and then to the hypothetical lunettes in the New Sacristy of San Lorenzo; or these connections have been avoided by dating it about 1530, that is, contemporaneously with the drawings for Cavalieri.

[141] British Museum, 1859, 6, 25, 553; ink; 8.5 × 12.1 cm. Has been related to a Samson and Delilah or to the cartoon for the Venus later painted by Pontormo. Cf. Berenson, N. 1504.

[142] Casa Buonarroti 35 F; sanguine and black pencil; 16.3 × 14.8 cm. Cf. Barocchi, 1962, N. 135.

[143] Casa Buonarroti 66 F; black pencil; 33.1 × 19.8 cm. Cf. Barocchi, 1962, N. 136. Long ago referred to the Christ of the Last Judgment; later, affinities have been seen with the Fall of Phaëthon. A penetrating analysis of the meaning of Michelangelo's conception of the Resurrection and of its development in various ways related to this whole series of drawings is in Tolnay, *Morte e Resurrezione in Michelangelo* in " Commentarii " 1964.

180 Sketch of Jupiter striking with lighting. Florence, Casa Buonarroti (153).

463

183　Three labours of Hercules. Windsor, Royal Library (160).

184　Salamander.　Oxford, Ashmolean Museum (160).

185　Salamander. London, British Museum (160).

[144] Casa Buonarroti 61 F r. and v.; black pencil; 38×25.2 cm. Cf. Barocchi, 1962, N. 137.

[145] Casa Buonarroti 32 F; sanguine; 13.5×19.5 cm. Barocchi (1964, N. 141) notes that "it bears witness to an extremely interesting stylistic phase in Buonarroti's gallery, a phase in which, with dolorous meditation, the artist subjectivizes the conquests of the New Sacristy, transforming its complex torsions and highly studied modeling into the tormented and dynamic sculpturalism of the Judgment."

[146] Louvre, 691 b; sanguine; 15.5×17.1 cm.

[147] Windsor, Royal Library N. 12767; charcoal and sanguine; 23.7×34.5 cm. Cf. Berenson, N. 1612.

[148] London, British Museum 1860, 6, 16, 133; black pencil; 32.6×28.6 cm.

[149] Windsor; Royal Library 12768; charcoal; 36.7×22 cm.

[150] London, British Museum 1895, 9, 15, 501; black pencil; 41.4×27.4 cm.; on the verso (Fig. 174) decorative sketches that have been called into question and related to the ornaments for the New Sacristy.

[151] British Museum, 1887, 5, 2, 119; charcoal; 40.5×27 cm.

[152] On the drawings for Cavalieri, see in particular Tolnay, III, pp. 111 ff., 199 ff., 220 ff. Missing here is the drawing of Ganymede, symbolic of union in mystic love, of which various copies exist, the best accredited being in Windsor Castle N. 13036 (Berenson, Fig. 633, N. 1614).

[153] Casa Buonarroti 4 F; sanguine; 11.5×7 cm.; a connection with the Fall of Phaëthon in the Venice Accademia version (Fig. 177) has been proposed by Tolnay.

[154] N. 1895, 9, 15, 517; black pencil; 31.3×21.7 cm. It has the following inscription in Michelangelo's hand (worked in): "Messer Tomaso, if this sketch does not please you, tell Urbino, so that I will have time to have another one made tomorrow evening, as I promised you and if you like it and wish me to finish it, send it back to me." Datable 1532-33.

[155] N. 177; black pencil; 39.4×25.5 cm. Written, in Michelangelo's hand but almost vanished: "I have drawn it as best I could, I therefore send it to you as yours, since I am your servant, to portray it another time." Date, 1532-33.

[156] N. 12766; charcoal; 41×23 cm. This must be the copy received by Tommaso Cavalieri on September 2, 1533: "Perhaps three days ago I got my Phaëthon, very well done, and it has been seen by the Pope, Cardinal de' Medici, and others: I do not know why it is desired to see it." On the verso, a bust of a woman that Berenson (N. 1617) would assign to "Andrea di Michelangelo," but is better judged by Tolnay (V, Fig. 112) as authentic.

¹⁵⁷ Royal Library 12771; black pencil; 19×33 cm. On the verso, a Christ rising again is obtained from the outline of the figure on the recto. 18736 F of the Uffizi (Barocchi, 1962, N. 132) may be a preparation for this. The drawing has been shown at Florence, in the 1964 Exposition (cf. Barocchi, *Catalogo*, N. 134).

¹⁵⁸ Royal Library, 12777; sanguine; 27×38.5 cm. For Tolnay, followed by others, this is a copy; the authenticity is asserted by Berenson (N. 1618), Wilde, etc.

¹⁵⁹ Royal Library, 12778; sanguine; 21.5×32 cm. Tolnay regards it as a replica. On the verso, a memorandum dated 1530, while the chronology is considered of the period of the drawings for Cavalieri (1532-33).

¹⁶⁰ Royal Library, 12770; sanguine; 27×41.7 cm. Berenson (N. 1611) takes it as somewhat earlier than the drawings for Cavalieri, "although it is tempting to imagine that it belonged to that series." In view of the hydra of Hercules, I have cited here two sketches of salamanders, believed to date about 1530 and perhaps related to the enterprise of Francis I. The first (Fig. 184) is Oxford 320 (charcoal; 13×21 cm.), cf. Berenson N. 1568; the second (Fig. 185) is British Museum N. 1895, 9, 15, 514 (charcoal; 9.2×12.7 cm.); cf. Berenson, N. 1533. As has been pointed out, there is also a relationship with the helmet of the so-called " Count of Canossa " in the British Museum, one of the " Divine Heads " spoken of in the text.

¹⁶¹ On the " divine heads " cf. Tolnay, V, pp. 165 ff. The author accepts as authentic his N. 145 (Kunsthalle, Hamburg), 146 (Boymans Museum), 152 (here Fig. 190), 153 (here Fig. 83), 154 (" Youth," in Windsor Castle, which Goldscheider has taken to be a portrait of Cavalieri); and he takes to be copies the " Count of Canossa " and " Marchioness of Pescara " of the British Museum (his N. 147, 148), the Florentine " Zenobia " (here Fig. 189), the " Damned " (here Fig. 186), the " Cleopatra " (here Fig. 187).

186 " The Damned Man." Florence, Uffizi (162).

187 Cleopatra. Florence, Casa Buonarroti (164).

188   Old Woman. Florence, Casa Buonarroti (165).

189   Zenobia. Florence, Uffizi (163).

190   Woman's head. Oxford, Ashmolean Museum (166).

¹⁶² Uffizi 601 E; black pencil; 29.8×20.5 cm. Bears the name of Gherardo Perini and a *me fecit* with Michelangelo's name. Another version at Windsor is preferred as original by Berenson (who later changed his mind) and others, while Wilde has come out for the Florentine sheet, dating it about 1525. Barocchi (1962, N. 187) continues to attribute it to Bachiacca, with Marcucci.

¹⁶³ Another drawing belonging to Perini is reasonably thought to be the so-called " Zenobia " (Fig. 189) of the Uffizi (598 E; black pencil; 35.7×25.1 cm.; the verso with sketches of heads and anatomical studies is evidently a school piece), which would represent " Venus, Vulcan, and Cupid " or " Venus, Mars, and Cupid." Those, like Wilde, who believe it authentic, have dated it in the third decade. Barocchi (1962, N. 185) accepts the attribution to Bachiacca.

¹⁶⁴ Casa Buonarroti 2 F; black pencil, 23.2×18.2 cm. Cited by Vasari as a gift from Cavalieri to Duke Cosimo (1562). There are copies of this drawing in existence (British Museum, Louvre, Boymans Museum), but the Florentine specimen is regarded as the original by Wilde (who dates it about 1533), followed by Barocchi (1962, N. 133).

¹⁶⁵ Casa Buonarroti, 3 F; black pencil, badly faded; 16.2×12 cm. Doubted by Berenson, Panofsky, and Dussler; Barocchi (1962, N. 190) attributes it to Bachiacca.

¹⁶⁶ Ashmolean Museum 315; sanguine; 20.5×16.5 cm. Copies at Oxford and in the Uffizi. Accepted as authentic by Berenson (N. 1552) and others, and finally by Tolnay as well (V, N. 152), who dates it about 1520-25.

¹⁶⁷ Also accepts the date about 1532-33 for the Sacrifice of Isaac (Fig. 191) of Casa Buonarroti (70 F; black pencil, ink and sanguine; 40.8×28.9 cm.). Cf. Barocchi, 1962, N. 140. " The swirling touch," however, is here joined with a still classicistic pictural softness.

191 Sacrifice of Isaac. Florence, Casa Buonarroti (167). ▷

Studies for the Last Judgment
(1534-41)

In the Last Judgment in the Sistine Chapel the theme itself set Michelangelo his ultimate goal beyond any contingent and earthly problems of form, passion, and culture. The action of masses that he had conceived of from the time of the Centauromachia, the titanic characters that he had learned to represent, starting by using Giotto and Masaccio as models, the nude human figure that he had endowed with the most powerful psychical meanings, and higher and more complex formalism: all were involved in a truly final drama, the Last Judgment, inspired by the most radical and exclusive ethical reason. In St. Bartholomew there is a significant figure, grotesque and tragic, of the artist himself, now a hollow shell perilously balanced on the edge of the abyss of the damned. Inasmuch as there evidently are some bonds of continuity between the evidence for the Judgment in the form of drawings (as usual, relatively scarce [168]) and the preceding graphic phase, it seems to me that critical evaluation should aim chiefly at this new element, which is basic in the " poetical " situation, and that, as is shown in fact by the later graphics of Michelangelo, it signifies the crisis of his drawing as well.

192 Studies for the Judgment. Florence, Casa Buonarroti (174).

193 Studies for the Judgment. Florence, Uffizi (175).

194 Thought for the Last Judgment. Florence, Casa Buonarroti (171).

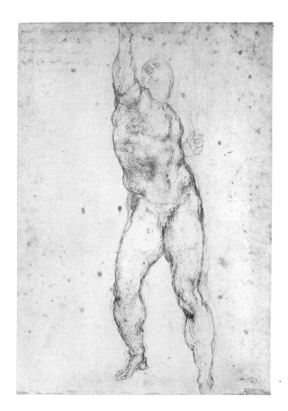

195 Risen man. Florence, Casa Buonarroti (171).

A preliminary study at Bayonne [169] still retains something of the soft drawings for Cavalieri; sheet 170 S of the Uffizi (a study of Christ and figures of the Elect) [170] " starts from the simpler arrangements of the Resurrections " of 1532-33 (Barocchi); but here we see an augmented " terribility " of form, which has changed from a long line to one that is heavier and more solid (e. g. the Christ); as is confirmed by the verso of Drawing 65 F of Casa Buonarroti (Fig. 195),[171] likewise a study of Christ risen, but now having a tragically massive anatomy, tormented as it were by the matter of the protagonists of the Judgment.

The recto of the same drawing 65 F (Fig. 194) is a first overall idea for the great composition. As has been remarked, in it Michelangelo still takes into account the existing condition of the wall of the Sistine Chapel, leaving room at the bottom for the altarpiece by Perugino that was in position there, and at the top leaving out the two lunettes on which he himself had painted the Forebears of Christ in the days of Pope Julius. The final solution was to be much grander and more complex, developing the right side in particular, but what is to be seen here in the vortex of damned and elect already follows a new rule, which is no longer the same as, for example, in the sketch for the Bronze Serpent (Fig. 176). There is a marked whirling centripetal force, urging toward Christ with his gesture of fulminating overwhelming judgment, a decisive moral significance involving every figure, those barely hinted at as well as those more emphasized.

In the London drawing, a study for the Martyrs and Damned to the left of Christ (Figs.

196 Study for St. Laurence in the Judgment. Haarlem, Teyler Museum (178).

469

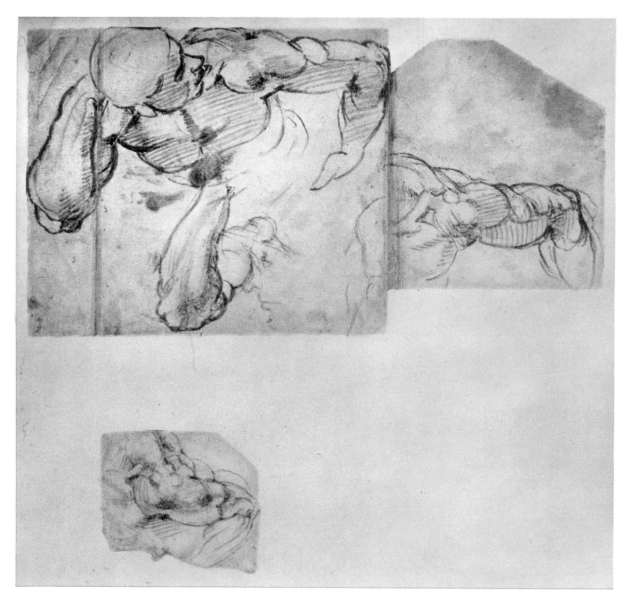

198 Studies for the Judgment. Haarlem, Teyler
Museum (179).

197 Martyrs and damned. London, British Museum (172).

199 Pietà. Haarlem, Teyler Museum (179).

200 Heads for the Judgment. London, British Museum (172).

197 and 200),[172] the choral feeling is more intense than in the corresponding section of the final fresco and the impression is that of a bunch (Fig. 197), but there still prevails the ethical subordination of the form of the group, and the two magnificent studies for heads on the verso (Fig. 200) achieve a mighty meditational synthesis.

A study at Windsor likewise deals with the risen, as they rise with difficulty out of the earth, or are drawn from it (Figs. 201, 202).[173] Others in Florence (Casa Buonarroti 69 F v., Fig. 192;[174] Uffizi 618 E, Fig. 193;[175] Casa Buonarroti 54 F, Fig. 203;[176] *ibid.* 46 F, Fig. 207[177]) relate to particulars. The splendid study for San Lorenzo in Haarlem (Fig. 196)[178] is a good instance of a detailed study of a single figure bringing out the enormous physical power of the personages of the Judgment, without any kind of pretentiousness, but rather tormented in shading and outline and with its face turned in anxiety toward the judgment from on high.

Cursory as this listing may have been, it may still have indicated how, in the Judgment, the return to titanic anatomism reaches a limit beyond which there can only be involution and dissolution (not in any negative sense, but referring only to formal structures). It seems fated that with time there is a gradual transition (Figs. 198, 199)[179] from studies still connected with the ideas of the Judgment to the last spiritualist drawing of Michelangelo, tremulous and defeated (cf. also Fig. 207).

201 Risen. Windsor, Royal Library (173).

471

204 Head and other sketches. Florence, Uffizi (177).

202 Studies for the Judgment. Windsor, Royal Library (173).

203 A damned man (?). Florence, Casa Buonarroti (176).

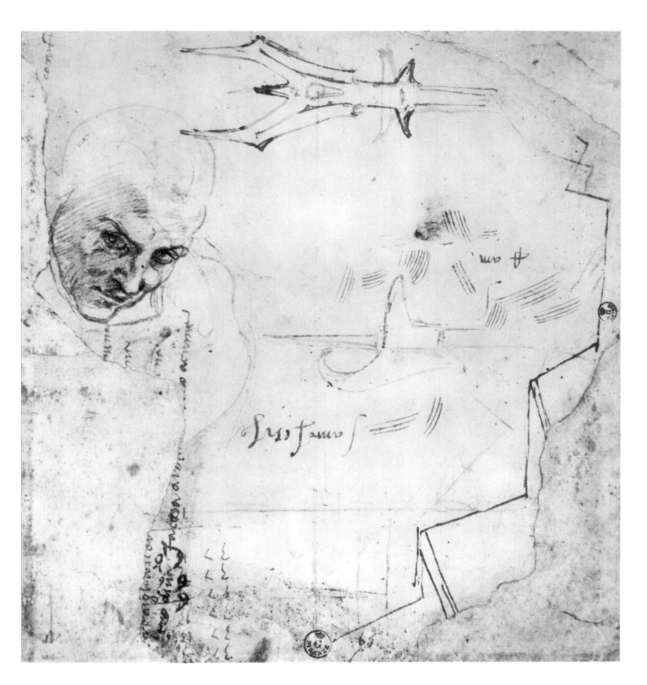

168 Tolnay, 1951, accepts as authentic only the first overall sketch of Casa Buonarroti (here, Fig. 194), the London one of Martyrs and Damned (here, Fig. 197), three sketches and two studies in the Vatican Library (in his Vol. V, Figs. 134-6 and 155-6) and a study at S. Marino, California.

169 Tolnay, V, Fig. 132 and No. 170.

170 Barocchi, 1942, No. 141, and Pl. CCX.

171 Black pencil with later retouching in ink; 41.8 × 28.8 cm. The recto is the first overall sketch for the Last Judgment, and can be dated 1533-34.

172 British Museum 1895, 9, 15, 518; black pencil and sanguine; 38.5 × 25.3 cm.

173 No. 12776; charcoal; 42.5 × 28 cm.

174 Black pencil; 39.8 × 28.2 cm. Cf. Barocchi, Exposition 1964, No. 147. The recto relates to a Pietà.

175 Ink; 9 × 6.5 cm. At least close to the studies for the Judgment. Barocchi, Exposition 1964, No. 148.

176 Black pencil; 25.8 × 15.7 cm. For Steinmann, relates to one of the damned; for Barocchi (Exposition 1964, No. 149), a little later in date, "forming as it were a passage from the plastic torment of the Sistine fresco to the meditative inwardness of maturer drawings."

177 Black pencil; 9.7 × 14.5 cm. Cf. Barocchi, 1942, No. 149. According to Frey, Berenson, and others, relating to the Judgment; for Wilde, Dussler and Barocchi, later, after 1550. We also give Drawing 14412 r. and v of the Uffizi (Figs. 204 and 206), in which the head "reveals the same mature torment as the studies for the faces of the Judgment," and the horseman "in his closed rotating form seems to prelude the models of the Cappella Paolina" (Barocchi, Exposition 1964, No. 150).

178 Teyler Museum, No. 13; charcoal; 24 × 18 cm.

179 The drawing (Haarlem, Teyler Museum 15 A; charcoal; 16.5 × 30.6 cm.) has been related (Marcuard) on the recto to the Judgment, on the verso to a Pietà (c. 1550). Cf. Tolnay, V, Nos. 244-5.

472

205 Detail of Fig. 206.

206 Horseman. Florence, Uffizi (177).

207 Figure for the Judgment (?). Florence, Casa Buonarroti (177).

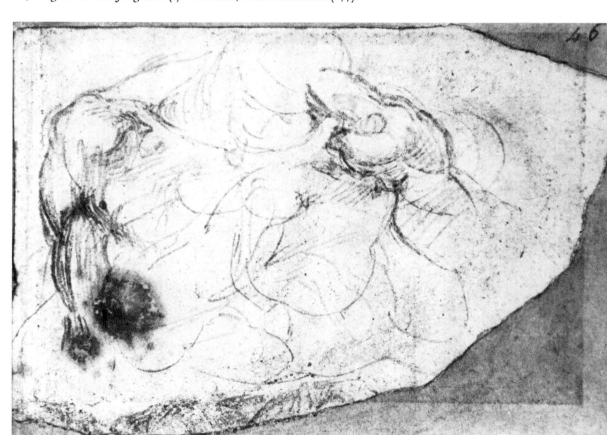

Architectural studies of the Roman period
(1541-64)

In Michelangelo's old age, while his vision turned inward in terms of figures, his mind, before which the whole world now bowed down in official reverence, turned to the great architectural creations of St. Peter's, the Campidoglio, etc. Frey and Tolnay note that " the language of architecture corresponded to the propensity of old age toward reasoning, abstraction, and synthesis."

Here only a few architectural drawings of the Roman period from 1541 on will be examined, referring to others that appear in the section on architecture; naturally, the interest is restricted to the exclusively graphic aspect.

In the sheet in Casa Buonarroti (Figs. 211 and 209) [180] for the tomb of Cecchino Bracci in Aracoeli (1544), the touch is certainly much livelier and more inventive than in the version by Pietro Urbano; in fact, the sureness is freer than it is in the drawings for the tombs of the Medici Sacristy, as for example the asymmetry with which the right side of the forms is more developed and stronger than the left. Compared with the edible gifts of Luigi Del Riccio and the almost openly artificial sonnets mourning the deceased youth with which Michelangelo paid for the food, these are certainly the frankest of the thoughts brought out on this occasion. " All of Rome mourns him, Messer M. is making me a drawing for a worthy marble tomb..."

Of the projects for St. Peter's and the Dome (1546 on), beginning with the sketch in the Vatican Library (cf. Tolnay, 1951, Fig. 357), not even the most representative sheets are shown here (see them in the architecture section), namely the one at Lille for the drum and dome (Lille, Musée des Beaux-Arts, Coll. Wicar 97), although sometimes attributed in part to assistants; and the one in the Teyler Museum at Haarlem (A 29), [181] likewise with the profile of the dome and the lantern, serves at least to recall Drawing 35 A of Casa Buonarroti (Fig. 210), [182] which has been discussed as documentation by Tolnay and Wittkower but, while cer-

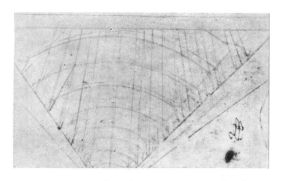

208 Perspective of vault. Paris, Louvre (184).

209 Studies for the Tomb of Cecchino Bracci and the Judgment. Florence, Casa Buonarroti (180).

474

211 Studies for the Tomb of Cecchino Bracci and the Judgment. Florence, Casa Buonarroti (180).

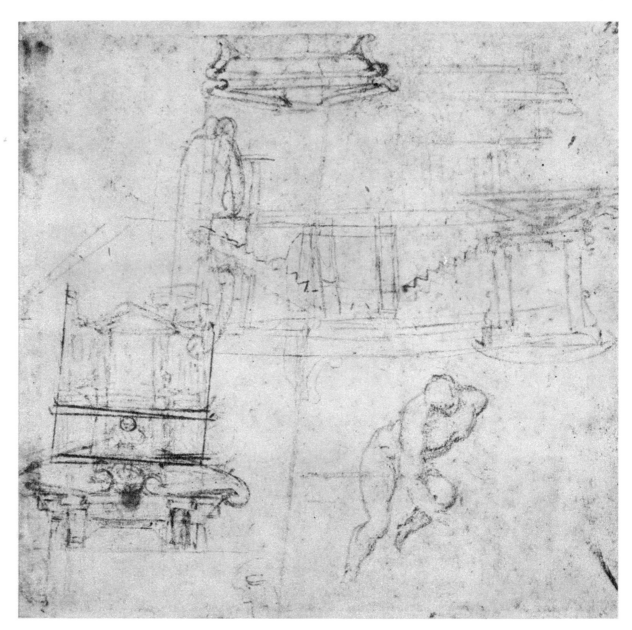

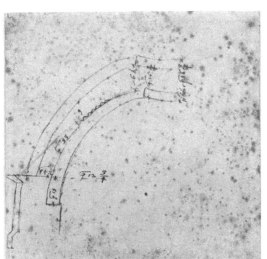

210 Section profile of dome. Florence, Casa Buonarroti (182).

tainly authentic calligraphically, must also be so in design.[183] As for a Louvre drawing (Fig. 208) [184] with a vault in foreshortening, it strangely suggests modern technocism with its deep perspective of a complex linear network.

In the section on architecture, note the beautiful plan drawings (dating 1559-60) for San Giovanni dei Fiorentini (especially Casa Buonarroti numbers 121 A, 120 A, 124 A), showing the transition from a static and subtle structure conceived first with an eye to the geometrically linear composition (Drawing 121 A) to a dynamic centrifugal conception of lines of force (Drawing 120 A) and finally, in Drawing 124 A, to a weighty sense of the matter deeply permeated by these forces, monumental and dramatic, in the contrast between the full water-color parts and the broken line, and the voids made dynamic by the guidelines marked out in pencil.

On the verso of the same Drawing 124 A (Fig. 214) [185] the upper portion of a portal likewise shows strong monumentality, with insistent linear tension in the moldings, as in another drawing (Fig. 212),[186] likewise with a doorway and a house plan for the so-called " Palazzo d'Altopascio."

For the studies for Porta Pia (c. 1561), another splendid series (in addition to those at Haarlem and Windsor, cf. 73 A bis of Casa Buonarroti; and *ibid.* 99 A, 84 A, 97 A, 102 A [see Plate XXVIII], 106 A r.), we refer again to the section on architecture. Here we can show only the little 84 A (Fig. 213),[187] with a highly suggestive line that, as in some figure studies, thinks in a flurry of ideas that superpose, intensifying the imaginative power, as is done here in the scaling of the two different pediments that then combine, and the studied balance between vertical drive and massive plastic solidity, extending horizontally. This series was conceived and drawn three years before Michelangelo's death, when he was eighty-six!

---

[180] Black pencil; 19.1 × 19.7 cm. The figures are studies for the Last Judgment; the staircase designs have been linked, though only hypothetically, with the Palazzo del Senatore on the Campidoglio, and with the Belvedere. Barocchi, Exposition 1964, No. 154.

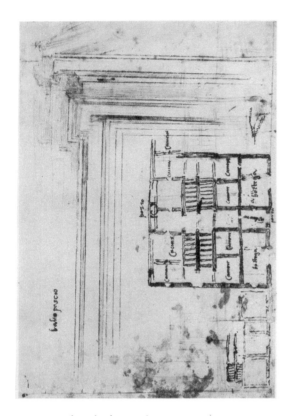

212 Portal and plan. Florence, Casa Buonarroti (186).

214 Studies of portal. Florence, Casa Buonarroti (185).

213 Study for Porta Pia. Florence, Casa Buonarroti (187).

181 Reproduced in Tolnay 1951, Fig. 359; included the tiny but splendid study for a portal of the type of Porta Pia, once in the upper right, but now detached.

182 Ink and black pencil; 16.1 × 16 cm. Barocchi, Exposition 1964, No. 155.

183 Also in Florence, Casa Buonarroti Drawing 31 A, with the plan of the drum of St. Peter's dome; 117 A v. (cross-section of the same dome?); and 118 A v., with important sketches for the lantern, related to Brunelleschi's for Santa Maria del Fiore (the first and the third of these drawings are reproduced in the section on architecture).

184 No. 842 verso; black pencil; 24.1 × 13.2 cm. (the recto corresponds to our Fig. 222). This verso was first published by Tolnay, V, 1960, No. 248.

185 Black pencil, ink, water color, with recto showing through strongly; 41.6 × 37.2 cm. Cf. Barocchi, 1962, No. 160, who links the idea of the portal to those of Drawings 118 A verso and 117 A recto (Fig. 212), and agrees with Dussler in giving a date later than 1540.

186 Casa Buonarroti 117 A; black pencil, ink; 27 × 40 cm. Cf. Barocchi, Exposition 1964, No. 159; the Palazzo Grifoni in the piazza of SS. Annunziata in Florence, to which the drawing has been referred in view of the annotation "d'Altopascio" (since Grifoni was administrator of the Ospedale di Altopascio), was not bought before 1549 and work on it began only in 1557. Plan of the same palace in Casa Buonarroti Drawing 118 A r. (shown in chapter on architecture).

187 Black pencil, ink; 11 × 8 cm. Cf. Barocchi, Exposition 1964, No. 170.

Figure drawings of the final period
(from about 1540)

A survey of the final period of Michelangelo's figure drawing may start with a consideration of the compositions done about 1540 for Vittoria Colonna, in which a noteworthy iconographic renewal shows the religious development that the noblewoman had inspired in the artist, but did not as yet bring about a decisive formal equivalent, in view of the conservative taste of Colonna (as of Cavalieri) for things "subtly and marvelously done," "finished."

It is doubtful, however,[188] that the Boston drawing (Gardner Museum) for the *Pietà*, documented as late 1546, is authentic. The authenticity proposed for the sanguine relating to the Madonna of Silence (c. 1538-40) in the Duke of Portland collection[189] may carry more conviction, especially in view of its provenance from the Casa Buonarroti. Doubts have also been voiced as to the London drawing for the Christ Crucified (Fig. 217)[190] for Colonna (c. 1540), " in which that body is seen not as falling like an abandoned dead man, but as feeling and tortured like a living person under the harsh torment " (Condivi). The reason for the doubts is the extreme finish of the drawing, and yet we know that it was precisely finish of this sort that the lady appreciated in the original. We have to accept this sheet dominated by its weighty Herculean figure, almost recalling the Crucifieds like sharks nailed out on boards of certain Romanesque paintings, in a posture producing great linear and plastic-chiaroscural tension that yet remains paganly material and rather indifferent, except for the pathos of the face; in fact, the Christ, especially from the waist up, owes much to the Lao-coön.

The rest of the paper, although all worked over in pencil, gives a feeling of the abstract void, with the great background of sky over the little arched patch of desert ground below, as well as the two grieving angels kept in a low tone.

We realize the development in the conception of the crucified figure that has taken place here when we consider a sketch still imbued with youthful classical harmony of proportions; dated in the second decade (c. 1515), at Christ Church, Oxford (Fig. 215).[191] Much more tragic, even though it is the torment of a thoroughgoing anatomical analysis of the muscles, is the

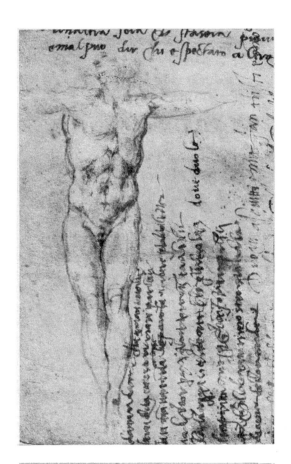

215 Crucifix. Oxford, Christ Church (191).
216 Crucifix. Vatican (193).

477

219 Crucifix. Haarlem, Teyler Museum (192).

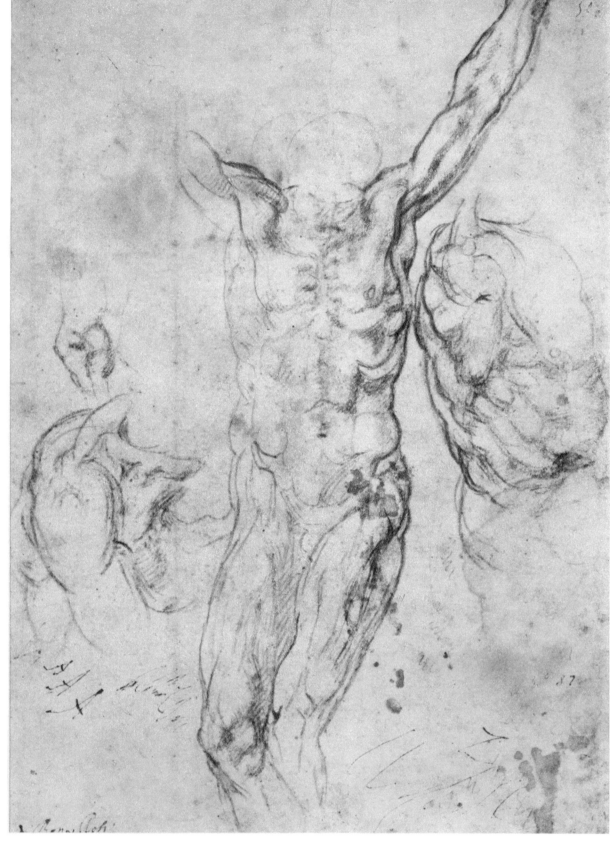

218 Sketch for the Sorrowing Virgin. Paris, Louvre (194).

◁ 217 Crucifix for Vittoria Colonna. London, British Museum (190).

Crucifix in a Haarlem drawing (Fig. 219),[192] dated by Tolnay about 1530-34, that is, at the end of the experience of the New Sacristy; whereas in a later sketch (c. 1557) on the back of a letter (Fig. 216) [193] the same arrangement takes on a direct spiritualized dramatic quality, even though the hand is now senile.

For the more elaborate version of the Christ Crucified for Vittoria Colonna, enriched by the figures of the two Mourners (c. 1538-41), the drawings that have the best title to be considered authentic (Figs. 218 and 221; [194] Fig. 220 [195]) embody various gradations of the figures: the sketch that for the Virgin (Fig. 218) is still indeterminate and roughed out will at the end (Fig. 221) have a powerful finish, both in the drapery swathing the anatomical structure and the psychological meanings of the face and hands; and at a point further back, the more fluid figure of St. John (Fig. 220) is still low in key and unfocused, perhaps, for present-day taste.

It is the last series of drawings for a Crucifixion (Figs. 222-230) that is thought to be of late conception, about 1555, possibly with a view to a projected sculptural group, that communicates the deepest impression. Tolnay has observed that the configuration of the figure seems to arise out of a truly mystical vision: " The images... are translucent, illumined by

221 Sorrowing Virgin. Paris, Louvre (194).

220 St. John in sorrow. Paris, Louvre (195).

223 Crucifixion. Paris, Louvre (200).

222 Crucifix. Paris, Louvre (197).

a veiled inner glow, and seem to give off a light vapor that makes their contours fluid and isolated.

By means of this phosphorescence the artist expresses the light that is peculiar to mystic visions... The bodies of the personages lose their materiality, their contours are simplified almost into straight lines; at the same time they are slightly evanescent, and the forces that once exalted them grow fainter and fade away..." [196] In a Louvre drawing (Fig. 222) [197] the figure as compared to previous ones (cf. Figs. 217 and 219) is shown simplified in its full-face view (barely bent to the left) and square, the limbs rather compact than articulated, and the outline has lost its analytical attack; the sculptural aspect is concentrated in the projection of the thorax over the sunken abdomen, the style expressing an inner vision, like that of the face of Christ. In an Oxford sheet (Figs. 228, 229) [198] the Crucified with face twisted to the right weighs down on the two mourners because He is low on the cross, the chest and legs jutting out boldly; an almost glowering frame of mind seems to have crept into the figures of the mourners, the nude apparently entering from the left, and the despairing man at the right with his head in his hands. There is something that even suggests Grünewald,

480

although of course far from the German's extreme expressionism. In another Windsor drawing (Fig. 224) [199] the crucified figure is low in pitch and rendered indistinct by variants, but the two mourners have formal finish and considerable psychological subtlety expressed in the studied attitudes of the Virgin hiding herself with her arms on her breast and of St. John looking on anxiously with both hands raised and pointing. Here too it seems to me we can perceive a sense, only a vague one, of affinity with the Northerners and their subtle feeling for psychology; although the Virgin recalls the figure in the Sistine Last Judgment, she now has a less proud majesty (still compassionate) than in the fresco, with the same humility and a

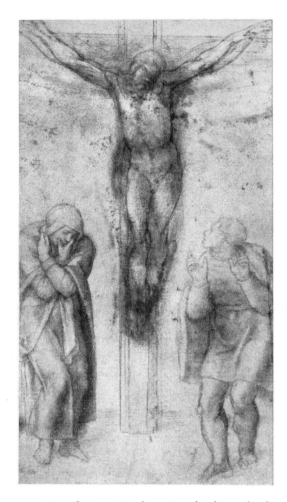

224 Crucifixion. Windsor, Royal Library (199).

226 Crucifixion. London, British Museum (201).

225 Crucifixion. Windsor, Royal Library (202).

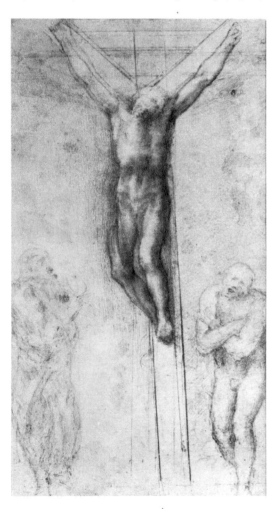

sort of equivocal nuance; so that this half-hidden face may recall, for example, the peering Madonna of Breughel's Adoration of the Magi in London.

On the other hand, dramatic power marks Louvre Drawing 700 (Fig. 223) [200] and one in London (Fig. 226).[201] In the Paris drawing the figure of Christ is given on the same plane as that of the two mourners, but the posture with the arms crucified on high gives it a vertical drive, with a dominant central axis along which the force of gravity runs but also an opposite force of elevation; that is, the horizontal components are reduced and the effect is more heroic, furthered by the intensified chiaroscuro treatment of this figure, which is dimin-

481

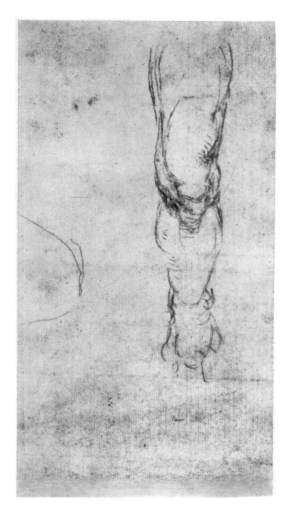

ished in the Virgin on the left and still more so in the St. John, which is only embryonic. Variants are hinted at in the chiaroscuro halo that surrounds the upper portion of the Christ in particular, as the left arm; rather than weakening the figure they enhance it, like a dark resonance effect of shadow or echo; and this is also true for the halo that enlarges the head and right edge of the Virgin. In the London sheet (Fig. 226), on the other hand, the dramatic effect is intensified by the play of diagonals from the angles, in the strange cross and the tightly folded arms of the Virgin. The figures of the mourners too reinforce this general rhythm, their slanting figures at an angle to the Christ, whose arms help in the spreading-out of the lines that are formed below by the outer contours of the two figures; that is, even laterally to the Christ the reference is to two triangles. Just at this point the accent is on the dynamically centrifugal elements, as if in an explosion of dramatic quality; the modeling of the Crucified one, which is rather precise in the arms and the Cross, is less in focus in the face and body, while the two mourners are echoed by a shadow halo; and indicative of the dynamic conception is the variant idea for the right arm of the Virgin, which would have had it outstretched. A Windsor drawing (Fig. 225) [202] is still at a less decisive stage; the Crucified seems to hint at twisting upon Himself, and likewise the two mourners are very vague but still suggestive.

Finally, in another London folio (Fig. 230) [203] the feeling is at last serene in the two figures holding together in contact with the Crucified, whose arms are horizontal once more and seem to be spread out in protection; the feeling of absolute inwardness is given by the three nude, somewhat tremulous figures:

> Let painting now and sculpture both be quiet
> The soul now turned toward that love Divine
> That opened, to take us in, Its arms on the Cross.

227 Back of drawing of Fig. 225.

228 Crucifix. Oxford, Ashmolean Museum (198).

482

229 Crucifixion. Oxford, Ashmolean Museum (198).

230 Crucifixion. London, British Museum (203).

Going back a step, there is a series of small sketches by Michelangelo (c. 1542-1550) that were used for paintings by Daniele da Volterra.[204] The Pierpont Morgan Library in New York has four tiny studies for a David and Goliath (Figs. 231-234)[205] that retain the *terribilità* and the feeling of the monumental. The same compositional idea of two men fighting, with one of them down (Figs. 231 and 235), recurs in a sheet of the Ashmolean Museum in Oxford, which, however, is for a Samson and a Philistine, and is considered to have a later date (Fig. 235).[206] In these two highly finished sketches, we still find a strong sculptural quality, heightened by the chiaroscuro and the complex organization of the composition.

In a private Swedish collection, and likewise for a painting by Daniele da Volterra, is a sketch of a Mercury (?) dragging Aeneas from the couch of Dido (Fig. 236),[207] on the verso of a sheet (Fig. 238) showing a figure of a prophet, which Tolnay believes was for a series (Christ, the Apostles, and Prophets) to be painted in niches in the interior of St. Peter's. To the same project is further referred a drawing in Haarlem (Fig. 237),[208] which could be dated 1547.

The Aeneas and Dido referred to above still has an extremely powerful pictural touch, as does the Prophet (Fig. 238), which equally expresses a vigilant, anxious feeling, one that 483

can therefore be connected with the Annunciation drawings (Figs. 247 and 250), dated about 1550; but in the sheets now being discussed the more sustained quality of the drawing suggests a slightly earlier date.

These drawings (Figs. 236 and 238) are evidently linked up as well with Michelangelo's last great undertaking in painting, the two episodes of the Pauline Chapel (1542-50), after which the seventy-five-year-old Titan refused to risk the hard labor of fresco anymore. But if we look at the Naples cartoon for the Crucifixion of St. Peter (Fig. 240),[209] we see that Michelangelo's monumental form had now reached its highest point in the Cappella Paolina. It is precisely the "drawing," an abstract mental conception expressed by the line, that alone sup-

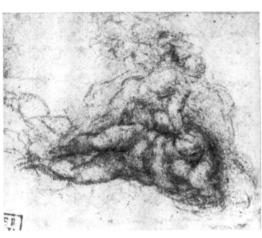

231-234 Sketches for a David and Goliath. New York, Pierpont Morgan Library (205).

236 Aeneas and Dido. Haarlem, Teyler Museum (207).

484

238 Prophet. Haarlem, Teyler Museum (207).

◁ 235 Samson and Philistine. Oxford, Ashmolean Museum (206).

237 Prophets in niches. Haarlem, Teyler Museum (208).

ports the weighty framework of these figures. The force of the edge of the line, without cutting in too deeply, defines the forms spread out over large plane areas, proceeding with a certain parallel squaring-off of the figures, which the drawing itself, with virtuoso curvilinear definition and discreet help from chiaroscuro, transforms into spatially defined, weighty sculptural masses.

Hence, the drawing emerges as a prehensile act of the mind, a technique that grasps and gives a figure to generic forms (legs, torsos, heads) that are elevated to expressive monumentality by the dignity of general "ideas"; and the drawing organizes and individualizes them sufficiently to obtain a dramatic significance, ideal but still concrete.

In the London cartoon with the so-called Epiphany (Fig. 239),[210] thought to date from about 1550, it seems that we can find a further liminal essential quality given the drawing. Although we owe the weak and feeble retouches to Condivi (as well as the addition of the three heads in the background), the original state must have had a form in which the contour line itself tended to be reabsorbed in the primary matrix of the figured idea modeled in pure *draftsman's chiaroscuro*, a sort of "lack of finish" in drawing, in which the first thing to emerge was the "total" imagined, as in fact we find it in some other drawings (cf. Fig. 251). The style therefore agrees admirably with the conception of the composition, the Child Jesus who has almost returned to his mother's womb, surrounded by the questioning of the figure to the left, and the curiosity of the Youthful St. John. "The presence of the Saviour is esoteric, in that

486

239 Holy Conversation. London, British Museum (210).

He exists only for the initiated, for those in whose souls He has been revealed, but He does not appear to those who seek him externally " (Tolnay): thus, the Michelangelesque form too now tends to exist only for those who are able to apprehend it in its ineffability, to discern

240 Cartoon for the Crucifixion of St. Peter. Naples, Museo di Capodimonte (209).

487

241 Sketches of apostles sleeping. Oxford, Ashmolean Museum (212).

242 Sleepers. London, British Museum (211).

it by active spiritual intuition and not merely by passive optics, within the opaque prison that matter makes for the profound idea.

Another set of late Michelangelo sketches (c. 1550-55) was used by Marcello Venusti. He painted a Christ in the Garden; the best version is in the Galleria Doria in Rome, while the drawing is in the Uffizi, a composition to which some sheets of Buonarroti refer. Thus, a very small, quick note in the British Museum, for the sleeping Apostles (Fig. 242),[211] figures turned in upon themselves; and another study in the Ashmolean Museum (Fig. 241),[212] in which it is mainly frontally that the figures are bent double, as the pencil notes them and envelops them in the shadowy halo. Finally, the problematical drawing in the Albertina (Fig. 243), in which Tolnay, with reason, sees as authentic only the sketch on the left, considering as school pieces the other three, which gradually define a female figure. I wonder, though, whether Michelangelo, now in extreme old age (the date of the inscription, by the way, is not absolutely probative), perhaps having been asked for the gift of a drawing, may not have started from a first conception of the type of an apostle asleep in the garden and then gradually repeated and developed it, certainly at some point resorting to firmer hands than his own, in other words, repeating in reverse the phases his drawing had passed through. Thus in the sketch furthest to the right, perhaps at least in part executing with his own hand after the type of Figs. 242 and 246, and then having it brought by others to the stage of the highly finished drawings for Cavalieri, in the uppermost figure: a woman sleeping in a robe that cloaks her face and takes the imprint of her bulk. This is a translation into the objective and decorous terms of the distant Cavalieri period of the late "haloes," and also a translation of the idea of form linked to matter that was basic in Buonarroti but that now was preferably expressed in tremulously sketched forms by the tired hand. It might also be that in 1560, on a sheet on which he himself had previously drawn, Michelangelo took up again, in the sketch on the left, the theme of a figure that formerly he could so fully master, but now could barely indicate.[213]

There are in existence other sketches for the Expulsion of the Moneychangers from the Temple from which Venusti derived his painting in the National Gallery in London. In three British Museum studies (Fig. 244, [214] Fig. 245, [215] Fig. 246 [216]) we see the image gradually broaden in conception, until a balance is achieved between the right and left sides of the composition and the details are defined, although the touch, even in the most developed sketch (Fig. 246), retains a vibrantly sketched and flaky quality, resistant to further detailing, especially when minute.

Venusti also made use of Michelangelo studies for an Annunciation (c. 1550) in two of his own compositions. In a British Museum drawing (Fig. 247) [217] the reference seems to be to Venusti's Annunciation in St. John Lateran, so that I am not at all sure of the connection (Wilde) drawn between the hand of the Angelo discernible on the right and the angel sketched on the back of another drawing in the British Museum,[218] who would seem to be in flight; accordingly, this most important variant could be eliminated from the picture in St. John Lateran, in which the angel is on earth. But confining ourselves to graphic considerations, the drawing is of the highest quality. Inside a diffuse chiaroscuro halo within which a variant for the right arm of the Virgin is hidden, there emerges the strong, sketched form, which the assumed adhesion of the drapery reduces to a sheathed nude treated with surface sensibility, and to which the sudden twisting movement and the interesting shading of the face give an emotional meaning of surprise and obedience. In the other British Museum drawing (Fig.

488

Micaelis Angeli manu Anno artatis suæ lxxx vij.
Roma 1560. xx vij. Martij.

243 Studies of sleeping figure. Vienna, Albertina (213).

250) [219] the reference is to the Annunciation of the Cappella Cesi (executed by Venusti and lost, but duplicated by Venusti himself in a small picture in the Galleria Nazionale in Rome, as well as in the cartoon in the Morgan Library), although the position of the figures is reversed; and the angel on the verso of this drawing is evidently for the same composition. Now, in this sheet, which might go back to 1547, the chiaroscuro is stronger, the embodiment of the form more pictural, as if in comment on a message whispered by the angel so close to the Annunziata.

When, over ten years later, Michelangelo was to return to this theme in the Oxford drawing (Fig. 249),[220] one of his very latest, the feeling for the pictural was to be even more spiritual, and the line, undone and worn out as it is, was to show as it were a differentiation between the Virgin, a creature of earth, a little more massive and charged by the chiaroscuro, and the long "ethereal" and "fluctuating" angel, like a phantom "that seems to come from far off" (Tolnay).

We are almost at the end of this survey of Michelangelo's drawing. The sixth decade of the century is probably the date of a sheet in the Fitzwilliam Museum in Cambridge, possibly referable to the "Christ Taking Leave of His Mother" that was the theme of a cartoon found in Michelangelo's house at his death, which later went to Cavalieri: "in which are drawn and sketched the figure of Our Lord Jesus Christ and that of the glorious Virgin Mary his mother" (Figs. 251, 252).[221] Here the stylistic manner of the recto (Fig. 251), sketchy but with an intense chiaroscural suggestiveness while the plastic mass of the figure is imbued with a skimming movement, is close to the drawings of the Crucifixion (cf. Fig. 223), which is believed to date from about 1555.

There are some valid reasons for doubting some sheets on a Descent from the Cross (Fig. 253) [222] and a Christ Borne to the Sepulcher (Fig. 254),[223] but now we see, derived from this theme, the Oxford drawing (Fig. 256),[224] in which two sketches deal with an action in the Descent and the other three with a Pietà, working out the idea that was to become the Rondanini Pietà. " Here the artist attacks the complex relationship between the dead and the living body, and, although facing up to the problem of multiple views, has not yet found that superhuman and primordial adhesion of the Mother to the Son that can be seen in the final sculptured version " (Barocchi); but what we gather is above all greater organization, due to spiritual intensification, of the massive conception that we have found in various late drawings of Michelangelo (cf. Figs. 241, 246, etc.). Where the two sketches for the Descent present a tight, frontally symmetrical group, as if developing the tragic late Crucifixions (cf. Fig. 230), with the body of Christ sunk with all its weight on the two mourners, keeping the cruciform opening of the arms, in the other three sketches the composition is conceived vertically, in an even more intimate and pathetic relationship of only two figures, one supporting and alive, the other abandoned and dead, studied in the meaningfulness of a diversity of views.

And, it has been said of the Rondanini Pietà, a further reversal, that " the faint torso of Christ... still rises despite everything, defying the laws of weight, while the figure of Mary must seek support on Him and seems to draw the warmth of life from that inert body " (Tolnay); that is, the image has been " transformed into the vision of the supreme consolation, thanks to the Divine love." But just at this point, when Michelangelo, repudiating in each and all of its consequences that very Form on whose uttermost enhancement he had labored all his life, was attaining absolute inwardness and in the face of imminent death a final " religious beatitude," now at last the masculine image that had always predominated in him and in his drawings, expressing a heroically active and severe ethics, was replaced by the ancestral female image; and the bulk that he had moved so much dissolves into a tremulous picturesqueness, recalling in a sense the old age of Titian and Renoir. It is touching to see how the drawing (Fig. 255) [225] that is thought to be the last one by him to come down to us is a Madonna and Child drawn by the shaky, old hand: behind the deformed appearance there is the intimacy of an absolute soliloquy, a fluttering idea of maternity, of contact no longer painful but an affectionate fusion, of origin and not of ending (or, at any rate, an ending that returns to the origin). And the shaky lines with which " the contour and the modeling suddivide into chiaroscural echos that now annul all the boundaries of the figure " (Barocchi) are waves of an energy that frees and perpetuates itself, the flow of a perennial fountain of physicality and spirituality.

After the longest of courses and the most sublime of experiments, Michelangelo's drawing, in a disintegration that has senile or even mortuary connotations, seems yet here to attain the ultimate secret of Life.

[188] Cf. Tolnay, V, p. 194, No. 197; and Fig. 159. According to Berenson, a copy.

[189] Cf. Tolnay, V, p. 193, N. 196; and Fig. 158.

[190] British Museum 1895, 9, 15, 504; black pencil; 37 × 27 cm. For this and the other related drawings cf. Tolnay, V, N. 198-201.

[191] Charcoal and bister; 16.5 × 10.5 cm. Cf. Berenson, N. 1578. This might relate to a " good thief," and there is some affinity to the Casa Buonarroti sketch 30 F, which Tolnay (V, N. 156, Fig. 161) refers to the fourth decade, while Dussler, followed by Barocchi, dates about 1520.

[192] Teyler Museum, N. 22; black pencil; 33.2 × 22.7 cm. On verso, sections of cornices. Not considered authentic by Berenson (" too fibrous and inept "), Knapp, and Panofsky; but accepted by Marcuard, Thode, Wilde (who dates 1535-40) and Tolnay (V, N. 157).

[193] Vatican Codex 3211, fol. 100 r.; black pencil. Cf. Tolnay, V, N. 258.

[194] Louvre, N. 720; black pencil; 23 × 10 cm. On recto the finished figure of the Virgin, on the verso the sketch. Tolnay (V, N. 199-200) doubts the authenticity, which is usually conceded.

[195] Louvre, N. 698; black pencil; 25 × 8.3 cm. Tolnay (V, N. 201) doubts the authenticity of this too, which is accepted by others.

[196] 1951, pp. 153 ff.

[197] N. 842; black pencil; 24.1 × 13.2 cm. Cf. Tolnay, V, N. 248. The verso is our figure 208.

245-246 Driving the merchants out of the Temple.
London, British Museum (215 and 216).

244 Driving the merchants out of the Temple.
London, British Museum (214).

[198] Ashmolean Museum, 72 r. (Fig. 229) and v. (Fig. 228); black pencil and white lead; 27.8×23.4 cm. The identification of the two mourners is controversial; the one to the right has been seen as the Madonna or St. John; to the left, the Madonna (?), St. John, or St. Peter. Cf. Tolnay, V, N. 254.

[199] Royal Library 12775; black pencil; 38.2×21 cm. Cf. Tolnay, V, N. 250.

[200] Black pencil and white lead; 43.2×28 cm. Tolnay, V, N. 249.

[201] British Museum 1895, 9, 15, 509; black pencil and white lead; 41.3×28.6 cm. Tolnay, V, N. 251.

[202] N. 12761; black pencil; 40.5×21.8 cm. On the back, a sketch of a block of marble important for the project of execution (Tolnay) and a study possibly for the left leg of the Crucified of the recto (Fig. 227). Cf. Tolnay, V, N. 252-3.

[203] British Museum, 1895, 9, 510; black pencil and white lead; 41.2×27.9 cm.

[204] Cf. Tolnay, V, pp. 199 ff.

[205] Black pencil; dimensions, in order: 4.9×6.6; 7.1×8.7; 5.1×8.4; 7×11.1 cm. Cf. Tolnay, V, N. 207.

[206] N. 69. Black pencil; 31×24.5 cm. The piece at the upper right, originally detached, relates to the composition of Christ driving the moneychangers from the Temple. The trend today is to give a date of about 1550. The verso is not believed to be authentic. Cf. Tolnay, V, N. 211.

[207] Haarlem, Teyler Museum, N. 18 verso; black pencil; 13.5×18 cm. Accepted by Berenson (N. 1470) and Tolnay (V, N. 209), who dates it about 1545, noting that the figure of Aeneas is very similar to that of the soldier at the left in the Conversion of St. Paul in the Cappella Paolina. Another study for the same composition is in the Coll. Bloch in London (Tolnay, *ibid.*, Fig. 193). The recto is our Fig. 238 (Tolnay, V, N. 215).

[208] N. 16 verso; 39.7×23.2 cm. Cf. Tolnay, V, N. 213. The recto relates to the dome of St. Peter's.

[209] Museo di Capodimonte 398; composed of 19 sheets attached to cloth; black pencil and water color; 263×156 cm. Source, like the London Epiphany, the Fulvio Orsini collection, from which it passed to the Farnese collection. Tolnay, V, N. 203; Barocchi, *Catalogo*, Exposition 1964, N. 151.

[210] British Museum 1895, 9, 15, 518; charcoal on brown paper (25 sheets); 232.7×165.5 cm. Cited in the Feb. 19,

1564 inventory: "another large paper, on which three large figures and two *putti* are drawn and sketched". Condivi, who drew from it the painting in Casa Buonarroti, retouched it and added some heads in the background. Cf. Tolnay, V, N. 236.

[211] N. 1885, 5, 9, 1894; black pencil; 6.6×10.1 cm. For these drawings, cf. Tolnay, V, N. 226-229 (this one is N. 228) and A. Perrig, "Michelangelo und M. Venusti" in *Wallraf-Richartz Jahrbuch* 1962. Formerly referred to the Last Judgment.

[212] N. 70-72; black pencil; 10.7×32.5 cm. Tolnay, V, N. 227.

[213] The disputed drawing in the Albertina (S. R. 169) is in charcoal, 17.3×19.8 cm. The ink inscription gives the date March 27, 1560, in Rome, when Michelangelo was 87. The one below, in pencil, reads (?): "February 17, at 23 hours, 1563 by Florentine usage, the year 1564 by Rome" (viz., the date of Michelangelo's death, as given in Vasari). For Berenson (N. 1606) the drawing could not go back further than 1540, and with its various stages may have been a lesson given to Cavalieri. The more sketchy figure at the left would be a pupil's work, a thesis directly the inverse of Tolnay's (V, N. 229), who as has been said considers it as the only one that is authentic.

[214] On these studies cf. Tolnay, V, N. 230-35, and his ideas on the dating. Our drawing, N. 1860, 6, 16, 2-1, is in charcoal, 13.9×13.7 cm. On the verso, four figures for the same theme. Tolnay, V, N. 233.

[215] 1860, 6, 16, 2-2; charcoal, 14×27 cm. Tolnay, V, N. 231. For the verso, *ibid.*, N. 230.

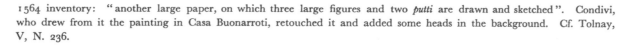

247 Our Lady of the Annunciation. London, British Museum (217).

248 Hand. Vatican (217).

249 Annunciation. Oxford, Ashmolean Museum (220).

250 Our Lady of the Annunciation. London, British Museum (219).

251 Christ taking leave. Cambridge, Fitzwilliam Museum (221).

253 Sorrowing Marys. London, British Museum (222).

252 Back of the drawing in Fig. 251 (221).

[216] 1860, 6, 16, 2-3; charcoal, 17.8×37.2 cm. Tolnay, V, N. 235.

[217] N. 1900, 6, 11, 1; black pencil; 34.8×22.4 cm. On verso, various non-authentic sketches. Cf. Tolnay, V, N. 220.

[218] Tolnay, V, Fig. 206; and cf. the two sheets side by side in Perrig, *art. cit.*, Fig. 167.

[219] N. 1859, 9, 15, 516; black pencil; 28.3×19.6 cm. For the verso, cf. preceding note. Tolnay, V, N. 221. The sketch in Codex Vaticanus 3211, fol. 74 r. (Fig. 248), has been related to the right hand of the Virgin; in connection with the letter on the back, it would date from 1547 (cf. Tolnay, V, N. 222).

[220] Ashmolean Museum N. 345, charcoal, 21.5×20 cm. The words written in above the Virgin and relating to the widow of Michelangelo's servant Urbino (died in December 1555), who lived at Casteldurante, date not earlier than 1556;

some put it as late as 1559-60 (when Michelangelo was eighty-five). Cf. Tolnay, V, N. 264, and his comment in the 1951 monograph, pp. 155-6.

[221] The Cambridge drawing, in black pencil, is 26.5×16.2 cm. Berenson (N. 1396 A) referred it to the *Noli me tangere* (1531) for Davalos, which Pontormo later executed, but the stylistic treatment is carried out differently, and despite the fact that one of the studies for a pointing left hand (recto, Fig. 251) much resembles the corresponding hand of the mourning Madonna in the Crucifixion for Vittoria Colonna (cf. Fig. 221), about 1540, our position should be not that they are contemporaneous but that here the motif was taken up again later (Tolnay, V, N. 224 and 225).

[222] British Museum, 1860, 6, 16, 4; charcoal; 21×14 cm. For Berenson (N. 1514), who appraises it with some reser-

493

254 Christ taken to the sepulchre. Paris, Louvre
(223).

255-256 Madonna and Child; Studies of Pietà.
London, British Museum (225), and
Oxford, Ashmolean Museum (224).

vations, the date should be about 1535. It seems to me that this group is certainly for the Marys of the Descent from the Cross relief (Daniele da Volterra?), of which there is a copy in Casa Buonarroti (Tolnay, VI, Fig. 215); an overall preparatory study for it is the Haarlem drawing (Tolnay, *ibid.*, N. 241 and Fig. 214) that Tolnay dates about 1536-40, and accepts. Others had previously attributed the Haarlem drawing to Sebastiano del Piombo or Daniele da Volterra.

[223] Louvre, N. 704 recto; sanguine; 29×18 cm. Accepted by Berenson (N. 1584) and others, and given various references and dates; Popp, however, attributes it to Rosso (Barocchi disagreeing, *Il Rosso Fiorentino*, 1950, p. 222); Tolnay questions it (V, No. 240). For the verso, cf. Berenson, *num. cit.*, and Barocchi, *op. cit.*, 1950, Fig. 212 (attributed to "Andrea di Michelangelo").
For two other drawings (Vienna, Oxford) attributed to Michelangelo and similar in theme, cf. Tolnay, V, N. 239 and 242, and Figs. 211-12.

[224] Ashmolean Museum 339; black pencil; 10.8×28.1 cm. Because of its technical and stylistic qualities, it has been linked to another Oxford sheet with studies for the Prayer in the Garden (here Fig. 241). Tolnay, V, N. 246 (the date is set in the monograph 1951, about 1555). For another study of Christ's descent from the Cross, cf. Tolnay, V, N. 244 and Fig. 217 (here Fig. 199).

[225] British Museum, 1859, 6, 25, 562; black pencil; 26.6×11.7 cm. Held to be even later than the late Crucifixions; Tolnay (V, N. 266) dates it (1951) between 1560 and 1564.

Bibliographical Note

General Review of the Drawings of Michelangelo:

B. Berenson: *The Drawings of the Florentine Painters* (1st ed. 1903; 2nd ed. Chicago 1938); 3rd ed. Milan 1961.
K. Frey: *Die Handzeichnungen Michelagniolos Buonarroti*, Berlin 1909-11.
H. Thode: *Michelangelo. Kritische Untersuchungen über seine Werke*, Berlin 1908-13.
E. Panofsky: *Handzeichnungen Michelangelos*, Leipzig 1922.
A. E. Brinckmann: *Michelangelos-Zeichnungen*, Munich 1925.
K. Frey-F. Knapp: *Die Handzeichnungen Michelagniolos Buonarroti*, Berlin 1925.

A. E. Popham: *Master Draughtsmen n. 1. Michelangelo*, London 1930.
M. Delacre: *Le Dessin de Michel-Ange*, Brussels 1938.
L. Goldscheider: *Michelangelo Drawings*, London 1951.
L. Dussler: *Die Zeichnungen des Michelangelo*, Berlin 1959.
C. Tolnay: *Michelangelo*, I-V, Princeton 1943-1960.
E. Borough-Johnson: *The Drawings of Michelangelo*, London s. d.
P. Barocchi: *Michelangelo. Mostra di disegni, manoscritti e documenti*, (*Catalogo*), Florence 1964.
M. Salmi, C. Tolnay, P. Barocchi: *Disegni di Michelangelo* (ed. Cassa di Risparmio di Firenze), 1964.
M. V. Brugnoli: *Michelangelo* (Drawings), Milan 1964.

In addition, for details:

F. Portheim: "Beiträge zu den Werken Michelangelos," *Repertorium für Kunstwissenschaft*, 1889.
F. Baumgart: "Die Jugendzeichnungen Michelangelos bis 1506," *Marburger Jahrbuch für Kunstwissenschaft* 1937.
A. E. Popp: *Die Medici-Kapelle Michelangelos*, Munich 1922.

SPECIAL WORKS

Florence

E. Jacobsen-P. N. Ferri: *Dessins inconnus de Michel-Ange*, Leipzig 1905.

C. Tolnay: " Die Handzeichnungen Michelangelos im Archivio Buonarroti " *Münchner Jahrbuch der bildenden Kunst*, 1928.

P. Barocchi: *Michelangelo e la sua scuola* (*I disegni di Casa Buonarroti e degli Uffizi*), vol. 2, Florence 1962.

P. Barocchi: *Mostra di disegni di Michelangelo* (*Catalogo*), Florence 1962.

M. Hirst: " Michelangelo Drawings in Florence, *Burlington Magazine* 1963.

Haarlem

F. Marcuard: *Die Zeichnungen Michelangelos im Museum Teyler zu Haarlem*, Munich 1901.

London

J. Wilde: *Italian Drawings in the British Museum, Michelangelo and his studio*, London 1953.

Oxford

J. A. Robinson: *A critical account of the drawings by Michelangelo and Raffaello in the University Galleries, Oxford*, Oxford 1870.

K. T. Parker: *Catalogue of the collection of drawings in the Ashmolean Museum, Vol. II. Italian Schools*, Oxford 1956.

Paris

L. Demonts: *Catalogue des dessins de Michel-Ange, Exposition*, Paris 1922.

The Vatican

C. Tolnay: " Die Handzeichnungen Michelangelos im Codex Vaticanus," *Repertorium für Kunstwissenschaft* 1927.

Vienna

F. Wickhoff: *Die italienischen Handzeichnungen der Albertina*, Vienna 1892.

Windsor

A. E. Popham-J. Wilde: *The Italian Drawings of the XV and XVI centuries in the Collection of His Majesty the King at Windsor Castle*, London 1949.

For a more detailed bibliography see the work of Dussler (1959), of Barocchi (1962), and always the Bibliography (1942-61, and including the former) in the monumental *Commento alla Vita vasariana* (1962, Vol. I); and now the recent compilation by Meller in this volume.

VI

MINOR WORKS

by Charles de Tolnay

What we know of Michelangelo's very sober private life indicates that by nature he must have had little interest in adorning his surroundings or in the artistic decoration of objects of everyday use. In this he was the antipode of Leonardo for whom adorning his surroundings was the natural thing to do, and who designed many objects of practical use with exquisite decoration. However, we cannot say that Michelangelo was opposed in principle to supplying designs for objects in the minor arts. When he made drawings for funerary monuments or chapels, or for such a library as the Laurentian, it was natural for him to make drawings for the secondary parts as well, like pavements, ceilings, sarcophagi, altars, fonts, coats of arms, etc., and, in the case of the library, even the furniture. He did this in order to achieve ab-

1-3 Left candelabrum on altar in the New Sacristy. Florence.

solute artistic unity in his work. Much less frequently, he designed isolated useful objects; but we do know of a dagger blade (1506-1507),[1] now lost, a marble " vase " or " plate " (possibly for a fountain), salt cellars, a bronze horse (probably the handle of an inkwell), for a bronze mortar for a pulpit (drawing, British Museum, No. 24) and two or three altar canopies. He made these objects either for friendship or for his patrons, to whom he felt indebted.

The formal genesis of these minor works of Michelangelo has not been investigated, although their history has been discussed by scholars such as Ronchini, Liverani, de Fabriczy, Thode, Schottmüller and Lavagnino, among others.

The problem of the altar tabernacle seems to have concerned Michelangelo at various times in his life. The earliest designs that have come down to us are two drawings for an altar canopy (and a design for a sarcophagus) on a sheet in Casa Buonarroti (Barocchi 36 r.; Fig. 15). On the other side of the sheet Michelangelo gives a summary of the history of the San Lorenzo façade from December 5, 1516 to February 25, 1518. The latter date would be, therefore, a *terminus post quem* for the sketches. It is not known whom they were meant for, but it is not impossible that, as Thode has suggested, they relate to the commission that Piero Soderini gave Michelangelo in May 1518 and the following months, for a reliquary to contain the head of St. John the Baptist, the patron saint of Florence, for an altar and for two sarcophagi (probably for S. Stefano and S. Silvestro) for the church of S. Silvestro in Capite in Rome.[2] Soderini was a Florentine, and it may not be fortuitous that Michelangelo chose for these projects an octagonal cupola on a drum with round windows, inspired by Santa Maria del Fiore.

The idea of the altar canopy as a little temple supported on a high shaft, as if suspended in the sky, is medieval in origin, familiar in Romanesque and Gothic art. The Florentine masters of the fifteenth century converted it into Renaissance forms, as for example Benedetto da Maiano did in the church of S. Domenico in Siena, 1475 (Fig. 13). Michelangelo must have gotten his idea from such a Quattrocento tabernacle, since the pattern of an octagonal small temple crowned by an octagonal dome with a lantern is repeated in his two sketches. In the fifteenth-century work, the shaft is broad and heavy and supports a narrow light temple; Michelangelo has the reverse, with the shaft relatively thin and its ascending movement accentuated by volutes, while the temple is broadened until it matches the breadth of the base.

498   4-5 Details of left candelabrum on altar in the New Sacristy.

6-9 Right candelabrum on altar in the New Sacristy.

Using repeated projecting moldings, accentuated shrines and alternating rectangular and broken pediments on the windows, the master succeeded in giving the temple a monumental aspect. To the same end, he inserted a drum under the cupola, a feature absent from the fifteenth-century work. Michelangelo placed the accents in such a way that the ascending movement of the ensemble took on the significance of an organic development, like that of a flower unfolding.

In a rapid sketch on the upper right of the same sheet the author varied the concept, giving the canopy the form of a cross, an invention that flourished in the sixteenth century, as is shown by a number of canopies, e. g. by Andrea Sansovino (Munich, Kupferstichkabinett) and Vasari (originally designed for the high altar of Santa Croce). However, the relative proportions of the slender high shaft and the broad temple remain about the same as in the first project.

A design for an altar, possibly related to the one for S. Silvestro in Capite, is preserved in Casa Buonarroti (Barocchi 98 r.).

Next come Michelangelo's designs for a canopy under a baldacchino on four columns, for the high altar of the church of San Lorenzo, between October 1525 and February 1526, which we identified (1928) in a sketch of the Archivio Buonarroti, Codex V, 29, folio 204 v. The design for the plan of this canopy is in the Casa Buonarroti drawing (Barocchi 96), identified by Geymüller. Instead of this canopy, which was never carried out, Michelangelo designed a shrine for relics over the main entrance of San Lorenzo, on the inner wall, which is still there.

Late in life Michelangelo made drawings and a model for a bronze canopy for S. Maria degli Angeli, which Vasari tells us (VII, 261) was later executed by Michelangelo's disciple Jacopo Del Duca. This work, in a fragmentary condition, is in the Museo di Capodimonte, Naples (Fig. 14). This canopy is mentioned not only by Vasari but also by Jacopo Del Duca in a letter to Leonardo Buonarroti (Daelli) dated March 15, 1565. The devoted pupil calls it a "metal tabernacle" and declares that in executing it he wanted to exalt Michelangelo's work rather than his own. This, too, consists of an octangle temple on a high base, one part of which is missing. The central part of the temple is covered by eight panels with reliefs telling the story of the Passion. Above it runs a strong circular cornice surmounted by a cupola with a scaled roof, today lacking its lantern and cross. To form an image of the original ap-

10 Ornamental vase with the Medici coat of arms. Florence, New Sacristy.

12 Michelangelo: designs for fountains. Florence, Casa Buonarroti.

11 Stoup. Florence, New Sacristy.

pearance, it must be filled in in imagination, with the base complete and the lantern, adorned with colored stones and glass in the circles and rectangles of the base, now empty, and eight lapis lazuli columns standing free in front of the pilasters. The temple thus seemed like a new version of Bramante's temple in S. Pietro in Montorio. This Bramantesque inspiration is characteristic of Michelangelo's old age. However, Del Duca does not seem to have followed the Master's design in the details, which are not characteristic of Michelangelo.[3]

A document dated August 3, 1574 describes a tabernacle with a bronze canopy by Jacopo Del Duca; this, too, octagonal and crowned by a globe supporting a risen Christ, designed by Michelangelo. This was three-quarters finished in February 1577 and was to have been bought by Philip II for the Escorial. But the negotiations broke down and ended on August 14, 1578 in a negative by the king.[4] There are two canopies in the Escorial: a marble

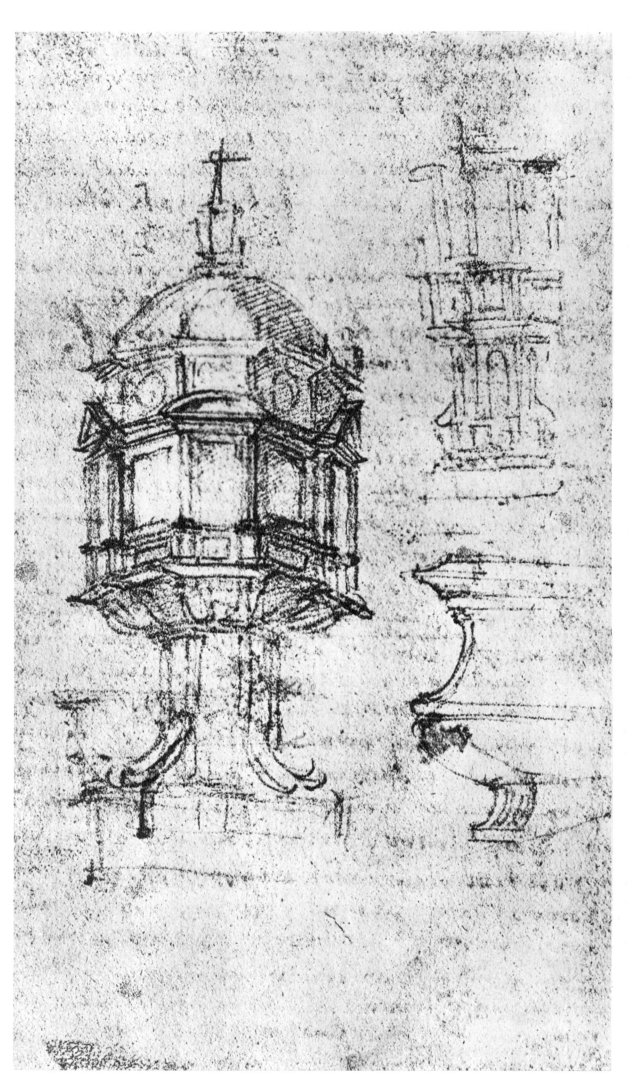

15 Michelangelo: designs for a canopy and sarcophagus. Florence, Casa Buonarroti.

13 Benedetto da Maiano: canopy. Siena, San Domenico.

14 Jacopo del Duca: canopy for Santa Maria degli Angeli in Rome. Naples, Capodimonte Museum.

model in the sacristy and a round temple with a hemispherical cupola on the high altar, also of marble. They do not accord with the description of Michelangelo's work, but both show the inspiration of Bramante's temple.[5] These canopies will be published by Xavier de Salas.

Thus, the idea of Michelangelo's canopy starts from the Quattrocento Florentine form and develops in the direction of Bramante's Roman conception, with a circle of detached columns around the temple.

16 Michelangelo and assistant: design for the Duke of Urbino's saltcellar (1537). London, British Museum.

18 Designs for bronze lamps. Cambridge, Mass., Fogg Museum of Art.

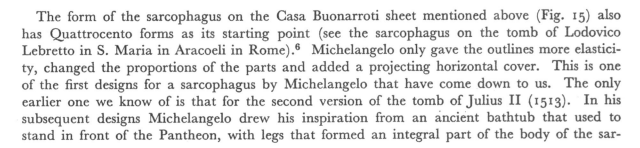

The form of the sarcophagus on the Casa Buonarroti sheet mentioned above (Fig. 15) also has Quattrocento forms as its starting point (see the sarcophagus on the tomb of Lodovico Lebretto in S. Maria in Aracoeli in Rome).[6] Michelangelo only gave the outlines more elasticity, changed the proportions of the parts and added a projecting horizontal cover. This is one of the first designs for a sarcophagus by Michelangelo that have come down to us. The only earlier one we know of is that for the second version of the tomb of Julius II (1513). In his subsequent designs Michelangelo drew his inspiration from an ancient bathtub that used to stand in front of the Pantheon, with legs that formed an integral part of the body of the sar-

17 and 19 Filippino Lippi: details of the top frame of the altar in the Chapel of St. Thomas. Rome, Santa Maria sopra Minerva.

20-21 Details of Julius II's Tomb. Rome, San Pietro in Vincoli.

cophagus. This is to be seen in the sarcophagi of the Medici Chapel and the projects for the tomb of Cecchino Bracci (Casa Buonarroti), which are not merely organized in horizontal zones but are also unified by the vertical lines of the legs. His contemporaries considered Michelangelo the insuperable Master in this domain. We know of about a dozen tombs that

24 Ornamental detail of one of the benches in the reading room of the Laurentian Library.

22 Detail of Julius II's Tomb. Rome, San Pietro in Vincoli.

503

25-26 Details of Julius II's Tomb. Rome, San Pietro in Vincoli.

27 Frieze of Benedetto Sopranzi's Tomb. Rome, Santa Maria sopra Minerva.

28 Mask on Giuliano de' Medici's armour. Florence, New Sacristy.

were either commissioned directly from him or executed by other masters who followed Michelangelo's directions after they had asked his advice.

We know from two letters that Michelangelo carved for Domenico Naldini a " vase " or " plate " at Carrara, probably for a fountain. Thode suggested that the three masterful ink sketches in Casa Buonarroti (Barocchi 97) might relate to this commission (Fig. 12).

The structure of the larger design corresponds to that of certain fifteenth-century fountains, for example the one attributed to Simone Ferrucci, originally in Villa Castello and now in the Pitti Palace. Here again, instead of piling unconnected forms one on top of the other, Michelangelo seeks the effect of an organic unity. The ascending movement becomes more effective because of the interruption caused by the horizontal bowl devoid of ornament. To attain his goal, the Master changed the proportions of every part: the low base of the fifteenth century becomes tall and slender with elastic contours; the heavy round stem is transmuted into a narrow neck, and the upper portion takes the aspect of a vase, reminiscent of the vase in the fountain attributed to Donatello or Verrocchio, in the space next to the choir of the Old Sacristy. To bring out the unity of the whole, Michelangelo has given up the Quattrocento ornament.

The two sketches to the right and left of the one mentioned above anticipate the development of the Roman fountains of the sixteenth and seventeenth centuries. In the sketch to the right a low basin is supported on a circular base that foreshadows certain Baroque fountains, such as the one facing the Medici Villa on the Pincio.

In the fragmentary sketch on the left we see a fountain in the form of a boat. This is ancient in origin, as is seen from a Renaissance copy of an ancient *ex voto* facing the entrance of S. Maria in Domnica in Rome. The boat shape is also found in fifteenth-century holy water stoups, for example in S. Maria Novella and in Santa Croce, the latter by Benedetto da Majano. Such later boat-shaped fountains as the one by Giacomo Della Porta in Piazza Colonna, or Pietro Bernini's ship in Piazza di Spagna, follow this tradition.

29 Mask drawings by Michelangelo. London, British Museum.

30-32 Friezes in the Medici Chapel. Florence.

33-35 Friezes in the Medici Chapel. Florence.

Because of the resemblance to the fountain in the Old Sacristy, it may well be that Michelangelo made these designs for the adjacent room, known as *lavamano*, in the New Sacristy. In any case, the powerful drive of the touch in these sketches indicates as their date the first period of the work on the Medici Chapel. This date is in agreement with the letters of Domenico Naldini and Giovanfrancesco Fattucci dated August 21, 1521.[7]

The holy water stoup of white marble in one corner of the Medici Chapel (Fig. 11) may likewise have been done from a design by Michelangelo. A remarkably small basin rests on a stem whose form derives from that of a baluster. The simplicity and unusual absence of ornament speak in favor of a hypothetical attribution to Michelangelo. Only, the moldings lack the keen finesse that Michelangelo favored in this period.

During the fifteenth century it was the fashion in Florence and Padua to make bronze inkstands, saltcellars, oil lamps and incense burners with statuettes, generally with satyrs or groups of satyrs, to which were added the vessels containing the incense, ink or salt. This tradition carried over into the sixteenth century, a celebrated example being the saltcellar that Benvenuto Cellini made for Francis I (about 1540). Here, too, the artist makes every effort to gloss over the practical purpose and give more relief to the mythological figures.

Michelangelo does not seem to have been satisfied by the duality between artistic form and utilitarian form. In the silver saltcellar he made for the Duke of Urbino, the heir of Pope Julius II, early in 1537, he tried to get a synthesis of the two forms. The starting point of his conception was the bowl of the cellar, to which he gave an organic aspect by adding claw feet (Fig. 16). The relatively small plastic figure on the top of the cover, a *putto* bending a bow, serves as a handle. The British Museum drawing of this cellar (Wilde, Catalogue of the British Museum, 66) is described in detail in a letter from Girolamo Staccoli, the Duke of Urbino's agent in Rome, dated July 4, 1537 (published by Vasari, ed. Milanesi, VII, 383): "In reply to a letter from Your Excellency...I can state that the model of the saltcellar in question has been finished for several months, and the silver work begun on certain animal claws, on which the bowl of the cellar is to rest, and around this bowl are certain festoons and masks, and on the cover a figure in the round, with certain other foliage, as Michelangelo ordered and as is shown on the model..." The drawing in question was probably executed by an assistant of Michelangelo and was used by the goldsmiths for the execution, but the figure of Cupid seems to have been added by Michelangelo himself.

A second saltcellar, now lost, which also was made from a design of Michelangelo's, was commissioned in 1567 from Manno, a Florentine goldsmith, by Cardinal Alessandro Farnese.

36 Detail of the floor of the Laurentian Library.

37 Detail of the floor of the Laurentian Library.

The goldsmith submitted two designs to the cardinal, a drawing on paper and a clay model, for him to choose the one he preferred. The author of the drawing is not named in the three letters sent to the cardinal—by his majordomo Lodovico Tedeschi, by Michelangelo's friend Tommaso de' Cavalieri and by Manno himself—concerning this work.[8] However, the letters clearly state that the clay model is Michelangelo's and that the figure on top, " where there are four tortoises," is missing. Cavalieri, too, states that the clay model was " made by order of Michelangelo " and adds that " certain things that did not please him [Michelangelo] have to be corrected, such as the tortoises on top, which are not right." No trace has ever been found of this second saltcellar by Michelangelo.

Two sketches for vases, inspired by ancient amphorae, are in the British Museum folio 27 v. This type was often followed in the fifteenth century as well. Michelangelo's sketches are distinguished by their vertical tension, which is expressed in the graceful, slim outlines, in the oval form of the principal part and in the elastic contour of the neck. These sketches are probably preparatory drawings for the vases decorating the corners of the shrines over the doors of the Medici Chapel, in which the silhouette becomes still more slender and elegant until it almost takes on the aspect of vases in the Louis XV style. Michelangelo decorated these vases with masks, fabulous dragons, swans and garlands without destroying the pure lines of their silhouettes.

Another small work, which Michelangelo did in 1537 for the Duke of Urbino, was a bronze horse that was probably used as the handle on the cover of an inkstand. Perhaps the life studies of horses in Casa Buonarroti and Oxford are related to this work.[9]

On a sheet, probably from the school of Michelangelo, now in the Fogg Museum in Cambridge, Massachusetts (Fig. 18), there are sketches in black pencil for little oil lamps; because

38 Sketch depicting Amor and Psyche for the floor of the Laurentian Library (see n. 40; relationship discovered by A. E. Popp). Florence, Casa Buonarroti.

39-45 Motifs of the floor of the Laurentian Library.

506

46-47 Benches, built to Michelangelo's design. Florence, Laurentian Library.

of their style, Wilde (Catalogue of the British Museum sub. 66) dates them prior to 1530. The upper sketch, representing a grotesque head with a very prominent jaw, is of a type that was well known in Padua in the Quattrocento, especially in the work of Riccio.[10] Michelangelo's drawing is distinguished from its model only by its freer imagination.

The fusion of the plastic and utilitarian forms is carried out in a more original way in the second sketch at the bottom of the sheet, which presents a satyr with a kind of yoke on his shoulder, blowing on a fire.

The coat of arms in the form of a *tête de cheval* or shield of the fifteenth and early sixteenth centuries recurs in two drawings by Michelangelo for the doorway of the Laurentian Library (about 1526), British Museum No. 37 r. and v. However, when in about 1530 the artist was making designs for the gallery of relics in San Lorenzo, he had a different idea and transformed the coat of arms over the doorway and under the gallery into a sort of horse's skull with the ears (Fig. 53). This motif is repeated even more abstractly on the tomb of Julius II in S. Pietro in Vincoli (Fig. 54), done in 1543 from a model by Michelangelo.[11] The center projects and becomes convex, while the circumference is concave. The lines are rounded out, no longer pointed; the material is soft, no longer " hard and fragile " (Wölfflin). What had been geometrical in the Quattrocento *tête de cheval* takes on an organic form. In the coat of arms over the main entrance of Palazzo Farnese, in which the forms soften, the convex center is framed by swellings reminiscent of ears in their shape (Fig. 55). These innovations of Michelangelo were very popular in coats of arms of the second half of the Cinquecento; for example, they were used in the coats of arms of the ceilings in Palazzo Farnese (Fig. 57, 58). The last form of coat of arms by Michelangelo that has come down to us is on Porta Pia, where the lower central portion is transformed into a lion's mask (Fig. 59).

507

48-50 Benches, built to Michelangelo's design. Florence, Laurentian Library.

Michelangelo's coats of arms are not only softer in substance than those of the fifteenth century, anticipating those of the Baroque, but are always inspired with a tension that assimilates them to living beings.

Candelabra by Michelangelo are known that date from both his youth and his old age. The one that the Angel on the tomb of St. Dominic in Bologna holds in his hands consists of a heavy stem with a spiral ornament. Those in the 1513 design for the tomb of Pope Julius show an altar base under the column. This is also the form given the candelabra on the altar

508

51 Frieze with masks. Rome, Palazzo Farnese (courtyard).

of the Medici Chapel. The one on the left is an original work (Figs. 1-5); the one on the right, according to Gori was broken about 1741 and restored by Ticciati. Bottari states, however, that it had been roughed out in Michelangelo's time and finished by Ticciati (Figs. 6-9). In the candelabra of the Quattrocento the base was low and the stem long; Michelangelo reversed the proportions so that the stem seems to be born from the base. The ornaments

52 Travertine frieze. Rome, Palazzo Farnese (courtyard).

54 Coat of arms on Julius II's Tomb.   Rome,
San Pietro in Vincoli.

55 Coat of arms over the great window in the
façade of Palazzo Farnese.

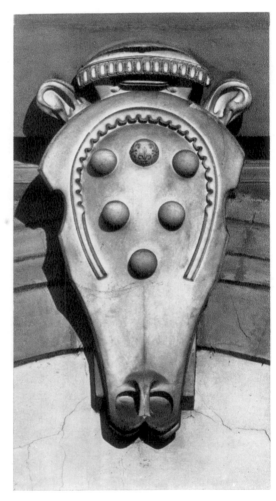

53 Coat of arms under the Tribune of the Relics.
Florence, Church of San Lorenzo.

56 Mask. Rome, Porta Pia.

58 Ceiling coat of arms in Palazzo Farnese.

59 Coat of arms. Rome, Porta Pia.

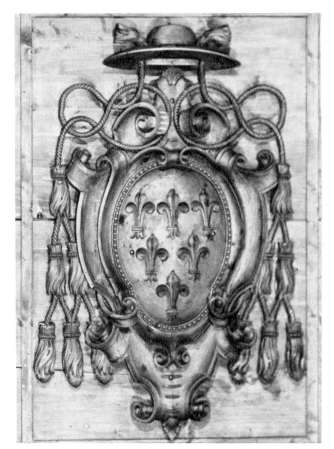

57 Ceiling coat of arms in Palazzo Farnese.

consist of masks, dragons, symbols of the vices, vases with flowers, the pelican with its young and pairs of birds—allusions to the salvation produced by Christ's sacrifice.

This form of candelabrum, inspired by the Roman candelabra of the Empire, was repeated by Michelangelo in the final version of the tomb of Julius (1542).[12] A sketch has been identified by us in Codex Vaticanus 3211 (fol. 25 v.). By now, in the later Roman period, the altar-shaped bases become broader and heavier.

The two large silver candelabra and the silver-gilt altar cross now in the Treasury of St. Peter's are by Antonio Gentili of Faenza (1581), but were attributed to Michelangelo as early as the end of the eighteenth century. Manno, a Florentine goldsmith, was the maker of the so-called Farnese Chest, executed in collaboration with Giovanni Bernardi di Castelbolognese

60 Wood ceiling (detail) of the Laurentian Library.

511

61 Wood ceiling (detail) of the Laurentian Library.

62 Floor (detail) of the Laurentian Library.

who did the crystal intaglios. It was already in process in 1540 and was delivered to Cardinal Alessandro Farnese at the end of 1547 (first mentioned in a letter of about 1540 of Claudio Tolomei; cf. Bottari, *Raccolta di lettere*, IV, p. 6 ff.). Although all the elements of these works are taken from Michelangelo, the ensemble lacks the sober structure that is characteristic of the Master. This is why the door knocker for the Jubilee of 1550, now in the Germanisches Museum (Figs. 63-65), Munich, cannot be attributed to Michelangelo either, but is a work inspired by him.

According to a statement by Bocchi in 1571, later repeated by Richa and Lalande, the pavement of the choir of S. Maria del Fiore was done from a design by Michelangelo. It was an octagon decorated in boxlike squares, diminishing toward the center as if in a soffited cupola. The colors, red, white and black, and the design are sober. The attribution to Michelangelo is not supported by other documents, but cannot be rejected out of hand, since the idea of a correspondence between the ceiling or vault and the pavement, which was ignored during the Middle Ages, was resumed by Michelangelo, as is seen, for example, in the pavement of the Laurentian Library. Here the ornament and structure correspond almost exactly to the wooden coffered ceiling, which was done after a drawing by the Master that is still preserved in Casa Buonarroti. The motifs of the decoration are ox skulls, dolphins, masks, garlands and emblems of the Medici family.

The use of masks in ornament is an important feature of Michelangelo's work. However, he was not the first to do this, since these motifs can already be seen in Quattrocento tombs and in frescoes by Pinturicchio and Filippino Lippi (Fig. 17). The paired masks seen in profile over the high altar of the Chapel of St. Thomas in S. Maria sopra Minerva (Figs. 17 and 19), seem to have been the direct stimulus for the paired masks in profile by Michelangelo that are seen on the left block (1505) of the tomb of Pope Julius (Fig. 21). Only, Michelangelo gave these aquiline-nosed masks a fierce expression, likewise transforming Pinturicchio's purely ornamental semicircle into flowing wind-blown hair and beards.

Full-face masks with a sort of diadem around the hair are also to be found prior to Michelangelo in the decorations of Roman tombs of the fifteenth century (Fig. 27). Michelangelo used this motif chiefly in the frieze of the Medici Chapel and later in the frieze of the courtyard of Palazzo Farnese (Figs. 30-35 and 51-52). It is only from him that these masks get the expression of terror that the Gothic masks had.

In Michelangelo's art, masks do not seem to be merely a decorative motif but are used to reflect and accentuate the sentiments animating the large figures situated near them.

67 Antonio Gentili of Faenza: silver candlesticks (1581).

66 Antonio Gentili of Faenza: silver cross (1581).

As we have seen, study of these minor works reveals some recurrent basic procedures that are, in essence, analogous to those of the monumental works; here too Michelangelo keeps going back to fifteenth-century conceptions, derived from antiquity as a rule, to give the traditional portions new proportions and redetermine their dynamic relationship. While the artists of the Quattrocento were content to superpose elements conceived separately, Michelangelo seems to seek to give the whole an organic unity. He subordinates the ornament to the essential structural lines. Although he sometimes enriches the ornament with new anthropomorphic or zoomorphic elements, he tries to keep, in the total effect, a severity and sobriety that is not without noble elegance, in contrast to the sometimes overburdened style of earlier and later decorative art. Michelangelo's ornament appears as no longer composed of heterogeneous elements, but rather of elements that are metamorphoses of a single vital force.

[1] To do a favor for his brother Buonarroto, Michelangelo had a dagger blade (or a dagger) made for Pietro Aldobrandini in Florence. This work is first mentioned in a letter from Michelangelo dated December 19, 1506 (Milanesi, *Lettere*, p. 61); the finished work is cited on March 6, 1507 (*ibid.*, p. 70). However, Aldobrandini was not satisfied with the

68-70 Manno and Giovanni Bernardi of Castelbolognese: Farnese jewel casket. Naples,
Capodimonte Museum.

dagger (*ibid.*, p. 71), and Michelangelo asked his brother Buonarroto to offer it to Filippo Strozzi (*ibid.*, p. 73). Nothing is known of what the work was like. Its story is told by Thode, *Kritische Untersuchungen*, II, (Berlin, 1908), p. 242 and Tolnay, *Michelangelo*, I, p. 223.

[2] Cf. K. Frey, *Sammlung ausgewählter Briefe an Michelangniolo Buonarroti*, Berlin 1899, p. 101 ff.

[3] See: A. Ronchini, *Atti e Memorie delle Regie Deputazioni di Storia Patria per le Provincie Modenesi e Parmensi*, VII, 1873. Liverani, *Maestro Giovanni Bernardo* (Faenza 1870). C. de Fabriczy, "Michelangelo Drawings for Goldsmith's Work," *Archivio Storico dell'Arte*, VII (1894), p. 151 ff. Thode, *op. cit.*, p. 225 ff. F. Schottmüller, *Michelangelo and the Ornament* in "Jahrb. d. Kh. Slg. (Vienna, 1926), p. 219 ff. E. Lavagnino, "Rivista del Regio Istituto d'Archeologia e di Storia dell'Arte" (Rome, 1930), p. 101 ff.

[4] Cf. Jean Babelon, *Jacopo da Trezzo et la construction de l'Escurial*, Bordeaux 1922, p. 135 ff.

[5] Photographs of the two canopies in the Escorial were kindly put at my disposal by Prof. Adele Condorelli, Rome.

[6] Cf. Baum, *Baukunst und dekorative Plastik der Frührenaissance* (Stuttgart, 1926), p. 262.

[7] Cf. K. Frey, *op. cit.*, p. 173.

[8] Cf. A. Ronchini, *op. cit.*, Note 3.

[9] The documents have been published by G. Gronau in *Jahrbuch der preussischen Kunstsammlungen*, XXVII (1906), Bh. p. 7 ff. The appearance of this work, probably a bronze inkstand, is as yet unknown. The two drawings that we think could relate to the horse that probably was used as a handle, are in Casa Buonarroti, Barocchi, No. 206, and Oxford, Parker, No. 293 r. Both have usually been dated about 1504 and related to the Battle of Cascina. However, the style of the drawings would suggest a later date, as has been observed by Popp, *Die Medici Kapelle* (Munich, 1922). The nature of the writing on the verso of the Oxford sheet also indicates dates much later than 1504, viz. about 1525 for the poetry and 1537 for the poetical fragments in the margins: the date of the bronze horse.

A terracotta model of a horse, formerly in the Volpi Collection, Florence, may be related to the two drawings mentioned above, and hence with the bronze inkstand for the Duke of Urbino. As for its authenticity, we are unable to express an opinion since we do not know the original. In any event this horse has no connection with those of Leonardo, as was supposed by W. Suida, *Leonardo und sein Kreis* (Munich, 1929), Pl. 45, but rather with Michelangelo, as was already held by Goldscheider, according to Parker, *Catalogo dei Disegni di Oxford*, sub No. 293 r.

[10] Cf. Planiscig, *A. Riccio*, Vienna 1927, p. 176.

[11] Cf. Milanesi, *op. cit.*, p. 719. Tolnay, *op. cit.* IV, p. 69.

[12] Cf. Milanesi, *op. cit.*, p. 717. Tolnay, *op. cit.* IV, p. 140.

VII

THINKER

by Eugenio Garin

Questions of method

Discussing a subject of this kind, already highly ambiguous in and of itself, calls for some preliminary clarifications. The effort must be made to determine, so far as possible, the limits within which the discussion intends to move, the sources to be referred to, the points to be concentrated on, the texts to be read.

The term " thought " is intrinsically equivocal and is constantly used in cases where it is desired to keep a halo of indefinite possibilities around the subject in question. It becomes even more equivocal when used of an artist who has shown his prowess in the figurative arts. It can then be taken as meaning several quite diverse things. In the first place, it may mean a philosophical or religious " conception " of reality that he explicitly expressed in writings of his own or in statements recorded by reliable witnesses, or even that he tried to articulate rationally in unified works. This was what Leon Battista Alberti did in his treatises and dialogues; and what Leonardo da Vinci did, even if not in systematic form. Actually, Leonardo set forth his ideas on all the great philosophical problems and erected a theory of the " science of the painter " and the techniques in general by means of which the work of art is made. In his manuscripts it is easy to identify not merely a philosophy and a physics but also a general theory of art.

In the second place, when we speak of the " thought " of an artist, we may mean a vision of reality expressed exclusively in his production as painter, sculptor or architect. In that case, the only texts to " read " are the art works themselves—the paintings, statues or buildings —with respect to which the term " reading " is already a metaphor, while the discrimination of general concepts by means of " texts " of this kind presupposes a highly complex series of intermediate transitions and theoretical justifications of those transitions.[1]

Taking for granted, as in the cases coming under the first hypothesis, the coexistence, in the activity of an artist, of explicitly literary or philosophical documents, that does not signify that the philosophical discourse of the artist, or some statement of his that puts down in writing a considered reflection, fully renders his " thought " as it inspired and fed his specific artistic work. It may even happen that in his writings he only reflected passively ideas that were current in one way or another in the circles in which he moved, fashionable or prevalent doctrines, perhaps at variance, and even foreign, in their substance, to what was expressed in his artistic production.

The fact that an artist moves in a group or a determinate historical context in which certain views predominate does not necessarily imply, even if he says so, that it was from those ideas that he actually drew inspiration and criteria for his specific activity. His primary work is of a different type; his expressive means and his commitment evolve on a different plane.

And not only that: even when there undoubtedly is an autonomous and reasoned acceptance of certain doctrines, as was the case with Alberti and Leonardo, or even a meditated and solid personal elaboration, as with them, the relationship between this " thought " and the significance of the artistic production is neither specific nor univocal and raises many major problems from the outset. In Leonardo da Vinci, who was so publicly engaged in an original, rigorous and conscious philosophical-scientific discourse, the link between the scientist and the painter is not very evident, unless one is content with approximation, for the most part predominantly rhetorical in nature.

In reality, the problem of the correspondence between artistic language and literary, scientific, philosophical language is a serious one; if you will, between thought and conceptions of reality as articulated in philosophical terms, and overall views and reflections on things as expressed in the rhythms of artistic productions. Nor is the problem, a very grave one in the field of the figurative arts, confined to them alone, for it recurs in the field of literary works, in poetry and in prose. It is beyond dispute that the *Paradiso* of Dante contains particularly lofty philosophical-theological conceptions; and yet " reading " them is singularly difficult, because that " reading " does not consist in picking out and identifying specific doctrines stated in the work, or does not consist only in that. The most original and most lofty aspect of Dante's thought is what develops beyond those theories and is released from them, setting forth in a form of their own conceptions of another sort, sometimes contradictory to the first ones, and in manners that are not conceptually mediated, or at least not mediated in the patterns of philosophical discourse of Dante's contemporaries. In other words, the " scholastic " doctrines that are expressed as content in passages of the *Paradiso* are one thing, and quite another thing is the vision of man and life that runs through the loftiest rhythms of the work and sustains them; this is a vision not expressed in the characteristic terms of discourse of the " schools " of the time. The two types of " thought " not only do not necessarily correspond, still less coincide; they may even be in flat contradiction. On the one hand Dante adopts, passively enough, doctrines of philosophers and theologians whose task he feels at bottom to be different from his; on the other, he expresses, in his own visions and in quite a different form, his relationship with reality. In clarifying this we are only partially helped, not only by the analysis of the theories and content in question, but even by recourse to such explicitly philosophical works as the *Convivio*.

At this point it seems obvious to fall back on the distinction between works of art and works of thought and so to call for consideration of poetry alone in poets and philosophy alone in philosophers. Matters are not so simple, unfortunately, nor are the distinctions so distinct. Analyzing the doctrines and the culture of artists is a necessary step to finding the situation and presuppositions of their work, and an indispensable one for commenting on their texts, by making explicit their intentions as well as the images and contents of the works. Apart from this labor, without which we run the risk of losing all the meaning of the works, every allusion in them, all their internal tension and all their flavor, it is a fact that in what is characteristic of the artist, in what nourishes the work of art as such, often in conflict with accepted ideas, there emerge views that are of importance in many ways for what we usually consider the essence of philosophical activity; namely, reflective thought. First of all, the deepest aspects and movements of the conscience of an era, those least dependent on preexisting formulas and patterns; in other words, the thought that is most authentic in its germination and most subtle manifestation. In the second place, syntheses and overall visions that are original and in advance of the movement of reflective thought and capable, even if only indirectly, of stimulating and feeding it on its path. In other words, the " thought " of the artist can in some cases be the most authentic of voices for grasping the sense of a society, of a historical moment, of a situation. It can be the most penetrating and valid of hypotheses, the most fruitful anticipation of future reflection, the most stimulating of ideas for the philosopher and the scientist. However this " thought " is not necessarily identified with the explicit " professions " set down in any literary works of the artist himself, or in contemporary testimony; nor should it be sought in the " contents " of his depictions, understood as more or less explicit " citations " from contemporary texts, unless we wish to impoverish a solemn vision by putting it into formulas that are all too often inadequate to hold it and from which, in fact, the artist's work tends to free itself, even if only unconsciously.

The consequences of these premises are fairly obvious. Reconstruction of the culture and ambience in which the work of an artist like Michelangelo came forth is of use for delineating a panorama and presuppositions, but is not sufficient even to provide us with the terminology in which to attempt a " translation " of his " thought," as he expresses it in his own manner in his course as an artist. This " thought," that is, his attitude towards reality, life and its problems, cannot be identified, insofar as it emerges in works of art, with a religious and philosophical credo, even if it is declared and professed explicitly in literary productions or documented by the testimony of reliable witnesses. The " conception " that the artist expresses in his works of art is not simply convertible into current " philosophical " or " religious " formulas. It is illicit to pass immediately from contemporary doctrines, even those widely diffused in the milieu in which the artist moved, to his works, assuming that those conceptions could be of use in commenting on some traits. Even correspondence between literary productions—in the case of Michelangelo, primarily poetical—and figurative productions must be made with great caution.

All this should be kept in mind in view of the frequent use made, in connection with Michelangelo without adequate justification, of insufficiently supported transitions. For example, the " thought " of Michelangelo as present in his compositions can be translated without discontinuity into a specific current " philosophy " (Platonism, Quattrocento Neoplatonism); that to define Michelangelo as a thinker it is enough to refer to his verses, to passages in his letters or to reliable testimony (Vasari, Condivi, Varchi, Francisco de Hollanda, Giannotti) which can be legitimately extended to the motive animating all his work; that a reconstruction of the substance of all his " thought," not merely the " culture," is possible by transferring into the confines of his specific activity ideas that were dominant in the circles in which he moved (Neoplatonism of the Medici court, Savonarola's prophetism, pre-Reformation and Reformation movements, political struggles in the Florentine crisis, religious inspirations in the circle of Vittoria Colonna).

In fact, at least a portion of these operations, when it has not broken down into a series of metaphors of vaguely allusive speeches and eloquent digressions, has proved to be of little value for comprehending the contributions of the artist. Any attempt to lead up to an understanding of the " thought " of Michelangelo will have to confine itself to modest tasks if it wants to escape the dangers we have referred to above: it can indicate the lines of cultural contexts in which the artist moved without pretending to define the extent to which he shared in them or attained them; it can outline his " ideas " to the extent that they can be found in the poetry, the letters and the accounts; it can identify, so far as possible, within the " contents " of his creations, the reflection of various doctrines circulating around him. All this, of course, without presuming to present the results of such a study as the " thought " of Michelangelo, but at most with the intention of indicating how much was, or could have been, consciously present in the mind of the artist.

In a research of this kind, obviously two themes will keep recurring: a statement of the sources and an examination of the overall interpretations that were made a long time ago. Such an examination and discussion cannot be exhausted at the outset, but will have to emerge throughout the course of the argument.

[1] Characteristic examples of the " transitions " referred to are given by Charles de Tolnay in his many and basic contributions to the study of Michelangelo. Speaking of him as architect, and resuming themes of his general work, *Michelangiolo*, Editore Del Turco (Florence, 1951), he observes, for example, in connection with St. Peter's: " This organism is an image-symbol of the universe. The lower part of the building is conceived as a symbol of the Earth, with the four cupolas representing the four cardinal points of the compass. Domes had, since time immemorial, been considered as a symbol of the celestial sphere, and this is evidently the idea that Michelangelo wished to express in his ' suspended dome,' crowned by the heavenly temple." (*Michelangelo architetto*, in the collective work, *Il Cinquecento*, [Florence, Sansoni, 1955], p. 119). Later, Tolnay says (pp. 126-7): " Architecture expressing spiritual concepts was not, however, an invention of Michelangelo's... In the churches of the Quattrocento the ideological content is less evident, but when Alberti requires that the temple, i. e. the church, be completely ' philosophical ' and ' mathematical,' he means to say that the temple, by its perfect form and proportions, should manifest the perfection of God and of our world, created by him. For Alberti, God is immanent in his creation; between man and the world, that is, God, there is a harmony. The architecture of Michelangelo, on the other hand, denotes a renewal of the tendency of the Middle Ages to create a metaphysical universe by means of the buildings. The harmony between God and the world is broken; the essence is once transcendent and incarnate in the edifice. But the building no longer represents the heavenly realm, as it did in the Middle Ages, but the true reality in all its grandeur and majesty, the true reality which, although not of our world, is still its essence."

Michelangelo as platonist

It has been said above that exposition and analysis of the interpretations of Michelangelo's thought will of necessity have to be considered step by step as the themes and particular questions recur. One exception will be made at the outset, however, in connection with what has been called Michelangelo's Platonism, or rather the manner in which it has often been asserted. It is customary, as if to stress the age of the evidence for it, to recall the fact that the recognition of a strong Platonic influence is found even among " Berni's Jests ":

> I have seen something of his painting work,
> > Ignorant as I am, I yet will say
> > I've read them all somewhere in Plato's quirk.
> Apollo and Apelles he is today.
> > Silence forever, all you violets pale
> > And liquid crystals and swift beasts of prey:
> He speaks in things and you but speak in words.[2]

In a well-known passage of Erwin Panofsky, in *Idea* (1924), we can read in peremptory form this very clear synthesis, which is at the same time an interpretative program: " After the studies of Ludwig von Scheffler, Borinski and Thode, there is no longer any doubt that the vision of the world expressed by Michelangelo was substantially inspired by the Neoplatonic metaphysics that had entered into his mentality, either directly or indirectly (directly by his familiarity with Dante and Petrarch, indirectly by the undeniable influence of the humanistic milieu of Florence and Rome)." [3]

In addition to the verses of Berni already mentioned, Panofsky was obviously referring to the passage in Condivi on the Platonic discourses on love. In this connection, it will be in order, putting Berni to one side for the time being, to look into the nature of Condivi's testimony. After having mentioned Michelangelo's interest in the " reasonings of learned men," and his great admiration for Dante and Petrarch, Condivi emphasized the influence that Savonarola had had on Buonarroti, inducing him to constant reading and meditation on the Old and the New Testaments. Condivi continues: " He even loved the beauty of the body, as a man who knew it best, and loved it in such a way that it gave certain carnal folk, who cannot understand any other love of beauty than a lascivious and dishonorable one, an occasion to think and speak ill of him; as though Alcibiades, that famous youth, had not been loved most chastely by Socrates, from whose side, when they were reposing together, he used to say he had arisen as though from the side of his father. I have heard Michelangelo several times speaking of and discussing love, and later heard those who were present say that he had not spoken otherwise of love than is written in Plato. For my part I know not what Plato says on that; but I know that having been in his company so long and so intimately, I never heard anything from that mouth other than most honorable words, capable of quenching in youth any disorderly and excessive desire that it might have."

Condivi then goes on: "And that ugly thoughts never were born in him can be known from this too, that he loved not only human beauty but universally every beautiful thing, a beautiful horse, a beautiful dog, a beautiful landscape, a beautiful mountain, a beautiful forest and every site and thing beautiful and rare of its kind, admiring them marvelously; selecting the beautiful in nature as bees collect the honey of flowers, then using it in their works: which all those have always done who have had some reputation in painting. That old master, in making a Venus, was not content to see a single virgin, but wanted to contemplate many; and taking the most beautiful and perfect part of each, made use thereof for his Venus."

The citation has been long, but it is necessary in order properly to evaluate it; to have all of its elements clearly in mind. Condivi begins by bringing out the presence in Michelangelo of a fervid religious feeling of Savonarolian pitch, which is not wanting in recognition of bodily beauty and love of it. This love, however, is not carnal but spiritual. Thus, with an evident recall of Ficino's *Sopra lo amore*, there is introduced the distinction between the two loves, connected, as in Ficino, with a theory of beauty as *idea*, manifested and resplendent in bodies. To confirm and integrate this, the discussion closes on the double example of the bee and the statue of Venus. Condivi declares that he is ignorant of Plato. Actually, the long text links Michelangelo to theories that were widespread ever since Ficino, and had become a sort of vogue from which, all through the Cinquecento, came innumerable lectures at the Academies, and interminable conversations at the Courts. An articulate commonplace, if you will, as to which it cannot even be said to be incompatible with Savonarola's starting point, since even among Savonarola's notes can be found careful extracts from works concerned with the theories of Plato's *Symposium*. Certainly Michelangelo discussed themes of this kind, and must have got from them the means of translating into an indirect and reflected form his way of understanding art and beauty, as the poetry shows. It will not be forgotten, however, in using an interpretative category of this type with respect to him, that the fact of his referring to it is not particularly significant since, as can never be repeated too often, the theme had become extremely banal by then. Furthermore, if we look a little closely at the poems, we shall indeed find a generically Platonic and, if you will, Plotinian and Ficinian aura; we shall not find, or find only rarely, more precise indications more technically attached to specific sources.

Thus, in the well-known verses,

> Love is an idea of loveliness
> > Imagined out or seen within the heart
> A friend of virtue and of gentleness...[4]

echoes of Ficino are easily found. But everyone will see that these are not themes peculiar to Ficino. The same is true of the other passage, which again has the characteristic image of the source of love:

> And to that pious fount, whence we are all,
> Repairs each lovely thing that here is seen.[5]

Another factor that should lead us to be more cautious in speaking of Michelangelo's Platonism is the very way in which it is generally introduced. Panofsky, in the text cited above, points to Dante and Petrarch as direct sources of Michelangelo's Platonism, a statement that calls for explanation, especially since in the same passage, Benedetto Varchi is called a " great Platonist, " whereas it is recognized later that his procedure is Aristotelian. Panofsky, writing on *The Neoplatonic Movement and Michelangelo* (1932, reprinted in 1962), harps again on the predominantly Platonic elements of Michelangelo's poetics, relying once more on the testimony of Berni and Condivi. " That Michelangelo's poetics, " he observes, " is full of ' Platonic ' conceptions was remarked by his contemporaries and has been almost unanimously recognized by modern students. " In this new essay by Panofsky the reference to Dante and Petrarch becomes secondary and is declared negligible as compared to the " genuine Platonism " with which " the pupil of Poliziano " had been said to have come in contact in youth. Panofsky now indicates the specific literary sources of these doctrines: Landino's commentary on Dante, all Platonic and Ficinian, plus, " if not Ficino's Latin works, Pico's Italian commentary on the *Canzone d'Amore* of Benivieni. "[6]

Undoubtedly Panofsky has done well to indicate Landino's voluminous commentary as one of the most important vehicles of Florentine Platonism and a line of penetration along which, really, Dante converges with the Neoplatonic renaissance.[7] On the other hand, grave doubts are raised by the further specifications of the Michelangelo-Platonism nexus, the documents of which are said to be traceable in his love for Tommaso Cavalieri and Vittoria Colonna, expressions " of the idea of Platonic love in its purest significance, " while the Neoplatonic conception of " a presence of the spiritual in the material," constituting the philosophical basis of an " esthetic and beauty-loving enthusiasm, " combined with the vision of the " unreality of human life," is said to be in harmony with the tormented discontent with the world and himself given as characteristic of Michelangelo's genius. Panofsky, indeed, goes so far as to assign a supposed anti-Platonism on the part of Leonardo as the source of his distance, as an artist, from Michelangelo; " the figures of Leonardo are as free from any repression as those of Michelangelo are inhibited." In support of his assertion he cites, among other things, the famous passage of Leonardo on " hope and repatriation " on the part of the soul, " as the butterfly is drawn to the light: " a text that could, without too much difficulty, be at least partly adduced as evidence of the contrary, namely the completely Neoplatonic nostalgia of the soul for its heavenly homeland. It is not at random that people have spoken of Leonardo's Platonism, and in some of his figures have been found the marks of a Platonic tone, very easily demonstrable, more so than in Michelangelo's bodies, so carnally terrestrial. These remarks, however, are not aimed at considerations of this kind, but at emphasizing the way in which many statements on Michelangelo's Platonism are based on and derive their substance from a panorama that is not altogether exact; a highly conventional and generic picture of the cultural currents in Italy, particularly in Florence, between the end of the Quattrocento and the middle of the Cinquecento. In this panorama Dante and Petrarch can become direct sources of Platonism, and Benedetto Varchi can be described as a great Platonist. As we shall see, the procedure is more or less as follows: in the decisive years of his life, Michelangelo was at the court of Lorenzo along with Ficino, Landino, Poliziano, Pico—all Platonists. He was influenced by them, thereby taking the first steps towards Platonism. In point of fact, he considered the body as an earthly prison; saw the idea as hidden in matter, felt the tension between the active and contemplative lives and understood the meaning of the form that emerges from the formless. Then he felt the counterblow, but also the appeal, of Savonarola's preaching. Thus, his inspiration was torn between the renaissance of Neoplatonism and the requirements of a lachrymose reform; and all this against the background of the last gasps of the civic humanism of the dying republic of Florence.

Leaving aside the external nature and naïveté of this profile, the Florentine culture of the end of the fifteenth century, even around Lorenzo, was torn by major differences; polemics that could not be passed over raged within it. Ficino was not Pico, nor Poliziano. Petrarch and Petrarchism were not the Neoplatonism of the Ficinians. Landino and his commentary on Dante had ways of their own; the return to the inspirations of the *dolce stile* had its own characteristics. On the other hand, the themes and " contents " of a certain Michelangelo can be reduced to an intrinsically Platonic manner only by means of arguments woven out of metaphors, whose basis is drawn predominantly from the poems. In connection with the poems, a closer examination should be made of the extent to which they embody current themes and motifs that were circulating during just those years to which they can be referred.

² F. Berni, *Prose e poesie*, a cura di E. Chiorboli (Florence, 1934), p. 168. Cf. G. Vasari, *La vita di Michelangelo nella redazione del 1550 e del 1568*, curata e commentata da Paola Barocchi (Milan and Naples, Ricciardi, 1962), Vol. II, p. 43 (reference will always be made to Barocchi's monumental work—text, comment, index—when referring to the Vasari " Life.") The reference to Berni's verses is *de rigueur*: see, e. g., R. J. Clements, *Michelangelo's Theory of Art* (New York, New York University Press, 1961), p. 4.
³ E. Panofsky, *Idea. Ein Beitrag zur Begriffengeschichte der älteren Kunsttheorie*, verbesserte Auflage (Berlin, Hessling, 1960), p. 64 (and Ital. translation of the first 1924 edition [Florence, La Nuova Italia, 1952], p. 87). The works referred to are: L. V. Scheffler, *Michelangelo. Eine Renaissancestudie* (Altenburg, 1892); K. Borinski, *Die Rätsel Michelangelos. Michelangelo und Dante* (Munich and Leipzig, 1908); H. Tode, *Michelangelo und das Ende der Renaissance* (Berlin, 1902-13). It is interesting that Panofsky, after having envisaged a possible Aristotelian interpretation of the " concetto," repeats his thesis of Michelangelo " als wirklichen Kenner des Neuplatonismus."
⁴ Michelangelo Buonarroti, *Rime*, a cura di Enzo Noè Girardi (Bari, Laterza, 1960), p. 20 (No. 38, vv. 9-11).
⁵ Buonarroti, *op. cit.* (No. 83, vv. 9-10).
⁶ E. Panofsky, *Studies in Iconology. Humanistic Themes in the Art of the Renaissance* (New York and Evanston, Harper and Row, 1962), pp. 171-230.
⁷ Cf. C. Dionisotti, " Leonardo uomo di lettere," in *Italia Medievale e Umanistica*, Vol. V (1962), (Padua, Antenore, 1964), p. 207. (" For forty years, between the Quattrocento and the Cinquecento, one of the books most read and most influential in Italian culture was undoubtedly Landino's Dante ").

The alleged platonic initiation of Michelangelo

Where Panofsky spoke of obvious Platonism, Charles de Tolnay, the outstanding exponent of Michelangelo, went still further. He has found in Michelangelo's entire work, at least up to a certain moment, the expression of a more articulate and clearer Neoplatonic conception of the world than even the one offered by the various philosophers found at the court of Lorenzo the Magnificent. And since we have here an interpretation on a large scale and of unusual importance, solidly put together and intended to embrace the entire work of the artist, it will have to be taken up by itself. The starting point is Condivi's narrative, which is rather lengthy on this point. Michelangelo goes from Ghirlandaio's *bottega* to the garden of the Medici " above the Piazza San Marco... all full of antiques and greatly adorned with excellent paintings, brought together in that place for beauty, for study, for pleasure." In the circle of Lorenzo the Magnificent, still following the well-known account of Condivi, the very youthful artist is said to have been very familiar with Poliziano, who was very fond of him and constantly urged him on, giving him many suggestions and instructions at every moment. That was the origin of the *Centauromachia*, Poliziano " explaining the entire story to him all the way through." The end of the work is said to coincide with the death of Lorenzo (April 8, 1492) and hence with Michelangelo's return to his father's house.[8]

The earliest activity of the artist, divided between ancient myths and religious themes, even though there have been serious doubts as to certain dates; his presence in the company of Lorenzo and Poliziano; and then the years of Savonarola, the political crisis in Florence and the stay in Bologna, in an atmosphere of dark forebodings and an uncertain future, which comes out well in Condivi's narrative: this entire complex of elements seems to facilitate a connection between the usual manner of interpreting the travail of the last decade in Florence and the analysis of Michelangelo's " mind," and at the same time to uncover in his works the sublimated expression of that dramatic moment. The tension between the court's " Platonism " and the tearful, austere religiosity seems to be the easiest category under which to place the " conception " of Michelangelo and the genesis of all his masterpieces.

With powerful eloquence, Charles de Tolnay, in the first volume of his great work dealing with the youth of Michelangelo picks up the saying by Proust that " great artists have never done more than a single work " and goes on to say that Buonarroti " was dominated by a single vision throughout his life. All his creations, all having the same unique quality, bear the message of a higher unknown world. " All, in other words, are said to be shot through with the Neoplatonic-Ficinian idea that " the true reality is beyond the appearance," that the body is " the image of the soul in which it participates," the " mortal veil," the earthly prison. Michelangelo's creations, centered around man, would therefore be the persistent depiction of the human drama in the higher reality of the cosmic drama, a formal reality in conflict with the weight of matter; of a soul of divine origin, imprisoned in an earthly body and struggling to liberate itself. More precisely, Michelangelo is said to have inserted his entire production into the effort to express this central sense of the dramatic nature of all his own tension, between the factor of contemplation of form and the tragic factor of the struggle of the form, of the idea, struggling to free itself from its prison. On this theory, the *Centauromachia* would already have been animated by a fundamental need to depict " life, as a continuous stream of energy, comprising within itself the various destinies of individual existences." " Bound to the original material and bound to one another, the figures " are said to be " like ramifications of a certain organic entity." [9] Forces and forms; matter and idea; ideal higher world, and terrestrial prison or veil; finally, Platonic myths and Christian faith, that is, essentially, convergence of sacerdotal influences and initiations into the Neoplatonic mysteries: these are the ingredients of an explanation of the stuff of which all of Michelangelo is made, as sculptor, painter and architect. When an equilibrium is reached, as in the Pietà, in which " the body is the image of the soul, and partakes of its most inmost qualities," then " the youth of the Virgin... expresses a beauty that is just as much physical as moral."

In the second volume of his monograph, *The Sistine Ceiling*, Tolnay stresses in detail this vision of another reality, consisting of the plane of the οὐσία, and sums up his point of view in very effective language. " The original iconographic program was made broader and deeper [by Michelangelo] by means of a philosophical conception of human existence ' that is not derived from the teachings of the Church ' but from the Platonic philosophy of the time.... The Biblical scenes are... transformed in accordance with the Platonic conception of the interior tragedy of the human soul, which despite its divine origin is condemned to the finitude of the prison of the earthly body.... The stories of the Creation are made deeper by means of the Platonic conception of the *return to God*, of the *deification* or *renovatio* of the soul...." And still more decisively: " The religious and philosophical beliefs of Humanism find their most perfect artistic embodiment: the conception of earthly beauty as manifestation of the divine idea; the belief in the inmost *renovatio* of the human soul, which is of divine nature; the belief in the possibility of its return to God (*deificatio*). But this is not merely an illustrative transcription into images of a given philosophical system. It is a philosophy on its own account—a creative synthesis of transcendental idealism in visual symbols. And the creative synthesis is much clearer and much more consistent than those that are found in the works of the philosophers and poets of the time. Writers like Landino, Ficino and Pico were unable to express their thoughts in unequivocal language and to arrive at a coherent synthesis. The fine arts must be considered as the fundamental language of sixteenth-century thought. The Sistine Chapel is the greatest *Summa* of Humanism's ideals of life, the perfect compendium of the artistic, philosophical and religious tendencies of the time, a true *Divina Commedia* of the Renaissance, as unique and representative as Dante's was for his epoch." [10]

In the Medici Chapels, by means of the rich expressive possibilities of a genre like the funerary monument, Michelangelo can offer us " a compendious image of the universe," in which " the ancient conception of Art fuses with the Christian beyond." But there is more: " since death, in Michelangelo's Platonic conception, is the liberation of the soul from everything that is extraneous to its nature, it is no wonder that the realm of death should become for him the realm of the true life of the soul." Further, whereas the Sistine Chapel would reflect " the triumph of the creative forces, of active life," and would constitute " the ideal portrait of the artist's soul " at the highest moment of his power, the Medici Chapels would represent the highest points of harmony and equilibrium. The break is said to have taken place at the moment when Michelangelo, " unable any longer to identify essence with beauty," had been driven to " renounce the archetypes of beauty, to express a new truth [religious and no longer philosophical] in new forms." This is said to have been in his last period in Rome, in a Europe profoundly travailed by a religious transformation. For from that time on, the dualism of philosophical and religious inspiration was bound to explode, even though, according to Tolnay, " the Platonism of the origins and the Christianity of the last years are not irreconcilable. Both imply detachment from the world, yearning for perfection, an enthusiastic drive toward ' higher regions.' They are united by a transcendent spirituality: and from this point of view Michelangelo's Platonism can be considered as a prelude to his final Christian spirituality. Michelangelo was mistaken in believing that he had to renounce his past, since that past was really a preparation for his last period." [11]

In the end, therefore, it is Michelangelo's entire life and his internal evolution that seem to Tolnay to symbolize the ascent of man. A " gradual catharsis " is said to mark " the development of his personality, as well as the structure of his various works."

It is difficult not to admire the effort that Tolnay has put into tracing a coherent line of thought in the work of the artist, and to locate within it, as chapters of a grand universal synthesis, the individual works, even though at bottom those chapters, translated into corresponding terms of thought, do not seem to be too different and certainly not more profound than those of any writer of the time along the common path from Plato to Christ, the stations of which had been situated with adequate precision by Canon Marsilio Ficino. Tolnay asserts, it is true, that Michelangelo's synthesis is richer and philosophically higher than that of his fellow-Platonists. When he presents it to us conceptually, however, making use of implicit or explicit references to the statements of various philosophers, its superiority to them does not consist in any conceptual superiority but in the figurative expression, that is, in something that goes beyond those conceptual schemes, or supposed schemes, which, if they really did reflect the considered thought of the artist, could at most help in interpretation, especially in understanding the " contents," the " matter," of his representations. Actually, then, when we come to set up a complex of precise correspondences, we have the impression that the general schemes are too general and are not always a reliable aid in interpretation, while all effective originality seems to disappear from them.

[8] For all this part, cf. in addition Charles de Tolnay, *Michelangelo I. The Youth of Michelangelo*, 2nd ed. (Princeton, 1947), p. 18 ff., A. Chastel, *Art et Humanisme à Florence au temps de Laurent le Magnifique* (Paris, Presses Univ. de France, 1959), p. 80 ff.

[9] Tolnay, *op. cit.*, p. 63 ff.; *Michelangiolo* (Florence, 1951), p. 15.

[10] Tolnay, *Michelangelo II. The Sistine Ceiling*, 2nd ed. (Princeton, 1949), pp. 24, 117.

[11] Tolnay, *Michelangelo III. The Medici Chapel* (Princeton, 1948), pp. 74-5, 84, 116-7; *Michelangelo IV. The Tomb of Julius II* (Princeton, 1954), pp. 74, 94.

The literary documents. The poems

In point of fact, the most solid pillars on which the various reconstructions of Michelangelo's " conception " rest are, as has been indicated, literary documents of two sorts: the poems and letters on the one hand, and on the other, primarily the two versions of the life by Vasari (those of 1550 and 1568), the biography by Condivi (1553) and the dialogues of Francisco de Hollanda and Donato Giannotti. In particular, attention should always be directed to the texts of Michelangelo himself, over which the light of his art plays and from which, by a singular cycle, light is sought to understand his art. Anthony Blunt, the author of a thoughtful analysis of Michelangelo's ideas on art, makes two highly judicious preliminary observations: first, that the letters contain hardly anything of importance from the point of view of theory, and deal almost exclusively with personal or family matters; and secondly, that the poems have few references to the arts. However, Blunt goes on to say, the verses, being for the most part love poems, enable the reader to form an idea as to Michelangelo's ideas concerning beauty.[12] To the letters and poems, Blunt continues, should be added the dialogues (*Dialogos em Roma*) of Francisco de Hollanda, Vasari and Condivi. Francisco de Hollanda was in Rome in 1538 and although not an intimate of Michelangelo's, frequented his circle for some time. The dialogues, composed mainly for self-glorification, must be taken with caution, but can be used for periods for which there is corroborating testimony.[13] The differences and divergences of Vasari's two versions have now been minutely analyzed and studied in their component parts, especially by Barocchi, and can be a useful source for reconstructing some aspects of Michelangelo's thinking and working. Condivi, who comes between Vasari's first and second biographies (correcting the first and serving as the basis for the second) is undoubtedly the most fruitful document, despite its simplicity.

But in defining the " Neoplatonic " conception of the artist, most constant reference is made to the poems, which Nesca A. Robb called " a kind of spiritual autobiography," whose cultural substratum should be sought in the ideas divulgated by Ficino, Pico, Benivieni, Diacceto.[14] More recently Robert J. Clements, in a huge treatise on *Michelangelo's Theory of Art*, has gone so far as to lay down as his starting point that " it would be hard to exaggerate the importance of these poems, especially the Neoplatonic ones, which shed light on the mind of the artist, his concept of beauty, his relation to his activity and his work." Clements, committed to rigorously defining the vocabulary used by Michelangelo himself, seeks the sources of his inspiration " in Plato, Aristotle, Plotinus and other Hellenic or Alexandrine writers translated or discussed during the Cinquecento, since it does not appear that Michelangelo knew Greek." Along with the Greek sources, he lists among the Latins, Horace, Ovid, Vitruvius, Ficino, Poliziano and other Latin and Neo-Latin writers. His purpose is to establish a relationship between Michelangelo's theories on art and beauty, and his works (" we shall study in what measure his theoretical ideas affected his technique and even his choice of subject matter... we shall hope to explain some of his persuasions about his art in the light of events of his life ").[15]

Blunt had already pointed out that the long life of the artist, from 1475 to 1564, extending over a period of profound changes and passing in culturally diverse centers, makes caution necessary in assigning environmental influences and in defining the periods. Even greater caution is required when reconstructing the extent of Michelangelo's reading, the temptation being to place it at a very high level. Robb cited Benci's *Pimandro* in Italian and Ficino's Italian *Convito*. Panofsky very astutely pointed out Landino's commentary on Dante, which Carlo Dionisotti recently suggested as a source of Leonardo's as well, showing how Landino's pages were likely to have been the most probable vehicle for wide diffusion of the Platonizing culture of the *fin de siècle* Florentine circles. To possible reading of this sort can be added conversations, " Academies," and sermons: a broadcast of themes, a climate, environments. On the other hand, it is not convincing, in commenting on Michelangelo's poems or his ideas on beauty, to have recourse to primary learned sources such as Plotinus or Plato himself or to use only two of the names emphasized by Clements. It is not convincing, nor does it seem to be necessary, since it would be much more fruitful to make the comparison with verses in the vernacular, even not on a very high level but circulating in the ambiences in which Michelangelo lived: numerous poems, which often seem to be fashionable exercises, the composition of which was in more than one case due to custom rather than to the urgency of an inspiration.[16]

Let us take one example. Our eyes fall on the youthful verses dropped off by Michelangelo among sketches and drawings, on the changefulness of mundane things:

> After many a happy year, in one
> Briefest moment a man will mourn and repine;
> Another is of famous lofty line
> And in a moment all his glory is gone.
>
> No changeful thing under the sun's so fine
> Death will not master it and bring it down.[17]

And here are the verses that Pico had written, probably some twenty years earlier:

> O wretched mortals, do not any more
> Put trustfulness of yours in fickle fate
> Which clips the wings of man in highest flight
> Turning them in an instant brown from white.
>
> There's nothing stable underneath the moon!
> And since we must live long with many woes
> And weal so fragile and so rarely found
> Happy is he whose life is ended soon.[18]

In a context of similar themes (fortune, death, the early loss of all things good, etc.), it is hard not to associate these verses: *No changeful thing under the sun's so fine/Death will not master it*, by Buonarroti, and Pico's *There's nothing stable underneath the moon*. Without a systematic exploration, which we have not by any means made, of Italian poetry of the fifteenth and sixteenth centuries, the time of Michelangelo, it is not easy to determine the extent to which a work takes up themes in general circulation and uses customary motifs and concepts, even though with original manner and accents, without thereby going back to primary sources that are too distant and without always necessarily expressing deeply-felt experiences.

Thus, in another place Michelangelo sketches on the back of a letter from Stefano di Tommaso in 1521, a lament over time, which is like a scythe, and we like the hay, while beauty does not last:

> Time marches on and measures out the hours
> Of this our life, a poisonous bitter day;
> It is a scythe and we are like the hay,
> ... Faith is short-lived and beauty does not last...[19]

The verses are not without power, but the Biblical inspiration is clear: *omnis caro foenum... exsiccatum est foenum, et cecidit flos* (Isaiah 40: 6-7); *omnis caro sicut foenum* (Eccles. 14, 18); *arescit foenum et flos ocius cecidit et decor vultus eius deperit* (James 1, 11). Undoubtedly the theme of death, meditation on death, dialogue with death ("my soul that speaks with death"), reflection on the transience of things, recur insistently in Michelangelo's poetry, and sometimes attain unusual force; but to what extent do they express personal travail and to what extent do they repeat commonplaces? There is the famous image of the hammer, and the sonnet in which it appears is famous:

> If my rough hammer to the stubborn stone
> Gives human shape, now this, now that, at will,
> Following his hand who wields and guides it still,
> It moves upon another's feet alone:

> But that which dwells in heaven, the world doth fill
> With beauty by pure motions of its own;
> And since tools fashion tools which else were none,
> Its life makes all that lives with living skill.[20]

Guasti already proposed an impossible reference of this to Plato's *Cratylus*, instead of the obvious citation from the second canto of the *Paradiso*, which corresponds perfectly to the passage from Michelangelo in meaning and value, and whose precise Aristotelian inspiration Landino had already pointed out. It would seem that the evident Peripateticism would offend the pan-Platonism that is the fashion today (the *Ottimo Commento* says: "It is taken from a material example in the work of the craftsman, where there are three things, the master, the hammer and the work. In the world God is the master, the heavens are the hammer, things below are the work."). Further, and even before Dante, why not recall the image in Jeremiah, 23, 29, in which the word of the Lord is "quasi malleus conterens petram." [21] The Biblical image, by way of Dante, fits into an exact Aristotelian profile with the theory of God as prime mover: which, of course, does not in any way legitimate speaking of Michelangelo as a Peripatetic.

Our purpose was merely to call for greater caution in exercising the tendency to assign a privileged position to Platonism, which, so far as the poems are concerned, must be spoken of, even when speaking of the theory of the beautiful, primarily in terms of a certain diffuse "atmosphere."

Without any doubt the "theory" delineated in a group of poems enables us to fix some "ideas": the artist, and Michelangelo refers to the sculptor in particular, sees a form within the block of marble, the form that he conceives in his mind. His hammer only removes the envelope and carves out what was contained hidden in the stone.

The texts are notorious:

> The best of artists does not have a concept
> That the marble itself does not contain within it
> Within its surface, and only that is reached
> By the hand obeying the intellect.

> Lady, as by removing do we place
> In hard and Alpine stone
> A living figure.
> Which grows the more, the less of stone is left;
> In some, likewise, good works
> By the still-trembling soul
> Are hid by the cover of its own flesh
> With its unpolished, rude, hard crust.[22]

This is a doctrine that has a precise echo in the well-known letter to Varchi, who had commented on the sonnet, "The best of artists does not have a concept," at the Florentine Academy on the second Sunday in Lent, 1546, in a lecture published together with the lecture "On Precedence in the Arts, and which is nobler, Sculpture or painting." Michelangelo's letter is an important document in this connection, precisely because of the contrast, which alert criticism has stressed, between his artist's "ignorance" and Varchi's "philosophy." On the point of slipping into the worn-out dispute of the "comparison" between painting and sculpture, Michelangelo says very resolutely:

"I say that painting is regarded as being better the more it approaches relief, and relief is regarded as being worse the more it approaches painting; and therefore I used to think that sculpture was the lantern of painting, and that the difference between the two is that between the sun and the moon. Now that I have read in your little book the part where you say that, philosophically speaking, those things that have the same end are one and the same thing, I have changed my mind; and I say, that if greater judgment and difficulty, hindrance and labor do not make greater nobility, then painting and sculpture are one and the same thing; and for that to be so, every painter should not fail to do sculpture as well as painting; and likewise the sculptor should do painting as well as sculpture. I mean by sculpture, that which is done by taking away; that which is done by adding, is like painting. 525

Well then, since both of them come from the same understanding, sculpture and painting that is, peace can well be made between them, and all these disputes can be dropped, because more time goes into them than into making works of art. As for the man who wrote that painting was nobler than sculpture, if he understood the other things he has written as well as he did that, my servant would have written them better." [23]

Various antecedents have been sought—and of course found—for these theses which Michelangelo, we should not forget, never went more deeply into. But it would be difficult to present these antecedents as anything more than an echo on the doctrinal plane, whereas his forthright note reflects an experience—his experience as a sculptor who, moreover, does not go basically into the theory of any of his most characteristic patterns, even when the occasion offers. Nor need anything much different be said concerning beauty, the relationship between God and the soul or between soul and body. Certainly beauty is for Michelangelo something mental, " spiritual "—"only rash and foolish judgments attribute beauty to sense." It is the intellect that brings out the internal form, the soul that is a divine spark, the work of God: that is under the corporeal husk (" I am shut in like the pulp in its rind... like spirits in a vial ").

The poet undeniably delights in a Platonizing terminology: " My soul is plucked and shaven of its plumes; " " The soul that fears and filters/What the eye does not see; " " Love wake and spur and fit my wings with plumes,/Nor bar the lofty flight to vain passion;/As the first step to take to its Creator,/From what were not, the soul mounts and goes upward; " " One draws toward heaven, and the other earthwards;/One in the soul resides, the other in the senses; " " The pilgrim soul."

The list could be extended; but it is always a list of general formulas, not gone into, not specified, on the doctrinal plane indicating nothing more than adherence to a certain taste, common to a widespread type of production. The higher accents, those more his own, are the echo of a laborious experience as artist and as man:

> For many years and in so many essays,
> Searching, the wise man, as death nears, attains
> The proper concept of a living image
> In hard and Alpine stone... [24]

" Difficulty, obstacles and toil; " this clash with the husk, this struggle towards liberation, this process of becoming tempered by discovering the transience of things, and the ever deeper sense of death are certainly interesting notes, as are the references to art conquering nature.

All these things make the poems a rarely human document, but in them the originality of the supreme artist does not in general break the *husk* of forms that are not always rare. Nor does it give an imprint of originality and integration to the Platonizing atmosphere in which it is located, nor to the rhythms which he most often takes over from a current manner. Extracting from the poems (and the letters) an articulated and precise theory of art which, even as compared with the ideas current at the time, would indicate the results of a meditation which had consciously reworked certain contemporaneous themes, does not seem to be an enterprise with any great chances of success. Even after we get beyond the hints, we sometimes do not know whether the primary inspiration is not a direct echo of images and commonplaces differing from those of Platonism and even of Aristotelianism.

The truth is that many themes whose models have been traced back to such writers as Ficino and the Ficinians can very well be taken as references to other poets—to Dante, to Dante's commentators. " You are right, " says Giannotti, " in saying of Michelangelo that he is a great Danteist; for I know no one who understands or possesses him better. He is so devoted to Dante that anything Dante wrote seems to him to have been revealed truth." [25] Dante and the Bible; Dante like the Bible; Dante and Petrarch and the other writers in Italian, and conversation with the learned. " I have always taken delight," he states in the dialogues of Giannotti, " in conversing with learned persons; and, if you remember, there was not a man of letters in Florence that was not my friend. So much so that as you see, I have learned a little, which helps me now when I read Dante, Petrarch and the other writers to be read in our Tuscan language." And a little further on: " Whenever I see someone who is good for something, who shows some power of the mind, who can do or say something better than the others, I am compelled to fall in love with him, and give myself to him as booty, so that I am no longer my own, but all his." [26]

This love of man, which made him see one thing always, namely man, led Michelangelo to talk with men and learn from them. But whether he took to anatomical drawings (" Who is there that, looking at the statues you have made... and the painted figures... will not conclude that you have a tremendous knowledge of anatomy? "), or cultivated learned discourse, the range of his experience seems definitely limited. The sources of his " ideas " are just those that emerge from these witnesses: the Bible, Dante and his commentators, Petrarch and " these other writers to be read in our Tuscan language."

His " philosophy " too had its sources in this milieu of a " vulgate " culture, of learned conversations, and is identifiable rather in a generic atmosphere than in theories carefully articulated on a high technical level. [27]

[12] Anthony Blunt, *Artistic Theory in Italy, 1450-1600*, 2nd ed. (Oxford, Clarendon Press, 1960), pp. 58-81.

[13] Cf. in the negative, H. Tietze, " Francisco de Hollanda und Donato Giannotti's Dialoge und Michelangelo," *Repertorium ür Kunstwissenschaft*, 28 (1905), pp. 295-320; C. Aru, " I Dialoghi Romani di Francisco de Hollanda," *L'Arte*, 21 (1928), pp. 117-28 (but against these, R. J. Clements, *op. cit.*, pp. 423-33 and ibid., *The Authenticity of Francisco de Hollanda*, PMLA, 61 [1946], pp. 1018-28).

[14] Nesca A. Robb, *Neoplatonism of the Italian Renaissance* (London, Allen and Unwin, 1935), p. 241.

[15] Clements, *op. cit.*, p. XX ff.

[16] Verses on the one hand, orations on the other, that is, sermons such as those given in the lay confraternities by Ficinians, by Neoplatonists; and the orations of Nesi are a typical case.

[17] Buonarroti, *op. cit.*, p. 3 (No. 1, vv. 1-6).

[18] G. Pico, *Sonetti*, XIII, L. Dorez, ed. (cited from *Nuova Rassegna*, II [1894], p. 10).

[19] Buonarroti, *op. cit.*, p. 9 (No. 17, vv. 5-7).

[20] *Ibid.*, pp. 23-4 (No. 16, vv. 1-8). Following Guasti, Frey maintained the derivation from the *Cratylus*. E. N. Girardi (p. 189) correctly refers to Dante, *Paradiso*, II, 127-32. Clements (p. 79), while rejecting the reference to the *Cratylus*, maintains the relation to Plato (" in any case, the idea of the divine hammer is an inevitable concomitant, with Platonic embellishments, of Michelangelo's certainty that God is the *summus artifex* ").

[21] We can hardly regret too much the failure of certain critics to refer to the book with which Michelangelo was most familiar, the Bible.

[22] Buonarroti, *op. cit.*, p. 82 (No. 151, vv. 1-4; No. 152, vv. 1-8).

[23] For the writings of Varchi and Michelangelo's letter, see *Trattati d'arte del Cinquecento fra umanesimo e controriforma*, a cura di Paola Barocchi, Vol. I (Bari, Laterza, 1960), pp. 1-91. Michelangelo's letter is on p. 82.

[24] Buonarroti, *op. cit.*, p. 113 (No. 241, vv. 1-4).

[25] *Dialogi di Donato Giannotti de' giorni che Dante consumò nel cercare i'Inferno e'l Purgatorio*. Edizione critica a cura di Deoclecio Redig de Campos (Florence, Sansoni, 1939), pp. 40, 88.

[26] Giannotti, *op. cit.*, pp. 66, 68.

[27] *Ibid.*, p. 41.

Michelangelo's cultural formation

If the poems are the major support for the Platonizing interpretation of Michelangelo's thought, the starting point is to found, in general, in the Florentine formation that had left indelible traces in his mind.

He was born in 1475 and the years of his adolescence coincided with the flowering of Lorenzo's circle, with the maturing of the views of Ficino and Pico. It was the golden age of collaboration of artists with literary men and philosophers. It was the moment, whose high point André Chastel places in 1490, of the " conscious reintegration of the ancient images in the ancient forms. ...Conceived in the circle of the Medici ' museum,' this ' reintegration ' tended to be carried out in Florence with the help of Careggi's humanism. And it is this that comes out clearly in the formation of the young Michelangelo." [28]

Chastel discerningly stresses the decisive experiences of the artist at Lorenzo's court: perfect competence in ancient art, in the ancient images, but also active participation in a vision of things in which " poetry and art, symbolic vision and the experiences of the expert " were organically linked.

The convergence between the work of art, which in a sort of meditation-creation captured from within the constructive processes of the ancients, and the historical and theoretical awareness of all their original meanings and speculative value, contributed to mold a most original personality—one that was rich with all the results obtained by classical times and at the same time remediated them through a renewed consciousness of the Christian sense of life. " Antiquity," Chastel says " no longer appears as a sequence of episodes and motifs, but as a totality, as an *historical cosmos*. Everything in it is linked: ideas, feelings, forms. This was the consequence of the respect that Lorenzo had for the architecture of the Ancients, Poliziano for their poetry, Ficino for their religion, Donatello and Bertoldo for their sculpture. Episodic imitation of a motif then becomes naïveté. It is emulation that counts. Michelangelo was always to maintain, as did Poliziano, that culture is nothing without the personal energy that vivifies it." [29]

The words of André Chastel are felicitous and effective. Without any doubt Michelangelo's attitude toward antiquity parallels that of those poets who refused to " ape " their models and vied with them, reaffirming the dignity of the moderns. In this sense young Michelangelo learned the lesson of Poliziano. But, it may be asked, did he also learn and make his own all the complex and muddy culture of Ficinian Neoplatonism and work out his synthesis of antiquity and Christianity in conformity with the modes and symbols of the great Platonist? To explain the genesis and significance of his works, is it required to make of him a thoroughgoing and conscious participant in that reality? That is precisely the problem: not to explain some of his images, as could easily be done, by referring back to writings of Ficino, Pico or others of their group, but to demonstrate that the vision of humanity—for that is what is involved—expressed in his " stones " and his pictures is translated into " words, " corresponding, even if on a higher level and with a better and deeper synthesis, to those of the *Theologia platonica*, or the *Disputationes Camaldulenses*. " It is not," Tolnay concedes, " a mere illustrative translation in imagery of a given philosophic system, but a philosophy in itself—a creative synthesis in visual symbols of the transcendent idealism." A synthesis, however, of Platonic idealism to be aligned in some way with those of the " Laurentian " philosophers. " The creative synthesis is much clearer and much more consistent... Writers like Landino, Ficino and Pico were unable to express their thoughts in unequivocal language and to arrive at a coherent synthesis." Greater clarity, note, and greater consistency and coherence; but what Michelangelo had within him, and which he uttered when he painted or carved, is said to be the same complex of ideas and problems, of questions and conflicts, that troubled Ficino. The Prisons, to give only one example, are said to be only the plastic representation of the soul bound to the body, " the image symbol of man in his corporeal enchainment, in the ' dark prison ' " : a gloss in stone, not of a text in the Greek tragedians, but in the *Republic* and the *Timaeus*. [30]

Probably this is just the point, Michelangelo's first formation, at which a discussion with much greater gradation is required. When historians of art refer to the cultural world of which Michelangelo formed part down to the death of Lorenzo the Magnificent, they like to show us the boyish artist as a serene table companion of Landino, Ficino and Pico, to reconstruct an ideal integrated context in which to locate that notorious Platonism. However, in those years the unity of that group, and of Florentine culture in general, was anything but solid and homogeneous. The political and economic tensions in the city, which were to explode shortly, agitated the learned men, thinkers, priests and ideologists of Medicean Florence. Savonarola, who precipitated the situation shortly thereafter, returned to San Marco in 1490. Poliziano was studying Aristotelian texts during the period when, according to Condivi, he was giving encouragement and suggestions to Michelangelo.[31] His famous inaugural lecture of 1492, the *Lamia*, is one long polemic, ironical but biting, against the learned " philosophers " that were criticizing him; perhaps against the Ficinians themselves. Only a little earlier were the anti-Ficinian sallies of Pico, to whom Poliziano came closer and closer, while Mirandola, who was very closely linked to Savonarola, made his visits to Lorenzo rarer and rarer. Nor should it be forgotten that Poliziano was reading the *Poetics*, discussing imitation, studying and commenting on Alexander of Aphrodisias.

Instead of a picture in manneristic style of a compact Florentine Neoplatonism, we have a much more changing panorama in which all the deep-lying divisions of the city, its entire economic, political and social crisis was mirrored in precise ideal contrasts. Very soon Savonarola was to insert his religious anxiety and gloomy prophecy into the clash between Mediceans and anti-Mediceans, between poor and rich; and his appeal was to be all the harsher in the disquiet of a world full of menaces, disturbed and uncertain in the face of a renovation whose consequences no one could calculate. It cannot be denied that ancient myths and Platonic fables were circulating in Florence. Giovanni Nesi, a Ficinian before he became a Savonarolian, was famous for the orations, in Italian as well as in Latin, that he went around making to lay confraternities: eloquent, full of Neoplatonic and hermetic themes, sometimes of baroque exuberance.

It was in these ways, and not by means that were too technically refined, that men like Michelangelo came into contact with Platonizing themes and images; but in these ways the sages of antiquity came in along with Moses and the Prophets, and were prophets themselves. And very soon they were overwhelmed by Savonarola's Biblical language and his apocalyptic pronouncements. Nesi has been mentioned precisely because he was a Platonist originally, because he was an admirer and imitator of Dante and the *Commedia*, because he wrote in the vernacular as well, and because he ended up as a fervent Savonarolian. In this version, moreover, which can be called educational and almost popular, Ficinian Neoplatonism changed its aspect and significance; while on the one hand it ran out in vague aspirations, on the other hand, starting as the ideology of the Medicean principate, it combined with republican nostalgias and finally was converted to the program of Savonarola.

Now, if we descend from the customary image of the Laurentian symposia, with high-level disputes on Platonic metaphysics, to the dramatic reality of Florence between the death of Lorenzo and the advent of Savonarola, with its culture refined to the point of decadence—against which the moralistic revolt was forming—and with its existence menaced at the roots, with its dreams of civic virtue, liberty and welfare, with its reality of crisis and misery, of internal and external menaces—in both Italy and Europe—in transformation, with new worlds on the horizon and implacable enemies at its borders, among intrigues and travail of all kinds; if we realize the harsh contradiction between the Platonic evasions and a tormented everyday life, then, perhaps we may find the ways along which Michelangelo's Florentine formation took place. Then we shall uncover all the tension over which the voice of the prophet of San Marco rose in hammer blows, against the bemused flutterings of the metaphysics of love and light triumphant in the sermons of the *Compagnia dei Magi*. And we shall also understand the passage of the young artist from Poliziano's Ovidian fables to the image of the world's sorrow collected and concentrated in the sorrow of the Virgin. We shall begin to understand his fleeings, between personal worries and catastrophic prophecies. We shall see summed up in the bulk of the *David* so many of the old civic myths of Florence; we shall find ideality and conflicts matured under the sign of the pages of the Bible and the tercets of Dante, interwoven with the " stories " of Rome and Athens. Through his fleeings we shall divine not only his fears, but also his experiences beyond the Florentine initiation; we shall divine his very awareness of the end of a primacy in the midst of a world that, despite the heights that had been reached, was crumbling. In this way his work becomes more and more profound in the measure in which it attains and expresses the drama of a tormented, menaced and sorrowing humanity, which sees not only its civic security disappear, but even its intellectual and moral refuges.

All in all, upon examination, this turns out to be a path along which the Platonic aura, which may help in some iconological researches, attenuates more and more and in reality yields its place to the greatest poetic depiction of the human tragedy in the world that Italian culture ever expressed in the visual arts.

In a well-known passage in Francisco de Hollanda's dialogues, Michelangelo, after justifying the " truth " of the depictions of the marvelous, the fantastic and the monstrous, goes on to that declaration of faith that is, at the same time, the definition of a precise program: the kind of painting he is praising consists in imitating, in depicting, the beings that God has created with infinite care and wisdom. The highest painting will consist in depicting, vying with the art of God, the most perfect of this creatures, the highest one and the most complex, the one he created in his own image and likeness: man. Certainly, no less skill is needed to depict a fish; but he who knows how to depict man has truly gathered in the microcosm the sense of the world.

Now, whether or not this dialogue be Michelangelo's, it is certain that his work, both as painter and as sculptor, was this: To render in human bodies, in their infinite individuations, the history and tragedy of man and his relations with God—that is, God himself and the divine world to the extent that it too enters into the human drama—since man participates therein to the extent to which the divine enters into history. The members, generally nude members, and the numberless faces, tell of dramas that are darker and darker, more and more sorrowful.

From the myths and civic ideals of the *David* to the tragic mass of the *Rondanini Pietà*, the entire struggle of men against men and against things is gone through, from the first emergence of the creation from nothing to the vertiginous damnation and redemption through the merit of the Son of Man, who, too, went through death, finding the wrath of the judge. And it is this sorrowing humanity that Michelangelo follows and depicts, with its saints and its prophets, saints and prophets of misfortune above all, in whom serenity, when it is attained, is an infinite nocturnal melancholy, or the " terribly " resigned reflection of misfortune, or the peace that comes from meditation on death.

Certainly, Michelangelo was born of the civilization that had engaged in so much rhetoric on man and his possibilities, on man as the center of the world, on man as the image of God. Without that culture, Michelangelo is simply unthinkable. Only, he no longer depicts a Platonic *idea*; he does not bend over the shadow of the cave in order to rise from the uncertain forms to the immortal essences. He carries all, Jesus included, along in the great whirlwind of history, which is sin, sorrow and expiation. Keen to detect the slightest movement of the soul in the vibration of a muscle, in that endless throng of bodies, almost always nude, solemn, isolated or in immense whirlwinds, he writes in the concrete individual flesh the entire story, divine and human, in a light that is more and more tragically apocalyptic as the composed and fragile initial calm gives place to a deeper and deeper awareness of sin and expiation. If there is a " history " that is far from the edifying evanescences of Platonic culture between the Quattrocento and the Cinquecento, it is certainly the art of Michelangelo, in which in the end everything is so tremendously earthly, sorrow and death, damnation and justice; where the Son of Man too, in all the splendor of his body risen from the dead, is present in man's tragic history, to provide its ultimate meaning: the justice of the executioner.

This is the point at which Tolnay's statement is most exact: the synthesis of Michelangelo like the *Commedia* of Dante; the great poem of man in the Renaissance, rooted in Florence, it is true, but then become the story of all the affairs of man, of all men, of the God-Man.[32] There, at a certain point, always under the wings of Death in the unfinished tombs or in judgment after death, man and God, united in the great drama, utter a word on all human history that is not rationally articulated but is not exhausted, as are the too many words of the philosophers.

[28] Chastel, *op. cit.*, p. 79.
[29] *Ibid.*, p. 82.
[30] Cf. Vasari, *op. cit.*, p. 296.
[31] V. Branca, " La incompiuta Seconda Centuria dei ' Miscellanea ' di Angelo Poliziano," *Lettere Italiane*, Vol. XIII (1961), pp. 137-77.
[32] On the " anthropomorphic " nature of Michelangelo's architecture as well, see the remarks of Tolnay, *Michelangelo architetto*, p. 125.

Concluding remarks

The researches of Edgar Wind in his *Pagan Mysteries in the Renaissance*[33] have shown once again, if it were needed, how necessary it is, for a precise commentary on the origins and significance of some of Michelangelo's images, to refer to certain literary works of the time, including the " Platonists. "

There is no need to go over that again. What was said here had a different purpose, obvious and banal, in a way: the statement that the vision of life implicit in the great procession of human figures set forth by Michelangelo in statues and paintings, goes beyond both the doctrinal terms that can be elicited from his poems (and the accounts of contemporaries) and the theoretical positions of contemporary thinkers, especially the " Platonists," to which he has always been referred. He goes beyond them and is separate from them. He is something else. While it is likely that on the technical plane of speculation he is much below a Ficino, it cannot be denied that the history of men and their passions that he put down in images is something quite different, with a quite different texture and a quite different meaning.

It is a meaning, however, that on the plane of thought, apart from the illustrative glosses of the erudite or the discourse of art critics, must be left to his language in stone and paints. It is not in conceptual terms; it speaks a language of its own. The translations into contemporary or subsequent speculative languages that have been attempted all finally leave us with the same disappointment as certain pages of Varchi or Vasari. They give the impression of an unbounded impoverishment, of a series of rhetorical or gratuitous digressions, of arbitrary excursuses, of baseless hypotheses as to the " ideas " of the author. True, he was deeply moved, and was aware of problems and conflicts, but he expressed the solutions in visual form. From these figures it is possible, in fact essential, to go back to the antecedents, human as well as technical and historical; we can run through once more the conflicts out of which they arose and, in a word, reevoke a cultural situation. To retranslate that work, which is properly called the " thought " of the artist, into pseudo-philosophical terms or into conceptual arguments turning around a " conception " of reality; to reduce it into patterns, even when he himself proposed them elsewhere, is probably meaningless labor. Certainly it is labor that up to now has been fruitless except for elegant pages and suggestive " appendices " to the work of art. If someone undertook to follow out the long series of strictly " philosophical " interpretations of the work of Michelangelo that have been made from the Cinquecento on, it would, no doubt, be an interesting and important task; but one of a different type and, of course, with a different goal.

[33] New Haven, Yale University Press, 1958.

VIII

WRITER

by Enzo Noè Girardi

Michelangelo as a writer of his time

AUTONOMY BETWEEN WRITER AND ARTIST

In trying to understand Michelangelo as writer, we must reject the obvious and easy assumption: that his literary activities were a secondary expression of his artistic life.

True the letters have to do with marbles, statues, stonecutters and apprentices, matters of contracts and jobs, while the poems speak of living stone, of hard mountain rock and are full of images, arguments, concepts and intuitions that have to do with art: the art of removing and of adding-on, of closed forms and open forms, of carved faces and painted faces and of the artist on his back under the vault of the Sistine Chapel and of the cathartic power and transcendence and immortality of the work of art, and so on. Nevertheless, neither the poems or the letters seem to have been written primarily for this purpose, although such specific references appear more frequently in the letters than they do in the poems.

In common with every writer, Michelangelo when he writes is writing of his own experience. Since so much of his life had to do with art and with things related to art, it is natural that art should play an important role in the poems and in the letters. But these were not, as has been said so many times, created above all for his own satisfaction and pleasure or to pass the time—a diversion on the fringes of his real work, nor as someone else has proposed, from the spiritual necessity to express thoughts that were too complex and deep to be trusted to the possibilities of stone and color, nor, finally are his words born from outbursts of temperament or love, but from the simple basic presence in Michelangelo of the true and genuine calling of writer. This can be determined by the fact that even the letters, though often written for practical purposes, are also stamped with that undeniable artistic quality which was so deeply rooted in the personality of the master.

The way in which this literary vocation is joined to the obviously primary one of fine-artist is readily understandable once we take into consideration the various possibilities of expression that were open to the individual in the humanistic-renaissance environment as compared to those which formed the framework of the romantic or post-romantic mentality. Although Michelangelo in some ways gives the impression of a man who is romantically committed and almost burned by his genius, that is, by his vocation as artist:

> That precious art in which one time I was
> Of so much reputation, now has made me
> A poor old man, a slave in others' hands
> I am undone, unless I perish soon,

still his personality in its essential nature was never so completely absorbed and imprisoned by this dedication to art as to eliminate other aspects of himself which he did not in any way consider subsidiary.

Not for nothing did Michelangelo belong to that unique phase of the Renaissance (prolonged in him far into the sixteenth century) in which the position of the artist long beyond academic specialization was also above the artisan phase of the fifteenth century. Writing to his nephew to tell him to address his letters not to " Michelangelo, sculptor " but to Michelangelo Buonarroti, he says, " I was never a painter or sculptor, like those who keep a studio and make a business of it. I always avoided that, for the honor of my father and my brothers although I served three popes, as I was forced to." This was that happy moment in which the man of genius, be he artistic, political, literary or whatever, far from exhausting himself or from totally identifying himself with any one function, had such broad and varied cultural interests within himself and around him such free conditions, in the uncrystallized forms of life and open cultural institutions, that he was able to express his intellectual and creative talents in various forms and directions without scattering his energies and without falling into superficial dilettantism.

It may be said with some truth that Michelangelo himself does not seem to give much importance to his work as a writer, preferring to have its worth evaluated within a restricted community of friends and colleagues and judging himself unfit, because of his " bad taste "[1] to make any pronouncement on poetry, as if he too, like Leonardo, were " an unlettered man." The phrases of the Letters will come to mind in which he tells of how difficult it was for him to write: " Writing is a great trial to me, since it is not my own art."; " I find writing a great annoyance and sorrow, etc... " [2]

Similar attitudes can be found towards painting:

> My painting dead
> Defend Giovanni, and my honor
> As painter too I am in sad estate;[3]

and it is clear that Michelangelo resists being categorized or boxed into any professional classification, so much so that he even feels the emphasis ought to be placed on the exercise of an art or on the art itself rather than on the artist. But even beyond these feelings, it is certain that Michelangelo not only recognizes the obvious differences which set him apart from those writers for whom writing was the sole mode of expression, or at least the most important, but realizes his own inadequacy in regard to that abstract idea of a perfect art of writing as well as to that line of taste which, codified by Bembo, was so widely accepted and used in prose, and even more so in poetry, as the norm or the official line; a style based on a compromise between the interior world of the writer and the custom of the time and above all on a regular education in humanistic rhetoric.

Michelangelo had not followed this usual curriculum of humanistic studies. His interior life was too rich, too strongly individual and too free of the restrictions of convention to allow himself to masquerade as that " character " or to put on that rigid and uniform mask which was the " correct " style as exemplified in the mediocrity of Bembo's work and in the half-truths which made up so much of the official culture.

All this obviously made him feel alien to the established literary order; the more so as this order became increasingly entrenched. But this did not prevent Michelangelo from going his own way, nor did it hinder his contemporaries such as Berni from using his example to silence the Bembists... (" Be silent eternal pallid violets," etc.). Nor can it keep us from admitting Michelangelo to full citizenship in literature for that personal inborn gift and for those habits and characteristic tendencies of taste and style which he, with conscious effort derived, interpreted and developed from other authors and which reflected so much of the ambience and cultural scene of Florence. That he, in common with the artists of his time and with the majority of artists of every time, had not gone through the normal course of studies and had remained outside of the predominant literary style of his day does not mean that he had not acquired certain fundamental learnings or that he had not been exposed to various cultural and literary influences. For these reasons, his experience as a writer fell at least partly within the general boundaries of common experience.

MICHELANGELO AND FLORENTINE CULTURE

Intelligent Florentines are in a special position with respect to the phenomenon of language, in that they have little or no need of a linguistic or rhetorical standard,[4] and enjoy special freedom because of their deep, native, unhampered mastery of the language. " Michelangelo," Bertoni says, " did not have a literary man's style, nor any words that were not his own, all his own, that is, rooted in his soul... "[5] This is true, but not only for Michelangelo, but also for a Machiavelli, a Guicciardini, a Cellini. It is true more or less for all the Tuscan writers, especially those of his generation, who had grown up in a climate of free development of forms. It is precisely this full and free possession of the tool of language, that is the source of that typical characteristic of Florentine literature, its apparent emphasis on content, its objectivism, not only in the more common meaning of the literature of things (whether those things pertain to the salvation of the soul or to intellectual speculation, to the government of the state or to family interests, to making works of art or to market operations), but also in the even more typically Florentine sense of making language itself an object, a content, a thing, whether in the form of the " ribobolo " slang or in all those other serious or burlesque forms of verbal and conceptual constructions and even play, examples of which are offered not only by a Burchiello, but more or less by all the Florentine writers, not excluding Dante, Boccaccio and Petrarch.

Both the letters and the poems of Michelangelo fit well into this doubly objectivist perspective. The letters deal more with things; the poems, despite Berni's opinion, are more concerned with the words; both, within the limits of their specific functions, offer us not only a vivid and faithful picture of the master's personality, but also reflect some typical aspects of Florentine literary culture.

Thus the letters, so many of which are concerned with the guidance and increase of the temporal and spiritual goods of the Buonarroti family, continue the tradition of familiar literature that inspires Alberti's *Family* book and Guicciardini's *Memoirs*, originating in the Dantesque myth of the family and civic traditions, the beautiful relaxed way of life of the citizens of Florence. While in the poems, the entire Tuscan lyric tradition, from the poets of the New Style through Petrarch down to the lyricists of the fifteenth century, reappears now recast, recapitulated and carried to an extreme point of development in an attempt at conceptual investigation and stylistic originality that have no analogues in contemporary poetry.

[1] Cf. M. Buonarroti, *Rime*, edited by E. N. Girardi, Bari 1960, p. 371.

[2] Phrases like this are the starting point for Giulio Bertoni in his essay on " The Prose of Michelangelo " in *Lingua e cultura*, Florence 1932, p. 153. I will remark that the phrases appear only in the letters of his old age, referring to the material labor of writing, more than to anything else.

[3] And so in the sonnet on his work in the Sistine Chapel (5); but he also speaks of it in a letter: " And this is the difficulty of the work, in addition to not being my profession."

[4] On this topic cf. the author's essay on " The Linguistic writings of G. B. Gelli " in *Ævum*, V-VI (1955), p. 469 ff.

[5] *Op. cit.*, p. 158.

Letters

GENERAL CHARACTER OF THE CORRESPONDENCE

Buonarroti's correspondence, as it comes to us today in Papini's reprint of the old edition of Milanesi,[6] comprises a little less than five hundred letters written by Michelangelo between 1486 and 1563.

A large group of them, almost half, seem to be written to members of the family: his father Lodovico (32), his brothers Buonarroto (56), Giovan Simone (9) and Gismondo (3) and his nephew Lionardo (130). A certain number were sent to persons linked to Michelangelo by friendship or association, such as Tommaso Cavalieri (3), Vittoria Colonna (2), Luigi del Riccio (27), and to administrators of the affairs of his family, such as G. F. Fattucci, chaplain of the cathedral of Florence (18), and Giovanni Spina (6). The remainder went to various illustrious or obscure addressees, among whom are artisans, apprentices and stonecutters, along with artists like Giuliano da Sangallo, Sebastiano del Piombo, Vasari, Cellini, Ammannati; men of letters like Aretino and Varchi; Popes Clement VII and Paul III, the king of France, Duke Cosimo de' Medici, Cardinals Giulio de' Medici and Dovizi da Bibbiena, Pio da Carpi, etc.

Naturally, not all these letters, whether relating to work, courtesy or family administration, are equally beautiful or even useful for defining Michelangelo's art as a writer to the same extent that they can be useful in biographical research. They are based, at least for the most part, not on care for writing well, but on practical matters; although it is true that the writer is always Michelangelo, we can not see the marks of genius or of remarkable style in many notes which the artist penned dealing with his interests.

1 Letter to father (October 1514).

Undoubtedly, this " worry and torment, without scornful posing in the modern manner," as Papini remarks, " about grandnephews and farms, and money and buying houses and choosing wives " [7] surprises us moderns, who are led by a persistent Romantic mentality to conceive of a genius as a kind of superman. It may be true that not all of Michelangelo's letters seem to be very important, but the correspondence as such can be said to be important, and especially the entire group, numerically the largest, of the letters concerning family administration. They are witnesses to a civilization in which genius does not represent itself as in opposition to other people, but rather in the willing acceptance of the responsibilities and the fate of all men; they attest the special intensity of moral and emotional participation that Michelangelo brought to everything he did.

FAMILY LETTERS

To initiate the discussion of these family letters, we may make a comparison with another " genius " of that period, Lodovico Ariosto, who was as opposed as Michelangelo to " scornful posing in the modern manner." Ariosto too accepts, more or less willingly, the practical labors involved in his post as a courtier and in ruling his family; his letters too meet these practical necessities, dealing simply and directly with the situation. But that is all the value they have; when we have said that they are simple and unadorned, there is nothing more to be said; clearly, the poet put into the relationship of letter-writing no more than the indispensable minimum of himself, and his heart was elsewhere.

Not so for Michelangelo. For him, the importance of communicating by letter is not confined to the momentary purpose of the letter itself. For him, writing means also and above all exercising the economic and spiritual government of the family, impressing the far-off members with the example of his own life and the authority of his judgment. He is thoughtful and loving in counsel, but if need be, severe in rebuke and violent in scorn and threats, always concerned that they should guide their conduct not so much by considerations of niggardly self-interest nor by the fear of losing the inheritance that he might leave them, but above all by dignity, disinterest, feelings of honor and religion.

He carried out this task with so much love, so much steadiness and consistency, that gradually, letter by letter, the correspondence takes on the guise of the basic law of the family organization, the moral foundation of the fortunes of the house, something to be not only preserved, but to be consulted long after; [8] and at the same time, it serves as a living autobiography, a psychological and moral self-portrait, drawn in simple outlines, without ostentation and flourishes, but not lacking in the touch of solemnity and grandeur befitting the founder of a house.

" We," he writes to his nephew in 1546 in connection with the advisability of buying a fine house in town, " are citizens descended from a most noble race... Some day when I have the time, I will tell you about our origins, where we came from and when [we came] to Florence, something that you may not know: but we do not wish to have taken from us that which God has given us."

The promise is kept, at least in part, in a later letter: " And about a year ago there came into my hands a hand-written book of Florentine chronicles, and there I found, about two hundred years ago, if I remember correctly, a Buonarroti Simoni several times on the Signoria, then a Simone Buonarroti, then a Michele di Buonarroto, etc." Like Dante, who only towards the end of his voyage, half-way through the *Paradiso*, feels that the time has come proudly to reveal the nobility of his blood, so Michelangelo goes about discovering the nobility of the family when he is already an old man, as if only the great name he had made for himself by his own merit could justify and make advisable, for the benefit of his heirs, the claim of the same nobility of blood. It is true that a concern for defending a family dignity that his own people did not seem to feel so intensely is seen vividly in the first letters written from Bologna to his father and his brother Buonarroto: " What happens to them is not our affair," he writes to his father, and repeats it to his brother, in connection with two workmen who had complained to them that Michelangelo had discharged them, and to whom Lodovico seemed to pay more attention than was fitting: " Tell Lodovico that you shouldn't talk about what happened to them by any means, because what happens to them is not our affir: and that's that."

Nor was it the affair of the Buonarroti what happened to that Piero Aldobrandini who had asked Michelangelo, through his relatives, to get him a chased dagger that he had ordered from an able Bologna master, but that did not turn out to his liking: " I want to write to you about this," Michelangelo writes to Buonarroto, "... don't have dealings with him, because that is not the kind of dealings for you: and that's that."

Nobility, as is well known, is also one of the conditions that Lionardo should require in choosing a wife: " It is up to you to take her or not to take her, or one rather than another, as long as she is noble and well-bred..." " You have to look for nobility, for good health, and more for goodness than anything else." And when the nephew objects that he is afraid of " seeming to want to ennoble himself," the answer is: " This doesn't count, because it is known that we are old citizens of Florence."

I do not believe that this matter of nobility can be considered as simply a mere weakness, one of the many that so often flourish even in the greatest men. In the first place, it is clear that when Michelangelo speaks of nobility he means ancient Florentine citizenship and important offices held in the city government. Secondly, if it is true, as has been said, that he did not let himself be taken in by the myth of the " divine " artist that soon formed around his name, it will not be surprising that quite the contrary took place, that is, that the dignity he had achieved in art should be the basis for augmenting and expanding his own person, and that this augmentation and expansion should take place in the sense called for by his Florentine cultural formation, comprising, among other things, that habit of municipal and family aristocracy that his association in Rome with the Strozzi, the Ridolfi, the Giannotti and the other anti-Medicean exiles would rather keep alive than attenuate.

In any case, nobility never became in Michelangelo a synonym for haughtiness or disdain. The friendly familiarity he employed with workingmen and artisans, and the paternal interest he had in his apprentices, are more than ample proof. If he is displeased that, for example, " people here keep saying that I have a brother (Gismondo) that follows the oxen at Settignano " (42) or that Lionardo forwards letters from strangers and inferiors, inclosing them in his own (" Don't put letters from anybody else in your letters, out of self-respect. Bugiardino is a good sort, but a simple man; and that's that. If you are asked to send me letters in yours, say that you don't have occasion to write me ") p. 73, he does not mean that nobility implies forgetting the lowly state the family was in before he brought it up by his labors, nor is it abandonment of simple habits.

" See to it," he keeps saying to Lionardo concerning a wife, " that you find one that won't be ashamed, if need be, to wash the dishes and other household things, so that you won't

534

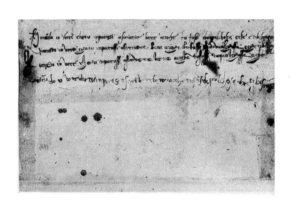

2 Note to his nephew Lionardo telling him to write better (1546?).

have to get poor by foolishnesses and showing off." And he had written to his father, at a time that was politically unfavorable to the family, "If you can not have worldly honors like the other citizens, be content to have bread and live well with Christ, poorly as I do here; I live a meager life and care not for honors, that is, for the world, and I live with tremendous labor and a thousand suspicions."

The spirit of poverty, if not poverty itself, is one of the themes that recurs most often and most vividly, and goes furthest towards determining the prudential nature and sententious tone of these family letters.

He advises his father to take care of Buonarroto, who had fallen ill, without thinking of the expense, because, he says, contradicting Machiavelli, [9] "men are worth more than money." Another letter says, in connection with his father's worries about "property": "Don't be dismayed at that, and don't have an ounce of melancholy, for if property is lost, life is not lost. I will make so much money for you that it will come to more than you will lose; but keep it well in mind not to have it too dear to your heart, for it is a deceitful thing... Take care of living, and never mind property, rather than have troubles, for I love you more living and poor; for if you died, all the gold in the world would not make it up to me." To Buonarroto, who has the chance of making a rich marriage, he recommends, among other things, not to consent out of avarice: "Avarice is a very great sin, and nothing that is sinful can come to a good end." And poverty is one of the prerequisites for the ideal wife that Michelangelo wants for Lionardo, along with nobility, health, kindness and simple ways; not only because if there is no dowry, "there will not be pride either," and because Lionardo needs a wife "that will stay home and that he can command, and that doesn't run around funerals and go to parties and weddings every day; because where there are festivities, it is an easy thing to become a whore," but also because in that way the nephew could make good use of the money he had not earned: "And this would please me greatly... that you would make the fortune of others, as others have done to you: but you find yourself rich, and don't know how... and so be grateful to God for the condition that you are in...," seeming to reflect a though of Dante's on "human probity": "and this is as He wishes that gives it, so that it may be asked of Him" (Purg. VII, 123).

Also frequent are religious recommendations and exhortations (to pray and have prayers said, to rely on the will of God, to think of one's soul, to take care to die with the sacraments, to give charity and give it well), not only in the later letters but all through the correspondence (which rules out the possibility of a supposed conversion of Michelangelo, presumably arising out of the artist's conversations with Vittoria Colonna); and they are such as to discourage any excessively complicated or heterodox interpretation of Michelangelo's religion either as a family habit derived solely from tradition and custom, or on the contrary as a spiritualism of Protestant type. Here are some instances.

At Bologna Michelangelo was casting the statue of Julius II. It came out badly. "Things went badly," he wrote his brother, and added: "Let us thank God for it, since I hold that all things are for the best." Some years later, at a hard time for everyone (Buonarroto seriously ill, Michelangelo without money to help him and forced to borrow from Fattucci): "Do not fret," is his exhortation, "for God did not create us to abandon us." On another occasion: "Do your work and thank God that, since this tribulation had to be, it came at a time when you could do better than you had done in the past."

Likewise in 1515, at another period of uncertainty over political events in Florence and in Italy, he recommends: "Take heed of your affairs, and most of all of your soul, for today that seems to be needful... Watch your soul, for things might go further than you think." In the following year, fearing that the death of Lodovico was near, he wrote to Buonarroto: "See to it that he lacks nothing of the things of the soul and the sacraments of the Church"; and later he writes to Lionardo, at Giovansimone's death: "Especially would I wish to know what kind of death he died, and whether he died confessed and communicate, with all the things ordained by the Church; because if he had this, and I knew it, I would be less desolate"; and on the death of Gismondo: "Since he died with a clear conscience and with all the sacraments that the Church ordains, God is to be thanked." He wrote something similar at the death of Paul III in November 1549: "He died a good death, with a good conscience down to his last word. God have mercy on his soul," adding, a propos of the conjectures as to the new pope "awaited at any moment": "God knows the needs of the Christians, and that's that." A few months later, after the election of Julius III, he writes to Fattucci: "All Rome is joyful, and nothing is expected but the greatest benefits, especially for the poor, because of his liberality." It was a simple, essential religion, without any pietism; once again, it suggests the teachings of Dante:

> You have the New and the Old Testament
> And the pastor of the Church that guides you:
> And that suffices you for your salvation.
> (Par. V, 76-78).

Thus, he says of a woman that wanted to give "a girl of the Capponi" in marriage to Lionardo and to that end "has written me a long gospel with a sermon exhorting me to live well and give charity... and she must have told you that God inspired her to give you that

535

3 Letter to Cornelia widow of Urbino (1557).

girl"; his judgment is that "she would do much better to be weaving or spinning than to go around spilling all that sanctity." When Lionardo informed him that he intended to make a pilgrimage to Loreto for the soul of his father, Michelangelo replied: "If it was a vow, I think it should be carried out by all means; if it is for help that you want to give his soul, I had rather give what you would spend on the way, down there for the love of God, for him, than do otherwise: for," he notes with a touch of anticlericalism that is quite normal in a man of the Cinquecento in the tradition of Savonarola, "giving money to the priests, the Lord knows what they do with it."

It is a religion that years and the approach of death make even more intimate and fervid, with a note of resignation to the divine will expressed no less vividly in the letters than in the last sonnets, whether he is calling on Lionardo (still in connection with the question of his wife) to "commend himself to God and have faith that He would send him something right," or to thank Him for his engagement to Francesca Ridolfi, "praying Him that this find grace with Him;" or referring to his last work, the structure of Saint Peter's, which he was slowly finishing in the midst of the tribulations of old age: "Because I am old and have nothing else to leave after me, I have not wished to give it up, and also because I serve for the love of God and in Him have all my hope."

We shall not take up the more exclusively economic or practical side of these family letters, even though they are not lacking in reflections and warnings, almost in the style of Guicciardini ("Never do anything in anybody's house unless you are entirely satisfied with it"; "Whatever you do, do it without passion, because there is no matter so great that if you do it without passion it will not seem small"; "There is nobody that loves others better

536

than himself"; "Going slowly you make fewer mistakes"; "If you have money in the house, one hand should not trust the other because the danger is extreme," etc.).

Instead, we shall deal rather with the letters that reflect moments of anger or indignation or bitterness. There are not many such, but they are undoubtedly among the finest; the excitement of his mind rouses him to a cold and cutting hardness, or to vibrant impassioned eloquence.

In 1544, hearing that Michelangelo was gravely ill, Lionardo rushed to Rome. Michelangelo had a suspicion that it was more concern over the will than love for his uncle that was driving him, and refused to see him. Instead, he wrote him this letter: " I was sick, and you in Sir Giovan Francesco's house came to give me death, and see whether I was leaving anything. Isn't there enough of mine in Florence to suffice you? You can't deny you're like your father, who chased me out of my house in Florence. I can tell you that I have made a will in such a way that you needn't worry anymore about what I own in Rome. God be with you and don't let me see you again and never write me, and do the way the priest does."

The next year, the nephew, just returned from a fresh visit to Rome, put pressure on him for the purchase of a certain property. Michelangelo reacted: " You were in quite a hurry to tell me about the Corboli's property: I hadn't thought you were in Florence yet. You must be afraid that I would change my mind, as if you had been instructed, and I say that I want to go slow, because that money, I earned it here with a kind of labor that someone like you will never know, that was born clothed and shod." He goes on: " As for rushing to Rome in such a fury, I don't know that you would have come so fast when I was poor and had nothing to eat... You are so afraid of losing this inheritance! and you say it was your duty to come here for the love you bear me: the love of the clothes-worm! If you loved me, you would have written me now: —Michelangelo, spend the three thousand scudos on yourself, because you have given us so much it is enough for us: your life is dearer to us than your possessions.— You have lived off me for forty years now, and I have never had even a kind word from you, let alone anything else! "

To his father too he had more than once written words of bitterness, even though they were filtered through filial love and respect. Thus, when Lodovico had complained that he could not recover certain rents from Monte and that his son had put the property in his own name, Michelangelo found himself forced even to reproach him with the poverty from which he had raised him: " I explained that thing about Monte and you can see him as you please; I have always done and undone as you have desired: I no longer know what you want of me. If I bother you by being alive, you have found the way to cure that, and you will get that key, of the treasure you say I have; and you will do well: for everyone in Florence knows that you were a man of great wealth and that I always robbed you, and deserve to be punished: you will get great praise for that! So shout and say what you will of me, but don't write to me any more, for you don't let me work... Take care of yourself and protect yourself from those you have to protect yourself from; for one only dies once, and one doesn't come back to repair things ill done. You have postponed death to do things like that! God be with you."

And so too to his brother Buonarroto, and so especially to Giovansimone, scapegrace and adventurer, who had gone so far as to raise his hand to his father. To him Michelangelo addressed the masterpiece of his eloquence: " I am sure that you are not my brother; because if you were, you would not threaten my father; you are a beast: and I shall treat you as a beast. I will tell you that anyone that sees his father threatened or struck has to defend him with his life: and that is that. I tell you that you have nothing in the world: and since I have the slightest interest in your affairs, I will come there posthaste and show you your error and teach you to waste your possessions and set fire to houses and properties that you didn't earn: you aren't where you think you are. If I come there, I'll show you something that will make you weep for fair, and you will find out what your arrogance is worth."

Then indignation gives way to affection somewhat: " ... but if you are willing to act right and honor and revere your father, I will help you like the others... "; but after the letter is finished and signed, Michelangelo feels he still has something to say to his scamp of a brother, and his indignation flares up again: " I can not help writing you another couple of lines; and that is that I have been wandering all over Italy for twelve years; subjected to all kinds of shame; made every effort, worn my body out in all kinds of labor; put my life in a thousand dangers, only to help my family; and now that I have started to get it up a bit, only you want to be the one that upsets and ruins, in an hour, what I have accomplished in so many years with so much toil; by the body of Christ, it shall not be so! I can take care of ten thousand like you, if I have to. Be sensible, and don't try the patience of someone of a different caliber."

" I can take care of ten thousand like you ": the expression is like one of Cellini's, but the tone is quite different. Michelangelo is genuine even in his exaggeration. For Cellini, talking of himself and his affairs in superlatives is a way of showing himself as worth more than he really is; for Michelangelo, it is one of many ways of showing what he is, possessed of a grandeur independent of his subjective attitude, useful to others and enjoyed in itself, and paid for with toil, worries and annoyances of every kind.

4 Letter to nephew Lionardo (June 1552).

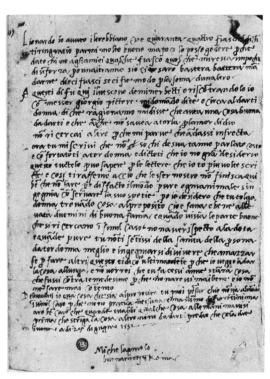

BUSINESS LETTERS

This is precisely the image of the artist as it appears in some letters to his family, when he chances to speak of a work in progress, and above all in the letters on his work, which are undoubtedly the most interesting, even from a literary point of view.

A good example is this which he writes from Bologna about the recasting of the great bronze statue of Julius II: "Here I am in the greatest distress and with extreme labors and all I do is work both day and night, and I have had so much labor, and still have, that if I had to make another, I don't think my life would be long enough to do it, because it was an enormous work; and if it had been in the hands of anyone else, he would have come to grief in it. But I hold that the prayers of certain persons have helped me and kept me well, because nobody in all Bologna thought I could ever bring it to completion."

This account is all superlatives; the distress is "greatest"; the labors, "extreme"; the work lasts "both day and night"; the work is "enormous," so that a lifetime would not be enough to make another like it; his own prowess is so great that "anyone else would have come to grief"; and finally, the skepticism as to the success of the enterprise, shared by "all Bologna." Everything is superlative except the measure of the boast. The idea that he was "helped and kept well" by the prayers of certain persons accentuates the feeling of the greatness of the work but removes any personal vanity, shows the sculptor as a man among men, needing their spiritual help to complete a work to which he lends his hand and mind, but which is essentially the work of God. And so he can say calmly that he will make things never seen in Italy before then ("I have spirit enough to make this work of the façade of San Lorenzo, so that it may be, in architecture and sculpture, the mirror of all Italy"; "I will make the most beautiful work ever made in Italy, if God help me") without a shadow of complacency or bombast between the lines of his sentences; and in the other direction, he can stress his own inadequacies and the most common and prosaic sides of his own activity without ever appearing less grand, less capable of domination and self-domination.

Whether he is retelling yet another time the chronicle of his altercation with Julius II and his flight from Rome, or restating his opinion on the dispute pending with the heirs of the pope; whether he is recounting the endless difficulties and incidents entailed in choosing and transporting the marble needed for the façade of San Lorenzo, or bewailing the unfaithfulness of his apprentices, the laziness of workmen, the thefts of master builders: one would say that he loves to depict himself, apart from the need to write about them, in these lesser aspects, as if to derive, even from this, his daily battle against the inadequacy of people and the hard materiality of things, a universal meaning: the very idea of human activity as gathered, not so much in its moment of victory, or as expressed in the beauty of the finished work, but in the human and religious dimension of its limits, in its essential inadequacy and irremediable incompleteness and innate fallibility.

Sometimes Michelangelo jests about his Sisyphus destiny: "As to doing or not doing the things that have to be done, which you say have to be overcome, it is better to leave them to be done by the man that has to do them, for I will have so much to do that I no longer worry about doing" (Letter to Fattucci, fall of 1525). Sometimes he rebels: "Painting and sculpture, labor and good faith, have ruined me, and things are still going from bad to worse. I would have done better in my first years to take to making sulfur sticks, and then I wouldn't be in such suffering!" "Here I have lost all my youth, tied down to this tomb... That was my fate! I see many men with two thousand and three thousand scudos of income idling in bed, and I, with enormous labor, manage to grow poorer." More often, though, he accepts his daily burden of toil, reliving in his letters the various events, the single cases, with his usual concreteness, with that intense participation that he brought to everything.

Here he is at Carrara to get marble, harried by constant urgings by the agents of Leo X, for the façade, or by the Della Rovere heirs, for the tomb of Julius. "I have located many marbles," he wrote to Domenico Buoninsegni, "and given money here and there, and had digging started in many spots. And in some places where I laid out money, the marble did not come out the way I wanted, because it is a tricky thing, and especially so in the big pieces that I need, if I want the fine ones as I do; and in one stone that I have had cut already, I came upon certain faults towards the Hill that could not have been anticipated, so that two columns that I wanted to make out of it did not come out well for me, and I had wasted half the expenditure on them." He then decided to have stone excavated at Serravezza. Here too he ran into difficulties. The stonecutters that he had sent for from Florence, he writes Buonarroto, "know nothing whatever about either quarrying or marble. They have already cost me more than a hundred thirty ducats, and they haven't yet got out a bit of marble that is good for anything, and they go around everywhere lying that they have found great things and they try to work for the Opera (of the cathedral of Florence) and for others with the money they have received from me..." "I undertook to bring the dead to life when I tried to tame these mountains and bring civilization into this region!" he comments finally; and the picture recurs in a letter to Berto da Filicaia: "The place to quarry here is very rugged, and the men very ignorant in this practice: so that great patience is needed for some months, until the mountains are tamed and the men trained..."

Organizing the transport of the blocks of marble caused him no less trouble. For those excavated at Carrara, Michelangelo had to go "as far as Genoa to get boats"; but the men of

5 Letter to Overseers of the building of St. Peter's (1560).

538

Carrara, among whom the artist had won " great enmity," perhaps because he had preferred the Serravezza quarries to theirs, " have corrupted the masters of the said boats and have cornered me so badly that I have to go to Pisa to get others." Back from Pisa, the days passed and the boats did not come, and Michelangelo exploded: " I think I have been rooked: and that is how everything goes for me. Oh, cursed a thousand times be the day I left Carrara! That is what has ruined me... "

At Serravezza, in the process of moving the rough-hewn blocks from the quarries to the boats (a road had to be made and a swamp filled in as best they could), other incidents occurred.

In lowering a column from the road to the canal, " some people were injured... and one had his neck broken and died on the spot, and I almost was killed."

In a similar operation on another occasion, " a link broke in the chain attached to the column, and the column fell down into the river in a hundred pieces." " That link," Michelangelo says in writing to his disciple Pietro Urbano, " Donato had had made by a crony of his, Lazzero the blacksmith; and as for its being suitable, if it had been well made it could have held four columns, and looking at it from the outside there seemed to be no doubt of it. After it broke, we saw what miserable work it was: there was nothing solid inside and there wasn't enough thickness of iron holding as there would be in the back edge of a knife; so that I am surprised it held as much as it did. All of us that were around it just escaped with our lives: and a marvelous stone was lost " (here there is a clear case of his feeling for materials, his love for good materials: the good iron, the marvelous stone, that is one of the outstanding traits of his poetry as well). Among the many long letters on his controversy with Julius II and his heirs, arising out of the need to justify the actual or alleged failures to perform his contract, or the use of the money received in advance for carrying on the work, we may mention the one in October 1525, in which we see Michelangelo greatly disturbed by the turn the dispute had taken (" I have had a report about these people... that has given me a great fright: and that is the ill will that Julius' relatives bear me: and not without reason... This has worried me greatly, and made me wonder what my position would be if the Pope let me down, this world would not be for me "), and in particular the letter believed to have been sent to Marco Vigerio, Bishop of Sinigaglia.

Asked by the prelate to paint the Pauline chapel, Michelangelo answered " that painting is done with the wits and not with the hands: and that he who can not have his wits about him shames himself: so that until my business is settled I can do nothing good." His " business " was the question of the tomb, for which " I am done to death every day as though I had crucified Christ " and " find I have lost all my youth," etc. Michelangelo writes at some length on this to his correspondent, as if to justify the conclusion: " I can refuse nothing to Pope Paul: I will paint ill-humoredly and do ill-humored things." However, his basic worry comes back to him and he dictates a postscript to him twice the length of the letter, in which, after denying the accusation of having lent out at usury the money given him by the Pope for the tomb (" I write what is true: before men, I will not say before God, I consider myself an honest man, for I never deceived anyone, and then to have to defend myself from the rogues I sometimes have to go out of my mind, as you see... I write what is true, and much less than I could, and I am not a usurious thief, but a Florentine citizen, noble, and son of a gentleman, and I am not from Cagli ") and reasserting that his conscience was clear, against the insinuations of the heirs (" The ambassador of Urbino came on an embassy to me... that if I wish rectification to be made, that I satisfy my conscience." " I say that he has manufactured a Michelangelo in his heart, of the stuff that he has in himself "), he recalls the episode in which he was driven from the papal palace and took refuge in Florence: " With the Pope pressing me to carry on as much as I could, he had me one day when I was there to talk to him about that matter (that is, to have money to pay for cartage of the marble), he had me put out by a footman. When a bishop from Lucca who saw this act, said to the footman: ' Don't you know him? ' And the footman said to me: ' Pardon me, noble sir, I am ordered to do thus.' I went home and wrote this to the Pope; ' Holy Father: This morning I was driven from the palace by order of your Holiness; whence I give you to know that from now on, if you require me, you will seek me elsewhere than in Rome.' And I handed this letter to Messer Agostino the steward to give to the Pope; and in the house I called one Cosimo the Joiner, who was with me and was making furniture for me, and a stonecutter, who is alive today, and I said to them: ' Go find a Jew, and sell what there is in this house, and come to Florence '; and I left, and took posthorses, and went off to Florence."

Once again there comes to mind, by way of contrast, the egotistic and imaginary exaggerations of Cellini's autobiography. In Michelangelo the feeling of offended dignity and of resentment towards the pope that had had him driven out by a footman appear all resolved in concrete decisions and facts, without any comment or emotional coloring, in a tone of calm objectivity which is reflected, for example, in his stressing the politeness of the footman. And this testimonial tone is maintained in his account of the subsequent events: the arrival at Poggibonsi of five horsemen sent by the Pope to order him to return to Rome at once; his reply in the negative; the pressure of the Pope on the Signoria and their intervention (" We do not want to get into a war with Pope Julius over you: you have to leave; and if you wish to go back to him, we will give you letters of such authority that if he should injure you it would be an injury to this Signoria."); his return to Rome. Merely the thought of the 539 losses suffered in this umpleasant episode (during his absence he had been robbed of virtually all the marble that he had had in Piazza S. Pietro) made him angry at his adversaries: "And he who has taken all my youth and honor and possessions calls me a thief!" And in concluding, making reference to "the envy of Bramante and Raffaello da Urbino" as cause of "all the disagreements that arose between Pope Julius and me," pride and bitterness well up at once: "And this was why he did not complete his tomb in his lifetime, to ruin me; and Raffaello had good reason for this, for what art he had, he had from me."

In this controlled and yet rich expressiveness of feeling, in this ability to portray himself, complete and living, without any rhetoric and yet with undoubted forensic power, lies, I should say, the greatest artistic significance of this second group of letters.

FORMAL LETTERS

As for the few letters of pure *politesse*, they represent, as a group, an intermediate phase between the direct matter-of-fact approach that characterizes most of the correspondence and the elevated, but sometimes studied and artful, intellectual meditation that is one of the most essential notes of the poems. In the letter to the King of France and in those to Duke Cosimo, Vasari and other important correspondents and friends, such as Aretino and Varchi, the rank of the addressees inspires a "decorousness" that, while not destroying the simplicity of the style, deprives the letters of the frank note of the personality. In others, and particularly in those to Vittoria Colonna and Tommaso Cavalieri, the style is so marvelously distilled and twisted, so crammed with tropes, plays on words and rhetorical figures, that the most studied poems seem simple by comparison.

The letter to the King of France is a model of elegance and sobriety. The monarch had expressed the desire of having something by his hand. Michelangelo's answer: "Now I am old and taken up for several months with work for Pope Paul; but if some time is left me to live after this occupation, what I have desired, as I have said, more time to work for Your Majesty, I will endeavor to put it into effect, that is, something in marble, something in bronze, a painting. And if death breaks in on this my desire, and it is possible to carve or paint in the other life, I shall not lack to do so there, where one no longer grows old."

The thought of death is likewise the conclusion of his answer to Duke Cosimo, who had written to him and had others write to him of his desire to have him back in Florence. Michelangelo could not accept the invitation until the chapel of the King of France in St. Peter's was redone: "The only thing I have left to do is to leave the model of the whole thing here... and then to go back to Florence with a mind to rest with death, to which I try to grow accustomed, day and night, so that it will not treat me worse than other old men."

Old age, the sadness of the times, the approach of death, are also the subject of considerations, sometimes grave and sometimes serene, in his letters to Vasari and other important friends or correspondents, in which his natural reflective and sententious disposition, divorced from any practical function, appears as a disinterested expression of his spirit, so as in some cases to constitute the reason for the letter itself. "I am old," he wrote to Luca Martini, "and death has taken from me the thoughts of youth; and he who does not know what old age is, let him have patience until it comes; for until then he can not know it." And to Vasari, to show how impossible it is for him to accede to the desire of the Duke of Florence: "My dear Messer Giorgio, I know that you realize from my writing that it is all over with me, and no thought arises in me that does not have death carved on it: and may God grant that I hold it off for some year or two."

On this subject, there are other famous things in the letters to Vasari: the judgment on the festivities his nephew had ordered for the birth of little Buonarroto: "This pomp displeases me much, for man should not laugh when all the world weeps; for which reason it seems to me that Lionardo does not have much judgment, and especially so for making so much rejoicing over a birth, with the joy that should be reserved for the death of one who has lived well," a thought that is a little strained; and the account of the death of his faithful servant Urbino: "You know that Urbino is dead; which was a very great grace of God to me, but a real loss and infinite sorrow. The grace was that whereas when alive he kept me alive, in dying he showed me how to die, not with displeasure but with the desire to die. I had him twenty-six years, and found him most diligent and faithful; and now that I had made him rich and hoped that he would be the staff and repose of my old age, he has gone from me; and no other hope is left me than to meet him again in Paradise. And God has given us a sign of this in the most happy death that he died: and even more than dying, he regretted leaving me alive in this traitorous world, with so many cares; so that the better part of me has gone with him, and nothing more is left to me than infinite misery."

These are the same accents and, in part, the same expressions that occur in so many of the poems inspired by his old age, by death, by the sorrow of living, in the poem on the death of his father ("... in thy death I learn to see my own; ... near the Divine seat / where, by the grace of God, I believe and think / and hope that I shall see thee..."); in the sonnet presumably dedicated to the death of Febo di Poggio ("Now there is gone from me..."); in the one sent to Mons. Beccadelli, which also speaks of the death of his servant ("... and then his death / spurs me on and draws to another road, / where he awaits me to harbor me with

6 Letter to Duke Cosimo (November 1559).

him "); to still others, especially the very late ones: all are elements of that essential colloquy with death and God that predominates in his last years and in which finally any substantial distinction between the letters and the poems disappears.

An analogous case, but one that is thoroughly negative esthetically, of the use in correspondence of the very language of the corresponding poems are the few letters we have of those sent to Cavalieri, of which the manuscripts contain no less than three versions (an obvious proof of the studied and labored nature of the missives): " Rashly, my dearest Tomao, I was moved to write to your Honor, not in reply to any letter of yours that I had received, but first to move, as if I had thought to pass over a little brook with dry feet, or the shallow water of a ford in full view. But once I had departed from the strand, it was not a little brook that I found, but the ocean with its towering waves appeared before me." The letter continues in this strain down to the end (" And if I should not have the skill to navigate the waves of the sea of your worthy genius, that genius will excuse me "; " the present time, with all that time that is still to come for me, I will give to your grace: and it will greatly grieve me that I may not have the past back, therewith to serve your grace so much longer than only with the future," etc., leaving you wondering whether you have a belated echo of the teachings of Guido Faba and Guittone d'Arezzo or an early form of baroque prose.

Some hyperbolic expressions of admiration and sympathy, acceptable and even felicitous in the framework of the sonnets, make a rather clumsy and strained effect here. " And I not born," another version of the same letter runs, " or born dead shall deem myself, and should say that I was in disgrace with heaven and earth, if by your grace I had not seen and believed your Honor willingly accept some works of mine: from which I had great astonishment and not little pleasure: and if it be true that your grace feels inwardly as she writes outwardly, namely to esteem my works; if it should happen that I should make one as I desire it, that should please your grace, I should call it much rather fortunate than good." And in a subsequent letter: " I know well that I can forget your name at the hour that I forget the food on which I live; rather, sooner can I forget the food on which I live, which nourishes only the body, unhappily, than your name, which nourishes the body and the soul, filling both with such sweetness that I can feel neither weariness nor fear of death while memory of you remains with me "; a conceit that is developed more briefly in another version: " I do not believe that you believe that I have forgotten or can forget the food on which I live, which is none other than your name." The two letters to Vittoria Colonna are colder and almost as artificial. In the second, assuring her of his intention to bring her in person the Crucifix he had designed or painted for her, he writes: " ... But the great press of business in which I have been and am made it impossible to inform your Honor thereof: and since I know that your grace knows that love will have no master, and that he who loves sleeps not, the means too were lacking: and although it might seem that I had not remembered, I did what I did not talk about, so as to arrive with a thing unexpected."

As for the reasons for the artificiality, they may be seen either in the exceptional nature and special elevation that characterize, for all their diversity, the affectionate relationships with these two correspondents, or as well in the aristocratic type of culture that both Vittoria Colonna and Cavalieri represented.

There are other cases in which politeness drives Michelangelo to muddy his own style with that of the addressee. For example, there are the letters to Sebastiano del Piombo and, in particular, the urbane commendation written on behalf of the same Sebastiano to the urbane Cardinal Bibbiena, when Sebastiano aspired to succeed Raphael in the project of the Palace: " ... And if your Honor should see its way to cast away service on one like me, I am minded that even in serving there are crazy ones, that rarely can any comfort be found; as someone who is fed up with capons will take to onions for a change," which takes us into the mocking and realistic atmosphere of the chapter replying to Berni in the name of Fra Bastiano.

---

[6] *Lettere di Michelangiolo Buonarroti*, with preface by G. Papini, 2 vols., Lanciano 1932.
[7] *Ibid.*, p. 5.
[8] He writes his brother Buonarroto from Rome in 1515: " I think that in a few years you will like the letters I have been writing you for the past four years better than you do now... " He would like to see as much love in those of his family when they write him; and so he scolds Lionardo who, by writing badly, shows " little love ": " I never get a letter from you but I get into a fever before I can read it: I don't know where you learned to write. Little love! "
[9] " Men forget the death of their fathers sooner than the loss of their property " (*Principe*, Ch. XVII).

Poems

RELATION BETWEEN THE LETTERS AND THE POEMS

While the letters primarily give the native side of the writer, the poems are substantially the product of literary research and construction.

This of course does not mean that the two worlds are absolutely separate. Just as there are (as we have pointed out) letters inspired by the most disinterested of themes, or by the most

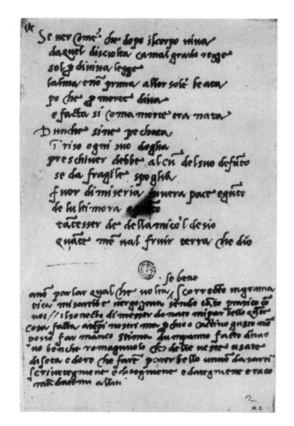

7 Rhymes, No. 192 (1544).

elaborate language of the poems, so are there verses of Michelangelo, especially of the initial period of his poetic activity, that deal with biographically circumstantial subjects in a manner so direct as to come very close to the manner of the letters. "Here one drowns in breast-plates," Michelangelo writes from Bologna; and a related expression: "Here helmets are made from chalices, and swords" opens the famous sonnet on the war preparations in Rome at the time of Julius II (*Rime*, 10). "And it has already been about fifteen years that I have not had a good hour," he writes from Rome again; and similar words come in the *canzoni Che fie di me?* (22, *40*): "for not an hour of all my years is mine," and *Oilmè, oilmè* (51, *12-15*): "... still reviewing / my past time do I go and do not find / in all that time an hour that was mine." And thus the various lamentations on the state of discomfort and solitude in which he had to work: "I am here unhappy and not too well and with great toil, with no guidance and with no money," "I am here in great trouble and with very great bodily toil, and I have no friends of any kind," "painting is done with the wits and not with the hands," etc., recur in the caudate sonnet on the work on the vault of the Sistine Chapel, *I' ho già fatto un gozzo* (5), in the sonnet "Here helmets are made" (10, cf. v. 9-11), in the autobiographical satire *I' sto rinchiuso* (267); and the expressions of indignation at the Florentines ("I never had to do with people that were more ungrateful or more arrogant than the Florentines") or at a friend or someone in the family, such as Giovansimone, Lionardo, or Riccio recur in the sonnet against the Pistoians, "envious, haughty, enemies of heaven" (71, *9*), as well as in the two in praise of Dante (248, 250) and the one attacking Riccio (251), which is a regular letter in verse; while in the cited satire "in the name of Fra Bastiano" we recognize, as has been said, the language and the jesting atmosphere of the letters to Bibbiena and to Sebastiano del Piombo himself.

But if we should conduct the comparison independently of any relatedness in the themes, but rather on the level of the tendencies and syntactic cadences governing the structural organization of the poems, we shall find that in fact they resemble one another much more often than the diversity of the subjects and the overall results might lead us to suppose.

Nonetheless, it is precisely the total result that leads us to make a sharp distinction between the two phenomena; for not only are the scope and method, and hence the accent of the poetical composition, different in compositions of similar theme; and not only is artistic research posited in the poems as the basis and synthesis of the biographical elements and the linguistic and cultural data that converge there; but here, in an unmistakable way, the influences of the Tuscan lyrical tradition are at work, assimilated in a thoroughly personal way, but nonetheless determinative in the very formation of this personal poetics.

LITERARY INITIATION OF MICHELANGELO: "POETS AND ORATORS IN THE VERNACULAR"

The fact is that reading the poets was the primary and decisive occasion of Michelangelo's discovering his own poetic leanings.

In the first years of the Cinquecento, probably around 1503, Michelangelo, according to the credible Condivi, suspended his activity as a sculptor and devoted himself to reading: "for some time he did almost nothing in that art," viz. sculpture, "to give himself to reading poets and orators in the vernacular, and to writing sonnets for his pleasure." [10]

Since the expression "writing sonnets for his pleasure" does not necessarily mean writing them "as a dilettante" in the modern sense of the word, it can reasonably be inferred from Condivi's assertion that this reading of the vernacular poets and orators is not to be regarded as a mere pastime or distraction on the edges of serious activity, but rather as a manifestation of a need for spiritual penetration and enrichment; and that this need, if the pause was not casual, was also noted, and especially noted, by the "sculptor" and was to have beneficial effects on the entire subsequent development of Buonarroti's life and work.

It is of course the task of the art historian or general biographer to determine how and to what extent this literary initiation influenced Michelangelo's later work in the visual arts, whether from the point of view of the thematic ideation of the figures or in the more important sense, though a less provable one, of a deepening of his work and his consciousness of his work. One thing is certain, that after Michelangelo had discovered, and tested within the framework of these general requirements of spiritual penetration, that he had a certain talent and taste for writing poetry, he never stopped writing it; from the approximate date of 1503 down to his last years this poetical activity appears, substantially independent of the fortunes of the artist. It is the story of a most original poetry, and yet one that in its traits followed the general outlines of sixteenth century lyrics.

The first question to be asked is who these vernacular poets and orators were, the reading of whom produced and also, in part, gave a certain orientation of taste to Michelangelo's poetical leanings.

As for the "orators" (as used at that time, the term is exactly equivalent to our "prose writers"), Papini believes they are the Florentine historians and such moralists as Alberti and Palmieri.[11] I think that to these should be added an orator in the true sense of the word, the Savonarola of the sermons and also perhaps of the *Triumph of the Cross;* writers of Platonic philosophy such as Ficino; Lorenzo the Magnificent; Bembo of the *Asolani;* and probably

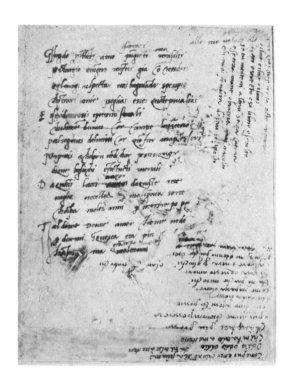

8 Rhymes, No. 3 (1504-1511).

Boccaccio and other Tuscan writers of fiction. But all this is pure conjecture; there is no document from which anything more definite can be derived.

For the poets, on the other hand, apart from Dante and Petrarch, whom Condivi mentions expressly (" he particularly admired Dante, delighted by the wonderful genius of that man, whom he knew almost all by heart; he held perhaps no less to Petrarch "),[12] their names can be recognized more or less surely to the extent that Michelangelo's poems show their traces.

The Politian of the *Stanze* and Lorenzo the Magnificent are clearly to be seen in the stanzas in praise of country life, *Nuovo piacere* (New pleasure) (67); the influence of Lorenzo in also frequently to be felt both in the poems of autobiographical meditation, such as the canzone *What will become of me?* (22) and the sestina *Then let there be, outside of my own* (33), inspired by themes of the fleetingness of time, of lost youth, of the approach of death, of adverse destiny, of the cruel tyranny of Love (cf. Lorenzo de' Medici, *Rime:* Nos. XVII, XVIII, XV, XLIX), and in the oldest love sonnets and madrigals as *Grato e felice* (3; cf. Lorenzo de' M., *Rime*, XXVIII), *Quanta dolcezza* (38; cf. L. d. M., *Rime*, CXXII), *Del fiero colpo* (39; cf. L. d. M., *Rime*, I), *Quand'amor* (40; cf. L. d. M., *Rime*, LXI, LXXXIX, *Comento*, V); *S'i'avessi creduto* (61; L. d. M., *Rime*, LI, 9-14), and in general in the compositions that take up the Platonic doctrine, as *Occhi miei* (229; cf. L. d. M., *Rime*, VII), and *Qual meraviglia* (166; cf. L. d. M., *Rime*, XII, XIII, CXXII), while many poetical themes and images and manners of speaking, spread more or less throughout the poems, such as the motif of " cruel fortune," the thematic pairs " heaven-earth," " night-day," " light-shadow," " hope-desire," the symbols of " Phoebus," " fire," " Love's arrow," the " little bird " caught in the " noose " and such expressions as " holy lights," " my sun," " clear star," while all having their origin in Petrarch or Dante or the *dolce stil nuovo*, appear here with the same intellectualistically stylized traits that they have in Lorenzo's poems.

The groups of stanzas *Tu ha' 'l viso* (20) and *I' crederrei* (54) evidently belong to the teasing style, and even outside of this manner signs are not wanting of an influence by the realistic playful poets of the Florentine Quattrocento from Burchiello to Pistoia, to Francesco Cei, especially in the sonnets *I' ho già fatto un gozzo* (5), *I' l'ho vostra mercè* (7) and in the satire *I' sto rinchiuso* (267).

It would be hazardous to affirm the existence of a direct relationship to non-Tuscan Quattrocento poets. It can be said, though, that some Buonarroti works in the popular style, such as *Chi è quel che per forza* (7), *Come può esser* (8), *Fuggite, amanti* (27), *S'i' avessi creduto* (61) recall the style and themes of such writers of *strambotti* as Panfilo Sasso and Cei; that the terza rima on the death of his father (86) could be said to be constructed in great part on the model of Bernardo Bellincioni's elegy on the death of Giuliano de' Medici; that the very fantasy that we might call phenomenalistic, which Michelangelo so often interlards with poetic conceits derived from object-symbols such as " rock," " iron," " fire," " sparks," " ashes," " coal," " dust," " smoke," or referring to the ideas of melting metal or the smith's working it, has ample precedents in the practice of a Gasparo Visconti, a Cei, a Tebaldeo; and finally that " seicentismo," or rather the discursive Petrarchism, of Tebaldeo and Aquilano and Cariteo is the source of many of the conceits and poetic attitudes that are dear to the difficult intellectualism of Michelangelo the poet.

DANTE AND PETRARCH

Into this framework of more or less contemporary suggestions, popular and learned, realistic and idealistic, are inserted with special emphasis, and quite different efficacy, the " readings " of the two major poets, the two " classics ": Dante and Petrarch.

As for Dante, his presence is in fact much less readily to be identified in the poetical work of Michelangelo than it is in the artistic work, even if we reject the elucubrations of Borinski and others. It is also true that for Michelangelo, as for every educated Florentine of that time, Dante was not only the master of style and poetic form, but also the father of the language and civilization, the first inspirer (the second being Savonarola) of that municipal *Weltanschauung*, compounded of non-clerical Catholicism, philosophizing somewhere between Neoplatonism and Aristotelianism, and democratic spirit, which in the atmosphere of the anti-Medicean exiles was readily colored by anti-tyrannical themes and polemics against the " native haunt " and its actual institutions.

This explains both Buonarroti's participation, as chief discussant, in Giannotti's Dantesque *Dialogi* [13] (in which among other things Brutus and Cassius are exalted and Dante is criticized for having condemned them) and the contemporaneous composition of the two sonnets *Dal ciel discese* (248) and *Quante dirne si può* (250), in which Dante is precisely the man—as we see in the first sonnet—who " wrongly illuminated the nest where I was born," whose works were " ill understood / ... by that ungrateful people / That is harsh only to the just," the man for whom Michelangelo would give " the happiest position " in the world to possess his virtue, his genius, his greatness even in the misfortune of exile:

> Were I but he / for born to such a fate
> for his harsh exile, with his virtue,
> I would exchange the world's most happy state.

543

This is rather an *imitatio virtutis*, therefore, than an *imitatio artis*, an instigation to great and strong thinking and feeling, rather than to writing.

But this does not exhaust the presence of Dante in Michelangelo's poetry, a most notable presence, but not on the plane of a reflective relationship, that is, not in the final phase of the poetical process, characterized by the stylistic choice, but rather (and here too a proof of the native, ethnic, radical nature of the Dantesque initiation can be seen) in the relatively unreflective phase, the prepoetic phase, so to speak, in which Michelangelo acquires his own interior set of idea-words.

In this sense, Condivi's report that Michelangelo had Dante "almost all by heart" is not a mere curiosity, but a valuable indication of what was certainly one of the chief, if not the chief linguistic and conceptual source of Michelangelo's culture. It is from Dante, and especially from the *Purgatorio* and the *Paradiso*, that most of the intellectual and metaphysical notions come that enrich his poetry, such as the idea of rising above the self, the sense of human insufficiency to salvation, the beatifying influence of woman, the theme of the ineffable and immemorial, Paradise as the world of light, the divine origin of the soul, etc. From it too come many of the verbal motifs of symbolic-ideal type, including, among those derived from the *Divine Comedy*, "holy eyes," "my eager eyes," "set my eyes on the sun like an eagle," "from the lowest part to the highest," "the blind world," "the soul suffices," "excessive light," "eternal light," "illuminate the pages," "a single point has ignited me," "lungs to make sighs," or psychological-emotional phrases, like the following, taken mostly from the shorter poems of Dante: "soul that trembles and fears," "biting file," "mortal blow," "unjust and beautiful lady," "cruel strong love," "cruel steel," "harsh fierce lady," "cruel fierce star," "anguish," "anguished lamentation," etc., which are less easy to identify, since they have also gone over into Petrarch.

Summing up, Dante provides many essential building materials for Michelangelo's poetry, but not its structural base; he provides terms and concepts, but not the method for organizing them. Michelangelo owes the structural base to Petrarch, whose effect on the poems of Buonarroti is more immediately apparent than that of any other poet (entire compositions seem to be modeled after the design of Petrarchan works, and even in the most original poems there are expressions, phrasings, hemistiches, entire lines, taken from Petrarch), and moreover offers more lasting resistance to Michelangelo's drive to remake and transform, getting the upper hand over it in the works of his extreme old age. Undoubtedly, Michelangelo's poetry is definitely a part of the great stream of Cinquecento Petrarchism, but it is a Petrarchism quite apart from Bembo's interpretation. Whereas for Bembo imitating Petrarch means essentially imitating his voice, that is, his style, music, tone, spiritual content, for Michelangelo it means merely making use of its structures, its discursive and constructive patterns. Bembo loves the soul of Petrarch to the point where he tries to make a similar one for himself, Michelangelo loves only his art, and uses that as the basis of a structural system aimed exclusively at reflecting his own soul, which is altogether unlike that of the poet of Vaucluse. The primacy of Petrarch in Michelangelo is not exclusive, therefore; not having sacrificed his mind, his voice, his sensibility to Petrarch, as Bembo had, Michelangelo can, so to speak, be unfaithful to him, by rejecting the entire idyllic, naturalistic, hedonistic aspect and instead seeking out and employing primarily the technically most ingenious elements and the symbolic themes and modes (and in particular those relating to the struggle against the passions, to the contrast between liberty and destiny, between grace and sin) in preference to naturalistic ones; and his treason, to use a strong word, is also seen in his introducing, on the level of the entire body of poetry and often even within individual works, elements derived from the other poets mentioned above: Dante, the poets of the *dolce stil nuovo* and the popular and learned versifiers of the Quattrocento.

It is a structural and not a tonal Petrarchism, therefore; one that is intellectual and symbolic, not sentimental and oratorical; objective, not subjective; a Petrarchism altogether consonant with the deep nature of the artist in Michelangelo, in whom art intervenes not only in the phase of execution, but already in the phase of thought. This gives rise to another, and not the least, aspect of his originality as compared with Bembo, Della Casa and all the other Petrarchists of his time: namely, that those poets usually give one the impression of translating into verse things that had first been thought, or at least could be thought, in prose, while on the contrary Michelangelo seems to think directly in poetry, his very ideas appear to be made poetically, and not only because the linguistic material of which they are made is poetical in its origin, but also, and above all, because of an irresistible trait in Michelangelo's mind, his tendency to transform every object and concept into a symbol, to make and to stamp with his own vigorous inner seal, the poetical elements of tradition.

THE ORIGINALITY OF MICHELANGELO'S POETRY

In this sense, and only in this sense, can we accept the judgment of Foscolo that "some of Michelangelo's works have the value of long-meditated thoughts," rather than being true poems.[14] Actually, in him concept and form, thing and word are identified; and to that extent his poems are thoughts, in that his thoughts are formed within a poetical tradition, with the very elements of the tradition. What counts, after all, is neither the perspicuity of the thought, which Foscolo says is at fault in Michelangelo "for want of practice in writing," nor the value of the thought as such, which has led some to the point of speaking of a philosophy of Michelangelo's.

What does count is the power with which Michelangelo, having absorbed into his own substance the data of the lyrical tradition, reworks them into concepts that are all the more highly and deeply significant precisely because of their inwardness. As the " inner fire " is to the " cold rock " that contains it,

> and from that time that it is hemmed about
> it burns and splits it, and in some way lives
> linking the others to it in eternity, (63)

so the poetic inspiration of the master operates with respect to the matter of the concepts and words of Dante, Petrarch and the others within which it burns: it envelops it, reworks it and makes it live with itself in eternity, that is, in poetical forms that are more intense, deeper, or even merely more complicated, ingenious and subtle.

Thus, for example, from the stale Petrarchan cliché of the lover who has the face of the beloved carved or painted on his heart, and from the myth itself of Laura, who is Medusa and can be Beatrice, turns to stone and can release from being stone (cf. *Canzoniere*, 197, 23, etc.), Michelangelo draws the idea of the affinity between the artistic process and the conquest of inner freedom that inspires some of his most significant lyrics (cf. Nos. 151, 152, 153); and from the notion, likewise derived from Petrarch, of the " hour and day that I opened my eyes " (*Canzoniere*, 29, etc.), of destiny sealed by " cruel stars " (*ibid.* 22, etc.), he forms the dolorous sense of his own total dedication to beauty in art and in life:

> As faithful example for my vocation
> Beauty was given me at birth; (164)

and also:

> If I was born not blind nor deaf to it,
> adapted to the one who burns and steals my heart,
> the fault is his who destined me to the fire. (97)

And so too the conceit of " dying in life " by reason of his lady, typical of the most superficial madrigal style, is transformed into the strangely deep and powerful theme of dying in life by reason of the sin that has taken hold of him in the most intimate fibers of his personality:

> I live by sin, dying to myself I live
> no longer my own life, but the life of sin, (32)

and Lorenzo's antithesis of days and nights (*Rime*, CVI) and the theme of sleep " the image of dying " (*ibid.*) become the origin of a theme with a series of variations (cf. 2, 101, 102, 103, 104) that vividly represent the dramatic and irreducibly dualistic way of feeling and thinking that is characteristic of Michelangelo.

His liberty with regard to the tradition of Tuscan lyric poetry does not always take the form of an enhancement of the moral meaning of these lyric themes, or a translation of them into more essential and deeply felt terms, but often appears by choice as play, as a search for sterile conceptual subtleties, for verbal complications for their own sake, or even (as in many of those epitaphs on the death of Cecchino Bracci that Riccio paid him for in mushrooms, figs and fish) ordinary puns, e. g.:

> Here there are arms (*Bracci*), feeble for the task
> of saving me from death, for against dying
> 'twere better to be on foot to help me fly
> than to have arms (*Bracci*) and not be helped by them;

this is precisely a confirmation of the background against which, it seems to us, the writer Buonarroti must be set if he is to be understood: that Florentinism or Tuscanism which, while attending to things, also likes to play with words, as if they too were things, matter; so that if the poet often becomes hermetic and abstruse or involved, the reason is not that he was helpless but that he had all too much competence, so much so that he took any and all liberties with words and sound standards of rhetoric.

POEMS OF THE FIRST PERIOD (1500-1532/34)

But the relationship between Michelangelo's poetical liberty and power and the lyric tradition is not merely the best criterion for understanding the literary significance of the individual poems but also the principle underlying the historical formation of the entire body of his poetry.

Michelangelo's poetical activity was carried out during three periods marked by the differing value assumed in each by Michelangelo's structural and reconstructing interest in the tradition. **545**

9 Rhymes, No. 6 (1511 ?).

In the first period, comprising the master's first poetical efforts, often written on the back of a sheet of paper with a drawing on it, or inscribed among the very lines of a sketch, as well as the poems written before his definitive trip to Rome (all in all, some ninety finished or fragmentary poems), the attitude of the poet is that of someone trying out various styles and various kinds of poetry: learned and popular, idealizing or realistic in taste, in short metrical forms (sonnets, quatrains, madrigals) and long ones (*canzoni, capitoli*, stanzas, sestinas in the Petrarchan manner), without showing any particular preference, and above all, without covering up, without reabsorbing the traces of the various influences that have been noted.

In addition to the compositions that we have already referred to in this connection (from the sonnet on the Sistine Chapel to the Politian-like or teasing stanzas, from the love madrigals of popular type to the tercets on the death of his father), mention may also be made of the jesting *Chiunche nasce* (21), lachrymose in inspiration, and the two sestinas *Sie pur* (33) and *Crudele stella* (70), in the latter of which there is perhaps not a single line that does not contain an expression or image from Petrarch. But make no mistake: saying that there are borrowings from other poets, as well as the characteristics of traditional styles does not by any means deny the imprint of Buonarroti, which often appears vigorously even in these early poems. For example, how can one doubt that the comic poem referred to is by Michelangelo, when one sees that it is dominated by the thoroughly Buonarrotian taste for antitheses, and in particular the contrasts of light and shadow, the sun and the earth, so typical of our poet:

> ..... and the sun
> leaves nothing alive.
> The mild man dies and he who sorrows,
> and the wisdom and the words;
> and our ancient progeny
> shade in the sun and smoke in the wind.
> Like you, we were men,
> gay and sad, as you are;
> and now we are, as you see,
> earth in the sun, deprived of life.

And how can one fail to see the originality of the stanzas *Nuovo piacere*, in which the classical elegance of Politian's idyll;

> What joy it is to see the goats depend
> on grass, and crop now this now that, (*Stanze*, I, 18, *1-2*)

is transmuted into a simpler and more direct taste, one more truly rustic:

> New Pleasure and of greater worth
> to see the daring goats ascend a rock,
> feeding on one peak now and then another;

and the " ungirt and barefoot little country girl " that " stays with her geese under a cliff and spins " (*Stanze*, I, 19, *7-8*) becomes " his charmer (the goatherd's beloved) who has a heart of steel " and stands " with the pigs, aloof, under an oak "?

And the same can be said of the elegy on his father's death, which adds to the same antithetical motifs of death-life, joy-sorrow, light-shade of the previous *barzelletta* and the theme of time that " distributes the hours " (cf. 17, *5*; *37*):

> Now you are dead to death and made divine
> nor longer fear to change your life or will,
> as hardly without envy can I write.
> Fortune and time within your threshold now
> no longer seek to pass, for which I waver
> between undoubted joy and certain sorrow.
> There is no cloud that now obscures your light,
> the changing hours have no power on you,
> chance or necessity no longer leads you.
> Your splendor is not paler with the night
> nor ever grows by day, however clear,
> or when the sun brings heat to us,

the theme, so insistent, especially in his last years, of initiation into death and the other life:

> In your dying have I learned my own decease,
> dear father mine, and in my thoughts I see you
> where the world rarely lets them pass.
> Death is not the worst of things, as some believe,
> for him whose last day goes beyond the first,
> by grace, etc.

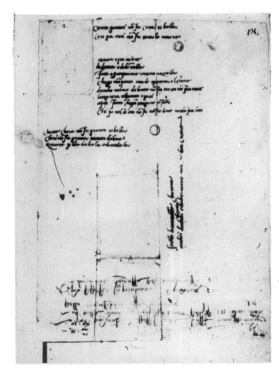

10 Rhymes, No. 19 (1522).

11 Rhymes, No. 86 (1534).

And the same is true, more or less, for all the other instances. And it may well be that Michelangelo's originality is shown, in this first phase, rather in the internal elements of the poem (such as the choice of vocabulary, which is immediate and realistic, and his preference for certain themes) than in the work in itself, in its basic physiognomy and literary character.

All in all, we should say that Michelangelo, not yet having a structural method of his own (something that in the next phase will be represented perfectly by the pattern of the madrigal ending in a rhymed couplet in sententious mood), here limits himself to searching, almost experimentally, for his own style, his own physiognomy as a poet operating on the patterns of others.

Within this perspective of unconscious seeking, an explanation is likewise found for some minutely descriptive, almost painter-like compositions, such as the sonnet for the " beautiful woman of Bologna," dating from 1507 (4), in which the writer strives to depict the enjoyment of the garland on the lady's head by means of the play of the flowers that go to make it up:

> one sends another still before the third
> so that he may be the first to kiss her head,

or, even more, the unfinished tercets on the human eye, *El ciglio col color* (35), in which the details of the human eye, its movement, its color, seem to be studied under a magnifying glass:

> The eye, moving slowly around underneath,
> shows but a little part of the great ball,
> its view serene now shifting much the less,
> and goes up less and down the while it covers,
> from which its eyelids all the shorter are,
> the less the wrinkles show the while it opens.
> The white so white, the dark more than funereal, etc.

and some isolated lines, like thematic and stylistic notes (" The will desires and then it has the sorrow," App. 2), and some fragmentary Petrarchan imitations (*Oltre qui fu*, 36, from the *Canzoniere*, 112, *5-13*; *L'ardente nodo*, App. 13, from *Canzoniere*, 271; *Signore, io fallo*, App. 31, from *Canzoniere*, 236), which are likewise characteristic of this first period of poetic activity.

If we regard the content, rather than the formal or strictly literary aspects; that is, if we follow the path pointed out by Foscolo and seek out the set of " thoughts," we have no difficulty in realizing that many of the themes dearest to Michelangelo's meditation are set forth here in their simplest form, as statements destined to be complicated and interpenetrated by each other and with still others in subsequent structural variations, which are precisely the most characteristic product of the second phase of his activity. Such, for example, are the themes of the transitoriness of life:

> No noble thing there is under the sun
> that death does not conquer it nor fortune change; (1, *5-6*)

of the alienating power of passion and guilt:

> How can it be I am no more my own? (8, *1*)
> I live by sin, dying to myself I live
> no longer my own life, but the life of sin; (32, *1-2*)

of the ambiguity of Love:

> Tis from a lovely and a pretty thing,
> from a true source of pity springs my woe, (16)

and its power:

> All wrath, all wretchedness and every form,
> he who is armed with love conquers all fates, (29)

and its philosophical significance:

> Love is a concept of what beauty is,
> imagined or seen within the heart,
> the friend of virtue and nobility; (38, *9-11*)

of the origin of beauty:

> The beauty that you see, it comes from her,
> but grows on rising to a better place,
> if through our mortal eyes it strikes the soul.
> There it becomes divine, noble and fair, etc.; (42, *9 ff.*)

547

of the power of virtue:

> As a flame grows the more it is opposed
> by the wind, each virtue that is raised by Heaven
> shines the more glorious when it is offended; (48)

of the correlation between good and evil:

> Where good endures not, evil does not last,
> but one is often changed into the other; (53, 5-6)

and it would be hard to find them set forth, these and other themes, as soberly and directly in the more complex and artistically more structural meditations of the following period.

POEMS OF THE SECOND PERIOD (1534-1547)

The period from 1534, in which year Michelangelo settled permanently in Rome, to 1547, when Vittoria Colonna died, marks the time when the artist was most involved with poetry. This involvement, furthered by the atmosphere of hard work and serene calm that characterizes these years, is shown primarily in the development and perfecting of a poetical process of meditation that from now on not only nourishes itself, substantially independent of biographical incidents (although they occur in that period as well, especially in relation to his friendships with Cavalieri, Vittoria Colonna, Riccio, Giannotti and others), but which is outstanding for a language and structural method of its own, now beyond the reach of suggestions from traditional modes.

The longer forms are now excluded, as being unsuited to the energetic and concentrated nature of his thinking and writing, and Michelangelo devotes himself exclusively to the forms of the sonnet, the epigrammatic quatrain and the madrigal. In the pattern of the sonnet his thought still finds some difficulty in arranging itself in such a way as to fill it out without leaving dead spots; and the epigrammatic meter runs the risk of accentuating rather than correcting his tendency to conceptual and verbal play; but the madrigal, varying in length and texture but invariably concluded by the poet with a rhyming couplet, almost always gnomic, seems to be the perfect instrument for elaborating the complex and subtle psychological and intellectual themes that the poetry of this period expresses.

Accordingly, the experience of art, meditation on existence, mere celebration of the various life relationships, of life, of love, or friendship with the persons mentioned before, now appear as involved and in part absorbed, if not ever dissolved, in the predominant and determining " poietic," constructive interest. Thus, the death of Bracci becomes the pretext for a good fifty variations on the themes of beauty, death, burial, time, eternity; and thus Platonic love for Cavalieri and spiritual friendship with Vittoria Colonna tend to lose their precise biographical and psychological outlines, turning into the terms of moral problems and the phenomenology of love, which are quite impersonal; and thus, finally, the experience of art, rather than being reflected directly in the verses, appears to be called on, by the poet's personal need to construct and express, to supply images, symbols, terms of comparison, and those conceptions of moral liberation, platonic transcendence, of struggle between beauty and time, between death and eternity, that have an essential part in the master's meditation.

A list of the poems (about 180 in number) of this period may begin with the group, mainly sonnets, dedicated to Cavalieri. Some of them were written even before 1534 (the unusual friendship goes back to 1532); they constitute, so to speak, the connecting link between the immediacy, realism and the sort of emotional effusiveness that are characteristic of the previous poetical phase, and the more intellectual, carefully constructed and sober language of this second period.

The most obvious characteristic of these sonnets is a remarkable emotional intensity, expressed not only through the more usual notions of fire, flame, ardor, wasting in tears or being fed by them:

> If I had thought to warm me at the fire
> at the first glimpsing of this phoenix soul... (61)
> I feel a cold countenance kindled by a fire
> burning me from afar... (88)
> I weep, I burn, I consume myself and his heart
> feeds... (74)
> If the heart is seen in the face through the eyes,
> I have no other sign more manifest
> of my flame... (72)
> Why should I, any more, intense desire
> vent with my weeping or my sorrowful words (97)

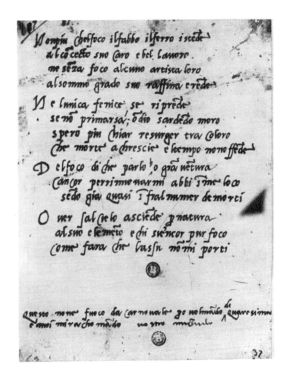

12 Rhymes, No. 62 (1532-1546).

but also with the traditional theme (cf. the sonnet *Quanto si gode*, 4) of the desire for physical contact with the beloved person:

> Let for a moment cease both time and hours,
> the daytime and the sun in its old course;
> that I may have, and not merely by my merit
> my very dear and much desired lord
> for ever in my ready unworthy arms, (72)

or even that perfect identification of personalities and vital functions, that reciprocal transformation of one into the other (cf. "if one lover be converted into the other," 193, *12*; 194, *4*), on the basis of which the poet says in one sonnet that he sees, feels, walks, suffers heat and cold, and even wishes, thinks and speaks with the members and the faculties of his friend:

> With your fair eyes I see a gentle light
> one that I can no longer with my blind ones;
> On your feet I can manage with a weight
> now unaccustomed to my halt and crippled state.
> I fly on your wings without having pinions;
> with your brain I have always soared to heaven;
> by your judgment I turn pale and red,
> cold in the sun, warm in the coldest mists.
> In your will only does my will reside,
> my thoughts take on their shape within your heart,
> it is with your breath that my words are said, (89, *1-11*)

while in another poem, *D'altrui pietoso* (94), it is the friend, so the poet hopes, that can put on *his* mortal vestment:

> And may my fate ordain it that my lord
> cover his living vestments with my dead;
> that, like a snake that sheds upon a rock,
> even by death I might amend my state.
> Oh, were it only mine, the hairy skin
> that woven of his skin makes such a tunic
> as has the fortune to wind so fair a breast, etc. (5-11)

These are certainly strong expressions, but any notion of realism would be highly misplaced with respect to them. Or rather, there is realism in them, but not in the romantic sense, as the reflection of an experience, but as the development of a literary theme, as the artistically heightened interpretation of a concept capable of being made poetry, and above all of lofty spiritualistic significance.

The sonnet *I' mi son caro* (90) is particularly indicative in this sense. Since I have known you, the poet says, I think more of myself and in fact am worth more, as a cut stone is compared to a rough one, as paper with writing or drawing on it is compared to a blank sheet; I am like someone that has a talisman with him that makes him invulnerable, I have power over water and fire, I restore sight to the blind and cancel the effects of poison:

> With such a seal I go in every place
> secure, like one having arms or spells with him,
> making to nought all perils that him meet.
> I have power against water and have strength against fire,
> with your sign I give light to all the blind,
> and with my spittle heal from every poison. (9-14)

Clearly, the interest of the poet lies entirely in poetic elaboration of the conceit of the heightened value produced by love, a glorification that here is effected by means of the pattern of examples, in a series of examples, as it is elsewhere, or for other conceits, by means of other patterns, such as metaphor, verbal or conceptual antithesis, apostrophe, iteration, etc.

These poems are particularly marked by another characteristic, of another nature than literary, or not exclusively literary, and serving to correct the first property: namely, moralism.

Michelangelo was not so indifferent to the possible, and indeed probable, embarrassment of Cavalieri at language such as this, nor so contemptuous of the public and of public opinion, that he failed to realize the advisability of frequently laying stress on the chaste nature of his affection for the young Roman nobleman, either by various summary expressions, such as "chaste will" (58), "chaste love" (59), "honorable desire" (83), "honorable fire" (72), or by treating the subject directly, as for example in the sonnet *Tu sa' ch'i' so* (60):

> If, my dear lord, I only love in thee
> what I love most in thee, take no offense
> in that one spirit is loving of another.

549

> That which I love and learn in your fair face,
> and is ill realized by mortal mind,
> he that would see it must first pass through death, (9-14)

and in *Non vider gli occhi miei* (105):

> Unbridled willfulness, not love, in sense,
> that slays the soul: and our love here perfects
> friends here, but even more by death in heaven; (12-14)

and even more clearly in *Veggio nel tuo bel viso* (83), which contrasts with the opinion of the "malicious, foolish and wicked rabble," which "points its finger at what others feel," the Platonic doctrine of love that is the mark of "the judicious":

> At that compassionate source whence we all spring,
> all beauty doth assemble that is seen
> more than all else by the judicious here;
> nor have we other taste, nor other fruits,
> of heaven here on earth; and he who loves you true
> ascends to God and makes death to be sweet. (9-14)

A second group of poems of this period comprises the sonnets and madrigals dedicated to, and in various ways inspired by, Vittoria Colonna. Apart from the substitution of "lady" for "lord" in the term of address, they differ from the poems of the previous group not so much in the themes in themselves, which are often similar, as in the case of those that derive from a single Petrarchan-Platonic mold (for example, the famous sonnet *Non ha l'ottimo artista* [151], written for Vittoria, is equivalent to the sonnet *Sì come nella penna* [84], written for Cavalieri), as in their greater emotional restraint, which in some of the poems, perhaps the first ones in the series, smacks of formal gallantry; but in the more elevated language and tone; in the afflatus of inner life that is characteristic of the last poems, we have a document of a true spiritual dialogue between the master and the noble lady.

For the most part Vittoria is addressed with various ceremonial epithets: "high and worthy lady," "divine lady," "high and godlike lady," "high lady"; and her actions are "divine," her eyes "holy," her beauty "supernal." She seems all but inaccessible in the poet's eyes, girt in a diadem of light:

> To thy most high and luminous diadem
> by the precipitous and lengthy path
> none can arrive, my lady,
> who does not come by way of humbleness and courtesy; (156, *1-4*)

the gift of her kindness is something "celestial," of which Michelangelo considers himself to be unworthy:

> The intellect and art and memory fail:
> he that is mortal can not with his own
> pay, by a thousand trials, a heavenly gift; (159, *11-14*)

her speech is like that of a god:

> A man speaks in a woman, rather a god
> speaks through her mouth,

having heard her has made the poet for ever not his own:

> whence I, for hearing her,
> have become such as nevermore to be my own; (235, *1-4*)

by her he is raised "above himself":

> So far above myself,
> lady, you make me rise,
> I can not speak thereof,
> I can not think it, for I am no more the same. (154, *1-4*)

All in all, it is the ancient theme of the *dolce stil nuovo*, the theme of the experience of the divine gained by way of the lady, mediated by the knowledge of the literature of Platonic love (the *Asolani* [of Bembo-Tr.] and Book IV of [Castiglione's] *Cortegiano* and to a great extent expressed in the language of Dante. On the one hand, however, this language is complicated by the experience of art in sculpture and painting, likewise taken to be an embodiment of things " divine," " eternal," in matter or with matter (cf. *Non ha l'ottimo artista*, 151; *Sì come per levar*, 152; *Non pur d'argento e d'oro*, 153; *Se ben concetto*, 236; *Com'esser donna può*, 239; etc.); on the other hand it is colored with more intimate tones, relating to the more personal motifs of sin, old age and death (*Per qual mordace lima*, 161; *Ora in sul destro, ora in sul manco piede*, 162; *Occhi mie, siate certi*, 229; *Come portato ho già*, 264).

Next follows a third group of poems, for the most part referring to a woman who is " beautiful and cruel," " unjust and beautiful," " harsh and fierce," " untamed and savage," and often addressed with a hurried " her ": all traits that can certainly not be fitted to Vittoria Colonna. They are in a way the most frivolous part of the poetical works. Platonism is entirely absent from them, and instead the dominant themes are unrequited love, placing in antithesis the lady's beauty and cruelty, as well as the contrast between her beauty and youth and the poet's age and ugliness.

The fact that we recognize here the taste, at once artificial and realistic, that is characteristic of Dante's poems for the " woman of stone " might go to support the theory that these are poems written in the first thirty years of the sixteenth century and reworked for printing in the years in question; for, as we know, Michelangelo expected to prepare an edition for publication with the aid of Riccio between 1544 and 1546. As a matter of fact, although the essential characteristics of this group are also to be found in a madrigal, *La nuova beltà d'una* (263), which certainly dates from the artist's old age:

> The fresh beauty of a woman
> spurs me on, unbridles me and scourges me;
> not only the third hour gone by,
> but nones and vespers, and soon it will be night, (1-4) [15]

it is not improbable that some of these poems were originally written at an early period. In any event, this does not impair the unity of the group, based as it is not on prepoetic data, on experience of life, but on the thematic and stylistic homogeneity of the poetical result. Among the most beautiful poems of the group are *Questa mie donna* (124), *Nel mie 'rdente desio* (169), *S'egli è che 'n dura pietra* (242), and most beautiful is the *Costei pur si delibra* (172), which is at the same time a synthesis of all the characteristic themes of the group:

> Thus she resolves,
> untamed and savage,
> that I should burn and die and droop
> to what in weight is not so much as an ounce;
> and my blood pound by pound
> she drains, and unnerves me, aborts my body from my soul.
> She rejoices, and preens
> in her trusty mirror,
> in which she sees herself like Paradise;
> then turns to me abusive
> in that since I am old,
> up against me her face appears lovely,
> and I more ludicrous
> for being ugly; and yet nature is my great fortune,
> if I succeed, in making her be beautiful.

I shall not dwell on the fourth group of poems, the epitaphs for the tomb of Cecchino Bracci, except to recall, in addition to my earlier remarks, that Michelangelo wrote them on several occasions, in place of a design for a monument that Riccio had asked him for and that he was unwilling or unable to make, and to pay his debt for the continual presents of foodstuffs that Riccio gave him. It is evident, however, that he would not have written so many if he had not found pleasure in doing so; they were to his taste, the taste that is characteristic of all this part, the largest one, of the poetical work: developing all the possibilities of a given theme, which can be reduced to the central motif of death, quite apart from the strict requirements of the occasion.

Of the same class as the epitaphs for Cecchino are the sonnet and epitaph on the death of Faustina Mancini Attavanti, dedicated to Gandolfo Porrino. The epitaph is a real " stunt," like the one cited above; the Mancini woman would not have died, Michelangelo says, if she had defended herself against Death's blows with her right hand. Why had she not done so? Just because she was " mancina " [left-handed].

> There lives in us, and lies here the divine
> beauty by death before her time offended.
> If with her right hand she had herself defended,
> she had escaped? Why did she not? She was *mancina*. (177)

The rest of the poems of this period can be put into a fifth and last group, from the two sonnets on Dante that have been cited (248, 250) to the famous epigram on Night in the Medici tombs (247) and the madrigal on Florence, victim of the tyrant (249), from the four sonnets on day and night (101-104) to all the other compositions with varying themes of meditation and confession: the sorrow of love, the habit of sin ("bad custom"), the relation between art and nature as against the work of time, the vanity of the world, old age, all developed with no special references to another person, or at least in such a way that the references are quite secondary to the subject. They are therefore poems that the artist wrote almost exclusively for himself; and as such are among the most clearly significant with respect to his ideal world of fantasy. In this frame of reference, special mention should be made of the few poems that bring out some fundamental ideas of Michelangelo on beauty and art, such as the madrigal *Per fido esemplo* (164), in which the artist reaffirms his radical dedication to beauty and defends its spiritual and transcendent essence:

> If there are reckless foolish judgments here
> to sense reducing beauty, which doth move
> and raise to heaven every healthy mind,
> weak eyes can not from mortal thing ascend
> to the divine, and strong ones always there
> where none without grace can hope to rise; (7-12)

the quatrains *Molto diletta* (237), in which he declares perishable the sculptured work, but not the beauty that is its object:

> Although injurious, harsh and base-born time
> ruins or twists it or dismembers all,
> its primal beauty still will be remembered
> and save the vain pleasure for a better place; (5-8)

and the madrigal *Negli anni molti* (241), which develops the theme, particularly dear to Michelangelo (cf. 278: "Let him who likes not leaves / not come to us in May," and Note 35: "Never full vestment comes / to anyone before the very end / of art and life."), of art as the expression of winning through to maturity, stressing the value of testing and research:

> Over the many years and many trials,
> seeking, the wise man reaches the true idea
> of a living image
> neighbor to death, in mountain rock and hard;
> for to things high and new
> one cometh late, and then it little lasts. (1-6)

POEMS OF THE THIRD PERIOD (1547-1560)

The project of printing his poems and the consequent work of preparation, collection and revision of the poems in which the master was engaged, with the aid of Luigi del Riccio, about 1546, crown and conclude Michelangelo's most intense poetical period.

Riccio's death, towards the end of the year, was probably the main cause for the failure of the publication project; but the death of the Marchioness of Pescara in February of the following year must have had even greater weight in bringing about not merely definitive abandonment of publication but also, and above all, a considerable decrease in Michelangelo's interest in poetry.

This relative detachment from poetry marks the third and last phase in the history of Michelangelo as poet, even more clearly than the almost exclusively religious content of the lyrics.

In and of itself, ending in piety is not distinctive only of Michelangelo's poetical work but is common to many other lyricists of those times, including of course Petrarch, the master of them all, who closes his "scattered poems" with the canzone *Alla Vergine*. Furthermore, Michelangelo had written poems of religious inspiration in his earlier periods as well: in 1524-1528 or shortly thereafter, the sestina *Sie pur fuor di mie propie* (33), in which he asks God for assistance against the habit of sin; in 1533, the sonnet *Forse perché d'altrui* (66), almost a penitential psalm in intonation, whose tercets:

> O flesh, O blood, O wood, O extreme sorrow,
> only by you my sin is done
> since I was born, and such my father was.
> Thou alone art good, etc.

have led to the idea that the master held the Protestant doctrine of justification by faith alone; [16] and a little later there is another sonnet *Vorrei voler, Signor* (87) in which God is invoked as the light and comfort of the besieged soul:

> Tear Thou the veil, O Lord, and break the wall
> whose hardness holdeth back and doth retard
> the sunshine of Thy light, lost to the world!

Send the predicted light to come to us
to Thy fair Consort, so that I may flame
at heart, full free of doubts, feeling Thee alone. (9-14) [17]

It is true that even in the last years of his friendship with Vittoria Colonna, and more and more after her death, the religious motif no longer appears sporadically, but becomes insistent and predominant, as they do in the letters of the same time to his nephew Lionardo; but this would not in itself be of importance outside of the merely biographical plane if it were not accompanied by a renunciation of art as such, which is not only stated here, with reference to the "content," but also has a noteworthy influence on the very form of the poetry.

The satire *I' sto rinchiuso* (267), the only long poem of these years, is a good expression of this crisis in art and in the will to artistic construction. After portraying himself at home, with desolation, in a state of physical decadence—here too he follows a literary pattern familiar to readers of Cecco Angiolieri and Pistoia, but with a grotesque-realistic accent that is all his own:

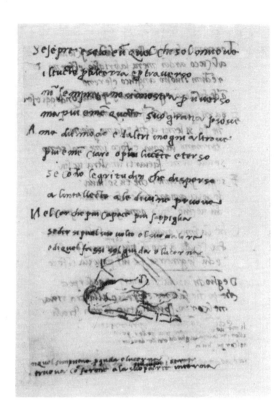

13 Rhymes, No. 273 (after 1546).

> Around the door I've giant heaps of droppings,
> and they that have eaten grapes or taken medicine
> go nowhere else to shit, the lot of them.
> And I have learned to recognize both urine
> and the spout that it comes out of, through the chinks
> that make the morning call in front of me.
> Dead cats or carrion, chanterelle mushrooms, offal,
> he who has them from the shambles or a lesser journey
> never comes a-visiting [18] me without such things.
>
> . . . .
>
> Back-strained and ruptured, undermined and cracked
> my toils have made me now, and my last inn
> is death, in which I live and eat on tick (7-15, 22-24)
>
> . . . .
>
> My face has taken on a scarecrow form;
> my clothes, without any other rags, would drive
> the crows into the wind from the dry sown field.
> A spider's web is hidden in one ear,
> in the other a cricket sings throughout the night;
> I do not sleep, and snore with catarrhal breath. (40-46)

Michelangelo goes on to refer to his activity and status as artist and poet in these terms:

> Love, and the Muses and the flowery grots,
> my scribblings, are reduced to cymbals and
> to scraps of paper, bones, offal and alleys.
> What good is it to make so many dolls,
> if they have brought me to my end, like one
> who has crossed the sea and then is drowned in snot?
> That precious art, in which one time I was
> of so much reputation, now has made me
> a poor old man, a slave in others' hands
> I am undone, unless I perish soon. (46-55)

Taken in isolation, these words might be but the expression of a moment of weariness, like some deprecations that frequently occur in the letters, or they might be merely a way of filling out the list of "annoyances." On the other hand, the theme returns, even more deeply, in tones of undoubted seriousness, in many of the latest poems, as in these two bits written in a 1552 letter:

> With so much servitude, with so much woe
> with false conceits and with the greatest peril
> of the soul to carve in this place things divine, (282)

> No, my dear lord, the fresh and verdant age
> can never feel how much, in the last phase,
> taste changes, love, desires change and thoughts.
> The soul acquires more, the more the world fades;
> and art and death go very ill together:
> what more indeed is there to hope from me? (283)

Hence, this is not a passing mood, but a meditated, ripened, etched-in conviction of the mind. Approaching the "last phase," Michelangelo realizes that the more the practice of art is oriented toward the perfection of its object, which is the work, the less it answers the purpose of the artist.

He had made divine things, and does not deny it, but how much " servitude," how much " woe," they had cost him; and with what a confusion of " false conceits," that is, of vain and erroneous thoughts, imbued with the spirit of the world, of " ruthless pride " and sensuality, and with what " peril of the soul " he had produced them! It is not only the weariness of old age that makes him feel thus, but the clarity of judgment that he has achieved: now he sees plainly how much error was contained in the passionate imagination with which he made art his idol and his tyrant:

> Whence the loving fancy
> that made of art my idol and my king,
> I know now well that it was full of wrong
> that which all men desire to their harm. (285, 5-8)

Certainly, it was God that gave him " at birth " his vocation to beauty and art; and beautiful things and beautiful faces and beautiful bodies are images of God. In the past he had not shrunk from holding God responsible for his sins as an artist:

> If I was born not deaf nor blind thereto,
> predestined to who burns and steals my heart,
> the fault is his who destined me to fire; (97)

now it is hard for him to admit that love for what reflects the image of the Creator may be a sin:

> If it be true the work is like its maker,
> what penalty can justice deal to me
> for that I love and burn, and for divine thoughts
> esteem and honor every noble person? (279, 5-8)

But death is near, and Michelangelo feels that now he must choose between the Creator and creatures. The time has passed for " poietic " mediation between earth and heaven, between world and God:

> and art and death go very ill together.

The time has passed for daring syncretisms, for Platonic-Christian ambiguities, for the indirect and impure prayer done with chisel, brush and pen. The time has come to love and pray without intermediates:

> The thoughts of love, that once were light and gay,
> What are they now, as I approach my death?
> . . . .
> Painting and sculpture shall no longer calm
> the soul turned to that love divine
> that spread its arms on the cross to take us in. (285, 9-14)

Now a single thought was to dominate in his mind; the thought of salvation:

> My thoughts unending, and with error full;
> in these the latest years of this my life
> must shrink themselves to one thought, that shall be
> a guide to His eternal days serene, (286, 1-4)

and therefore Michelangelo asks God to free him from any remaining attachment to the world, to beauty, to art:

> Make me to hate whate'er the world is worth
> and all its beauties that I love and cherish
> that rather death earn me eternal life. (288, 12-14)

How many writers, how many artists have there been that, having come to this point, were no longer able or willing to carry on? But Michelangelo worked down to the end; and down to the end, although much less frequently, he wrote poetry. Nonetheless, the change was a radical one: art, which had been the primary interest, the " idol and king " of his life, now becomes but a means to serve God humbly. If this does not entail any visible consequences in the work of the architect offered to St. Peter, " for the love of God," the incidence of the new attitude in the style of the sculptor and poet is quite another matter.

The sculptor, who formerly had sought, in marble, the fullness and splendor of form and of forms, now seeks the certainty of pardon there, beyond form and as it were beyond the very law of art, in the abnormal, wasted and incomplete forms of the Rondanini Christ. In the

554

same way the poet, who formerly had delighted in ingenious construction of conceits, now recovers the simple, poor, heartfelt words of the Christian speaking with God:

> I speak to you, O Lord, for all my trials
> outside thy blood does not make man be blessed:
> have mercy on me... (280, *5-7*)

> Prepare for me the way that leads to Heaven,
> O my dear Lord... (288, *9-10*)

> When will that come, O Lord, that he awaits
> who trusts in Thee?...; (295, *9-10*)

if formerly he had disdained the way of the " voice " of common Petrarchism, pathetic and oratorical, he now seems to have no further motive for not himself adopting the method of prayer that Petrarch had taught to all the poets of his time.

> Burdened with years and full of sins
> and with ill custom rooted deep and strong,
> I see myself full near to double death,
> my heart, laden with poison, bursts in two,

is the beginning of one of the latest sonnets (293); and one thinks of Gaspara Stampa:

> Sad and repentant of my grave mistakes
> and of my great and vain frivolity,
> and for having wasted this my little time
> of fleeting life in frivolous amours...

It does not matter that when we look more closely, we see at once how different they are: one always rough, dense, immediate and personal, the other delightfully conventional; the important thing is that now a comparison is at least possible, on the basis of a certain common oratorical rhythm.

Michelangelo's strength, his poetry, is always there; but I should say it is attained here anew, as in his letters, in its native state, no longer with that love of employing it in a sealed-off exercise, involving rare and prideful ideas, but rather with the desire to make it serve the recognition of God, in all simplicity and humility.

Thus the arc of Michelangelo's poetry, begun at the dawn of the century in forms that were still of the Quattrocento, ends up in the patterns of the spiritual Petrarchism·of the second half of that century, after having reached the peak of its own possibilities in a most remarkable manifestation of Renaissance freedom.

[10] Ascanio Condivi, *Vita di M. Buonarroti*, Milan 1964, p. 38.
[11] G. Papini, *Vita di Michelangelo*, Milan 1949, p. 111.
[12] *Op. cit.*, p. 81.
[13] D. Giannotti, *Dialogi de' giorni che Dante consumò nel cercare l'inferno e 'l purgatorio*, edited by D. Redig de Campos, Florence 1939.
[14] U. Foscolo, *Opere*, Vol. X, p. 447.
[15] Papini conjectures that a woman had reawakened Michelangelo's heart about 1558: the Cremona painter Sofonisba Anguissola (cf. *Vita di Michelangelo, op. cit.*, chapter on " The Last Woman "). In that case, the madrigal might refer to her.
[16] The reformistic interpretation now reappears in the essays of Binni (see the Bibliographical Note) and of C. Mutini " Le ultime rime di M." in *Filologia e Letteratura*, a. XI (1965), fasc. I, No. 41, p. 84 ff. That a leaning towards Valdesianism is found in the fundamentally Catholic spirituality of Michelangelo is undeniable, but it is equally undeniable that such an inclination cannot form the same interpretative foundation of his art, poetic and otherwise. But, on the methodological limits of a criticism which tends to ideological qualifications of the poetry, see my *Studi sulle Rime di Michelangelo* (cit. in Biographical Note) p. 15.
[17] It is hard to accept Papini's opinion (*Vita di Michelangelo, op. cit.*, p. 590), that these verses " would suggest that he, like his Dante, was tempted by the Joachimite hope of the Third Kingdom." Contrary to what he believes, the " predicted light " is not the Holy Ghost but simply " the sunshine of Thy light, lost to the world " of the line above, and " predicted " and " to come to us " because we shall see it on the Day of Judgment. And the " fair Consort " can not be the Church here, but only the soul, in Platonic language, the soul of Michelangelo, to which all the sonnet refers.
[18] Instead of " mutarmi ". I agree with the reading suggested by G. Vigolo in *Il Mondo*.

Conclusion

It can be said that, with the last portion of his poetical work, Michelangelo had himself given the start to the critical history of his art and of his poetry as a whole.

As Petrarch, asking pardon of his readers for the " varied style " of his wailing and reasoning in verse, thereby identifies its significance and sums it up in relation to his own human life, to his own reality and interior history: so, and much more in anguish, because without any comfort of participation by his readers, Michelangelo here defines his poetry as the mirror of his own life, and in it the life of every man.

How different, and hence how false, is the judgment of the master's great-nephew, Michelangelo the Younger, intent on reducing the existential exemplariness of this poetry to a petty

14 Rhymes, No. 228 (1555).

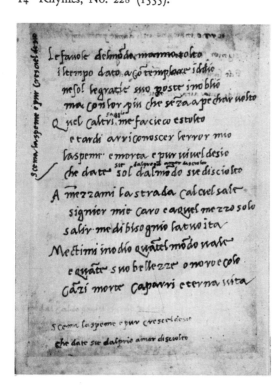

moral, or rather moralistic, exemplarity: " Of Michelangelo's poems it can be said that, in that they are grave and not lascivious and not ornate, they would not be expelled from good republics." [19] And for his part, the nephew turned editor will leave nothing undone, censuring everything he could lay his hands on, to deform, for purposes of moral and grammatical edification, the strong, rugged and contradictory image of a man that the great master had put into the poems.[20]

Rediscovery of the writer in his authenticity and entirety was the task of the scholars of the Romantic age: Guasti, the first critical editor of the poems,[21] and Milanesi, who first published the correspondence.[22] And obviously, Romantic critics and readers were the first to understand the " Romantic " sides of Michelangelo's personality, as reflected in the work of the " writer " as well: his pessimism, his religiosity, his dramatic sense of existence as the scene of battle between spirit and matter, between God and the world, his realism, his taste for the bizarre, grotesque and obscure.

But beyond these marks of genius, judgment of the writer remains uncertain and reserved: a poet, but an improviser; inspired, but lacking the requisite technique; a setter-forth of strong and deep thoughts, but not a composer of harmonious verses, an author of remarkable fragments but not of finished poems: in a word, a dilettante of genius. And such, more or less, is the judgment current in the manuals.

I do not mean to say, and have not said, that Michelangelo's poetical writings are free of defects, that they are not often obscure, hard, uneven, over-subtle. It only seemed to me that a quite different motivation should be given than the one beloved of the " technicians," the " hard workers " of every century: Bemboists, Cruscans, Neoclassicists, historians, all equally incapable of judging on any other bases than the grammatical, poetical, esthetic and other respectable but always inadequate tables of the law applicable in the republic of letters. It seemed to me, and some of the most recent studies led to this, that it was necessary to form a judgment on the basis of history, to compare Michelangelo not with the conventional and academic tradition that was predominant and still forms our taste to a great extent, but with an older tradition, more alive and free, which he followed. In this perspective, the limits of Michelangelo are not those of a dilettante, of one who abuses his language and who is pardoned only by virtue of his authority in other fields; in this perspective they appear as the limits of a great writer who rises above the *aurea mediocritas* of the contemporary writers of poetry to the degree that his roots go down to a glorious tradition of literary, artistic and civic culture.

[19] Cf. my " Philological Note " in the edition of the *Rime, op. cit.*, pp. 495-496.
[20] *Rime di Michelangelo Buonarroti raccolte da Michelangelo suo nipote*, Florence MDCXXIII.
[21] *Le rime di Michelangelo Buonarroti*, Florence MDCCCLXIII.
[22] Florence 1875.

Bibliographical Note

B. Varchi: " Lezione sul sonetto ' Non ha l'ottimo artista,' " in *Le rime di M. Buonarroti*, cit., Florence 1863, pp. 85-92.

U. Foscolo: " Michelangelo," in *New-Monthly Magazine*, Vol. IV, 1822, and " Poems of M.," in *Retrospective Review*, Vol. XIII, October 1826. See both writings in the original English work and translated into Italian by U. Foscolo, in *Opere*, Vol. X, p. 333 ff.

C. Guasti: " Di Michelangelo come poeta," foreword to edition of the *Rime*, Florence 1863, cit., pp. 7-49.

W. Pater: " The poetry of Michelangelo," in *Fortnightly Review*, Oct. 1871, then in *Studies in the history of the history of the Renaissance*, London 1873.

J. A. Symonds: *The sonnets of M. Buonarroti and Campanella*, London 1878.

G. Klaczko: *Causeries florentines*, Paris 1880.

C. Boito: *Leonardo, Michelangelo, A. Palladio. Studi artistici*, 2nd ed., Milan 1883, p. 119 ff.

C. Frey: foreword to the critical edition of the rhymes: *Dichtungen des M. B.*, Berlin 1897.

A. Farinelli: " Michelangelo poeta," in *Raccolta di studi dedicata ad Alessandro d'Ancona*, Florence 1901; last edition in *Michelangelo e Dante. Michelangelo poeta*, Turin 1943.

T. Parodi: " Michelangelo Buonarroti," in *Poesia e letteratura*, Bari 1916.

F. Rizzi: *Michelangelo poeta*, Milan 1924.

G. Bertoni: " La prosa di Michelangelo," in *Lingua e pensiero*, Florence 1932.

G. G. Ferrero: *Il petrarchismo del Bembo e le rime di Michelangelo*, Turin 1935.

G. Contini: " Il senso delle cose nella poesia di Michelangelo," in *Rivista rosminiana*, Oct.-Dec. 1937, then in *Esercizi di lettura*, Florence 1947.

V. Mariani: *Poesia di Michelangelo*, Rome 1941.

H. Sckommodau: " Die Dichtungen Michelangiolos," in *Romanische Forschungen*, 56 (1942), pp. 49-104.

C. E. Gilbert: " Michelangelo's madrigal ' Gli sguardi che tu strazi,' " in *The Art Bulletin*, 26, March 1944, pp. 48-51.

T. Mann: " La concezione dell'amore nella poesia di Michelangelo," in *Letterature moderne*, I, 1950, p. 427 ff; now in *Scritti Minori*, Milan 1958.

L. Baldacci: " Lineamenti della poesia di Michelangelo," in *Paragone*, 1955, No. 72, pp. 27-45.

G. Di Pino: " Le rime di Michelangelo," in *Umanità e stile*, Florence 1957.

E. N. Girardi: " Michelangelo Buonarroti," in *Letteratura italiana — I Minori*, Milan 1960 and *Studi sulle Rime di Michelangiolo*, Milan 1964.

L. De Vecchi: " Sulla poesia di Michelangelo," in *Giornale storico della letteratura italiana*, CXL (1963), pp. 30-66; 364-402.

W. Binni: " Michelangelo scrittore," in *La Rassegna della letteratura italiana*, 68, s. VII, Nos. 2-3 (May-December 1964), p. 213 ff.

H. Friedrich: *Epochen der italienischen Poesie*, Frankfurt a. M., 1964.

IX

LANGUAGE

by Giovanni Nencioni

The cooperative pattern of this miscellany seems to be made to order to stimulate a spirit of contradiction. It is virtually an invitation, after centuries of interpretation of Michelangelo in the titanic mode, to consider him in a centripetal, sociological perspective, as a norm rather than as an exception. We will do so linguistically, of course, within the bounds of our interests and competence, and without the censorious intent of a Marinoni, who aimed, with good reason, at deflating the myth of a Leonardo da Vinci who was a grammarian and lexicographer, in addition to being everything else, by giving us the grammatical and lexical exercises of an " unlettered " artist; although, to tell the truth, Michelangelo criticism has kept its universalism and titanism within more reasonable and acceptable limits, and has not exaggerated the relatively modest dimensions of Michelangelo as a poet.

It is not the poet in verse that we shall discuss here, even though it is certainly in order to look for adherence to a standard or custom in the poems; this has already been done by able critics of poetry, who have brought out, from various points of view, Michelangelo's more or less active participation in the language of Petrarchism, in that of Berni, and in the " stony " language of Dante. But we know that literary standards are so optional that a strictly linguistic study would not yield fruits of any importance. The best it could do would be to lead us to take note of the persistence, within a more or less ennobled mixture, of elements of the current Florentine language in the less adaptable sectors of the linguistic system.

We therefore take up the artist's letters. The extemporaneous nature of most of them has been pointed out on various occasions, and recently by Pier Luigi De Vecchi in his excellent *Studi sulla poesia di Michelangelo*.[1] For the modern reader, this extemporization is a pleasant contrast to much Cinquecento correspondence written for publication. In addition, being in prose relieves them of the syntactic and phono-syntactical alterations imposed by the meter and the tradition of a poetical taste.

Now, even the writing, the most external and least essential aspect of a language, gives us important guidelines. Lucilla Ciulich, a very young scholar who has made a careful study of Michelangelo's handwriting,[2] has discerned in it the limits of his culture, which had scant humanistic foundations, a fact of which he was deeply aware. His sparing use of etymological or pseudo-etymological forms, his adoption of practical solutions (e. g., *ct* for double *t* even in phonosyntactical doubling), the very frequent running-on of words, the abundance of apheresis and apocope exactly as in the patterns of speech, the absence of the principal spelling innovations proposed by grammarians during the Cinquecento, and the modest extent of Michelangelo's undoubted progress as a result of his contacts with friends possessing a literary culture: all this has led Ciulich to describe his writing as spontaneous, practical and often approximate, and hence calling for the collaboration of the reader's intuition, even though it also shows revisions of thought aimed at seeking relatively constant solutions. Ciulich points out repeatedly that the increased intensity or co-presence of these modes of writing, obviously shared by the manuscripts of the poems, characterizes the letters to the family, i. e., the more extemporaneous writings.

We know that during the Quattrocento Florence went a different way, linguistically, from the rest of Italy. Although other centers of culture in Italy guided and modeled themselves on the fourteenth century Florentine of the three great authors Dante, Petrarch, Boccaccio, freeing themselves from dialect as a national unity was formed on the basis of these models, Florence went through a phase of grammatical and rhetorical laxity induced by the indifference or reaction of its humanists to those models, at the same time feeling pressure from

557

large-scale immigration from the country. As a result, it rapidly modified many characteristics of its idiom, not only the most superficial and changeable but also those inherent in the phonological and morphological structures, to the point where Cesare Segre can speak of a transformation of the linguistic system. On the national scale, this transformation became a competition that ended in the defeat of living Florentine, that is, in its redialectization.

One of the most frequent phenomena in Florentine writing around 1500, found even in the prose and poetry that were not written for the common people (this was in a center in which the divergence between spoken and literary language operated within a unitary tradition, and at a time at which Florence still combined a taste for the living language with a conviction that it could use it as a tool of vernacular literature), is the tendency to phonological assimilation in the case of enclitic attachment of pronouns to infinitives and verbals, or to adverbs ending in *m* or *n*, and in the case of proclitic attachment of prepositions, articles, etc. As early as Michelangelo's first letters (1496-97, pp. 3-5, 375 ff.) [3] we find *avello* (averlo), *accordalla, tenello, dagli* (dargli), *no' mi, no 'gli, noll'ò, gra' maestri, i' modo;* at the same time that we find *dargli, acattargli, non gli,* and, to point up the limits of the phenomenon, *non vi, non si.* In the letters [1508] to his father Lodovico on the misconduct of his brother Giovan Simone (p. 13 ff.) and to that brother (p. 150 ff.), which are among the most impromptu and impetuous of the entire correspondence, we find *i' mano, u' minimo, i' mentre che;* in the latter, note the development of the adverb into an adverbial phrase, typical of the spoken language, as is the accumulation of prefixes. Ciulich points out the contiguity of "*comperallo e pagarlo*" in a 1550 letter to his nephew Leonardo (Milanesi, p. 265, reads "*comperarlo e pagarlo*"), and a reconsideration as shown by an *r* over the double letters of *maravigliassi* (maravigliarsi) and also *ritornalla,* in a [1533] letter to Bartolomeo Angiolini (for which Milanesi, p. 469, reads *maravigliarsi* and *ritornalla*). She further points out *'mparentassi* (1549 letter to Leonardo, p. 237), *parvo'gli* (p. 225), and various analogous cases, such as *togga* (tolga, 1548 and 1556, pp. 230 and 321), *maninconico* (1556, p. 319); to which I might add *ma' g[i]udicare* (1512?, p. 43), *u' mal segnio* (letter to his brother Buonarroto, Aug. 11, 1515 [Milanesi, p. 121, does not list it]), *no' guardassi* (1549, p. 237), *no' prestar* (1556, p. 316), *noi sia' certi* (1549, p. 245), *e' banbino* alongside *el banbino* in the letter to Lorenzo di Pier Francesco de' Medici dated July 2, 1496 (not listed by Milanesi), *e' loro* (el loro, about 1521) in folio 1859-6-25-543 of the British Museum, *i' libretto* (il libretto, in a letter to his nephew Leonardo, 1551, p. 273). But the importance of these facts can become clear only within a framework of correlations, that is, remembering that they are absent from Guicciardini's *Ricordi*,[4] that they are infrequent in Michelangelo's letters as compared with analytical forms, and that, on the other hand, they are frequent in the letters of Antonio Mini, an uneducated disciple of his: *no' si, ridesene* (ridersene) *co' vostr[e], no' vo, no' sono, e' re* (el re, 4 times), *no.llo* (3 times), *no' rie[m]pie, a' Rosso* (al Rosso), *soci* (sonci), *i' luogho* (in luogo), *no' vole, i' voi* (2 times), *a' re* (al re, 2 times), *no' maravilglia, e' suo* (el suo), *co' Betuccio, no.ssa* (another case of assimilation), *co' Michelagniolo, no' sia, no' meritava, vederllo, i' sere* (in sere), *no' sapete, e' male* (el male), *de' Beni* (del Beni), *no' rispondevo.* All are taken from a single letter (to Francesco Tedaldi, [1532],[5] which, however, also contains unassimilated forms (*el vero, spregiarla, non vi, songli, el mio, con ta[n]ti, avermi,* etc.). It would be interesting to determine whether the phenomena we are speaking of also appear in the letters written by Michelangelo to eminent persons, and other more carefully written letters. In point of fact, the stilted letters to Tommaso Cavalieri and those to Clement VII, Francis I and Cosimo I are free of traits; but they contain some of another sort, perhaps more intrinsically derived from the system and hence less likely to be refined out by the writer, as we shall see.

In the opposite area of dissimilation, and in the area of metathesis and paretymological attraction, we find a few examples, but typical ones. *Propio* (for proprio) is dominant, but it does not appear that *drieto, adrieto, drento* (which are the rule in Machiavelli and Guicciardini) prevail, to go by Ciulich's results, over *dietro* and *dentro,* nor is *albitrio* favored over *arbitrio.* A curious instance, even lexically, is *alberinto* (labirinto, p. 54). To this may be added the constant *obrigo* (always *obligo* in Guicciardini; and I find *prenaria* in a letter from Buonarroto to Michelangelo dated December 1515; and I find *sempice* in Michelangelo himself, p. 247, an obvious reaction, like the preceding instances, to an offensive group of a consonant plus *l*), the equally constant *scarpellino* (for scalpellino), and the *reallissimo* (lealissimo) in a letter to Vasari dated 23.II.1556;[6] and also the *alturità* in a letter to his brother Buonarroto (p. 134; but also in one to Clement VII, p. 424) and *araudo* alternating with *araldo,* and *utimo* in a 1563 letter to his nephew Leonardo (p. 369) in contrast to the prevalence of *ultimo.* All these examples indicate the interweaving of popular and hyper-correct trends around a crisis of the group *l* plus consonant, much more common in the letters of Michelangelo's correspondents, whether educated or not. Thus I find *autra, aultare,* along with *altra* and *altare,* in letters of the ecclesiastic Giovan Francesco Fattucci (cf. *altentico* in Cellini, *Vita,* p. 830 of the Cordié edition); *vota* (volta), *otre* (oltre), *atro* (altro), *ischutore* (iscultore) in letters of Piero Roselli and Tommaso di Balduccio; *utimo* in letters from Ludovico and Buonarroto Buonarroti, Bernardo Niccolini, etc.[7] But we must not overlook two telltale Michelangelisms, not listed by Milanesi (pp. 14 and 70): *un'anltra* in the letter to his brother Buonarroto dated March 6, 1507, and *l'arltra* in a letter to his father [June-July 1509].

We shall not dwell on such other uses as the insertion of a consonant in *Pagolo, pagonazzo, strasordinario* (and on the other hand such reductions as *aoperato,* p. 366, *i' beo,* p. 245, etc.), or the addition of a final *e*-vowel in *none* (the only case I have found; but this phenomenon does not occur in Guicciardini's *Ricordi*, and is rare even in the uneducated correspondents),[8] or the constant elimination of the labial element in the labiovelars of *chiunque, dunque, ovunque* (*chiunche, dunche, ovunche* are also exclusively present in Guicciardini and are accepted by the Florentine literary men open to the feeling for the living language, e. g. Varchi). Emphasis should be placed, instead, on the ferment in one of the most movable and restless sectors of the consonantal system, the palatals. The flattened *gn* (prevalent but alternating with *ng* in Machiavelli, exclusive in Guicciardini) in Michelangelo's letters is constant in words as important as *dipignere* and in the very name *Michelagniolo*. In other words *gn* oscillates not only with *ng* but also with *gl* in *gniene* for *gliele*, a demotic form in which a parallel is found, in the artist's correspondents, in *gni* for *gli*. The plural of nouns ending in -*ello* usually ends in -*egli* (*modegli*, always *frategli* and *begli*, etc.; Ciulich); the accusative plural article and pronoun *li* almost always appears as *gli* (*lavorargli, ve gli manderò, no' gli avete, quegli disegni, gli à fatti*, etc.; an analogous situation in Guicciardini). There are instances of oscillation between a sibilant pronunciation and its absence (*risucitare, laciarla, nutri[s]ce, stracinare, vicitare* [Ciulich]; but also *riscievuta, e[s]cie, u[s]cì, discie*, etc., in Michelangelo's correspondents), and there is also a tendency for the undermined consonant group *schj* to become occluded into *stj* (*arristiare, stiavo, mastio;* thus in Machiavelli, but in Guicciardini *schiavo, maschio*). As early as the Quattrocento all these distinguish Florentine usage from that which had become established in literature in the Trecento, and are considered lower-class characteristics in subsequent grammatical codification.

In this connection, it is of interest that *mugg[h]iato* (1549, p. 242) and *Fegg[h]ine* (1561, p. 360) have been retained when the type of *mugliare, Figline* was becoming established as a "reaction to the rural pronunciation of the type of *migghia* for *miglia*."[9] Was it a stand in favor of the mother tongue spoken at home, or merely a consequence of the isolation of the old artist from his native linguistic center, which he had finally abandoned in 1534? There seems to be a stand, but an anti-vernacular one, in the answer to a letter from Ser Marcantonio del Cartolaio, Cancelliere to the Nine during the siege of Florence (1529), Michelangelo using *voce mia* to reply to the chancellor's *boce vostra*. But in the letter to his nephew Leonardo dated April 7, 1548, he writes *boto* for *voto* (p. 222).

We now leave the consonants for the vowels, if only to point out the absence of assimilatory and dissimilatory forms of a demotic nature (such as *uchupatissimo, achupato* [occupato], *ugnuno*, etc., which can be found in Bernardo Niccolini, Lodovico Buonarroti, Cellini, etc.); the presence of undiphthongized forms such as *omo, vòi, pòi, foco, core, loco, scafaioli, renaiolo, gioco*, alternating (except in the case of *voto* and the three last; Ciulich) with the diphthongized forms; and the preponderance of *prego* and *breve* over *priego* and *brieve*, but on the other hand, *truovo* and *pruovo* rather than *trovo* and *provo* (Ciulich). While for the first series (except for the case of the reduction after the consonant *v*, in which there may be a graphic element, as is shown by an author's correction[10]) Michelangelo is in accord with a tendency visible already in non-courtly prose writers of the Quattrocento (e. g., Vespasiano da Bisticci, where it is not uncommon to find *bono*, etc.) and hence characteristic of spoken usage, with respect to the second series he is affected by a state of crisis that extends to even the greatest Florentine writers of the Cinquecento.[11] One clear case of yielding to the spoken language is in the forms *quante, quande*—which are supported by indubitable documentary evidence, apart from instances that can be analyzed and are therefore ambiguous (such as *quante gli altri* [Milanesi, p. 8, *quant'è gli altri*], *quande nulla avenissi* [Milanesi, p. 9, *quand'e' nulla avenissi*]; *quande si truovassi* [Milanesi, p. 275, *quand'e' si truovassi*], etc.)—in such groups as *quande ciò avenissi* (p. 43), *quante puoi* (p. 125), *quande bene, quande tu truovi* (p. 237), *fa' tanto quante conosci* (p. 257), *quante l'uomo* (p. 293), etc. These forms are certainly less frequent than the standard ones, but they persist down into the old age of the artist and are also present, at least *quante*, in the poetry.

Ciulich has shrewdly remarked that the various modes of phonetic joinings in the syntactical chain, such as apheresis, apocope, elision, are frequent in Michelangelo's letters to his family and most intimate friends, in which the writer "can let himself go in the confidential tone... employing the discursive course of the spoken language," a tone and course that, as Ciulich has stressed, correspond to a more rapid tempo of discourse and rhythmic requirements of special expressiveness. We add that the fact is all the more interesting in a dialect whose tempo is notoriously slow, as the Florentine is, and in an author who, as Ciulich shows, prefers full forms to syncopated ones in prose (*offerire, comperare, anderai, diriza, medesimo, opera*, etc.) and makes much use of prosthesis (*per istiavo, per iscusato, in ispesa, grande ispesa, voglio iscrivere, sei iscudi*, etc.). Although the aphereses assume the forms common in literary texts (*lo 'ntesi, a 'mparare, la redità*, etc.), Ciulich's results show that apocope takes on special extent and intensity: *io, ei, noi, poi, mai, fui, sei, assai*, in addition to the prepositions with the article, often lack the final vowel; and the same for the future, conditional and past definite tenses in their enclitic forms *dara'gli, portera'gli, vedra'lo, manda'ne, porta'le, lascia'vi, fare'la;* and likewise without enclisis: *sare'* (sarei), *sare'* (sarebbe, p. 467), *saré'* (sarete, p. 67: *se sare' savi*), *simil cose* (p. 56), not to speak of shortened infinitives and such instances as *son, sien, siàn, par, vien, tien, vadin, sarebon, eron, guaston*, etc., which make an impressive series, which yet is not exclusive nor dominant, since even in the most confidential and agitated letters we always find apocopated and full forms side by side.

But it is in morphology that the greatest change in structure takes place in Florentine between the second half of the fifteenth and the first half of the sixteenth centuries; to be more precise, in the declension of nouns and conjugation of verbs, in which analogy finally gets the better of many etymological forms or forms set by a previous analogical phase. This is a continuation of a process going on in informal language, beginning in vulgar Latin and developing further in the post-Roman period, ceasing temporarily during the victory of Florentine in literature in the thirteenth and fourteenth centuries and then beginning afresh, now in dialectical relationship with the "literary" structures, during the age of humanism and the rise of the cities. Analogical forms like *ero, stimavo* (for *era, stimava*), *venissino* (from the now predominant third person *venissi*; no longer *venisseno* or *venissono*), *rispondino, sappino, venghino* (from the prevalent third person *sappi, facci, abbi*, and the expansion of *amino, pensino*, etc.), *andorono, lavororono* (p. 141), and likewise *lasciorno, presentorno* (pp. 398, 493) and often *furno, vennono, feciono, leverebbono* (and no longer *feceno, leverebbeno*), *consigliono, gittono, erono, piacevono* (and, vice versa, *vogliano* for *vogliono*, p. 249), the first plurals *siàno, facciàno, andereno*, the analogical futures and conditionals *scriverrò, troverrei*: all are forms, exclusive or alternating with the literary forms, but in any case dominant by and large, that bring Michelangelo's letters into line with current Florentine spoken usage, with vernacular touches (but excluding certain extremes, like the haplologies of the type of *avamo*, etc., occurring in Buonarroto, etc.). It was a usage not unknown to such literarily cultivated and perceptive writers as Machiavelli and Guicciardini, except that in them the assimilation and consequent presence of the literary tradition makes the dosage different, indicating greater cultural complexity. In Michelangelo, we have rather a tendency to avoid plebeian traits than a tendency to seek out courtly ones. If, for example, we find, along with the usual and constant *arò, arei, arranno*, etc., the archaic *àve* in a note dated April 3, 1524 (*àve facto*, Archivio Buonarroti I, 38, 93), the old short forms of the unsuffixed participle are almost entirely confined to the cases in which they coincide with the adjectival forms (*io gli ebbi scarichi*, p. 6; *io ò conto*, p. 155; *avete aconcio*, p. 176; *la m'à straco*, p. 290; *è stato guasto*, p. 545). It is regular to have the second person plurals looking like singulars (*voi dovevi, desideravi, facessi*) that had become established in the Quattrocento by virtue of the interchangeability of the final *-e / -i* (*avesse / avessi, scriveste / scrivesti*), but along with cases of strenuous analogy, such as *siate* (for *siete*) and *sendo*, there are isolated queer forms like *dolfe* and *dolfono*, and cases of non-popular choice, like the constant *stato* instead of *suto* (which is absent in Guicciardini too, while being frequent in Machiavelli). It is rare that we find the conditional in *-ia* (*[io] renderia*, p. 375, *reggierieno*, p. 403), much more rare than in Cellini's *Vita* or the prose of Vasari.

A confirmation of what we have said is found in the numerals, where *dua* is far more common, in any combination or position, than *due*, in accordance with the Florentine usage common to the great writers of the early Cinquecento (Machiavelli, Guicciardini),[12] while I have not encountered the more demotic *duoi* (in frequent spoken use, as Caro testifies, and to be found, without leaving Florence, in Vasari's letters and Lives, in the letters of Vincenzio Borghini, in Cellini, etc.), nor *duo, dui, doi*. In the possessives, on the other hand, we note the heterogeneous series, known as early as the Trecento: *mie, tuo, suo* for both genders and both numbers (*la tuo lettera*, p. 162; *e' tuo bisogni*, p. 157; *e' mie panni*, p. 157; *un mie pari* in the letter to Francis I, p. 519, etc.) but not in the tonic position, where instead we have *mia, tua, sua* for the plural of both genders (*e' fatti mia*, p. 3; *e' mia*, p. 108; and at the same time *e' mia marmi*, p. 7; *le mia lettere*, p. 261; *per le tua ultime*, p. 132; *delle sua cose*, in the same letter to the King of France, p. 519). Naturally, the normal declined forms are not lacking, but they are very rare, especially the plurals (*cogli ochi tuoi*, p. 286), which are rare indeed. This confirms the Cinquecento situation that, with a few modifications, continues into the present-day Florentine vernacular.

For the article, the outstanding fact is the absence of analytical prepositional forms of the type *in ello, a il*, etc., which are present in Cellini and in plebeian writers and which lead up to today's situation in the vernacular, while the old alternation continues between *el* and *il*, *e'* and *i*. One would be led to say that the second form becomes more frequent in the later letters and in those written with more care. For example, in a letter to his nephew Leonardo dated March 29, 1544 (p. 173), there is a sequence *i marmi, il frutto, e' danari, il podere, il papa;* but in a letter of [August 1508] to his father there was the sequence *i casi, il tempo, el contrario, il fargli, il dì, el podere, e' danari, il meglio, il vostro, el piato* (p. 13 ff.). And while in the elaborate letter to Tommaso Cavalieri [January 1, 1533] we have *il tempo, il passato, il cuore* (p. 462), the letter to Cosimo I dated November 1, 1559 (p. 551) contains *i Fiorentini, e' quali, i sopradetti, el quale, el più onorevole, el quale*. Certainly the presence, or rather the frequency of *el, e'*, forms unknown to or condemned by the grammarians and increasingly rare in writers,[13] constitutes a conservative trait in the Michelangelo mixture of articles, but one common to Machiavelli and Guicciardini. Conservative traits are also present in the morphology of the noun: *opinione* and *orazione* are masculine (*un altro openione*, p. 128; *l'openione mio*, p. 225; *gli orazioni*, p. 88; *agli orazioni*, p. 248); the plural in *-e* is vigorous (*molte cagione*, p. 4; *le leggie*, p. 145; *delle possessione*, p. 189; *le parte buone* alternating with *le parti buone* in a single short letter dated October 17, 1551 to his nephew Leonardo, p. 276; *troppe grande*, also noteworthy for the agreement, p. 84; etc.); plurals in *-a* are present (*quante staiora*, p. 143, as well as *le vista*, p. 10, and perhaps *mie scusa* [14]).

In the personal pronouns, on the other hand, the tendency is toward innovation. Here, although old forms, which had penetrated sporadically into literary usage as well, are conserved (e. g. *gli* for " *le, a lei* " [cf. however *che io le facci*, p. 15] but not for " *a loro* " [cf. *presti loro*, p. 65; *scrivere loro*, p. 86; *dar loro*, p. 388; *diciate loro*, p. 389; *ne sa loro male*, p. 393; etc.]), the overall impression bears the imprint of the late Quattrocento whose usages were consolidated in the following century and were handed down to the present-day dialect. Also striking is the fact of quantity, i. e. frequency. There are sequences of sentences with elliptical subjects (*Gli scarpellini che vennono qua non iscontorono niente. Lavororono solamente...; poi s'andorono con Dio... Sandro s'è partito ancora lui di qua. È stato qua parechi mesi... atteso a pescare e a vaghegiare. Àmmi buttato via cento ducati. À lasciato qua una certa quantità di marmi...* p. 141), but often the ellipsis of the noun or its equivalent is made good by the pronoun of the third person, especially in the short forms *e', gli, la, le*, very close to the spoken rhythm, in fact derived from it: *perché e'* (*egli*) *non si crucci meco*, p. 6; *quando e'* (*essi*) *si dolfono di me*, p. 8 (cf. *in modo che egli sperassino*, p. 13); *duolmi che gli* (*egli*) *abbi di mio sette ducati*, p. 9; *quanto gli* (*essi*) *erano stati con meco*, p. 8; *s'egli è vero che gli* (*essa*) *abbi sì grande bisognio*, p. 15; *la mi donò*, p. 272; *di che sorte le sono*, p. 267. Particular and significant cases of this frequency of pronouns are prolepsis and pleonastic emphasis, in which the form *e'* usually, if not always, is plurivalent: *se e' vi bisognia danari*, p. 11; *e' non è sì gran faccenda che...*, p. 12; *quando e' non ci fia da spendere*, p. 12; *se e' non venissi la state*, p. 13 (cf. *egli è dua mesi che...*, p. 70); *che e' no' ne vadi male una minima carta*, p. 6; *io e' so che...*, p. 395; *e' me n'era uscito la voglia*, p. 237; *le non sono le terre che...*, p. 143; *le son quelle di sopra*, p. 143; *e' quali io te gli mando*, p. 109; *a l'Ammannati vorrei che gli dicessi*, p. 348; *gli puoi involtargli*, p. 263; *a lui digli*, p. 161; *duolmi a me*, p. 551; *come la cosa e' va*, p. 138; *in qualche altra cosa che e' l[a] abbi fantasia*, p. 296; *con quello che io vi darò io*, p. 13. Also noteworthy is the use of *lui, lei, loro* as subjects, a usage that took firm root in the Quattrocento and was vainly ostracized by the grammarians,[15] and also the archaic use of *uomo* with the value of the indefinite *si*: *inanzi che l'uomo comperi*, p. 42; *abiate cura comprare da giente che a un bisognio l'uomo possa combattere con esso lui*, p. 105; *parmi sia da ringraziarne Idio... quante l'uomo sa e può*, p. 293.

We should consider the vocabulary, pointing out elements that are at once archaic and popular, such as *piova* (p. 267), *tornarsi* in the sense of " to take lodgings " (p. 5), or of Quattrocento exuberance, such as *francioso* (p. 75; common to the humorous writings of Piovano Arlotto [p. 174, ed. Folena], to Pulci and later to Cellini), *alie* (which goes back to the Trecento [16]), *imburiassare* " to teach, prompt, suborn " (*imburiassato*, p. 187), of familiar use and tone in the fifteenth and sixteenth centuries (cf. *Vocabolario della Crusca*, 5th ed., s. v.) and cited as a typically Florentine word by Varchi in the *Ercolano* (p. 85, ed. Dal Rio); picturesque and sometimes crudely vulgar locutions of an obviously provincial stamp (*far lo scoppio e il baleno*, p. 61; *lasciar cotesto tristo col culo i' mano*, p. 14; *questa merda seca di questo fanciullo*, p. 27); or formal alternations that betray the co-presence of diverse stylistic levels (*confessore* and *confessoro* in the same letter, p. 321); or the extensive polysemia, characteristic of spoken language, of the most common words (*dire, fare, avere, dare*, etc.); leaving out of account the artisan's terminology that flourished in the workshops which, unlike modern technical jargon, had such deep roots in metaphorical inventiveness. But we shall go on to the syntax, which more clearly exhibits the limits of the relationship between the individual and the institution.

As for the particular constituent factors, precedence in the topological order must go to one of the best-defined of syntactical institutions, the so-called Tobler-Mussafia law; we should say that, although it is no longer observed as a " law," it is retained as preference for enclisis in the old positions, especially after the conjunction *e*, and as a traditional background to make expressive innovations stand out. The letter to Michelangelo's father Lodovico dated January 31, 1507 shows the following alternations in a few linea: *Pregovi che voi pigliate... Vi prego che vo' gniene rammentiate, e ancora prego voi che...*, p. 6 ff.: these alternations are indicative of syntactical liberty, played on the keyboard of emotional mobility. In another letter dated February 8 of the same year, and much more agitated in tone, there are similar phenomena: *Io gli risposi e dissigli che... Mi rispose...*, p. 10. Sometimes the oscillation is within a single sentence: *Se mi trovassi danari, m'informerei se si potessi..., e bisognierebemi fare...*, p. 11; and of course the encliticism is retained more, by inertia, in such fossilized formulas as *Avvisovi, Parmi, Piaceravvi* (in an order to pay, p. 521). One fact that weakens and reduces the application of enclisis is without doubt the very frequent explicit statement of the subject pronoun, arising out of psychological motivations of the same kind as those leading to proclisis; so that where we might expect *Pregovi, Racomandovi, Mandovi, Sonmi resoluto, Parebbemi*, etc., we often find *Io vi prego, Io vi racomando, Io vi mando, Io mi son resoluto, E' mi parebbe*, etc.; but often the choice seems to be quite arbitrary (*Ti scrissi de' dua brevi*, p. 264; *Scrissiti ultimamente d'una serva*, p. 265). All in all, this goes to show that this phenomenon in Michelangelo does not depart from the current usage of the time; and the same is true for the mere juxtaposition of two clauses usually connected by a declarative or non-restrictive *che*, a usage most especially practiced in completive clauses with subjunctive, governed by such verbs as *pregare, chiedere, volere*, etc., and after demonstrative pronouns (*quello mi chiederete*, p. 5; *quello n'avete a fare*, p. 10; *non so quello s'arà fatto*, p. 7; *prego lo scriviate*, p. 7; *credo gli abbiate ricievuti*, p. 19;

dei servizii m'avete fatti e delle noie avete ricevute, io lo so.., p. 399; *poi* [poiché] *avete avuta tanta pazienza*, p. 399; but also *di quello che lui mi domanda*, p. 61; *io prego che voi andiate*, p. 9, etc.), all by and large backward steps from Quattrocento usage. By no means absent is the repetition of the declarative *che* (*ringraziate Idio che, poi che questa tribulazione aveva a venire, che la sia venuta in un tempo...*, p. 32; *ditegli che, se si rià questi dua poderi, che la potrà tenere una serva*, p. 155; *penso che, ancora nel servire e' matti, che rare volte si potrebe trovare qualche dolceza*, p. 413; *e dico che, se maggiore iudicio et difficultà, impedimento et fatica non fa maggiore nobiltà, che la pittura et scultura è una medesima cosa*, p. 522); this repetition is even more frequent in other texts, for example, in Michelangelo's correspondents and in Vasari's letters. Also present is the anacoluthic, plurivalent relative *che* (*aresti domandato di quello che e' si dolevano*, p. 8; *in qualche luogo che voi stiate bene*, p. 14; *in qualche altra cosa che e' l'abbi fantasia*, p. 296; *ti scrissi sabato passato..., che ne attendo risposta*, p. 186; *io gli darei e' danari che la togliessi*, p. 10); and the *che* that, as written, is not clearly either declarative, causal, of result or relative, but is determined by the intonation, that is, a tonally defined morpheme, one therefore that is characteristic of the spoken language and still subsistent in the Florentine dialect: *non v'è da dire altro per ora, perché non sono ancora risoluto di cosa nessuna che io vi possa avisare*, p. 15; *mancavami facienda oltre quella che i' ò avuta poi che io tornai! che ho avuto el mio garzone... amalato...* p. 27; *già sono stato così circa di quindici anni, che mai ebbi un'ora di bene*, p. 47; *e non correte a furia, che noi non fussimo gabati*, p. 105; *fallo tanto che io sia costà, che stimo tornare infra quindici o venti dì*, p. 142. Another indication of colloquial usage, especially but not exclusively Tuscan, is the *che* introducing a direct question (*Che à' tu paura che io non mi penta...?*, p. 187), found in our prose from the Trecento on. On the other hand, the pseudohypotactic *che* does not occur, a *che* that appears to be a conjunction but is really a means of transition from one episode to another of the discourse, independent of the actual logico-syntactical connections, a point of rest and repetition of a substantially paratactic chain of statements. I take an instance from Francesco da Sangallo's letter to Varchi on the question of the " precedence of the arts: " " *Questo è quello che ha confortato assaissimi pittori; con questa speranza, non che una volta, ma molte hanno fatto e rifatto le loro opere infino che a loro sono sadisfatti; e così vivano opere onorate che laldevole, solo causate da questa benigna proprietà e benignità di natura di essa arte, del potere disfare e in brieve potere rifare. Che ancora hanno un altro diletto, quale non è piccolo...*" [17]

Michelangelo's sentence structure is the product of too clear and consistent a mind to yield to such typical instances of agglutination and indistinctness; and this apart from any cultural preparation or linguistic reflection. The very rare use made of the accusative with the, infinitive, even in the most commonly occurring case, i. e., depending on verbs of saying (*udendo dire dal detto capitano, voi essere unico al mondo e così essere tenuto in Roma*, p. 446); the extensive use of the infinitive as a noun, familiar to both the relaxed and the humanistic prose of the Quattrocento (*io non ò pecato nessuno... se non del fare più che mi si conviene*, p. 8; *mi vo afaticando... per alungare la vita mia*, p. 473; *benché io parli molto prosuntuosamente, per esser molto inferiore*, p. 468; *nel ricever della vostra lettera... sonmi molto allegrato, per venire da voi*, p. 472; *per rispondere allo scrivere di me, ibid.*; *il vostro non voler capitare a Roma, ibid.*; *per conto del veder la pittura, ibid.*); the flexibility of agreement in number and gender (*gli era stato tolto la cappa*, p. 3; *m'è dato buone parole*, p. 25; *e' viene costà certi scarpellini*, p. 412; *quando si trovassi che le fussi cose sicure*, p. 189; *se non v'era cose o lettere che importassino, non è da pensarvi più; e se v'erano...* p. 171; something that occurs even in the careful and very logical Guicciardini): these and other facts mentioned above are undoubtedly evidence of reliance on a time-honored tradition and of minimum participation in the new grammatical logicism and the laws it was imposing. But by way of contrast there are other facts that are not derived from precepts of symmetry or more or less assimilated cultural superpositions, but from an internal order, from a discourse that unfolds in operations that are not desultory, rarely interjective, mostly organized and categorized. The elementary manifestations of this internal order appear with negative or positive sign.

To the first category belongs the rarity of grave anacoluthon, as it can be seen in some of Michelangelo's correspondents (e. g. Topolino or Antonio Mini). Except for the cases coming under the heading of the polyvalent relative *che* (some of which have been accepted in literary usage), Michelangelo's anacoluthon is not so much lack of syntactic connection as it is anticipation by segmentation of the clause, i. e., a typical expressive procedure: *El salario, gli darò quello mi scrivesti*, p. 26; *Il cacio che tu m'ài mandato, io ò avuto la lettera, ma non ò già avuto il cacio*, p. 236; *E' mille ducati overo scudi che io t'ò mandati... tu comprerai più presto la possessione*, p. 188. Note the rigorous concatenation of this sentence, going straight to its goal, without parentheses or interruptions: *Io vi scrissi che voi domandassi Bonifazio a chi e' faceva pagare a Lucca quegli cinquanta ducati che io mando a Carrara a Matteo di Cucherello, e che voi iscrivessi el nome di colui che gli à a pagare in sulla lettera che io vi mandai aperta, e che voi la mandassi a Carrara al detto Matteo, acciò che e' sapessi a chi egli aveva a andare in Luc[c]a per e' detti danari* (p. 7). This deductive directness is dated 1507, prior to Michelangelo's cultivated sojourn in the Roman literary milieu, and is carried through unchanged down to the last years: *Intendo per la tua come ài ricevuti i cento scudi che io ti ò mandati, e come ài inteso per la mia quello che tu n'ài a fare, cioè a mandarmi dicianove palmi di rascia pagonazza scura, e del resto farne limosine dove e come pare a te, e darmene aviso* (1555, p. 303). When he uses parataxis, it is not a mere enumeration; its absence of articulation does not denote missing connections, but silences that are semantically and expressively eloquent: *Sandro si è partito ancora lui di qua. È stato qua parechi mesi con un mulo e con un muletto in sulle pompe, atteso a pescare e a vaghegiare. Àmmi buttato via cento ducati. À lasciato qua una certa quantità di marmi, con testimoni che io pigli quegli che fanno per me. Io non ve ne trovo tanti per me che vaglino venti cinque ducati...* (p. 141). It would be hard to find a more strictly connected paratactic procedure than this, in which the logical links arise out of compressed irony and moral condemnation.

The artist who called himself " incorrect in grammar " took pleasure in verbal play, which shows how much attention he paid to the rhythmic and formal resources of the language (*Del fare o del non fare le cose che s'ànno a fare, che voi dite che ànno a soprastare, è meglio lasciarle fare a chi l'à fare...*, p. 449; *Scrivetegniene e ditegniene e dategniene e racomandatemi a lui*, p. 504); and he was perfectly capable of balancing a wearisome statement of expedients and domestic warnings against his lazy brother Giovan Simone with the unforgettable finale: *e lasciar cotesto tristo col culo i' mano* (p. 14). But the most complex effects of Michelangelo's prose are obtained subjecting the hypotactic structures to a melodic tablature, which lends dimensions of depth and duration to the network of the logical operation. Take for example the postscript to the rebuke to his brother Giovan Simone dated [July 1508]: *Io non posso fare che io non ti scriva ancora dua versi; e questo è che io son ito da dodici anni in qua tapinando per tutta Italia, sopportato ogni vergognia, patito ogni stento, lacerato il corpo mio in ogni fatica, messa la vita propria a mille pericoli, solo per aiutar la casa mia; e ora che io ò cominciato a rilevarla un poco, tu solo voglia esser quello che scompigli e rovini in una ora quel che i' ò fatto in tanti anni e con tante fatiche: al corpo di Cristo che non sarà vero! ché io sono per iscompigliare diecimila tua pari, quando e' bisognierà. Or sia savio, e non tentare chi à altra passione* (p. 151). Here we feel the echo of a celebrated grieving passage in Dante's *Convivio* (I, iii, 3-6), and admire the inventive syntax, which after reaching halfway turns about, moving back from the ruler to the ruled and as it were seeking its own source, with a step that is difficult but supported by a solid melodic framework. Another example is a [1545] letter to Vittoria Colonna, much more closely studied but no less inventive, which juxtaposes three short sentences, each in a different tense (imperfect, present, future) and all three merged in a process that is restrained and as it were suspended by incidental phrases, graver and by and large more futile than the principal ones: *Volevo, Signora, prima che io pigliassi le cose che vostra Signoria m'à più volte volute dare, per riceverle manco indegnamente che io potevo, far qualche cosa a quella di mia mano. Dipoi, riconosciuto e visto che la grazia di Iddio non si può comperare, e ch'el tenerla a disagio è peccato grandissimo, dico mia colpa e volentieri dette cose accetto. E quando l'arò, non per averle in casa, ma per essere io in casa loro, mi parrà essere in paradiso; di che ne resterò più obrigato, se più posso essere di quel ch'i' sono, a vostra Signoria* (p. 514). The technique is that of the most correct, in fact the most academic school of letter-writing, but the extraordinary effect of depth is due to a poetically practiced ear.

Buonarroti's fancy in syntax reaches a high point in the letter to Vasari on the project for the staircase of the Laurentian Library, or rather on the memory of the project, drawn up thirty years previously and never built. The exposition is in the tone of an anamnesis rising from the distant past, and thus moves uncertainly and vaguely (*Mi torna bene nella mente come un sogno una certa scala, ma non credo che sia appunto quella che io pensai allora, perché mi torna cosa goffa; pure la scriverò qui...*); the description, at first tinted and as it were toned down by the imperfect subjunctives, becomes more precise and peremptory as it goes along, and didactically takes on the present tense of the same mood; it works itself out by way of a technical vocabulary presented along a rigorous logico-syntactical design, and its concreteness gives it the value of a plastic material taking on force and form of model: *...pure la scriverò qui: Cioè, che i' togliessi una quantità di scatole aovate, di fondo d'un palmo l'una, ma non d'una lunghezza e larghezza; et la maggiore et prima ponessi in sul pavimento, lontana dal muro della porta tanto quanto volete che la scala sia dolce e cruda; e un'altra ne mettessi sopra questa, che fussi tanto minore per ogni verso, che in sulla prima disotto avanzassi tanto piano quanto vuole il piè per salire, diminuendole et ritirandole verso la porta fra l'una et l'altra, sempre per salire; et che la diminuzione dell'ultimo grado sia quant'è 'l vano della porta; et detta parte di scala aovata habbi come dua ale, una di qua et una di là, che vi seguitino i medesimi gradi et non aovati. Di queste serva il mezzo per il signore dal mezzo in su di detta scala, et [le] rivolte di dette alie ritornino al muro. Dal mezzo in giù insino in sul pavimento si discostino con tutta la scala dal muro circa tre palmi, in modo che l'imbasamento del ricetto non sia occupato in luogo nessuno, et resti libera ogni faccia. Io scrivo cosa da ridere; ma so ben che voi troverrete cosa al proposito.*[18]

One who, speaking of the poems, defined Michelangelo's vocabulary as a vocabulary of " substances " could concede that in another sense this substantial quality is confirmed by a syntax that while never enfeebling the semantic backbone of the word, not even in the melodious passages, makes the word into a solid palpable being, a visual datum.

But here we have gone beyond the norm, beyond custom, that is, beyond language as a sociological fact; here we are in the realm of the exceptional, in the sphere of Michelangelo's most individual language. We have come on to the king's highway of syntax, which in Michelangelo (so frank but also so pure and luminous a user of the living Florentine of the turn of the century) is free from the diffractions and immixtures that mark the demotic level, as well as from the architectural efforts that appear on the rhetorical plane; instead, it draws itself from a constructiveness that is an unconditioned and impelling stylistic vocation.

[1] *GSLI*, Vol. CXL, 1963, p. 63 ff.

[2] Her extensive article " On Michelangelo's Writing, " published in the *Atti del Congresso per il IV Centenario della morte di Michelangelo, Firenze-Caprese-Roma, 1964*, was preceded by a summary that appeared in *Lingua Nostra* (Vol. XXV, 1964, pp. 74-78).

[3] References are to the pages of the celebrated edition by G. Milanesi, *Le lettere di M. B.*, Florence, 1875, almost always reliable linguistically.

[4] For the linguistic data concerning Guicciardini (*Ricordi*) and Machiavelli (*Principe*) we make use of the results of R. Spongano in his wellknown edition of the *Ricordi*, Florence, 1951, and of F. Chiapelli in his *Studi sul linguaggio del Machiavelli*, Florence, 1952.

[5] I use the text prepared by G. Chiarini for the volume *Michelangelo. Mostra di disegni, manoscritti e documenti*, Florence, 1964, p. 144 ff.

[6] K. Frey, *Der literarische Nachlass Giorgio Vasaris*, Vol. I, Munich, 1923, p. 433.

[7] For the letters of Michelangelo's correspondents, I also make use of the *Sammlung ausgewählter Briefe an M. B.*, ed. K. Frey, Berlin, 1899.

[8] E. g., I find *sue, òne, piue, ène, àne* in Piero Roselli's letter to Michelangelo dated May 10, 1506.

[9] B. Migliorini, *Storia della lingua italiana*, Florence, 1960, p. 387.

[10] As Ciulich correctly points out.

[11] Migliorini, *op. cit.*, p. 385.

[12] Migliorini, *op. cit.*, p. 390.

[13] Migliorini, *op. cit.*, p. 389.

[14] Frey, *Der literarische Nachlass Giorgio Vasaris, cit.*, I, p. 433.

[15] Migliorini, *op. cit.*, pp. 288, 390.

[16] Frey, *op. cit.*, I, p. 420.

[17] *Trattati d'arte del Cinquecento. Fra Manierismo e Controriforma*, edited by P. Barocchi, I, Bari, 1960, p. 72.

[18] Frey, *op. cit.*, I, p. 419 ff.

X

BIOGRAPHICAL NOTE

by Francesco De Feo

Michelangelo was born at Caprese in Val Tiberina on March 6, 1475, the second of five children, to Ludovico di Leonardo di Buonarroto Simoni and Francesca di Neri di Miniato del Sera. Ludovico Buonarroti's six-month term as *podestà* was completed at the end of March, and he then brought his family back to Settignano, near Florence, his native city, where he had a house and lands. At Settignano Michelangelo was given out to nurse with a woman who was the wife and daughter of stonecutters. Much later the artist jested with Vasari about these two events, saying: "Giorgio, if my mind isn't good for anything, that comes from being born in the thin air of your country Arezzo, just as I got from my nurse's milk the chisels and hammer with which I make my statues." [1]

His first and only grammar master was the humanist Francesco Galeata da Urbino, but young Buonarroti did not profit much from his schooling. He liked drawing and, above all, he "was fonder of going into churches to draw the paintings than of going to school to learn grammar, and very often he would play truant from school to go to see painters at work, and he would rather associate with those who drew than with those who studied." [2] This early vocation for art soon found encouragement in his friend Francesco Granacci but was fought hard by his family, "so that his father and his father's brothers, who hated that art, disliked him and very often gave him good beatings, for to them, being unaware of the excellence and nobility of art, it seemed a disgrace that such a thing should be in his house." [3] And one can hardly say that there were no reasons for this "disgrace," in the context of a family reduced to the brink of poverty, trying desperately to retain their social position and faced with the prospect of sinking to a lower level. The idea of having a "stonecutter" son could certainly not attract a family of "ancient Florentine citizens," [4] which had a distinguished past and which, apart from the unproved claim to be descended from the Counts of Canossa, had been connected with oligarchical political traditions since the previous century. The financial disasters of Michelangelo's grandfather Leonardo had not attenuated his son Ludovico's feeling for a respectable life based on the modest resources derived from public office, which may have been the only source of income of a family by now reduced to the meager revenues of a small rural property. This was the basis of Ludovico's reproaches for the evil ways his son had fallen into, reproaches often repeated and always justified by fidelity to family tradition and the specter of poverty, two themes that had a deep effect on the spiritual formation of the artist. [5]

It was by the advice and insistence of Granacci, who was older than Michelangelo, that Ludovico decided to have Michelangelo attend the *bottega* of Domenico and David di Tommaso Bigordi, known as del Ghirlandaio, who, around 1488, were painting the choir of the church of S. Maria Novella in Florence. The contract, signed April 1, 1488, bound Michelangelo to an apprenticeship for three years. But a year had hardly gone by until young Buonarroti began to haunt the garden of Lorenzo de' Medici in Piazza San Marco. Relations with Domenico Ghirlandaio had meanwhile become a bit strained. Michelangelo had done some drawings from Giotto and Masaccio (a copy of *St. Anthony Tormented by Demons* from the engraving of the German, Martin Schongauer, and other drawings), but the talent that the young apprentice showed had soon aroused dismay and envy in Ghirlandaio, rather than admiration. Probably, as Condivi says, [6] it was Granacci again who introduced Michelangelo into the milieu of the artists that frequented the garden of the Medici; a garden museum, almost an art school, taught by old Bertoldo di Giovanni, who had been a pupil of Donatello's. 565

In the garden Benedetto da Maiano, Andrea Sansovino, Lorenzo di Credi, Rustici, Baccio da Montelupo and Giuliano Bugiardini, some of the best sculptors and painters of the time, worked for the Magnificent Lorenzo de' Medici. From Bertoldo, and perhaps from Benedetto da Maiano as well, Michelangelo learned the technique of sculpture. Some terracotta figures date from this period, as well as a head of a Faun, now lost.

In the garden of Lorenzo de' Medici, Michelangelo also made the acquaintance of Pietro Torrigiano, a proud hot-tempered youth, who was the main actor in an unpleasant episode.

In the church of the Carmine, where Michelangelo often went to study the paintings in Masaccio's chapel, Torrigiano, enraged by Buonarroti's japes and sarcasms, once punched Michelangelo in the nose so hard that " he was carried home as if he were a dead man," as Condivi says.[7] His nose was " twisted " for the rest of his life, and the deformity helped to make his complex of physical inferiority even more acute.

Lorenzo the Magnificent felt Michelangelo's extraordinary talent and was enthusiastic about it. Early in 1490, with Ludovico's permission, he invited him to live with him, almost like an adopted son, thus giving him the opportunity of coming into contact with that refined court of erudite humanists that had such a deep influence on his human and spiritual development. In the palace on Via Larga, around the poet prince in an atmosphere of courteous simplicity, there gathered Poliziano, Marsilio Ficino, Cristoforo Landino, Pico della Mirandola and Domenico Benivieni. Although Michelangelo had never read the classics in the original, he must have absorbed the humanistic culture and Neoplatonic philosophy of those learned men; but it is not easy to determine to what extent those academic discussions and those trends of thought influenced his artistic formation. Inspired by Poliziano, who had told him " the entire fable bit by bit," he did at that time the bas-relief depicting the *Battle of Hercules against the Centaurs*. Also dating from the period in which he lived in the Medici house were the *Madonna della Scala* and, between 1493 and 1494, a *Crucifix* in wood for the prior of the church of Santo Spirito—in gratitude for being allowed to make studies of anatomy by " cutting up bodies " in the hospital for the poor attached to the church.

Michelangelo was deeply grieved by the death of Lorenzo the Magnificent in 1492. Piero, his successor, was not the peer of his father in love, arts and letters or political sagacity. It was unwillingly that Michelangelo went back to live in the house of the Medici when Piero called him there in the winter of 1493 after a heavy snowfall to make a snow statue in the court of the Medici palace. A feeling of unease and dislike for the dissolute conduct of the new prince soon took the form of a desire to flee from the city. An obscure presentiment of the precarious position of the Medici family in ruling Florence, due to the ineptitude and dissoluteness of Lorenzo's eldest son, and sensitivity to the prophetic visions of the courtier Andrea Cardiere concerning the imminent expulsion of the Medici from the city, led Michelangelo, a few weeks before Charles VIII's entry into Florence in 1494, to escape to Venice. After a brief stay there, he went to Bologna, where he accepted the hospitality and friendship of the noble Gianfrancesco Aldovrandi. In Bologna he remained for a little over a year, assisting Aldovrandi in his reading and, we may imagine, in his commentaries on the great Tuscans of the fourteenth century, as well as working on a commission of his own, completing the Arca (Tomb) of St. Dominic by executing the three marble statues missing from the work that Niccolò dell'Arca had left unfinished: an angel, *St. Petronus* and *St. Proclus*. He returned to Florence in November 1495 and did two statuettes, now lost: a *Youthful St. John* and a *Sleeping Cupid*, for Pierfrancesco de' Medici, who was opposed to Piero and had sympathized with the popular revolt.

At that time Florence was in the throes of the polemic centering around Savonarola, and Michelangelo, who had diligently listened to the sermons of the Dominican friar ever since the years he had lived with the Medici, had already made up his mind. For Savonarola, Condivi tells us, " he always had a great affection, the memory of his living voice still being fresh in his mind." [8] The artist's admiration for Savonarola, however, never went so far as to place the artist in the ranks of the true *frateschi* in the political struggle within Florence.

Michelangelo did not take part in the Savonarolan movement, and during the years when the popular party was in power, he was out of the city. There is no doubt, however, that his religious and austere spirit must have been deeply impressed by the fiery words of the Dominican in his sermons in Florence on the Apocalypse, Genesis, and the Lamentations of Jeremiah. It would also seem likely that expectation of the afflictions that were to purify and renew the Church and Italy, which were predicted so often and so eloquently in the friar's preaching, helped, along with other events, to increase the disquiet in Buonarroti that led him to flee Florence in October 1494.[9]

In July 1496, a few months after his return from Bologna, Michelangelo had to make his first trip to Rome. The occasion was his need to justify himself to the Cardinal of San Giorgio, Raffaele Riario, to whom Baldassarre del Milanese had sold the *Cupid*, passing it off as an antique work. Riario had sent the statuette back to Michelangelo on discovering the fraud. Buonarroti remained in Rome until 1501. There, in addition to Riario, of whom he soon became a friend and guest, he met the banker Iacopo Galli, for whom he made a *Bacchus* (now in the Bargello) and a *Cupid* (lost). Through Galli he was presented to the Cardinal of St. Denis, Jean Bilhères de Lagraulas, and got from him a commission to carve a Pietà, which Galli guaranteed would be " the finest work in marble that there is in Rome today

1 Francesco Furini: Michelangelo's mother falls from her horse during the journey to Caprese in Casentino. Florence, Casa Buonarroti.

and that no master would do better today." [10]   To choose the marble for this work, the famous *Pietà* of the Vatican Basilica, Michelangelo made his first trip to Carrara, in November 1497. The commission for the work goes back to this period, while the contract was drawn on August 27, 1498.   The *Pietà* was completed in 1499 and made him famous.   This was the second Pietà he had carved, the first being the one in 1496 for the church of S. Maria a Marcialla in Valdelsa.

Michelangelo's life in Rome was hard and aggravated by the requests for money that his family made on him.   As early as 1497 his father had asked for help to meet a payment to a creditor (Consiglio d'Antonio Cisti, haberdasher) and Michelangelo had answered affectionately and regretfully that he had had many expenses (among them the purchase of marbles) and that " although I have little money—I shall get hold of it... so that you must believe that I too have expenses and troubles, but all the same, what you ask me for, I shall send you, if I have to sell myself as a slave." [11]   Ludovico was sensitive to the difficulties of his far-off son and reproved him affectionately (" I am worried that you have been there so long and, as you write me, have nothing to eat.   If you were in your own home, perhaps you would have something...") [12]   He praised him for his sacrifices in helping his brothers Buonarroto and Giovan Simone set up a shop and was not sparing of advice concerning his health.   When he learned from Buonarroto, who had been in Rome, that Michelangelo was destitute, Ludovico warned him that " poverty is bad because it is a fault that displeases God and people in the world, and in addition will do you harm in body and soul.   While you are young, you can stand this for a while, but when the strength of youth is gone, maladies and infirmities will turn up that are bred by the said difficulties and by living poorly or in destitution... But above all do not be niggardly.   Live moderately and without ostentation, and above all avoid difficulties because your art, if you should fall sick (God preserve you from it), you would be done for... " [13]

Early in 1501 Michelangelo returned to Florence;   the fame of his success in Rome had gone before him.   In Florence, after the fall of Savonarola, a republic had been set up under strong influence by the optimates, whose representative was the Gonfaloniere, Pier Soderini.   Although Michelangelo had listened to Savonarola's preaching, as has been said, and had had high esteem for the friar as master of the spiritual life, he had not followed the party of the " piagnoni " in politics, and after the defeat of the popular party, he allied himself unreservedly with the republican regime that was set up.   He was on excellent terms with Soderini and the richest families in Florence, and they showed their esteem for him, which he reciprocated by doing some of the most important works connected with his name to exalt the new regime. Up to 1505 he had a period of intense activity in Florence accepting commissions that were offered him in great numbers.

From the Consuls of the Arte della Lana and from the Operai di S. Maria del Fiore he received a commission on August 16, 1501 to carry to completion a work in marble that had

2 Matteo Rosselli: Michelangelo is received with great honours by the Priors of the Florentine Republic. Florence, Casa Buonarroti.

been roughed out for some time, " a certain man called the *Giant*." [14] It was a large marble block that had been rough hewn by a Maestro Bartolomeo di Pietro, called Baccellino.[15] The *David* was practically completed by the beginning of 1504, and its emplacement was decided on January 25 of that year.[16] A commission for a bronze *David* was given him by the Signoria on August 12, 1502, on the condition that it should resemble Donatello's work of the same name. The work, intended for Cardinal Pierre de Rohan, was still unfinished in 1508 and was completed in the following year by Benedetto da Rovezzano. The Signoria also commissioned him to do the fresco on one of the walls of the Sala del Consiglio in Palazzo Vecchio; the order for the cartoon of the *Battle of Cascina* was given him by Soderini in the second half of 1504. With the parallel picture of the *Battle of Anghiari* entrusted to Leonardo da Vinci it was intended to celebrate the idea of republican independence. The cartoon was well advanced by the time of Michelangelo's departure for Rome, but both cartoons were broken up shortly thereafter.

During this period Michelangelo did four Madonnas and Child, three sculptures and one painting. The *Bruges Madonna*, a bronze sculpture, begun in the spring of 1501, was completed and sent to the brothers Mouseron of Bruges in 1506, most probably. The Pitti Tondo (*Madonna with Child* and the *Youthful St. John*) was carved for Bartolomeo Pitti between 1503 and 1504; the Taddei Tondo was executed for Taddeo Taddei, perhaps after the Pitti Tondo; the Doni Tondo, the only panel painting depicting the Holy Family, seems to have been done between 1503 and 1504 and is thought to have been completed on the occasion of the marriage of Agnolo Doni to Maddalena Strozzi.

Through Galli, Michelangelo was commissioned by Cardinal Piccolomini, in 1501, to make fifteen small statues for the Piccolomini altar in Siena Cathedral. He did only four (*St. Peter, St. Paul, St. Gregory*, and *St. Pius*), which were completed in 1504. Because of the conditions laid down by the cardinal (small size of the statues, rigidity of the figures because of the narrowness of the niches, and previous approval of the drawings by the cardinal for fear of excessive nudity), Michelangelo took up the work against his will and left it as soon as he got work more suitable to his uncompromising and intolerant artistic spirit.

Again from the Arte della Lana and the Opera di S. Maria del Fiore, on April 24, 1503, he received a commission for twelve statues of the Apostles for S. Maria del Fiore. Of these, Michelangelo began only one, the *St. Matthew*; the figure was already roughed out in March 1505, as appears from a reference to it by Michelangelo in a letter to Giovan Francesco Fattucci in 1524.[17]

In March 1505, probably through Giuliano da Sangallo, Pope Julius II invited Michelangelo to Rome to intrust him with the erection of his tomb. The project for the work, " which for beauty and pride, and great ornament and richness of the statues surpassed every ancient and imperial tomb," as Vasari tells us,[18] was approved by the pontiff, and Michelangelo spent eight months (May to December 1505) in Carrara having the marble quarried for the great work which he had undertaken with unmatched enthusiasm. Back in Rome, he found that the pope had changed his mind, probably because of the imminent military operations against Perugia and Bologna, and because of his desire to build the new church of St. Peter at Bramante's suggestion and design. In compensation, he was entrusted with decorating the vault of the Sistine Chapel. Michelangelo asked for an audience with the pope, but it was not granted: " ... I was put out, that is driven away, and the fellow that was sent to me said that he knew me, but that such was his commission. So that I... went off in great despair," he wrote to Giuliano da Sangallo.[19] On the next day, April 18, 1506, Michelangelo, offended by the affront, fled from Rome, vainly pursued and overtaken at Poggibonsi by five couriers of the pope sent to dissuade him from leaving the city. This was the beginning of what was to be called " the tragedy of the tomb," that was to be on his mind for forty years. The grand plan was to be gradually cut down in the successive contracts with the pontiff's heirs, and Michelangelo was to bear forever within him the torment of not having performed a work in which he could have given full expression to his vocation as a sculptor.

Back in Florence, he resumed work on the cartoon for the *Battle of Cascina* and on the *St. Matthew*. Possibly with the intention of doing something that would please the pontiff, he toyed with the idea of accepting the invitation received from the Turkish Sultan, through the Franciscan friars, to go to Turkey to build a bridge between Constantinople and Pera. Meanwhile, the pope was putting constant pressure on Soderini to persuade Michelangelo to return to Rome. Finally Buonarroti yielded to the imperious insistence of Soderini, to whom Julius II had written three times (July 8 [20] and August 18,[21] and November 21,[22] from Bologna) and for whom it was important to remain on good terms with the pontiff. He agreed to be reconciled with the pope, and submissive but not repentant, went to meet him at Bologna on November 29 of the same year, 1506, bearing a letter of recommendation by Soderini himself, dated November 27, to his brother Francesco, Cardinal of Volterra. In the letter were testimonials to the worth and character of Buonarroti, with words that seem like a prophecy, certifying " him [Michelangelo] to be a fine youth and in his craft unique in Italy, perhaps *etiam in universo*. We can not recommend him too highly," Soderini continued. " He is of such a nature that with fair words and kindness, if he is given them, he will do everything. He must be shown love and favor, and he will do things that will amaze him that sees them. Informing Your Excellency that he has begun a work for the public that will be admirable, namely XII Apostles, 4 ½ ells in V each, which will be a noble work." [23] Michelangelo

3 Giovanni Bilivert: Michelangelo declines the invitation of the Sultan's messengers to go to Constantinople. Florence, Casa Buonarroti.

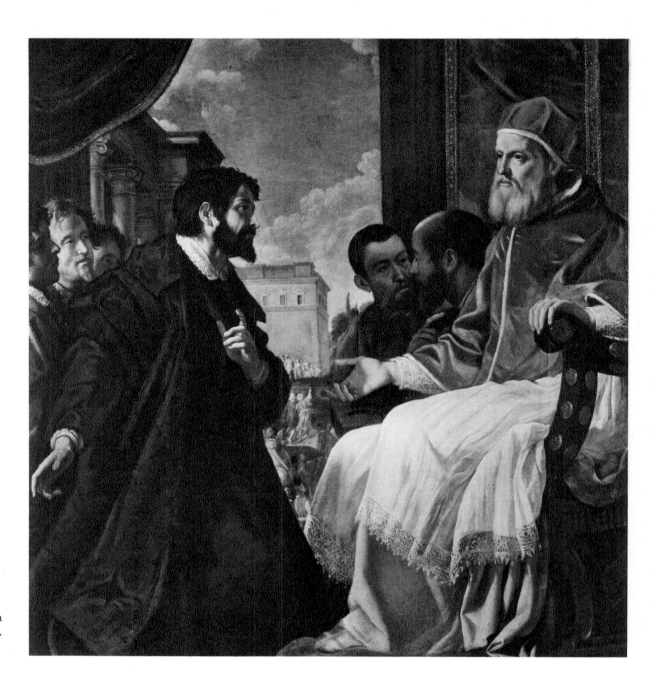

4 Anastasio Fontebuoni: Michelangelo makes an act of submission to Pope Julius II in Bologna. Florence, Casa Buonarroti.

stayed sixteen months in Bologna to complete a large statue of Julius II that the Pontiff had commissioned him to do, a bronze for the façade of the Cathedral of S. Petronio. The statue, finished in January 1508, was destroyed three years later after the return of the Bentivoglios to the city.

Buonarroti returned to Florence at the end of February and Soderini commissioned him to carve a *Hercules and Cacus*. To this end he had written to Alberigo Malaspina, lord of Carrara, on May 10, to reserve for him a certain block of marble, being sure that Michelangelo, who had returned to Rome in April, would turn down the work on the Sistine Chapel. But, on the same day of May 10, Michelangelo signed the contract for the frescoes on the vault of the chapel of Sixtus IV.

For four years Buonarroti labored uninterruptedly and virtually unaided, in the midst of deep solitude. The hardships of a murderous task were made worse by economic difficulties and the thought that he had to help his relatives, to whom he was bound by great love. " I expect to work as long as I can," he wrote to his father in June 1508. " I have not had any money from the pope for thirteen months now and I expect to get some in a month and a half in any case, for I shall have earned much more than what I have got. If they don't give me any, I shall have to borrow money to get back home, for I don't have a cent." [24] On September 18, 1512 he warned his brother Buonarroto " I don't have a farthing and am, so to speak, barefoot and naked, and can not have my balance until I have finished the work, and I have great discomforts and labors." [25]

While he was working on the Sistine Chapel, however, his thoughts were constantly on Florence, concerned both with his father's finances and with the health and establishment of his brothers and the purchase of lands. With great sacrifices, he sent his father a hundred gold ducats on January 1510 for the purchase of the shop " for Buonarroto and the others," and added: " I have no money. What I am sending you I am cutting out of my heart, and I don't feel I have the right to ask for any, because I don't get others to work and I myself work little." [26] The work on the Sistine ground him down. There were phases of discouragement ("... it is a year now that I have not had a farthing from this pope and I don't ask him for any, because my work is not going ahead in a way that makes me feel I deserve any ") [27] alternating with apprehension (" I am in great trouble here and enormous physical labor and have no friends of any kind, so that no more difficulties should be made me, because I couldn't stand another drop.") [28]

When his father told him of a law suit he was involved in for a question of interest on money, Michelangelo replied with generous words of consolation: " I see from your last letter how things are going. I feel badly about it. I can't help you in any other way, but don't let that discourage you, and don't be sad a bit, because if you lose property, you don't lose life. I will earn so much for you that it will be more than you will lose. But I remind you not to think too much of it, for it is a deceptive thing... Think of living and let property go rather than suffer sorrows, for I would rather see you alive and poor, and if you died, I would not want all the gold in the world... " [29]

While always kind and thoughtful towards Ludovico, Michelangelo avoided any expressions of tenderness. His salutations were " Most reverend father " or " Dearest father " and sometimes " To Ludovico," as in two letters dated 1516 and June 1523, harsh and hard in anger. In the first one Michelangelo, hurt and surprised by Ludovico's sudden departure from Florence for Settignano, reacted to his father's accusation of having driven him out of the house for reasons not clearly stated and rejected the calumny, stressing once again that he had always worked to help his father and brothers. He ended by asking humble pardon and inviting him to return: " ... I ask your pardon. Act as though you were forgiving a son of yours that always led a bad life and did you all the harm that can be done in this world. And so I beg you again to pardon me, like the rascal that I am, and don't give me the reputation up there that I drove you away, because that means more to me than you think. I am your son after all!... I beg you to drop all resentment and come." [30] There was a reconciliation, but some years later, for money matters, Ludovico started again to make accusations against his son immediately provoking a strong reaction. After stating the actual terms of the question, Michelangelo expressed his anger in violent terms: " ... I don't know any more what you want of me. If I bother you by living, you have found the way of solving that, and you will get back the keys to the treasure you say I have, and you will be doing right, because all Florence knows that you were a very rich man and that I have always robbed you and deserve to be punished. Great praise you will have for that! Scream and say anything you want about me but don't write to me any more, because you don't let me work." Summarizing how much he had done in the past, he writes " I would have to count up all you have got from me for twenty-five years. I wouldn't want to tell you ... And you put off death to do things like that! God help you! " [31]

Michelangelo was also interested in Giovan Simone, the dissipated and rebellious brother to whom in 1507, from Bologna, he promises that on his return he will do " everything I promised to do for all of you, that is, help you with what I have, as you will desire and as our father will desire. But be of good cheer and tend the *bottega*, as or as much as you can, because I hope you will soon have a *bottega* of your own. If you learn art and are able, it will help you a great deal... " [32] But he is not sparing of the sharpest rebukes when he learns that Giovan Simone has rebelled against his father's advice and even threatened the old man. He writes him a moving letter, full of affectionate anger: " I have been trying for years with good words and deeds to get you to live right and at peace with your father and all of us, and you are still getting worse... Now I am sure you are not my brother, because if you were, you would not threaten my father. You are a beast, and I will treat you like a beast. Know that anyone who sees his father threatened or hurt has to defend him with his life, and that's that... If I come up there, I'll show you things that will make you cry your eyes out and realize what your arrogance is based on... " After the rebuke comes the promise to continue helping him, if he will reform: " ... if you are willing to do right and honor and revere your father... I will help you like the others and in a little while I will make you have a good *bottega*." And in the end he warns him not to destroy in a short time all his labors and sacrifices for the twelve years " that I have been going... in wretchedness all over Italy, submitting to all kinds of indignity, made every effort, worn out my body in all kinds of labor, put my life into a thousand perils, only to help my family..." just when he had succeeded in putting it on its feet financially. [33]

His brother Buonarroto's illness disturbed him deeply and made him realize, in those days of most anxious concern, his love for the sick man and nostalgia for his distant home. He exhorted his father to take good care and not to spare the money needed and to keep him informed about the illness, "... because, if you think it best, I will take post horses and be there in two days, for men are worth more than money." [34] Buonarroto recovered, and firm bonds of affection remained between him and Michelangelo as the many letters exchanged between them attest.

Living a very simple, modest and even frugal life, as can be seen from his letters and from two humble sheets of paper on which the artist carefully notes the pieces of laundry he was having done, [35] Michelangelo managed to send his father, on a number of occasions, considerable sums of money to be invested in houses and farms and thereby provide his family a certain measure of prosperity. Ludovico was free to act as he pleased: "Then do what seems best to you and buy what you please, because what pleases you will please me too," he wrote in 1512. [36] As early as 1506, on his return from Carrara, he had bought a farm in the village of S. Stefano a Pozzolatico, a farm that he was to assign as dowry on June 2, 1537, to his niece Francesca, Buonarroto's daughter. [37] Other farms and houses were bought in 1507, 1508, 1512 and subsequent years (as appears from the report made in 1534) at Settignano, in Via Ghibellina, at S. Stefano in Pane, and at S. Pier Maggiore, [38] and it can be said that on the eve of his leaving for Rome in 1534 he left his brothers in a solid financial position.

The period during which he was working on the frescoes of the Sistine vault was also a period of religious meditation for Michelangelo. His study of the Bible and the physical suffering he had to undergo brought home to him with special force the old call of Savonarola to despise the things of this world and indignation at the flagrant immorality that prevailed at the Roman Curia. In a letter written in October 1512, he recommends to his father: "See to it that you live, and if you can not have earthly honors, as other citizens do, be satisfied with little and live well with Christ and poorly, as I do here, living meanly and paying no attention to life or prestige, that is, to the world, and I live with enormous labor and a thousand suspicions." [39] In these years the artist, sorely tried by labor and sorrows, was haunted by the thought that was to become dominant for the entire course of his long life: the thought of God, the idea of a Divine will operating in reality, a mysterious will present throughout life. The vision of a good and merciful God was always the basis of Michelangelo's thinking and working. He wrote his father on September 5, 1510: "Don't fret, for God did not create us to abandon us." [40] Michelangelo would never cease turning trustfully to the Lord ("I am here unhappy and not in too good health and with much labor and with no guidance and no money, yet I have good hope that God will help me," [41] to thank Him for benefits received, to beg mercy and to pray for a serene and holy death that would give his soul eternal peace.

On October 11, 1512 the tremendous work in the Sistine Chapel was completed and the fresco was unveiled on November 1. In order to execute it, Michelangelo had to study the Bible carefully, and he must have done so in the Jenson edition or that of Nicolò de' Mallermi or de' Mallerbi, both poor editions, reworkings of the old medieval translations based on St. Jerome's Vulgate. But in the Genesis story he seems in a way to have gone beyond the limits of this purely popular culture, so that it seems reasonable to suppose that in painting the Sistine vault frescoes Michelangelo wanted to express his point of view on the polemic that had been raging among the Neoplatonists in the last decades of the fifteenth century concerning the doctrines, of Aristotelian origin, that denied the creation of the world and the immortality of the soul and cast doubt on the credibility of the Bible account; disputes that he must have been aware of, even if superficially. [42]

6 Iacopo da Empoli: Michelangelo submits the plans for the Laurentian Library to Pope Leo X. Florence, Casa Buonarroti.

The political events of 1512 (Spanish invasion of Tuscany, sack of Prato and end of the republican regime in Florence) greatly increased the spiritual stress of the artist. Terrified and dismayed by the course of events, he recommended that his family look to saving his life without delay: "... be the first to flee," he wrote to his brother Buonarroto. [43] When the danger of the Spanish occupation of Florence had passed and Giuliano de' Medici, who had come back to Florence on September 1, had restored Medici rule of the city, Michelangelo took care to recommend prudent conduct: "I do not believe that it is necessary to leave any more, but lay low and do not be friendly or familiar with any one except God, and do not say anything, either good or bad, about any one, because how things will turn out is still unknown. Just tend to your own affairs." [44] He was to feel the same dismay in 1529 during the siege of Florence. In the face of the vague menace of personal danger from an unknown person, of whom he was later to wonder whether he was an emissary of God or the Devil, Michelangelo was to flee in terror to Venice without hesitating.

The Medici's return to Florence brought fears to Ludovico, who lamented of it to Michelangelo; either because being suspect to the Medici he would no longer be able to round out the family revenues with the proceeds of public office (Ludovico had often obtained minor positions in offices and small towns) or because of the levy of sixty ducats that the new lords had imposed on him. Michelangelo promised his father to help him financially and intercede for him with Giuliano de' Medici; and admonished him: "One must have patience and put oneself in God's hands and repent one's errors, for these adversities come solely and mostly through pride and ingratitude, and there never were people prouder or more ungrateful than the Florentines. So if punishment comes, there is good reason. As to the sixty ducats you tell me you have to pay, it seems to me a dishonorable thing and I was indignant about it. Yet 571 we must have patience, since this is God's pleasure....Still, if you should see that you were treated worse than others, go ahead and refuse to pay and rather let what you have be taken and let me know. But if they treat the others the way they do you, have patience and trust in God." [45] These words undoubtedly reflect Michelangelo's conviction that the misfortunes of Florence were a just punishment by God for the sins of the Florentines, misfortunes that had to be borne patiently, without rebelling, but with the intention of repenting; and it certainly is not out of the question that Buonarroti was writing under the influence of the preaching of Savonarola, and that in all the events of his times he believed he saw the accomplishment of the friar's prophecies and that in the face of the Divine wrath he felt, each time, the impulse to humble himself and flee.[46]

On March 6, 1513, a few days after the death of Julius II, a new contract for the Pontiff's tomb was signed between Michelangelo and the pope's heirs, the Della Rovere family. The grandiose original project, which was to have been a structure with four faces, eighteen ells long and twelve wide, at the crossing of the new church of St. Peter's, and with forty statues in addition to ornaments, was reduced to only three sides, with twenty-eight statues. Michelangelo began to carve three figures, the two *Slaves* or *Prisons*, and the *Moses*, the execution of which is not generally thought to antecede 1513.

Michelangelo was in Carrara selecting the marble for the statues of the tomb when he received an invitation from the new pope Leo X (Giovanni di Lorenzo de' Medici) to go to Rome for the commission of designing the façade of the church of San Lorenzo in Florence. He left Carrara December 5, 1516, and presented a drawing to the pope in which the pontiff himself made changes, and a model which was made by Baccio d'Agnolo. Michelangelo, not satisfied with this model, made another in terracotta and sent it to the pope at the end of December 1517, with further changes from the design previously agreed on. Under the contract entered into on January 19, 1518, Michelangelo undertook to execute the work in eight years, for the price of forty thousand gold ducats. Also included in the project were twenty-two statues, including six in bronze, and seven bas-reliefs. Between January 1517 and March 1520 Michelangelo made many trips to Carrara, Pietrasanta and Serravezza to select marbles for this, his first architectural work, which he entered into with great enthusiasm: "... I have spirit enough to make this work, the façade of San Lorenzo, the mirror of all Italy for architecture and sculpture," he wrote from Carrara to Domenico Buoninsegni on May 2, 1517.[47] In December of that year he had already had the ground in front of the church excavated, and the foundations and vaults to support the steps erected. Soon, however, his enthusiasm had to give way to the bitterness of being unable to carry out the work for which he had worked and sacrificed himself for more than three years; on March 10, 1520 the pontiff rescinded the contract and released the artist from all obligation, producing in him resentment for "the enormous insult"[48] he had received. The reason for this unilateral decision was probably not shortage of funds, as Vasari gives us to understand,[49] but the altered attitude of the pope and his cousin Cardinal Giulio, archbishop of Florence, after the death of Lorenzo de' Medici, Duke of Urbino, on May 4, 1519. This loss, which struck the Medici family only a few years after the death of Giuliano, Duke of Nemours, was like a funeral veil thrown over the Medici hopes, as if to warn them that the time had come to turn their minds to funerary undertakings and erect a mausoleum for the remains of the deceased members of their family, rather than to erect works celebrating their power.[50] This explanation can be maintained with great probability on the basis of a very valuable piece of testimony, a "Memory" by Giovan Battista Figiovanni, canon of San Lorenzo, a familiar and table companion of Cardinal Giulio de' Medici, the future Pope Clement VII.[51] In 1519 Cardinal Giulio confided secretly to Figiovanni that he had in mind "spending about 50,000 ducats on San Lorenzo, the library and the sacristy, to accompany the one already [made] and it will be called a chapel, with many tombs to bury the deceased ancestors that are in storage: Lorenzo and Giuliano, our forebears, and Giuliano and Lorenzo, brothers and nephews."[52]

Leo X's changed intentions as to the construction of the façade caused new bitterness for Michelangelo, who was under suspicion, as voiced in a letter from Cardinal Giulio, of having preferred the Carrara quarries (belonging to Marquis Alberigo Cybo Malaspina, lord of that city) to those of Pietrasanta (under Medici jurisdiction) in order to get illicit gains. This was one more hard blow to Buonarroti, already hard hit by his disappointments over the tomb of Julius II and Bramante's rivalry. Attesting this sorrow is a letter dated December 21, 1518, to his friend Leonardo di Compagno, a saddler, who had urged him to come back to Rome to answer the accusations and slanders going the rounds concerning him: "I am urged in your last letter, and I appreciate it greatly, because I see that you do this for my sake. But I tell you plainly, from another point of view, that these urgings are so many stabs for me, because I am dying of grief at not being able to do what I should like to have done, by my bad luck."[53] Cardinal Giulio, by order of the pope, had directed him to select the marble from the quarries at Pietrasanta and Serravezza in territory under Florentine dominion, and Michelangelo considered these marbles to be inferior in quality to those of Carrara from which, moreover, transportation to Florence was easier.

We see from Figiovanni's "Memory" that the idea of constructing the New Sacristy and the Library had been born at the same time in the mind of Cardinal Giulio, although the two structures were begun at different times; the first, as is seen from the same "Memory," on

7 Matteo Rosselli: Michelangelo directs the works for the fortifications of San Miniato during the siege of Florence. Florence, Casa Buonarroti.

8 Valerio Marucelli: Michelangelo, in Venice, is asked by the Doge Gritti to make the plan of the Rialto Bridge. Florence, Casa Buonarroti.

November 4, 1519, and the second in August 1524, when work on the Sacristy had reached the lantern.[54] Michelangelo was entrusted with both commissions. The sculptures for the new " chapel," which initially were to have been six in number (Lorenzo the Magnificent and Giuliano de' Medici, Giuliano Duke of Nemours and Lorenzo Duke of Urbino, Leo X and Cardinal Giulio), were reduced to two, those of the two dukes, with the allegories of *Day* and *Night*, *Dawn* and *Twilight*. The statues were finished, not all of them entirely, between 1524 and 1534. Construction of the Library, begun in 1524, was only partly directed by Michelangelo, and was terminated much later by Vasari and Ammannati. It was only in 1559 that Michelangelo, urged and entreated by Vasari, many Florentine friends and Duke Cosimo himself, consented to send Bartolomeo Ammannati " a little clay model of the Library staircase." [55]

The only work completed by Buonarroti during the four years in which he was occupied on the projects for the façade of San Lorenzo was the *Christ Risen* for the church of S. Maria sopra Minerva in Rome, commissioned by Bernardo Cencio and Metello Vari in 1514. A first version of the work, presented to Vari because of imperfections in the marble, has been lost.

In 1523, with the support of Adrian VI, the new pope, the heirs of Julius II directed Michelangelo to bring the tomb to completion according to the project contemplated in the contract dated July 8, 1516 (which had taken the place of, and further reduced, the project of the 1513 contract), providing for the work to be completed in nine years. Michelangelo, although once more busy with the work on San Lorenzo, confirmed to him by Clement VII, successor to Adrian VI, sent a new design to Rome in 1526, one simpler and of more rapid execution. But it did not please the Della Rovere. Thus, the 1516 design was not carried out either. Meanwhile, the political events of 1527 in Rome intervened, resulting in the overthrow of Medici rule in Florence. All work on the church of San Lorenzo was suspended, as Figiovanni's " Memory " confirms.[56] Michelangelo put himself at the service of the restored republican regime and on August 22, 1528 received a commission from Gonfaloniere Niccolò Capponi to carve a *Hercules and Cacus* from a block of marble that Clement VII had entrusted to Baccio Bandinelli to make into a Hercules. Michelangelo transformed the design into the group representing Samson with two Philistines. Meanwhile, the republican government had to defend itself from the pope's armies, and Michelangelo was called in by Capponi on October 3, 1528 as fortifications expert. Some months later, on January 10, 1529, he was elected a member of the Magistracy of the Nine for Ordinance and Militia and prepared a number of designs for the defense of Florence, especially in the region of the hill of San Miniato where it

573

9 Cristofano Allori: Michelangelo seeks inspiration for his poems. Florence, Casa Buonarroti.

was most exposed. These drawings, both for quantity and quality, undoubtedly have a political component. Subsequent events disappointed his dream of making Florence a bulwark of republican liberties and saddened him deeply. Michelangelo, probably out of desire for honor or out of dislike for Capponi, decided not to go with the oligarchs, who had gone over to the side of the pontiff, but to continue to prepare the defense of the city, thus giving support, in the most evident way, to the popular party, the direct heir of the Piagnoni and the most resolute in defense to the death. And the popular party took him into its ranks, precisely because he had been " created by the Medici."

On April 6, 1529 the Signoria elected him " Governor and Procurator General for the fortifications." In that capacity Michelangelo was sent in June to Pisa and Livorno to direct the defense works of those cities. In the following month he was sent to Ferrara to study those fortifications. He returned to Florence in September and stayed there only a few days. " On September twenty-first," he wrote to Giovan Battista della Palla, " a man came out of the Porta a San Nicolò, where I was on the bastions, and whispered in my ear that he was not going to wait any longer to save his life, and he came home with me, and there he dined and brought me mounts, and never left me until he got me out of Florence, showing me that that was best for me. Whether God or the Devil sent him, I do not know." [57] So Michelangelo fled from Florence and went to Venice, with the intention of going to France. On September 30 the republic declared him a rebel and outlawed him. What Michelangelo wrote to della Palla is hardly credible; the motives for his flight are generally considered to be Buonarroti's conviction of the imminent treason of Malatesta Baglioni, commander of the Florentine militia. Figiovanni's " Memory " (which, incidentally, is wrong as to the place to which Michelangelo fled; it gives Ferrara, perhaps confusing it with Buonarroti's previous trip to that city) tells us that the reason for the artist's sudden flight was his desire to put his own money in a place of safety: " He had absented himself," Figiovanni relates, " going to Ferrara to save his treasure threatened by the people for the needs of the war." [58] And it may well be that this was what he did, either to make sure that his family, whose prosperity had always been close to his heart, should not be deprived of the fruits of his labors, or to prevent his money from being taken to meet the expenses of the war.[59]

Back in Florence towards the middle of November, after the Signoria had sent him a safe conduct to enter the city, he immediately resumed his position as governor of the fortifications: on November 23 his outlawry was commuted to a lesser penalty—exclusion from the Consiglio Maggiore for three years. In December he lent the Signoria a thousand ducats. On August 12; 1530 the besieged Florentine republic surrendered. Fleeing the revenge of the victors, Michelangelo hid, not in the tower of San Nicolò Oltrarno as Vasari states, but in Figiovanni's house in the cloister of San Lorenzo. Figiovanni's " Memory " finally sheds light on this disputed incident, telling how he gave Michelangelo asylum and got his property to safety. Up to that point Figiovanni's relations with Michelangelo had not been of the best (" Chief of the architecture [of the chapel] was Michelangelo Simoni alone, with whom Job could not have patience for a single day," he says of Buonarroti at another point in his " Memory.") [60] But it is due to him that the artist's life was saved in escaping from Alessandro Corsini, " tool of the pope," who wanted to kill him by order of Baccio Valori, undoubtedly acting for Alessandro de' Medici. Michelangelo asked " a thousand pardons " [61] of Figiovanni who showed himself a true and generous friend in this emergency. Certainly, this attempt on his life weighed heavily in Buonarroti's life and was the main reason why the artist refused to return to Florence after 1534; the reason for his being " bitter " towards " that ungrateful people/where only the just are unsafe." [62]

A short time later Michelangelo was pardoned by Clement VII. With the skies clear at last, he resumed work on the statues of the Sacristy and the Library. The pontiff had ordered Figiovanni, who in the meantime had become Prior of San Lorenzo and Superintendent of the Work, to continue to pay Buonarroti the 50 scudi a month that he had received in the period prior to the assault. A letter from Sebastiano del Piombo, dated April 29, 1531, attests

10 Francesco Furini: Michelangelo refuses the money sent to him by Paul III as payment for the plans of the building of St. Peter's. Florence, Casa Buonarroti.

574

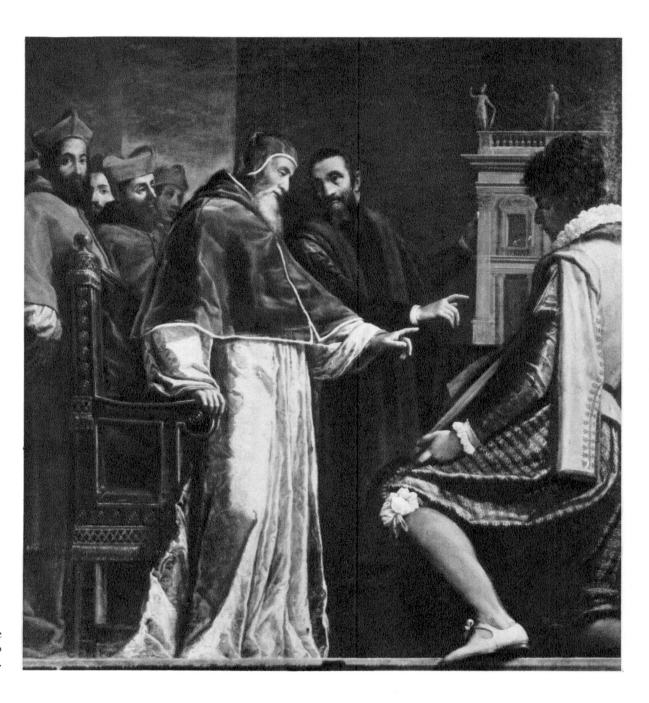

Fabrizio Boschi: Michelangelo submits the
model for the layout of the Campidoglio to
Pope Giulio III. Florence, Casa Buonarroti.

the pontiff's good will towards Michelangelo: "... for he loves you, knows you, and adores
your things, and enjoys them as much as any man has ever enjoyed them... And he speaks
of you with so much honor and affection, as he says," adding in connection with Buonarroti's
republican position in 1527-1530: " It is true that on some occasions [Clement VII] was
saddened by some slanders related to him, at the time of the siege of Florence: he shrugged
his shoulders and said, ' Michelangelo is wrong, don't do him any harm.' But, brother, learn
to know him and take things by the good side and be of good cheer." [63]

In 1531 Michelangelo was very sick, so much so that his friends feared for his life. He was
working very hard and neglected food and rest. The pontiff was informed of this and ordered
him, on pain of excommunication, not to engage in any other work of painting or sculpture
except on the Medici tombs, in order to enable him to recover his health and cope with the
work on San Lorenzo with a tranquil mind.

During the siege Michelangelo had done the " tempera colored " painting of *Leda* for Duke
Alfonso d'Este of Ferrara, but the painting was not delivered because of an act of discourtesy
by the Duke's messenger who had come to Florence to take it. Instead, it was presented, along
with a number of cartoons and drawings, to Antonio Mini, who took it to France. He had
also carved an *Apollo* for Baccio Valori in 1530, and in April of the following year did the
cartoon with " Noli me tangere " for the Marquis D'Avalos, which was to be painted by
Pontormo. In addition, he accepted a commission for a drawing of the *Madonna and Child* for a
gentleman of Bologna. Another commission for San Lorenzo was the *Reliquary Tribune*, earlier
designed as a ciborium for the high altar; the Tribune was erected between October 1531
and July 1532 on the inner wall of the façade.

In April 1532 Michelangelo went to Rome to be present at the final negotiations between
the pontiff and Giovanni Maria Della Porta, representing Francesco Maria Della Rovere,
Duke of Urbino, for the tomb of Julius II; the negotiations led to the new contract (the fourth
one) dated April 29. However, Michelangelo was not present at the signing of the contract,
having been sent to Florence by the pope. Superseding all previous agreements, the contract
stipulated that Michelangelo was to undertake to make a new design for the tomb, with six
statues, and to complete it, along with the architectural portions, in three years. The monument, which was thus still further reduced from the original project, was to be located in the
church of S. Pietro in Vincoli.

12 Domenico Cresti known as Passignano: Michelangelo shows Pope Paul IV the model of the dome of St. Peter's. Florence, Casa Buonarroti.

After a brief interlude in Florence, Michelangelo returned to Rome on August 25, and remained there until the end of June, 1533. On September 25, 1533, he met at San Miniato al Tedesco with Clement VII, on his way to France.

Almost certainly, the first understanding with the pope for the frescoes of the *Last Judgment* in the Sistine Chapel, and hence the first studies for the second great painting enterprise of the artist, go back to a period prior to the pontiff's voyage to France. When the pope came back to Rome on December 10, 1533, where Michelangelo had been since the end of October, the project had already been agreed on. The choice of subject, which was justified formally by contemporary biographers, has been reevaluated in modern times as the result of the pontiff's personal initiative, not only structurally new but fully in tune with the moment in history. Condivi relates that the pope " having thought of more and more things about this, as a man of good judgment would, finally decided to have him do the day of the Last Judgment." [64] Michelangelo was not too pleased to accept this new and exacting commission, especially because of the further delay it would involve in the tomb of Julius II, according to the 1532 contract. As Condivi relates, he tried to " get out of it as best he could, and when he could not, postponed it; and pretending to be busy on the cartoon, as he was in part, he secretly worked on the statues that were to go on the tomb." [65]

During this period another great sorrow was added to the loss of his brother Buonarroto, dead of the plague in 1528; this was the death of his father, who died in the villa at Settignano toward the end of 1533. Now that his father was dead, staying in Florence meant less to Michelangelo. His relations with his other brothers, Giovan Simone and Gismondo (Leonardo had become a Dominican monk), had never been as affectionate as those with Ludovico and Buonarroto; but that was not to exempt him from feeling himself obligated to help them as in the past. In April 1532 he wrote to Giovan Simone, who had returned after twenty years of seeking his fortune in Lisbon, that he was ready to help him in case of need: "... and when you will need help, while I am not there, write to me and I will always help you wherever I am." [66] In the following year, after recalling how much hardship he had gone through for the sake of his family, he declared " I will never fail you with what I can, for I consider my duty and not your words," [67] and he did not neglect to recommend that faithful " mona Margherita " should not be forgotten.

Moreover, the situation in Florence was particularly ticklish for him. Michelangelo still

13 Cosimo Gamberucci: Michelangelo and Francesco di Cosimo de' Medici in Rome. Florence, Casa Buonarroti.

576

14 Francesco Furini: Michelangelo's death. Florence, Casa Buonarroti.

feared the vengeful wrath of Duke Alessandro, now absolute master of the city. It is not hard to imagine that the prospect of working outside of the city was not displeasing to him. Evidently, his relations with the Duke were none of the best. As Condivi reports, Michelangelo " was in deadly fear because Duke Alessandro hated him, being, as everyone knows, a fierce and vindictive young man. There is no doubt that, except for the pope, he would have got rid of him." [68] Things became still more strained after an incident arose to complicate matters. The Duke had had Michelangelo asked to advise him in connection with the construction of a fortress designed to hold the people in check and increase the security of the regime. Michelangelo had refused, objecting that this work had not been commissioned of him by the pope, an answer that definitively exasperated the already hostile attitude of the Duke. " And certainly [Michelangelo] was helped by the Lord God," Condivi adds, " in that he was not in Florence at the death of Clement." [69] Clement VII had protected him and helped get back from Duke Alessandro the money lent to the Signoria during the siege; it may well be that this victory of the artist was not unconnected with the attempt on his life in 1530.

In September 1534 Michelangelo settled permanently in Rome, where the job of painting the Sistine fresco awaited him, and where he was called by his affectionate friendship with Tommaso de' Cavalieri.

A few days after Michelangelo's arrival in Rome Clement VII died and was succeeded by Paul III Farnese. Michelangelo hoped to be free at last to devote himself to work on the tomb of Julius II, but despite his remonstrances the new pontiff confirmed the old project of his predecessor, who had had it in mind for thirty years, as Condivi tells us, and which he would not allow to be neglected. And Michelangelo had to obey, although he had ideas of escaping to Genoa or withdrawing to Urbino.

In August 1532 he met in Rome Tommaso de' Cavalieri, a young Roman patrician of unusual intelligence and a lover of art, famous for the beauty and harmony of his person. Sentiments of admiration, sympathy and esteem marked their relations, which were primarily relations between two artists; between master and disciple. Vasari tells how, knowing him " much inclined to these *virtù* (viz., the arts), in order for him to learn to draw he made him many of the most wonderful drawings in black and red pencil of divine heads; and then he drew for him a Ganymede carried off to heaven by Jove's bird; a Tityus with the vulture eating his heart; the fall of the sun's chariot with Phaethon into the Po and a Bacchanalia of *putti*, each of which is a most splendid thing in itself, and drawings never seen before or since." [70] Thus, Michelangelo was his drawing master, but he certainly was fascinated by Cavalieri's physical beauty, so much so that he did for him what he never was willing to do for anyone else, a portrait, for, Vasari says, " he abhorred making a likeness unless it was of infinite beauty." [71]

For Tommaso, Michelangelo wrote letters and poems of Petrarchian inspiration, full of love and passion, while Cavalieri's letters show respectful veneration and affectionate gratitude for the old master. Buonarroti's love for young Tommaso was a pure and totally disinterested love, a love of beauty as a witness of God; it was a love entirely spiritual and almost sacred, understood as a high and noble sentiment of friendship for the virtues and beauty of the youth, for his eloquence and intelligence, for his culture. It was the agreement of two souls that felt each needed the other. And the best proof of the purity of their feelings is the duration of this mutual affection; it lasted until the death of the artist. Cavalieri was of help to him in business as well; it was thanks to him that the master, now very old, completed the wood model for the dome of St. Peter's. It was Cavalieri who was with him at the moment of death and jealously preserved Michelangelo's drawings for the Campidoglio.

On September 1, 1535 Paul III named Michelangelo painter, sculptor and architect of the apostolic palace. The work on the *Judgment*, begun in the summer of that year, was completed in six years. The work was finished in 1541, unveiled on November 1, and opened to the public for Christmas of that year.

During the period of the *Judgment*, Michelangelo worked on only a single piece of sculpture, certainly after 1539. This was the *Brutus* (later finished by Tiberio Calcagni), at the invitation of his friend Donato Giannotti, who had commissioned it for Cardinal Niccolò Ridolfi, a Florentine exile in Rome. Carved only two years after the assassination of Duke Alessandro by Lorenzino, this work has a significance that leaves no doubts as to the inclination of the 577

15 Agostino Ciampelli: Solemn funeral of Michelangelo in San Lorenzo in Florence. Florence, Casa Buonarroti.

artist's mind almost ten years after the siege. Since that stormy period, Michelangelo had remained substantially on his republican position of Soderini's time. At Rome he had friendly relations not only with the *émigrés* of the popular party but also with those of the oligarchical party that had opposed the republic and who, in exile, had joined forces with the republican exiles. These were the Strozzi, the two Ridolfi cardinals, Salviati and Gaddi, Donato Giannotti, Luigi Del Riccio, Baccio Valori himself and even descendants of the Medici—Cardinal Ippolito and Lorenzino. During the period of illness that struck him between 1544 and 1546, Michelangelo was the guest of Luigi Del Riccio at the Roman house of the Strozzi, to whom Del Riccio was attached, and it can be said that it was the care that his friend lavished on him that enabled him to get through the crisis. Buonarroti repaid the kindness by presenting the Strozzi with two *Prisons* he had carved for the tomb of Julius II, " a truly princely gift that proves the warmth of Michelangelo's feelings towards this house of unshakable adversaries of Cosimo I." [72] Nonetheless, Michelangelo, writing to his nephew Leonardo in March 1548, said he had broken off all connections with the Strozzi,[73] but this must have been a statement designed to calm his family and prevent reprisals against them by the Duke, who on March 11 of that year had outlawed conspirators and rebels and their descendants. In point of fact, as late as 1560 Roberto Strozzi was acting as intermediary between Michelangelo and Catherine de' Medici, queen of France, who had wanted Buonarroti to make a monument to her late husband, Henry II.[74] Michelangelo never accepted Duke Cosimo's repeated invitations to return to Florence, although always making courteous replies. Nor did he yield to flattering offers of the highest offices in the state, which came to him indirectly, as can be seen from a letter sent by Bishop Alfonso Tornabuoni to Giovan Francesco Lottini, secretary of Cosimo I, on October 8, 1546: " This morning I did not get to say all that I had to say, and I say it now. I asked His Excellency for a letter of credentials for Michelangelo, the divine sculptor, and request him to give me authority or commission to promise him great things to get him to return, perhaps a place on the 48 (i. e., in the Senate of 48), exempt, or any office he might wish..." [75]

The period of Michelangelo's work on the fresco on the back wall of the Sistine Chapel was also a period of intense spiritual travail, in which a most important role was played by Vittoria Colonna, Marchioness of Pescara.

Vittoria Colonna, widow of Ferrante Francesco d'Avalos since 1525, was a Roman noblewoman, not beautiful, it would seem, but gifted with remarkable intelligence and nobility of character. She was fifteen years younger than Buonarroti, who made her acquaintance in Rome almost certainly between 1536 and 1538. Endowed with ardent Christian faith, Vittoria Colonna had had restless years of disappointing religious experiences, at first following the lectures of the Spaniard Francesco Valdès at Ischia, where she was living with her family, and then, in Rome, being attracted by the preaching of Bernardino Ochino. Between 1536 and 1537 she had had her first contacts with Ignatius Loyola; then came three years that were decisive for her interior life, years spent in the convent of S. Caterina in Viterbo, from which she often went to Rome to meet Buonarroti. At the end of 1544 she moved to Rome permanently, being now attracted to the charitable activities of the Company of Grace instituted by Loyola. Here liberal, humanist, cultured Catholicism had changed into the militant Catholicism of the Jesuits; her spirit was serene at last, and she spent her last years in the convent of the Benedictine nuns of S. Anna de' Funari. She had in common with Michelangelo an ardent faith in Christ and a deeply felt aspiration to the inner purification and reform of the Church. Between the two there was affectionate friendship, and not what malicious tongues said of them at the time. Michelangelo summed up their relations in a letter to Fattucci three years after Colonna's death: " I am sending you one or two of the tales I wrote for the Marchioness of Pescara, who loved me greatly and I her no less. Death took a great friend from me." [76] The verses that Michelangelo wrote for her, in addition to his few letters, attest his " honorable and most sweet " love, sublimated into a more and more intense spirituality, from the suffering of earthly love and tormenting sense of inferiority to awareness of the illuminating beauty of the beloved, the mediatrix between man and God.[77] It has been said that a religious conversion matured in Buonarroti's mind during the period of the *Last Judgment* and thereafter; but it would be more exact to speak of a higher spiritualization,

16 Tiberio Titi: Leonardo Buonarroti has the monument erected to Michelangelo in Santa Croce in Florence. Florence, Casa Buonarroti.

579

17 Inside of Casa Buonarroti in Florence.

a deepening of religious feeling in Michelangelo's mind under the influence of Vittoria Colonna's Jesuit Catholicism. Her influence on him consisted " above all in this deepened Catholicism, oriented towards reform of the souls of the faithful and towards internal reform of the Church." [78]

In the poems he wrote her, there is still the soaring Platonism of the poems written for Cavalieri, but now purified of all sensual elements; in them the love for Vittoria Colonna appears as an image of the love of God.[79] Testimony to this purest of loves, to Michelangelo's devotion to the noble poetess and to her admiration for him is to be seen in some sections of the *Dialoghi* of Francisco de Hollanda.

Michelangelo executed some works for Vittoria Colonna that are now lost: a *Pietà*, a *Christ Crucified* and a *Samaritan Woman*. She gave him a collection of over a hundred sonnets. The two often met to hear the reading of the *Letters of St. Paul* in the church of S. Silvestro al Quirinale. Buonarroti grieved deeply at her death, towards the end of February 1547. " He did not complain of anything," Condivi relates, " except that when he went to see her as she departed this life, he did not kiss her forehead and face as he kissed her hand." [80]

The *Last Judgment* aroused much criticism. It was admired by those who realized its artistic value but censured by the supporters of the Counter Reformation. Michelangelo was deeply hurt, and his bitterness was increased by the insults and insolence of Pietro Aretino in his famous letter in November 1545, accusing him of impiety for having profaned with obscene figures " the major temple of God." [81]

After finishing the fresco of the *Judgment* Michelangelo hoped once more to be able to go back to work on the tomb of Julius II, but again was frustrated by Paul III's desire to have him paint the altar wall of the Cappella Paolina, construction of which had recently been completed. As long ago as 1536 the pontiff, by a Brief dated November 17, had expressly released Michelangelo, who had been forced to devote himself to the *Judgment*, from any responsibilities assumed under the 1532 contract. On November 23, 1541, after the fresco had been unveiled, the pope intervened with Guidobaldo, Duke of Urbino and heir of the Della Rovere, to get him to agree to have other artists finish the tomb under Michelangelo's direction, in order to enable Michelangelo to work on the Cappella Paolina fresco. The Duke proved amenable and consented to having Michelangelo do only three of the six statues contemplated. This led to the new contract, the last in the series, on August 20, 1542, providing that only one statue was to be completed by Michelangelo, the *Moses* (which, incidentally, had already been carved at the time of the 1513 contract), while the other two (no longer the two *Prisons*, but those of *Leah*, or the *Active Life*, and *Rachel*, or the *Contemplative Life*, according to a wish of Michelangelo expressed to the pope and accepted by Guidobaldo) would be finished by Raffaello da Montelupo. The architectural part was done at the end of 1544; the statues, probably in February of the following year. Thus ended, after forty years, the " tragedy of the tomb," a long period of sufferings, frustrations and humiliations for Michelangelo (" It would have been better for me to have been put out to make matchsticks in my early years, and then I would not have had so much sorrow... ") [82]—a period in which he had seen the great dream of his youth vanish. He put the blame for his misfortunes on Bramante and Raphael, as he wrote in October 1542, perhaps to Bishop Marco Vigerio or a prelate of the Roman Curia: " All the discord between Pope Julius and me was [due to] the envy of Bramante and Raphael da Urbino; and that was the reason why he never carried out his tomb in his lifetime, to ruin me, and Raphael had good reason for that, for what art he had, he had got from me." [83]

Michelangelo took on the two frescoes in the Cappella Paolina against his will: " ...I shall paint without satisfaction and do discontented things," he wrote in the same letter of October 1542. [84] He completed the work in about eight years, doing the *Conversion of St. Paul* between 1542 and 1545 and the *Crucifixion of St. Peter* between 1546 and 1550. Over this long period, in addition to completion of the tomb of Julius II, he had to engage in three architectural projects of considerable importance: the fabric of St. Peter's, the Campidoglio complex and completion of Palazzo Farnese.

After the death of Antonio da Sangallo the Younger, the pontiff in October 1546 named Michelangelo " *commissarium, praefectum, operarium et architectorem quoad vixeret.*" [85] Buonarroti, in his old age, was once more forced to accept. " I call God to witness," he wrote Vasari in May 1557, " that I was against my will with the utmost force put by Pope Paul on the fabric of St. Peter's in Rome ten years ago." [86] However, the artist laid down as his conditions that he should be free to alter existing designs and that he should not receive any compensation. Under his direction work on the Vatican Basilica went forward as it never had for the previous forty years. Despite the trouble and bitternesses caused him by the disciples of Sangallo, Buonarroti brought about a great change in the design of the edifice, bringing it back faithfully to the primitive design of Bramante, as a Greek cross with a central dome, resulting in a church that was " clear, open, luminous and freestanding." [87] He took on the task almost as though it were a religious mission, " because, as many believe, and I, too, I had been assigned it by God." [88] In the seventeen years that he was in charge of work on the cathedral, he had to cope with and overcome the annoyances and slanders from the side of the " Sangallo sect " (which included, among others, Nanni di Baccio Bigio and Pirro Ligorio) going so far as to accuse him of having gone astray in the construction of the windows so that one of the chapels was dark. But his character was not one that was given to making concessions; the opposition of the Sangallo faction made him feel a greater attachment to the work and did not lead him to yield to the temptation of giving up the enterprise, either because he feared that his design would be altered by others, or in order not to " give occasion for the thieves to come back to rob, as they used to, and still hoped to." [89]

As for the Campidoglio, which was then a mass of structures without any relationship to the city below, Michelangelo had been called in as early as 1537. At that time he had been consulted with reference to the pontiff's intention to transfer the statue of Marcus Aurelius to the square in front of the Senatorial Palace. Michelangelo had opposed the transfer, showing that he already had in mind an arrangement of the Capitoline region into which the statue could not have been set without spoiling the architectural structure of the square. The statue was later set up by Michelangelo in 1538, on a rectangular base in the center of the square, facing as it does today.

Buonarroti designed a unified group of three buildings to surround the square on three sides; the staircase that takes up the fourth side was begun in 1544 and completed in 1552.

On March 20, 1546, Buonarroti was granted Roman citizenship. In the same year the project he presented for completing the Palazzo Farnese was chosen by the pontiff over those of other artists, such as Sebastiano del Piombo, Perino del Vega and Giorgio Vasari. Buonarroti's share in the building consisted in completing the cornice and the second story.

In the meantime, his mind, already sorely tried by the sorrows of life, had new sufferings to cope with: in January 1544, the death of young Francesco (Cecchino) Bracci, nephew of Luigi del Riccio, of whom Buonarroti was very fond; in June of the same year, a serious illness that threatened his own life; in 1546 the death of his friend Del Riccio, followed soon (February 1547) by that of Vittoria Colonna; in 1548 and 1555, the loss of his two brothers Giovan Simone and Gismondo; and on December 3, 1555, the death of the faithful Urbino.

Michelangelo had deep feelings of gratitude and esteem for his servant and right-hand man, Francesco d'Amadore di Casteldurante, known as Urbino; he had a delicate, almost fatherly affection for him because of his care and attention over the long period they were together. The letter of February 23, 1556 in which Michelangelo gave Vasari the sad news is one of the most beautiful and moving he had ever written, bringing out what the dominant motives of his life were, the thought of God and the desire for death. " You know," he wrote Vasari, " that Urbino is dead, which has been a very great grace of God to me but to my grave loss and infinite sorrow. The grace is that while he was alive he kept me alive, and in dying has taught me to die, not with displeasure but with desire for death. I had him twenty-six years and found him always most helpful and faithful, and now that I had made him rich and hoped to have him the staff and support of my old age, he has gone, and I have no other hope than to see him again in Paradise. And God has shown me a sign of this in the most happy death he had. More than dying he regretted leaving me alive in this traitorous world with so many cares, although the best part of me has gone with him, and all I have left is infinite misery..." [90] The year before, on June 22, 1555, he had confided to Vasari that " no thought is born in me that does not have death carved on it, and may it please God to hold

18 Lorenzo Lotto: Portrait of a man, believed to be Michelangelo. Nancy, Musée des Beaux Arts.

19 Jacopino del Conte (attribution): Portrait of Michelangelo. Florence, Casa Buonarroti.

it off a year or two." [91] With the death of Urbino, the thought of death was reinforced in him, and with it concern for the salvation of his soul.

Of the family in Florence, once so numerous, there were left two children of Buonarroto, Francesca and Leonardo, whom he did not forget and was ready to help whenever they needed it. Leonardo was his agent and counselor in distributing charity in Florence. Michelangelo was as generous to the poor as he had been to his family, and in his letters to Leonardo makes many references to "alms." With great delicacy he sought out particularly "some needy citizen who has girls to marry or place in a convent... citizens... who in need would be ashamed to go begging." [92] And in 1552, he directs that his property should go to the "ashamed, that is to poor citizens" [93] if there were no heirs. Nor does he neglect to recommend to Leonardo that the charity should be given "secretly," so that no one should know the name of the benefactor. But not trusting the nephew, he requires that receipts be sent him, and knowing how much he liked money, scolds him: "As to alms, it seems to me that you neglect it more than you should. If you don't give my money for the soul of your father, you should at least give of your own." [94]

Leonardo had grown up in the school of Gimondo and Giovan Simone. He was not an evil man, but rather coarse, incapable of understanding his uncle's great heart and need for affection, and often earned rebukes, as when in 1540 he sent him three shirts "so coarse that there is not a peasant here that would not be ashamed to wear them," [95] or when in 1546, being sick and seeing the indecent haste with which Leonardo had come to Rome to see him, he wrote him: "As to your rushing up to Rome, I don't know whether you would have come so fast if I had been poor and had nothing to eat... You are so anxious not to lose this heritage! And you said that it was your duty to come here because of the love you bear me. The love of the clothesmoth!" [96]

A very moving aspect of Michelangelo's relations with Leonardo was his concern over the many marriage projects of his nephew. Michelangelo wanted his nephew to marry "so that our being should not finish here, although," he adds bitterly, "it would not mean the end of the world. And yet every animal tries to perpetuate his species." [97] In the spring of 1553 Leonardo married Cassandra Ridolfi, to whom Michelangelo gave a dowry and two rings, one with a diamond and the other of rubies. The birth of Buonarroto in the following year brought a ray of serenity into the last years of the artist. "God be thanked," Michelangelo wrote to Leonardo, "and make him good, so that he may do us honor and maintain our house." [98]

His last years saw his activities as architect and sculptor multiplied, although he did not neglect the onerous tasks he had already taken on. In 1552 it was the design for the staircase of the Belvedere courtyard in the Vatican; in 1559, the designs for the church of S. Giovanni de' Fiorentini and the Cappella Sforza in S. Maria Maggiore; in 1559-60, designs for an equestrian monument to Henry II, commissioned by Catherine de' Medici, and for the tomb of the Marquis di Marignano, the latter probably in the form of advice or recommendations to Leone Leoni, who executed the work; in 1560, the design for Porta Pia; and, in the year after, the design for the church of S. Maria degli Angeli to be built on the ruins of the Baths of Diocletian.

Michelangelo had not left Rome since 1534, with the sole exception of a trip in 1556 with the intention of going to Loreto. However, the voyage of the now octogenarian Buonarroti was cut short on the mountains of Spoleto, where he was overtaken, something more than a month later, by an invitation from the pope to come back to Rome and resume work on St. Peter's. Probably this was a "flight" from Rome, as Vasari says, motivated by the approach of the Spanish army commanded by the Duke of Alva and fear of a sack of the city. The reason may possibly have been something different, something that Michelangelo found it necessary to confide to Vasari a little later, writing him on December 18 of that year: "These days, with great trouble and expense, I had great pleasure in the mountains of Spoleto, visiting those mountains, so that I have only half come back to Rome, for truly there is no peace to be found except in the woods." [99] The naturalistic tinge in this passage of the letter, linked to the temperament of the artist, had led modern criticism to justify this last voyage of Michelangelo, interpreting it "either as the relief of excessive tension or as an inextinguishable idyllic aspiration or, finally, as the conquest in old age of a simplicity and tenderness unknown during the heroic phase." [100]

The decade 1550-1559 comprises his final sculptures, in which a single theme recurs, the Pietà. About 1550 he began to carve the *Pietà*, now in the cathedral at Florence, that was intended for his tomb; between 1555 and 1559 the *Pietà* known as the *Pietà di Palestrina* and, finally, the *Rondanini Pietà*, barely rough-hewn.

On February 18, 1564, almost 90, Michelangelo died in Rome, in his Macel de' Corvi house, surrounded by a few friends, including Cavalieri, who had helped him during his brief illness. His nephew wanted to carry out his wish to be buried in Florence and had the body transported there secretly; it arrived on March 11 and was buried in Santa Croce.

On July 14, at the desire of the Accademia delle Arti del Disegno, solemn funeral rites were held, and Benedetto Varchi pronounced the official oration in the church of San Lorenzo.

[1] G. Vasari, *La Vita di Michelangelo Buonarroti nelle redazioni del 1550 e del 1568*, edited by P. Barocchi, Naples 1962, Vol. I. p. 5 (1568).

[2] B. Varchi, *Orazione funerale fatta e recitata da lui pubblicamente nell'essequie di Michelagnolo Buonarroti in Firenze nella chiesa di S. Lorenzo*, Florence, 1564, p. 12.

[3] A. Condivi, *Michelangelo, la vita raccolta dal suo discepolo*, edited by P. D'Ancona, Milan 1928, p. 35.

[4] M. Buonarroti, *Le Lettere pubblicate coi ricordi e i contatti artistici*, edited by G. Milanesi, Florence 1875, p. 237. Letter to nephew Leonardo February 1, 1549.

[5] G. Spini, "Politicità di Michelangelo," *Rivista Storica Italiana*, A. LXXVI, No. 3, September 1964, p. 560-67.

[6] Condivi, *op. cit.*, p. 37.

[7] *Ibid.*, p. 200.

[8] *Ibid.*, p. 192.

[9] Spini, *op. cit.*, p. 572.

[10] Buonarroti, *op. cit.*, p. 614. *Allogazione a Michelangelo del gruppo di marmo della Pietà*, August 27, 1498.

[11] *Ibid.*, p. 5. Letter August 19, 1497.

[12] Coll. H. Hertz, in Pogatscher *Dok. z. Sixtin Kapelle*, p. 787-88. Letter from Ludovico to Michelangelo February 14, 1500.

[13] Letter from Ludovico to Michelangelo December 19, 1500 in A. Gotti, *Vita di Michelangelo Buonarroti narrata con l'aiuto di nuovi documenti*, Florence 1875, p. 23.

[14] G. Gaye, *Carteggio inedito d'artisti dei secoli XIV, XV, XVI*, Florence 1840, Vol. II, p. 454.

[15] A. Fortuna, *Cronologia Michelangiolesca*, in *Il Vasari*, A. XV (N. S. T.), n. 3 (1957), p. 110.

[16] Gaye, *op. cit.*, Vol. II, p. 455-62; Buonarroti, *op. cit.*, p. 620-22.

[17] Buonarroti, *op. cit.*, p. 426; Fortuna, *op. cit.*, A. XVI (N. S. II), n. 1 (1958), p. 40-41. Letter January 1524.

[18] Vasari, *op. cit.*, Vol. I, p. 28.

[19] Buonarroti, *op. cit.*, p. 377. Letter May 2, 1506.

[20] G. G. Bottari, *Raccolta di lettere sulla pittura, scultura e architettura scritte dai più celebri professori che in dette arti fiorirono dal secolo XV al XVII*, Rome 1759, T. III, p. 320-21.

[21] A. De Zahn, *Notizie artistiche tratte dall'archivio segreto vaticano*, in: *Archivio storico italiano*, S. III, T. 6, pt. I, 1867, p. 180, note 1.

[22] Gaye, *op. cit.*, Vol. II, p. 91. Letter from the Cardinal of Pavia to the Signoria of Florence.

[23] *Ibid.*, Vol. II, p. 91-92.

20 Detail of the Last Judgment, believed to be a self-portrait of Michelangelo. Vatican, Sistine Chapel.

22 Federico Zuccari: Michelangelo watches Taddeo Zuccari painting the façade of Palazzo Mattei in Rome. Vienna, Albertina.

21 Head of Nicodemus, in the Santa Maria del Fiore Pietà, believed to be a self-portrait of Michelangelo. Florence, Santa Maria del Fiore.

[24] Buonarroti, *op. cit.*, p. 11.

[25] *Ibid.*, p. 108.

[26] *Ibid.*, p. 29.

[27] *Ibid.*, p. 27. Letter to Ludovico January 27, 1509.

[28] *Ibid.*, p. 97. Letter to brother Buonarroto October 17, 1509.

[29] *Ibid.*, p. 32. Letter to Ludovico September 15, 1509 (not 1510): cf. Fortuna, *op. cit.*, A. XVII, (N. S. III), n. 1 (1959) p. 60.

[30] Buonarroti, *op. cit.*, p. 49.

[31] *Ibid.*, p. 55-56. Letter June 1523.

[32] *Ibid.*, p. 147. Letter April 20, 1507.

[33] *Ibid.*, p. 150-51.

[34] *Ibid.*, Letter September 7, 1510.

[35] E. Steinmann, "Due conti di bucato di Michelangelo Buonarroti," *Bollettino d'Arte del Ministero della Pubblica Istruzione*, 1921, p. 31-35.

[36] Buonarroti, *op. cit.*, p. 39.

[37] *Archivio di Stato di Firenze*, *Archivio della Decima Granducale, Arroti del Quartiere di Santo Spirito del 1537 e c. 122*.

[38] *Archivio di Stato di Firenze*, *Archivio della Decima Granducale, Campione del Quartiere di S. Croce, Lion Nero, del 1534, cc. 41-42*.

[39] Buonarroti, *op. cit.*, p. 47.

[40] *Ibid.*, p. 30.

[41] *Ibid.*, p. 11. Letter to Ludovico June 1508.

[42] Spini, *op. cit.*, p. 578-79.

[43] Buonarroti, *op. cit.*, p. 107. Letter September 5, 1512.

[44] *Ibid.*, p. 108. Letter to brother Buonarroto September 18, 1512.

[45] *Ibid.*, p. 47. Letter October 12, 1512.

[46] Spini, *op. cit.*, p. 582-83.

[47] Buonarroti, *op. cit.*, p. 383.

[48] *Ibid.*, p. 416. Letter to Sebastiano del Piombo in 1520.

[49] Vasari, *op. cit.*, Vol. I, p. 56-57 (red. 1568).

[50] A. Parronchi, " Michelangelo al tempo dei lavori di S. Lorenzo in una ricordanza del Figiovanni," in: *Paragone (Arte)*, Milan, July 1964, p. 11.

[51] G. B. Figiovanni, " Una ricordanza di Giovan Battista Figiovanni," edited by G. Corti, in: *Paragone (Arte) op. cit.*, p. 24-31.

[52] Figiovanni, *op. cit.*, p. 27.

[53] M. Buonarroti, *op. cit.*, p. 398.

[54] Figiovanni, *op. cit.*, p. 28.

[55] Buonarroti, *op. cit.*, p. 550.   Letter to Bartolomeo Ammannati.

[56] Figiovanni, *op. cit.*, p. 29.

[57] Buonarroti, *op. cit.*, p. 457.   Letter September 25, 1529.

[58] Figiovanni, *op. cit.*, p. 29.

[59] Parronchi, *op. cit.*, p. 11 ff.

[60] M. Buonarroti, *Le Rime*, edited by E. N. Girardi, Bari 1960, p. 117.

[61] Figiovanni, *op. cit.*, p. 29.

[62] *Ibid.*, p. 28.

[63] G. Milanesi, *Les corrispondents de Michel-Ange, I—Sebastiano del Piombo*, Paris 1890, p. 44.

[64] Condivi, *op. cit.*, p. 146.

[65] *Ibid.*

[66] Buonarroti, *op. cit.*, p. 152.   Letter of 1533 from Florence.

[67] Buonarroti, *op. cit.*, p. 153.

[68] Condivi, *op. cit.*, p. 138-39.

[69] *Ibid.*, p. 139.

[70] Vasari, *op. cit.*, Vol. I, p. 118.

[71] *Ibid.*

[72] Spini, *op. cit.*, p. 599.

[73] Buonarroti, *op. cit.*, p. 221.

[74] Gotti, *op. cit.*, Vol. II, p. 146.

[75] Archivio di Stato di Firenze, *Archivio Mediceo del Principato, f. 380, c. 218;* cf. also G. Gaye, *op. cit.*, Vol. II, p. 352.

[76] Buonarroti, *op. cit.*, p. 528.   Letter August 1, 1550.

[77] Note by P. Barocchi in: Vasari, *op. cit.*, Vol. IV, p. 2006-2007.

[78] C. de Tolnay, *Michelangiolo*, Florence 1951, p. 150.

[79] *Ibid.*, p. 135.

[80] Condivi, *op. cit.*, p. 186.

[81] Gaye, *op. cit.*, Vol. II, p. 333.

[82] Buonarroti, *op. cit.*, p. 488.   Letter to Luigi del Riccio October 1542.

[83] *Ibid.*, p. 494.

[84] *Ibid.*, p. 490.

[85] Gotti, *op. cit.*, Vol. II, p. 134.

[86] Buonarroti, *op. cit.*, p. 544.

[87] *Ibid.*, p. 535.   Letter to Bartolomeo Ammannati of 1555.

[88] *Ibid.*, p. 336.   Letter to nephew Leonardo July 1557.

[89] *Ibid.*

[90] *Ibid.*, p. 539.

[91] *Ibid.*, p. 538.

[92] *Ibid.*, p. 213.

[93] *Ibid.*, p. 279.   Letter February 20.

[94] *Ibid.*, p. 206.   Letter of 1547.

[95] *Ibid.*, p. 162.   Letter July 1540.

[96] *Ibid.*, p. 187.   Letter February 6, 1546.

[97] *Ibid.*, p. 282.   Letter June 24, 1552.

[98] *Ibid.*, p. 300.   Letter April 21, 1554.

[99] *Ibid.*, p. 541.

[100] Note by P. Barocchi in: Vasari, *op. cit.*, Vol. IV, p. 1642-44.

XI

BIBLIOGRAPHY

by Peter Meller

The enormous bibliography on Michelangelo was first systematized by Ernst Steinmann and Rudolf Wittkower, *Michelangelo Bibliographie 1510-1926*, Leipzig, 1927, brought up to date in a supplement compiled by H. W. Schmidt as an appendix to E. Steinmann, *Michelangelo im Spiegel seiner Zeit*, Leipzig, 1930. This in turn was continued by P. Cherubelli (" Supplemento alla bibliografia michelangiolesca 1931-1942," in *Centenario del Giudizio* [1942] p. 270-304) and finally by P. Barocchi, *Giorgio Vasari: La vita di Michelangelo nelle redazioni del 1550 e del 1568*, Milan and Naples, 1962, Vol. I, p. 338-376.

The present supplement begins with 1961, pointing out some items omitted in previous summaries.

Ackerman J. S., *Renaissance News* XV, 1962, p. 139-142: review of R. J. Clements, *Michelangelo's theory of art*, New York and Zürich, 1961.
— *The architecture of Michelangelo*, London 1961; for review, cf.: *Architectural Record*; Coffin D. R.; *The Connoisseur*; Murray P.; Pope-Hennessy J.; Schulz J.; Sypher W.; Watterson J.; Zucker P.
— " Reports on scholarship in the renaissance," *Renaissance News*, XVIII, 1965, 1, p. 73-79.
Adhemar J., " Aretino: Artistic Adviser to Francis I," *Journal of the Warburg and Courtauld Institutes*, XVIII, 1954, p. 311-318.
Agasso D., " Michelangelo. La bastonata del Papa," *Epoca*, XV, No. 704, 1964, p. 26.
Alexander S., *Michelangelo the Florentine. A Novel*, New York, 1957.
— " Michelangelo Buonarroti," article in: *New Collier's Encyclopedia*, New York, 1963.
Alhadeff A., " Michelangelo and the Early Rodin," *The Art Bulletin*, XLV, 1963, p. 363-367.
" Amazing art fund," *Daily Mail*, October 26, 1963.
American Institute of Architects Journal, 34, November 1960, p. 57; review of C. H. Morgan, *The Life of Michelangelo*, New York, 1960.
" A missing Michelangelo? A Crucifix found in Florence may be a youthful work by the Master," *Life International*, April 20, 1964.
" Anatomia degli edifici," *Architettura*, 8, 1963, p. 689.
Architectural Record, 130, 1961, p. 48; review of J. S. Ackerman, *The architecture of Michelangelo*, London, 1961.
Argan G. C., " La tomba di Giulio II," in: Portoghesi P.-Zevi B., *Michelangelo architetto*, Turin, 1964, p. 61-94.
— " Materia e furore," in: *Michelangelo scultore*, series *Civiltà dell'immagine*, ed. E. Battisti, Rome, 1964, p. 111-120.
— " Del Genio," *Il Messaggero*, February 18, 1964.
Arthos J., *Dante, Michelangelo and Milton*, London, 1963; for review, cf.: Moores S. D.
Baldini U., " È pronto per il centenario il Crocifisso di Michelangiolo," *La Nazione*, February 1, 1964.
— " Il Crocifisso di Michelangiolo," *La Nazione*, February 23, 1964.
— " Precisazione su due opinioni," *La Nazione*, March 5, 1964.
— " Specchio magico," *La Nazione*, July 26, 1964.
Barbieri F.-Putti L., *Tutta l'architettura di Michelangelo*, Milan, 1962.
— " Catalogo delle opere architettoniche di Michelangelo," in: Portoghesi P.-Zevi B., *Michelangelo architetto*, Turin, 1964, p. 813-947.
Bargellini P., see: Michelangiolo.
Barocchi P., *Giorgio Vasari: La vita di Michelangelo nelle redazioni del 1550 e del 1568*, Vol. 1-5, *Documenti di Filologia*, 5, Milan and Naples, 1962; for review, cf.: Gilbert C.; Hirst M.; Pittaluga M.; Rossi A.
— " Michelangelo e la sua scuola. I disegni dell'archivio Buonarroti," *Accademia toscana di scienze e lettere " La Colombaria,"* *Studi*, 8, Vol. 3, Florence, 1964; for review of Vols. 1 and 2, see: Hirst M.
— *Trattati d'arte del Cinquecento*, Bari, 1960-62; for review, see: Previtali G.
— " Due frammenti michelangioleschi," *Il Vasari* XXI, 1963, 1, p. 15.
— " Michelangelo e il manierismo," *Arte Antica e Moderna*, 27, 1964, p. 260-280.
— see: *Disegni di Michelangelo*.
Barocchi P.-Bianchini A.-Forlani A.-Fossi M., *Mostra di disegni dei Fondatori dell'Accademia delle Arti del Disegno. Catalogo a cura di*, Florence, 1964.
Barocchi P.-Chiarini G., *Michelangelo. Mostra di disegni, manoscritti e documenti. Catalogo a cura di*, Florence, 1964.
Bassi E., " Dal Diario di Antonio Canova," I, *Critica d'Arte Nuova*, V, 1958, p. 325-326.

Battisti E., " Michelangelo e l'antico," in: *Resümees. 21. Internationaler Kongress für Kunstgeschichte*, Bonn, September 1961, p. 65.

— " Come Michelangelo elabora i suoi progetti," *ivi*, p. 101.

— " Premessa," in: *Michelangelo scultore*, series *Civiltà dell'immagine*, ed. E. Battisti, Rome, 1964, p. 9-12.

— " Magia e non-finito," *ibid.*, p. 87-110.

— see: Michelangelo.

Bean J. (=J. B.), *Master Drawings*, II, 1964, 4, p. 420: review of M. V. Brugnoli, " Michelangelo," *I Grandi Maestri del Disegno*, Milan, 1964.

Beck J. H., *Arte Antica e Moderna*, 27, 1964, p. 360: review of S. Bottari, *L'arca di S. Domenico in Bologna*, Bologna, 1964.

Beck J. H.-Fanti M., " Un probabile intervento di Michelangelo per la ' porta magna ' di San Petronio (Documenti)," *Arte Antica e Moderna*, 27, 1964, p. 349-354.

Berenson B., *Italian pictures of the renaissance, a list of the principal artists and their works with an index of places. Florentine School*, 2 Vol., London, 1963 (new ed.); for review, see: *Listener; Times Literary Supplement*.

— *I disegni dei pittori fiorentini*, Vol. 1-3, Milan, 1961; for review, see: Pouncey Ph.

Bergsträsser G., *Zeichnungen alter und neuer Meister aus dem Hessichen Landesmuseum in Darmstadt*, Darmstadt, 1964; for review, see: Vitzthum W.

Bernardi M., " Michelangelo," *La Stampa*, February 18, 1964.

Berti L., " Michelangelo: le tombe medicee," series *Forma e Colore*, Florence, 1965.

— see: Salmi M.

Bertini A., *Arte Antica e Moderna*, 17, 1962, p. 106-109: review of R. Bonelli, *Da Bramante a Michelangelo*, Venice, 1960.

— " La facciata e la Sacrestia Nuova di San Lorenzo," in: Portoghesi P.-Zevi B., *Michelangelo architetto*, Turin, 1964, p. 121-208.

Bertram A., *Michelangelo*, London, 1965.

Bessone Aureli A. M., *Dialoghi michelangioleschi a Francesco d'Olanda*, Rome, 1953.

Bettini S., " La fabbrica di S. Pietro," in: Portoghesi P.-Zevi B., *Michelangelo architetto*, Turin, 1964, p. 497-608.

Bianchini A., see: Barocchi P.

Binni W., " Le lettere (Michelangelo storicizzato)," *Marcatrè*, 11/12/13, 1964, p. 81-102.

— " Michelangelo scrittore," *La Rassegna della letteratura italiana*, 68, ser. VII, 1964, 2/3, p. 213-255.

Bonelli R., " La piazza Capitolina," in: Portoghesi P.-Zevi B., *Michelangelo architetto*, Turin, 1964, p. 425-496.

— " Palazzo Farnese," *ibid.*, p. 609-650.

— *Da Bramante a Michelangelo*, Venice, 1960; for review, see: Pertini A.

Borea E., *The High Renaissance: Italian Painting*, London and New York, 1963.

— " Mostra dei disegni dei Fondatori della Accademia delle Arti del Disegno a Firenze," *Arte Antica e Moderna*, 21, 1963, p. 88-89.

Borgese L., " Michelangelo," *Il Corriere della Sera*, February 18, 1964.

Borland P., " A copy by Venusti after Michelangelo," *The Burlington Magazine*, CIII, 1961, p. 433-444.

— " La Mostra di Michelangelo a Roma," *Arte Antica e Moderna*, 25, 1964, p. II-III.

Botto I. M., " Alcuni aspetti dell'architettura fiorentina della seconda metà del Cinquecento," *Proporzioni*, IV, 1963, p. 25-45.

Bousquet J., *Il Manierismo in Europa*, Milan, 1963.

— *La peinture maniériste*, Neuchâtel, 1964.

Brandes G. M. C., *Michelangelo: his life, his times, his era*, translated from the Danish and with a foreword by H. Norden, London, 1963; for review, see: Read H., Smart A., Wall B., Wedgewood C. V.,

Brandi C., " Forma e compiutezza in Michelangelo," in: *Resümees. 21. Internationaler Kongress für Kunstgeschichte*, Bonn, September 1964, p. 67 (report of address).

Briganti G., *Italian mannerism*, translated by M. Kunzle, London, 1963.

Brugnoli M. V., " Mostra commemorativa di Michelangelo in Varsavia," *Il Vasari*, XXI, 1963, 4, p. 183.

— " Michelangelo," *I Grandi Maestri del Disegno*, Milan, 1964; for review, see: Bean J.; (L. S.).

Buonarroti M., see: Michelangelo; Michelangiolo.

Burchard L.-d'Hulst R. A., *Rubens Drawings*, Brussels, 1963. (Copies of Michelangelo: No. 17-20).

Busch H.-Lohse B., *Renaissance Sculpture; European Sculpture*, translated from the German by P. George, London, 1964.

Busignani A., " Preistoria di Michelangelo," *Bollettino degli Ingegneri*, Collegio degli Ingegneri di Firenze, 1965, 2/3, p. 11-14.

" Butchered to make a Roman Holiday (Picasso and Michelangelo)," *Apollo*, LVII, August 1953, p. 33.

Calvesi M., " Michelangelo in Vaticano," *Marcatrè*, 4/5, 1964, p. 97-106.

Camesasca E., " Sulla scia del Piombo," *Il Vasari*, XXI, 1963, 1, p. 16-22.

Cardellini I., see: D'Ancona P.

Carli E., *La pittura fiorentina*, Novara, 1962.

— *Florentine painting*, translated by P. S. Hamlyn, London, 1963.

— *Michelangelo a Siena*, Rome, 1965.

Castelfranco G., *Arte Antica e Moderna*, 23, 1963, p. 267-268: review of D. Durbé, " Raffaello," *I Grandi Maestri del Disegno*, Milan, 1962.

Cataldi F., see: Portoghesi P.

— *Catalogue of Important Old Master Drawings*, London, Sotheby & Co., Sale: September 12, 1964, p. 16: Michelangelo Buonarroti: *Ascanius pulling Aeneas from Dido's Bed*.

Chastel A., *Italian art*, translated by P. and L. Murray, London, 1963; for review, see: *Listener; Russel J.*

— *Arte e Umanesimo a Firenze* (=*Art et Humanisme à Florence au temps de Laurent le Magnifique*, Paris, 1959), translated by R. Federici, Turin, 1964.

Chiarini G., see: Barocchi P.

Clark K., " Johannes Wilde," *The Burlington Magazine*, CIII, June 1961, p. 205.

— " Michelangelo pittore," *Apollo* LXXX, December 1964, p. 436-446.

Clements R. J., *Michelangelo. A self-portrait*. Englewood Cliffs, N. Y., 1963.

— *Michelangelo's theory of art*, New York and Zürich, 1961; for review, see: Ackerman J. S., Gilbert C., Newton E., Schulz J., Smart A.

— *Journal of Aesthetics and Art Criticism*, 22, 1963, p. 231-232 (reply by Clements to review by Schulz).

— *The Art Bulletin*, 45, 1963, p. 173-177 (reply by Clements to review by Gilbert).

— *Michelangelo* (=*Michelangelo's theory of art*, New York and Zürich, 1961), translated by E. Battisti, Milan, 1964.

— *The poetry of Michelangelo*, Milan, 1964.

— " Idee artistiche e temi figurativi," in: *Michelangelo scultore*, series *Civiltà dell'immagine*, ed. E. Battisti, Rome, 1964, p. 13-42.

Coffin D. R., *Society of Architectural Historians Journal*, 21, 1962, p. 103-104; review of J. S. Ackerman, *The architecture of Michelangelo*, London, 1961.

— " Pirro Ligorio on the nobility of the arts," *Journal of the Warburg and Courtauld Institutes*, XXVII, 1964, p. 191-210.

Contelli Isola M., see: Rotili M.

D'Ancona P.-Pinna A.-Cardellini I., *Michelangelo*, Milan, 1964.

De Angelis D'Ossat G., see: *Il Campidoglio di Michelangelo.*

Del Debbio E., see: *ibid.*

De Maffei F., *Michelangelo's lost St. John. The Story of a Discovery*, New York, 1964.

De Vecchi P. L., " Studi sulla poesia di Michelangelo," *Giornale storico della letteratura italiana*, 1963, p. 420-431.

Díaz Gonzáles J., *Il linguaggio segreto del " Giudizio " di Michelangelo*, Rome, 1964; for review, see: (L. S.).

Disegni di Michelangelo. 103 disegni in facsimile. Foreword by M. Salmi, introduction by C. de Tolnay, comments by P. Barocchi. Milan, 1964.

" Disegni di Michelangelo a Firenze," *Domus*, 388, 1962, p. 57.

Di Stefano R., *La cupola di S. Pietro*, Naples, 1963.

Durbé D., *Raffaello*, " *I Grandi Maestri del Disegno*," Milan, 1962; for review see: Castelfranco G.

Dussler L., *Pantheon*, III, 1961, p. 225; review of A. Perrig, *Michelangelo Buonarrotis letzte Pietà-Idee*, Berne, 1960.

— *Pantheon*, IV, 1963, p. 247; review of K. Frey, *Briefe des Michelangelo Buonarroti*, Berlin, 1961 (3rd ed.).

— " Michelangelos Spätwerke," in: *Michelangelo Buonarroti*, Würzburg, 1964, p. 115-156.

" Earliest Michelangelo perhaps discovered," *Art News*, 62, December 1963, p. 8.

Eggleshaw S. R., " Michelangelo frescoes (Letter to the Editor)," '*Apollo*, LVIII, September 1953, p. 75.

von Einem H., *Michelangelo*, Dutch translation by M. B. A. Laffree, Antwerpen, 1962.

— *Zeitschrift für Kunstgeschichte*, 25, 1962, I, p. 80-85: review of Ch. Tolnay, *Michelangelo, vol. V.: The final period. Last Judgment, frescoes of the Paoline Chapel, last Pietàs.* Princeton, 1960.

Eisler C., " The athlete of virtue. The Iconography of Asceticism," in: *De Artibus Opuscula XL*, Essays in Honor of E. Panofsky, New York, 1961, p. 82-97.

— " The Madonna of the Stairs — Problem of Date and Style," in: *Resümees. 21. Internationaler Kongress für Kunstgeschichte*, Bonn, September, 1964 p. 71-73.

— " Michelangelo and the North " (report of address in *Renaissance Symposium*, State University of New York, Albany), *Renaissance News*, XVII, 1964, 4, p. 354.

Emiliani A., *Rinascimento e Barocco in Italia*, Novara, 1963.

Ettlinger L. D., *Reflections on a New History of Italian Sculpture* (review of J. Pope-Hennessy, " An Introduction to Italian Sculpture," I-III, London, 1955-63), *The Burlington Magazine*, CVII, March 1965, p. 139-142.

— " Exibition of drawings at the British Museum," *Museums Journal*, 53, 1953, p. 60; *Studio*, 146, 1953, p. 28.

Fasolo V., " Michelangelo architettor poeta," *Architettura*, series edited by L. Vagnetti, Saggi I, Genova, 1965.

Ferbach M., *Die Kunstpolitik gegen Michelangelo*, Abhandlungen des Institutes für Michelangelo-Forschung, Vienna, 1960.

— *Michelangelo und der geistige Umbruch der Zeiten. Michelangelo und Raffael 1508-1511.* Abhandlungen des Institutes für Michelangelo-Forschung, Vienna, 1960.

— *Die Peterskirche im Forschungschaos. Julius II. bis Paul III.* Abhandlungen des Institutes für Michelangelo-Forschung, Vienna, 1960.

Fernandez J., " Miguel Ángel de su alma," *Instituto de Investigaciones Estéticas, Universidad nacional autónoma de México*, Mexico, 1964.

Florence, see: Michelangelo.

Forlani A., *I disegni italiani del Cinquecento*, Venice, 1962; for review, see: Pittaluga M.

— " Michelangelo," series *Forma e Colori*, Milan, 1963.

Formaggio D., *Michelangelo*, Novara, 1955.

Forster K. W., " Pontormo and Michelangelo," in: *Resümees. 21. Internationaler Kongress für Kunstgeschichte*, Bonn, September 1964, p. 100.

Fortuna A., " Cronologia michelangiolesca," *Il Vasari*, XXI, 1963, 1, p. 30-38; 2/3, p. 94-104.

Fossi M., *Mostra di chiaroscuri italiani dei secoli XVI, XVII, XVIII. Catalogo a cura di*, Florence, 1956.

Foster K., " Michelangelo's failure," *Blackfriars*, September 1963, p. 355-363.

Francia E., *San Pietro*, Milan, 1963.

Francisco de Hollanda, *Dialoghi romani con Michelangelo*, translated by L. Marchiori, introduction and notes by E. Spina Barelli, Milan, 1964.

Freedberg S. J., " Drawings for Sebastiano " or " drawings by Sebastiano ": the problem reconsidered, *The Art Bulletin*, 45, 1963, p. 256-258.

Frey K.-Frey H. W., *Die Briefe des Michelangelo Buonarroti*, Berlin, 1961.

— *Die Dichtungen des Michelangiolo Buonarroti*, Berlin, 1964 (new edition).

Friedrich H., *Epochen der Italienischen Lyrik*, Frankfurt a/M., 1964.

Frommel Ch. L., " Antonio da Sangallos Cappella Paolina. Ein Beitrag zur Baugeschichte des Vatikanischen Palastes," *Zeitschrift für Kunstgeschichte*, 27, 1964, 1, p. 1-42.

— " S. Eligio degli Orefici und die Kuppel der Medici-Kappelle," in: *Resümees. 21. Internationaler Kongress für Kunstgeschichte*, Bonn, September 1964, p. 30-32.

Frosali S., " Al Convegno Michelangiolesco," *La Nazione*, June 18, 1964.

Fulini M., " Michelangiolo fu anche poeta?," *La Stampa*, February 27, 1964.

Galassi Paluzzi C., *San Pietro in Vaticano (Le Chiese di Roma Illustrate, No. 74)*, Rome, 1963.

Galasso E., see: Rotili M.

Gazette des Beaux-Arts, Supplement: *La Chronique des Arts*, No. 1154, March 1965, p. 11-12; review of V. Mariani, *Michelangelo pittore*, Milan, 1964.

Gaynor J. S., see: Toesca I.

van Gelder J. G., "Two aspects of the Dutch Baroque. Reason and Emotion", in: *De Artibus Opuscola XL*; Essays in Honor of E. Panofsky, New York, 1961, p. 445-453.

Gendel M., "Michelangelo year opens in Rome at the Exhibition palace," *Art News*, 63, April 1964, p. 26-28.

Gere J. A., see: Pouncey Ph.

Gerosa G., "Il mistero di Michelangelo," *Epoca*, XV, No. 704, 1964, p. 23-30.

Gerstenberg K., *Pantheon*, XVIII, 1960, p. 260-262: review of L. Dussler, *Die Zeichnungen des Michelangelo. Kritischer Katalog*, Berlin, 1959.

Gilbert C., "A Sarasota notebook, 2.: A 'new' work by Sebastiano del Piombo and an offer by Michelangelo, *Arte Veneta*, 15, 1961, p. 33-45.

— *The Art Bulletin*, XLIV, December 1962, p. 347-355: review of R. J. Clements, *Michelangelo's theory of art*, New York and Zürich, 1961.

— *The Art Bulletin*, XLVI, June 1964, p. 247-251: review of *Michelangelo Buonarroti. The letters of Michelangelo*. Translated, edited and annotated by E. H. Ramsden, Stanford University Press, 1963; P. Barocchi, *Giorgio Vasari: La Vita di Michelangelo nelle redazioni del 1550 e del 1568*, Milan and Naples, 1962.

Gioseffi D., "San Giovanni dei Fiorentini," in: Portoghesi P.-Zevi B., *Michelangelo architetto*, Turin, 1964, p. 651-680.

— "Porta Pia," *ibid.*, p. 725-760.

Girardi E. N., "La poesia di Michelangelo," in: *Resümees. 21. Internationaler Kongress für Kunstgeschichte*, Bonn, September 1964, p. 94.

— "Michelangelo poeta (Michelangelo storicizzato)," *Marcatrè*, 11/12/13, 1964, p. 74-77.

— *Studi sulle rime di Michelangelo*, Milan, 1964.

Gloton S. I., "Longhi, Mascherino et Fontana, trois architects de la Contre-Réforme face à la tradition de Michel-Ange," *Resümees. 21. Internationaler Kongress für Kunstgeschichte*, Bonn, September 1964, p. 25-26.

Goez W., "Annotationes zu Michelangelos Mediceergräbern," in: *Festschrift für Haral Keller*, Darmstadt, 1963, p. 235-254.

Goldscheider L., *A survey of Michelangelo's models in wax and clay*, London, 1962.

— "Sechs Terrakotten von Michelangelo in Montreal (Die Sammlung P. I. und I. P. Le Booy)," *Die Weltkunst*, 32, 1962, No. 24, p. 11.

— *Michelangelo. Gemälde, Skulpturen, Architekturen. Gesamtausgabe.* Cologne, 1964.

— *Michelangelo's bozzetti for statues in the Medici Chapel*, London, 1957; for review, see: Perrig A., *The Connoisseur*.

Gombrich E. H., "Recent concepts of mannerism. Introduction: the historical background," in: *Studies in Western Art II.: The Renaissance and Mannerism*. Acts of the twentieth international congress of the history of art, Princeton, 1963, II, p. 163-173.

Gosebruch M., "Zum 'Disegno' des Michelangelo," in: *Michelangelo Buonarroti*, Würzburg, 1964, p. 51-114.

Gould C., "Leonardo's great battle-piece, a conjectural reconstruction," *The Art Bulletin*, XXXVI, January 1954, p. 125-129.

Gramberg W., "Ein wenig beachtetes Planstudium in der Entstehungsgeschichte der Medicikapelle," *Mitteilungen des Kunsthistorischen Instituts*, Florenz, 1955, II, p. 151-160.

Graščenkov V. N., *Risunok Masterov Italjanskogo Vozroždenija* (Drawings of Italian Renaissance masters), Moscow, 1963.

Grassi L., *Introduzione all'arte di Michelangelo*. Issues by C. Falcidia. Università degli Studi di Roma, Facoltà di Magistero, Rome, 1964.

Grimm H., *Michelangelo*, translation by G. Varchi, Milan, 1964.

Grohn H. W., "Die Schule der Welt. Zu Michelangelos Karton der Schlacht bei Cascina," *Il Vasari*, XXIV, 67/68, 1963, p. 63-79.

Guerra C., *Statica e tecnica costruttiva delle cupole antiche e moderne*, Naples, 1958.

Gutman H. B., "Michelangelo Botschaft in der Sixtinischer Kapelle," *Archivum Franciscanum Historicum*, 56, 1963, p. 258-283.

Guzzi V., "Genio di Michelangelo," *Il Tempo*, February 18, 1964.

Hager W., "Zur Raumstruktur des Manierismus," in: *Festschrift M. Wackernagel*, Cologne and Graz, 1958, p. 112-140.

Hartt F., *Michelangelo pittore*, Milan and New York, 1964.

Haug H., "Schongauer et Michel-Ange," *Cahiers alsaciens d'archéologie, d'art et d'histoire*, IV, 1960, p. 71-77.

Hauser A., *Der Manierismus*, Munich, 1964.

Heikamp D., *Scritti d'arte di Federico Zuccaro. Fonti per lo studio della storia dell'arte inedite o rare.* Florence, 1961.

Hibbard H., "Michelangelo and Maderno," in: *Resümees. 21. Internationaler Kongress für Kunstgeschichte*, Bonn, September 1964, p. 27-28.

Hirst M., "Chigi chapel in S. Maria della Pace," *Journal of the Warburg and Courtauld Institutes*, XXIV, 1961, p. 161-181.

— "Francesco Salviati's Visitation," *The Burlington Magazine*, CIII, June 1961, p. 236-240.

— *The Burlington Magazine*, CV, 1963, p. 166-171: review of P. Barocchi, *Michelangelo e la sua scuola. I disegni di Casa Buonarroti e degli Uffizi*. Vol. 1-2. Florence, 1962.

— *The Burlington Magazine*, CVI, December 1964, p. 576: review of P. Barocchi, *La Vita di Michelangelo nelle redazioni del 1550 e del 1568*, Milan and Naples, 1962.

Hoogewerff G., "L'ispirazione romana di Martino van Heemskerck," in: *Scritti di Storia dell'Arte in onore di M. Salmi*, Rome, 1963, Vol. III p. 163-167.

Hubala E., "Eine Anmerkung zu Michelangelos Grundriss-Skizze für die Medici-Kapelle in Florenz," *Kunstchronik*, 18, 1965, 2, p. 37-46.

— "Michelangelo und die Florentiner Baukunst," in: *Michelangelo Buonarroti*, Würzburg, 1964, p. 157-190.

Il Campidoglio di Michelangelo, texts by De Angelis D'Ossat G., Pietrangeli C.; surveys by Del Debbio E., Perugini G.; photos by Von Matt L., Milan, 1965.

(Il Tiberino), "Michelangelo alla ribalta," *Palatino*, VIII, 3rd series, 1964, 7-8, p. 184.

Isermeyer Ch. A., "Die Arbeiten Leonardos und Michelangelos für den grossen Ratsaal in Florenz: Eine Revision der Bild- und Schriftquellen für ihre Rekonstruction und Geschichte," in: *Studien zur Toskanischen Kunst. Festschrift L. H. Heydenreich*, Munich, 1963, p. 83-130.

van Isselt D., " La fresque ' La Conversion de Saül ' de Michelangelo dans la Cappella Paolina du Vatican," in: *Actes du XVIIe Congrès International d'Histoire de l'Art*, 1955, p. 315-322 (see original Dutch text in: *Mededeelingen van het Nederlands Historisch Instituut te Rome*, 3, VII, 1953, p. 169-180).

Ivanoff N., " Leopoldo Cicognara ed il gusto dei Primitivi (Canova e Michelangelo)," *Critica d'Arte Nuova*, IV, 1957, p. 32-46.

Karlinger F., " Michelangelo in der Musik," in: *Michelangelo Buonarroti*, Würzburg, 1964, p. 215-224.

Keller H., " Ein früher Entwurf des Pietro de Cortona für SS. Martino e Luca in Rom," in: *Miscellanea Bibliothecae Herzianae zu Ehren von Leo Bruhns*, Munich, 1961, p. 375-385.

Keutner H., " Über den Florentiner Beitrag zu Michelangelo Jahr," *Kunstchronic*, 17, 1964, 9, p. 233-237.

Klein R., *Bibliothèque d'Humanisme et Renaissance*, tome XXIV, 1962, p. 268-271: review of P. Barocchi, *Trattati d'Arte del Cinquecento*, I-II, Bari, 1960-61.

Kroll J., *Art News*, 60, September 1961, p. 39: review of J. Stone, *Agony and Ecstasy, a novel of Michelangelo*, New York, 1961.

Kultzen R., *Kunstchronik*, 16, 1963, 12, p. 339-346: review of Ph. Pouncey-J. A. Gere, *Italian Drawings in the Department of Prints and Drawings in the British Museum. Raphael and his Circle*, London, 1962.

Kunoth G., " Francisco Pacheco's Apotheosis of Hercules," *Journal of the Warburg and Courtauld Institutes*, XXVII, 1964, p. 335-337.

Künzle P., " Die Aufstellung des Reiters vom Lateran durch Michelangelo," in: *Miscellanea Bibliothecae Herzianae in Ehren von Leo Bruhns*, Munich, 1961, p. 255-270.

Lavagnino E., *La chiesa di Santo Spirito in Sassia*, Turin, 1962.

Lavin J., " Working procedure in the sculpture of Michelangelo and Bernini," in: *Resümees. 21. Internationaler Kongress für Kunstgeschichte*, Bonn, September 1964, p. 105-106.

Levie S. H., " Die portretten van Michelangelo door Daniele da Volterra," *Nederlands Kunsthistorisch Jaarboek*, 6, 1955, p. 119-130.

Lewin M. J., " Roman Architectural Practice during Michelangelo's Maturity, in: *Resümees. 21. Internationaler Kongress für Kunstgeschichte*, Bonn, September 1964, p. 23-24.

Lindahl G., " Michelangelos erster Entwurf des Juliusgrabes," *Konsthistorisk Tijdskrift*, 32, 1963, p. 65-79.

Lisner M., " Der Kruzifixus Michelangelos im Kloster Santo Spirito in Florenz," *Kunstchronik*, 16, 1963, 1, p. 1-2.

— " Michelangelos Kruzifixus aus S. Spirito," *Münchener Jahrbuch der Bildenden Kunst*, 3rd series, XV, 1964, p. 7-31.

— " Michelangelo und das Quattrocento " in: *Resümees. 21. Internationaler Kongress für Kunstgeschichte*, Bonn, September 1964, p. 66 (report of address).

— " Zum Rahmen von Michelangelo's Madonna Doni," *Studien zur Geschichte der Europäischen Plastik, Theodor Müller*, Munchen, 1965.

Listener, August 8, 1963, p. 210: review of B. Berenson, *Italian pictures of the renaissance*, London, 1963 (new edition); A. Chastel, *Italian art*, translated by P. Murray, London, 1963.

Lohse B., see: Busch H.

Lotz W., " Mannerism in Architecture: changing aspects " in: *Studies in Western Art II: The Renaissance and Mannerism*, Acts of the twentieth international congress of the history of art, Princeton, 1963, p. 239-246.

— " La Libreria di San Marco e l'urbanistica del Rinascimento," *Bollettino del Centro Internazionale di Studi di architettura A. Palladio*, III, 1961, p. 85-88.

— " Zu Michelangelos Kopien nach dem Kodex Coner " in: *Resümees. 21. Internationaler Kongress für Kunstgeschichte*, Bonn, September 1964, p. 22 (report of address).

— " Zu Michelangelos Christus in S. Maria sopra Minerva " in: *Festschrift H. von Einem*, Berlin, 1965, p. 143-150.

Lowry Bates, *Renaissance Architecture*, New York and Toronto, 1962.

(L. S.) *Palatino*, VIII, series 3rd, 1964, 7/8, p. 187: review of J. Díaz Gonzáles, *Il linguaggio segreto del " Giudizio " di Michelangelo*, Rome, 1964; M. V. Brugnoli, " Michelangelo," *I Grandi Maestri del Disegno*, Milan, 1964.

Maltese C., see: Portoghesi P.

Marcucci L., *David di Michelangiolo Buonarroti*, Milan, 1963.

Mariani V., *Michelangelo*, Naples, 1964.

— " Michelangelo a Roma " in: *Studi Romani*, XII, 1964, I, p. 1-11.

— *Michelangelo pittore*, Milan, 1964; for review, see: *Gazette des Beaux-Arts*.

— see: Rotili M.

Mariani V.-von Matt L., *Rom in der Renaissance*, Zürich, 1961.

Martin J. R., " Butcher's shop of the Caracci," *The Art Bulletin*, XLV, 1963, p. 263-266.

Martini M., " Osservazioni di uno scultore sul Crocifisso ' ritrovato '," *Giornale del Mattino*, April 8, 1964.

Mascherpa G., " Michelangelo e il mito," *Arte Club*, June 20, 1964.

von Matt L., see: Mariani V., *Il Campidoglio di Michelangelo*.

Maurer E., " Pontormo and Michelangelo " in: *Resümees. 21. Internationaler Kongress für Kunstgeschichte*, Bonn, September 1964, p. 91-93.

Melchiori G., " William Blake and Michelangelo," *Pubblicazioni dell'Istituto Italiano di Cultura di Londra*, 4. Rome, 1960.

Meller P., " Leonardo da Vinci's Drawings to the Divine Comedy," *Acta Historiae Artium Academiae Scientiarum Hungaricae*, II, Budapest, 1955, p. 135-168.

Messerer W., " Zur Datierung von Michelangelos Moses," *Kunstchronik*, 15, 1962, 9, p. 284.

" Michelangelo at the 1964-65 New York Fair," *Architectural Forum*, 116, May 1962, p. II.

Michelangelo Buonarroti. The Letters of Michelangelo. Translated from the original Tuscan, edited and annotated by E. H. Ramsden. Stanford University Press, 1963; for review, see: *Art and Architecture*: Gilbert C.; Read H.; Smart A.; Wedgewood C. V.

Michelangelo Buonarroti, Würzburg, 1964; with articles by: Dussler L., Gosebruch M., Hubala E., Karlinger F., Rauhut F., Tolnay Ch.; cf. under the names of the authors.

Michelangelo, *Disegni di*, see *Disegni...*; *Tekeningen...*

" Michelangelo for study and pleasure," *The Illustrated London News*, No. 223, December 26, 1953.

" Michelangelo Fund. Venus im Schatten. *Der Spiegel*, June 2, 1958.

" Michelangelo's drawings at the British Museum," *Art News*, 52, 1953, p. 38.

" Michelangelo's great drawing at the British Museum," *The Illustrated London News*, No. 222, April 25, 1953.

" Michelangelo Scandal," *Art News*, 23, May 1962, p. 62.

" Michelangelo scultore " series *Civiltà dell'immagine* ed. E. Battisti, Rome, 1962; with articles by: Argan C. C., Battisti E., Clements R. J., Negri-Arnoldi F.; see under names of authors.

Michelangelo sculptor: an autobiography through letters, edited by I. and J. Stone, from the translation by Ch. Speroni, London, 1963; for review, see: Jennings E.; *Times Literary Supplement*.

" Michelangelo Zeichnungen," *Pantheon*, XX, 1962, I, p. 66-67: review of Mostra Gabinetto Disegni e Stampe della Galleria Uffizi, Florence, December 1961.

Michelangiolo. Les sculptures – Las esculturas – The sculptures – Die Skulpturen. Rome, 1963.

Michelangiolo. Dono del Sindaco di Firenze. Text by P. Bargellini, Florence, 1964.

Migliorini B., " Dialoghetto su Michelangelo," *Corriere della Sera*, January 15, 1964.

Millar O., *Italian Drawings and Paintings in the Queen's Collection*, London, 1965.

Mondrone D., " Divagazioni su Michelangelo," *La civiltà cattolica*, 115, 1964, 6, p. 539-552.

Montagu J., " A Renaissance Work Copied by Wedgewood," *Journal of the Warburg and Courtauld Institutes*, VIII, 1955, p. 380-81.

Moores J. D., *Italian Studies*, XIX, 1964, p. 108: review of J. Arthos, *Dante, Michelangelo and Milton*, London, 1963.

v. Moos S., " Rom: Mostra critica delle opere michelangiolesche," Museo Nazionale delle Esposizioni, *Das Werk*, 51, 1964, p. 165-166.

Morgan C. H., *The Life of Michelangelo*, New York, 1960; for review, see: *American Institute of Architects Journal*.

Morozzi C., " Michelangelo architetto," *Bollettino degli Ingegneri*, Collegio degli Ingegneri di Firenze, 1965, 2/3, p. 4-10.

Murray P., *The Burlington Magazine*, CIV, 1962, p. 306-307; review of J. S. Ackerman, *The architecture of Michelangelo*, London, 1961.

— *The Architecture of the Italian Renaissance*, London, 1963.

— " Bramante and Michelangelo," *Resümees. 21. Internationaler Kongress für Kunstgeschichte*, Bonn, September 1964, p. 33.

Müller Hofstede J., " Some Early Drawings by Rubens," *Master Drawings*, II, 1964, I, p. 3-17.

Negri-Arnoldi F., " La formazione, in: Michelangelo scultore," series *Civiltà dell'immagine*, ed. E. Battisti, Rome, 1964, p. 43-64.

Newton E., *New Guardian*, June 5, 1963: review of R. J. Clements, *Michelangelo's theory of art*, New York and Zürich, 1961.

Nicolosi G., " Il consolidamento della cupola di Michelangelo durante il pontificato di Pio XII," *Bollettino Centro Studi di Storia dell'architettura*, Rome, 8, 1953.

Noehles K., " Die Louvre-Projekte von Pietro da Cortona und Carlo Rainaldi," *Zeitschrift für Kunstgeschichte*, 24, 1961, p. 70-74.

Oberhuber K., " Michelangelo und Raffael," in: *Resümees. 21. Internationaler Kongress für Kunstgeschichte*, Bonn, September 1964, p. 95-96.

— " A Drawing by Raphael Mistakenly Attributed to Bandinelli," *Master Drawings*, II, 1964, 4, p. 398-400.

Orozco Díaz E., " Barroquismo y religiosidad en el ' Judicio final ' de Miguel Angel," *Revista de ideas esteticas*, 21, 1963, p. 121-144; 203-213.

Paladini G., " Pellegrinaggio a Caprese," *Bollettino degli Ingegneri*, Collegio degli Ingegneri di Firenze, 1965, 2/3, p. 15-28.

Pane R., *Andrea Palladio*, Turin, 1961.

— " L'architettura della volta sistina," in: Portoghesi P.-Zevi B., *Michelangelo architetto*, Turin, 1964, p. 95-120.

Panofsky E., " The Mouse that Michelangelo failed to carve," in: *Essays in memory of Karl Lehmann*, New York, 1964, p. 242-251.

— *Tomb sculpture*, New York, 1964.

Papini G., " Come nacquero i capolavori," *Epoca*, XV, No. 704, 1964.

Parronchi A., " Il modello michelangiolesco del David bronzeo per Pietro di Roano," *Arte Antica e Moderna*, 5, 1962, p. 170-180.

— " Tutto su Michelangelo," *La Nazione*, December 23, 1962.

— " Inizi di Michelangelo," in: *Studi fiorentini. Libera Cattedra di Storia della Civiltà Fiorentina*, Florence, 1963, p. 235-270.

— " Il più bel ritratto di Michelangelo," *La Nazione*, January 16, 1964.

— " Michelangelo invertebrato," *La Nazione*, February 21, 1964.

— " L'altare di S. Spirito," *La Nazione*, February 27, 1964.

— " Attribuzioni a Michelangelo," *La Nazione*, March 18, 1964.

— " Il non-finito come sogno," *La Nazione*, April 3, 1964.

— " La Vergine della Pietà," *La Nazione*, June 15, 1964.

— " La croce e lo specchio," *La Nazione*, July 3, 1964.

— " L'Amore dormente," in: *Resümees. 21. Internationaler Kongress für Kunstgeschichte*, Bonn, September 1964, p. 74.

— " Un attentato a Michelangelo," *La Nazione*, September 25, 1964.

— " Titulus crucis," *La Nazione*, November 4, 1964.

— " Crocifisso attribuito a Michelangelo Buonarroti (1493)," in: *Mostra del Restauro. Pisa, Museo Nazionale di S. Matteo*, April 1964, p. 22-25.

— " Michelangelo al tempo dei lavori di San Lorenzo in una Ricordanza del Figiovanni," *Paragone*, XV, 1964, No. 175, p. 9-24.

— " Sul probabile tipo del ' Cupido dormente ' di Michelangelo," *Arte Antica e Moderna*, 27, 1964, p. 281-294.

Pecchiai P., " Palazzo Taverna a Monte Giordano." *Quaderni di Storia d'arte III.* Rome, 1963.

Peman y Pemartin C., " La portée de l'influence de Michel-Ange dans le temps et dans l'espace: ' La bataille des anges ' de Juan Martínez Montañés (Séville 1671-73)," in: *Resümees. 21. Internationaler Kongress für Kunstgeschichte*, Bonn, September 1964, p. 77-78.

Perrig A., *Pantheon*, III, 1961, p. 154-155: review of L. Goldscheider, *Michelangelo's bozzetti for statues in the Medici Chapel*, London, 1957.

— " Michelangelo und Marcello Venusti. Das Problem der Verkündigungs- und Ölberg-Konzeptionen Michelangelos," *Wallraf-Richartz Jahrbuch*, 24, 1962, p. 261-294.

— " Bemerkungen zur Freundschaft zwischen Michelangelo und Cavalieri," in: *Resümees. 21. Internationaler Kongress für Kunstgeschichte*, Bonn, September 1964, p. 97.

Perugini G., see: *Il Campidoglio di Michelangelo*.

Pica A., " Apparato per una nuova lettura di Michelangelo: la mostra al Palazzo delle esposizioni a Roma," *Domus*, No. 415, June 1964, p. 56-58.

Pietrangeli C., " I palazzi capitolini nel Rinascimento," *Capitolium*, XXXIX, 1964, p. 195.
— see: *Il Campidoglio di Michelangelo*.
Pinna A., see: D'Ancona P.
Piola Caselli Chiovenda L., " Una copia ad affresco inedita del Giudizio di Michelangelo," *Palatino* VIII, 3rd series, 1964, 7/8, p. 149-151.
Pittaluga M., " Vasari e Michelangelo," *Il Vasari*, XXI, 1963, 4, p. 190-193: review of P. Barocchi, *Giorgio Vasari: La Vita di Michelangelo nelle redazioni del 1550 e del 1568*, Milan and Naples, 1962.
— *Bollettino d'Arte*, XLIV, 1964, II, p. 189-190: review of A. Forlani, *I disegni italiani del Cinquecento*, Venice, 1962.
Plesters J., see: Ruhemann H.
Poggi F., " Michelangelo e la sua casa," *Bollettino degli Ingegneri*, Collegio degli Ingegneri di Firenze, 1965, 2/3, p. 34-38.
Pommer R., *Renaissance News*, 15, 1962, p. 317-320: review of J. Stone, *Agony and ecstasy, a novel of Michelangelo*, New York, 1961.
Pope-Hennessy J., *Italian High Renaissance and Baroque Sculpture*, London, 1963; for review, see: Ettlinger L. D., *New Guardian, Times Literary Supplement*.
— *Art News*, 60, 1962, p. 43: review of J. S. Ackerman, *The architecture of Michelangelo*, London, 1961.
— " The Palestrina Pietà," in: *Resümees. 21. Internationaler Kongress für Kunstgeschichte*, Bonn, September 1964, p. 70 (report of address).
Popham A. E., *Raphael and Michelangelo: selected drawings in the Royal Collection at Windsor*, London, 1954.
Portoghesi P., " La Biblioteca Laurenziana," in: Portoghesi P.-Zevi B., *Michelangelo architetto*, Turin, 1964, p. 209-376.
— " Mostra critica delle opere michelangiolesche al Palazzo delle esposizioni a Roma," *Architettura*, 10, 1964, p. 84-91.
— " La Biblioteca Laurenziana e la critica michelangiolesca alla tradizione classica," in: *Resümees. 21. Internationaler Kongress für Kunstgeschichte*, Bonn, September 1964, p. 21 (report of address).
Portoghesi P.-Zevi B., " Michelangelo architetto." *Collana Storica di architettura*, 6, Turin, 1964 (with articles by: Argan G. C., Bertini A., Bettini S., Bonelli R., Gioseffi D., Pane R., Portoghesi P., Zevi B.; Catalogue of architectural works by Barbieri F. and Puppi L.: cf. under names of authors).
Portoghesi P.-Maitese C.-Cataldi F., *Mostra critica delle opere michelangiolesche. Catalogo a cura di*, Rome, 1964.
Pouncey Ph., *Master Drawings*, II, 1964, 3, p. 278-293: review of B. Berenson, *I disegni dei pittori fiorentini*, Milan, 1961.
Pouncey Ph.-Gere J. A., *Italian Drawings in the Department of Prints and Drawings in the British Museum. Raphael and his Circle*, London, 1962; for review, see: Kultzen R., Shearman J.
Previtali G., " Alle origini del primitivismo romantico," *Paragone*, 149, 1962, p. 32-51.
— *Paragone*, 151, 1962, p. 74-82: review of P. Barocchi, *Trattati d'arte del Cinquecento*, Bari, 1960-62.
— " Michelangelo demistificato " *Paragone*, 179, 1964, p. 56-62.
" Proposta per Michelangelo," *Il Vasari*, XXI, 1963, 4, p. 186-187.
Procacci U., " Parla Michelangelo (Michelangelo storicizzato)," *Marcatrè*, 11/12/13, 1964, p. 56-60.
— " Postille al Condivi," *Bollettino degli Ingegneri*, Collegio degli Ingegneri di Firenze, 1965, 2/3, p. 3.
Puppi L., see: Barbieri F.
(R.), " Mostra di disegni di Michelangelo in Olanda," *Il Vasari*, XXI, 1963, 4, p. 183.
Raggio O., " The Myth of Prometheus. Its survival and metamorphoses up to the eighttenth century," *Journal of the Warburg and Courtauld Institutes*, XXI, 1958, p. 44-62.
Ramsden E. H., see: Michelangelo.
Rauhut F., " Michelangelo als Dichter," in: *Michelangelo Buonarroti*, Würzburg, 1964, p. 191-214.
Read H., *Listener*, December 5, 1963; review of G. M. C. Brandes, *Michelangelo: his life, his times, his era*, London, 1963.
Recupero J., *Michelangelo*, Rome, 1964.
Redig de Campos D., " Un ritratto satirico di Michelangelo attribuito al Bandinelli," *Rendiconti della Pontificia Accademia Romana di Archeologia*, XIX, 1942, p. 397-405 (new version in: *Raffaello e Michelangelo*, cap. VIII).
— " La Pietà di Michelangelo in San Pietro," *Ecclesia*, II, 1943, p. 18-27 (new version in: *Raffaello e Michelangelo*, cap. VI).
— *Die Fresken Michelangelos in der Sixtinischen Kapelle*, Zürich, 1947.
— " Ricordare con una lapide il soggiorno a Roma di Michelangelo," *Il Quotidiano*, August 22, 1948.
— " Note sulla Pietà Rondanini," *Ecclesia*, V, 1950, p. 245-248.
— " Michelangelo Buonarroti," article in: *Enciclopedia Cattolica*, Vol. VIII, 1952, coll. 935-946.
— *Michelangelo Buonarroti*, Rome, 1956.
— " Trois aspects du Judgment Dernier de Michel-Ange," *La Table Ronde*, 110, February 1957, p. 85-95.
— " Un nuovo aspetto della Pietà di Michelangelo in San Pietro," *Capitolium*, XXXVIII, 1963, p. 188-191.
— *La Pietà giovanile di Michelangelo*, Milan, 1964.
— *Itinerario pittorico dei Musei Vaticani* (3rd ed.), Rome, 1964.
— " Michelangelo pittore in Vaticano," *L'Osservatore Romano*, February 23, 1964.
— " Il Crocifisso di Michelangelo per Vittoria Colonna," *L'Osservatore Romano*, June 20, 1964.
— " Das Kruzifiz Michelangelos für Vittoria Colonna," in: *Resümees. 21. Internationaler Kongress für Kunstgeschichte*, Bonn, September 1964, p. 102 (report of address).
— " Drei Bedeutungen des Jüngsten Gerichts Michelangelos," *Römische Quartalschrift*, LIX, 1964, p. 230-242.
— *Il " Giudizio Universale " di Michelangelo*, Milan, 1964.
— " Miguel-Ángelo pintor," *Estudos italianos em Portugal*, 24, 1965.
— " Das Porträt Michelangelos mit dem Turban von Giuliano Bugiardini," in: *Festschrift H. von Einem*, Berlin, 1965, p. 49-51.
Reff Th., " Degas, Copies of Older Art," *The Burlington Magazine*, CV, June 1963, p. 241-251.
van Regteren Altena J. Q., " Zu Michelangelos Zeichnungen von der Reise nach Venedig (1529) bis zum Jüngsten Gericht," in: *Resümees. 21. Internationaler Kongress für Kunstgeschichte*, Bonn, September 1964, p. 98-99.
— *Michelangelo na vier eeuwen. Rede*, Haarlem, 1965.
Robertson M., " Michelangelo and Seurat," *The Burlington Magazine*, CV, November 1953, p. 371: review of J. Wilde, *Italian Drawings in the Department of Prints and Drawings in the British Museum. Michelangelo and his studio*, London, 1953.

" Romulus," " Michelangelo, Cerano and the expressionists." *Apollo*, LXXX, October 1964, p. 318-319.

Rosenthal E. E., " Michelangelo's: Moses, dal di sotto in sù," *The Art Bulletin*, XLVI, December 1964, p. 544-550.

Rossi A., *Paragone* (Letteratura), No. 178, 1964, p. 71-80; review of P. Barocchi, *Giorgio Vasari: La vita di Michelangelo nelle redazioni del 1550 e del 1558*, Milan and Naples, 1962.

Rotili M.-Contelli Isola M.-Galasso E., *Fortuna di Michelangelo nell'incisione. Catalogo della mostra a cura di*, Introduction by V. Mariani, Benevento, 1964.

Ruhemann H.-Plesters J., " The Technique of Painting in a ' Madonna ' attributed to Michelangelo," *The Burlington Magazine*, CVI, 1964, p. 546-554.

Russel J., *Sunday Times*, August 25, 1963: review of A. Chastel, *Italian art*, London, 1963.

Russoli F., *All the sculpture of Michelangelo* (=*Tutta la scultura di Michelangelo*, Milan 1953), London, 1963.

Safarik E. A., " Contributi all'opera di Sebastiano del Piombo," *Arte Veneta*, XVII, 1963, p. 64-78.

Salmi M.-Berti L., *Mostra del Pontormo e del primo manierismo fiorentino. Catalogo a cura di*, Florence, 1956.

— see: *Disegni di Michelangelo*.

Sandström S., " Levels of Unreality. Studies in Structure and Construction in Italian Mural Painting during the Renaissance," *Uppsala Studies in the History of Art*, New Series, 4, Uppsala, 1963; for review, see: Wohl H.

Sanminiatelli B., *Vita di Michelangelo*, Rome, 1964.

Sanpaolesi P., *Brunelleschi*, Milan, 1962.

— " Il Non Finito (Michelangelo storicizzato)," *Marcatrè* 11/12/13, 1964, p. 64-65.

— " Le strutture della Laurenziana," *Bollettino degli Ingegneri*, Collegio degli Ingegneri di Firenze, 1965, 2/3, p. 29-33.

" Scatenati i critici: Michelangelo oppure no?," *Panorama*, April 19, 1964.

Schiavo A., " Il modello della cupola di S. Pietro nel suo IV. Centenario," *Studi Romani*, 9, 1961, p. 519-532.

— " Il Campidoglio di Michelangelo e dei continuatori," *Capitolium*, XXXIX, 1964, p. 199.

Schott R., *Michelangelo*. Translated and adapted from the German by C. McNab, London, 1963.

Schulz J., *Journal of Aesthetics and Art Criticism*, 1962, I, p. 91-94; review of R. J. Clements, *Michelangelo's theory of art*, New York and Zürich, 1961.

— *ibid.*: review of J. S. Ackerman, *The architecture of Michelangelo*, London, 1961.

— " Pinturicchio and the Revival of Antiquity," *Journal of the Warburg and Courtauld Institutes*, XXV, 1962, p. 35-55.

— *The Art Bulletin*, XLV, 1963, 2, p. 159-163; review of S. J. Freedberg, *Painting of the High Renaissance in Rome and Florence*, Cambridge (Mass.), 1961.

Schultz W., " Michelangelo, der Künstler und der Mensch," *Archiv für Kulturgeschichte*, 42, 1960, p. 76-104.

Schwager K., " Unbekannte Zeichnungen Jacopo del Ducas," in: *Resümees. 21. Internationaler Kongress für Kunstgeschichte*, Bonn, September 1964, p. 34-35.

Sckommodau H., " Michelangelo und der Neuplatonismus," *Jahrbuch für Ästhetic und allgemeine Kunstwissenschaft* 7, 1962, p. 28-47.

Sedlmayr H., " Michelangelo. Ein Zugang zu seiner Kunst," *Universitas*, 16, 1961, p. 137-150.

Semi F., *Storia del Duomo di Padova fino al sec. XVI*. Thesis presented at " Istituto superiore universitario di architettura, 1962/63.

Seymour Ch. jr.; " Homo Magnus et Albus. The Quattrocento Background for Michelangelo's David 1501-1504," in: *Resümees. 21. Internationaler Kongress für Kunstgeschichte*, Bonn, September 1964, p. 68-69.

Shearman J., " Maniera as an aesthetic ideal," in: *Studies in Western Art II: The Renaissance and Mannerism*. Acts of the twentieth international congress of the history of art, Princeton, 1963, p. 200-221.

— *The Burlington Magazine*, CVII, January 1965, p. 34-36; review of Ph. Pouncey-J. A. Gere, *Italian Drawings in the Department of Prints and Drawings in the British Museum. Raphael and his Circle*, London, 1962.

Siebenhüner H., " Umrisse zur Geschichte der Ausstattung von St. Peter in Rom von Paul III bis Paul V (1547-1606), in: *Festschrift H. Sedlmayr*, Munich, 1962, p. 229-320.

" Sistina restoration rumored," *Art Digest*, May 29, 1955, p. 5.

Smart A., *Apollo*, LXV, May 1964, p. 436-437; review of G. M. C. Brandes, *Michelangelo: his life, his times, his era*, London, 1963; R. J. Clements, *Michelangelo's theory of art*, New York, 1961; " Michelangelo Buonarroti ": *The Letters of Michelangelo*, translated by E. H. Ramsden, Stanford University Press, 1963; R. and M. Wittkower, *The divine Michelangelo*, London, 1964.

Smyth C. H., " Mannerism and Maniera," in: *Studies in Western Art II: The Renaissance and Mannerism*. Acts of the twentieth international congress of the history of art, Princeton, 1963, p. 174-199.

Spini G., " Michelangelo e la Bibbia (Michelangelo storicizzato)," *Marcatrè* 11/12/13, 1964, p. 66-73.

— " Politicità di Michelangelo," *Rivista storica italiana*, 1964, p. 557.

Stechow W., " Letter to the Editor," *The Art Bulletin*, XXXV, September 1953, p. 263-264.

— " Joseph of Arimathia or Nicodemus? " in: *Studien zur Toskanischen Kunst. Festschrift L. H. Heydenreich*, Munich, 1963, p. 289-302.

Sterba R.-Sterba E., " Observações sobre a personalidade de Michelangelo Buonarroti," *Habitat*, 70, December 1962, p. 55-59.

Stone J., *Agony and ecstasy, a novel of Michelangelo*, New York, 1961; for review, see: Kroll J., Pommer R., Watterson J.

Sutherland A. B., " A new Michelangelo Drawing in the Louvre?," *The Burlington Magazine*, CVI, December 1964, p. 572-575.

Sypher W., *Arts*, 36, 1961, p. 68: review of J. S. Ackerman, *The architecture of Michelangelo*, London, 1961.

Sztuka Czasów Michala Aniola, Wystawa w czterechtna rocznice smerci artyst. Museum Narodowe w Warszawie (*The times of Michelangelo. Commemorative exhibition in the fourth centenary of the artist's death*), Warsaw, December 1963-March 1964.

Tekeningen van Michelangelo, Teylers Museum, Haarlem 1964.

Thoenes Ch., " Studien zur Geschichte des Petersplatzes," *Zeitschrift für Kunstgeschichte*, XXVI, 1963, p. 97-145.

Times Literary Supplement, May 17, 1963: review of G. Briganti, *Italian Mannerism*, London, 1963.

— October 13, 1963, p. 684: review of B. Berenson, *Italian pictures of the Renaissance*, London, 1963 (new ed.).

Toesca I., *Le vicende architettoniche*, in: Gaynor J. S. and Toesca I., *San Silvestro in Capite*, Rome, 1964, p. 36-118,

Tolnay Ch., *Michelangelo, Vol. V. The final period. Last Judgment, frescoes of the Paoline Chapel, last Pietàs*, Princeton 1960; for review, see: von Einem H.

— " Michel-Ange dans son atelier par Delacroix," *Gazette des Beaux-Arts*, 6, LIX, January 1962, p. 43-52.

— " Un ritratto sconosciuto di Michelangelo dipinto da Raffaello," in: *Festschrift F. Gerke*, Baden-Baden, 1962, p. 167-172.

— " Poussin, Michel-Ange et Raphael," *Art de France*, 2, 1962, p. 260-262.

— " Michelangelo Buonarroti," article in: *Enciclopedia Universale dell'Arte*, Vol. IX, coll. 263-306, Venice and Rome, 1963.

— " Morte e Resurrezione in Michelangelo," *Commentari*, XV, 1964, p. 3-20.

— " Tod und Auferstehung bei Michelangelo," in: *Michelangelo Buonarroti*, Würzburg, 1964, p. 7-50.

— " Un simbolo di Firenze (Michelangelo storicizzato)," *Marcatrè*, 11/12/13, 1964, p. 60-63.

— " Newly Discovered Drawings Related to Michelangelo: the ' Scholz-Scrapbook ' in the Metropolitan Museum of Art," in: *Resümees. 21. Internationaler Kongress für Kunstgeschichte*, Bonn, September 1964, p. 29.

— " L'Hercule de Michel-Ange à Fontainebleau," *ibid.*, p. 75-76, cf.: *Gazette des Beaux-Arts*, 6, LXIV, September 1964, p. 125-140.

— *The art and thought of Michelangelo*, New York, 1964.

— " A forgotten architectural project by Michelangelo: the Choir of the Cathedral of Padua," in: *Festschrift H. von Einem*, Berlin, 1965, p. 247-251.

— " Michelangelo," article in: *Encyclopedia of World Art*, New York - Toronto - London, 1964, Vol. IX, coll. 861-914.

— see: *Disegni di Michelangelo*.

Turcio G., " Le vicende storiche della ' Pietà ' di Michelangelo," *Fede e Arte*, 10, 1962, p. 292-301.

Valentiner W. R., " Il cupido dormiente di Michelangelo," *Commentari*, VII, 1956, p. 236-248.

Viera J. G., " Miguel Ángelo no quarto centenario de sua morte," *Habitat*, No. 76, March 1964, p. 66-71.

Vitzthum W., " Exhibition of Italian Drawings," *Master Drawings*, 1963, 1, p. 54: review of Mostra di disegni di Michelangelo, Florence, Uffizi-Casa Buonarroti.

— (W. V.), *Master Drawings*, II, 1964, 4, p. 424; review of G. Bergsträsser, *Zeichnungen alter und neuer Meister aus dem Hessischen Landesmuseum in Darmstadt*, Darmstadt 1964.

Wall B., *Observer*, December 29, 1963; review of G. M. C. Brandes, *Michelangelo: his life, his times, his era*, London, 1963.

Ward-Jackson P., " Vasari the Biographer," *Apollo*, LXXVII, May 1963, p. 376-378.

Watterson J., *American Institute of Architects Journal* 36, 1961, p. 80-81; review of J. S. Ackerman, *The architecture of Michelangelo*, London, 1961; J. Stone, *Agony and ecstasy, a novel of Michelangelo*, New York, 1961.

Wedgewood C. V., *Daily Telegraph*, December 20, 1963; review of G. M. C. Brandes, *Michelangelo: his life, his times, his era*, London, 1963.

Wethey H. E., " Michelangelo e El Greco," *Palatino*, VIII, 3rd series, 1964, 7/8, p. 144-148.

Whiting F. A., " Royal Academy tondo by Michelangelo," *The Connoisseur*, CLVI, May 1964, p. 44-45.

Wilde J., *Le Triomphe du Maniérisme européen de Michel-Ange au Greco*, Amsterdam, 1955.

— see: Clark K.

Wind E., *Pagan Mysteries in the Renaissance*, New Haven, 1958.

Wirch C., " Study by Tintoretto after Michelangelo: drawing of the figure of Day from the tomb of Giuliano de' Medici," *Metropolitan Museum of Art Bulletin*, new series, 15, December 1956, p. 111-116.

Wittkower R., " La cupola di S. Pietro di Michelangelo (Riesame critico delle testimonianze contemporanee)," *Arte Antica e Moderna*, 20, 1962, p. 390-437.

— *ibid.*, Florence, 1964.

Wittkower R.-Wittkower M., " The divine Michelangelo," *The Florentine Academy's Homage on his death in 1564. A facsimile edition of " Esequie del Divino Michelangelo Buonarroti," Florence 1564. Introduced, translated and annotated by*, London, 1964; for review, see: Smart A.

Wohl H., *The Burlington Magazine*, CVII, February 1965, p. 92-93: review of S. Sandström, *Levels of Unreality. Studies in Structure and Construction in Italian Mural Painting during the Renaissance*, Uppsala, 1963.

Wolff-Metternich F., Graf, " San Lorenzo in Mailand, Sankt Peter in Rom," *Kunstchronik*, 15, 1962, 9, p. 285-286.

— " Le premier projet pour St. Pierre de Rome," in: *Studies in Western Art II: The Renaissance and Mannerism*. Acts of the twentieth international congress of the history of art, Princeton, 1963, p. 70-81.

— " Zur Aufstellung des Juliusgrabes nach dem Entwurf von 1513," in: *Der Mensch und die Künste. Festschrift H. Lützeler*, Düsseldorf, 1962, p. 443-450.

— " Eine Vorstufe zu Michelangelos Sankt Peter Fassade," in: *Festschrift H. von Einem*, Berlin, 1965, p. 162-170.

Wölfflin H., *Renaissance und Barock. Eine Untersuchung über Wesen und Entstehung des Barockstils in Italien*, Basel and Stuttgart, 1961.

Würtenberger F., *Il Manierismo*, Milan, 1964 (orig. ed.: Vienna, 1962).

Zevi B., " Michelangelo in prosa (with English translation). L'opera architettonica di Michelangelo nel quarto centenario della morte: modelli, fotografie e commenti degli studenti dell'Istituto di architettura di Venezia," *Architettura*, 9, 1964, p. 650-712.

— " Le fortificazioni fiorentine," in: Portoghesi P.-Zevi B., *Michelangelo architetto*, Turin, 1964, p. 377-424.

— " S. Maria degli Angeli," *ibid.*, p. 761-812.

— see: Portoghesi P.

Zucker P., *Progressive Architecture*, 43, 1962, p. 206; review of J. S. Ackerman, *The architecture of Michelangelo*, London, 1961.

CONTENTS

IV – GUGLIELMO DE ANGELIS D'OSSAT

Architecture

V – LUCIANO BERTI

Drawings

Plates

Acknowledgments

The photographs illustrating these volumes have been kindly furnished by:

A.C.L., Bruxelles – Alinari, Florence – Anderson, Rome – F. Arborio Mella, Milan – Archivio fotografico Gallerie Musei Vaticani – Ashmolean Museum, Oxford – Bayerisches Nationalmuseum, Munich – Bazzechi, Florence – C. Bevilacqua, Milan – British Museum, London – Brogi, Rome – Bulloz, Paris – B. Del Priore, Rome – Ch. de Tolnay – The Detroit Institute of Arts – Ferruzzi, Venice – The Fogg Art Museum, Harvard University, Ch. A. Loeser Bequest – Gabinetto fotografico della Soprintendenza alle Gallerie, Florence – Gabinetto Fotografico Nazionale, Rome – A. Garuti, Florence – Giraudon, Paris – Grassi, Siena – G. Guzzoni, Florence – Istituto Geografico De Agostini, Novara – Laboratoire et Studio Gérondal, Lille – La Photothèque, Paris – Lombardi, Siena – L. Marchese, Milan – The Metropolitan Museum of Art, New York – National Gallery, London – National Gallery of Ireland, Dublin – Novosti Press Agency, Moscow – Cav. Uff. U. Orlandini, Modena – R. Pedicini, Naples – Photo Studios Ltd. (by courtesy of the Royal Academy of Arts), London – The Pierpont Morgan Library, New York – Royal Library (by gracious permission of Her Majesty Queen Elizabeth II), Windsor – O. Savio, Rome – Scala, Florence – Stearn & Sons (by courtesy of the Fitzwilliam Museum), Cambridge – Teylers Stichting, Haarlem – Victoria and Albert Museum, London – L. Von Matt, Buochs – Walker Art Gallery, Liverpool.

A special acknowledgment is made to the Azienda Autonoma del Turismo of Florence for the kind permission granted us to publish the photographs taken by A. Garuti, Florence.

Printed and bound in Italy
by Istituto Geografico De Agostini - Novara - 1966